The Myth and Ritual Theory

The Myth and Ritual Theory

An Anthology

Edited by
Robert A. Segal

BLACKWELL
Publishers

Copyright © Robert A. Segal 1998

First published 1998

2 4 6 8 10 9 7 5 3 1

Blackwell Publishers Inc.
350 Main Street
Malden, Massachusetts 02148
USA

Blackwell Publishers Ltd
108 Cowley Road
Oxford OX4 1JF
UK

Library of Congress Cataloging-in-Publication Data has been applied for.

ISBN 0631 206795 (Hbk) 0631 206809 (Pbk)

British Library Cataloguing in Publication Data

A CIP catalogue record for this book is available from the British Library.

Typeset in 10½ on 12 pt Ehrhardt
by Graphicraft Typesetters Ltd., Hong Kong
Printed and bound in Great Britain by MPG Books Ltd, Bodmin, Cornwall

This book is printed on acid-free paper

CONTENTS

ACKNOWLEDGMENTS

The authors and publishers gratefully acknowledge the following for permission to reproduce copyright material:

American Anthropological Association for William Bascom: "The Myth-Ritual Theory" from *Journal of American Folklore*, 70:276, April–June 1957; and Stanley Edgar Hyman: "The Ritual View of Myth and Mythic" from *Journal of American Folklore*, 68:270, October–December 1955. Not for further reproduction.

E. J. Brill Publishers for H. J. Rose: "The Evidence of Divine Kings in France" from *The Sacral Kinship/ La Regalita Sacra*, VIIIth International Congress for the History of Religions (Brill, 1959); and H. S. Versnel: 'Prospects' from *Transition and Renewal in Myth and Ritual* (Brill, 1993).

Cambridge University Press for Jane Harrison: chapter from *Themis* 1st edition (1912); Gilbert Murray: "Excursus on the Ritual Forms Preserved in Greek Tragedy" also from *Themis* (1912); extract from William Ridgeway: *The Dramas and Dramatic Dances of Non-European Races* (1915); extract from Jessie L. Weston: *From Ritual to Romance* (1920); and F. M. Cornford: "A Ritual Basis for Hesiod's Theogony" from *The Unwritten Philosophy and Other Essays* (1950), this last also by permission of the Trustees of Dr F. M. Cornford.

The Centennial Review and the author for Herbert Weisinger: "The Myth and Ritual Approach to Shakespearean Tragedy" first published in *The Centennial Review*, Winter 1957 (1:1).

Doubleday, a division of Bantam Doubleday Dell Publishing Group, Inc. for extracts from Theodore H. Gaster: *Thespis: Ritual, Myth, and Drama in the*

Ancient Theatre (rev. ed. Doubleday, 1961), copyright © 1950 by Theodore Herze Gaster.

HarperCollins Publishers, Inc. for extract from Mircea Eliade: *Myth and Reality* translated by Willard R. Trask (HarperTorch Book, 1968), copyright © 1963 by Harper & Row, Publishers, Inc. Copyright renewed; and Claude Levi-Strauss: "Structure and Dialectics" from *Structural Anthropology*, translated by Claire Jacobson and Brooke Grundfest Schoepf (Basic Books, 1963), English translation copyright © 1963 by Basic Books, Inc.

Harvard University Divinity School for Clyde Kluckhohn: "Myth and Rituals: A General Theory" from *Harvard Theological Review* 35, (1942), copyright © 1942 by the President and Fellows of Harvard College.

Harvard University Press for James E. Frazer: Introduction from Appollodorus: *The Library*, Vol. 1, copyright © 1921 by the President and Fellows of Harvard College.

The Johns Hopkins University Press for extract from Rene Girard: "What is a Myth?" from *The Scapegoat* translated by Yvonne Freccero (Johns Hopkins University Press, 1986), pp. 24–44, copyright © 1986 The Johns Hopkins University Press.

The Kenyon Review for Northrop Frye: "The Archetype of Literature" first published in *The Kenyon Review*, Winter 1951, OS Vol. XIII, No. 1, copyright © The Kenyon Review.

Oxford University Press for S. H. Hooke: "The Myth and Ritual Pattern of the Ancient East" from *Myth and Ritual* edited by S. H. Hooke (1933); and S. G. F. Brandon: "The Myth and Ritual Position Critically Examined", copyright © Oxford University Press 1958, from *Myth, Ritual and Kingship* edited by S. H. Hooke (1958).

Penguin Books Ltd for Claude Levi-Strauss: "Structure and Dialectics" from *Structural Anthropology*, translated by Claire Jacobson and Brooke Grundfest Schoepf (Allen Lane, The Penguin Press, 1963), English translation copyright © 1963 by Basic Books, Inc.

Princeton University Press for Frances Ferguson: *The Idea of a Theater* (Princeton 1949), copyright © 1949 by Princeton University Press.

Routledge for E. O. James: *The Beginnings of Religion* (Routledge); and A. M. Hocart: "The Life-giving Myth" from *The Life-giving Myth and Other Essays* (Methuen, 1952).

The Society for Promoting Christian Knowledge for extracts from Bronislaw Malinowski: "Myth in Primitive Psychology" (1926) from *Magic, Science and Religion and Other Essays* (Doubleday Anchor Books 1954 [1948]).

University of California Press for extract from Walter Burkert: *Homo Necans: The Anthropology of Ancient Greek Sacrificial Ritual and Myth* translated and edited by Peter Bing (University of California Press, 1983), copyright © 1983 The Regents of the University of California; and extract from Joseph Fontenrose: *The Ritual Theory of Myth* (University of California Press, 1966), copyright © 1966.

Vanderbilt University Press for extract from Ivan Engell: *A Rigid Scrutiny* translated and edited by John T. Willis (Vanderbilt, 1969), copyright © 1969 Vanderbilt University Press.

A. P. Watt Ltd on behalf of Trinity College, Cambridge for Sir James Frazer: extract from *The Golden Bough* (Macmillan, 1922), and Introduction from Appollodorus: *The Library*, Vol. 1.

The publishers apologize for any errors or omissions in the above list and would be grateful to be notified of any corrections that should be incorporated in the next edition or reprint of this book.

INTRODUCTION

Among the many theories of myth and many theories of ritual, the myth and ritual theory is distinctive in connecting myths to rituals. The myth and ritual, or myth-ritualist, theory maintains that myths and rituals operate together. The theory claims not that myths and rituals happen to go hand in hand but that they must. In its most uncompromising form, the theory contends that myths and rituals cannot exist without each other. In a milder form, the theory asserts that myths and rituals originally exist together but may subsequently go their separate ways. In its mildest form, the theory maintains that myths and rituals can arise separately but subsequently coalesce.

Original Formulation

In a few introductory pages of his *Lectures on the Religion of the Semites* the Victorian biblicist and Arabist William Robertson Smith pioneered the myth-ritualist theory.[1] Smith begins by warning against the anachronistic "modern habit . . . to look at religion from the side of belief rather than of practice" (*Lectures*, First Series, 1st edn, p. 17). Smith's approach to ancient religion is behaviorist. Instead of first looking for the "creed" that will provide "the key to ritual and practice" (p. 18), he does the reverse: he first finds the ritual, which will then unlock the creed. Indeed, he cautions against even expecting to find a creed, for "the antique religions had for the most part no creed; they consisted entirely of institutions and practices" (p. 18). Smith grants that ancients, whom he compares with primitives, doubtless performed rituals for some

[1] See William Robertson Smith, *Lectures on the Religion of the Semites*, First Series, 1st edn (Edinburgh: Black, 1889).

reason: "No doubt men will not habitually follow certain practices without attaching a meaning to them" (p. 18). But he claims that the meaning was secondary and could even fluctuate: "as a rule we find that while the practice was rigorously fixed, the meaning attached to it was extremely vague, and the same rite was explained by different people in different ways, without any question of orthodoxy or heterodoxy arising in consequence" (p. 18).

In classical Greece, for example, "certain things were done at a temple, and people were agreed that it would be impious not to do them. But if you had asked why they were done, you would probably have had several mutually exclusive explanations from different persons, and no one would have thought it a matter of the least religious importance which of these you chose to adopt" (p. 18). Moreover, the explanations given for a ritual did not stir strong feelings. Rather than formal declarations of belief – creeds – the various explanations were stories, or myths, which simply described "the circumstances under which the rite first came to be established, by the command or by the direct example of the god" (p. 18). "The rite, in short, was connected not with a dogma [i.e., creed] but with a myth" (p. 18). "In all the antique religions, mythology takes the place of dogma" (p. 18).

At the same time, ritual was much more important in ancient religion than myth: "this mythology was no essential part of ancient religion, for it had no sacred sanction and no binding force on the worshippers. The myths connected with individual sanctuaries and ceremonies were merely part of the apparatus of the worship; they served to excite the fancy and sustain the interest of the worshipper; but he was often offered a choice of several accounts of the same thing, and provided that he fulfilled the ritual with accuracy, no one cared what he believed about its origin" (p. 19). Consequently, Smith spurns the attention conventionally accorded not only creed but also myth in ancient religion: "mythology ought not to take the prominent place that is too often assigned to it in the scientific study of ancient faiths" (p. 19). Smith goes as far as to declare that "ritual and practical usage were, strictly speaking, the sum total of ancient religions" (p. 21).

According to Smith, "in almost every case the myth was derived from the ritual, and not the ritual from the myth" (p. 19). Myth arose only once the reason for the ritual had somehow been forgotten: "Now by far the largest part of the myths of antique religions are connected with the ritual of particular shrines, or with religious observances of particular tribes and districts. In all such cases it is probable, in most cases it is certain, that the myth is merely the explanation of a religious usage; and ordinarily it is such an explanation as could not have arisen till the original sense of the usage had more or less fallen into oblivion" (p. 19). Myth was superfluous as long as the reason for the ritual remained clear. Only once the reason was lost was myth created to explain and perhaps to justify the ritual, which might nevertheless have continued to be practiced anyway.

Smith's brand of myth-ritualism is tame. Rituals antedate myths and thereby do not initally require myths. Conversely, myths can eventually flourish apart from rituals. But Smith remains the pioneering myth-ritualist because he was the first to propose that the earliest myths arose in connection with rituals. While myth-ritualism requires some indispensable connection between myth and ritual, it does not require a link of equality. For Smith, ritual is conspicuously more important than myth, which he calls "secondary" (e.g., p. 20). He proposes the myth-ritualist theory to explain myth, not ritual. Myth depends on ritual, even if ritual comes to depend on myth. Without ritual there would be no myth, whether or not without myth there would cease to be ritual.

In claiming that myth is an explanation of ritual, Smith is denying that myth is an explanation of the world – the standard conception of myth, espoused classically by Edward Tylor.[2] For Tylor, myth is an account of events in the physical world. Myth is more important than ritual, which is the *application*, not the *subject*, of myth. Myth constitutes creed, which is merely expressed in the form of a story. For Tylor, myth serves the same function as science. Indeed, myth is the ancient and primitive counterpart to modern science. For both Smith and Tylor, science has neither myths nor rituals.

Development of the Theory

In the several editions of *The Golden Bough* the classicist and anthropologist James Frazer developed the myth-ritualist theory far beyond that of his close friend Smith.[3] While Frazer is best known for his tripartite division of all culture into the stages of magic, religion, and science, the bulk of his tome is devoted to an intermediate stage between religion and science – a stage of magic and religion combined. In this in between stage is to be found myth-ritualism, for only here do myths and rituals work together. In the stage of sheer magic there are rituals – the routines involved in carrying out the directions – but no myths, for there are no gods. In the stage of religion there are both myths and rituals, but they are barely connected. Myths describe the character and behavior of gods. Rituals seek to curry divine favor. Rituals may presuppose myths, which would suggest what activities would most please the gods, but they are otherwise independent of myths.

---

[2] See E. B. Tylor, *Primitive Culture*, 1st edn (London: Murray, 1871), vol. I, chs 8–10. On Tylor see my "Tylor's Theory of Myth as Primitive Science," in *The Sum of Our Choices: Essays in Honour of Eric J. Sharpe*, ed. Arvind Sharma (Atlanta: Scholars Press, 1996), 70–84.

[3] See J. G. Frazer, *The Golden Bough*, 1st edn, 2 vols (London: Macmillan, 1890); 2nd edn, 3 vols (London: Macmillan, 1900); 3rd edn, 12 vols (London: Macmillan, 1911–15); abridged edn (London: Macmillan, 1922).

By contrast, in the following stage of magic and religion combined, myths and rituals work together. Frazer, rarely consistent, in effect presents two distinct versions of myth-ritualism. In the first version myth describes the life of the god of vegetation, and ritual enacts the myth, or at least that portion of the myth describing the death and rebirth of the god. The ritual operates on the basis of the Law of Similarity, according to which the imitation of an action causes it to happen. The ritual does not manipulate vegetation directly. Rather, it manipulates the god of vegetation. But as the king goes, so goes vegetation. The assumption that vegetation is under the control of a god is the legacy of religion. The assumption that vegetation can be controlled, even if only through the king, is the legacy of magic. The combination of myth and ritual is the combination of religion and magic: "Thus the old magical theory of the seasons was displaced, or rather supplemented, by a religious theory. For although men now attributed the annual cycle of change primarily to corresponding changes in their deities, they still thought that by performing certain magical rites they could aid the god who was the principle of life, in his struggle with the opposing principle of death. They imagined that they could recruit his failing energies and even raise him from the dead" (*Golden Bough*, abridged edn, p. 377). In the ritual a human being plays the role of the god and acts out what he magically causes the god to do. While the actor may be the king, Frazer does not strongly tie this version of myth-ritualism to kingship.

In Frazer's second version of myth-ritualism the king is central. In the first version the king, even when the actor in the ritual, merely plays the part of the god of vegetation. In the second version the king is himself divine, by which Frazer means that the god resides in him. Just as the health of vegetation depends on the health of its god, so now the health of the god depends on the health of the king: as the king goes, so goes the god of vegetation and so, in turn, goes vegetation itself. To ensure a steady supply of food, the community kills its king while he is still in his prime and thereby safely transfers the soul of the god to his successor: "For [primitives] believe . . . that the king's life or spirit is so sympathetically bound up with the prosperity of the whole country, that if he fell ill or grew senile the cattle would sicken and cease to multiply, the crops would rot in the fields, and men would perish of widespread disease. Hence, in their opinion,the only way of averting these calamities is to put the king to death while he is still hale and hearty, in order that the divine spirit which he has inherited from his predecessors may be transmitted in turn by him to his successor while it is still in full vigour and has not yet been impaired by the weakness of disease and old age" (pp. 312–13).

The king is killed either at the end of a fixed term or at the first sign of infirmity. Certainly the sudden death of a king can never be precluded, but the killing of the king before his likely passing guarantees as nearly as possible the continuous health of the god and so of vegetation. The aim is to fend off winter. The withering of vegetation during the winter of even a year-long reign is ascribed to the weakening of the king.

This second version of myth-ritualism has proved the more influential by far, but it in fact provides only a tenuous link between myth and ritual and in turn between religion and magic. Instead of enacting the myth of the god of vegetation, the ritual simply changes the residence of the god. The king dies not in imitation of the death of the god but as a sacrifice to preserve the health of the god. What part myth plays here, it is not easy to see. Instead of reviving the god by magical imitation, the ritual revives the god by a transplant. It would therefore be better to restrict the term myth-ritualism to Frazer's first version of the theory.

In Frazer's true myth-ritualist scenario, myth arises prior to ritual rather than, as for Smith, after it. The myth that gets enacted in the combined stage emerges in the stage of religion and therefore antedates the ritual to which it is applied. In the combined stage, myth, as for Smith, explains the point of ritual, but not only once the meaning of ritual has been forgotten. Rather, myth *gives* ritual its meaning. In the combined stage, ritual would not be undertaken without myth: one would not ritualistically enact the death and rebirth of the god of vegetation without the myth of the death and rebirth of that god.

Myth for Frazer, as for Tylor, serves to explain the world, but for Frazer explanation is only a means to an end: controlling the world. Myth for Frazer, no less than for Tylor, is the ancient and primitive counterpart to modern science, but for Frazer it is the counterpart to applied science and not primarily, as for Tylor, to scientific theory.

For all Frazer's extension of the myth-ritualist theory beyond Smith, he gradually became an ever more vociferous Tylorean and even a critic of the very ritualists inspired by him.[4] In turn, he came to be condemned by some myth-ritualists for exactly his Tylorean stance. Far purer exemplars of the myth-ritualist theory than he are Jane Harrison and S. H. Hooke, the leaders of the initial main groups of myth-ritualists: classicists and scholars of the ancient Near East.[5] Their positions are close and constitute the strongest form of myth-ritualism. Fittingly, they disagree most sharply over the status of Frazer: where Harrison lauds him as her mentor, Hooke lambastes him as the arch-Tylorean.

[4] See J. G. Frazer, Introduction to Apollodorus, *The Library*, Loeb Classical Library (London: Heinemann; New York: Putnam, 1921), vol. I, esp. xxvii–xxviii.

[5] See Jane Ellen Harrison, *Themis*, 1st edn (Cambridge: Cambridge University Press, 1912); *Epilegomena to the Study of Greek Religion* (Cambridge: Cambridge University Press, 1921); S. H. Hooke, "The Myth and Ritual Pattern of the Ancient East," in *Myth and Ritual*, ed. Hooke (London: Oxford University Press, 1933), ch. 1; Introduction to *The Labyrinth*, ed. Hooke (London: SPCK, 1935), v–x; *The Origins of Early Semitic Ritual*, Schweich Lectures 1935 (London: Oxford University Press, 1938); "Myth, Ritual and History" and "Myth and Ritual Reconsidered," in Hooke, *The Siege Perilous* (London: SCM, 1956), chs 3 and 12; "Myth and Ritual: Past and Present," in *Myth, Ritual, and Kingship*, ed. Hooke (Oxford: Clarendon Press, 1958), ch. 1.

Harrison and Hooke begin by pitting their theory against the intellectualist one of Tylor and others. Referring to the peoples of the ancient Near East, especially those of Egypt and Mesopotamia, Hooke says that they "were not occupied with general questions concerning the world but with certain practical and pressing problems of daily life. There were the main problems of securing the means of subsistence, to keep the sun and moon doing their duty, to ensure the regular flooding of the Nile . . . . In order to meet these needs the early inhabitants of Egypt and Mesopotamia developed a set of customary actions directed towards a definite end" ("The Myth and Ritual Pattern of the Ancient East," pp. 2–3). Those actions were rituals. What Hooke says of the ancient Near East, Harrison says of ancient Greece.

In explaining how rituals served to control the otherwise uncontrollable forces of nature, Hooke and Harrison follow Frazer. Ritual works on the basis of the Law of Similarity. The ritual acts out the death and rebirth of the god of vegetation, who, as for Frazer, is the chief god of the pantheon. While the god is dead, the land is infertile; when he is revived, so is the land. The ritual is performed at the end of winter – better, at the point when one wants winter to end. A human being plays the part of the god.

Unlike Frazer, Hooke and Harrison postulate no distinct, prior stages of magic and religion and begin instead with the equivalent of Frazer's stage of magic and religion combined. For them, myth-ritualism is likely the earliest stage of religion. For Hooke and Harrison, no less than for Frazer, myth-ritualism is the ancient and primitive counterpart to modern science. For them, as for Frazer, modern science replaces not only myth-ritualism but myth and ritual per se.

As a myth-ritualist, Hooke, who scorns Frazer as a Tylorean, is ironically even closer to Frazer than Harrison, who applauds him. For Hooke stresses the role of the king, which Harrison downplays. Sometimes for Hooke, as sometimes for Frazer, the king is only the human representative of the god of vegetation. The king imitates the death and rebirth (as well as the victory, marriage, and inauguration) of the god and thereby automatically causes the god and in turn vegetation to do the same. Other times for Hooke, as other times for Frazer, the king is himself divine, in which case the ritual is the actual killing and replacement of him. Yet Hooke still places the ritual at the end – the would-be end – of winter rather than, as for Frazer, at the end of a king's prescribed reign or at the onset of weakness. Hooke thus faces the same inconsistencies as Frazer over the status of the king.

Venturing beyond both Frazer and Hooke, Harrison, inspired by thinkers ranging from Henri Bergson to Emile Durkheim, adds to the ritual of the renewal of vegetation the ritual of initiation into society. Indeed, she argues that the original ritual, while still performed annually, was exclusively initiatory. There was no myth. God was only the projection of the euphoria produced by the ritual – a straight application of Durkheim. Subsequently, god became a god of vegetation, the myth of the death and rebirth of that god arose, and the ritual of initiation became an agricultural ritual as well. Just as the initiates symbolically died and were reborn as full-fledged members of society, so the god of vegetation and in turn crops literally died and were reborn. Eventually, the initiatory side of the combined ritual faded, and only the Frazerian ritual of vegetation remained.

Harrison and Hooke alike deny vigorously that myth is an explanation of even ritual, much less of the world. "The myth," states Harrison, "is not an attempted explanation of either facts or rites" (*Epilegomena to the Study of Greek Religion*, p. 32). In denying that myth is an explanation of ritual, she and Hooke really mean no more than Frazer the myth-ritualist: that myth flourishes alongside ritual to provide its script rather than, as for Smith, arising only after the meaning of ritual has been forgotten. Myth can still, then, be regarded as an explanation of ritual, but of *living* ritual. Myth is recited as the ritual is enacted, just as for Frazer. Myth is therefore like the sound in a film or the narration of a pantomime. Says Hooke: "In general the spoken part of a ritual consists of a description of what is being done . . . This is the sense in which the term 'myth' is used in our discussion" ("The Myth and Ritual Pattern of the Ancient East," p. 3). Says Harrison: "The primary meaning of myth . . . is the spoken correlative of the acted rite, the thing done . . ." (*Themis*, 1st edn, p. 328).

Where for Smith myth arises later than ritual, and where for Frazer ritual arises later than the myth used with it, for Harrison and Hooke myth and ritual arise simultaneously. "It has been much disputed," notes Harrison, "whether the myth arises out of the rite or the rite out of the myth . . . As a matter of fact the two operations arose together and are practically inseparable" (*Epilegomena*, p. 27). Elsewhere, however, Harrison places ritual prior to myth.

Harrison and Hooke carry myth-ritualism further than Frazer in conferring on myth the same magical power contained in the ritual. Where for Frazer the power of myth is merely dramatic, for Harrison and Hooke it is outright magical. "The spoken word," says Hooke, "had the efficacy of an act . . ." ("The Myth and Ritual Pattern of the Ancient East," p. 3). "A myth," says Harrison, "becomes practically a story of magical intent and potency" (*Themis*, p. 330). We have here word magic – and perhaps a glint of the notion of "speech acts."

Application of the Theory to the Ancient World

With Harrison and Hooke the development of the theory of myth–ritualism peaked. The next stage was the application of the theory. The initial application was still to the ancient world. Most famously, the classicists Gilbert Murray, F. M. Cornford, and A. B. Cook applied Harrison's theory to such ancient

Greek phenomena as tragedy, comedy, the Olympic games, science, and philosophy.[6] These seemingly secular, even anti-religious phenomena were interpreted as latent expressions of the myth of the death and rebirth of the god of vegetation.

Among biblicists, Ivan Engnell, Aubrey Johnson, and Sigmund Mowinckel accepted Hooke's formulation of the myth-ritualist theory but differed over the extent to which ancient Israel in particular adhered to the myth-ritualist pattern.[7] Engnell saw an even stronger adherence than Hooke; Johnson and especially Mowinckel, a weaker one. Hooke was never the mentor of the biblicists, the way Harrison was for the classicists, but he was still the key figure among them. He was their myth-ritualist stalwart.

Application of the Theory Worldwide

More broadly, the anthropologist A. M. Hocart and the historian of religion E. O. James applied the myth-ritualist theory to cultures around the world.[8] Hocart uses a simplified version of myth-ritualism – the lowest common denominator of Frazer, Hooke, and Harrison. James' more complicated version combines Frazer's two versions of myth-ritualism. The extension of myth-ritualism by Hocart and James, while worldwide, was less radical than that of Harrison's followers because the application was to manifestly religious phenomena – that is, to overt myths and rituals.

[6] See Gilbert Murray, "Excursis on the Ritual Forms Preserved in Greek Tragedy," in Harrison, *Themis*, 341–63; *Euripides and His Age*, 1st edn (New York: Holt; London: Williams and Norgate, 1913), 60–8; *Aeschylus* (Oxford: Clarendon Press, 1940); F. M. Cornford, "The Origin of the Olympic Games," in Harrison, *Themis*, ch. 7; *The Origin of Attic Comedy* (London: Arnold, 1914); "A Ritual Basis for Hesiod's *Theogony*" (1941), in Cornford, *The Unwritten Philosophy and Other Essays*, ed. W. K. C. Guthrie (Cambridge: Cambridge University Press, 1950), 95–116; *Principium Sapientiae*, ed. W. K. C. Guthrie (Cambridge: Cambridge University Press, 1952), 191–256; A. B. Cook, *Zeus*, 3 vols (Cambridge: Cambridge University Press, 1914–40).

[7] See Ivan Engnell, *Studies in Divine Kingship in the Ancient Near East*, 1st edn (Uppsala: Almqvist & Wiksells, 1943); *A Rigid Scrutiny*, ed. and tr. John T. Willis (Nashville: Vanderbilt University Press, 1969) (retitled *Critical Essays on the Old Testament* [London: SPCK, 1970]); Aubrey R. Johnson, "The Role of the King in the Jerusalem Cults," in *The Labyrinth*, ed. Hooke, 73–111; "Hebrew Conceptions of Kingship," in *Myth, Ritual, and Kingship*, ed. Hooke, 204–35; *Sacral Kingship in Ancient Israel*, 1st edn (Cardiff: University of Wales Press, 1955); Sigmund Mowinckel, *The Psalms in Israel's Worship*, tr. D. R. Ap-Thomas, 2 vols (New York: Abingdon, 1962 [1951]); *He That Cometh*, tr. G. W. Anderson (Nashville: Abingdon, 1954 [1951]), ch. 3.

[8] See A. M. Hocart, *The Life-giving Myth and Other Essays*, ed. Lord Raglan (London: Methuen, 1952), chs 1, 4, 5; *Kingship* (Oxford: Oxford University Press, 1927); *The Progress of Man* (London: Methuen, 1933), chs 13, 19; E. O. James, *Christian Myth and Ritual* (London: Murray, 1933); *Comparative Religion*, 1st edn (London: Methuen, 1938), ch. 4; *The Beginnings of Religion* (London: Hutchinson, 1948), ch. 7; "Myth and Ritual," *Eranos-Jahrbüch* 17 (1949), 79–120; *Myth and Ritual in the Ancient Near East* (London: Thames and Hudson, 1958), esp. ch. 9.

Invoking Frazer, the anthropologist Bronislaw Malinowski applied his own, qualified version of the theory to the myths of native peoples worldwide.[9] Malinowski argues that myth gives rituals a hoary origin and thereby sanctions them, but he argues that myth sanctions many other cultural phenomena as well. Society depends on myth to encourage obedience to rules and customs of all kinds, not merely to rituals. The historian of religion Mircea Eliade applied a similar form of the theory to the myths of all cultures.[10] Myth for him, too, sanctions phenomena of all kinds, not merely rituals, by giving them a primeval origin. Yet Eliade goes beyond Malinowski in stressing the importance of the ritualistic enactment of myth in the fulfillment of the the ultimate function of myth: carrying one back to the time of the myth and thereby bringing one close to the gods.

Application of the Theory to Literature

The most notable application of the myth-ritualist theory outside of religion has been to *secular* literature. Harrison herself boldly derived all art, not just literature, from ritual. She speculates that eventually people ceased believing that the imitation of an action caused that action to occur. Yet rather than abandoning ritual, they now practiced it as an end in itself. Ritual for its own sake became art, her clearest example of which is drama. More modestly than she, Murray and Cornford rooted specifically Greek epic, tragedy, and comedy in myth-ritualism. Murray then extended the theory to Shakespeare.[11]

Other standard-bearers of the theory – derived from Frazer, Harrison, or Hooke – have included Jessie Weston on the Grail legend, E. M. Butler on the Faust legend, C. L. Barber on Shakespearean comedy, Herbert Weisinger on Shakespearean tragedy and on tragedy per se, Francis Fergusson on tragedy, Lord Raglan on hero myths and on literature as a whole, C. M. Bowra on primitive song, and Stanley Edgar Hyman and Northrop Frye on literature

[9] See Bronislaw Malinowski, *Myth in Primitive Psychology* (London: Routledge & Kegan Paul; New York: Norton, 1926) (reprinted in his *Magic, Science and Religion and Other Essays* [Glencoe, IL: Free Press, 1948], 72–124); "Magic, Science and Religion," in *Science, Religion and Reality*, ed. Joseph Needham (London: Sheldon Press; New York: Macmillan, 1925), esp. 76–8 (reprinted in *Magic, Science and Religion and Other Essays*, 1–71).

[10] See Mircea Eliade, *The Sacred and the Profane*, tr. Willard R. Trask (New York: Harcourt, Brace, 1959 [1957]), ch. 2; *Myth and Reality*, tr. Willard R. Trask (New York: Harper & Row, 1963); *Patterns in Comparative Religion*, tr. Rosemary Sheed (London: Sheed and Ward, 1958 [1949]), esp. ch. 15.

[11] See Jane Ellen Harrison, *Ancient Art and Ritual* (New York: Holt; London: Williams and Norgate, 1913); in addition to the references in note 6 above, see Gilbert Murray, "Hamlet and Orestes: A Study in Traditional Types," Annual Shakespeare Lecture, 1914, *Proceedings of the British Academy* 6 (1913–14) (London: Oxford University Press, 1914), 389–412.

generally.[12] As literary critics, these myth–ritualists have understandably been concerned less with myth itself than with the mythic origin of literature. Works of literature are interpreted as the outgrowth of myths once tied to rituals. For those literary critics indebted to Frazer, as the majority are, literature harks back to myths that were originally the scripts of the key primitive ritual of regularly killing and replacing the king in order to ensure crops for the community. "The king must die" becomes the familiar summary line.

For literary myth–ritualists, myth becomes literature when it is severed from ritual. Myth tied to ritual is religious literature; myth cut off from ritual is secular literature, or mere literature. When tied to ritual, myth can serve any of the active functions ascribed to it by the myth–ritualists. Myth bereft of ritual is demoted to mere commentary. To paraphrase Marx and Engels, myth linked to ritual can change the world, where myth severed from ritual can only interpret it.

Independently of Frazer and others, René Girard has proposed his own linkage of myth, ritual, and literature.[13] For him, literature is the legacy of myth, which recounts, albeit in distorted form, the ritual sacrifice of an innocent victim. The central connection for him between myth and the killing of a figure celebrated as a savior is reminiscent of the myth–ritualism of Frazer. While Girard seeks to show how literature reflects myth, he goes beyond

---

[12] See Jessie L. Weston, *From Ritual to Romance* (Cambridge: Cambridge University Press, 1920); E. M. Butler, *The Myth of the Magus* (New York: Macmillan, 1948); C. L. Barber, *Shakespeare's Festive Comedy* (Princeton: Princeton University Press, 1959); Herbert Weisinger, *Tragedy and the Paradox of the Fortunate Fall* (London: Routledge & Kegan Paul; East Lansing: Michigan State College Press, 1953); "The Myth and Ritual Approach to Shakespearean Tragedy," *Centennial Review* 1 (1957), 142–66; "An Examination of the Myth and Ritual Approach to Shakespeare," in *Myth and Mythmaking*, ed. Henry A. Murray (New York: Braziller, 1960), 132–40; *The Agony and the Triumph* (East Lansing: Michigan State University Press, 1964); Francis Fergusson, *The Idea of a Theater* (Princeton: Princeton University Press, 1949); *Dante's Drama of the Mind* (Princeton: Princeton University Press, 1953); "'Myth' and the Literary Scruple," *Sewanee Review* 64 (1956), 171–85; Lord Raglan, "The Hero of Tradition," *Folk-Lore* 45 (1934), 212–31; *The Hero* (London: Methuen, 1936); "Myth and Ritual," *Journal of American Folkore* 68 (1955), 454–61; C. M. Bowra, *Primitive Song* (London: Weidenfeld and Nicolson, 1962); Stanley Edgar Hyman, "Myth, Ritual, and Nonsense," *Kenyon Review* 11 (1949), 455–75; "The Ritual View of Myth and the Mythic," *Journal of American Folkore* 68 (1955), 462–72; Northrop Frye, "The Archetypes of Literature," *Kenyon Review* 13 (1951), 92–110; *Anatomy of Criticism* (Princeton: Princeton University Press, 1957), 131–239; "Myth, Fiction, and Displacement," *Daedalus* 90 (1961), 587–605; "Literature and Myth," in *Relations of Literary Study*, ed. James Thorpe (New York: Modern Language Association, 1967), 27–55.

[13] See René Girard, *Violence and the Sacred*, tr. Patrick Gregory (London: Athlone Press; Baltimore: Johns Hopkins University Press, 1977 [1972]); *"To double business bound"* (London: Athlone Press; Baltimore: Johns Hopkins University Press, 1978); *The Scapegoat*, tr. Yvonne Freccero (London: Athlone Press; Baltimore: Johns Hopkins University Press, 1986 [1982]); *Things Hidden since the Foundation of the World*, trs. Stephen Bann and Michael Metteer (London: Athlone Press; Stanford: Stanford University Press, 1987 [1978]); *Job, the Victim of his People*, tr. Yvonne Freccero (London: Athlone Press; Stanford: Stanford University Press, 1987 [1985]).

other literary myth-ritualists in proposing his own theory of myth and ritual. The function of myth is to cover up the memory of the dastardly killing and thereby preserve the stability of society. Girard roots sacrifice not, like Frazer, in hunger, but in aggression.

Revisions of the Theory

Working on their own, the biblicist Theodor Gaster and the anthropologist Adolf Jensen independently proposed versions of myth-ritualism which make myth more important than ritual.[14] Whether or not their contention that their fellow myth-ritualists downplay myth is correct, they offer a new twist to the relationship between myth and ritual.

The anthropologist Clyde Kluckhohn went much further.[15] He tempered the myth-ritualist dogma that myths and rituals are inseparable. He argued that, operating separately or together, myth and ritual serve a psychological function: that of alleviating anxiety. Myth provides prescribed ways of understanding; ritual, prescribed ways of behaving. When, for Kluckhohn, myths and rituals do operate together, they operate in the same general manner as for Harrison and Hooke: the myth explains what the ritual enacts.

While allowing, like Kluckhohn, for the independence of myth and ritual, the classicist Walter Burkert maintains that when the two do come together, they reinforce each other.[16] Myth links rote human behavior to the behavior of gods. Ritual links a mere story to prescribed behavior of the most dutiful kind. Like Girard, Burkert roots myth in sacrifice and roots sacrifice in aggression, but he does not limit sacrifice to human sacrifice, and he roots sacrifice itself in hunting – the original expression of aggression. Moreover, myth for Burkert functions not to hide the fact of sacrifice but to preserve it and its role in enabling human beings to cope with the guilt and anxiety they feel over their own aggression and mortality. Finally, Burkert connects myths not only to

---

[14] See Theodor H. Gaster, "Divine Kingship in the Ancient Near East: A Review Article," *Review of Religion* 9 (1945), 267–81; *Thespis*, 1st edn (New York: Schuman, 1950); "Myth and Story," *Numen* 1 (1954), 184–212; *The New Golden Bough* (New York: Criterion, 1959), 462–4; Adolf E. Jensen, *Myth and Cult among Primitive Peoples*, trs. Marianna Tax Choldin and Wolfgang Weissleder (Chicago: University of Chicago Press, 1963).

[15] See Clyde Kluckhohn, "Myths and Rituals: A General Theory," *Harvard Theological Review* 35 (1942), 45–79; Kluckhohn and Dorothea Leighton, *The Navaho*, rev. edn (Cambridge, MA: Harvard University Press, 1974), 229–40.

[16] See Walter Burkert, *Structure and History in Greek Mythology and Ritual* (Berkeley: University of California Press, 1979), esp. 56–8, 99–101; *Homo Necans*, tr. Peter Bing (Berkeley: University of California Press, 1983 [1972]), esp. 29–34; *Ancient Mystery Cults* (Cambridge, MA: Harvard University Press, 1987), 73–8; *Creation of the Sacred* (Cambridge, MA: Harvard University Press, 1996), ch. 3.

rituals of sacrifice but also, like Harrison, to rituals of initiation. Myths here serve the same socializing function as rituals.

By far the most radical and influential contemporary variety of myth-ritualism has been structuralism, pioneered by the anthropologist Claude Lévi-Strauss.[17] While Lévi-Strauss focuses overwhelmingly on myth, he does consider ritual as well. According to Lévi-Strauss, all human beings think in the form of classifications and project them onto the world. Humans think specifically in the form of pairs of appositions, which Lévi-Strauss calls "binary opposi-tions." Not only myths but all other human activities as well display humanity's pairing impulse.

Myth is distinctive in not only expressing oppositions, which are equivalent to contradictions, but also resolving them: "the purpose of myth is to provide a logical model capable of overcoming a contradiction" ("The Structural Study of Myth," p. 443). Myth resolves a contradiction dialectically, by providing either a mediating middle term or an analogous, but more easily resolved, contradiction.

Not only do whole myths have the same dialectical relationship to one another that the parts of each have internally, but so do myths and rituals. Rather than mirroring each other, as for other myth-ritualists, myth and ritual oppose each other. Lévi-Strauss thus presents a new, structuralist slant to the relation-ship between myth and ritual. As he says in contrasting his brand of myth-ritualism to prior ones, "The current [i.e., nonstructuralist] theory, according to which a [chronological] term-to-term correspondence exists between two orders (whether the rite acts out the myth, or the myth explicates the rite), is redu-cible to the particular case of a more general [structuralist] relation. The study of individual cases makes myths and rites appear as different transformations of identical elements" (*Structural Anthropology*, II, pp. 65–6).

As influential as the myth-ritualist theory has been among not only theorists of myth or ritual but also specialists in the myths and rituals of individual cultures, most theorists of myth and most theorists of ritual have rejected the theory in any of its forms.[18] They maintain that myths and rituals exist largely independently of each other. Most theorists of myth continue to focus on myth

[17] See Claude Lévi-Strauss, "The Structural Study of Myth," *Journal of American Folklore* 68 (1955), 428–44 (reprinted in his *Structural Anthropology*, tr. Claire Jacobson and Brooke Grundfest Schoepf [New York: Basic Books, 1963 (1958)], ch. 11); "Structure and Dialectics," in his *Structural Anthropology*, ch. 12; "Comparative Religions of Nonliterate Peoples," in his *Structural Anthropology II*, tr. Monique Layton (New York: Basic Books, 1976 [1973]), ch. 5.

[18] To cite a single example of the influence of the theory on specialists: "Modern research stresses the connection between *myth and ritual*: The myths are stories explaining the rites enacted in the *sacred dramas* of the great festivals. Above all the *creation drama* of the *New Year Festival* has been of great importance in the whole Ancient Near East, and through the medium of Canaan it has also gained a firm footing in Israel" (Aage Bentzen, *Introduction to the Old Testament*, 5th edn [Copenhagen: Gad, 1959], vol. I, 242). John Rogerson pointed out this example to me.

alone, and most theorists of ritual continue to focus on ritual alone. Even those theorists of myth or of ritual who accept some linkage between myth and ritual usually limit the tie to a fraction of myths and rituals.[19]

Whatever the actual nexus between myths and rituals turns out to be, the myth-ritualist theory remains valuable. It suggests aspects of myth that might otherwise get overlooked – notably, the relationship between belief and practice, between narrative and action. The theory also suggests parallels between myth and other cultural phenomena like science and literature that might otherwise get missed.[20]

Acknowledgment

For their helpful comments on the introduction, I want to thank Robert Ackerman, C. Robert Phillips III, and John Rogerson. An earlier version of the introduction appeared as "The Myth and Ritual Theory: An Overview" in the *Journal of Jewish Thought and Philosophy*, vol. 6 (1997), pp. 1–18, and is reprinted here with permission.

[19] Criticisms of the myth-ritualist theory abound. In addition to Frazer's criticism cited in note 4 above, see esp. William Ridgeway, *The Dramas and Dramatic Dances of Non-European Races* (Cambridge: Cambridge University Press, 1915), 41–64; Norman H. Snaith, *The Jewish New Year Festival* (London: SPCK, 1947); Henri Frankfort, *Kingship and the Gods* (Chicago: University of Chicago Press, 1948); *The Problem of Similarity in Ancient Near Eastern Religions*, Frazer Lecture 1950 (Oxford: Clarendon Press, 1951); Haskell M. Block, "Cultural Anthropology and Contemporary Literary Criticism," *Journal of Aesthetics and Art Criticism* 11 (1952), 46–54; Wallace W. Douglas, "The Meanings of 'Myth' in Modern Criticism, "*Modern Philology* 50 (1953), 232–42; Stith Thompson, "Myths and Folktales," *Journal of American Folklore* 68 (1955), 482–8; William Bascom, "The Myth-Ritual Theory," *Journal of American Folklore* 70 (1957), 103–14; S. G. F. Brandon, "The Myth and Ritual Position Critically Examined," in *Myth, Ritual, and Kingship*, ed. Hooke, 261–91; H. J. Rose, "The Evidence for Divine Kings in Greece," in *The Sacral Kingship/La Regalità Sacra*, VIIIth International Congress for the History of Religions (Leiden: Brill, 1959), 371–8; Joseph Fontenrose, *Python* (Berkeley: University of California Press, 1959), ch. 15; *The Ritual Theory of Myth* (Berkeley: University of California Press, 1966); Francis Lee Utley, "Folklore, Myth, and Ritual," in *Critical Approaches to Medieval Literature*, ed. Dorothy Bethurum (New York: Columbia University Press, 1960), 83–109; A. N. Marlow, "Myth and Ritual in Early Greece," *Bulletin of the John Rylands Library* 43 (1961), 373–402; G. S. Kirk, *Myth* (Berkeley: University of California Press, 1966), 12–31; *The Nature of Greek Myths* (Harmondsworth, Middlesex: Penguin, 1974), ch. 10; Hans H. Penner, "Myth and Ritual: A Wasteland or a Forest of Symbols?" *History and Theory*, Beiheft 8 (1968), 46–57.

[20] The fullest presentations of the myth-ritualist theory are to be found in Richard F. Hardin, " 'Ritual' in Recent Criticism: The Elusive Sense of Community," *PMLA* 98 (1983), 846–62; H. S. Versnel, "What's Sauce for the Goose Is Sauce for the Gander: Myth and Ritual, Old and New," in *Approaches to Greek Myth*, ed. Lowell Edmunds (Baltimore: Johns Hopkins University Press, 1990), ch. 1 (revised version in Versnel, *Transition and Reversal in Myth and Ritual* [Leiden: Brill, 1993], ch. 1); Robert Ackerman, *The Myth and Ritual School* (New York: Garland Publishing, 1991).

Part I

ORIGINAL FORMULATION
OF THE THEORY

1

Lectures on the Religion of the Semites

William Robertson Smith

The pioneering myth-ritualist was the Scottish biblicist and Arabist William Robertson Smith (1846–94), who began his career as Professor of Hebrew and Old Testament Exegesis at the Free Church College, Aberdeen, and ended it as Professor of Arabic at Cambridge University. In his most famous work, Lectures on the Religion of the Semites, Smith asserts that in ancient religion ritual was primary and belief secondary. Ritual originally provided its own explanation, but that explanation was eventually forgotten, and myth was invented to explain the ritual. While Smith grants that myth subsequently developed independently of ritual, his stress on the initial dependence of myth on ritual constitutes the earliest version of the myth-ritualist theory. The following selection is the first lecture of the First Series of the Lectures on the Religion of the Semites (1st edn, Edinburgh: Black, 1889), 1–28. See also the last lecture of the Third Series of the Lectures, ed. John Day (Sheffield: Sheffield Academic Press, 1995), 96–112, where Smith discusses myth on its own, apart from ritual. On Smith see John Sutherland Black and George Chrystal, The Life of William Robertson Smith (London: Black, 1912); T. O. Beidelman, W. Robertson Smith and the Sociological Study of Religion (Chicago: University of Chicago Press, 1974); William Robertson Smith: Essays in Reassessment, ed. William Johnstone (Sheffield: Sheffield Academic Press, 1995); and J. W. Rogerson, The Bible and Criticism in Victorian Britain (Sheffield: Sheffield Academic Press, 1995), Part II.

Lecture I

Introduction: the subject and the method of enquiry

The subject before us is the religion of the Semitic peoples, that is, of the group of kindred nations, including the Arabs, the Hebrews and Phœnicians,

Original publication: William Robertson Smith, *Lectures on the Religion of the Semites*, 1st edn (Edinburgh: Black, 1889), lecture 1 (pp. 1–28).

the Aramæans, the Babylonians and Assyrians, which in ancient times occupied the great Arabian Peninsula, with the more fertile lands of Syria Mesopotamia and Irac, from the Mediterranean coast to the base of the mountains of Iran and Armenia. Among these peoples three of the great faiths of the world had their origin, so that the Semites must always have a peculiar interest for the student of the history of religion. Our subject, however, is not the history of the several religions that have a Semitic origin, but Semitic religion as a whole in its common features and general type. Judaism, Christianity and Islam are *positive* religions, that is, they did not grow up like the systems of ancient heathenism, under the action of unconscious forces operating silently from age to age, but trace their origin to the teaching of great religious innovators, who spoke as the organs of a divine revelation, and deliberately departed from the traditions of the past. Behind these positive religions lies the old unconscious religious tradition, the body of religious usage and belief which cannot be traced to the influence of individual minds, and was not propagated on individual authority, but formed part of that inheritance from the past into which successive generations of the Semitic race grew up as it were instinctively, taking it as a matter of course that they should believe and act as their fathers had done before them. The positive Semitic religions had to establish themselves on ground already occupied by these older beliefs and usages; they had to displace what they could not assimilate, and whether they rejected or absorbed the elements of the older religion, they had at every point to reckon with them and take up a definite attitude towards them. No positive religion that has moved men has been able to start with a *tabula rasa*, and express itself as if religion were beginning for the first time; in form, if not in substance, the new system must be in contact all along the line with the older ideas and practices which it finds in possession. A new scheme of faith can find a hearing only by appealing to religious instincts and susceptibilities that already exist in its audience, and it cannot reach these without taking account of the traditional forms in which all religious feeling is embodied, and without speaking a language which men accustomed to these old forms can understand. Thus to comprehend a system of positive religion thoroughly, to understand it in its historical origin and form as well as in its abstract principles, we must know the traditional religion that preceded it. It is from this point of view that I invite you to take an interest in the ancient religion of the Semitic peoples; the matter is not one of mere antiquarian curiosity, but has a direct and important bearing on the great problem of the origins of the spiritual religion of the Bible. Let me illustrate this by an example. You know how large a part of the teaching of the New Testament and of all Christian theology turns on the ideas of sacrifice and priesthood. In what they have to say on these heads the New Testament writers presuppose, as the basis of their argument, the notion of sacrifice and priesthood current among the Jews and embodied in the ordinances of the Temple. But, again, the ritual of the Temple was not in its origin an entirely novel thing; the precepts of the Pentateuch did not create a priesthood and a sacrificial service on an altogether independent basis, but only reshaped and remodelled, in accordance with a more spiritual doctrine, institutions of an older type, which in many particulars were common to the Hebrews with their heathen neighbours. Every one who reads the Old Testament with attention is struck with the fact that the origin and *rationale* of sacrifice are nowhere fully explained; that sacrifice is an essential part of religion is taken for granted, as something which is not a doctrine peculiar to Israel but is universally admitted and acted on without as well as within the limits of the chosen people. Thus when we wish thoroughly to study the New Testament doctrine of sacrifice, we are carried back step by step till we reach a point where we have to ask what sacrifice meant, not to the old Hebrews alone, but to the whole circle of nations of which they formed a part. By considerations of this sort we are led to the conclusion that no one of the religions of Semitic origin which still exercise so great an influence on the lives of millions of mankind can be studied completely and exhaustively without a subsidiary enquiry into the older traditional religion of the Semitic race.

You observe that in this argument I take it for granted that, when we go back to the most ancient religious conceptions and usages of the Hebrews, we shall find them to be the common property of a group of kindred peoples, and not the exclusive possession of the tribes of Israel. The proof that this is so will appear more clearly in the sequel; but, indeed, the thing will hardly be denied by any one who has read the Bible with care. In the history of old Israel before the captivity, nothing comes out more clearly than that the mass of the people found the greatest difficulty in keeping their national religion distinct from that of the surrounding nations. Those who had no grasp of spiritual principles, and knew the religion of Jehovah only as an affair of inherited usage, were not conscious of any great difference between themselves and their heathen neighbours, and fell into Canaanite and other foreign practices with the greatest facility. The significance of this fact is manifest if we consider how deeply the most untutored religious sensibilities are shocked by any kind of innovation. Nothing appeals so strongly as religion to the conservative instincts; and conservatism is the habitual attitude of Orientals. The whole history of Israel is unintelligible if we suppose that the heathenism against which the prophets contended was a thing altogether alien to the religious traditions of the Hebrews. In principle there was all the difference in the world between the faith of Isaiah and that of an idolater. But the difference in principle, which seems so clear to us, was not clear to the average Judæan, and the reason of this was that it was obscured by the great similarity in many important points of religious tradition and ritual practice. The conservatism which refuses to look at principles, and has an eye only for tradition and usage, was against the prophets, and had no sympathy with their efforts to draw a sharp line between the religion of Jehovah and that of the foreign gods. This is a proof that what I may call the natural basis of Israel's worship was very closely akin to that of the neighbouring cults.

The conclusion on this point which is suggested by the facts of Old Testament history, may be accepted the more readily because it is confirmed by presumptive arguments of another kind. Traditional religion is handed down from father to child, and therefore is in great measure an affair of race. Nations sprung from a common stock will have a common inheritance of traditional belief and usage in things sacred as well as profane, and thus the evidence that the Hebrews and their neighbours had a large common stock of religious tradition falls in with the evidence which we have from other sources, that in point of race the people of Israel were nearly akin to the heathen nations of Syria and Arabia. The populations of this whole region constitute a well-marked ethnic unity, a fact which is usually expressed by giving to them the common name of Semites. The choice of this term was originally suggested by the tenth chapter of Genesis, in which most of the nations of the group with which we are concerned are represented as descended from Shem the son of Noah. But though modern historians and ethnographers have borrowed a name from the book of Genesis, it must be understood that they do not define the Semitic group as coextensive with the list of nations that are there reckoned to the children of Shem. Most recent interpreters are disposed to regard the classification of the families of mankind given in Genesis x. as founded on principles geographical or political rather than ethnographical; the Phœnicians and other Canaanites, for example, are made to be children of Ham and near cousins of the Egyptians. This arrangement corresponds to historical facts, for, at a period anterior to the Hebrew conquest, Canaan was for centuries an Egyptian dependency, and Phœnician religion and civilisation are permeated by Egyptian influence. But ethnographically the Canaanites were akin to the Arabs and Syrians, and they spoke a language which is hardly different from Hebrew. On the other hand, Elam and Lud, that is, Susiana and Lydia, are called children of Shem, and doubtless these lands were powerfully influenced by Semitic civilisation, but there is no reason to think that in either country the mass of the population belonged to the same stock as the Syrians and Arabs. Accordingly it must be remembered that when modern scholars use the term Semitic, they do not speak as interpreters of Scripture, but as independent observers of ethnographical facts, and include all peoples whose distinctive ethnical characters assign them to the same group with the Hebrews, Syrians, and Arabs.

The scientific definition of an ethnographical group depends on a variety of considerations; for direct historical evidence of an unimpeachable kind as to the original seats and kindred of ancient peoples is not generally to be had. The defects of historical tradition must therefore be supplied by observation, partly of inherited physical characteristics, and partly of mental characteristics habits and attainments such as are usually transmitted from parent to child. Among the indirect criteria of kinship between nations, the most obvious, and the one which has hitherto been most carefully studied, is the criterion of language; for it is observed that the languages of mankind form a series of natural groups, and that within each group it is possible to arrange the several languages which it contains in what may be called a genealogical order, according to degrees of kinship. Now it may not always be true that people of the same or kindred speech are as closely related by actual descent as they seem to be from the language they speak; a Gaelic tribe, for example, may forget their ancient speech, and learn to speak a Teutonic dialect, without ceasing to be true Gaels by blood. But, in general, large groups of men do not readily change their language, but go on from generation to generation speaking the ancestral dialect with such gradual modification as the lapse of time brings about. As a rule, therefore, the classification of mankind by language, at least when applied to large masses, will approach pretty closely to a natural classification; and in a large proportion of cases, the language of a mixed race will prove on examination to be that of the stock whose blood is predominant. Where this is not the case, where a minority has imposed its speech on a majority, we may safely conclude that it has done so in virtue of a natural pre-eminence, a power of shaping lower races in its own mould, which is not confined to the sphere of language, but extends to all parts of life. Where we find unity of language, we can at least say with certainty that we are dealing with a group of men who are subject to common influences of the most subtle and far-reaching kind; and where unity of speech has prevailed for many generations, we may be sure that the continued action of these influences has produced great uniformity of physical and mental type. When we come to deal with groups which have long had separate histories, and whose languages are therefore not identical but only cognate, the case is not so strong. A Scot, for example, whose blood is a mixture of the Teutonic and Celtic, and a North German, who is partly Teutonic and partly Wendish, speak languages belonging to the same Teutonic stock, but in each case the non-Teutonic element in the blood, though it has not ruled the language, has had a perceptible effect on the national character, so that the difference of type between the two men is greater than the difference of their dialects indicates. It is plain, therefore, that kinship in language is not an exact measure of the degree of affinity as determined by the sum of race characters; but on the whole it remains true, that the stock which is strong enough, whether by numbers or by genius, to impress its language on a nation, must exercise a predominant influence on the national type in other respects also; and to this extent the classification of races by language must be called natural and not artificial. Especially is this true for ancient times, when the absence of literature, and especially of religious books, made it much more difficult than it has been in recent ages for a new language to establish itself in a race to which it was originally foreign. All Egypt now speaks Arabic – a Semitic tongue – and yet the population is very far from having assimilated itself to the Arabic type. But this could not have happened without the Coran and the religion of the Coran, which have given what I may call an artificial advantage to the Arabic language. In very ancient times the language of a conquering people had no such artificial help in preserving and propagating itself. A tongue which is spoken and not written makes way only in proportion as those who speak it are able to hold their own without assistance from the literary achievements of their ancestors.

As regards the Semitic nations, which, as I have already said, are classed together on the ground of similarity of language, we have every reason to recognise their linguistic kinship as only one manifestation of a very marked general unity of type. The unity is not perfect; it would not, for example, be safe to make generalisations about the Semitic character from the Arabian nomads, and to apply them to the ancient Babylonians. And for this there are probably two reasons. On the one hand, the Semite of the Arabian desert and the Semite of the Babylonian alluvium lived under altogether different physical and moral conditions; the difference of environment is as complete as possible. And on the other hand, it is pretty certain that the Arabs of the desert have been from time immemorial a race practically unmixed, while the Babylonians, and other members of the same family settled on the fringes of the Semitic land, were in all probability largely mingled with the blood of other races, and underwent a corresponding modification of type.

But when every allowance is made for demonstrable or possible variations of type within the Semitic field, it still remains true that the Semites form a singularly well marked and relatively speaking a very homogeneous group. So far as language goes the evidence to this effect is particularly strong. The Semitic tongues are so closely related to one another, that their affinity is recognised even by the untrained observer; and modern science has little difficulty in tracing them back to a common speech, and determining in a general way what the features of that speech were. On the other hand, the differences between these languages and those spoken by other adjacent races are so fundamental and so wide, that no sober philologist has ventured to lay down anything positive as to the relation of the Semitic tongues to other linguistic stocks. Their nearest kinship seems to be with the languages of North Africa, but even here the common features are balanced by profound differences. The evidence of language therefore tends to show that the period during which the original and common Semitic speech existed apart, and developed its peculiar characters at a distance from languages of other stocks, must have been very long in comparison with the subsequent period during which the separate branches of the Semitic stock, such as Hebrew Aramaic and Arabic, were isolated from one another and developed into separate dialects. Or, to draw the historical inference from this, it would appear that before the Hebrews, the Aramæans, and the Arabs spread themselves over widely distant seats, and began their course of separate national development, there must have been a long period in which the ancestors of all these nations lived together and spoke with one tongue. And as Hebrew Aramaic and Arabic are all much liker to one another than the old common Semitic can possibly have been to any of the languages of surrounding races, it would seem that the separate existence of the several Semitic nations up to the time when their linguistic distinctions were fully developed, can have been but short in comparison with the period during which the undivided Semitic stock, living in separation from other races, formed its peculiar and distinctive type of speech.

The full force of this argument can hardly be made plain without reference to philological details of a kind unsuited to our present purpose; but those of you who have some acquaintance with the Semitic languages will readily admit that the development of the common Semitic system of triliteral roots, not to speak of other linguistic peculiarities, must have been the affair of a number of generations vastly greater than was necessary to develop the differences between Hebrew and Arabic. If, now, the fathers of all the Semitic nations lived together for a very long time, at the very ancient date which preceded the separate history of Hebrews Aramæans and Arabs, – that is, in the infancy of the races of mankind, the period of human history in which individuality went for nothing, and all common influences had a force which we moderns can with difficulty conceive, – it is clear that the various swarms which ultimately hived off from the common stock and formed the Semitic nations known to history, must have carried with them a strongly marked race character, and many common possessions of custom and idea, besides their common language. And further let us observe that the dispersion of the Semitic nations was never carried so far as the dispersion of the Aryans. It we leave out of account settlements made over the seas, – the South Arabian colonies in East Africa, and the Phœnician colonies on the coasts and isles of the Mediterranean, – we find that the region of Semitic occupation is continuous and compact. Its great immovable centre is the vast Arabian peninsula, a region naturally isolated, and in virtue of its physical characters almost exempt from immigration or change of inhabitants. And from this central stronghold, which the predominant opinion of modern scholars designates as the probable starting-point of the whole Semitic dispersion, the region of Semitic speech spreads out round the margin of the Syrian desert till it strikes against great natural boundaries, the Mediterranean, Mount Taurus, and the mountains of Armenia and Iran. From the earliest dawn of history all that lies within these limits was fully occupied by Semitic tribes speaking Semitic dialects, and the compactness of this settlement must necessarily have tended to maintain uniformity of type. The several Semitic nations, when they were not in direct contact with one another, were divided not by alien populations but only by the natural barriers of mountain and desert. These natural barriers, indeed, were numerous, and served to break up the race into a number of small tribes or nations; but, like the mountains of Greece, they were not so formidable as to prevent the separate states from maintaining a great deal of intercourse, which, whether peaceful or warlike, tended to perpetuate the original community of type. Nor was the operation of these causes disturbed in ancient times by any great foreign immigration. The early Egyptian invasions of Syria were not accompanied by any attempt at colonisation; and though the so-called Hittite monuments, which have given rise to so much speculation, may afford evidence that a non-Semitic people from Asia Minor at one time pushed its way into Northern Syria, it is pretty clear that the Hittites of the Bible, i.e., the non-Aramaic communities of Cœle-Syria, were a branch of the Canaanite stock, and that the utmost concession that can be made to modern theories on this subject is that they may for a time have been dominated by a non-Semitic aristocracy. At one time it was not uncommon to represent the Philistines as a non-Semitic people, but it is now generally recognised that the arguments for this view are inadequate, and that, though they came into Palestine from across the sea, from Caphtor, i.e., probably from Crete, they were either mainly of Semitic blood or at least were already thoroughly Semitised at the time of their immigration, alike in speech and in religion.

Coming down to later times, we find that the Assyrian Babylonian and Persian conquests made no considerable change in the general type of the population of the Semitic lands. National and tribal landmarks were removed, and there were considerable shiftings of population within the Semitic area, but no great incursion of new populations of alien stock. In the Greek and Roman periods, on the contrary, a large foreign element was introduced into the towns of Syria; but as the immigration was practically confined to the cities, hardly touching the rural districts, its effects in modifying racial type were, it would seem, of a very transitory character. For in Eastern cities the death-rate habitually exceeds the birth-rate, and the urban population is maintained only by constant recruital from the country, so that it is the blood of the peasantry which ultimately determines the type of the population. Thus it is to be explained that after the Arab conquest of Syria, the Greek element in the population rapidly disappeared. Indeed, one of the most palpable proofs that the populations of all the old Semitic lands possessed a remarkable homogeneity of character, is the fact that in them, and in them alone, the Arabs and Arab influence took permanent root. The Moslem conquests extended far beyond these limits, but except in the old Semitic countries, Islam speedily took new shapes, and the Arab domination soon gave way before the reaction of the mass of its foreign subjects.

Thus the whole course of history, from the earliest date to which authentic knowledge extends down to the time of the decay of the Caliphate, records no great permanent disturbance of population to affect the constancy of the Semitic type within its original seats, apart from the temporary Hellenisation of the great cities already spoken of. Such disturbances as did take place consisted partly of mere local displacements among the settled Semites, partly, and in a much greater degree, of the arrival and establishment in the cultivated lands of successive hordes of Semitic nomads from the Arabian wilderness, which on their settlement found themselves surrounded by populations so nearly of their own type that the complete fusion of the old and new inhabitants was effected without difficulty, and without modification of the general character of the race. If at any point in its settlements, except along the frontiers, the Semitic blood was largely modified by foreign admixture, this must have taken place in prehistoric times, or by fusion with other races which may have occupied the country before the arrival of the Semites. How far anything of this sort actually happened can only be matter of conjecture, for the special hypotheses which have sometimes been put forth – as, for example, that there was a considerable strain of pre-Semitic blood in the Phœnicians and Canaanites – rest on presumptions of no conclusive sort. What is certain is that the Semitic settlements in Asia were practically complete at the first dawn of history, and that the Semitic blood was constantly reinforced, from very early times, by fresh immigrations from the desert. There is hardly another part of the world where we have such good historical reasons for presuming that linguistic affinity will prove a safe indication of affinity in race, and in general physical and mental type. And this presumption is not belied by the results of nearer enquiry. Those who have busied themselves with the history and literature of the Semitic peoples, bear uniform testimony to the close family likeness that runs through them all.

It is only natural that this homogeneity of type appears to be modified on the frontiers of the Semitic field. To the West, if we leave the transmarine colonies out of view, natural conditions drew a sharp line of local demarcation between the Semites and their alien neighbours. The Red Sea and the desert north of it formed a geographical barrier, which was often crossed by the expansive force of the Semitic race, but which appears to have effectually checked the advance into Asia of African populations. But on the East, the fertile basin of the Euphrates and Tigris seems in ancient as in modern times to have been a meeting-place of races. The preponderating opinion of Assyriologists is to the effect that the civilisation of Assyria and Babylonia was not purely Semitic, and that the ancient population of these parts contained a large pre-Semitic element, whose influence is especially to be recognised in religion and in the sacred literature of the cuneiform records.

If this be so, it is plain that the cuneiform material must be used with caution in our enquiry into the type of traditional religion characteristic of the ancient Semites. That Babylonia is the best starting-point for a comparative study of the sacred beliefs and practices of the Semitic peoples, is an idea which has lately had some vogue, and which at first sight appears plausible on account of the great antiquity of the monumental evidence. But, in matters of this sort, ancient and primitive are not synonymous terms; and we must not look for the most primitive form of Semitic faith in a region where society was not primitive. In Babylonia, it would seem, society and religion alike were based on a fusion of two races, and so were not primitive but complex. Moreover, the official system of Babylonian and Assyrian religion, as it is known to us from priestly texts and public inscriptions, bears clear marks of being something more than a popular traditional faith; it has been artificially moulded by priestcraft and statecraft in much the same way as the official religion of Egypt; that is to say, it is in great measure an artificial combination, for imperial purposes, of elements drawn from a number of local worships. In all probability the actual religion of the masses was always much simpler than the official system; and in later times it would seem that, both in religion and in race, Assyria was little different from the adjacent Aramaic countries. These remarks are not meant to throw doubt on the great importance of cuneiform studies for the history of Semitic religion; the monumental data are valuable for comparison with what we know of the faith and worship of other Semitic peoples, and peculiarly valuable because, in religion as in other matters, the civilisation of the Euphrates-Tigris valley exercised a great historical influence on a large part of the Semitic field. But the right point of departure for a general study of Semitic religion must be sought in regions where, though our knowledge begins at a later date, it refers to a simpler state of society, and where accordingly the religious phenomena revealed to us are of an origin less doubtful and a character less complicated. In many respects the religion of heathen Arabia, though we have few details concerning it that are not of post-Christian date, exhibits an extremely primitive character, corresponding to the primitive and unchanging character of nomadic life. And with what may be gathered from this source we must compare, above all, the invaluable notices, preserved in the Old Testament, of the religion of the small Palestinian states before their conquest by the great empires of the East. For this period, apart from the Assyrian records, we have only a few precious fragments of evidence from inscriptions, and no other literary evidence of a contemporary kind. At a later date the evidence from monuments is multiplied and Greek literature begins to give important aid; but by this time also we have reached the period of religious syncretism – the period, that is, when different faiths and worships began to react on one another, and produce new and complex forms of religion. Here, therefore, we have to use the same precautions that are called for in dealing with the older syncretistic religion of Babylonia and Assyria; it is only by careful sifting and comparison that we can separate between ancient use and modern innovation, between the old religious inheritance of the Semites and things that came in from without.

Let it be understood from the outset that we have not the materials for anything like a complete comparative history of Semitic religions, and that nothing of the sort will be attempted in these Lectures. But a careful study and comparison of the various sources is sufficient to furnish a tolerably accurate view of a series of general features, which recur with striking uniformity in all parts of the Semitic field, and govern the evolution of faith and worship down to a late date. These widespread and permanent features form the real interest of Semitic religion to the philosophical student; it was in them, and not in the things that vary from place to place and from time to time, that the strength of Semitic religion lay, and it is to them therefore that we must look for help in the most important practical application of our studies, for light on the great question of the relation of the positive Semitic religions to the earlier faith of the race.

Before entering upon the particulars of our enquiry, I must still detain you with a few words about the method and order of investigation that seem to be prescribed by the nature of the subject. To get a true and well-defined picture of the type of Semitic religion, we must not only study the parts separately, but must have clear views of the place and proportion of each part in its relation to the whole. To this end it is very desirable that we should follow a natural order of enquiry and exposition, beginning with those features of religion which stood, so to speak, in the foreground, and therefore bulked most largely in religious life. And here we shall go very far wrong if we take it for granted that what is the most important and prominent side of religion to us was equally important in the ancient society with which we are to deal. In connection with every religion, whether ancient or modern, we find on the one hand certain beliefs, and on the other certain institutions ritual practices and rules of conduct. Our modern habit is to look at religion from the side of belief rather than of practice; a habit largely due to the fact that, till comparatively recent times, almost the only forms of religion which have attracted much serious study in Europe have been those of the various Christian Churches, and that the controversies between these Churches have constantly turned on diversities of dogma, even where the immediate point of difference has been one of ritual. For in all parts of the Christian Church it is agreed that ritual is important only in connection with its interpretation. Thus within Christendom the study of religion has meant mainly the study of Christian beliefs, and instruction in religion has habitually begun with the creed, religious duties being presented to the learner as flowing from the dogmatic truths he is taught to accept. All this seems to us so much a matter of course that, when we approach some strange or antique religion, we naturally assume that here also our first business is to search for a creed, and find in it the key to ritual and practice. But the antique religions had for the most part no creed; they consisted entirely of institutions and practices. No doubt men will not habitually follow certain practices without attaching a meaning to them; but as a rule we find that while the practice was rigorously fixed, the meaning attached to it was extremely vague, and the same rite was explained by different people in different ways, without any question of orthodoxy or heterodoxy arising in consequence. In ancient Greece, for example, certain things were done at a temple, and people were agreed that it would be impious not to do them. But if you had asked why they were done, you would probably have had several mutually contradictory explanations from different persons, and no one would have thought it a matter of the least religious importance which of these you chose to adopt. Indeed the explanations offered would not have been of a kind to stir any strong feeling; for in most cases they would have been merely different stories as to the circumstances under which the rite first came to be established, by the command or by the direct example of the god. The rite, in short, was connected not with a dogma but with a myth.

In all the antique religions, mythology takes the place of dogma, that is, the sacred lore of priests and people, so far as it does not consist of mere rules for the performance of religious acts, assumes the form of stories about the gods; and these stories afford the only explanation that is offered of the precepts of religion and the prescribed rules of ritual. But, strictly speaking, this mythology was no essential part of ancient religion, for it had no sacred sanction and no binding force on the worshippers. The myths connected with individual sanctuaries and ceremonies were merely part of the apparatus of the worship; they served to excite the fancy and sustain the interest of the worshipper; but he was often offered a choice of several accounts of the same thing, and provided that he fulfilled the ritual with accuracy, no one cared what he believed about its origin. Belief in a certain series of myths was neither obligatory as a part of true religion, nor was it supposed that, by believing, a man acquired religious merit and conciliated the favour of the gods. What was obligatory or meritorious was the exact performance of certain sacred acts prescribed by religious tradition. This being so, it follows that mythology ought not to take the prominent place that is too often assigned to it in the scientific study of ancient faiths. So far as myths consist of explanations of ritual their value is altogether secondary, and it may be affirmed with confidence that in almost every case the myth was derived from the ritual, and not the ritual from the myth; for the ritual was fixed and the myth was variable, the ritual was obligatory and faith in the myth was at the discretion of the worshipper. Now by far the largest part of the myths of antique religions are connected with the ritual of particular shrines, or with the religious observances of particular tribes and districts. In all such cases it is probable, in most cases it is certain, that the myth is merely the explanation of a religious usage; and ordinarily it is such an explanation as could not have arisen till the original sense of the usage had more or less fallen into oblivion. As a rule the myth is no explanation of the origin of the ritual to any one who does not believe it to be a narrative of real occurrences, and the boldest mythologist will not believe that. But, if it be not true, the myth itself requires to be explained, and every principle of philosophy and common sense demands that the explanation be sought, not in arbitrary allegorical theories, but in the actual facts of ritual or religious custom to which the myth attaches. The conclusion is, that in the study of ancient religions we must begin, not with myth, but with ritual and traditional usage.

Nor can it be fairly set against this conclusion, that there are certain myths which are not mere explanations of traditional practices, but exhibit the beginnings of larger religious speculation, or of an attempt to systematise and reduce to order the motley variety of local worships and beliefs. For in this case the secondary character of the myths is still more clearly marked. They are either products of early philosophy, reflecting on the nature of the universe; or they are political in scope, being designed to supply a thread of union between the various worships of groups, originally distinct, which have been united into one social or political organism; or, finally, they are due to the free play of epic imagination. But philosophy politics and poetry are something more, or something less, than religion pure and simple.

There can be no doubt that, in the later stages of ancient religions, mythology acquired an increased importance. In the struggle of heathenism with scepticism on the one hand and Christianity on the other, the supporters of the old traditional religion were driven to search for ideas of a modern cast, which they could represent as the true inner meaning of the traditional rites. To this end they laid hold of the old myths, and applied to them an allegorical system of interpretation. Myth interpreted by the aid of allegory became the favourite means of infusing a new significance into ancient forms. But the theories thus developed are the falsest of false guides as to the original meaning of the old religions.

On the other hand, the ancient myths taken in their natural sense, without allegorical gloss, are plainly of great importance as testimonies to the views of the nature of the gods that were prevalent when they were formed. For though the mythical details had no dogmatic value and no binding authority over faith, it is to be supposed that nothing was put into a myth which people at that time were not prepared to believe without offence. But so far as the way of thinking expressed in the myth was not already expressed in the ritual itself, it had no properly religious sanction; the myth apart from the ritual affords only a doubtful and slippery kind of evidence. Before we can handle myths with any confidence, we must have some definite hold of the ideas expressed in the ritual tradition, which incorporated the only fixed and statutory elements of the religion.

All this, I hope, will become clearer to us as we proceed with our enquiry, and learn by practical example the use to be made of the different lines of evidence open to us. But it is of the first importance to realise clearly from the outset that ritual and practical usage were, strictly speaking, the sum total of ancient religions. Religion in primitive times was not a system of belief with practical applications; it was a body of fixed traditional practices, to which every member of society conformed as a matter of course. Men would not be men if they agreed to do certain things without having a reason for their action; but in ancient religion the reason was not first formulated as a doctrine and then expressed in practice, but conversely, practice preceded doctrinal theory.

Men form general rules of conduct before they begin to express general principles in words; political institutions are older than political theories, and in like manner religious institutions are older than religious theories. This analogy is not arbitrarily chosen, for in fact the parallelism in ancient society between religious and political institutions is complete. In each sphere great importance was attached to form and precedent, but the explanation why the precedent was followed consisted merely of a legend as to its first establishment. That the precedent, once established, was authoritative did not appear to require any proof. The rules of society were based on precedent, and the continued existence of the society was sufficient reason why a precedent once set should continue to be followed.

Strictly speaking, indeed, I understate the case when I say that the oldest religious and political institutions present a close analogy. It would be more correct to say that they were parts of one whole of social custom. Religion was a part of the organised social life into which a man was born, and to which he conformed through life in the same unconscious way in which men fall into any habitual practice of the society in which they live. Men took the gods and their worship for granted, just as they took the other usages of the state for granted, and if they reasoned or speculated about them, they did so on the presupposition that the traditional usages were fixed things, behind which their reasonings must not go, and which no reasoning could be allowed to overturn. To us moderns religion is above all a matter of individual conviction and reasoned belief, but to the ancients it was a part of the citizen's public life, reduced to fixed forms, which he was not bound to understand and was not at liberty to criticise. Society demanded of each of its members the observance of the forms, not for his sake but for its own, for if its religion was tampered with the bases of society were undermined, and the favour of the gods was forfeited. But so long as the prescribed religious forms were duly observed, a man was recognised as a pious man, and no one asked how his religion was rooted in his heart or affected his reason. Religious like political duty, of which indeed it was a part, was entirely comprehended in the observance of certain fixed rules of outward conduct.

The conclusion from all this as to the method of our investigation is obvious. When we study the political structure of an early society, we do not begin by asking what is recorded of the first legislators, or what theory men advanced as to the reason of their institutions; we try to understand what the institutions were, and how they shaped men's lives. In like manner, in the study of Semitic religion, we must not begin by asking what was told about the gods, but what the working religious institutions were, and how they shaped the lives of the worshippers. Our enquiry therefore, will be directed to the religious institutions which governed the lives of men of Semitic race.

In following out this plan, however, we shall do well not to throw ourselves at once upon the multitudinous details of rite and ceremony, but to devote our

attention to certain broad features of the sacred institutions which are sufficiently well marked to be realised at once. If we were called upon to examine
the political institutions of antiquity, we should find it convenient to carry with
us some general notion of the several types of government under which the
multifarious institutions of ancient states arrange themselves. And in like manner it will be useful for us, when we examine the religious institutions of the
Semites, to have first some general knowledge of the types of divine gover-
nance, the various ruling conceptions of the relations of the gods to man, which
underlie the rites and ordinances of religion in different places and at different
times. Such knowledge we can obtain in a provisional form, before entering on
a mass of ritual details, mainly by considering the titles of honour by which men
addressed their gods, and the language in which they expressed their dependence on them. From these we can see at once, in a broad, general way, what
place the gods held in the social system of antiquity, and under what general
categories their relations to their worshippers fell. The broad results thus
reached must then be developed, and at the same time controlled and rendered
more precise, by an examination in detail of the working institutions of religion.

The question of the metaphysical nature of the gods, as distinct from
their social office and function, must be left in the background till this whole
investigation is completed. It is vain to ask what the gods are in themselves till
we have studied them in what I may call their public life, that is, in the stated
intercourse between them and their worshippers which was kept up by means
of the prescribed forms of cultus. From the antique point of view, indeed, the
question what the gods are in themselves is not a religious but a speculative
one; what is requisite to religion is a practical acquaintance with the rules
on which the deity acts and on which he expects his worshippers to frame
their conduct – what in 2 Kings xvii. 26 is called the "manner" or rather the
"customary law" (*mishpat*) of the god of the land. This is true even of the religion of Israel. When the prophets speak of the knowledge of God, they always
mean a practical knowledge of the laws and principles of His government in
Israel,[1] and a summary expression for religion as a whole is "the knowledge
and fear of Jehovah,"[2] i.e., the knowledge of what Jehovah prescribes, combined with a reverent obedience. An extreme scepticism towards all religious
speculation is recommended in the Book of Ecclesiastes as the proper attitude
of piety, for no amount of discussion can carry a man beyond the plain rule to
"fear God and keep His commandments."[3] This counsel the author puts into
the mouth of Solomon, and so represents it, not unjustly, as summing up the
old view of religion, which in more modern days had unfortunately begun to
be undermined.

---

[1] See especially Hosea, chap. iv.
[2] Isaiah xi. 2.
[3] Eccles. xii. 13.

The propriety of keeping back all metaphysical questions as to the nature of the gods till we have studied the practices of religion in detail, becomes very apparent if we consider for a moment what befel the later philosophers and theosophists of heathenism in their attempts to construct a theory of the traditional religion. We find that they were not able to give any account of the nature of the gods from which all the received practices of worship could be rationally deduced, and accordingly those of them who had any pretension to be orthodox were compelled to have recourse to the most violent allegorical interpretations in order to bring the established ritual into accordance with their theories.[4] The reason for this is obvious. The traditional usages of religion had grown up gradually in the course of many centuries, and reflected habits of thought characteristic of very diverse stages of man's intellectual and moral development. No one conception of the nature of the gods could possibly afford the clue to all parts of that motley complex of rites and ceremonies which the later paganism had received by inheritance, from a series of ancestors in every stage of culture from pure savagery upwards. The record of the religious thought of mankind, as it is embodied in religious institutions, resembles the geological record of the history of the earth's crust; the new and the old are preserved side by side, or rather layer upon layer. The classification of ritual formations in their proper sequence is the first step towards their explanation, and that explanation itself must take the form, not of a speculative theory, but of a rational life-history.

I have already explained that, in attempting such a life-history of religious institutions, we must begin by forming some preliminary ideas of the practical relation in which the gods of antiquity stood to their worshippers. I have now to add, that we shall also find it necessary to have before us from the outset some elementary notions of the relations which early races of mankind conceived to subsist between gods and men on the one hand, and the material universe on the other. All acts of ancient worship have a material embodiment, the form of which is determined by the consideration that gods and men alike stand in certain fixed relations to particular parts or aspects of physical nature. Certain places, certain things, even certain animal kinds are conceived as holy, i.e., as standing in a near relation to the gods, and claiming special reverence from men, and this conception plays a very large part in the development of all religious institutions. Here again we have a problem that cannot be solved by à priori methods; it is only as we move onward from step to step in the analysis of the details of ritual observances that we can hope to gain full insight into the relations of the gods to physical nature. But there are certain broad features in the ancient conception of the universe, and of the relations of its parts to one another, which can be grasped at once, upon a merely preliminary survey,

---

[4] See, for example, Plutarch's *Greek* and *Roman Questions*.

and we shall find it profitable to give attention to these at an early stage of our discussion.

I propose, therefore, to devote my second lecture to the nature of the antique religious community and the relations of the gods to their worshippers. After this we will proceed to consider the relations of the gods to physical nature, not in a complete or exhaustive way, but in a manner entirely preliminary and provisional, and only so far as is necessary to enable us to understand the material basis of ancient ritual. After these preliminary enquiries have furnished us with certain necessary points of view, we shall be in a position to take up the institutions of worship in an orderly manner, and make an attempt to work out their life-history. We shall find that the history of religious institutions is the history of ancient religion itself, as a practical force in the development of the human race, and that the articulate efforts of the antique intellect to comprehend the meaning of religion, the nature of the gods, and the principles on which they deal with men, take their point of departure from the unspoken ideas embodied in the traditional forms of ritual praxis. Whether the conscious efforts of ancient religious thinkers took the shape of mythological invention or of speculative construction, the raw material of thought upon which they operated was derived from the common traditional stock of religious conceptions that was handed on from generation to generation, not in express words, but in the form of religious custom.

In accordance with the rules of the Burnett Trust, three courses of lectures, to be delivered in successive winters, are allowed me for the development of this great subject. When the work was first entrusted to me, I formed the plan of dividing my task into three distinct parts. In the first course of lectures I hoped to cover the whole field of practical religious institutions. In the second I proposed to myself to discuss the nature and origin of the gods of Semitic heathenism, their relations to one another, the myths that surround them, and the whole subject of religious belief, so far as it is not directly involved in the observances of daily religious life. The third winter would thus have been left free for an examination of the part which Semitic religion has played in universal history, and its influence on the general progress of humanity, whether in virtue of the early contact of Semitic faiths with other systems of antique religion, or – what is more important – in virtue of the influence, both positive and negative, that the common type of Semitic religion has exercised on the formulas and structure of the great monotheistic faiths that have gone forth from the Semitic lands. But the first division of the subject has grown under my hands, and I find that it will not be possible in a single winter to cover the whole field of religious institutions in a way at all adequate to the fundamental importance of this part of the enquiry.

It will therefore be necessary to allow the first branch of the subject to run over into the second course, for which I reserve, among other matters of interest, the whole history of religious feasts and also that of the Semitic priesthoods. I hope, however, to give the present course a certain completeness in itself by carrying the investigation to the end of the great subject of sacrifice. The origin and meaning of sacrifice constitute the central problem of ancient religion, and when this problem has been disposed of we may naturally feel that we have reached a point of rest at which both speaker and hearers will be glad to make a pause.

Part II

DEVELOPMENT OF THE THEORY

2

THE GOLDEN BOUGH

James Frazer

James Frazer's *The Golden Bough* (1st edn, 1890, 2 vols) remains the most popular work of anthropology ever written. The Scottish classicist and anthropologist Frazer (1854–1941), who was a Fellow of Trinity College, Cambridge University, wrote ever longer editions of the tome (2nd edn, 1900, 3 vols; 3rd edn, 1911–15, 12 vols) and then a one-volume abridgment (1922). The heart of *The Golden Bough* is the analysis of the myths of Adonis, Attis, Osiris, and Dionysus. For Frazer, these figures are gods of vegetation, whose death and rebirth are annually enacted to spur their rebirth and, with it, the rebirth of vegetation. This version of myth-ritualism centers on the god and not on the king, who may or may not play the role of the vegetation god in the annual ritual. Frazer's alternative version of myth-ritualism, which appears here only in passing, centers on the king, who is himself killed and replaced to ensure the health of the vegetation god residing in him. The king is killed either annually or at the end of a fixed term. On this version of myth-ritualism see Frazer, *Lectures on the Early History of the Kingship* (London: Macmillan, 1905), which is incorporated in *The Magic Art and the Evolution of Kings*, the first two volumes of the third edition of *The Golden Bough* (London: Macmillan, 1911). The following selection from the abridged edition of *The Golden Bough* (London: Macmillan, 1922) presents the myth and ritual of Osiris (chs 38–40). For the unabridged presentation of Osiris from the third edition of *The Golden Bough* see volume 6, entitled *Adonis Attis Osiris* (London: Macmillan, 1914), 1–218. On Frazer see R. R. Marett, "James George Frazer, 1854–1941," *Proceedings of the British Academy* 27 (1941), 379–91; Edmund R. Leach, "Golden Bough or Gilded Twig?," *Daedalus* 90 (1961), 371–87; John B. Vickery, *The Literary Impact of "The Golden Bough"* (Princeton: Princeton University Press, 1973); Jonathan Z. Smith, "When the Bough Breaks," in his *Map Is Not Territory*

Original publication: James Frazer, *The Golden Bough*, abridged edn (London: Macmillan, 1922), chs 38–40 (pp. 420–43).

(Leiden: Brill, 1978), ch. 10; Robert Ackerman, *J. G. Frazer* (Cambridge: Cambridge University Press, 1987); Ackerman, *The Myth and Ritual School* (New York: Garland Publishing, 1991), ch. 4; Robert Fraser, *The Making of "The Golden Bough"* (London: Macmillan, 1990); and *Sir James Frazer and the Literary Imagination*, ed. Robert Fraser (London: Macmillan, 1990).

The Myth of Osiris

In ancient Egypt the god whose death and resurrection were annually celebrated with alternate sorrow and joy was Osiris, the most popular of all Egyptian deities; and there are good grounds for classing him in one of his aspects with Adonis and Attis as a personification of the great yearly vicissitudes of nature, especially of the corn. But the immense vogue which he enjoyed for many ages induced his devoted worshippers to heap upon him the attributes and powers of many other gods; so that it is not always easy to strip him, so to say, of his borrowed plumes and to restore them to their proper owners.

The story of Osiris is told in a connected form only by Plutarch, whose narrative has been confirmed and to some extent amplified in modern times by the evidence of the monuments.

Osiris was the offspring of an intrigue between the earth-god Seb (Keb or Geb, as the name is sometimes transliterated) and the sky-goddess Nut. The Greeks identified his parents with their own deities Cronus and Rhea. When the sun-god Ra perceived that his wife Nut had been unfaithful to him, he declared with a curse that she should be delivered of the child in no month and no year. But the goddess had another lover, the god Thoth or Hermes, as the Greeks called him, and he playing at draughts with the moon won from her a seventy-second part of every day, and having compounded five whole days out of these parts he added them to the Egyptian year of three hundred and sixty days. This was the mythical origin of the five supplementary days which the Egyptians annually inserted at the end of every year in order to establish a harmony between lunar and solar time. On these five days, regarded as outside the year of twelve months, the curse of the sun-god did not rest, and accordingly Osiris was born on the first of them. At his nativity a voice rang out proclaiming that the Lord of All had come into the world. Some say that a certain Pamyles heard a voice from the temple at Thebes bidding him announce with a shout that a great king, the beneficent Osiris, was born. But Osiris was not the only child of his mother. On the second of the supplementary days she gave birth to the elder Horus, on the third to the god Set, whom the Greeks called Typhon, on the fourth to the goddess Isis, and on the fifth to the goddess Nephthys. Afterwards Set married his sister Nephthys, and Osiris married his sister Isis.

Reigning as a king on earth, Osiris reclaimed the Egyptians from savagery, gave them laws, and taught them to worship the gods. Before his time the Egyptians had been cannibals. But Isis, the sister and wife of Osiris, discovered wheat and barley growing wild, and Osiris introduced the cultivation of these grains amongst his people, who forthwith abandoned cannibalism and took kindly to a corn diet. Moreover, Osiris is said to have been the first to gather fruit from trees, to train the vine to poles, and to tread the grapes. Eager to communicate these beneficent discoveries to all mankind, he committed the whole government of Egypt to his wife Isis, and travelled over the world, diffusing the blessings of civilisation and agriculture wherever he went. In countries where a harsh climate or niggardly soil forbade the cultivation of the vine, he taught the inhabitants to console themselves for the want of wine by brewing beer from barley. Loaded with the wealth that had been showered upon him by grateful nations, he returned to Egypt, and on account of the benefits he had conferred on mankind he was unanimously hailed and worshipped as a deity. But his brother Set (whom the Greeks called Typhon) with seventy-two others plotted against him. Having taken the measure of his good brother's body by stealth, the bad brother Typhon fashioned and highly decorated a coffer of the same size, and once when they were all drinking and making merry he brought in the coffer and jestingly promised to give it to the one whom it should fit exactly. Well, they all tried one after the other, but it fitted none of them. Last of all Osiris stepped into it and lay down. On that the conspirators ran and slammed the lid down on him, nailed it fast, soldered it with molten lead, and flung the coffer into the Nile. This happened on the seventeenth day of the month Athyr, when the sun is in the sign of the Scorpion, and in the eight-and-twentieth year of the reign or the life of Osiris. When Isis heard of it she sheared off a lock of her hair, put on a mourning attire, and wandered disconsolately up and down, seeking the body.

By the advice of the god of wisdom she took refuge in the papyrus swamps of the Delta. Seven scorpions accompanied her in her flight. One evening when she was weary she came to the house of a woman, who, alarmed at the sight of the scorpions, shut the door in her face. Then one of the scorpions crept under the door and stung the child of the woman that he died. But when Isis heard the mother's lamentation, her heart was touched, and she laid her hands on the child and uttered her powerful spells; so the poison was driven out of the child and he lived. Afterwards Isis herself gave birth to a son in the swamps. She had conceived him while she fluttered in the form of a hawk over the corpse of her dead husband. The infant was the younger Horus, who in his youth bore the name of Harpocrates, that is, the child Horus. Him Buto, the goddess of the north, hid from the wrath of his wicked uncle Set. Yet she could not guard him from all mishap; for one day when Isis came to her little son's hiding-place she found him stretched lifeless and rigid on the ground: a scorpion had stung him. Then Isis prayed to the sun-god Ra for help. The god hearkened to her and staid his bark in the sky, and sent down Thoth to teach her the spell by which she might restore her son to life. She uttered the words of power, and straightway the poison flowed from the body of Horus, air passed into him, and he lived. Then Thoth ascended up into the sky and took his place once more in the bark of the sun, and the bright pomp passed onward jubilant.

Meantime the coffer containing the body of Osiris had floated down the river and away out to sea, till at last it drifted ashore at Byblus, on the coast of Syria. Here a fine *erica*-tree shot up suddenly and enclosed the chest in its trunk. The king of the country, admiring the growth of the tree, had it cut down and made into a pillar of his house; but he did not know that the coffer with the dead Osiris was in it. Word of this came to Isis and she journeyed to Byblus, and sat down by the well, in humble guise, her face wet with tears. To none would she speak till the king's handmaidens came, and them she greeted kindly, and braided their hair, and breathed on them from her own divine body a wondrous perfume. But when the queen beheld the braids of her handmaidens' hair and smelt the sweet smell that emanated from them, she sent for the stranger woman and took her into her house and made her the nurse of her child. But Isis gave the babe her finger instead of her breast to suck, and at night she began to burn all that was mortal of him away, while she herself in the likeness of a swallow fluttered round the pillar that contained her dead brother, twittering mournfully. But the queen spied what she was doing and shrieked out when she saw her child in flames, and thereby she hindered him from becoming immortal. Then the goddess revealed herself and begged for the pillar of the roof, and they gave it her, and she cut the coffer out of it, and fell upon it and embraced it and lamented so loud that the younger of the king's children died of fright on the spot. But the trunk of the tree she wrapped in fine linen, and poured ointment on it, and gave it to the king and queen, and the wood stands in a temple of Isis and is worshipped by the people of Byblus to this day. And Isis put the coffer in a boat and took the eldest of the king's children with her and sailed away. As soon as they were alone, she opened the chest, and laying her face on the face of her brother she kissed him and wept. But the child came behind her softly and saw what she was about, and she turned and looked at him in anger, and the child could not bear her look and died; but some say that it was not so, but that he fell into the sea and was drowned. It is he whom the Egyptians sing of at their banquets under the name of Maneros.

But Isis put the coffer by and went to see her son Horus at the city of Buto, and Typhon found the coffer as he was hunting a boat one night by the light of a full moon. And he knew the body, and rent it into fourteen pieces, and scattered them abroad. But Isis sailed up and down the marshes in a shallop made of papyrus, looking for the pieces; and that is why when people sail in shallops made of papyrus, the crocodiles do not hurt them, for they fear or respect the goddess. And that is the reason, too, why there are many graves of Osiris in Egypt, for she buried each limb as she found it. But others will have it that she buried an image of him in every city, pretending it was his body, in order that Osiris might be worshipped in many places, and that if Typhon searched for the real grave he might not be able to find it. However, the genital member of Osiris had been eaten by the fishes, so Isis made an image of it instead, and the image is used by the Egyptians at their festivals to this day. "Isis," writes the historian Diodorus Siculus, "recovered all the parts of the body except the genitals; and because she wished that her husband's grave should be unknown and honoured by all who dwell in the land of Egypt, she resorted to the following device. She moulded human images out of wax and spices, corresponding to the stature of Osiris, round each one of the parts of his body. Then she called in the priests according to their families and took an oath of them all that they would reveal to no man the trust she was about to repose in them. So to each of them privately she said that to them alone she entrusted the burial of the body, and reminding them of the benefits they had received she exhorted them to bury the body in their own land and to honour Osiris as a god. She also besought them to dedicate one of the animals of their country, whichever they chose, and to honour it in life as they had formerly honoured Osiris, and when it died to grant it obsequies like his. And because she would encourage the priests in their own interest to bestow the aforesaid honours, she gave them a third part of the land to be used by them in the service and worship of the gods. Accordingly it is said that the priests, mindful of the benefits of Osiris, desirous of gratifying the queen, and moved by the prospect of gain, carried out all the injunctions of Isis. Wherefore to this day each of the priests imagines that Osiris is buried in his country, and they honour the beasts that were consecrated in the beginning, and when the animals die the priests renew at their burial the mourning for Osiris. But the sacred bulls, the one called Apis and the other Mnevis, were dedicated to Osiris, and it was ordained that they should be worshipped as gods in common by all the Egyptians, since these animals above all others had helped the discoverers of corn in sowing the seed and procuring the universal benefits of agriculture."

Such is the myth or legend of Osiris, as told by Greek writers and eked out by more or less fragmentary notices or allusions in native Egyptian literature. A long inscription in the temple at Denderah has preserved a list of the god's graves, and other texts mention the parts of his body which were treasured as holy relics in each of the sanctuaries. Thus his heart was at Athribis, his backbone at Busiris, his neck at Letopolis, and his head at Memphis. As often happens in such cases, some of his divine limbs were miraculously multiplied. His head, for example, was at Abydos as well as at Memphis, and his legs, which were remarkably numerous, would have sufficed for several ordinary mortals. In this respect, however, Osiris was nothing to St Denys, of whom no less than seven heads, all equally genuine, are extant.

According to native Egyptian accounts, which supplement that of Plutarch, when Isis had found the corpse of her husband Osiris, she and her sister Nephthys sat down beside it and uttered a lament which in after ages became the type of all Egyptian lamentations for the dead. "Come to thy house," they wailed. "Come to thy house. O god On! come to thy house, thou who hast no foes. O fair youth, come to thy house, that thou mayest see me. I am thy sister, whom thou lovest; thou shalt not part from me. O fair boy, come to thy house. . . . I see thee not, yet doth my heart yearn after thee and mine eyes desire thee. Come to her who loves thee, who loves thee, Unnefer, thou blessed one! Come to thy sister, come to thy wife, to thy wife, thou whose heart stands still. Come to thy housewife. I am thy sister by the same mother, thou shalt not be far from me. Gods and men have turned their faces towards thee and weep for thee together. . . . I call after thee and weep, so that my cry is heard to heaven, but thou hearest not my voice; yet am I thy sister, whom thou didst love on earth; thou didst love none but me, my brother! my brother!" This lament for the fair youth cut off in his prime reminds us of the laments for Adonis. The title of Unnefer or "the Good Being" bestowed on him marks the beneficence which tradition universally ascribed to Osiris; it was at once his commonest title and one of his names as king.

The lamentations of the two sad sisters were not in vain. In pity for her sorrow the sun-god Ra sent down from heaven the jackal-headed god Anubis, who, with the aid of Isis and Nephthys, of Thoth and Horus, pieced together the broken body of the murdered god, swathed it in linen bandages, and observed all the other rites which the Egyptians were wont to perform over the bodies of the departed. Then Isis fanned the cold clay with her wings: Osiris revived, and thenceforth reigned as king over the dead in the other world. There he bore the titles of Lord of the Underworld, Lord of Eternity, Ruler of the Dead. There, too, in the great Hall of the Two Truths, assisted by forty-two assessors, one from each of the principal districts of Egypt, he presided as judge at the trial of the souls of the departed, who made their solemn confession before him, and, their heart having been weighed in the balance of justice, received the reward of virtue in a life eternal or the appropriate punishment of their sins.

In the resurrection of Osiris the Egyptians saw the pledge of a life ever-lasting for themselves beyond the grave. They believed that every man would live eternally in the other world if only his surviving friends did for his body what the gods had done for the body of Osiris. Hence the ceremonies observed by the Egyptians over the human dead were an exact copy of those which Anubis, Horus, and the rest had performed over the dead god. "At every burial there was enacted a representation of the divine mystery which had been performed of old over Osiris, when his son, his sisters, his friends were gathered round his mangled remains and succeeded by their spells and manipulations in convert-ing his broken body into the first mummy, which they afterwards reanimated and furnished with the means of entering on a new individual life beyond the grave. The mummy of the deceased was Osiris; the professional female mourners were his two sisters Isis and Nephthys; Anubis, Horus, all the gods of the Osirian legend gathered about the corpse." In this way every dead Egyptian was identified with Osiris and bore his name. From the Middle Kingdom onwards it was the regular practice to address the deceased as "Osiris So-and-So," as if he were the god himself, and to add the standing epithet "true of speech," because true speech was characteristic of Osiris. The thousands of inscribed and pictured tombs that have been opened in the valley of the Nile prove that the mystery of the resurrection was performed for the benefit of every dead Egyptian; as Osiris died and rose again from the dead, so all men hoped to arise like him from death to life eternal.

Thus according to what seems to have been the general native tradition Osiris was a good and beloved king of Egypt, who suffered a violent death but rose from the dead and was henceforth worshipped as a deity. In harmony with this tradition he was regularly represented by sculptors and painters in human and regal form as a dead king, swathed in the wrappings of a mummy, but wearing on his head a kingly crown and grasping in one of his hands, which were left free from the bandages, a kingly sceptre. Two cities above all others were associated with his myth or memory. One of them was Busiris in Lower Egypt, which claimed to possess his backbone; the other was Abydos in Upper Egypt, which gloried in the possession of his head. Encircled by the nimbus of the dead yet living god, Abydos, originally an obscure place, became from the end of the Old Kingdom the holiest spot in Egypt; his tomb there would seem to have been to the Egyptians what the Church of the Holy Sepulchre at Jerusalem is to Christians. It was the wish of every pious man that his dead body should rest in hallowed earth near the grave of the glorified Osiris. Few indeed were rich enough to enjoy this inestimable privilege; for, apart from the cost of a tomb in the sacred city, the mere transport of mummies from great distances was both difficult and expensive. Yet so eager were many to absorb in death the blessed influence which radiated from the holy sepulchre that they caused their surviving friends to convey their mortal remains to Abydos, there to tarry for a short time, and then to be brought back by river and interred in the tombs which had been made ready for them in their native land. Others had cenotaphs built or memorial tablets erected for themselves near the tomb of their dead and risen Lord, that they might share with him the bliss of a joyful resurrection.

The Ritual of Osiris

The popular rites

A useful clue to the original nature of a god or goddess is often furnished by the season at which his or her festival is celebrated. Thus, if the festival falls at the new or the full moon, there is a certain presumption that the deity thus honoured either is the moon or at least has lunar affinities. If the festival is held at the winter or summer solstice, we naturally surmise that the god is the sun, or at all events that he stands in some close relation to that luminary. Again, if the festival coincides with the time of sowing or harvest, we are inclined to infer that the divinity is an embodiment of the earth or of the corn. These presumptions or inferences, taken by themselves, are by no means conclusive; but if they happen to be confirmed by other indications, the evidence may be regarded as fairly strong.

Unfortunately, in dealing with the Egyptian gods we are in a great measure precluded from making use of this clue. The reason is not that the dates of the festivals are always unknown, but that they shifted from year to year, until after a long interval they had revolved through the whole course of the seasons. This gradual revolution of the festal Egyptian cycle resulted from the employment of a calendar year which neither corresponded exactly to the solar year nor was periodically corrected by intercalation.

If the Egyptian farmer of the olden time could get no help, except at the rarest intervals, from the official or sacerdotal calendar, he must have been compelled to observe for himself those natural signals which marked the times for the various operations of husbandry. In all ages of which we possess any records the Egyptians have been an agricultural people, dependent for their subsistence on the growth of the corn. The cereals which they cultivated were wheat, barley, and apparently sorghum (*Holcus sorghum*, Linnaeus), the *doora* of the modern fellaheen. Then as now the whole country, with the exception of a fringe on the coast of the Mediterranean, was almost rainless, and owed its immense fertility entirely to the annual inundation of the Nile, which, regulated by an elaborate system of dams and canals, was distributed over the fields, renewing the soil year by year with a fresh deposit of mud washed down from the great equatorial lakes and the mountains of Abyssinia. Hence the rise of the river has always been watched by the inhabitants with the utmost anxiety; for if it either falls short of or exceeds a certain height, dearth and famine are the inevitable consequences. The water begins to rise early in June, but it is not until the latter half of July that it swells to a mighty tide. By the end of September the inundation is at its greatest height. The country is now submerged, and presents the appearance of a sea of turbid water, from which the towns and villages, built on higher ground, rise like islands. For about a month the flood remains nearly stationary, then sinks more and more rapidly, till by December or January the river has returned to its ordinary bed. With the approach of summer the level of the water continues to fall. In the early days of June the Nile is reduced to half its ordinary breadth; and Egypt, scorched by the sun, blasted by the wind that has blown from the Sahara for many days, seems a mere continuation of the desert. The trees are choked with a thick layer of grey dust. A few meagre patches of vegetables, watered with difficulty, struggle painfully for existence in the immediate neighbourhood of the villages. Some appearance of verdure lingers beside the canals and in the hollows from which the moisture has not wholly evaporated. The plain appears to pant in the pitiless sunshine, bare, dusty, ash-coloured cracked and seamed as far as the eye can see with a network of fissures. From the middle of April till the middle of June the land of Egypt is but half alive, waiting for the new Nile.

For countless ages this cycle of natural events has determined the annual labours of the Egyptian husbandman. The first work of the agricultural year is the cutting of the dams which have hitherto prevented the swollen river from flooding the canals and the fields. This is done, and the pent-up waters released on their beneficent mission, in the first half of August. In November, when the inundation has subsided, wheat, barley, and sorghum are sown. The time of harvest varies with the district, falling about a month later in the north than in the south. In Upper or Southern Egypt barley is reaped at the beginning of March, wheat at the beginning of April, and sorghum about the end of that month.

It is natural to suppose that the various events of the agricultural year were celebrated by the Egyptian farmer with some simple religious rites designed to secure the blessing of the gods upon his labours. These rustic ceremonies he would continue to perform year after year at the same season, while the solemn festivals of the priests continued to shift, with the shifting calendar, from summer through spring to winter, and so backward through autumn to summer. The rites of the husbandman were stable because they rested on direct observation of nature: the rites of the priest were unstable because they were based on a false calculation. Yet many of the priestly festivals may have been nothing but the old rural festivals disguised in the course of ages by the pomp of sacerdotalism and severed, by the error of the calendar, from their roots in the natural cycle of the seasons.

These conjectures are confirmed by the little we know both of the popular and of the official Egyptian religion. Thus we are told that the Egyptians held a festival of Isis at the time when the Nile began to rise. They believed that the goddess was then mourning for the lost Osiris, and that the tears which dropped from her eyes swelled the impetuous tide of the river. Now if Osiris was in one of his aspects a god of the corn, nothing could be more natural than that he should be mourned at midsummer. For by that time the harvest was past, the fields were bare, the river ran low, life seemed to be suspended, the corn-god was dead. At such a moment people who saw the handiwork of divine beings in all the operations of nature might well trace the swelling of the sacred stream to the tears shed by the goddess at the death of the beneficent corn-god her husband.

And the sign of the rising waters on earth was accompanied by a sign in heaven. For in the early days of Egyptian history, some three or four thousand years before the beginning of our era, the splendid star of Sirius, the brightest of all the fixed stars, appeared at dawn in the east just before sunrise about the time of the summer solstice, when the Nile begins to rise. The Egyptians called it Sothis, and regarded it as the star of Isis, just as the Babylonians deemed the planet Venus the star of Astarte. To both people apparently the brilliant luminary in the morning sky seemed the goddess of life and love come to mourn her departed lover or spouse and to wake him from the dead. Hence the rising of Sirius marked the beginning of the sacred Egyptian year, and was regularly celebrated by a festival which did not shift with the shifting official year.

The cutting of the dams and the admission of the water into the canals and fields is a great event in the Egyptian year. At Cairo the operation generally takes place between the sixth and the sixteenth of August, and till lately was attended by ceremonies which deserve to be noticed, because they were probably handed down from antiquity. An ancient canal, known by the name of the Khalíj, formerly passed through the native town of Cairo. Near its entrance the canal was crossed by a dam of earth, very broad at the bottom and diminishing in breadth upwards, which used to be constructed before or soon after the Nile began to rise. In front of the dam, on the side of the river, was reared a truncated cone of earth called the 'arooseh or "bride," on the top of which a little maize or millet was generally sown. This "bride" was commonly washed down by the rising tide a week or a fortnight before the cutting of the dam. Tradition runs that the old custom was to deck a young virgin in gay apparel and throw her into the river as a sacrifice to obtain a plentiful inundation. Whether that was so or not, the intention of the practice appears to have been to marry the river, conceived as a male power, to his bride the cornland, which was so soon to be fertilised by his water. The ceremony was therefore a charm to ensure the growth of the crops. In modern times money used to be thrown into the canal on this occasion, and the populace dived into the water after it. This practice also would seem to have been ancient, for Seneca tells us that at a place called the Veins of the Nile, not far from Philae, the priests used to cast money and offerings of gold into the river at a festival which apparently took place at the rising of the water.

The next great operation of the agricultural year in Egypt is the sowing of the seed in November, when the water of the inundation has retreated from the fields. With the Egyptians, as with many peoples of antiquity, the committing of the seed to the earth assumed the character of a solemn and mournful rite. On this subject I will let Plutarch speak for himself. "What," he asks, "are we to make of the gloomy, joyless, and mournful sacrifices, if it is wrong either to omit the established rites or to confuse and disturb our conceptions of the gods by absurd suspicions? For the Greeks also perform many rites which resemble those of the Egyptians and are observed about the same time. Thus at the festival of the Thesmophoria in Athens women sit on the ground and fast. And the Boeotians open the vaults of the Sorrowful One, naming that festival sorrowful because Demeter is sorrowing for the descent of the Maiden. The month is the month of sowing about the setting of the Pleiades. The Egyptians call it Athyr, the Athenians Pyanepsion, the Boeotians the month of Demeter. . . . For it was that time of year when they saw some of the fruits vanishing and failing from the trees, while they sowed others grudgingly and with difficulty, scraping the earth with their hands and huddling it up again, on the uncertain chance that what they deposited in the ground would ever ripen and come to maturity. Thus they did in many respects like those who bury and mourn their dead."

The Egyptian harvest, as we have seen, falls not in autumn but in spring, in the months of March, April, and May. To the husbandman the time of harvest, at least in a good year, must necessarily be a season of joy: in bringing home his sheaves he is requited for his long and anxious labours. Yet if the old Egyptian farmer felt a secret joy at reaping and garnering the grain, it was essential that he should conceal the natural emotion under an air of profound dejection. For was he not severing the body of the corn-god with his sickle and trampling it to pieces under the hoofs of his cattle on the threshing-floor? Accordingly we are told that it was an ancient custom of the Egyptian corn-reapers to beat their breasts and lament over the first sheaf cut, while at the same time they called upon Isis. The invocation seems to have taken the form of a melancholy chant, to which the Greeks gave the name of Maneros. Similar plaintive strains were chanted by corn-reapers in Phoenicia and other parts of Western Asia. Probably all these doleful ditties were lamentations for the corn-god killed by the sickles of the reapers. In Egypt the slain deity was Osiris, and the name *Maneros*, applied to the dirge, appears to be derived from certain words meaning "Come to thy house," which often occur in the lamentations for the dead god.

Ceremonies of the same sort have been observed by other peoples, probably for the same purpose. Thus we are told that among all vegetables corn, by which is apparently meant maize, holds the first place in the household economy and the ceremonial observance of the Cherokee Indians, who invoke it under the name of "the Old Woman" in allusion to a myth that it sprang from the blood of an old woman killed by her disobedient sons. After the last working of the crop a priest and his assistant went into the field and sang songs of invocation to the spirit of the corn. After that a loud rustling would be heard, which was thought to be caused by the Old Woman bringing the corn into the field. A clear trail was always kept from the field to the house, "so that the corn might be encouraged to stay at home and not go wandering elsewhere." "Another curious ceremony, of which even the memory is now almost forgotten, was enacted after the first working of the corn, when the owner or priest stood in succession at each of the four corners of the field and wept and wailed loudly. Even the priests are now unable to give a reason for this performance, which may have been a lament for the bloody death of Selu," the Old Woman of the Corn. In these Cherokee practices the lamentations and the invocations of the Old Woman of the Corn resemble the ancient Egyptian customs of lamenting over the first corn cut and calling upon Isis, herself probably in one of her aspects an Old Woman of the Corn. Further, the Cherokee precaution of leaving a clear path from the field to the house resembles the Egyptian invitation to Osiris, "Come to thy house." So in the East Indies to this day people observe elaborate ceremonies for the purpose of bringing back the Soul of the Rice from the fields to the barn. The Nandi of East Africa perform a ceremony in September when the eleusine grain is ripening. Every woman who owns a plantation goes out with her daughters into the cornfields and makes a bonfire of the branches and leaves of certain tress. After that they pluck some of the eleusine, and each of them puts one grain in her necklace, chews another and rubs it on her forehead, throat, and breast. "No joy is shown by the womenfolk on this occasion, and they sorrowfully cut a basketful of the corn which they take home with them and place in the loft to dry."

The conception of the corn-spirit as old and dead at harvest is very clearly embodied in a custom observed by the Arabs of Moab. When the harvesters have nearly finished their task and only a small corner of the field remains to be reaped, the owner takes a handful of wheat tied up in a sheaf. A hole is dug in the form of a grave, and two stones are set upright, one at the head and the other at the foot, just as in an ordinary burial. Then the sheaf of wheat is laid at the bottom of the grave, and the sheikh pronounces these words, "The old man is dead." Earth is afterwards thrown in to cover the sheaf, with a prayer, "May Allah bring us back the wheat of the dead."

The official rites

Such, then, were the principal events of the farmer's calendar in ancient Egypt, and such the simple religious rites by which he celebrated them. But we have still to consider the Osirian festivals of the official calendar, so far as these are described by Greek writers or recorded on the monuments. In examining them it is necessary to bear in mind that on account of the movable year of the old Egyptian calendar the true or astronomical dates of the official festivals must have varied from year to year, at least until the adoption of the fixed Alexandrian year in 30 BC. From that time onward, apparently, the dates of the festivals were determined by the new calendar, and so ceased to rotate throughout the length of the solar year. At all events Plutarch, writing about the end of the first century, implies that they were then fixed, not movable; for though he does not mention the Alexandrian calendar, he clearly dates the festivals by it. Moreover, the long festal calendar of Esne, an important document of the Imperial age, is obviously based on the fixed Alexandrian year; for it assigns the mark for New Year's Day to the day which corresponds to the twenty-ninth of August, which was the first day of the Alexandrian year, and its references to the rising of the Nile, the position of the sun, and the operations of agriculture are all in harmony with this supposition. Thus we may take it as fairly certain that from 30 BC onwards the Egyptian festivals were stationary in the solar year.

Herodotus tells us that the grave of Osiris was at Sais in Lower Egypt, and that there was a lake there upon which the sufferings of the god were displayed as a mystery by night. This commemoration of the divine passion was held once a year: the people mourned and beat their breasts at it to testify their sorrow for the death of the god; and an image of a cow, made of gilt wood with a golden sun between its horns, was carried out of the chamber in which it stood the rest of the year. The cow no doubt represented Isis herself, for cows were sacred to her, and she was regularly depicted with the horns of a cow on her head, or even as a woman with the head of a cow. It is probable that the carrying out of her cow-shaped image symbolised the goddess searching for the dead body of Osiris; for this was the native Egyptian interpretation of a similar ceremony observed in Plutarch's time about the winter solstice, when the gilt cow was carried seven times round the temple. A great feature of the festival was the nocturnal illumination. People fastened rows of oil-lamps to the outside of their houses, and the lamps burned all night long. The custom was not confined to Sais, but was observed throughout the whole of Egypt.

This universal illumination of the houses on one night of the year suggests that the festival may have been a commemoration not merely of the dead Osiris but of the dead in general, in other words, that it may have been a night of All Souls. For it is a widespread belief that the souls of the dead revisit their old homes on one night of the year; and on that solemn occasion people prepare for the reception of the ghosts by laying out food for them to eat, and lighting lamps to guide them on their dark road from and to the grave. Herodotus, who briefly describes the festival, omits to mention its date, but we can determine it with some probability from other sources. Thus Plutarch tells us that Osiris was murdered on the seventeenth of the month Athyr, and that the Egyptians accordingly observed mournful rites for four days from the seventeenth of Athyr. Now in the Alexandrian calendar, which Plutarch used, these four days corresponded to the thirteenth, fourteenth, fifteenth, and sixteenth of November, and this date answers exactly to the other indications given by Plutarch, who says that at the time of the festival the Nile was sinking, the north winds dying away, the nights lengthening, and the leaves falling from the trees. During these four days a gilt cow swathed in a black pall was exhibited as an image of Isis. This, no doubt, was the image mentioned by Herodotus in his account of the festival. On the nineteenth day of the month the people went down to the sea, the priests carrying a shrine which contained a golden casket. Into this casket they poured fresh water, and thereupon the spectators raised a shout that Osiris was found. After that they took some vegetable mould, moistened it with water, mixed it with precious spices and incense, and moulded the paste into a small moon-shaped image, which was then robed and ornamented. Thus it appears that the purpose of the ceremonies described by Plutarch was to represent dramatically, first, the search for the dead body of Osiris, and, second, its joyful discovery, followed by the resurrection of the dead god who came to life again in the new image of vegetable mould and spices. Lactantius tells us how on these occasions the priests, with their shaven bodies, beat their breasts and lamented, imitating the sorrowful search of Isis for her lost son Osiris, and how afterwards their sorrow was turned to joy when the jackal-headed god Anubis, or rather a mummer in his stead, produced a small boy, the living representative of the god who was lost and was found. Thus Lactantius regarded Osiris as the son instead of the husband of Isis, and he makes no mention of the image of vegetable mould. It is probable that the boy who figured in the sacred drama played the part, not of Osiris, but of his son Horus; but as the death and resurrection of the god were celebrated in many cities of Egypt, it is also possible that in some places the part of the god come to life was played by a living actor instead of by an image. Another Christian writer describes how the Egyptians, with shorn heads, annually lamented over a buried idol of Osiris, smiting their breasts, slashing their shoulders, ripping open their old wounds, until, after several days of mourning, they professed to find the mangled remains of the god, at which they rejoiced. However the details of the ceremony may have varied in different places, the pretence of finding the god's body, and probably of restoring it to life, was a great event in the festal year of the Egyptians. The shouts of joy which greeted it are described or alluded to by many ancient writers.

The funeral rites of Osiris, as they were observed at his great festival in the sixteen provinces of Egypt, are described in a long inscription of the Ptolemaic period, which is engraved on the walls of the god's temple at Denderah, the Tentyra of the Greeks, a town of Upper Egypt situated on the western bank of the Nile about forty miles north of Thebes. Unfortunately, while the information thus furnished is remarkably full and minute on many points, the arrangement adopted in the inscription is so confused and the expression often so obscure that a clear and consistent account of the ceremonies as a whole can hardly be extracted from it. Moreover, we learn from the document that the ceremonies varied somewhat in the several cities, the ritual of Abydos, for example, differing from that of Busiris. Without attempting to trace all the particularities of local usage I shall briefly indicate what seem to have been the leading features of the festival, so far as these can be ascertained with tolerable certainty.

The rites lasted eighteen days, from the twelfth to the thirtieth of the month Khoiak, and set forth the nature of Osiris in his triple aspect as dead, dismembered, and finally reconstituted by the union of his scattered limbs. In the first of these aspects he was called Chent-Ament (Khenti-Amenti), in the second

Osiris-Sep, and in the third Sokari (Seker). Small images of the god were moulded of sand or vegetable earth and corn, to which incense was sometimes added; his face was painted yellow and his cheek-bones green. These images were cast in a mould of pure gold, which represented the god in the form of a mummy, with the white crown of Egypt on his head. The festival opened on the twelfth day of Khoiak with a ceremony of ploughing and sowing. Two black cows were yoked to the plough, which was made of tamarisk wood, while the share was of black copper. A boy scattered the seed. One end of the field was sown with barley, the other with spelt, and the middle with flax. During the operation the chief celebrant recited the ritual chapter of "the sowing of the fields." At Busiris on the twentieth of Khoiak sand and barley were put in the god's "garden," which appears to have been a sort of large flower-pot. This was done in the presence of the cow-goddess Shenty, represented seemingly by the image of a cow made of gilt sycamore wood with a headless human image in its inside. "Then fresh inundation water was poured out of a golden vase over both the goddess and the 'garden,' and the barley was allowed to grow as the emblem of the resurrection of the god after his burial in the earth, 'for the growth of the garden is the growth of the divine substance.'" On the twenty-second of Khoiak, at the eighth hour, the images of Osiris, attended by thirty-four images of deities, performed a mysterious voyage in thirty-four tiny boats made of papyrus, which were illuminated by three hundred and sixty-five lights. On the twenty-fourth of Khoiak, after sunset, the effigy of Osiris in a coffin of mulberry wood was laid in the grave, and at the ninth hour of the night the effigy which had been made and deposited the year before was removed and placed upon boughs of sycamore. Lastly, on the thirtieth day of Khoiak they repaired to the holy sepulchre, a subterranean chamber over which appears to have grown a clump of Persea-trees. Entering the vault by the western door, they laid the coffined effigy of the dead god reverently of a bed of sand in the chamber. So they left him to his rest, and departed from the sepulchre by the eastern door. Thus ended the ceremonies in the month of Khoiak.

In the foregoing account of the festival, drawn from the great inscription of Denderah, the burial of Osiris figures prominently, while his resurrection is implied rather than expressed. This defect of the document, however, is amply compensated by a remarkable series of bas-reliefs which accompany and illustrate the inscription. These exhibit in a series of scenes the dead god lying swathed as a mummy on his bier, then gradually raising himself up higher and higher, until at last he has entirely quitted the bier and is seen erect between the guardian wings of the faithful Isis, who stands behind him, while a male figure holds up before his eyes the *crux ansata*, the Egyptian symbol of life. The resurrection of the god could hardly be portrayed more graphically. Even more instructive, however, is another representation of the same event in a chamber dedicated to Osiris in the great temple of Isis at Philae. Here we see the dead body of Osiris with stalks of corn springing from it, while a priest waters the stalks from a pitcher which he holds in his hand. The accompanying inscription sets forth that "this is the form of him whom one may not name, Osiris of the mysteries, who springs from the returning waters." Taken together, the picture and the words seem to leave no doubt that Osiris was here conceived and represented as a personification of the corn which springs from the fields after they have been fertilised by the inundation. This, according to the inscription, was the kernel of the mysteries, the innermost secret revealed to the initiated. So in the rites of Demeter at Eleusis a reaped ear of corn was exhibited to the worshippers as the central mystery of their religion. We can now fully understand why at the great festival of sowing in the month of Khoiak the priests used to bury effigies of Osiris made of earth and corn. When these effigies were taken up again at the end of a year or of a shorter interval, the corn would be found to have sprouted from the body of Osiris, and this sprouting of the grain would be hailed as an omen, or rather as the cause, of the growth of the crops. The corn-god produced the corn from himself: he gave his own body to feed the people: he died that they might live.

And from the death and resurrection of their great god the Egyptians drew not only their support and sustenance in this life, but also their hope of a life eternal beyond the grave. This hope is indicated in the clearest manner by the very remarkable effigies of Osiris which have come to light in Egyptian cemeteries. Thus in the Valley of the Kings at Thebes there was found the tomb of a royal fan-bearer who lived about 1500 BC. Among the rich contents of the tomb there was a bier on which rested a mattress of reeds covered with three layers of linen. On the upper side of the linen was painted a life-size figure of Osiris; and the interior of the figure, which was waterproof, contained a mixture of vegetable mould, barley, and a sticky fluid. The barley had sprouted and sent out shoots two or three inches long. Again, in the cemetery at Cynopolis "were numerous burials of Osiris figures. These were made of grain wrapped up in cloth and roughly shaped like an Osiris, and placed inside a bricked-up recess at the side of the tomb, sometimes in small pottery coffins, sometimes in wooden coffins in the form of a hawk-mummy, sometimes without any coffins at all." These corn-stuffed figures were bandaged like mummies with patches of gilding here and there, as if in imitation of the golden mould in which the similar figures of Osiris were cast at the festival of sowing. Again, effigies of Osiris, with faces of green wax and their interior full of grain, were found buried near the necropolis of Thebes. Finally, we are told by Professor Erman that between the legs of mummies "there sometimes lies a figure of Osiris made of slime; it is filled with grains of corn, the sprouting of which is intended to signify the resurrection of the god." We cannot doubt that, just as the burial of corn-stuffed images of Osiris in the earth at the festival of sowing was designed to quicken the seed, so the burial of similar images in the grave was meant to quicken the dead, in other words, to ensure their spiritual immortality.

The Nature of Osiris

Osiris a corn-god

The foregoing survey of the myth and ritual of Osiris may suffice to prove that in one of his aspects the god was a personification of the corn, which may be said to die and come to life again every year. Through all the pomp and glamour with which in later times the priests had invested his worship, the conception of him as the corn-god comes clearly out in the festival of his death and resurrection, which was celebrated in the month of Khoiak and at a later period in the month of Athyr. That festival appears to have been essentially a festival of sowing, which properly fell at the time when the husbandman actually committed the seed to the earth. On that occasion an effigy of the corn-god, moulded of earth and corn, was buried with funeral rites in the ground in order that, dying there, he might come to life again with the new crops. The ceremony was, in fact, a charm to ensure the growth of the corn by sympathetic magic, and we may conjecture that as such it was practised in a simple form by every Egyptian farmer on his fields long before it was adopted and transfigured by the priests in the stately ritual of the temple. In the modern, but doubtless ancient, Arab custom of burying "the Old Man," namely, a sheaf of wheat, in the harvest-field and praying that he may return from the dead, we see the germ out of which the worship of the corn-god Osiris was probably developed.

The details of his myth fit in well with this interpretation of the god. He was said to be the offspring of Sky and Earth. What more appropriate parentage could be invented for the corn which springs from the ground that has been fertilised by the water of heaven? It is true that the land of Egypt owed its fertility directly to the Nile and not to showers; but the inhabitants must have known or guessed that the great river in its turn was fed by the rains which fell in the far interior. Again, the legend that Osiris was the first to teach men the use of corn would be most naturally told of the corn-god himself. Further, the story that his mangled remains were scattered up and down the land and buried in different places may be a mythical way of expressing either the sowing or the winnowing of the grain. The latter interpretation is supported by the tale that Isis placed the severed limbs of Osiris on a corn-sieve. Or more probably the legend may be a reminiscence of a custom of slaying a human victim, perhaps a representative of the corn-spirit, and distributing his flesh or scattering his ashes over the fields to fertilise them. In modern Europe the figure of Death is sometimes torn in pieces, and the fragments are then buried in the ground to make the crops grow well, and in other parts of the world human victims are treated in the same way. With regard to the ancient Egyptians we have it on the authority of Manetho that they used to burn red-haired men and scatter their ashes with winnowing fans, and it is highly significant that this barbarous sacrifice was offered by the kings at the grave of Osiris. We may conjecture that the victims represented Osiris himself, who was annually slain, dismembered, and buried in their persons that he might quicken the seed in the earth.

Possibly in prehistoric times the kings themselves played the part of the god and were slain and dismembered in that character. Set as well as Osiris is said to have been torn in pieces after a reign of eighteen days, which was commemorated by an annual festival of the same length. According to one story Romulus, the first king of Rome, was cut in pieces by the senators, who buried the fragments of him in the ground; and the traditional day of his death, the seventh of July, was celebrated with certain curious rites, which were apparently connected with the artificial fertilisation of the fig. Again, Greek legend told how Pentheus, king of Thebes, and Lycurgus, king of the Thracian Edonians, opposed the vine-god Dionysus, and how the impious monarchs were rent in pieces, the one by the frenzied Bacchanals, the other by horses. The Greek traditions may well be distorted reminiscences of a custom of sacrificing human beings, and especially divine kings, in the character of Dionysus, a god who resembled Osiris in many points and was said like him to have been torn limb from limb. We are told that in Chios men were rent in pieces as a sacrifice to Dionysus; and since they died the same death as their god, it is reasonable to suppose that they personated him. The story that the Thracian Orpheus was similarly torn limb from limb by the Bacchanals seems to indicate that he too perished in the character of the god whose death he died. It is significant that the Thracian Lycurgus, king of the Edonians, is said to have been put to death in order that the ground, which had ceased to be fruitful, might regain its fertility.

Further, we read of a Norwegian king, Halfdan the Black, whose body was cut up and buried in different parts of his kingdom for the sake of ensuring the fruitfulness of the earth. He is said to have been drowned at the age of forty through the breaking of the ice in spring. What followed his death is thus related by the old Norse historian Snorri Sturluson: "He had been the most prosperous (literally, blessed with abundance) of all kings. So greatly did men value him that when the news came that he was dead and his body removed to Hringariki and intended for burial there, the chief men from Raumariki and Westfold and Heithmörk came and all requested that they might take his body with them and bury it in their various provinces; they thought that it would bring abundance to those who obtained it. Eventually it was settled that the body was distributed in four places. The head was laid in a barrow at Steinn in Hringariki, and each party took away their own share and buried it. All these barrows are called Halfdan's barrows." It should be remembered that this Halfdan belonged to the family of the Ynglings, who traced their descent from Frey, the great Scandinavian god of fertility.

The natives of Kiwai, an island lying off the mouth of the Fly River in British New Guinea, tell of a ceratin magician named Segera, who had sago for his totem. When Segera was old and ill, he told the people that he would soon die, but that, nevertheless, he would cause their gardens to thrive. Accordingly, he instructed them that when he was dead they should cut him up and place pieces of his flesh in their gardens, but his head was to be buried in his own garden. Of him it is said that he outlived the ordinary age, and that no man knew his father, but that he made the sago good and no one was hungry any more. Old men who were alive some years ago affirmed that they had known Segera in their youth, and the general opinion of the Kiwai people seems to be that Segera died not more than two generations ago.

Taken all together, these legends point to a widespread practice of dismembering the body of a king or magician and burying the pieces in different parts of the country in order to ensure the fertility of the ground and probably also the fecundity of man and beast.

To return to the human victims whose ashes the Egyptians scattered with winnowing-fans, the red hair of these unfortunates was probably significant. For in Egypt the oxen which were sacrificed had also to be red; a single black or white hair found on the beast would have disqualified it for the sacrifice. If, as I conjecture, these human sacrifices were intended to promote the growth of the crops – and the winnowing of their ashes seems to support this view – red-haired victims were perhaps selected as best fitted to personate the spirit of the ruddy grain. For when a god is represented by a living person, it is natural that the human representative should be chosen on the ground of his supposed resemblance to the divine original. Hence the ancient Mexicans, conceiving the maize as a personal being who went through the whole course of life between seed-time and harvest, sacrificed new-born babes when the maize was sown, older children when it had sprouted, and so on till it was fully ripe, when they sacrificed old men. A name for Osiris was the "crop" or "harvest"; and the ancients sometimes explained him as a personification of the corn.

Osiris a tree-spirit

But Osiris was more than a spirit of the corn; he was also a tree-spirit, and this may perhaps have been his primitive character, since the worship of trees is naturally older in the history of religion than the worship of the cereals. The character of Osiris as a tree-spirit was represented very graphically in a ceremony described by Firmicus Maternus. A pine-tree having been cut down, the centre was hollowed out, and with the wood thus excavated an image of Osiris was made, which was then buried like a corpse in the hollow of the tree. It is hard to imagine how the conception of a tree as tenanted by a personal being could be more plainly expressed. The image of Osiris thus made was kept for a year and then burned, exactly as was done with the image of Attis which was attached to the pine-tree. The ceremony of cutting the tree, as described by Firmicus Maternus, appears to be alluded to by Plutarch. It was probably the ritual counterpart of the mythical discovery of the body of Osiris enclosed in the *erica*-tree. In the hall of Osiris at Denderah the coffin containing the hawk-headed mummy of the god is clearly depicted as enclosed within a tree, apparently a conifer, the trunk and branches of which are seen above and below the coffin. The scene thus corresponds closely both to the myth and to the ceremony described by Firmicus Maternus.

It accords with the character of Osiris as a tree-spirit that his worshippers were forbidden to injure fruit-trees, and with his character as a god of vegetation in general that they were not allowed to stop up wells of water, which are so important for the irrigation of hot southern lands. According to one legend, he taught men to train the vine to poles, to prune its superfluous foliage, and to extract the juice of the grape. In the papyrus of Nebseni, written about 1550 BC, Osiris is depicted sitting in a shrine, from the roof of which hang clusters of grapes; and in the papyrus of the royal scribe Nekht we see the god enthroned in front of a pool, from the banks of which a luxuriant vine, with many bunches of grapes, grows towards the green face of the seated deity. The ivy was sacred to him, and was called his plant because it is always green.

Osiris a god of fertility

As a god of vegetation Osiris was naturally conceived as a god of creative energy in general, since men at a certain stage of evolution fail to distinguish between the reproductive powers of animals and of plants. Hence a striking feature in his worship was the coarse but expressive symbolism by which this aspect of his nature was presented to the eye not merely of the initiated but of the multitude. At his festival women used to go about the villages singing songs in his praise and carrying obscene images of him which they set in motion by means of strings. The custom was probably a charm to ensure the growth of the crops. A similar image of him, decked with all the fruits of the earth, is said to have stood in a temple before a figure of Isis, and in the chambers dedicated to him at Philae the dead god is portrayed lying on his bier in an attitude which indicates in the plainest way that even in death his generative virtue was not extinct but only suspended, ready to prove a source of life and fertility to the world when the opportunity should offer. Hymns addressed to Osiris contain allusions to this important side of his nature. In one of them it is said that the world waxes green in triumph through him; and another declares, "Thou art the father and mother of mankind, they live on thy breath, they subsist on the flesh of thy body." We may conjecture that in this paternal aspect he was supposed, like other gods of fertility, to bless men and women with offspring, and that the processions at his festival were intended to promote this object as well as to quicken the seed in the ground. It would be to misjudge ancient religion to denounce as lewd and profligate the emblems and the ceremonies which the Egyptians employed for the purpose of giving effect to this conception of the divine power. The ends which they proposed to themselves in these rites were natural and laudable; only the means they adopted to compass them were mistaken. A similar fallacy induced the Greeks to adopt a like symbolism in their Dionysiac festivals, and the superficial but striking resemblance thus produced between the two religions has perhaps more than anything else misled enquirers, both ancient and modern, into identifying worships which, though certainly akin in nature, are perfectly distinct and independent in origin.

Osiris a god of the dead

We have seen that in one of his aspects Osiris was the ruler and judge of the dead. To a people like the Egyptians, who not only believed in a life beyond the grave but actually spent much of their time, labour, and money in preparing for it, this office of the god must have appeared hardly, if at all, less important than his function of making the earth to bring forth its fruits in due season. We may assume that in the faith of his worshippers the two provinces of the god were intimately connected. In laying their dead in the grave they committed them to his keeping who could raise them from the dust to life eternal, even as he caused the seed to spring from the ground. Of that faith the corn-stuffed effigies of Osiris found in Egyptian tombs furnish an eloquent and unequivocal testimony. They were at once an emblem and an instrument of resurrection. Thus from the sprouting of the grain the ancient Egyptians drew an augury of human immortality. They are not the only people who have built the same lofty hopes on the same slender foundation.

A god who thus fed his people with his own broken body in this life, and who held out to them a promise of a blissful eternity in a better world hereafter, naturally reigned supreme in their affections. We need not wonder, therefore, that in Egypt the worship of the other gods was overshadowed by that of Osiris, and that while they were revered each in his own district, he and his divine partner Isis were adored in all.

3

THEMIS

Jane Harrison

Jane Harrison (1850–1928), who was affiliated with Newnham College, Cambridge University, for much of her life, was the leader of the group of classicists known as the Cambridge Ritualists, whose other members were F. M. Cornford, A. B. Cook, and Oxford's Gilbert Murray. Harrison took Frazer's myth-ritualism and applied it in detail to ancient Greek religion. At the same time she introduced a sociological dimension to myth-ritualism. On the one hand Harrison follows Frazer in postulating an annual ritual enacting the myth of the death and rebirth of the god of vegetation. As for Frazer, so for her, this ritual is intended to imitate and thereby magically induce the resurrection of the god, on whose health vegetation depends. The king, whose overall place Harrison downplays, either plays the role of the god in the ritual or is himself killed and replaced – the same options as for Frazer. On the other hand Harrison goes beyond Frazer in interpreting the annual ritual of physical renewal as simultaneously a ritual of initiation into society. Like the god, members of society die – die symbolically to childhood – and are reborn as adults. The following selection is the first chapter of Harrison's key myth-ritualist work, *Themis* (1st edn, Cambridge: Cambridge University Press, 1912). See also her *Epilegomena to the Study of Greek Religion* (Cambridge: Cambridge University Press, 1921); *Ancient Art and Ritual* (New York: Holt; London: Williams and Norgate, 1913); and *Alpha and Omega* (London: Sidgwick & Jackson, 1915), ch. 6. Her earlier *Prolegomena to the Study of Greek Religion* (1st edn, Cambridge: Cambridge University Press, 1903) considers only ritual, not myth. See also Harrison's autobiography, *Reminiscences of a Student's Life* (London: Hogarth, 1925). On Harrison see Jessie Stewart, *Jane Ellen Harrison* (London: Merlin Press, 1959); Sandra J. Peacock, *Jane Ellen Harrison* (New Haven: Yale University Press, 1988); Renate Schlesier, "Jane Ellen Harrison," in

Original publication: Jane Harrison, *Themis*, 1st edn (Cambridge: Cambridge University Press, 1912), ch. 1 (pp. 1–29).

Classical Scholarship, eds Ward W. Briggs and William M. Calder III (New York: Garland Publishing, 1990), 127–41; Robert Ackerman, The Myth and Ritual School (New York: Garland Publishing, 1991), chs 5–7; and Hugh Lloyd-Jones, "Jane Ellen Harrison, 1850–1928," in Cambridge Women, eds Edward Shils and Carmen Blacker (Cambridge: Cambridge University Press, 1996), ch. 2.

The Hymn of The Kouretes

Ζεῦ πάντων ἀρχά,
πάντων ἀγήτωρ,
Ζεῦ, coι πέμπω ταύταν γμνων ἀρχάν.

Zeus, the Father of Gods and Men, was born, men fabled, in the island of Crete. So far there was substantial agreement. It may be that this uniformity reflects some half-unconscious tradition that in Crete were the beginnings of that faith and practice which if it cannot be called Hellenic religion was at least the substratum on which Hellenic religion was based. No one now thinks he can have an adequate knowledge of Greek art without a study of the Mycenaean and Minoan periods, and, since the roots of religion strike as deep as or deeper than the roots of art, no one now will approach the study of the Olympian Zeus without seeking for the origin of the god in his reputed birth-place.

By the most fortunate of chances, at Palaikastro on the eastern coast of Crete, just the very material needed for this study has come to light, a ritual Hymn commemorating the birth of the infant Zeus. The Hymn itself is, as will be seen, late, but it embodies very early material, material indeed so primitive that we seem at last to get back to the very beginnings of Greek religion, to a way of thinking that is not in our sense religious at all, but that demonstrably leads on to religious faith and practice. This primitive mode of faith and practice it is, I believe, of the first importance that we should grasp and as fully as may be realise. It lets us see myth as well as ritual in the making, it will even disclose certain elements that lie deep embedded in early Greek philosophy. The new, or at least partially new, outlook opened by the Hymn is easy to misconceive, and, in the first flush of discovery, easy perhaps to over-emphasize. It needs patient scrutiny and some effort of the historical imagination. To such a scrutiny and to conclusions arising from it the following chapters will be devoted.

Before the meaning of the Hymn is discussed the circumstances of its finding must be made clear. This Hymn, about which our main enquiry into the origins of Greek religion will centre, was not found at Knossos nor even at Phaestos, places whose names are now in every man's mouth, but at the remote

Figure 3.1 Map of Crete

seaport town of Palaikastro, a name familiar only to archaeologists. If Palaikastro should ever be a household word to classical scholars in general, it will be as the place of the finding of this Hymn. The marshy plain out of which Palaikastro rises is almost certainly the ancient Heleia, known to us through inscriptions[1] as a tract of land over which the dwellers in Itanos and Hierapytna disputed. Near to Heleia these same inscriptions tell us lay the sanctuary of Diktaean Zeus.

Our Hymn bids the god come to Dikte. The two great mountain peaks of Crete, Ida and Dikte, both claimed to be the birth-place of Zeus. Dikte, though less splendid and dominant, has the earlier and better claim. Hesiod,[2] our earliest authority, places the birth-story at Lyktos on the north-western spur of Dikte.

> To Lyktos first she came, bearing the child
> As black night swiftly fell.

There is a shade of suspicious emphasis on the "first," as of one whose orthodoxy is impeached. When the glory of Cnossos overshadowed and over-whelmed lesser and earlier sanctities, Ida was necessarily supreme, and it required some courage to support the claims of Dikte. Diodorus[3] with true theological tact combines the two stories: the god was born indeed on Dikte but educated by the Kouretes on Mount Ida.

But Palaikastro, as a glance at the map[4] in figure 3.1 will show, is not Dikte – not even near Dikte. All eastern Crete with its towns of Itanos and Praisos,

---

[1] Dittenberger, II. 929, line 37 Ἰτάνιοι πόλιν οἰκοῦντες ἐπιθαλάσσιον χώραν ἔχοντες προγονικὴν γειτονοῦσαν τῶι τοῦ Διὸς τοῦ Δικταίου ἱερῶι, and see lines 45 and 65.

[2] Hes. *Theog.* 481

ἔνθα μὲν Ἴκτο φέρουσα θοὴν διὰ νύκτα μέλαιναν
πρώτην ἐς Λύκτον.

[3] v. 70 κατὰ δὲ τὴν Ἴδην, ἐν ἧ συνέβη τραφῆναι τὸν θεόν . . . ἀνδρωθέντα δ' αὐτόν φασι πρῶτον πόλιν κτίσαι περὶ τὴν Δίκταν, ὅπου καὶ τὴν γένεσιν αὐτοῦ γενέσθαι μυθολογοῦσιν. . . .

[4] Reproduced with slight modifications from *B.S.A.* VIII. p. 287, Fig. 1.

where dwelt the Eteokretans, and the modern sites of Zakro and Palaikastro
are cut off from the mountain mass of Dikte by the low narrow isthmus[5] that
joins the trading towns of Minoa (Gournia) and Hierapytna (Hierapetra). How
comes it then that in remote Palaikastro Diktaean Zeus is worshipped, that in
Palaikastro the ruins of his temple have come to light? This brings us to the
question of chronology.

Strabo[6] in discussing the origin of Cretan institutions makes an interesting
remark. "Among the Cretans," he says, "when their warlike cities, and especially that of Knossos, were ravaged, certain of their customs were kept up
among the inhabitants of Lyttos and Gortyna and other of the lesser towns
rather than by the Knossians." Here we have much history in a nutshell.
Conspicuous cities pay the toll of their splendour. Palaikastro is but a lesser
town ($\pi o\lambda i\chi\nu\iota o\nu$): there we may hope to find customs surviving that had died
down at Knossos.

In the Hymn before us just such customs are enshrined. The actual stele
was engraved in the second or third century after Christ;[7] that is clear from the
very cursive character of the letters. But the poem inscribed is much earlier,
probably about 300 BC. We have oddly enough two copies on the back and face
of the same stone. It seems to have presented serious difficulties to the stone-
mason. The first copy whether from another stone or from a MS. was so faulty
that it had to be redone. This looks as if matter and language were unfamiliar.
For some reason which now escapes us, an old ritual hymn was revived. How
far it was rewritten we cannot now say. Its material is, as will presently be
shown, primaeval; we cannot date it, it is $\nu \acute{o}\mu\iota\mu o\nu$.

The cave on Dikte where Zeus was born has been identified and thoroughly
excavated.[8] It is a large double cavern about 500 feet above the modern village
of Psychro in the upland of Lasithi. Lyttos, of which the ruins still remain, lies
on one spur of the north-western peak of Dikte (Lasithi); on the opposite spur
is the Psychro cave. In the lowest stratum of the deposit in the cave is found
Kamares ware, above that Mycenaean ware, and so on in regular sequence to
the geometric period, i.e., about the eighth century BC. After that, save in quite
sporadic cases the votive offerings cease. It is impossible to avoid the conclusion
that the cult in the cave came to an end. Dikte it is probable was superseded

---

[5] Strabo, x. 475 $\pi\lambda\alpha\tau\upsilon\tau\acute{\alpha}\tau\eta$ $\delta\grave{\epsilon}$ $\kappa\alpha\tau\grave{\alpha}$ $\tau\grave{o}$ $\mu\acute{\epsilon}\sigma o\nu$ $\acute{\epsilon}\sigma\tau\acute{\iota}$, $\pi\acute{\alpha}\lambda\iota\nu$ δ'$\acute{\epsilon}\nu\tau\epsilon\hat{\upsilon}\theta\epsilon\nu$ $\epsilon\grave{\iota}\varsigma$ $\sigma\tau\epsilon\nu\acute{\omega}\tau\epsilon\rho o\nu$ $\tau o\hat{\upsilon}$
$\pi\rho o\tau\acute{\epsilon}\rho o\upsilon$ $\sigma\upsilon\mu\pi\acute{\iota}\pi\tau o\upsilon\sigma\iota\nu$ $\grave{\iota}\sigma\theta\mu\grave{o}\nu$ $\alpha\grave{\iota}$ $\mathring{\eta}\acute{o}\nu\epsilon\varsigma$ $\pi\epsilon\rho\grave{\iota}$ $\acute{\epsilon}\xi\acute{\eta}\kappa o\nu\tau\alpha$ $\sigma\tau\alpha\delta\acute{\iota}\omega\nu$, $\tau\grave{o}\nu$ $\acute{\alpha}\pi\grave{o}$ $M\iota\nu\acute{\omega}\alpha\varsigma$ $\tau\hat{\eta}\varsigma$
$\Lambda\upsilon\tau\tau\acute{\iota}\omega\nu$ $\epsilon\grave{\iota}\varsigma$ $\acute{I}\epsilon\rho\acute{\alpha}\pi\upsilon\tau\nu\alpha\nu$ $\kappa\alpha\grave{\iota}$ $\tau\grave{o}$ $\Lambda\iota\beta\upsilon\kappa\grave{o}\nu$ $\pi\acute{\epsilon}\lambda\alpha\gamma o\varsigma$.

[6] Strabo, x. 481 $\kappa\alpha\kappa\omega\theta\epsilon\iota\sigma\hat{\omega}\nu$ $\tau\hat{\omega}\nu$ $\pi\acute{o}\lambda\epsilon\omega\nu$ $\kappa\alpha\grave{\iota}$ $\mu\acute{\alpha}\lambda\iota\sigma\tau\alpha$ $\tau\hat{\eta}\varsigma$ $K\nu\omega\sigma\sigma\acute{\iota}\omega\nu$, $\tau\hat{\omega}\nu$ $\pi o\lambda\epsilon\mu\iota\kappa\hat{\omega}\nu\cdot$
$\mu\epsilon\hat{\iota}\nu\alpha\iota$ $\delta\acute{\epsilon}$ $\tau\iota\nu\alpha$ $\tau\hat{\omega}\nu$ $\nu o\mu\acute{\iota}\mu\omega\nu$ $\pi\alpha\rho\grave{\alpha}$ $\Lambda\upsilon\tau\tau\acute{\iota}o\iota\varsigma$ $\kappa\alpha\grave{\iota}$ $\Gamma o\rho\tau\upsilon\nu\acute{\iota}o\iota\varsigma$ $\kappa\alpha\grave{\iota}$ $\mathring{\alpha}\lambda\lambda o\iota\varsigma$ $\tau\iota\sigma\grave{\iota}$ $\pi o\lambda\iota\chi\nu\acute{\iota}o\iota\varsigma$
$\mu\hat{\alpha}\lambda\lambda o\nu$ $\mathring{\eta}$ $\pi\alpha\rho$' $\acute{\epsilon}\kappa\epsilon\acute{\iota}\nu o\iota\varsigma$. Clement, citing as his authority the *Nostoi* of Antikleides, says that
human sacrifice was offered by the Lyctii, a Cretan tribe (Book III. 4).

[7] See Prof. Bosanquet, *B.S.A.* xv. 1908–1909, p. 347, and Prof. Gilbert Murray, p. 364.

[8] For full description see Mr D. G. Hogarth, *The Dictaean Cave, B. S. A.* VI. p. 94 and
especially p. 115.

by Ida. In a treaty[9] between Lyttos and Olous, Zeus is sworn by, but his title is Βιδάτας "Zeus of Ida," not Δικταῖος. On his own mountain "He of Dikte" was superseded.

Central Crete in her public documents swears by Zeus of Ida, but a little group of cities in the remote eastern district held to the earlier cult. Itanos, the northernmost of the towns on the east coast, was said to have been founded by one of the Kouretes. In an inscription[10] found on the modern site (Erimopolis) the citizens swear first of all by Zeus Diktaios and Hera and the gods in Dikte. At Eteokretan Praisos, Strabo,[11] quoting Staphylos, says there was the sanctuary of Diktaean Zeus. Athenaeus[12] notes that the Praisians sacrifice *to* a sow, and he connects the custom with the "unspeakable sacrifice" which took place on Dikte in commemoration of the fact that Zeus was suckled by a sow. Settlers from Hierapytna[13] take their oath by two Zeuses, Zeus Oratrios and Zeus Diktaios.

It is clear then that though in classical days central Crete was dominated by the Zeus of Ida, Zeus of Dikte,[14] whose worship went on during the bronze and iron ages in the great cave at Lyttos, was a living power in the eastern and especially the north-eastern extremity of Crete.

Zeus of Ida might and did dominate central Crete, but in the eastern and especially the north-eastern extremities Zeus of Dikte, Zeus of the Birth-cave, lived on in classical and even post-classical days. His was a name to swear by and at Palaikastro he had a temple and a precinct. It is this temple that has been recovered for us by the excavations of the British School[15] carried on in 1902–1905. These excavations have abundantly shown that in the third Late-Minoan period (after 1500 BC) Palaikastro was the seat of a ruling prince, after Knossos, Phaistos and Gournia had been destroyed. Not a stone of the temple was standing, but from architectural fragments found scattered on the site some notion of its size and its decoration can be gleaned. The temenos

[9] *C.I.A.* ii. 549, and see R. C. Bosanquet, op. cit. p. 349.

[10] Blass (in Collitz-Bechtel, iii².), 5058 [Τά]δε ὤμοσαν τοι Ἰτάνιοι πά[ντες] Δία Δικταῖον καὶ Ἥραν καὶ θ[εο]ὺς τοὺς ἐν Δίκται καὶ. . . .

[11] Strabo, x. 475 . . . ὧν (τῶν Ἐτεοκρήτων) εἶναι πολίχνιον Πρᾶσον ὅπου τὸ τοῦ Δικταίου Διὸς ἱερόν. For an inscription of Praisos in which "Diktaios" may be with great probability restored see Prof. Bosanquet, op. cit. p. 350.

[12] Athen. ix. 375, quoting Agathocles, Μυθεύουσιν ἐν Κρήτῃ γενέσθαι τὴν Διὸς τέκνωσιν ἐπὶ τῆς Δίκτης ἐν ᾗ καὶ ἀπόρρητος γίνεται θυσία . . . Πραίσιοι δὲ καὶ ἱερὰ ῥέζουσιν ὑὶ καὶ αὕτη προτελὴς αὐτοῖς ἡ θυσία νενόμισται.

[13] Blass, 5039 Ὁμνύω τὰν Ἑστίαν καὶ Ζῆνα Ὁράτριον καὶ Ζῆνα Δικταῖον.

[14] It is even probable that the name of Dikte was transferred to one of the peaks, perhaps the cone of Modhi near Praisos and Palaikastro. Strabo expressly states that Dikte is only 100 stadia from Salmonion, the north-east promontory of Crete, and that it is not "as Aratus alleges" near Ida, but distant from it 1000 stadia towards the east. Aratus is probably describing the old Dikte of the cave. Strabo must intend some more easterly peak. The conjecture is due to Prof. Bosanquet, op. cit. p. 351.

[15] See *Excavations at Palaikastro*, iv. B.S.A. xi. p. 299, Pl. ix.–xv.

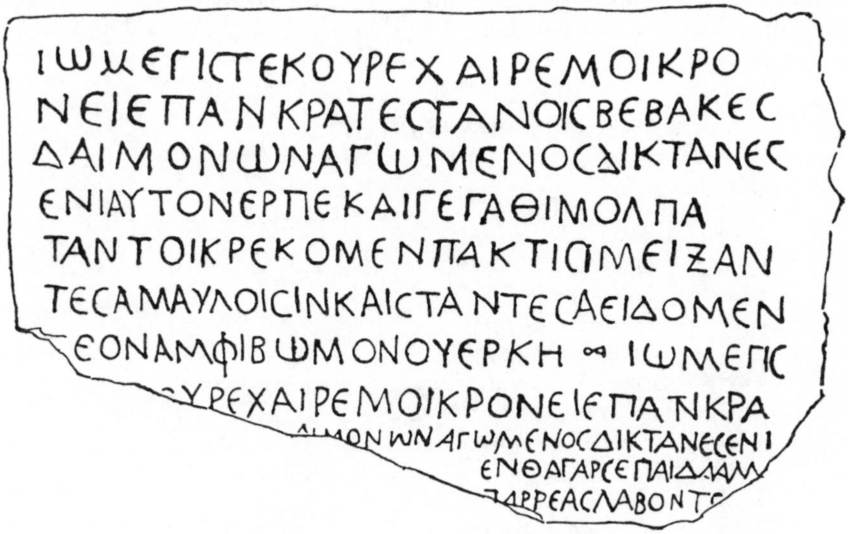

Figure 3.2 Fragment of Hymn of the Kouretes

wall[16] can be traced for about thirty-six metres. The temple stood not as the Hellenic temples of Troy and Mycenae at the summit of the hill, but on a platform artificially levelled, about half-way down. The bulk of the votive offerings belong to the archaic period and show that the sanctuary was in full prosperity from the seventh to the fifth century BC. Bronze shields of the same style and date as those found in the cave on Mt. Ida have also come to light.

The three main fragments of the inscribed Hymn were found a little to the south of the temple in a deep pocket of earth and stones which had been dug right down into the Minoan strata, probably in some recent search for building stones. The missing pieces were carefully searched for over the whole field of excavation, but they have either been destroyed or carried away as building material. They may still come to light built into churches or houses in the neighbourhood. More than half the stele is missing, but, thanks to the fact that there are two copies of the text back and front, not nearly half of the text. One of the fragments, that which contains the opening lines in the fair copy, is reproduced in figure 3.2.

For what precise occasion our Hymn was written we shall probably never know, but the fact that it was found near a temple of Diktaean Zeus in a place remote from Dikte, the significant fact too of the double copy, show clearly that the Hymn is essentially a revival, and that we may expect to find in it

---

[16] This temenos wall is mentioned in an inscription (Dittenberger, II. 929, l. 75) τὸ δὲ ἱερὸν καὶ τὸν περίβολον αὐτοῦ ἰδίοις σημείοις καὶ περιοικοδομήμασιν περιεχόμενον.

fossilised ways of thinking. This will emerge more clearly in the sequel. We must first consider the general structure and character of the Hymn. The text[17] is as follows.

RESTORED TEXT.

Ἰώ,
Μέγιστε Κοῦρε, χαῖρέ μοι,
Κρόνιε, παγκρατὲς γάνους,
βέβακες
5 δαιμόνων ἀγώμενος·
Δίκταν ἐς ἐνιαυτὸν ἔρ-
πε καὶ γέγαθι μολπᾷ,
Τάν τοι κρέκομεν πακτίσι   ⏓ – ∪ ∪   ⏓ – ∪ ∪
μείξαντες ἅμ᾽ αὐλοῖσιν,   ⏓ – ∪ ∪   ⏓ – – ⏒
10 καὶ στάντες ἀείδομεν τεὸν   ⏓ – ∪ ∪   ⏓ ∪ – ⏓⏒
ἀμφὶ βωμὸν εὐερκῆ.   ⏓ ∪ – ∪   ⏓ – –
Ἰώ, κ.τ.λ.
Ἔνθα γὰρ σέ, παῖδ᾽ ἄμβροτον,   ⏓ ∪ – ∪   ⏓ – ∪ ∪
ἀσπιδ[ηφόροι τροφῆες]   ⏓ ∪ – ∪   ⏓ ∪ – ⏒
15 παρ Ῥέας λαβόντες πόδα   ⏓ ∪ – ∪   ⏓ – ∪ ∪
κ[ρούοντες ἀπέκρυψαν].   ⏓ – ∪ ∪   ⏓ – –
Ἰώ, κ.τ.λ.

.   .   .   .   .

TRANSLATION.

"Io, Kouros most Great, I give thee hail, Kronian, Lord of all that is wet and gleaming, thou art come at the head of thy Daimones. To Dikte for the Year, Oh, march, and rejoice in the dance and song,

That we make to thee with harps and pipes mingled together, and sing as we come to a stand at thy well-fenced altar.

Io, etc.

For here the shielded Nurturers took thee, a child immortal, from Rhea, and with noise of beating feet hid thee away.

Io, etc.

.   .   .   .   .   .

RESTORED TEXT (continued).

20 .   .   .   .
.   .   . τᾶ]ς καλᾶς Ἀο(ῦ)ς   ∪   ⏓ – –
Ἰώ, κ.τ.λ.
[Ὧραι δὲ βρ]ύον κατῆτος   – – ∪ ∪   ⏓ ∪ – ⏒
καὶ βροτο(ὺ)ς Δίκα κατῆχε   ⏓ ∪ – ∪   ⏓ ∪ – ⏒

[17] As restored by Prof. Gilbert Murray. See B.S.A. xv. 1908–1909, p. 357.

25 [πάντα τ᾽ ἄγρι᾽ ἄμφεπ]ε ζῷ᾽   ⏒ ⏑ _ ⏑   ⏒ ⏑ _ ⏑
     ἁ φίλολβος Εἰρήνα.   ⏒ ⏑ _ ⏑   ⏒ _ _
     Ἰώ, κ.τ.λ.
     Ἄ[μιν θόρε, κὲς στα]μνία,   ⏒ ⏑ _ _   ⏒ _ ⏑ ⏑
     καὶ θόρ᾽ εὔποκ᾽ ἐ[ς ποίμνια,   ⏒ ⏑ _ ⏑   ⏒ _ ⏑ ⏑
30 κὲς λήϊ]α καρπῶν θόρε,   ⏒ _ ⏑ ⏑   ⏒ _ ⏑ ⏑
     κὲς τελεσ[φόρους σίμβλους.]   ⏒ ⏑ _ ⏑   ⏒ _ _
     Ἰώ, κ.τ.λ.
     Θόρε κὲς] πόληας ἁμῶν,   ⏒ ⏑ _ ⏑   ⏒ _ ⏑ ⏑
     κὲς ποντοφόρο(υ)ς νᾶας,   ⏒ _ ⏑ ⏑   ⏒ _ _ ⏑
35 θόρε κὲς [νεοὺς πολ]είτας,   ⏑ ⏑ _ _   ⏒ ⏑ _ ⏑
     θόρε κὲς Θέμιν κ[αλάν].   ⏑ ⏑ _ ⏑   ⏒ _ _

TRANSLATION (*continued*).

. . . . of fair dawn?
Io, etc.
And the Horai began to be fruitful year by year (?) and Dikè to possess
mankind, and all wild living things were held about by wealth-loving Peace.
Io, etc.
To us also leap for full jars, and leap for fleecy flocks, and leap for fields of
fruit, and for hives to bring increase.
Io, etc.
Leap for our Cities, and leap for our sea-borne ships, and leap for our young
citizens and for goodly Themis."

Our Hymn is obviously a Hymn of Invocation of a ritual type fairly well
known,[18] though the instances extant are unfortunately rare. It opens with a
refrain in ordinary lyric (di-iambic)[19] metre and this refrain is repeated before
each of the (di-trochaic) stanzas. The structure of the Hymn is of importance
and should be clearly realised. It falls into three parts.

[18] Our earliest instance is the invocation of the Bull-god by the women of Elis; the Delphic
Paean to Dithyrambos presents a later and closer analogy. See my *Prolegomena*, pp. 438 and 417.
[19] I call the metre of the refrain iambic because this seems simplest. But of course the
difference between iambics and trochees is often only nominal. Wilamowitz considers it more
consonant with the rest of the hymn to scan trochaically:

ἰ-ώ, μέγιστε Κοῦρε,   _   _ ⏑   _ ⏑   _ ⏑
χαῖρέ μοι, Κρόνειε, (sic lapis)   _ ⏑   _ ⏑   _ ⏑
παγκρατὲς γάνος, βέβακες   _ ⏑   _ ⏑   _ ⏑   _ _
δαιμόνων ἀγώμενος,   _ ⏑   _ _   _ ⏑   _
Δίκταν [ἐς] ἐνιαυτὸν ἔρπε   _ _   ⏑ ⏑   _ ⏑   _ ⏑
καὶ γέγαθι μολπᾷ,   _ ⏑   _ ⏑   _ _

This involves treating ἰ ⏑ ώ as = a cretic, keeping the very questionable form Κρόνειε (Κρονεῖον
= temple of Kronos in Pap. Grenf. I. 11 is of course different): and deleting ἐς before ἐνιαυτόν.
Otherwise it has great advantages (G.M.).

First we have in the refrain the actual invocation; the god is addressed by his various titles and instructed how, where and when to come – he is invoked as "Kouros most Great," as "Kronian,"[20] as "Lord of all that is wet and gleaming"[21] – it is in these capacities he is wanted and expected. He is further bidden to come at the head of his *Daimones*, he is to come to Dikte and for the year, he is to come marching and rejoicing. So far for the god.

Next by an easy transition we have a statement of the ritual performed. The god is adjured to rejoice in the dance and song which the worshippers make to him "with harps and pipes mingled together, and which they sing as they come to a stand at his well-fenced altar." We have clearly a ritual dance accompanying a song. The reason, or rather the occasion, of this dance and song is next stated. We have in fact what would usually be called an "aetiological" myth. The worshippers dance round the altar of the Kouros because "here the shielded Nurturers took the Kouros, an immortal child from Rhea, and with noise of beating feet hid him away."

Next follows a lamentable gap. When the text re-emerges we are midway in the third factor, the statement of the benefits which resulted from the events recounted in the myth, benefits which clearly it is expected will be renewed in the annual restatement and ritual re-enactment of this myth. The coming Seasons are to be fruitful, Dikè is to possess mankind, the Kouros by leaping in conjunction with his worshippers is to bring fertility for flocks and fields, prosperity to cities and sea-borne ships, and young citizens.

---

[20] The order of the words is, I think, conclusive against taking μέγιστε Κοῦρε Κρόνιε together, "greatest Kronian youth," "greatest son of Kronos" (G.M.).

[21] Both reading and translation are doubtful. Wilamowitz and Mr A. B. Cook independently suggest γάνος. The stone has γάνους three times, which is strong evidence of what the stone-cutter meant to write, and is not really weakened by the fact that in one case the Υ is crowded in between the Ο and Σ, as if it had been omitted and then inserted; παγκρατὲς γάνος, "Almighty Gleam" or "Radiance," would be simple and good: but παγκρατὲς γάνους seems to be quite good Greek for "Lord of all γάνος." Any compound of -κρατής would take the genitive, like ἐγκρατής, ἀκρατής. Cf. the gen. with παμμήτωρ, παναίτιος, πάνδοκος.

But what is the meaning of γάνος? The Etymologicum Magnum has a gloss: γάνος· ὕδωρ χάρμα φῶς λίπος αὐγή λευκότης λαμπηδών. "γάνος: *water joy light grease gleam candor fulgor*." (I am reduced to Latin for the last two equivalents.) It starts with "water" and it ends with "light" or "gleam." I translate "*wet and gleaming*."

It has been suggested by Mr Cook that perhaps the Kouros is only Lord of the Bright Sky, like a Sun God, and that γάνος is *hoc sublime candens*, The Aether. Now it is quite true that γάνος never means simply *water*, without any "gleam," while instances can easily be found in which it means only "gleam" or "glory" with no sense of wetness, e.g., Aesch. *Ag.* 579 λάφυρα – δόμοις ἐπασσάλευσαν ἀρχαῖον γάνος. If the context required it we could certainly leave out the wetness. But (1) the wetness is normally present: it is κρηναῖον γάνος, Ἀσωποῦ γάνος, βότρυος or ἀμπέλου γάνος, ξουθῆς μελίσσης γάνος, γάνος Ἠριδανοῖο and the like; and (2) the context here seems to me not to reject but rather to welcome the connotation of moisture. It is not mere sunlight that the Kouros brings; it is fruitful Spring as a whole, with dew and showers and young sap as well as sunshine. Γάνος in its ordinary sense exactly hits off the required meaning (G.M.).

The full gist of the Hymn will not appear till all three factors have been examined in detail, but already, at the first superficial glance, we note certain characteristics of a Hymn of Invocation that may help to its understanding. The god invoked is not present, not there in a temple ready waiting to be worshipped; he is bidden to come, and apparently his coming, and as we shall later see his very existence, depends on the ritual that invokes him. Moreover the words addressed to him are not, as we should expect and find in the ordinary worship addressed to an Olympian, a prayer, but an injunction, a command, "come," "leap." Strangest of all, the god it would seem performs the same ritual as his worshippers, and it is by performing that ritual that he is able to confer his blessings. He leaps when his attendant worshippers leap and the land is fertile. All this as will later appear lands us in a region rather of magic than religion.

It will now be necessary to examine in detail the three[22] factors of the Hymn – the introductory refrain, the aetiological[23] myth, and what for convenience we may call "the resultant blessings." The gist of the ritual will be found in the second factor, the aetiological myth, but we begin with the first.

The Invocation

Μέγιστε Κοῦρε, χαῖρέ μοι,
Κρόνιε.

The opening words are enough to startle the seven mythological sleepers. From the circumstances of the finding of the Hymn in the temple of Diktaean Zeus and from the title Kronian, it is clear that Zeus[24] the Father of gods and men, is addressed as "Kouros most Great," greatest of grown-up youths. To our unaccustomed ears the title sounds strange and barely reverent. "Father," still more "Mother," and even "Babe" are to us holy words, but a full-grown youth has to us no connotation of sanctity. Moreover the words Full-grown Youth go ill with "Kronian," a title of reverend association. How these two dissonant titles come to be unequally yoked together will appear in the sequel.

[22] The first two factors only will be examined at this point; the third factor, the "resultant blessings and their relation to Themis," is reserved for chapter x.

[23] I use the current term "aetiological" provisionally, for convenience. Its inadequacy will be shown later.

[24] It should, however, be definitely noted at the outset, for the fact is of ordinal importance, that nowhere, neither in the refrain nor in the body of the poem, does the actual name *Zeus* appear.

When the Hymn was first discovered, the opening words as was natural at once arrested attention, but – so crusted and stiffened is the mind with traditional thinking – the full significance of the title could not at first be seen. Zeus the Father was firmly rooted in our minds, so it was natural at first to think, here we have the young Zeus, Zeus the Divine Son. The Christian religion has accustomed us to a god as Son. But it should at once be noted, Kouros is not υἱός, not *son*, nor is it even παῖς, *child*. Kouros connotes[25] no relationship to a parent, it is simply *young man just come to maturity*. Hence it is that Kouros with a capital is in English practically untranslatable save by periphrasis. "Greatest of Youths" is intolerably clumsy, "Prince of Youths," which perhaps might serve, introduces an alien association. Nothing is more stimulating to enquiry than an untranslatable word, since underlying it we may hope to find something new, unknown. We have no sacred Kouros now, we have got to rediscover what caused the sanctity of the Kouros.[26] We shall find it in the aetiological myth, but before we examine this, another statement in the Invocation yet remains and one scarcely less surprising.

The Kouros, the young Zeus, is hailed as coming "at the head of his *daimones*" (δαιμόνων ἀγώμενος). This brings us to a curious and, for our investigation, cardinal point. Nowhere save in this Hymn do we hear of Zeus with attendant *daimones*.[27] He stands always alone, aloof, approached with awe, utterly delimited from his worshippers. One god only, Dionysos, and he but a half-bred Olympian, is attended by *daimones*. We can scarcely picture Dionysos without his attendant *thiasos*, be they holy women, Maenads, be they the revel rout of Satyrs. We think of this *thiasos* of *daimones* as attendants, inferior persons, pale reflections, emanations as it were from the god himself. It seems appropriate that he should be surrounded by attendants (προπόλοι): superior persons, high officials, always are. If this be all, how strange, how even unseemly is it that Zeus, the supreme god, Father of Gods and Men, should have no *thiasos*, no escort. The Hymn brings us face to face with the fact that Zeus once had a *thiasos*, once when he as a young man, a Kouros. When he grew up to be the Father, it seems, he lost his *thiasos* and has gone about unattended ever since. If we can once seize the meaning of this *thiasos* and its relation to the god we shall have gone far to understand the making of Greek theology.

[25] The word κοῦρος is of course often used as the rough equivalent of παῖς or υἱός, cf. Eur. *El.* 463 τῷ Μαίας ἀγροτῆρι κούρῳ, but I suspect that in this and similar passages it covers an earlier and different relation.

[26] Some survivals of initiation-rites and of the Kouros idea will be considered in chapters IX. and X.

[27] Mr Cook kindly reminds me that this rule has one singular and beautiful exception. In the *Phaedrus* of Plato (246 E) we read ὁ μὲν δὴ μέγας ἡγεμὼν ἐν οὐρανῷ Ζεὺς ... πρῶτος πορεύεται ... τῷ δ᾽ ἕπεται στρατιὰ θεῶν τε καὶ δαιμόνων ... θείου χοροῦ. ... The passage reads almost like a reminiscence of a ritual-procession similar to that headed by the greatest Kouros (δαιμόνων ἀγώμενος).

The Aetiological Myth

The presence of the Kouros is confidently claimed and with it all the blessings to flocks and herds that attend his coming. The god will come, *is* come, to Dikte for the year and the produce of the year; and the reason is clearly stated. The worshippers "come to a stand" at the altar and there recite and probably enact the myth.

For here the shielded Nurturers took thee, a child immortal and with noise of beating feet hid thee away.

The text at this point is unfortunately defective,[28] but enough remains to make it clear, beyond the possibility of doubt, that the story told is the familiar myth of the birth of Zeus and his nurture by the Kouretes.[29] The myth is obviously "aetiological." The worshippers of the Kouros say they invoke the Kouros because of the myth (ἔνθα γάρ). We may of course safely invert the order of things, the myth arose out of or rather together with the ritual, not the ritual out of the myth.

The myth of the birth of Zeus and its ritual enactment is recounted by Strabo[30] as follows. After mentioning the mysteries of Demeter and Dionysos, he says, "These things in general and the sacred ceremonies of Zeus in particular, are performed with orgiastic rites and with assistance of attendants (πρόπολοι) similar to the Satyrs that attend Dionysos. *These attendants they call Kouretes*; they are certain young men who perform armed movements accompanied by dancing. *They allege as their reason the myth about the birth of Zeus*, in which Kronos is introduced with his habit of swallowing his children immediately after birth, and Rhea trying to conceal her birth-pangs and to get the new-born child out of the way and doing her utmost to save it. With a view to this she enlists the help of the Kouretes. They surround the goddess and with drums and with the din of other instruments try to strike terror into Kronos and to escape notice whilst trying to filch away the child. The child is then given over to them to be reared with the same care by which it was rescued."

A little earlier in his discussion of the functions of the Kouretes he says[31] they are "*daimones* or attendants (πρόπολοι) on the gods, similar to Satyroi,

[28] Prof. Murray writes, op. cit. p. 359 " 'L. 14 ἀσπιδ[ηφόροι Κούρητες] Bosanquet.' The sense seems certain but the metrical license _ _ _ _ for _ ∪ _ ∾ is doubtful and does not occur elsewhere in the hymn. Hence I prefer τροφῆες: ἀσπίδ[εσσι | Κού ∪ ρητες] however would correspond neatly with μείξαντες ἄμ' | αὖ ∪ λοῖσιν."

[29] In the similar ritual at Ephesus as Prof. Murray points out (op. cit. p. 359) the Kouretes in like fashion "come to a stand" round the altar. See Strabo, p. 640, init. ὄρος, ὅπου στάντας φασὶ τοὺς Κούρητας τῷ ψόφῳ τῶν ὅπλων ἐκπλῆξαι. . . .

[30] x. 468 . . . προστησάμενοι μῦθον τὸν περὶ τῆς τοῦ Διὸς γενέσεως, ἐν ᾧ τὸν μὲν Κρόνον εἰσάγουσιν εἰθισμένον καταπίνειν τὰ τέκνα κ.τ.λ.

[31] x. 466 . . . τοιούτους γάρ τινας δαίμονας ἢ προπόλους θεῶν τοὺς Κούρητας φασὶν οἱ παραδόντες τὰ Κρητικὰ καὶ τὰ Φρύγια, ἱερουργίαις τισιν ἐμπεπλεγμένα ταῖς μὲν μυστικαῖς ταῖς δ' ἄλλαις περί τε τὴν τοῦ Διὸς παιδοτροφίαν τὴν ἐν Κρήτῃ καὶ τοὺς τῆς μητρὸς τῶν θεῶν ὀργιασμοὺς ἐν τῇ Φρυγίᾳ καὶ τοῖς περὶ τὴν Ἴδην τὴν Τρωικὴν τόποις.

Seilenoi, Bacchoi and Tityroi, and this is expressly stated by those who hand down the tradition of Cretan and Phrygian ceremonies, these being involved with certain sacred rites, some of them mystical, others relating to the child-nurture of Zeus and the orgiastic rites of the Mother of the Gods in Phrygia and in the region about the Trojan Ida.

Strabo thought that the child reared and protected by the Kouretes was Zeus, but our ritual Hymn knows him only as Kouros. It need not therefore surprise us that the Kouros appears elsewhere with other names. He is sometimes Dionysos, sometimes Zagreus.

The mysteries of Dionysos (Zagreus) are, says Clement of Alexandria, "utterly inhuman." He then proceeds to recount them. Utterly inhuman they are as Clement understood or rather utterly misunderstood them: very human indeed, social and civilising through and through if my interpretation be correct, so human and social that a very considerable portion of humanity thinks it well to practise analogous rites to-day.

Let Clement[32] tell his story:

"The mysteries of Dionysos are wholly inhuman, for while he was still a child and the Kouretes were dancing round him their armed dance the Titans came stealthily upon him and lured him with childish toys and tore him limb from limb while he was yet a babe. Thus does the Thracian Orpheus, the poet of the Rite recount.

The cones, the rhombos and the limb-bending toys,
And the fair gold apples of the Hesperides."

Other authorities add other details. The wicked Titans who stole the child away were painted over with white clay, gypsum[33] (τίτανος). Moreover, and this is of cardinal importance, there is a sequel to the story. After the child has been made away with (ἀφανισμός), swallowed by his father (τεκνοφαγία) or torn to pieces (διασπαραγμός), he comes back to life again: there is a coming to life again (ἀναβίωσις), a resurrection (παλιγγενεσία),[34] how and when we

---

[32] Abel, Orphica, 196 τὰ γὰρ Διονύσου μυστήρια τέλεον ἀπανθρωπα, ὅν εἰσέτι παῖδα ὄντα, ἐνόπλῳ κινήσει περιχορευόντων Κουρήτων, δόλῳ δὲ ὑποδύντων Τιτάνων, ἀπατήσαντες παιδαριώδεσιν ἀθύρμασιν, οὗτοι δὴ οἱ Τιτᾶνες διέσπασαν, ἔτι νηπίαχον ὄντα, ὡς ὁ τῆς τελετῆς ποιητής Ὀρφεύς φησιν ὁ Θράκιος.

κῶνος καὶ ῥόμβος καὶ παίγνια καμπεσίγυια
μῆλά τε χρύσεα καλὰ παρ᾽Ἑσπερίδων λιγυφώνων.

[33] Harpocrat. s.v. ἀπομάττων: ὡς ἄρα οἱ Τιτᾶνες τὸν Διόνυσον ἐλυμήναντο γύψῳ καταπλασάμενοι.

[34] Plut. De Is. et Os. xxxv. and De Ei ap. Delph. ix. Διόνυσον δὲ καὶ Ζαγρέα καὶ Νυκτέλιον καὶ Ἰσοδαίτην αὐτὸν ὀνομάζουσι, καὶ φθοράς τινας καὶ ἀφανισμούς, καὶ τὰς ἀναβιώσεις καὶ παλιγγενεσίας, οἰκεῖα ταῖς εἰρημέναις μεταβολαῖς αἰνίγματα καὶ μυθεύματα παραίνουσι.

are not told. Some said[35] the child's heart was saved and then put back into a figure made of gypsum. In some versions[36] the wicked giants or white-clay-men are struck[37] with lightning by Zeus and burnt to ashes and from these ashes sprang the human race.

The cardinal elements of the story whether told of the infant Zeus, Dionysos, Zagreus or the Kouros are:

(1) A child is taken from his mother and carefully tended by men called Kouretes. To guard him they dance over him an armed dance (παιδοτροφία).

(2) The child is hidden, made away with, killed, dismembered by men sometimes called Titans, "white-clay-men" (ἀφανισμός, σπαραγμός).

(3) The child reappears, is brought to life again. Sometimes this is effected by the white-clay-men, sometimes the child reappears as a white-clay-man himself, his heart being put into a figure of gypsum (ἀναβίωσις, παλιγγενεσία).

Of these elements only the first, the Child-Nurture, appears in the Hymn. This need not surprise us. Literature, even hieratic literature, tends to expurgate savage material, the death and resurrection ritual was well enough as a mystery, but in the third century AD not for publication even in a ritual Hymn.

In the study of Greek religion it is all important that the clear distinction should be realized between the comparatively permanent element of the ritual and the shifting manifold character of the myth. In the case before us we have a uniform ritual, the elements of which we have disentangled – the armed dance over the child, the mimic death and rebirth; but the myth shifts; it is told variously of Zagreus, Dionysos, Zeus, and there is every variety of detail as to how the child is mimetically killed and how the resurrection is effected. To understand the religious intent of the whole complex it is all important to seize on the permanent ritual factors.

This does not, however, imply, as is sometimes supposed, that ritual is prior to myth; they probably arose together. Ritual is the utterance of an

---

[35] Firmicus Mat. *De Err. Prof. Relig.* 6 . . . imaginem eius ex gypso plastico opere perfecit et cor pueri, ex quo facinus fuerat sorore deferente detectum, in ea parte plastae conlocat, qua pectoris fuerant lineamenta formata. Possibly the *imago* may have been like the παίγνια καμπεσίγυια and similar in character to the jointed terracotta dolls with movable arms and legs, found in Greek tombs.

[36] The sources for all these details are collected in Abel's *Orphica*, pp. 224 ff. and in Lobeck's *Aglaophamus*, pp. 553 ff. The Zagreus story is told in minute detail in the *Dionysiaka* of Nonnus, VI. 155 ff.

[37] The thunder-element in the story and the myth of the swallowing of the thunder-stone by Kronos will be discussed in chapter III.

emotion, a thing felt, in *action*, myth in words or thoughts. They arise *pari passu*. The myth is not at first *aetiological*, it does not arise to give a reason; it is representative, another form of utterance, of expression. When the emotion that started the ritual has died down and the ritual though hallowed by tradition seems unmeaning, a reason is sought in the myth and it is regarded as aetiological.[38]

We have now to ask what is the meaning of this extraordinary ritual. Why is a child or young man subjected to mimic rites of death and resurrection?

The orthodox explanation is that the child is a sort of vegetation spirit or corn-baby, torn to pieces in winter, revived in spring. I do not deny that in the myth there is an element of Corn- or rather Year-baby, but the explanation cannot be regarded as satisfactory, as it fails to explain the Kouretes, and the Titans disguised with white clay.

I offer a simpler and I think more complete explanation. Every single element, however seemingly preposterous, in both the ritual and myth of Zagreus can be explained I believe by the analogy of *primitive rites of tribal initiation*.

This I had long suspected because of the white-clay-men. These I have already fully discussed elsewhere[39] and I need now only briefly resume what is necessary for the immediate argument. The word Titanes (white-clay-men) comes of course from τίτανος, white earth or clay, gypsum. The Titanes, the white-clay-men, were later, regardless of quantity, mythologized into Τῑτᾶνες, Titans, giants. Harpocration,[40] explaining the word ἀπομάττων, says that the Titans, when they tore Dionysos to pieces, were covered with a coat of gypsum in order that they might not be recognized. Later, people when they were initiated went on doing the same thing and for the same reason that most people do most things nowadays, because "it was the thing to do." Nonnus[41] also says that the Titans were "whitened with mystic gypsum."

A coat of white paint was a means of making yourself up as a bogey or ghost; by disguising your real character as a common human man you reinforced your normal personality. A coat of white or sometimes black paint is the frequent disguise of savages to-day when in ceremonies of initiation for the edification of their juniors they counterfeit their tribal ancestors.

---

[38] This point will become clearer when (in chapter II.) the psychology of the δρώμενον, the ritual act, is examined. The general relation of myth to ritual is reserved for chapter VIII.

[39] *Prolegomena*, p. 492.

[40] ἐκμιμούμενοι τὰ μυθολογούμενα παρ᾽ ἐνίοις, ὡς ἄρα οἱ Τιτᾶνες τὸν Διόνυσον ἐλυμήναντο γύψῳ καταπλασάμενοι ἐπὶ τῷ μὴ γνώριμοι γενέσθαι. τοῦτο μὲν οὖν τὸ ἔθνος ἐκλιπεῖν, πηλῷ δὲ ὕστερον καταπλάττεσθαι νομίμου χάριν.

[41] Nonn. *Dionys.* XXVII. 228

ἐλευκαίνοντο δὲ γύψῳ
μυστιπόλῳ.

The Titans then, the white-clay-men, are real men dressed up as bogies to perform initiation rites. It is only later when their meaning is forgotten that they are explained as Tītānes, mythological giants. This much was clear to me years ago: i.e., that under the myth of Zagreus lay some form of initiation rite. What I then did not see, though my blindness seems to me now almost incredible, was the significance of the child and the toys[42] and above all why the child was first killed and then brought back to life.

Again light came to me unexpectedly from a paper kindly sent to me by Dr Frazer[43] containing an account of certain initiation ceremonies among the Wiradthuri tribe of New South Wales. This account must be briefly resumed:

> At a certain stage in the initiation ceremonies of these tribes the women and children huddled together and were securely covered up with blankets and bushes. Then a number of men came from the sacred ground where the initiation ceremonies were performed. Some of them swung bull-roarers, and some of them took up lighted sticks from a fire, and threw them over the women and children "to make them believe that Dhuramoolan had tried to burn them." At a later period of the ceremonies the boys were similarly covered up with blankets, a large fire was kindled near them, and when the roaring of the wood and the crackling of the flames became audible, several old men began to swing bull-roarers, and the lads were told that Dhuramoolan was about to burn them. These performances were explained by a legend that Dhuramoolan, a powerful being, whose voice sounded like the rumbling of distant thunder, had been charged by a still more powerful being called Baiamai, with the duty of taking the boys away into the bush and instructing them in all the laws, traditions, and customs of the community. So Dhuramoolan pretended that he always killed the boys, cut them up, and burnt them to ashes, after which he moulded the ashes into human shape, and restored them to life as new beings.

With the Cretan ritual in our minds it is clear that the Wiradthuri rites present more than an analogy; *mutato nomine* the account might have been written of Zagreus.

I have chosen the account of the Wiradthuri out of countless other instances, because in it we have the definite statement that the boys were burnt to ashes and Zagreus-like remodelled again in human shape. But everywhere, in Africa, in America, in Australia, in the South Pacific Islands, we come upon what is practically the same sequence of ceremonies. When a boy is initiated,

---

[42] A child's "toys" in antiquity were apt to be much more than mere playthings. They were charms inductive of good, prophylactic against evil, influences. Thus *crepundia*, from *crepere* "to rattle," served to amuse the child but also to protect him. For this whole subject see R. Wünsch, *Charms and Amulets*, in Hastings' Encyclopaedia of Religion and Ethics.

[43] *On some Ceremonies of the Central Australian Tribes*, Melbourne, 1901. Dr Frazer's authority is R. H. Matthews, *The Burbung of the Wiradthuri Tribes*, Journal of Anthropological Institute, xxv. (1896), pp. 297 f., 308, 311.

that is when he passes from childhood to adolescence, this pantomime, this terrifying (ἔκπληξις), this pretended killing of the child, this painting him with clay and bringing him back to life again as a young man, is everywhere enacted. Till the boy has died and come to life again, till he has utterly "put away childish things" he cannot be a full member of the tribe, he may not know the tribal secrets or dance the tribal dances, he may not handle bull-roarers, he cannot perform any of the functions of the full-grown man.

At and through his initiation the boy is brought into close communion with his tribal ancestors: he becomes socialized, part of the body politic. Henceforth he belongs to something bigger, more potent, more lasting, than his own individual existence: he is part of the stream of the totemic life, one with the generations before and yet to come.

So vital, so crucial is the change that the savage exhausts his imagination and his ingenuity in his emphasis of death and new birth. It is not enough to be killed, you must be torn to pieces or burnt to ashes. Above all you must utterly forget your past life. The precautions taken to secure this completeness of death and resurrection and consequent oblivion are sometimes disgusting enough. Murder is carefully counterfeited with the help of bladders of blood and the like. Sometimes the details are amusing: not only does the boy forget his own name that in this his social baptism he may receive a new one, but he does not know his own mother, he has forgotten how to speak and can only stammer, he cannot even swallow, he has to be artificially fed. He cannot come in straight at the door but must stumble in backwards. If he forgets and stupidly recognizes his mother or eats his food like a Christian he is taken back and "huskinawed" again.[44] All this is of course much more than mere pretence, it is a method of powerful suggestion.

The ritual, then, commemorated and perhaps in part enacted in our Hymn is the ritual of tribal Initiation. The Kouretes are Young Men who have been initiated themselves and will initiate others, will instruct them in tribal duties and tribal dances, will steal them away from their mothers, conceal them, make away with them by some pretended death and finally bring them back as newborn, grown youths, full members of their tribe. The word *Koures* is simply a specialized derivative of Kouros, as γυμνής of γυμνός, and perhaps γόης of γόος. It is, like Kouros, a word impossible to translate, because we have lost the social condition expressed. Young Men (*Kouroi*) we know, but Initiated Young Men (*Kouretes*) are gone for ever.

[44] For details as to Death and Resurrection elements in Initiation Ceremonies see H. Schurtz, *Altersklassen und Männerbünde*, 1902; H. Webster, *Primitive Secret Societies*, 1908; H. Hubert and M. Mauss, *Mélanges d'Histoire des Religions*, 1909, pp. 144 ff.; A. van Gennep, *Les Rites de Passage*, 1909, pp. 93 ff.; L. Lévy-Bruhl, *Les fonctions mentales dans les Sociétés Inférieures*, 1910, pp. 409 ff.; and, especially, Dr J. G. Frazer, *Golden Bough*,[2] III. pp. 423 ff. and *Totemism and Exogamy*, IV. p. 228.

The Kouretes are young men full-grown, but it will have been already noted that in the Hymn we have a child, and in the Zagreus myth a babe.[45] This brings us to an important point. It is not only the passage from childhood to adolescence that among savages is marked by rites of initiation, of death and resurrection. As Monsieur van Gennep[46] has well shown in his suggestive book, the ceremonies that accompany each successive stage of life, ceremonies, i.e., of birth, of marriage, of ordination as a medicine-man, and finally of death, are, no less than the ceremonies of adolescence, one and all *Rites de Passage*, ceremonies of transition, of going out from the old and going in to the new.[47]

Myths, then, which embody the hiding, slaying and bringing to life again of a child or young man, may reflect almost any form of initiation rite. It is not always possible to distinguish very clearly. Later[48] we shall see that the Kouretes had to do with a rite of the initiation of a sort of medicine-man, a rite nearer akin to our Ordination than to either Baptism or Confirmation. When the Greeks lost touch with the tribal customs which involved the rite of adolescence, we may suspect that they invented or at least emphasized Infant-Initiation. Later theologians entirely forgot the Kouros, and even the infant Zeus presented somewhat of a difficulty if not a scandal. A babe is rather the attribute of the divine Mother than the divine Father, and in patriarchal times, once the cult of the Mother was overshadowed, the infant Zeus needed apology. He was consigned to "local legend" and was held to be due to "*contaminatio* with the child Dionysos."

A clear and striking instance of a Second Birth in early childhood is reported by Mr and Mrs Routledge[49] as practised among the Akikúyu of British East Africa. It is known as "To be Born Again" or "To be Born of a Goat," and

---

[45] Thus Nonnus, *Dionysiaka*, VI. 179

ἄλλοτε ποικιλόμορφον ἔην βρέφος, ἄλλοτε κούρῳ
εἴκελος οἰστρηθέντι,

whereas Lucretius, II. 635

Dictaeos referunt Curetas . . .
Cum *pueri* circum *puerum*.

[46] *Les Rites de Passage*, Paris, 1909.

[47] For the psychology of initiation rites see Mr Marett's very interesting analysis in *The Birth of Humility*, Inaugural Lecture before the University of Oxford, 1910.

[48] Chapter III.

[49] *With a Prehistoric Race*, 1910, p. 151. Neither Mr nor Mrs Routledge could obtain permission actually to witness the rite. The custom is one of the oldest among the Akikúyu customs and universal among them. There is great reluctance to talk of the ceremony, and the knowledge of it was only obtained from natives who had broken with their own traditions and come under the influence of Christianity. Till a boy has been born again he cannot assist at the burial rites of his father. He is not part of the clan.

takes place when the boy is about ten years old or even younger if the father can afford the necessary goat for sacrifice. The goat is killed, a piece of skin cut in a circle and passed over one shoulder of the candidate and under the other arm. No men are allowed inside the hut, but women are present. The mother sits on a hide on the floor with the boy between her knees, the goat's gut is passed round the woman and brought in front of the boy. The woman groans as in labour, another woman cuts the gut, and the boy imitates the cry of a new-born infant, the women present all applaud and afterwards the assistant and the mother wash the boy. That night the boy sleeps in the same hut as the mother. On the second day the boy stays with his mother in the homestead. On the third day food is brought, and the relatives and friends come to a feast in the evening, but no native beer is drunk. After all is over the hut is swept out. The boy again sleeps in the mother's hut, and that night the father sleeps in the hut also.

The Akikúyu rite presents one feature of great interest. The boy is "Born of a Goat." It is nowhere stated that he is called a Goat, but the child of a goat must surely in some sense have been regarded as a Kid. We are irresistibly reminded of the Kid-Dionysos (Eriphios),[50] of the Horned Child and of the Baby Minotaur. The notion lingers on in the beautiful thought that at Baptism a child becomes one of the lambs of Christ the Lamb of God. At present among the Akikúyu the boy who is "Born of a Goat" is regarded as fit to tend goats, but behind a ceremony so emphatic and so expensive must, it would seem, lie some more serious significance.

The Akikúyu rite contains no mimic death. Death indeed seems scarcely an integral part of initiation, it is only a preparation for, an emphasis of, the new Life.[51] But an element like this of a striking and dramatic nature tends in myth sometimes to swamp the really integral factor. We hear more for example of the sufferings ($\pi\acute{a}\theta\eta$) of Dionysos than of his rebirth; the death of the child in such myths as those of Atreus and Thyestes, Demeter and Demophon[52] obscures the element of Resurrection. But there can be little doubt that originally the New Birth and Resurrection lay behind. Lucian[53] in his account of the strange solecisms committed by dancers says that he remembers how a man who was supposed to be "dancing the Birth of Zeus and the Child-Eating of Kronos actually *danced by mistake the calamities of Thyestes*, deceived by their similarity." The mistake is at least highly suggestive; the ritual dance of the two myths must have been almost identical.

---

[50] Hesych. s.v.

[51] The Orphic Hymn, xxxviii. 14, misunderstanding inverts the sequence. The Kouretes are . . . τροφέες τε καὶ αὖτ' ὀλετῆρες.

[52] Mr W. R. Halliday has shown clearly that the story of Demeter passing Demophon through the fire is the survival of an infant initiation-rite.

[53] de Salt. 80 τὰς γὰρ γονὰς ὀρχούμενός τις καὶ τὴν τοῦ Κρόνου τεκνοφαγίαν παρῳρχεῖτο καὶ τὰς Θυέστου συμφορὰς τῷ ὁμοίῳ παρηγμένος.

Anthropologists have been sometimes blamed,[54] and perhaps with justice, for the fiendish glee with which, as though they were Christian Fathers, they seize on barbarous survivals in Greek religion or literature. Zagreus dismembered by the Titans, the cannibal feasts of Thyestes and Lycaon, Demeter burning Demophon – these and a host of other stories are "survivals of human sacrifice."[55] It is only a little anthropology that is a dangerous thing. Men will kill and eat each other and especially their enemies for many and diverse reasons, but actual Human Gift-Sacrifice, and especially child-sacrifice, is rare among savages. Many a cannibal is a kind and good father; adorned with a necklace of skulls he will sit playing with the child on his knee. But, rare though Human Sacrifice is, and rarer still its survivals, the mock slaying of a boy in initiation rites is so common as to be almost universal, and in a large number of instances it is the memory of this mock slaying, misunderstood, that survives. By way of placation, of palinode, we offer to the humanist the mysteries of Zagreus made harmless, humanized by anthropology. Dhuramoolan *"pretended* that he killed the boys."

Primarily then the Kouretes are, in their capacity of Initiators, Child-Nurturers, Guardians (Παιδοτρόφοι, Φύλακες). Strabo[56] is on this point emphatic. "In the Cretan discourses," he says, "the Kouretes are called the nurses and guardians of Zeus," and again[57] in trying to explain the word Kouretes he says, "they were so called either because they were young and boys, or because of their rearing of Zeus." They earned this title, he adds, through being "as it were Satyrs attendant on Zeus. . . ." In the light of this initiation nurture the other functions of the Kouretes fall easily and naturally into place.

The Kouretes are *armed and orgiastic dancers* (ὀρχηστῆρες ἀσπιδηφόροι). Strabo[58] says they are certain youths who execute movements in armour; it is especially as inspired dancers that they fulfil their function as ministers in sacred rites. "They inspire terror by armed dances accompanied by noise and hubbub of timbrels and clashing arms and also by the sound of the flute and shouting." Nursing young children or even drilling young boys are functions that seem to us scarcely congruous with the dancing of armed dances. On the terracotta relief[59] in figure 3.3 we see the Kouretes armed with shields and

---

[54] See Prof. Murray, *Olympian Houses* in Albany Review, 1907, p. 205.

[55] A like explanation is often given of the rites of the Lupercalia, but see Warde-Fowler, *Roman Festivals*, p. 316 "The youths were never actually killed but were the figures in a kind of acted parable."

[56] x. 472 ἐν δὲ τοῖς Κρητικοῖς λόγοις οἱ Κουρῆτες Διὸς τροφεῖς λέγονται καὶ φύλακες.

[57] x. 468 ὥσθ᾽ οἱ Κουρῆτες ἤτοι διὰ τὸ νέοι καὶ κόροι ὄντες ὑπουργεῖν ἢ διὰ τὸ κουροτροφεῖν τὸν Δία (λέγεται γὰρ ἀμφοτέρως) ταύτης ἠξιώθησαν τῆς προσηγορίας, οἱονεὶ Σάτυροί τινες ὄντες περὶ τὸν Δία.

[58] op. cit.

[59] *Annali d. Inst.* XII. (1840), Tav. d᾽ agg. K. I am uncertain where the relief now is. E. Braun, who publishes it, says it passed from the Palazzo Colonna to royal castle of Agliè near Turin.

Figure 3.3 The Kouretes and the infant Zeus

short spears dancing over the infant Zeus, and if we try to realize the scene at all it seems to us absurd, calculated rather to scare the child to death than to defend him. But the Kouretes as Initiators continue their incongruous functions. Pantomimic dancing is of the essence of each and every mystery function. To disclose the mysteries is as Lucian[60] puts it "to dance out the mysteries." Instruction among savage peoples is always imparted in more or less mimetic dances.[61] At initiation you learn certain dances which confer on you definite social status. When a man is too old to dance, he hands over his dance to another and a younger, and he then among some tribes ceases to exist socially. His funeral when he dies is celebrated with scanty and perfunctory rites; having lost his dance he is a negligible social unit.[62]

The dances taught to boys at initiation are frequently if not always *armed* dances. These are not necessarily warlike. The accoutrement of spear and shield was in part decorative, in part a provision for making the necessary hubbub. Conspicuous in their dancing gear are the great ceremonial dancing shields and the long staves. They are painted in zigzag with white paint, and

[60] *Pisc.* 33 ἤν τινα καὶ τῶν μεμυημένων ἰδὼν ἐξαγορεύοντα τοῖν θεοῖν τὰ ἀπόρρητα καὶ ἐξορχούμενον ἀγανακτήσω. . . .

[61] Webster, op. cit. pp. 50, 51.

[62] R. Hertz, *Contribution à une étude sur la représentation collective de la mort.* Année Sociologique, x. 1905–6.

wear tails and skins of monkey and wild cat. To be allowed to dance it is essential that a boy be "painted with a particular pattern" of divine institution, "he must wear a particular dress and carry certain articles."[63]

The ancient Kouretes were not merely young men; they were half divine, *Daimones*. The Kouros in the Hymn is bidden to come at the head of his *Daimones* (δαιμόνων ἀγώμενος). As *daimones* the Kouretes resembled, Strabo[64] says, Satyrs, Seilenoi, Bacchoi, Tityroi. Divine but not quite gods, they are as we shall presently see the stuff of which ancient gods are made. Hesiod,[65] and Hesiod only, calls them actually gods. He tells of

> . . . the worthless idle race of Satyrs
> And the gods, Kouretes, lovers of sport and dancing.

In the light of initiation ceremonies we understand why the Kouretes and Korybantes though they are real live youths are yet regarded as δαίμονες, as half divine, as possessed (ἔνθεοι), enthusiastic, ecstatic, and why their ceremonies are characterized by Strabo[66] as orgiastic. The precise meaning of orgies will concern us later; for the present it is enough to note that in most savage mysteries it is a main part of the duty of initiators to impersonate gods or demons. The initiators dress up as the ancestral ghosts of the tribe, sometimes even wearing the actual skulls[67] of their ancestors, and in this disguise dance round the catechumens and terrify them half out of their senses. It is only when fully initiated that the boys learn that these terrific figures are not spirits at all but just their living uncles and cousins.[68] The secret is never imparted to women and children. To do so would be death.

As δαίμονες whether wholly or half divine the Kouretes *have all manner of magical capacities*. These capacities are by Strabo rather implied than expressly stated and are especially noticeable in their Phrygian equivalents, Korybantes. The Korybantes bind and release men from spells, they induce madness and heal it. The chorus asks[69] the love-sick Phaedra

[63] op. cit. p. 156.
[64] x. 466 ἔοικε δὲ μᾶλλον τῷ περὶ Σατύρων καὶ Σειλήνων καὶ Βακχῶν καὶ Τιτύρων λόγῳ.
[65] Frg. CXXIX.

καὶ γένος οὐτιδανῶν Σατύρων καὶ ἀμηχανοεργῶν
Κουρῆτές τε Θεοί, φιλοπαίγμονες ὀρχηστῆρες.

[66] x. 465 ὡς δὲ τύπῳ εἰπεῖν καὶ κατὰ τὸ πλέον ἐνθουσιαστικούς τινας καὶ Βακχικούς.
[67] H. Schurtz, *Altersklassen und Männerbünde*, 1902, p. 38. For the functions of ancestral ghosts see chapter 273.
[68] H. Webster, *Primitive Secret Societies*, pp. 101 and 187.
[69] Eur. *Hip.* 141

ἦ σύ γ' ἔνθεος, ὦ κούρα,
εἴτ' ἐκ Πανὸς εἴθ' Ἑκάτας
ἢ σεμνῶν Κορυβάντων φοι-
τᾷς ἢ ματρὸς ὀρείας;

Is this some Spirit, O child of man?
Doth Hecat hold thee perchance, or Pan?
Doth She of the Mountains work her ban,
Or the dread Corybantes bind thee?

The Kouretes are also, as all primitive magicians are, seers (μάντεις). When
Minos in Crete lost his son Glaukos he sent for the Kouretes to discover where
the child was hidden.[70] Closely akin to this magical aspect is the fact that they
are metal-workers.[71] Among primitive people metallurgy is an uncanny craft,
and the smith is half medicine man. The metal-working side of these figures
comes out best in the kindred Daktyls and Telchines. A step more and the
magicians become Culture-Heroes, inventors of all the arts of life, house-
building, bee-keeping, shield-making and the like.[72] As culture-heroes they
attend the Kouros in the Hymn. This development of the *daimon* and the
culture-hero will be discussed later.

Just such functions are performed to-day among primitive peoples by the
Initiated Young Man. If the investigations of recent anthropologists[73] are correct, it is not so much about the family and the domestic hearth that the
beginnings of the arts cluster, as about the institution known as the Man's
House.[74] Here, unencumbered by woman, man practises and develops his
diverse crafts, makes his weapons, his boats, his sacred images, his dancing
masks. Even after marriage when he counts as an elderly man he returns to the
Man's House[75] to keep in touch with civilization and the outside world. He is
a Culture-Hero in the making.

To resume the results of our enquiry.

The worshippers in the Hymn invoke a Kouros who is obviously but a
reflection or impersonation of the body of Kouretes. They "allege as their

---

[70] Apollod. 3. 2. 2.

[71] Soph. *ap.* Strabo, x. 473 says of the Idaean Daktyls οἳ σίδηρόν τε ἐξεῦρον καὶ εἰργάσαντο
πρῶτοι καὶ ἄλλα πολλὰ τῶν πρὸς τὸν βίον χρησίμων.

[72] Diod. Sic. v. 64. Idaean Daktyls are described as γόητες who superintend ἐπῳδὰς καὶ
τελετὰς καὶ μυστήρια. They invent fire and the use of iron. The magical functions of the
Kouretes and their aspect as medicine-men will be discussed in chapter III.

[73] See especially H. Schurtz, *Altersklassen und Männerbünde*, p. 48.

[74] H. Webster, *Primitive Secret Societies*, ch. I. The ancient Kouretes seem to have had a sort
of Man's House at Messene; it was a *megaron* not a temple. See Pausanias, IV. 31. 7 Κουρήτων
μέγαρον ἔνθα ζῷα τὰ πάντα ὁμοίως καθαγίζουσιν.

[75] That institutions analogous to those of the Man's House among savages lived on in Crete
we have abundant evidence in Strabo's account (x. 483) of Cretan institutions. The Ἀγέλαι with
their ἄρχοντες, the συσσίτια, the ἀνδρεῖα, clearly belong to the same social morphology as the
Männerhaus. It is probable that the ἁρπαγή and the custom ἀποκρύπτειν τὸν παῖδα (Strabo,
483) is a misunderstanding and in part a corruption of primitive initiation ceremonies. For
a discussion of some part of these Cretan customs and their religious origin see Dr E. Bethe,
Die dorische Knabenliebe, ihre Ethik und ihre Idee in Rhein. Mus. LXII. p. 438.

reason" an aetiological myth. This myth on examination turns out to be but the mythical representation of a rite of mimic death and resurrection practised at a ceremony of initiation. Now the Kouros and the Kouretes[76] are figures that belong to cultus; they are what would in common parlance be called religious. We are face to face with the fact, startling enough, that these religious figures arise, not from any "religious instinct," not from any innate tendency to prayer and praise, *but straight out of a social custom*. Themis and Dike, invoked by the Kouretes, lie at the undifferentiated beginnings of things when social spelt religious. They are not late abstractions, but primitive realities and sanctities.[77]

This contradicts, it is clear, many preconceived notions. We are accustomed to regard religion as a matter intensely spiritual and individual. Such undoubtedly it tends to become, but in its origin, in the case under investigation, it is not spiritual and individual, but social and collective. But for the existence of a tribe or group of some kind, a ceremony of initiation would be impossible. The surprise is all the greater because the particular doctrine in question, that of the New Birth, is usually held to be late and due to "Orphic," i.e., quasi Oriental influence. It is held to have affinities with Christianity, and is a doctrine passionately adhered to by many sects and establishments in the present day. It may indeed – in some form or another – as Conversion or as Regeneration – be said to be *the* religious doctrine par excellence.

Now it has of late been frequently pointed out that the god in some sense always "reflects" the worshipper, takes on the colour of his habits and his thoughts. The morality of a god is not often much in advance of that of his worshippers, and sometimes it lags considerably behind. The social structure is also, it is allowed, in some sense reflected in the god: a matriarchal society will worship a Mother and a Son, a patriarchal society will tend to have a cult of the Father. All this is true, but the truth lies much deeper. Not only does the god reflect the thoughts, social conditions, morality and the like, but in its origin his substance when analysed turns out to be just nothing but the representation, the utterance, the emphasis of these imaginations, these emotions, arising out of particular social conditions.

Long ago Robertson Smith[78] noted that among the ancient Semites or indeed everywhere antique religion "was essentially an affair of the community rather than of individuals"; the benefits expected from the gods were of a public character, affecting the whole community, especially fruitful seasons, increase of flocks and herds, and success in war. The individual sufferer, who to us is the special object of Divine protection, was more or less an outcast.[79]

---

[76] For the meagre survivals of the actual worship of the Kouretes in historical times as attested by inscription see Prof. Bosanquet, op. cit. p. 353.

[77] For fuller discussion of this point see chapter x.

[78] *Religion of the Semites*, 1889, pp. 211, 240.

[79] It is when the old tribal sanctions are broken down that Aidos and Nemesis of and for the individual come into force. See Prof. Murray, *Rise of the Greek Epic*,[2] p. 103.

"Hannah with her sad face and silent petition was a strange figure at the sanctuary of Shiloh; the leper and the mourner alike were unclean and shut out from the exercises of religion as well as from the privileges of social life." But necessarily at the time when Robertson Smith wrote he conceived of a god as something existing independently of the community, though very closely related. This brings us to our last point.

So long as religion was defined by its object it was, to the detriment of science, confused with theology. It was currently supposed that religion was a kind of instinct of the soul after some sort of god or spirit or – as the doctrine became more rarefied – some innate power of apprehending the infinite.[80] The blunder here made was an elementary one, and took small account of facts. The most widespread and perhaps potent of all religions, Buddhism, knows no god. The error arose partly from ignorance or carelessness as to facts, and partly from the mistake in method common to all pre-scientific enquiry, the mistake of starting with a general term *religion* of which the enquirers had a preconceived idea, and then trying to fit into it any facts that came to hand.

In the present enquiry we shall at the outset attempt no definition of the term *religion*, but we shall collect the facts that admittedly are religious and see from what human activities they appear to have sprung. The Kouros and the Kouretes are such facts. They sprang, we have just seen, from certain social interests and activities. The worshippers, or rather the social agents, are prior to the god. The ritual act, what the Greeks called the δρώμενον, is prior to the divinity.

---

[80] This error, originated I believe by Max Müller and adopted with various modifications and extensions by M. Réville in his *Prolégomènes à l'histoire des religions*, and by Morris Jastrow in his *Study of Religions*, has been well exposed by Prof. Durkheim in his article *De la définition des phénomènes religieux* in Année Sociologique, II. (1898), pp. 4 ff.

4

THE MYTH AND RITUAL PATTERN
OF THE ANCIENT EAST

S. H. Hooke

The English biblicist S. H. Hooke (1874–1968), who was Professor of Old Testament Studies in the University of London, edited three collections of essays that sought to establish the existence of a myth-ritualist pattern in the ancient Near East. Hooke's brand of myth-ritualism comes from Frazer. The core of the pattern is the enactment of the myth of the death and rebirth of the god of vegetation. The ritual works magically to effect the myth. Sometimes the king merely plays the part of the god. More often the king is the god. No more than Frazer, from whom he gets both options, does Hooke reconcile the two. Despite Hooke's indebtedness to Frazer, he dismisses him as a Tylorean intellectualist rather than a myth-ritualist. The real difference between Hooke and Frazer is over the source of the pattern. Hooke, confining the pattern to a single area, attributes it to diffusion, most likely from Mesopotamia. Frazer, postulating a worldwide pattern, attributes it to independent invention by each culture. Hooke's original presentation of the pattern, which follows, is from the first of his three myth-ritualist collections: *Myth and Ritual* (London: Oxford University Press, 1933), ch. 1. See also his "Traces of the Myth and Ritual Pattern in Canaan," in *Myth and Ritual*, ch. 4; Introduction to *The Labyrinth*, ed. Hooke (London: SPCK, 1935), v–x; "The Myth and Ritual Pattern in Jewish and Christian Apocalyptic," in *The Labyrinth*, ch. 6; *The Origins of Early Semitic Ritual*, Schweich Lectures 1935 (London: Oxford University Press, 1938); "Myth, Ritual and History" and "Myth and Ritual Reconsidered," in his *The Siege Perilous* (London: SCM, 1956), chs 3 and 12; and "Myth and Ritual: Past and Present," in *Myth, Ritual, and Kingship*, ed. Hooke (Oxford: Clarendon Press, 1958), ch. 1. On Hooke see *Promise and Fulfilment: Essays*

Original publication: S. H. Hooke, "The Myth and Ritual Pattern of the Ancient East," in *Myth and Ritual*, ed. Hooke (London: Oxford University Press, 1933), pp. 1–14.

Presented to Professor S. H. Hooke, ed. F. F. Bruce (Edinburgh: T. & T. Clark, 1963); and E. C. Graham, *Nothing Is Here for Tears: A Memoir of Samuel Henry Hooke* (Oxford: Blackwell, 1969).

The meaning of the terms "myth" and "ritual" – Early ritual concerned with practical problems of daily life – Myth the spoken part of ritual – The spread of culture patterns from one country to another – The three processes accompanying the spread of culture patterns – Adaptation – Disintegration – Degradation – The king the central feature of the ritual – The annual festival the centre and climax of the ritual – Its main elements – Dramatic representation of the death and resurrection of the god – Symbolic representation of the myth of creation – The ritual combat – The sacred marriage – The triumphal procession – Influence of this ritual pattern upon the religious practices of the Hebrews – The Hebrew prophets and the conception of the King-god – Moses as the originator of Hebrew hostility to this conception – Features of the Hebrew Seasonal Feasts which imply the influence of the ritual pattern – The Creation Myth and the ritual combat – The implications of early ritual prohibitions – Sun- and Moon-cults dealt with in later Essays, not of the essence of the pattern.

Since the terms "myth" and "ritual" will be constantly used in the following pages, it will be well to state briefly the particular sense in which they will be so used. In his recent book, *Myths of the Origin of Fire*, Sir James Frazer defines mythology as the philosophy of primitive man: "It is his first attempt to answer those general questions concerning the world which have doubtless obtruded themselves on the human mind from the earliest times and will continue to occupy it to the last." He also describes myths as "documents of human thought in the embryo". Now the expression "primitive man" is almost as vague as the phrase "the man in the street". To describe the myths and practices of Australian aborigines or Polynesian islanders as representing the behaviour and mentality of primitive man is a question-begging process.

The term "primitive" is a purely relative one. The only kind of behaviour or mentality which we can recognize as "primitive" in the strict sense is such as can be shown to lie historically at the fountain-head of a civilization. The earliest civilizations known to us are those of Egypt and Mesopotamia, and the earliest evidence which we can gather concerning the beliefs and practices there prevalent constitutes for us what is "primitive" in the historical sense.

To the educated reader the word "myth" probably suggests familiar and often very beautiful Greek stories, the themes of poet and dramatist, such as the myths of Zeus and Semele, Theseus and the Minotaur, Perseus and the Gorgon Medusa. But as soon as these stories are examined we find that they all contain some thread which, like the clue which Ariadne gave to Theseus, leads back to the centre, to the original or primitive significance of the story, to the home of the myth. From Perseus we find a thread leading back to the Canaanite god, Resheph. Sir Arthur Evans, in *The Palace of Minos*, has said: "We see the Minotaur himself on the way to Crete, but if he reached the Island from the Delta, his starting-point was still the Euphrates." In both Dionysiac myth and ritual we find clues pointing back to Egypt and Osiris. Hence behind the myths of Greece, in the region of the world's most ancient civilizations, there lie those modes of behaviour which are primitive for us in the sense that they are the source of the great body of myth and ritual characteristic of ancient culture.

When we examine these early modes of behaviour we find that their originators were not occupied with general questions concerning the world but with certain practical and pressing problems of daily life. There were the main problems of securing the means of subsistence, to keep the sun and moon doing their duty, to ensure the regular flooding of the Nile, to maintain the bodily vigour of the king who was the embodiment of the prosperity of the community. There were also individual problems, how to ward off disease and ill fortune, how to acquire a knowledge of the future. In order to meet these needs the early inhabitants of Egypt and Mesopotamia developed a set of customary actions directed towards a definite end. Thus the coronation of a king, both in Egypt and Babylon, consisted of a regular pattern of actions, of things prescribed to be done, whose purpose was to fit the king completely to be the source of the well-being of the community. This is the sense in which we shall use the term "ritual".

Moreover, we find that these early ritual patterns consisted not only of things done but of things said. The spoken word had the efficacy of an act, hence the magic value of the many punning allusions which we find in early Egyptian ritual texts, a point which will be abundantly illustrated by Dr Blackman in his essay. In general the spoken part of a ritual consists of a description of what is being done, it is the story which the ritual enacts. This is the sense in which the term "myth" is used in our discussion. The original myth, inseparable in the first instance from its ritual, embodies in more or less symbolic fashion, the original situation which is seasonally re-enacted in the ritual.

Thus in the Egyptian Coronation ritual contained in the Ramesseum Papyrus, with which Dr Blackman will deal in his essay, the spoken part of the ritual embodies the myth of Osiris. Again, to take an example from the Babylonian New Year ritual, when Marduk is lying dead in the "mountain", the recitation of the Creation myth, the *enuma elish*, is an essential part of the ritual for restoring life to the dead god. But the *enuma elish* contains the description of the situation which is being enacted in the ritual, the triumph of Marduk over his enemies, and the fixing of destinies.

Accordingly the origin of such actions as may be classed as ritual lies in the attempt to deal with or control the unpredictable element in human experience. Since in the early stages of man's knowledge of the universe the realm of the unpredictable was almost co-extensive with human life, and even the

Figure 4.1   Examples of winged disks: (i) Egypt, (ii) Assyria, (iii) Cappadocia, (iv) Persia

simplest acts might have unforeseen and undesirable consequences, the range of ritual activities was far larger than it is to-day. As far back as evidence for such activities in Egypt or Mesopotamia exists, that is, between three and four millenniums before Christ, we find that they had assumed a pattern which was adapted to the needs of an urban civilization and a social structure of which the king was the centre. This pattern will be discussed at a later stage.

In the myths of Greece, as we have already observed, there is a clue, a connecting thread, which leads back to this ancient myth and ritual pattern just referred to. This raises the question of the transmission of such patterns from one culture area to another. Since Goblet d'Alviella's pioneer work on the subject, the fact of the migration of symbols has been generally accepted. But a symbol is merely a detached fragment of myth or ritual which has acquired a separate life of its own. If it be recognized that a fragment of a myth or ritual may travel far from its original setting, as has happened, for instance, in the case of the familiar winged disk (see figure 4.1), it is also possible to conceive of the carrying of the larger ritual pattern with its associated myth from one country to another by one of the various ways of "culture spread", such as commerce, conquest, or colonization.

We are on sure ground in asserting that there is abundant evidence for the interchange of many culture elements throughout the ancient East. In *The Palace of Minos* Sir Arthur Evans repeatedly stresses the cultural interchange between Crete, Egypt, and Mesopotamia. The relation between Hittite,

Elamite, and early Babylonian seals, as indeed between most of the early seals from the culture area which we are considering, is very striking both in technique and content. The new material from Mohendjodaro[1] increases the possible range of such a "culture spread".

Now it may be said that in general, when such a transmission of culture patterns takes place, three processes are set in motion, namely, adaptation, disintegration, and degradation.

In the first place there is always an adaptation of borrowed cultural elements to their new environment. The bold and original way in which Minoan artists dealt with Egyptian culture motifs abundantly illustrates the principle. A simple and familiar example is furnished by the winged solar disk already referred to. In Assyria the place of the solar disk is taken by the figure of Asshur, in Persia by that of Ahura Mazda. Indeed, the presence of a cultural element which is clearly alien to its environment is often a sure indication of borrowing. For example, the representation of the god in his sacred bark is at home in Egypt, where the funeral procession of Osiris by river to Abydos was part of the regular ritual pattern. We also find it in Babylon where it is not alien to the conditions of a river-valley culture, and where, even if it was originally borrowed, it has been completely assimilated. But when we find a Hebrew seal from Jerusalem, depicting a god in his sacred bark, we have a clear case of a borrowed cultural element in an alien environment, for that of Palestine is least of all a riverine civilization.

Next we have another process, one which is specially illustrated in the field of Canaanite and Hebrew culture, but is found throughout the world, the process of disintegration. In the first place it is clear that a very large part of Egyptian ritual was based on the practice of mummification. Hence, when the ritual was carried to an environment where mummification was the exception, much of it would tend to disappear as meaningless or be adapted to altered conditions. It would disintegrate. Mr A. M. Hocart's valuable book *Kingship* contains overwhelming evidence of the way in which the original pattern of the elaborate ritual of coronation could be broken up in the course of its migration into various parts of the world.

Mummification was not practised in Sumer and Akkad; hence the general ritual pattern which developed there was more readily adaptable to the Semitic environment of Canaan, and its influence there is more easily traced. But the same process of disintegration took place, though to a lesser degree. The theory of culture-borrowing which we are endeavouring to establish in no way conflicts with the fact that borrowing may exist side by side with the development of independent ideas and institutions. Hence we get the peculiar mingling of cultures which is characteristic of Canaanite civilization.

---

[1] See Sir John Marshall, *Mohendjodaro*, 1932.

But the process, that of disintegration, appears even more clearly in the breaking up of myth. The Greek myths, as we know them, are fragments of an original pattern which have taken on a separate existence as literary forms. Both the Minotaur and the Perseus myths involve an underlying ritual pattern of human sacrifice, and take us back to a stage in which the myth and ritual were united. In Mr Hartland's *Perseus* we can see the gradual disintegration and dispersion of the severed members of the myth.

The third process, of degradation, often takes place simultaneously with adaptation and disintegration. Though it is more noticeable in the material and artistic side of culture, it is not without influence upon the content of myth and ritual. The gods and their representations in any cultural area are not isolated conceptions but form part, and indeed are the product, of the original ritual pattern.

Hence the borrowing and interchange of gods, their names and attributes, is an important part of the process we are discussing. But it is here that degradation is particularly observable. Degradation may appear as actual loss of skill and artistic feeling, as for instance, in the representation of the Hathor head-dress in the many figurines of Astarte found in Canaanite excavation.[2] It may also consist of loss of meaning, as when a symbol or a fragment of ritual persists after its original meaning has been lost. In Canaan, the region with which we are specially concerned, the pervading influence of the culture of Egypt and Babylon was bound to be felt in a marked degree owing to the fact that Canaan was a dependency of one or other of these two powers from 2000 to 1000 BC. This is fully discussed below in the fourth essay.

The distinctive features of the Egyptian and Babylonian ritual systems are described in the next two essays. Hence it is only necessary here to give an account of the pattern assumed by the common elements of all these early rituals.

The central feature is the importance of the king for the well-being of the community – it may be a coincidence, it may be more than a coincidence, that some of the finest descriptions of the Golden Age to Come, written by Hebrew prophets and apocalyptists, had as their essential point the figure of a king, now only human, now semi-divine or more. It lies beyond the scope of our inquiry to discuss the origin of this conception. But in the earliest ritual material at our disposal from Egypt and Babylon, the king is already the focus of those activities which we have described as ritual. In both Egypt and Babylon the king is regarded as divine. He represents the god in the great seasonal rituals.

The annual festival which was the centre and climax of all the religious activities of the year contained the following elements:

---

[2] See Gressmann, *Texte und Bilder zum Alten Testament*, 1927, vol. ii, pl. 118, figs. 279–84.

(*a*)   The dramatic representation of the death and resurrection of the god.

(*b*)   The recitation or symbolic representation of the myth of creation.

(*c*)   The ritual combat, in which the triumph of the god over his enemies wad depicted.

(*d*)   The sacred marriage.

(*e*)   The triumphal procession, in which the king played the part of the god followed by a train of lesser gods or visiting deities.

These elements might vary in different localities and at different periods, some being more strongly stressed than others, but they constitute the underlying skeleton, so to speak, not only of such seasonal rituals as the great New Year Festivals, but also of coronation rituals, initiation ceremonies, and may even be discerned in occasional rituals such as spells against demons and various diseases.

We have seen that the origin of ritual in general lies in the attempt to control the unpredictable element in human experience. The ritual pattern represents the things which were done to and by the king in order to secure the prosperity of the community in every sense for the coming year. Behind the dramatic representation of the death and resurrection of the king lies the original custom of killing the king when his physical vigour showed signs of diminishing, a custom which still survives among the Shilluk of the Upper Nile.[3]

The widespread occurrence of the myth of creation in connexion with this ritual pattern suggests the recall or re-enactment of the original situation out of which the civilization of the community, with its institutions, its customs, and its gods, came into existence. This situation always involved a struggle of some kind, either against material difficulties, river-floods, drought, or early political conflicts, such as the struggle between the North and the South of Egypt before the united monarchy came into existence. In the ritual this struggle is represented by the ritual combat. In the inscription of I-khernofret, a high Egyptian official of the time of the Twelfth Dynasty, occurs the passage: "I avenged Un-Nefer on the day of the Great Battle, I overthrew all his enemies on the dyke (?) of Netit."[4] In the Babylonian New Year Festival the ritual takes the form of a foot-race between Zu and Ninurta, in which Zu is defeated and afterwards, apparently, slain. In the myth the counterpart of the ritual is the story of the struggle between Horus and Set, between Marduk and Tiamat, or between Jahweh and the dragon.

One of the earliest elements in the ritual pattern was the sacred marriage. Sir James Frazer has interpreted the processional scene in the rock sculpture of Boghaz Keui as the representation of a sacred marriage:

[3] Sir James Frazer, *The Golden Bough*, abridged edn, 1923, pp. 293–5.

[4] Sir E. A. Wallis Budge, *Osiris and the Egyptian Resurrection*, 1911, vol. ii, p. 10.

We may conjecture that it is the rite of the Sacred Marriage, and that the scene is copied from a ceremony which was periodically performed by human representatives of the deities. . . . If this was so at Boghaz Keui, we may surmise that the chief pontiff and his family annually celebrated the marriage of the divine powers of fertility, the Father God and the Mother Goddess, for the purpose of ensuring the fruitfulness of the earth and the multiplication of men and beasts.[5]

The cylinder inscription B of Gudea contains an account of the sacred marriage of the god Ningirsu with the goddess Bau, the daughter of heaven. The text describes how the warrior Ningirsu enters like a whirlwind into his temple, and how Bau, like the rising sun, comes in to him to his couch, and how their union, like the Tigris in flood, brings prosperity to Lagash.[6]

Not the least important part of the ritual, and one of the most widespread, was the triumphal procession, the epiphany of the god, his public manifestation as risen, triumphant, possessing all power to determine the destinies of his people for the coming year.

There are many other features of early ritual. We have not mentioned them since our purpose has been simply to give the general outline of the central elements of the myth and ritual characteristic of the ancient East.

There now arises the question whether the religious practices of the Hebrews show traces of this prevalent ritual pattern. More detailed discussions of the problem and fuller statements of the evidence will be found in the later essays of this volume. We confine ourselves here to a general statement of the position.

At the outset a fact is evident which might seem at first sight fatal to the suggestion that Hebrew religion received the imprint of this ancient ritual pattern. It is the fact that the theory of divine kingship was definitely rejected by the prophets who gave to Hebrew religion its permanent form and character.[7] That the conception of a king-god was not unknown to them we learn from a remarkable passage in the book of Ezekiel. Here is a part of his description of the king-god of Tyre:

Son of man, say unto the prince of Tyre, Thus saith the Lord God: Because thine heart is lifted up, and thou hast said, I am a god, I sit in the seat of God, in the midst of the seas; yet thou art man, and not God, though thou didst set thine heart as the heart of God . . . thou sealest up the sum, full of wisdom, and perfect in beauty. Thou wast in Eden the garden of God; every precious stone was thy covering . . . Thou wast the anointed cherub that covereth: and I set thee, so that thou wast upon the holy mountain of God; thou hast walked up and down in the midst of the stones of fire. (Ezek. xxviii. 1–14.)

---

[5] *Adonis, Attis, Osiris*, 1906, pp. 58–9.

[6] F. Bohl, *Z.A.*, Oct. 1929, p. 91.

[7] For a discussion of this subject see C. R. North, *The Old Testament Estimate of the Monarchy*, in *The American Journal of Semitic Languages and Literature*, vol. xlviii, pp. 1 ff.

It is clear that the prophet and, no doubt, his readers, were familiar with the conception of a king-god and with the ritual of the deification of the king.[8] Doubtless we should have had many more references to this circle of ideas but for its partial eclipse – though no more than a *partial* one – at a comparatively early period. This latter may well be attributed to the influence of Moses himself. There does not seem to be any reason for rejecting the tradition that Moses, the traditional founder of Hebrew religion, spent the first part of his life in the environment of the Egyptian Court. Here he would be familiar with the ritual pattern of which the divine king was the centre in its most elaborate form. When he was obliged to leave Egypt, he spent some years among the pastoral tribes who occupied the steppes of Midian. Here he passed through the experience which is symbolized by the story of the burning bush. This seems to have impressed upon his mind a conception of the nature of God wholly incompatible with the conception of the Egyptian divine king. This might well have produced in him a strong revulsion against the whole ritual system of Egypt and especially against everything in it that implied the idea of making a man into a god.

Hebrew ritual, more especially early Hebrew ritual, is dealt with in the sixth and seventh essays. Hence it is only necessary here to refer to certain features of the early Seasonal Feasts which seem to imply the influence of the ritual pattern discussed above.

(*a*) We find a parallel to the double observance of the New Year Festival in Babylonia – in Nisan and in Tishrit – in the existence in the Hebrew Festival Calendar of the double New Year celebration of Passover and Unleavened Bread in Nisan, and of *Rosh Hashanah* in Tishri.

(*b*) The Feast of Ingathering, later called the Feast of Tabernacles, was also clearly a New Year Festival, as is shown by the expression "at the out-going of the year".[9]

(*c*) A characteristic feature of the Feast of Tabernacles was the booths of greenery. This, although it belongs to the priestly account of the feast, may very well be of far earlier origin. It is probably connected with the conception of the sacred marriage and the ceremony of decorating the *gigunu*, or bridal-chamber, of the god in the *ziqqurat* with greenery.[10]

(*d*) The slaying of the first-born in Egypt, which in Exodus appears as an aetiological myth explaining Jahweh's claim to all first-born, probably goes back to the ritual of the slaying of the king; in its Hebrew form it may be connected with the night of slaughter referred to in the inscription of I-khernofret mentioned above, as part of the Osiris ritual.

---

[8] C. R. North, *The Religious Aspects of Hebrew Kingship*, Z.A.W., 1932, pp. 21–38.

[9] See G. B. Gray, *Sacrifice in the Old Testament*, 1925, pp. 300–1.

[10] See the article by Mr Sidney Smith in *The Journal of the Royal Asiatic Society*, 1928, pp. 849–68.

There are many features of the early Seasonal Feasts which suggest that we have to do here with the phenomenon already referred to, namely, the breaking up of the ritual pattern in the course of its passage into a fresh environment. The ritual pattern was probably transmitted indirectly to the Hebrews through the medium of the Canaanites – whatever may have been added afterwards.

It has long been recognized that in the various references to the fight between Jahweh and the dragon preserved in Hebrew literature, we have the survival of the Creation Myth and the fight between Marduk and Tiamat. But what has not been so generally recognized is that the myth thus preserved is the counterpart of the ritual combat, and constitutes a vital part of the whole ritual pattern – hence the importance of all that Mr Gadd has written below.

Old Testament scholars have been rather reluctant to accept Mowinckel's theory that the Processional Psalms imply the existence among the Hebrews of a New Year Festival of the enthronement of Jahweh. But the existence of such a ceremony in the earlier stages of Hebrew religion seems to be extremely probable, when it is recognized that the epiphany of the god and his triumphal procession attended by a train of lesser gods is also a part of this general ritual pattern of which we have seen traces in other elements of early Hebrew ritual.

It seems possible to draw similar conclusions from an examination of a number of ritual prohibitions in early Hebrew religious legislation. We have merely indicated its general trend. While a large number of such prohibitions are evidently due to the later prophetic attack on every religious custom which bore the stamp of Canaanite origin, there is a group of ritual prohibitions, some of which belong to the earliest stage of Hebrew religious legislation, pointing to the existence of the king-god ritual pattern. This group includes certain laws which have offered considerable difficulty to commentators, but which appear in a new light when they are related to the ritual system which sprang from the conception of the divine king. Such, for example, are the prohibitions against steps up to the altar, against seething a kid in its mother's milk, against incest, sacred prostitution, interchange of clothing between the sexes, and a number of similar instances. This point is dealt with in the fourth essay.

Lastly a word must be said about Sun-worship and Moon-worship. These cults were very prevalent throughout the cultural areas with which we are concerned. But here they can only be mentioned in passing since neither of them exercised a formative influence upon the main outlines of the ritual pattern which has been the chief subject of this essay. Those cults, however, in their relation to Jahwism, are by no means neglected in the essays which follow.

Part III

APPLICATION OF THE THEORY TO THE ANCIENT WORLD

5

EXCURSUS ON THE RITUAL FORMS PRESERVED IN GREEK TRAGEDY

Gilbert Murray

The Australian-born Gilbert Murray (1866–1957), who was Regius Professor of Greek at Oxford University, was an ally of Harrison's in postulating a primitive, pre-Homeric stage of Greek religion. In this stage the gods, initially unnamed, are earth rather than sky gods and can be magically controlled rather than merely beseeched. The god who most fully embodies this stage is Dionysus. Murray views tragedy as the legacy of the ritualistic enactment of the myth of the death and rebirth of Dionysus, taken as a vegetation god. To be sure, Murray does not equate tragedy with myth and ritual. He merely derives tragedy from myth and ritual. His evidence is the similarity between the plot of Greek tragedy and the myth of the life of Dionysus. Tragic heroes are symbolic substitutes for Dionysus. In addition to the following "Excursus" on Greek tragedy written for Harrison's *Themis* (pp. 341–63), see also Murray, *Four Stages of Greek Religion* (New York: Columbia University Press; London: Oxford University Press, 1912; 2nd edn, retitled *Five Stages of Greek Religion* [New York: Columbia University Press; Oxford: Clarendon Press, 1925]); *Euripides and His Age* (1st edn, New York: Holt; London: Williams and Norgate, 1913), 60–8; "Hamlet and Orestes: A Study in Traditional Types," Annual Shakespeare Lecture, 1914, *Proceedings of the British Academy* 6 (1913–14) (London: Oxford University Press, 1914), 389–412, which is reprinted in his *The Classical Tradition in Poetry* (Cambridge, MA: Harvard University Press; London: Oxford University Press, 1927), ch. 8; *Aeschylus* (Oxford: Clarendon Press, 1940); and "Dis Geniti," *Journal of Hellenic Studies* 71 (1951), 120–8. See also his *An Unfinished Autobiography*, ed. Jean Smith and Arnold

Original publication: Gilbert Murray, "Excursus on the Ritual Forms Preserved in Greek Tragedy," in Harrison, *Themis*, pp. 341–63.

Toynbee (London: Allen and Unwin, 1960). On Murray see Arthur Pickard-Cambridge, *Dithyramb, Tragedy and* Comedy (1st edn, Oxford: Clarendon Press, 1927); *Essays in Honour of Gilbert Murray*, eds J. A. K. Thomson and A. J. Toynbee (London: Allen and Unwin, 1936); J. A. K. Thomson, "Gilbert Murray, 1866–1957," *Proceedings of the British Academy* 43 (1957), 245–70; Francis West, *Gilbert Murray* (New York: St Martin's Press; London: Croom Helm, 1984); Duncan Wilson, *Gilbert Murray OM, 1866–1957* (Oxford: Clarendon Press, 1987); Robert L. Fowler, "Gilbert Murray," in *Classical Scholarship*, eds Ward W. Briggs and William M. Calder III (New York: Garland Publishing, 1990), 321–34; and Robert Ackerman, *The Myth and Ritual School* (New York: Garland Publishing, 1991), 128–38, 145–52, 167–74.

The following note presupposes certain general views about the origin and essential nature of Greek Tragedy. It assumes that Tragedy is in origin a Ritual Dance, a *Sacer Ludus*, representing normally the Aition, or supposed historical Cause, of some current ritual practice: e.g., the *Hippolytus* represents the legendary death of that hero, regarded as the Aition of a certain ritual lamentation practised by the maidens of Trozên. Further, it assumes, in accord with the overwhelming weight of ancient tradition, that the Dance in question is originally or centrally that of Dionysus, performed at his feast, in his theatre, under the presidency of his Priest, and by performers who were called $\Delta\iota\upsilon\upsilon\sigma\upsilon$ $\tau\epsilon\chi\nu\hat{\iota}\tau\alpha\iota$. It regards Dionysus in this connection as an "Eniautos-Daimon," or vegetation god, like Adonis, Osiris, etc., who represents the cyclic death and rebirth of the Earth and the World, i.e., for practical purposes, of the tribe's own lands and the tribe itself. It seems clear, further, that Comedy and Tragedy represent different stages in the life of this Year Spirit; Comedy leads to his Marriage Feast, his $\kappa\hat{\omega}\mu os$ and $\gamma\acute{\alpha}\mu os$, Tragedy to his death and $\theta\rho\hat{\eta}\nu os$. See Mr Cornford's *Origin of Attic Comedy*.[1]

These conceptions, it will be seen, are in general agreement with the recent work of Dieterich (*Archiv für Religionswissenschaft*, XI. pp. 163–196), also with that of Usener (*ib.* VII. pp. 303–313), as developed by Dr Farnell (*Cults*, vol. V. p. 235, note A), and the indications of the Macedonian mummeries described by Mr Dawkins and others. I must also acknowledge a large debt to Prof. Ridgeway's Tomb-theory, the more so since I ultimately differ from him on the main question, and seek to show that certain features in tragedy which he regards as markedly foreign to Dionysus-worship are in reality natural expressions of it.

---

[1] It is worth remarking that the Year-Daimon has equally left his mark on the New Comedy. The somewhat tiresome foundling of unknown parentage who grows up, is recognized, and inherits, in almost every play of Menander that is known to us, is clearly descended from the foundling of Euripidean tragedy who turns out to be the son of a god and inherits a kingdom. And that foundling in turn is derived from the Year-Baby who grows up in such miraculous fashion in the Mummers' Play. These babies are always bastards and always divine; also they are generally twins. One need only recall the babies of the *Ichneutae*, the *Ion*, the *Augê*, the *Alopê*, the *Oedipus* (esp. *O.T.* 1086–1109); the twins of Antiopê and Melanippê, of Alcmena, and Leda, and Leto, and Iphimedeia and Rhea Silvia. In Menander the foundlings are prevailingly twins.

It is of course clear that Tragedy, as we possess it, contains many non-Dionysiac elements. The ancients themselves have warned us of that. It has been influenced by the epic, by hero cults, and by various ceremonies not connected with Dionysus. Indeed the actual Aition treated in tragedy is seldom confessedly and obviously Dionysiac. It is so sometimes, as sometimes it is the founding of a torch-race or the original reception of suppliants at some altar of sanctuary. But it is much more often the death or *Pathos* of some hero. Indeed I think it can be shown that every extant tragedy contains somewhere towards the end the celebration of a tabu tomb. This point we must gladly concede to Professor Ridgeway. I wish to suggest, however, that while the content has strayed far from Dionysus, the forms of tragedy retain clear traces of the original drama of the Death and Rebirth of the Year Spirit.

Dieterich has already shown that a characteristic of the Sacer Ludus in the mysteries was a Peripeteia, or Reversal. It was a change from sorrow to joy, from darkness and sights of inexplicable terror to light and the discovery of the reborn God. Such a Peripeteia is clearly associated with an Anagnorisis, a Recognition or Discovery. Such formulae from the mysteries as Θαρσεῖτε, Μύσται, τοῦ θεοῦ σεσωσμένου – Ηὑρήκαμεν, συγχαίρομεν – Ἔφυγον κακόν, ηὗρον ἄμεινον, imply a close connection between the Peripeteia and the Anagnorisis, and enable us to understand why these two elements are regarded by Aristotle as normally belonging to Tragedy. Now Peripeteia of some kind is perhaps in itself a necessary or normal part of any dramatic story. But no one could say the same of Anagnorisis. It must come into Greek tragedy from the Sacer Ludus, in which the dead God is Recognized or Discovered.

So far Dieterich. But we may go much further than this. We have the actual testimony of Herodotus.

A well-known passage in Hdt. 5, 67 tells how at Sicyon they used to honour "Adrastus" instead of Dionysus, celebrating his πάθεα with tragic choruses. Ordinary people, therefore, in their tragic choruses, may be supposed to have celebrated the πάθεα of Dionysus.

Now it is strange that, while we have such masses of material about Dionysus-worship, we are never explicitly told what these πάθεα were. We are faced therefore with two questions: (1) Why is the "fate" of Dionysus so hidden? (2) What was it? The answer to both is the second book of Herodotus.

(1) The "fate" of Dionysus was ἄρρητον and was kept unspoken through εὐφημία. Herodotus is explicit. In speaking of the mourning for Osiris which took place at the Feast of Isis he says: τὸν δὲ τύπτονται (= mourn) οὔ μοι ὅσιόν ἐστι λέγειν 2, 61.

2, 132 ἐπεὰν δὲ τύπτωνται τὸν οὐκ οὐνομαζόμενον ὑπ’ ἐμεῦ θεὸν ἐπὶ τοιούτωι πρήγματι . . .

2, 170 ταφαὶ τοῦ οὐκ ὅσιον ποιοῦμαι ἐπὶ τοιούτωι πρήγματι ἐξαγορεύειν τοὔνομα. In 2, 86 there is similar language about the mummy of this god whose name must not be mentioned in connection with death. The god in question was of course Osiris. Now apparently it was not forbidden in Egypt to mention Osiris' death; but to Herodotus Osiris is Dionysus, and if he treats the death of Osiris as ἄρρητον that must be because the death of Dionysus was so.

Cf. 2, 144 Ὄσιρις δέ ἐστι Διόνυσος κατ᾽ Ἑλλάδα γλῶσσαν.

2, 42 Ὀσίριος, τὸν δὴ Διόνυσον εἶναι λέγουσιν (where observe the apologetic τὸν δή, "whom of course"). In other passages Herodotus simply uses the name "Dionysus" for "Osiris."

We need not therefore be surprised that we have no direct statement about the fate of Dionysus, or even that no tragedy ever depicts that fate. It was ἄρρητον.

But (2) can we tell what it must have been? Can we, for example, argue that the πάθος of Dionysus was the same in kind as that of Osiris? Yes. Herodotus again is explicit. He says of the Osiris Feast in the month Athyr τὴν δὲ ἄλλην ὁρτὴν ἀνάγουσι τῶι Διονύσωι, πλὴν χορῶν, κατὰ ταὐτὰ σχεδὸν πάντα Ἕλλησι 2, 48. The Egyptians did not have τραγικοὶ χοροί, "but in almost all other respects the ritual was identical." At any rate the gist of the δρώμενον was the same. Thus we may conclude that the fate of Dionysus, in Herodotus' time as well as later, was a *Sparagmos*: doubtless he had, like the other Year-Daimons, a special enemy; was torn in pieces, scattered over the fields, lost, sought for, discovered and recognized, just as Osiris was. This forms the normal pattern for the fate of the Year-Daimon; the other representatives of that being go through similar experiences, but Dionysus, the most typical of them, has the most typical and complete cycle of πάθεα. Cf. Frazer, *Adonis Attis Osiris* pp. 244 ff.; esp. 267 on the *Sparagmos*.

If we examine the kind of myth which seems to underlie the various "Eniautos" celebrations we shall find:

1 An *Agon* or Contest, the Year against its enemy, Light against Darkness, Summer against Winter.

2 A *Pathos* of the Year-Daimon, generally a ritual or sacrificial death, in which Adonis or Attis is slain by the tabu animal, the Pharmakos stoned, Osiris, Dionysus, Pentheus, Orpheus, Hippolytus torn to pieces (σπαραγμός).

3 A *Messenger*. For this Pathos seems seldom or never to actually performed under the eyes of the audience. (The reason of this is not hard to suggest, and was actually necessary in the time when there was only one actor.) It is announced by a messenger. "The news comes" that Pan the Great, Thammuz, Adonis, Osiris is dead, and the dead body is often brought in on a bier. This leads to

4 A *Threnos* or Lamentation. Specially characteristic, however, is a clash of contrary emotions, the death of the old being also the triumph of the new: see Plutarch's account of the Oschophoria.

5 and 6 An *Anagnorisis* – discovery or recognition – of the slain and mutilated Daimon, followed by his Resurrection or Apotheosis or, in some sense,

his Epiphany in glory. This I shall call by the general name *Theophany*. It naturally goes with a *Peripeteia* or extreme change of feeling from grief to joy.

Observe the sequence in which these should normally occur: *Agon, Pathos, Messenger, Threnos, Theophany*, or, we might say, *Anagnorisis* and *Theophany*.

First, however, there is a difficulty to clear away. Peripeteiai are of course common in tragedy: both from joy to grief, as in *O.T.* 920 ff., where the Corinthian Stranger seems to come as a blessed answer to prayer but really brings calamity, or the similar scene in Soph. *El.* 665; and from grief to joy, as in various Recognition scenes, such as Soph. *El.* 1210 ff., *I.T.* 770–850. But in the ritual there seems to have been a special final Peripeteia, from grief to joy, in connection with the Anagnorisis and Theophany. Now our tragedies normally, or at least commonly, end with a comforting Theophany but not with an outburst of joy. – No, but it looks as if they once did. We know that they were in early times composed in tetralogies consisting of three tragedies and a Satyr-play.

This is no place to discuss the Satyr-play at length. But those who have read Miss Harrison's article on the Kouretes (*B.S.A.* xv. and *Themis*, chapter I) will recognize that the Satyrs are the πρόπολοι δαίμονες in the rout of Dionysus, especially associated with his "initiations and *hierourgiai*" – that is, exactly with our Sacer Ludus of Dionysus. Strabo, pp. 466–8, makes this pretty clear. Hence comes their connection with the dead and with the anodos of Korê. The subject could easily be illustrated at length, but probably the above point, as it stands, will hardly be disputed. The Satyr-play, coming at the end of the tetralogy, represented the joyous arrival of the Reliving Dionysus and his rout of attendant daimones at the end of the Sacer Ludus.

It has however been argued, and by so high an authority as Mr Pickard-Cambridge,[2] that the Satyr-play though very early associated with tragedy was not so in its first origin. He points out that no Satyr-plays are attributed to Thespis, that it is difficult to make out tetralogies for any writer before Aeschylus, and that it was Pratinas who πρῶτος ἔγραψε Σατύρους (Suidas). I take this to mean that Pratinas was the first person to *write words* for the rout of revelling masquers to learn by heart. Thespis, like many early Elizabethans, had been content with a general direction: "Enter Satyrs, in revel, saying anything." I do not, however, wish to combat this view. It would suit my general purpose equally well to suppose that the Dionysus-ritual had developed into two divergent forms, the Satyr-play of Pratinas and the tragedy of Thespis, which were at a certain date artificially combined by a law. In any case there must have been close kindred between the two. The few titles of tragedies by Thespis which are preserved by tradition are unfortunately not well attested: but even if they are all forgeries by Heraclides Ponticus it is perhaps significant that he

---

[2] In a public lecture at Oxford in 1910. It may be worth mentioning that the new fragments of Sophocles' *Ichneutae* (Oxyrhynchus Papyri, vol. IX.) are markedly tragic in metre and diction.

thought such names plausible. They are Ἱερεῖς, Ἤιθεοι, Πενθεύς, Φόρβας ἢ Ἄθλα ἐπὶ Πελίᾳ. All bear the mark of the initiation *drômenon* or Sacer Ludus. *The Priests; The Youths*, or Kouroi; *Pentheus*, the torn Dionysus; *Phorbas*, the battling King who slew or was slain – to a reader of the present volume these tell their own tale. And after all Aristotle has told us that Tragedy ἐκ τοῦ Σατυρικοῦ μετέβαλεν (*Poet.* 4). It "developed out of the Satyric" – at the very least, from something akin to the Satyrs. I therefore continue – provisionally – to accept as a starting-point some tragic performance ending in a Satyr-play.

Now we know that in the historical development of Tragedy a process of differentiation occurred. The Satyr-play became more distinct and separate from the tragedies and was eventually dropped altogether; and, secondly, the separate Tragedies became independent artistic wholes.

This process produced, I conceive, two results. First, the cutting-off of the Satyr-play left the tragic trilogy without its proper close. What was it to do? Should it end with a threnos and trust for its theophany to the distinct and irrelevant Satyr-play which happened to follow? or should it ignore the Satyr-play and make a theophany of its own? Both types of tragedy occur, but gradually the second tends to predominate.

Secondly, what is to happen to the Anagnorisis and Peripeteia? Their proper place is, as it were, transitional from the Threnos of tragedy to the Theophany of the Satyr-play; if anything, they go rather with the Satyrs. Hence these two elements are set loose. Quite often, even in the tragedies which have a full Theophany, they do not occur in their proper place just before the Theophany, yet they always continue to haunt the atmosphere. The poets find it hard to write without bringing in an Anagnorisis somewhere.

Before tracing the Forms in detail, let us take some clear and typical instances of the sequence of all the five elements together, Agon, Pathos, Messenger, Threnos, Theophany. I take three plays which, though not early, are very strict in structure, and I begin with the *Bacchae*. For, if there is any truth in this theory at all, our one confessedly Dionysiac play ought to afford the most crucial test of it.

The latter half of the *Bacchae* divides itself thus:

787–976. A long Agon, divided by a Choric dance, 862–911. Dionysus pleads with Pentheus in vain, then at 819 begins to exert the Bacchic influence upon him till Pentheus follows him into the house, already half-conquered: after the Chorus, the two come out, the Contest already decided and Pentheus in his conqueror's power; they go out to the mountain.

Chorus, then 1024–1152 Pathos, Σπαραγμός of Pentheus, narrated by a Messenger and received with violent clash of emotion.

1153–1329. Elaborate Threnos, which consists first of a mad dance of triumph ἀντὶ θρήνου, then of a long Threnos proper, and contains in the midst of it – exactly in the proper place – the collection of the fragments of Pentheus' body and the Anagnorisis of him by Agave.

1330, or rather in the gap before 1330. Epiphany of Dionysus.

Now, when we remember that Pentheus is only another form of Dionysus himself – like Zagreus, Orpheus, Osiris and the other daimons who are torn in pieces and put together again – we can see that the *Bacchae* is simply the old Sacer Ludus itself, scarcely changed at all, except for the doubling of the hero into himself and his enemy. We have the whole sequence: Agon, Pathos and Messenger, Threnos, Anagnorisis and Peripeteia, and Epiphany. The daimon is fought against, torn to pieces, announced as dead, wept for, collected and recognized, and revealed in his new divine life. The *Bacchae* is a most instructive instance of the formation of drama out of ritual. It shows us how slight a step was necessary for Thespis or another to turn the Year-Ritual into real drama.

Hippolytus.

902–1101. Clear and fierce Agon between Theseus and Hippolytus.

Short Chorus, Threnos-like.

1153–1267. Σπαραγμός of the Hero by his own horses: Pathos, narrated by a Messenger.

Short Chorus, hymn to Cypris ἀντὶ θρήνου.

1283–end. Epiphany of Artemis, curiously mixed with the Threnos, and bringing with it the Anagnorisis (1296–1341).

We are just one step further from the original ritual. For who was Hippolytus? He was, ritually, just another form of the same Year-Daimon, who is torn to pieces and born again. When we remember the resurrection of Hippolytus in legend, we shall suspect that in an earlier form of the Hippolytus-*drômenon* there may have been a resurrection or apotheosis of the hero himself together with his protectress Artemis. Drama has gained ground upon ritual. Hippolytus has been made a mortal man. And we now have a Theophany with Artemis immortal in the air and Hippolytus dying on the earth.

Andromache.

547–765. Agon between Peleus and Menelaus.

An interrupting scene containing the appearance of Orestes and flight of Hermione; Chorus.

1070–1165. Pathos – stoning – narrated by Messenger.

1166–1225. Threnos.

1226. Theophany of Thetis, bringing comfort.

The Theophanies of Euripides almost always bring comfort, and thus conserve an element of the old Peripeteia from grief to joy. The sequence in the *Andromache* is very clear, but has one interrupting scene. This interrupting scene will find its explanation later. For the present we merely notice that it is concerned with Orestes and that it falls naturally into the following divisions: 802–819, Nurse as Exangelos or Messenger from within; 825–865, Threnos of Hermione; 879–1008, Appearance of Orestes, who saves and comforts Hermione, and expounds the death of Neoptolemus, which is the Aition of the play.

The above cases are merely illustrations of the way in which the Dionysus ritual has adapted itself to the reception of heroic myths. The chief modification is that other persons and events are put into the forms which originally belonged to the Daimon. In the *Bacchae* it is Pentheus who is torn, but Dionysus who appears as god. In the *Hippolytus* it is not Hippolytus who appears as god but Artemis, his patroness. In the *Andromache* the persons are all varied: it is Peleus and Menelaus who have the contest; it is Neoptolemus who is slain and mourned; it is Thetis who appears as divine. This substitution of persons undoubtedly occurs and is certainly very curious. I suspect that it comes from the fact, noticed above, that the real death of Dionysus himself was ἄρρητον and though it had to be somehow shown in the *Sacer Ludus* it could only be shown δι' αἰνιγμῶν. It may well be, for instance, that when Drama became public entertainment rather than religious celebration, objection was felt to an actual public mention or representation of the God's death.

We will now consider the various Forms, and see how far they are constant or usual, and what modifications they undergo. And first for the most crucial of them, the Theophany. This subject has been excellently treated by Eric Müller, *De Deorum Graecorum Partibus Tragicis*, Giessen, 1910.

Theophany

We all know that most of the extant plays of Euripides end with the appearance of a god (*Hipp., Andr., Suppl., Ion, El., I.T., Hel., Or., Bac., I.A., Rhes.*). But it has not been observed that in this, as in so many of his supposed novelties, Euripides is following the tradition of Aeschylus. The reason of this is, first, that the technique of Aeschylus is not so clear-cut and formal as that of Euripides. His gods do not so definitely proclaim themselves as such, and probably did not appear from quite so effective a μηχανή. Second, and more important, Aeschylus was still operating with trilogies, not with single plays, so that his Theophanies are normally saved up to the end of the trilogy and then occur on a grand scale.

To take the extant plays first:

The Oresteia has no gods till the *Eumenides* (unless we count a vision of the Furies at the end of the *Choephoroi*), but then we have a great Theophany of Apollo, Athena and the Furies in procession together.

The Supplices trilogy, *Supplices, Aegyptii, Danaides*: we know that this ended with an epiphany of Aphrodite, whose speech, founding the institution of marriage based on consent, is preserved (Nauck, fr. 44). This is evidently a full-dress Theophany in the style afterwards followed by Euripides, in which the god solemnly founds an institution and gives the Aition of the performance.

The Persae trilogy consisted of the *Phineus, Persae, Glaucus* (*Pontius?*), that is, it seems not to have been a continuous treatment of one subject leading up to one final Epiphany, like the Oresteia and the Danaid-trilogy. It falls apart into separate plays, and each play will be found to have in it some divine or supernatural apparition.

Persae: the Hero or, as he is called, the God (θεός 644, etc., δαίμων 642) Darius is evoked from his sacred tomb.

Phineus: the end, or at any rate the *dénouement*, of the play consisted in the chasing away of the Harpies by the Sons of the North-wind – that is, in a great apparition of winged supernatural shapes.

Glaucus Pontius: it contained, probably at the end, a prophecy spoken by Glaucus; and in it Glaucus, half-man, half-beast, appeared rising from the sea. (N. 26.) This seems like a regular Theophany with a prophecy. (If the third play was the other *Glaucus*, called *Potnieus*, then we have no evidence.)

Prometheia Trilogy. This stands somewhat apart for two reasons. First, its Aition is not any Year-ritual or Tomb-ritual but definitely the institution of the Torch-race at the Prometheia. Secondly, all the characters are divine, so that there can hardly be question of an epiphany in the ordinary sense. The reconstruction of the trilogy is still doubtful, but it seems unlikely that the ultimate reconciliation of Prometheus and Zeus can have been dramatically carried out without some appearance of Zeus in his glory.

Theban Trilogy. *Laius, Oedipus, Septem.* Here we possess the third play and it ends not in a Theophany but in a Threnos.[3] That is, it belongs to the first type mentioned above. The Satyr-play belonged to the same cycle of saga. It was called Sphinx. It would be interesting to know how Dionysus and his train were brought into connection with the Sphinx and Oedipus and whether there was any appearance of the God as deliverer or bringer of new life. In any case the same conjunction appears on the Vagnonville Crater; a Sphinx is sitting on a χῶμα γῆς which Satyrs are hammering at with picks, as though for the Anodos of Kore. (See J. E. Harrison, *Delphika*, J.H.S. xix. 1899, p. 235, and *Prolegomena*, p. 211, fig. 45; cf. also the krater in *Monumenti dell' Inst.* ii. pl. lv.)

Thus we find that of the five trilogies of Aeschylus which are represented in our extant plays, two end with a final epiphany, one has an epiphany in each play, one is uncertain but most likely had a grand final appearance of Zeus in state; one ends with a Threnos.

What of the fragmentary plays? I will not attempt to discuss them at length, but will merely mention those which *prima facie* seem to have contained an epiphany. I refer throughout to Nauck's *Fragmenta*.

---

[3] I do not mean by this to suggest that the final scene is spurious. On the contrary. The Aition is the grave-ritual of Eteocles and Polynices, and the last scene is quite correct and normal in stating that Aition.

Amymône: the heroine attacked by satyrs Ποσειδῶνος δὲ ἐπιφανέντος ὁ Σάτυρος μὲν ἔφυγεν. Epiphany of Poseidon.

Bassarai: 2nd of the Lycurgus trilogy, *Edoni, Bassarai, Neaniskoi*. The *Neaniskoi* I take to be the converted *Edoni*; they form a band of Kouroi initiated into the worship of Dionysus. Thus the whole trilogy had probably an epiphany at the end, with Dionysus instituting his own ritual worship. But also the separate plays seem to have had epiphanies.

Êdôni: king Lycurgus acts the part of Pentheus: Dionysus is on the stage, as in the *Bacchae*, fr. 61: he makes an earthquake, as in the *Bacchae*, fr. 58: and, since his enemy Lycurgus was ultimately confounded, it is practically certain that in the end, as in the *Bacchae*, he appeared in glory.

Bassarai: Orpheus, a rebel of a different sort, was torn to pieces by the Maenads (Bassarids) for worshipping the Sun, αἱ δὲ Μοῦσαι συναγαγοῦσαι ἔθαψαν Eratosth. *Catast*. 24. This suggests a great epiphany of the Muses. The play must have been very close to the original Dionysiac ritual, like the *Bacchae*. The Daimon (Dionysus-Orpheus) is torn to pieces, collected and recognized, mourned for, and then revealed in glory.

Other Dionysiac plays are *Pentheus*, of which we are definitely told that its plot was the same as that of Euripides' *Bacchae; Dionusou Trophoi*, plot not known: evidently the nursing of the young Year-Daimon in some form; and lastly, *Bacchae*.

See also, for other Year-Daimon plays, the *Krêssai*, and the *Nemea-Hypsipyle* trilogy below.

Ixîon: perhaps the third play of the same trilogy as the *Perrhaebides*. The last scene seems to have shown Ixîon bound by Zeus to the burning wheel in the sky. See Diod. Sic. 4. 69. 3, *ap*. N. This would give a great epiphany of Zeus and the gods.

Eurôpê or *Kâres*: see N. The play seems to have ended by the arrival through the air of the gods Sleep and Death, bearing the body of Europa's son, Sarpêdôn, for burial in his native land.

Kabîrî: plot uncertain, but we know that the Kabiri themselves made an appearance. Plutarch, *ap*. N. 97.

Memnon: at the end Memnon is slain by Achilles. His goddess mother, Eôs, goes to Zeus and obtains the gift of immortality which she brings to him. Epiphany of Eôs. Proclus, *ap*. N.

Niobê: no direct evidence, but it is difficult to see how this plot can have been completed without the appearance of a god.

Pentheus: same plot as the *Bacchae*. Epiphany of Dionysus. See above.

Xantriai, "The Rending Women": possibly another name for the *Pentheus*: in any case it seems to have dealt with the same story.

Semele or *Hydrophoroi*. The "Water-bearers" are those who try to put out the conflagration of the palace owing to the epiphany of Zeus.

Toxotides: Actaeon transformed into a stag. Probably epiphany of Artemis.

Phineus:

Psychostasia: the epiphany here was famous and elaborate. Zeus appeared on the "theologeion," Thetis on one side of him and Eos on the other, weighing the souls of Achilles and Memnon. Pollux, 4. 130. Eos, we are told, came down on a γέρανος.

Ôreithuia: she was carried off by Boreas. The passages from Longinus and John of Sicily about the extravagance or ἀτοπία of the poet suggest that Boreas appeared in person when he "stirred the sea by blowing with his two cheeks."

The following are less clear.

Heliades: their transformation into poplars was foretold or explained. This suggests an epiphany. Such things are usually done by a divine being.

The Achilles trilogy, *Myrmidones, Nereides, Phryges* or *Hector's Ransom*. In the first Thetis seems to have appeared to provide the arms, in the second the Chorus consists of Nereids and it is difficult to imagine the play without Thetis. In the third we know that Hermes appeared at the beginning. It seems possible that the council of the gods described in *Il.* XXIV. as insisting on the ransoming of Hector made an appearance.

Hoplôn Krisis, the Adjudgement of the Arms of Achilles: it appears from N. 174 that Thetis was summoned to come with her attendants to preside over the trial. No doubt she came.

Lastly, there are some plays in which our supposed Year-Daimon makes his epiphany not as a celestial god but as a ghost or a hero returned from the grave. It is obvious that he is quite within his rights in so appearing: he is essentially a being returned from the dead, and his original ritual epiphany was a resurrection.

Persae: after the Pathos narrated by the Messenger comes a Thrênos and an *evocation of the dead king or god*, Darius.

Krêssai: the subject seems to have been the restoration to life of Glaucus, son of Minos, by Polyidus. (This Glaucus, restored to life by snakes, may well have been a form of Year-Daimon.)

Psychagôgoi: the plot is unknown, except that the title is said to have denoted "persons who by charms of some sort resurrect the souls of the dead." Bekk. *Phryn.* p. 73, 13.

Nemea and *Hypsipyle* probably belong to a trilogy on the death and heroization of Archemorus-Opheltes, who is a typical Year-Daimon, appearing as a Snake or a Baby.

We do not know whether there was an appearance of Heracles at the end of Aeschylus' *Philoctetes*, as there was in that of Sophocles. But it is perhaps worth remembering that Aeschylus was supposed to have revealed "certain lore of the mysteries" in the *Toxotides, Hiereiai, Sisyphus Petrocylistes, Iphigenia* and *Oedipus*. The extremely close connection between the mysteries and the Year-daimon will be in the minds of all who have read the present volume.

A numerical tabulation of the above results would be misleading, both because most of the conclusions are only probabilities, and still more because we cannot generally constitute the trilogies to which the various lost tragedies belong. If we could, the final Theophanies would probably be still more numerous. There remain outside the above plays some 23 of which our knowledge is so scanty that no *prima facie* conclusions can, as far as I can see, be drawn. But it can hardly be disputed that in a surprising number of Aeschylus' tragedies we have found signs of either a definite epiphany of a god or the resurrection of a dead hero, or lastly the direct worship of a Year-Daimon. We cannot be certain, but we may surmise that some such epiphany or resurrection was quite as common in Aeschylus as in Euripides.

I will leave out the question of such Epiphanies in the fragments of Sophocles: the evidence would take very long to state. His extant plays will be briefly treated below. In general the result is that in this, as in so many other particulars, Sophocles is influenced more by the Ionian Epic and less by the Attic Sacer Ludus than the other two tragedians. It is just the same with the other Forms. Sophocles deliberately blurs his outlines and breaks up his Agôn and Messenger and Prologue into what we may almost call continuous dramatic conversation; Euripides returns to an extreme clarity and articulateness and stiffness of form in all three. The discussion of Euripides' technique is of course another story, but so much will, I think, hardly be denied either by his friends or his enemies.

Passing on, then, to Euripides, what is it that he did about his epiphanies? In especial, why is he ridiculed by comedy for his use of the *Deus ex machina*, if Aeschylus really used such epiphanies as much or more?

The answer, I think, is not that he invented the introduction of gods: he clearly did not: but that, *more suo*, he introduced them in a sharply defined manner, always at the end of the play, and, it would seem, with some particularly smooth and effective machinery. (Perhaps an invention made about the year 428, see Bethe, *Prolegomena*, pp. 130–141.) The general purpose for which he used them – (1) to console griefs and reconcile enmities and justify *tant bien que mal* the ways of the gods, and (2) to expound the Aition of the play, and the future fates of the characters – was, I believe, part of the tradition. In these respects his gods play exactly the parts of Athena in the *Eumenides* or Aphrodite in the *Danaides*, probably even of Zeus in the *Prometheus Unbound*.

The Theophanies in the extant plays of Euripides are as follows:

Hippolytus: Artemis appears, (1) comforts and reconciles Theseus and Hippolytus, and (2) founds the ritual of Hippolytus at Trozên.

Andromache: Thetis appears, (1) sheds comfort on the suffering Peleus and Andromache, and (2) orders that Neoptolemus be laid in his tabu tomb at Delphi.

Supplices: Athena appears, (1) comforts the Argives by foretelling the expedition of the Epigoni to conquer Thebes, and (2) bids Theseus consecrate the brazen tripod at Delphi which is witness to the oath of eternal friendship to Athens sworn by the Argives.

Ion: Athena appears, (1) comforts Ion and Creusa, and (2) ordains the founding of the four Attic tribes.

Electra: the Dioscoroi appear, (1) condemn the law of vengeance, comfort Electra and Orestes, and (2) expound the origin of the Areopagus, of the Oresteion in Arcadia, and of the tabu tombs of Aegisthus and Clytemnestra (cf. Paus. II. 16. 7).

Iphigenia Taurica: Athena appears, (1) appeases Thoas, promises comfort to Orestes, and (2) founds the worship of Artemis-Iphigenia at Halae and Brauron.

Helena: the Dioscoroi appear, (1) appease Theoclymenus, (2) found the worship of Helen (in conjunction with their own), explain the name of the island Helene, and promise immortality to Menelaus.

Orestes: Apollo appears, striking (as I hope to show elsewhere) his hearers into a trance; (1) makes peace between Menelaus and Orestes, (2) explains the origin of the Oresteion in Arcadia and of the Areopagus and proclaims the worship of Helen.

Bacchae: Dionysus appears, (1) judges his enemies, consoles Cadmus and (2) establishes his worship. See above.

Iph. Aul.: end lost: Artemis seems to have appeared, (1) saved Iphigenia, comforted Agamemnon, and (2) doubtless ordained the Brauron rite.

Rhesus: the Muse, mother of Rhesus, appears, (1) laments her son, and (2) establishes his worship as an "anthropodaimon."

If this were free and original composition the monotony would be intolerable and incomprehensible: we can understand it only when we realize that the poet is working under the spell of a set traditional form.

The Euripidean plays which do not end with a god are the following: *Cyclops, Alcestis, Medea, Heracleidae, Hecuba, Heracles, Troades, Phoenissae*.

These require special consideration. It is no part of my case to argue that all plays necessarily conform to the same type. The sacer ludus of a Torch-race, like the Prometheia, or the sacer ludus of some Altar of Sanctuary like the various Suppliant Plays, has no particular reason for conforming to the scheme of the Dionysus-play, except the influence of custom and analogy. But we shall find even in these plays which have no obvious Theophanies some curious traces of the Theophany-form.

The *Cyclops* is a Satyr-play, and does not come into question.

The *Alcestis* is, I think, also in form a Satyr-play. (See Argument, also Dieterich, *Pulcinella*, p. 69.) Yet we must note that it ends with a Resurrection.

Medea: it ends with a scene in which Medea appears on a height (Schol. *ad* 1317), and then rides through the air uttering prophecies and founding the rite of her children's worship. When we remember that Medea was really a goddess, and that she and her children received worship in Greece, we can see that this scene is really a faded or half-humanized Theophany. Cf. the treatment of Hippolytus.

Heracleidae: who is, in the ritual sense, the "hero" of the *Heracleidae*? Without doubt Eurystheus; it is the Ἄγος of his death and his sacred grave or "place of burial" (1040 ff.) that constitute the Aition of the play. The end in our MSS. seems to be incomplete, but it clearly contains the foundation by the Hero himself of his own tabu ritual. This is not far removed from the original daimon-rite or theophany.

Hecuba: it ends with the prophecies of the fey and dying Thracian hero, and his announcement of the Aition of the *Kunos Sêma* (1273).

Heracles: Theseus is of course not a god, but he is a worshipped hero: and his function in this play is just that of the ordinary *Deus*. He comforts Heracles, sends him away from Thebes, describes his future life, and lastly ordains his worship with its proper honours and ritual. (See esp. 1322–1340: just like a speech *ex machina*.)

Troades: it ends with a pure Threnos. See above. It is interesting to note that the Theophany, omitted here, comes by its rights at the beginning of the play.

Phoenissae: a curious question arises. The play apparently ends with a Threnos, which is legitimate enough. But the last scene also contains the driving out of Oedipus to Mt Kithairon. Now Oedipus was a daimon who haunted Mt Kithairon. (See Roscher; also my Introd. to Sophocles' *Oed. Rex*.) He goes out to Kithairon in this play, 1751 f. Also in *Oed. Rex*, 1451 ff. he expresses his wish to go out to "yonder Kithairon that is called mine own." When we remember that the connection of Oedipus with the Attic Colônus is probably a late Attic invention (*Phoen*. 1704 ff.) and reflect on the curious "passing" of Oedipus in the *Coloneus*, a suspicion occurs that the true ritual end of the Oedipus-dromenon was the supernatural departure of the hero-daimon to his unknown haunt on the mountain. In this case the sending forth to Kithairon – otherwise almost unmotived – is again a faded remnant of what we have called the Theophany-form. This argument is strengthened by the generally admitted fact that the pair Oedipus-Jocasta are a vegetation pair, like Adonis-Aphrodite, Hippolytus-Artemis, etc. But it cannot be pursued further here.

To sum up, we find that the tragedies of Euripides usually end with a Theophany of a markedly formal and ritual character, closely suiting our conception of the Sacer Ludus of Dionysus, as daimon of the Year-Cycle of death and rebirth; further, that in those tragedies which do not end in a confessed Theophany there are at any rate curious resemblances to the typical Theophany-form; furthermore, the evidence of the extant and fragmentary plays of Aeschylus, though often uncertain, seems to show that a Theophany of a similar sort was also usual in them, either at the end of a trilogy or in the separate plays. About Sophocles we shall say something later: the evidence is not very conclusive, but the indications are not at all inconsistent with the above results.

Let us now consider the other forms, especially the group.

Agon, Pathos, Messenger, Threnos

Pathos and Messenger almost always go together; the Agon is doubtless less characteristically ritual than the other parts, as arguments and spirited dialogue scenes naturally tend to occur in any drama. With respect to the Agon and Threnos we will chiefly notice how they stand in relation to the Messenger, and how far the supposed original order of sequence is preserved in each play.

Euripides being the clearest and most definite in his ritual forms, we will take him first.

Alcestis: being a Satyr-play it need not conform to the tragic type. It has, however, in the proper place the Agon (Heracles and Death), Threnos and Resurrection.

Medea: typical, with the necessary modifications. Agon, Medea against herself 1020–1080. (The scene before has also been an Agon, Medea outwitting Jason.) Pathos and Messenger 1121–1230; quasi-Threnos in the frightful scene (1251–1292) where the children are murdered behind the barred door: quasi-Theophany, as explained above. (There cannot be a real Threnos because that is definitely forbidden by Medea 1378 ff. We may conjecture that there was no θρῆνος in the Corinthian rite: cf. Paus. II. 3. 6 and Schol. *Med.* 273. If it was intended to mitigate infant mortality, this would be natural.)

Heracleidae: see above on Eurystheus. The Pathos-Messenger (799–866) announces the battle and the capture of Eurystheus: there then follows an Agon-scene, apparently out of its order; the end is incomplete, but it contained the establishment of the funeral rite by Eurystheus himself, as Hero.

Hippolytus: typical. Agon, Messenger with Pathos, Threnos, Anagnorisis, Theophany. See above.

Andromache: typical: same order. See above.

Hecuba: the Messenger comes early in the play, hence we cannot have a Theophany immediately following it. In compensation a Ghost appears at the beginning. We have Agon between Odysseus and Hecuba-Polyxena (218–440): Messenger with Pathos 484–582: then Threnos in Hecuba's speech. Then the course of the play interrupts. On the end see above.

Supplices: clear sequence. Agon between Herald and Theseus-Adrastus (399–597); Messenger announcing the Battle 634–777; then Threnos. This Threnos is enormously developed and practically includes the rest of the play up to the Theophany, except that it is interrupted by the Euadne scene. (That curious scene seems to have been inserted to fill up the interval while the slain men are cremated and their bones made ready for burial. But it must, no doubt, have some ritual explanation also.)

Heracles: the sequence is peculiar. The Messenger bursts out from the ruined house at 909. The scene before has been the divine apparition of Lyssa, which, however, is quite different in character from the regular Theophanies. I am inclined to think that technically the attack of Lyssa upon Heracles is an Agon; see below on the *Iph. Aul.*, *Persae* and *Septem*. The scene before has certainly been an Agon between Heracles and Lycus (cf. 789, 812). Thus we get the sequence Agon (Agon), Pathos and Messenger, Threnos, and, clearly, Anagnorisis 1089–1145: then, instead of a god, Theseus appears, *ex machina* as it were: see above.

Ion: typical. Great Agon scene, Creusa against Apollo 859–922, or one may perhaps count it as lasting till 1047; then Pathos-Messenger 1106–1228, brief Threnos 1229–1250; then second Agon 1250–1394 and Anagnorisis 1395–1549 (with Peripeteia): then Theophany.

Troades: the form in many ways peculiar, but the latter part has the sequence: Agon of Helen against Hecuba-Menelaus 860–1060; Choric ode, then Messenger 1123–1155, then great Threnos to the end.

Electra: Agon of Electra and Clytemnestra 997–1146: then the Messenger is omitted, the Pathos is αὐτάγγελον, announced by the shriek of Clytemnestra and the return of the murderers with bloody swords 1147–1176: then Threnos (with a Repentance-scene which forms a spiritual Anagnorisis and Peripeteia), then Theophany. The Messenger-form, omitted here, has occurred earlier in the play 761–858.

Iphigenia Taurica: the end is clear: Agon, Thoas and Iphigenia 1152–1233: Messenger (with a kind of Anagnorisis 1318, 1361): no Threnos, unless we may take the Chorus' two lines of lamentation, 1420, 1421, as an atrophied Threnos: Theophany. The real Threnos of the play has come earlier, as it tends to come in plays about Orestes.

Helena: Agon with Theoclymenus (I take the diplomatic contest with these dangerous barbarians to be a clear form of Agon) 1186–1300: continued in 1369–1450: then Messenger 1512–1618: no Threnos is possible; instead we have a brief Agon, Theoclymenus against the Servant at the door 1621–1641: then Theophany.

Phoenissae: there are two Messengers, each with a double speech. We take at present only the second. The great Agon of the play has occurred much earlier, 446–637, between Eteocles and Polynices. The sequence at the end is merely Messenger 1356–1479, Threnos 1485–1580, and 1710–end, interrupted by an Agon between Creon and Antigone. As Aitia we have the burial arrangements of Eteocles and Polynices and the expulsion of Oedipus to Mt Kithairon – perhaps a faded Theophany, see above. The tabu tombs of the two princes form also the end of the *Septem*. The general structure of the *Phoenissae* is highly formal under its cover of Epic expansion, but we will not discuss it here.

Orestes: in the conclusion of the play I think we must recognize the Phrygian as an Exangelos. That is, his dramatic function is to relate what has taken place inside the house. The lyrical form is merely chosen for variety's sake. This gives us the sequence: Messenger combined with Threnos: Agon between Orestes and Menelaus: Theophany of Apollo. There has been an ordinary Messenger earlier 852–956: also a Threnos 960–1012. Also an Evocation of the dead Agamemnon, much atrophied 1225–1240. (These atrophied evocations of Agamemnon are of course derived from the great evocation in the *Choephori*: one would like to know if that scene itself is softened down from some still more complete predecessor, in which Agamemnon actually rose from the tomb.)

Bacchae: absolutely typical: see above.

Iphigenia Aulidensis: the end is lost, but the present traces suggest a pretty typical sequence: Agon, Achilles pelted by the troops, argument between Achilles and Clytemnestra 1337–1432: Threnos of Iphigenia 1475–1531: Messenger 1532–? Then perhaps Threnos, certainly Theophany.

Rhesus: the Hêniochos is clearly a Messenger. So we end with the sequence Agon 675–727, fight of Diomedes and Odysseus with the Guards: Messenger 728–819, continuing into a short Agon between Hêniochos and Hector 820–881: then Theophany combined with Threnos.

But let us consider one particular point more closely. If we notice the plays in which Orestes occurs we shall find that that hero always produces a peculiar disturbance in the Forms. Now Orestes is traditionally a figure of strongly marked type – the beloved hero who is reported dead and then returns in triumph. I strongly suspect that his reported death, lamentation and reappearance alive were in origin exactly parallel to the reported death, lamentation and reappearance alive of the Daimon, Dionysus, Osiris, etc. In Sophocles the false death is described in detail: it is a σπαραγμός, like that of Hippolytus, and at the Pythian games! As Orestes became thoroughly humanized, the supernatural element dwindled away. But we shall see that his appearance, though it mostly comes early in the play and does not count – so to speak – as a real final Theophany, is apt to come in conjunction with Messenger and Threnos and Invocation of the Dead. It bears traces of its original theophanous glory.

Usener has argued on other grounds (*Archiv*, *l.c.* pp. 332 ff.) that Orestes at Delphi was a winter daimon and "Doppelgänger" to Dionysus, as Neoptolemus was to Apollo. And it is worth noting that the same line of thought possibly supplies a clue to a puzzling and tiresome scene in Euripides' *Electra*, 771–858. The ritual described in the messenger's speech seems extraordinarily like a reflection of a *Bouphonia* at an Eniautos festival. Orestes is made to act as *Daitros* for the communal *Dais* – one might say, as some reminiscence of a daimon of the New Year who in human form slays the Old Year in bull form. As such he is recognized (*v.* 852 ἐγνώσθη δ᾽ ὑπὸ | γέροντος . . .) and they crown and lead him with acclamation (*v.* 854 στέφουσι δ᾽ εὐθὺς σοῦ κασιγνήτου κάρα | χαίροντες ἀλαλάζοντες). However this may be, Orestes is the most typical of Greek tragic heroes and occurs in more (extant) plays than any other. See my *Hamlet and Orestes, a Study in Traditional Types*, Proceedings of British Academy 1912.)

Iph. Taur.: besides the final sequence we have an opening Orestes-sequence: Threnos for Orestes 136–235: Messenger announcing Pathos (*Stoning*) of Orestes: then Appearance of Orestes, in a great scene 472–900, involving an Agon and an Anagnorisis and Peripeteia.

Eur. *Electra*: after Prologue, we have Threnos 112–212 (on Orestes and Agamemnon): then Appearance of Orestes, with Agon leading to Anagnorisis 487–595. Oddly enough this is followed by an Evocation of the Dead, and a Messenger. The various elements of the death and resurrection of the Daimon are all there, but scattered and broken since the conception which held them together has been lost.

We noticed above in the *Andromache* that the interrupting Orestes-scene came with a sequence Messenger, Threnos, Epiphany of Orestes, and that, much in the manner of a *deus ex machina* he (1) saved and consoled Hermione, and (2) announced the Aition of the play.

In the *Orestes* the hero does not return from the dead, and the sequence is quite confused, but our supposed original Daimon-Orestes appears possibly to have left two rather curious traces. 1. He is shown at the beginning of the play *lying like a dead man* (83 ἀθλίωι νεκρῶι· νεκρὸς γὰρ οὗτος κτλ., 385 τίνα δέδορκα νερτέρων;), is *roused by the women wailing round him* and rises.

2. At the end, just before the full-blooded Theophany of Apollo, we see Orestes appearing on the roof of the Palace, a place generally appropriated to divine beings. See also below on the *Choephori* and Soph. *Electra*.

Turning from Euripides to the less formal tragedians, we shall not of course expect to find in them the same clear-cut sequences of unmistakable Agon, Messenger-Pathos, Threnos, Anagnorisis, Theophany. But I think we shall find that these Forms, a little less stark and emphatic, a little more artistically modified, are usually present in both Aeschylus and Sophocles.

Aeschylus:

Supplices: we have seen that the whole trilogy ended in a typical Theophany, so we need not expect one here. But we have a clear Agon (Maidens against Herald) 826–910, followed by arrival of the Basileus with a Peripeteia; then Messenger (Danaus as Messenger 980–1014); then not exactly a Threnos, but a song of prayer (1018–end).

Persae: the Forms come early. Messenger 249–514, Threnos 515–597, Evocation of dead "god" 598–680: epiphany 681–842. The rest to the end is Threnos. This gives us a perfect typical sequence, except that the Agon seems to be absent. If we look for it in its proper place we shall find it, not acted indeed but described. In 176–214 we have Atossa's dream of the Agon between Europe and Asia, the Agon which was actually taking place but could not be represented on the stage. Cf. *Alc., Heracles, Iph. Aul.*

Septem: here also the Agon takes place "off," after 718. Then Messenger 792–822: then Threnos 831–1009, and, instead of a Theophany, an enactment of the Aition of the ritual. (Grave-worship of Eteocles and Polynices.)

Prometheus: a passionate little scene between Prometheus and the Chorus just before 940 might possibly be described as an Agon, though the greater Agon comes earlier; then 944–1035 Messenger (Hermes, cf. 943) mixed with Agon: then, as substitute for the Theophany, a supernatural earthquake involving the cleaving of Earth and the revealing of Hell.

Agamemnon: in this trilogy the full Theophany is reserved for the last play and consequently the sequence in the individual plays is upset and confused. We have, however, Messenger 550–680: Agon of Clytemnestra and Agamemnon 810–975: then the Cassandra scene, foretelling the Pathos; then Pathos αὐτάγγελον, another Agon and Threnos.

Choephori: as in other Orestes-plays we have a Threnos and Anagnorisis quite early 165–244: Evocation of dead 315–510: Agon (Orestes and Clytemnestra) 674–930, with a Messenger (Exangelos) in the midst of it 875–886, combined with Pathos αὐτάγγελον: Threnos, consisting of mixed joy and woe and culminating in long speeches over the dead bodies 935–1047: lastly a Vision of the Furies, which may possibly have involved a real epiphany.

Eumenides: Agon 566–680, or perhaps to 750, with Athena making an Aition-speech in the style of a *Deus ex machina* in the middle 681–710: then new Agon with a reconciliation (886 ff.) and Peripeteia; then great Procession of gods. No Messenger. The whole play is really the Theophany of the Oresteia trilogy.

Sophocles:

It is especially interesting to see how Sophocles has broken down the stiff lines of the ritual Theophany into scenes of vague supernatural grandeur.

Oedipus Rex: fairly clear end. Agon (short but involving Anagnorisis and Peripeteia) between Oedipus and the Herdsman 1123–1185: Exangelos or Messenger with Pathos 1223–1296: then Threnos with suggestion of Oedipus' flight to Kithairon to become a daimon (1451 ff.).

Oedipus Coloneus: Agon between Oedipus and Polynices 1254–1396: slight Threnos and last speech of Oedipus. This last speech is very supernatural; it consists of prophecies and Aitia, and is spoken amid continuous lightning and thunder (1514 f.): then Messenger 1579–1666, and final Threnos over Oedipus' passing. A faded Theophany is pretty visible here.

Antigone: enormous Agon scene, Creon v. Antigone, then v. Haemon, then v. Antigone again 384–943: Tiresias bringing a kind of Discovery (?) and Peripeteia 988–1114: Messenger with Pathos 1155–1256, small Threnos: Second Messenger (Exangelos) 1278 and greater Threnos. The Aition is the same as that of the *Septem*, some Theban hero-ritual commemorating the children of Oedipus and their unhallowed ends – the buried living and the unburied dead.

Ajax: a curious question suggests itself. All the latter part of the play, 1046–1401, is occupied with an Agon (in three stages, ending in a reconciliation) about the burial of Ajax. It is triumphantly decided that he is to be buried. Is that the end? Or was he really buried? Was there not some great final pomp representing the burial? – In considering the prolonged emphasis laid on this burial question in the *Ajax*, we should remember that among the dromena of the Aianteia was a πομπή and that the funeral bier of Ajax μετὰ πανοπλίας κατεκοσμεῖτο. (Hesych., vid. Pauly s. *Aianteia*.) The play is close to the old hero-cult; and perhaps the hero-cult itself not quite unrelated to some "Year-ritual," if the dead hero re-appeared in the spring flower that was marked with his name.

In any case the sequence is rather curious: Theophany at beginning 1–133. Later on we get a much atrophied Messenger 719–783, who foretells the Pathos which then proceeds to follow 815–865. Then a scene of search and Anagnorisis 866–890: then Threnos 891–1040: then the great Agon, Reconciliation and – on some scale or other – Heroic Funeral.

Electra: an Orestes-play, with the usual special characteristics. It begins, after the Prologue, with a Threnos 86–250, then an Agon 328–471 (Chrysothemis) and a greater Agon 516–633 (Clytemnestra): then an Invocation of the dead Agamemnon 634–659: this is answered by the arrival of the Messenger announcing the death of Orestes 660–763, short Agon and Threnos 822–870: then, after Agon which is almost part of the Threnos, 871–1057, Appearance of Orestes, with Anagnorisis, Peripeteia and final settlement of the play.

Trachiniae: the same question arises here as in the *Ajax*. The burning of Heracles on Mt Oeta was in ancient tradition and art closely associated with his Apotheosis. Was this burning and apotheosis represented on the stage? It definitely is so in Seneca's imitation, *Herc. Oet.* ad fin. In any case, whether represented or not, I think it must have been suggested to the minds of all spectators. The sequence is fairly typical: Agon of Hyllus and Deianira 734–820, Messenger (Exangelos) 870–946, Threnos, interrupted by the Appearance of Heracles, his Self-Lamentation and Burning – i.e., Apotheosis.

Philoctetes: this play has a definite Theophany at the end, but otherwise its sequence is rather far from any type. One might divide it thus: Agon 865–1080, including an Anagnorisis 895–926: Threnos 1081–1217: fiercer Agon (Odysseus v. Neoptolemus and Philoctetes) 1222–1302: Reconciliation 1308–1408: Theophany 1400–1471.

Prologues

We have hitherto considered the Forms that come towards the end and build up the conclusion of a tragedy. In any true work of art the end is always specially important and significant. It is the last act that chiefly determines the character of a play. It is the end of the verse that best indicates the metre. But there is one important form which belongs necessarily to the beginning.

Dieterich is doubtless right in comparing the Prologue of tragedy with the Prorrhêsis of the hierophant before a sacred Drômenon. What such a prorrhêsis was like we can only guess. There are a few small phrases of ritual preserved: there is the parody of a prorrhêsis given by the Hierophant in the *Frogs*, 354 ff.; there are a few lines spoken by Iphigenia as priestess before her tabu procession starts (*I.T.* 1226 ff.). It certainly gave orders for Euphemia, or solemn silence: it probably also said something about the sacred dance which was to follow. *"Make room for a Dance of Mystae! And do you begin the singing and the all-night dances that are meet for this festival"* (Ar. *Frogs*, 370 f.). When the nature of the dance was something obviously dictated by the occasion – e.g., when it was the celebration of a particular Festival on the proper day – there was no need for any further explanation. But as soon as anything like tragedy began, the case was different. The sacred dance of Dionysus might be about Agamemnon, or Oedipus, or the Daughters of Danaus, or what not. Consequently there was need of a *Pro-logos*, of something *spoken before*. The word suggests prose rather than verse. We know that the sacred Herald proclaimed – in an audience which had no knowledge of what play or what poet was coming – *"O Theognis, lead on your Chorus!"* (Ar. *Ach.* 11). We know that – in a certain Proagon, whatever that was – Sophocles led on his Chorus in black. What was the poet supposed to do when he "led on" his Chorus? Did he just bow and retire, leaving the audience to guess as best they could from the play itself what it was all about? Or did he use this opportunity and tell them? Anyhow the prologos is defined as "all the part before the dancers come on," and it seems quite likely that originally it was not regarded as part of the sacred dance at all, but was something informal spoken by the poet. If our knowledge were a little fuller we should very likely be told who πρῶτος ἔγραψε προλόγους, and be able to assume that when Aeschylus "led on" his Chorus for the *Persae* and the *Suppliant Women* he told the audience what the play was to be. Then the development would be like that of the Dithyramb, of Comedy, of the Satyr-play, perhaps of the Apotheosis-scenes at the end: a Form that was first merely improvised or built up by scenic effects without written verses, grew gradually to be "written" and regarded as an integral part of an artistic whole. Mediaeval prologues and clown-scenes would afford good parallels, and we should understand why Euripides was so proud that οὑξιὼν πρώτιστά μοι τὸ γένος ἂν εἶπεν εὐθὺς τοῦ δράματος. He, more than either of his predecessors, made a character in the play do all the Prologue for him, and that in a thorough and clear manner. For clearness, σαφήνεια, was to the age of the Sophists the first virtue of λέξις.

But this is conjectural: what development is traceable in our extant remains? I think we can see that the Prologue, still rather fluid in the hands of Aeschylus, grew first in the direction of mere drama, and then turned aside towards a definite religious form.

For instance, in Aeschylus we have the stages:

1   No written Prologue: *Supplices* and *Persae*;
2   Simple Prologue of one speaker: *Agamemnon, Choephori* (with Pylades dumb);
3   Complete exposition-scene with two or more characters:
     Septem: Eteocles and Messenger.
     Eumenides: Pythia: change of Scene: Apollo, Orestes and Ghost. (Unless indeed the Dance in the strict sense begins by the Chorus being seen within about v. 35.)
     Prometheus: the elaborate scene with Kratos and Bia has apparently been introduced to meet the need of nailing the gigantic figure on the rock.

In Sophocles stage (1) disappears altogether, and so practically does (2). All the plays without exception begin with regular exposition-scenes involving two or more characters. It is noticeable, however, that two of the latest plays, *Trachiniae* and *Philoctetes*, start this exposition-scene with a quasi-Euripidean Prologue, addressed confessedly or half-confessedly to the audience. That is, Sophocles regularly works in stage (3), but in his latest work begins to be influenced by a further stage. What this is we shall find in Euripides.

Euripides has practically always an exposition-scene – so much is a natural concession to the growing complexity of drama – but in front of the exposition-scene he has a formal speech addressed to the audience by one quiet and solitary figure; a figure, also – and this is what I wish to emphasize – which is either confessedly supernatural or at least somehow charged with religious emotion.

Let us take first the plays which happen to omit the exposition-scene altogether. To do so is, of course, a kind of archaism: a return to a less complex kind of drama, in which the sacred dance followed immediately on the Prologue-speech. It occurs, if we disregard the *Cyclops* as not being a tragedy, in only two dramas, and those naturally enough the very two that are most formal and nearest to their respective forms of Sacer Ludus, the *Bacchae* and the *Supplices*. The *Bacchae* has been already dealt with: the Sacer Ludus behind all the Suppliant Plays seems to me to have been a ritual only second in its influence on tragedy to that of the Year-cycle itself. I will not now discuss the subject at length, but I can understand the origin of the Suppliant Plays best as a ritual intended to keep alive the right of sanctuary attached to some particular altar or tomb or the like, very much as we keep alive the control over a right of way. On one day in the year some fugitives take refuge at the altar, some pursuer tries to drag them away, and some high authority, god or king or people, forbids him. This is notoriously a very common motive in Greek tragedy, and was used, as recent finds have shown us, in the romantic comedy of the fourth century. (Pap. Ox. VI. 855, a scene which I should now explain differently.) I suspect that this ritual is also at the back of various rites which have generally been interpreted as survivals of human sacrifice, rites in which some one is pursued with weapons and is supposed to be killed unless he reaches a certain place of refuge.

However that may be, let us consider the actual Prologue-speakers. We may start with *Alcestis*, Apollo (and Death): *Hippolytus*, Aphrodite: *Hecuba*, the Ghost of Polydorus: *Ion*, Hermes: *Troades*, Poseidon (and Athena): *Bacchae*, Dionysus: all these are supernatural. Next observe *Heracleidae*, Iolaus suppliant at an altar: *Andromache*, the heroine suppliant at an altar: *Supplices*, Aithra, surrounded by a band of women suppliant at an altar: *Heracles*, Amphitryon and Megara, suppliants at an altar: *Helena*, the heroine suppliant at an altar: *Iph. Taur.*, the half-divine priestess of a strange and bloodstained Temple rising from a dream of death. The religious half-supernatural atmosphere is unmistakable.

The only exceptions are *Medea, Phoenissae, Electra, Orestes*, though in the two last the exception is more apparent than real. We must remember the curious traces of the daimon that cling about Orestes. In any case, both openings produce a decidedly uncanny atmosphere – the lonely woman in the night uttering curses against her mother, and the woman sitting alone by her brother who is mad and perhaps dead.

There remain two peculiar cases, the *Rhesus* and *Iphigenia in Aulis*. We know that the *Rhesus* had in Alexandrian times three different Prologues, while the *Iphigenia* has two in our present MSS. I will not discuss them further than to point out that they seem to represent a new form of Prologue, which starts with a lyric scene. The lyric Prologues of both are very similar and exceedingly beautiful, and I may say in passing that I have long been inclined to think that we have in them the hand of the original producer of *Iphigenia*, Euripides the younger. In the *Iph. Aul.*, according to our MSS., the Prologue proper follows the lyrical scene. This order seems to be taken from the New Comedy: Menander usually made his expository Prologue the second scene of the play.

What is the explanation of these facts? It seems to me that the old Sacer Ludus has reasserted itself: the Prologue, after passing into a mere dramatic exposition-scene between ordinary people, returns again to be a solemn address spoken to the audience by a sacred or mysterious figure. The differences are, first, that it is now integral in the whole play as a work of art, and secondly, that it has been markedly influenced by the speech of the god at the end. It is the same story with other elements of the drama. The language and metre get freer in Sophocles, and return to formality in Euripides. The dialogue becomes irregular and almost "natural" in Sophocles, and then returns to a kind of formal antiphony of symmetrical speeches or equally symmetrical *stichomythiae*. The Chorus itself first dwindles to a thing of little account and then increases again till it begins once more to bear the chief weight of the tragedy. Something like the old hierophant reappears at the beginning, something like the old re-risen god at the end; and, as we have seen, it is in plays of Euripides, and most of all in the very latest of his plays, that we find in most perfect and clear-cut outline the whole sequence of Contest, Tearing-asunder, Messenger, Lamentation, Discovery, Recognition, and Resurrection which constituted the original Dionysus-mystery.

Thus the death of Dionysus is ἄρρητον. It was blasphemous, if not impossible, to speak seriously of the death of the Life of the World. This fact seems to me to have had important consequences, differentiating Dionysus from the other Year-Daimons and incidentally explaining some peculiarities of Greek Tragedy.

The ordinary Year-Daimon arrived, grew great and was slain by his successor, who was exactly similar to him. But Dionysus did not die. He seemed to die, but really it was his enemy, in his dress and likeness, it was Pentheus or Lycurgus who died while Dionysus lived on in secret. When the world seemed to be dead and deprived of him, he was there in the ivy and pine and other evergreens; he was the secret life or fire in wine, or other intoxicants. By this train of ideas Dionysus comes to be regarded not as a mere vegetation-spirit or Year-Daimon, but as representing some secret or mysterious life, persisting through death or after death.

An outer shape dominated by tough and undying tradition, an inner life fiery with sincerity and spiritual freedom; the vessels of a very ancient religion overfilled and broken by the new wine of reasoning and rebellious humanity, and still, in their rejection, shedding abroad the old aroma, as of eternal and mysterious things: these are the fundamental paradoxes presented to us by Greek Tragedy. The contrasts have their significance for other art also, perhaps for all great art. But aesthetic criticism is not the business of the present note.

6

A RITUAL BASIS FOR HESIOD'S *THEOGONY*

F. M. Cornford

The English classical philosopher F. M. Cornford (1874–1943), who was Professor of Ancient Philosophy at Cambridge University, devoted himself to two main issues in ancient Greek culture: the relationship between religion and science, and the relationship between myth and ritual. Cornford argued that Greek science did not arise *ex nihilo* but instead grew out of Greek religion and only subsequently severed its ties to religion and became empirical science (see *From Religion to Philosophy* [London: Arnold, 1912]). Later he argued more radically that Greek science never severed its ties to religion. Cornford simultaneously argued that Greek myth grew out of ritual and only subsequently lost its ties to ritual and became an explanation of the world, as Smith, Harrison, and Hooke also maintain. Cornford's myth-ritualism, which comes ultimately from Frazer but directly from Hooke, centers on the annual killing and replacement of the king, who is divine, to ensure the renewal of vegetation. Unlike Hooke, Cornford says that the ritual came first and that the myth arose only once the god had been differentiated from the king, who then became his mere representative. The myth of the death and rebirth of the god of vegetation now provided the script for the ritual, with the king playing the role of the god. By distinguishing two stages of the ritual, one prior to myth and one directed by myth, Cornford avoids the inconsistency facing both Hooke and Frazer over the status of the king. In the following essay on "A Ritual Basis for Hesiod's *Theogony*" (1941) (in *The Unwritten Philosophy and Other Essays*, ed. W. K. C. Guthrie [Cambridge: Cambridge University Press, 1950], 95–116), Cornford works back from the extant creation myth to the original myth accompanying the ritual. For a fuller reconstruction of the *Theogony*

Original publication: F. M. Cornford, "A Ritual Basis for Hesiod's *Theogony*" (1941), in his *The Unwritten Philosophy and Other Essays*, ed. W. K. C. Guthrie (Cambridge: Cambridge University Press, 1950), pp. 95–116.

see Cornford, *Principium Sapientiae*, ed. W. K. C. Guthrie (Cambridge: Cambridge University Press, 1952), 191–256. Cornford's other, somewhat less original myth-ritualist endeavor was the reconstruction of a comparable myth-ritualist scenario for Aristophanic comedy – an endeavor less original only because Murray had recently done the same for Greek tragedy. See Cornford, *The Origin of Attic Comedy* (London: Arnold, 1914). See also his "The Origin of the Olympic Games," in Harrison, *Themis* (Cambridge: Cambridge University Press, 1912), ch. 7. On Cornford see Gilbert Murray, "Francis Macdonald Cornford, 1874–1943," *Proceedings of the British Academy* 29 (1943), 421–32; W. K. C. Guthrie, Memoir, in Cornford, *The Unwritten Philosophy and Other Essays*, vii–xix; Theodor H. Gaster, Editor's Foreword to Cornford, *The Origin of Attic Comedy* (Garden City, NY: Doubleday Anchor Books, 1961), xiii–xxvii; Douglas Kellogg Wood, "F. M. Cornford," in *Classical Scholarship*, ed. Ward W. Briggs and William M. Calder III (New York: Garland Publishing, 1990), 23–36; and Robert Ackerman, *The Myth and Ritual School* (New York: Garland Publishing, 1991), 111–13, 138–44.

Professor Mazon has recently described Hesiod's *Theogony* as "a genealogy interrupted by episodes". These episodes are myths, and Professor Mazon rightly remarks that their authenticity ought not to be suspected merely because they interrupt the genealogy, or because they are not consistent with one another. The texts produced by higher critics, who have given rein to such suspicions, leave the impression that the poem consists mainly of interpolations, like a bad sponge consisting mostly of holes. They are approaching the point at which the critics of the Pauline Epistles, having condemned them all, one after another, were left with no means of knowing what a genuine Pauline Epistle would be like. If the game was to go on, it was necessary to restore at least one to serve as a criterion for rejecting the remainder; and when that had been done, most of the others crept back again one by one into the canon.

This paper is inspired by the hope of rescuing some of the so-called episodes now jettisoned from the *Theogony*. I shall call in question what seems to be the current view, that the narrative parts of the poem are a mere patchwork of unconnected stories drawn from a variety of sources: Homer's account of the Olympian society; local cult-legends; other myths universally current in Greece; and a few stories too crudely indecent to be acknowledged as Hellenic.[1] I shall argue that the bulk of the episodes fit into the pattern of a very old myth of Creation, known to us from eastern sources and ultimately based on ritual.

Hesiod's own programme, laid down in the prelude, mentions three elements that are to figure in the poem: (1) theogony proper, i.e., the generations of the gods; (2) cosmogony, or the formation of the physical world-order and the creation of mankind; and (3) the story of how the gods took possession of

---

[1] So Ziegler in Roscher, *Lex. Myth.* s.v. "Theogonien".

Olympus under the supreme kingship of Zeus, who apportioned to the other gods their several provinces and honours.

(1)   We can quickly pass over the first element – the genealogies of the gods. Hesiod gives three main lines of descent: (*a*) The children of Night prove to be a list of allegorical abstractions: Death, Sleep, the Fates, and all the afflictions which plague mankind. (*b*) The children of the Sea (Pontos), including a Dragon of the Waters with a brood of monsters, of whom we shall hear more later on. (*c*) Finally there are the offspring of Ouranos and Gaia: the earlier generation of Titans, Cyclopes, and the Hundred-Armed, and the second generation of the sons of Cronos, Zeus and the other Olympians and their descendants. These genealogies, though bewilderingly complicated, can be understood as an effort to combine in one pantheon a very miscellaneous collection of supernatural beings, ranging from the most concrete and anthropomorphic to the barest allegorical abstractions.

(2)   Setting aside the genealogies, we come next to the second factor, cosmogony: "how at the first the gods and earth came into being, and the rivers, and the swelling rage of the boundless sea, and the shining stars, and the broad heaven above" (108–10). The cosmogony, so announced in the prelude, follows immediately. It is quite short, occupying seventeen lines of which three of four are possibly spurious (116–32).

We are here told how the main divisions of the existing cosmos came into being: the earth with its dry land and seas, and the sky above with its stars. The veil of mythological language is so thin as to be quite transparent. Ouranos and Gaia, for instance, are simply the sky and the earth that we see every day. They are not here supernatural persons with mythical biographies and adventures. Even when Earth is said to "give birth" to the mountains and the sea, Hesiod himself tells us that this is conscious metaphor: a "birth" can only follow upon a marriage, but here it occurs "without love or marriage", ἄτερ φιλότητος ἐφιμέρου (132). The metaphor means no more than that this cosmogony is of the evolutionary type. There are no personal gods to make the world out of pre-existing materials according to the alternative pattern, the creational. The personal gods come later, when the world-order is already complete.

At that moment (132) Gaia and Ouranos suddenly become mythical persons, who marry and have children – Gaia is now a goddess, who can plot with her son Cronos to mutilate her husband Ouranos. We have passed into the world of myth, where the characters acquire the solidity and opaqueness of anthropomorphic individuals, with the whole apparatus of human motive and action.

(3)   The remainder of the poem – the third of our three elements – moves in this genuine mythical atmosphere. It is a story of the adventures which led from the birth of the earliest gods to the final establishment of Zeus, triumphant over his enemies, as king of the gods and of the universe.

My object is to show that we have here not "a genealogy interrupted by episodes", but a sequence of episodes, most of which once formed parts of a connected pattern, interrupted by genealogies, which serve to explain how the characters in the mythical action came into existence. The sequence of episodes itself constitutes what is, in essence, a hymn to Zeus and also a hymn of Creation – a mythical account of the beginning of things, immeasurably more primitive in character than the evolutionary cosmogony that precedes it. These two elements – the cosmogony and the hymn of Creation – are not in origin what Hesiod has made them, two chapters in a single story. The hymn is based on a genuine myth of enormous antiquity, itself founded on ritual. The cosmogony, on the other hand, has almost completely emerged from the atmosphere of myth. It is only just on the wrong side of the line we draw between mythical thinking and the earliest rational philosophy – the system of the Milesians.

Contents of the Cosmogony

Let us look first at the cosmogony.

I can only deal very shortly with its contents. I think it can be shown to conform to a pattern which also appears in the Orphic cosmogonies and underlies the Ionian systems of philosophy from Anaximander onwards.

(1) *"First of all Chaos came into being."* There should be no doubt about the meaning of Chaos.[2] Etymologically, the word means a yawning gap; and in the Greek poets, including Hesiod himself (*Theog.* 700), it denotes the gap or void space between sky and earth. Bacchylides (v, 27) and Aristophanes (*Birds*, 192) speak of birds as flying in or through this space (διὰ τοῦ χάους, ἐν χάει).

A gap or yawn *comes into being* (Hesiod says γένετο, not ἦν) by the separation of two things that were formerly together. What these things were we learn from a fifth-century Ionian system, preserved by Diodorus (I, 7).[3] It opens with the words: "Originally, heaven and earth had one form (μίαν ἰδέαν), their natures being mingled; then, when these bodies had taken up their stations apart from one another, the world embraced the whole order now seen in it." Diodorus cites as parallel the famous lines of Euripides' Melanippe: "The tale is not mine – I had it from my mother: how heaven and earth were once one form, and when they were separated apart, they gave birth to all things."

[2] Most modern discussions of this term are vitiated by the introduction of the later idea of infinite empty space, and by modern associations with disorder. I do not think Chaos is ever described as ἄπειρον, and if it were, that would mean no more than "immeasurable", as when the word is used of the earth or the sea.

[3] This system is now ascribed (Diels-Kranz *Vors.*[5], II, 135) to Democritus; but there is no mention of atoms.

Orpheus (Apollonius Rhodius, *Argon*. I, 496) sang "how earth and heaven and sea were once joined together in one form, and by deadly strife were separated from each other", then the heavenly bodies, mountains and rivers (dry land and water) were formed; and finally all living things.

Thus all these cosmogonies begin with a primal unity, which is separated apart, when the sky is lifted up from the earth, leaving the yawning gap of void or air between.

(2) By the opening of the gap, the broad bosom of Earth is revealed ($\gamma\alpha\tilde{\iota}\alpha$ $\epsilon\mathring{v}\rho\acute{v}\sigma\tau\epsilon\rho\nu o\varsigma$), and Eros. Eros is an allegorical figure. His function is to reunite the sundered parents, Heaven and Earth, in the marriage from which all life, mortal and immortal, is born. So we are told in the parabasis of the *Birds*: "Before that there was no race of immortals, until Eros mixed all things together", $\sigma\upsilon\nu\acute{\epsilon}\mu\epsilon\iota\zeta\epsilon\nu$: the use of $\mu\iota\gamma\tilde{\eta}\nu\alpha\iota$ for marriage needs no illustration. Eros is the allegorical image of that intercourse of the separated opposites which will generate life.

His physical equivalent is the rain, the seed of the Heaven-father which fertilises the womb of mother Earth.

(3) Another physical consequence of the opening of the gap is that light is let in between the sundered parts. Accordingly we hear next of the appearance of light out of darkness. In genealogical terms, Darkness, as the male Erebos and the female Nyx, generates Light as the male Aither and the female Hemera. Day dawns from Night.

In one form of the Orphic cosmogony Eros is replaced by the spirit of light, Phanes, who appears when the world-egg is separated apart, the upper half forming the dome of heaven, the lower containing the moist slime from which the dry earth and the sea will emerge.

(4) The next event is startling. In spite of the fact that the gap separating heaven and earth has already come into being, we now hear that "Earth first generated the starry heaven, equal to herself, to envelop her all round, that there might be for the blessed gods a seat secure for ever".

Here is another separation of heaven from earth duplicating the opening of the gap. We shall soon encounter this duplication again, and when we get back to the original myth we shall be able to explain it.

Meanwhile let us note the epithet of heaven – "starry" ($\mathring{\alpha}\sigma\tau\epsilon\rho\acute{o}\epsilon\iota\varsigma$). This is expanded in Hesiod's proem: "the shining stars of the broad heaven above" (110). Strange as it seems to us, the Ionian philosophers likewise regard the heavenly bodies as derived from the earth. They were explained mechanically as huge rocks, flung off to a distance, which became incandescent because of the speed of their motion.

(5) Then comes the distinction of the dry land from the sea: "Earth gave birth to the high hills and to the sea (Pontos) with swelling waves." This was *not* the result of a marriage, but $\mathring{\alpha}\tau\epsilon\rho$ $\phi\iota\lambda\acute{o}\tau\eta\tau o\varsigma$ $\mathring{\epsilon}\phi\iota\mu\acute{\epsilon}\rho o\upsilon$, another act of separation.

So again, in the Ionian systems, the last stage is the separation of dry from moist, when part of the earth is dried by the sun's heat, and the seas shrink into their beds.

The world-order is now complete as we see it, with its four great divisions: earth, sea, the gap of air, and starry sky above. From first to last the process is the separation or division, out of a primal indistinct unity, of parts which successively became distinct regions of the cosmos.

This cosmogony, as I have remarked, is not a myth, or rather it is *no longer* a myth. It has advanced so far along the road of rationalisation that only a very thin partition divides it from those early Greek systems which historians still innocently treat as purely rational constructions. Comparison with those systems shows that, when once the cosmic order has been formed, the next chapter should be an account of the origin of life. In the philosophies, life arises from the interaction or intercourse of the separated elements: animal life is born of the action of the heavenly heat on the moist slime of earth. This is the rationalised equivalent of the marriage of Heaven and Earth. And sure enough this marriage follows immediately in Hesiod: Gaia lay with Ouranos and brought forth the Titans. And so the genealogies begin – the theogony proper.

But here comes the sudden change I mentioned.

These gods are supernatural persons, with human forms and characters and well-known biographies. So at this point we turn back into that world of mythical representation which the rationalised cosmogony had left so far behind. Sky and Earth are re-transformed into a god and goddess, whose love and hate are depicted in all too human terms.

Here, where the mythical hymn to Zeus begins with the birth of the eldest gods, we must leave Hesiod for the moment to note a curiously close parallel to this sudden shift from rationalised cosmogony back to pure myth.

The first three chapters of Genesis contain two alternative accounts of Creation. The first account, in its present form, was composed not earlier than the Exile; it is considerably later than Hesiod, it may even be later than Anaximander. In this Hebrew cosmogony, moreover, we find nearly the same sequence of events. Let us recall what happened on the six days of Creation.

(1) There is the original confusion, the unformed watery mass wrapped in darkness. Light appears, divided from darkness, as day from night. (So Hesiod's gap opened and Day was born from Night.)

(2) The sky as a solid firmament ($\sigma\tau\epsilon\rho\epsilon\omega\mu\alpha$) is lifted up to form a roof separating the heavenly waters, whence the rain comes, from the waters on the earth. (This corresponds to Hesiod's Earth generating the sky as a secure seat for the gods. There is the same duplication that we noted.)

(3) The dry land is separated from the sea, and clothed with plants and trees.

(4) The heavenly bodies, sun, moon, and stars are made.
(As in the Greek myths and philosophies, their formation follows that of the earth.)

(5) & (6) Then came the moving creatures with life – birds, fishes, and creeping things – and finally man.
(Thus life appears when the cosmic frame is complete.)

The most striking difference from the Greek cosmogonies is that Hebrew monotheism has retained the Divine Creator as the sole first cause. Otherwise there are no mythical personifications, no allegorical figures like Eros or Phanes. And the action of the Elohim is confined to the utterance of the creative word. He has become extremely abstract and remote. If you eliminate the divine command: "Let there be" so-and-so, and leave only the event commanded: "There was" so-and-so, and then link these events in a chain of natural causation, the whole account is transformed into a quasi-scientific evolution of the world-order. The process is the same as in the Greek cosmogonies – separation or differentiation out of a primitive confusion. And as measured by the absence of allegorical personifications, Genesis is less mythical than Hesiod's *Theogony*, and even closer to the rationalised system of the Milesians.

When we turn to the second account of Creation in Genesis ii–iii, we find ourselves back once more in the world of myth. The utterly remote Elohim of the first chapter is replaced by an anthropomorphic Jahweh, who moulds man out of dust, breathes life into his nostrils, plants a garden with trees, takes the man's rib and makes out of it a woman, walks in the garden in the cool of the day, and speaks to Adam with a human voice. The substance of the story also is composed of genuine myths: the woman Eve and the trouble she brings recall Hesiod's Pandora; there is the myth explaining man's mortality by failure to eat the fruit of the tree of life; and so on.

These myths may represent the concluding episodes in a primitive Creation myth. The earlier part, dealing with the formation of the world-order before man was made, has been suppressed by the priestly compilers of Genesis. They substituted for it their own expurgated and semi-philosophical cosmogony in the first chapter.

There is thus a curious parallel between Hesiod and Genesis. In both we find a prosaic cosmogony followed by a shift back into the world of poetry, peopled by the concrete human figures of mythical gods. This is no mere accident. In each case the cosmogony is the final product of a long process of rationalisation, in which the expurgation of mythical imagery has been carried so far that the result might almost be mistaken for a construction of the intellect reasoning from observation of the existing world. Only when we reflect on certain features do we realise that it can be nothing of the kind.

There is nothing whatever in the obvious appearance of the world to suggest that the sky ever had to be lifted up from the earth, or that the heavenly bodies were formed after the earth, and so on. The same remark applies to the slightly more rationalised cosmogonies of the Ionian philosophers. They follow the same pattern, which pattern could never have been designed by inference from the observation of nature.

Now the value of the parallel I have drawn with Hebrew cosmogony lies in the fact that the Old Testament has preserved elsewhere other traces of the original myth of Creation which the priestly authors of Genesis have largely obliterated. This myth has been restored by scholars, and, what is more, traced to its origin in ritual. And behind this Palestinian myth and ritual lie the Babylonian Hymn of Creation and the corresponding New Year rites. If we follow this track, we shall, I believe, discover the framework of those episodes which make up the third element in Hesiod's *Theogony* – the mythical hymn to Zeus.

The Opening of Chaos

We may start from that curious feature I have emphasised: the fact that, both in Hesiod and Genesis, the separation of sky from earth occurs twice over. We will take the two versions of this event separately.

First there is the opening of the gap and the appearance of light in the primaeval darkness. Turning from Hesiod's cosmogony to the hymn which follows, we find that this event has its counterpart in the first episode of the myth. Fifty years ago Andrew Lang pointed out that the mutilation of the sky-god by his son Cronos could be "explained as a myth of the violent separation of the earth and sky, which some races, for example the Polynesians, supposed to have originally clasped each other in a close embrace". I quote these words from Frazer's *Adonis* (I, 283); and this explanation is adopted by Nilsson in his *History of Greek Religion* (p. 73).

After mentioning the Orphic world-egg, Nilsson writes: "Still more crude is the cosmogonic myth in Hesiod. Ouranos (the sky) settled down upon Gaia (the earth), completely covering her, and hid their children in her entrails. Gaia persuaded her son Kronos to part them by cutting off the genitalia of Ouranos. There are curious parallels in the Egyptian myth of Keb and Nut, the earth-god and the goddess of heaven, and in the Maori myth of Rangi and Papa."

In this myth we read:[4] "From Rangi, the Heaven, and Papa, the Earth, sprang all men and things; but sky and earth clave together, and darkness

---

[4] Tylor, *Primitive Culture* I. 322.

rested upon them and the beings they had begotten, till at last their children took counsel whether they should rend apart their parents or slay them."

Tane Mahute separated them and raised up the sky. The gods then departed each to his separated place in air, earth, and sea, and thus the world was established. We may note further that as, in Hesiod's Cosmogony, the opening of the gap is followed by the appearance of Eros, so in his myth the sundering of Ouranos and Gaia is followed by the birth of Aphrodite, who has Eros and Himeros in her train and whose prerogative ($\tau\iota\mu\acute{\eta}$ and $\mu o \widetilde{\iota} \rho a$) is to preside over marriage (201–6).

The Polynesian myth brings out more clearly than Hesiod does the purpose for which heaven and earth were forced apart: it was to give the gods room in which to be born and distinct regions they could occupy in a world-order. In the language of myth, it enables Gaia to give birth to her children, Pontos and the other gods. In the language of rationalised cosmogony, it is followed by the separation of the sea from the dry land and the appearance of living things. Once you have granted the fundamental axiom that "heaven and earth were once one form" (or, as the philosophers put it, "all things were together", $\mathring{\eta}\nu$ $\acute{o}\mu o \widetilde{\upsilon} \pi\acute{a}\nu\tau a$), theogony and cosmogony alike must begin with the separation of the two parents of the gods or the two primary regions of the cosmos.

The agent in the mythical version is Cronos, instigated by Gaia herself. To that extent Cronos fills the role of creator. Also he was the king, who originally distributed among the Titans their privileges and provinces in the order of the world (*Theog.* 392 ff.). But his reign has receded into the dim past. In the hymn the foreground is occupied by his son, the young king, Zeus. Zeus is the hero whose exploits established the world as it now is.

The Dragon

So much, then, for the original opening of the gap. We will now go on to the second version of this act of separation. In Hesiod, Earth gives birth to the heaven and the shining stars. In Genesis, Elohim lifts up the firmament to support the heavenly ocean and creates the sun, moon, and stars. What is the mythical counterpart of this episode in cosmogony?

Once more the answer is to be found in the pages of the *Golden Bough*. Frazer writes:

> The Babylonian myth relates how in the beginning the mighty god Marduk fought and killed the great dragon Tiamat, an embodiment of the primaeval watery chaos, and how after his victory he created the present heaven and earth by splitting the huge carcase of the monster into halves and setting one of them up to form the sky, while the other half apparently he used to fashion the earth.

Thus the story is a myth of creation. . . . The account of creation given in the first chapter of Genesis, which has been so much praised for its simple grandeur and sublimity, is merely a rationalised version of the old myth of the fight with the dragon, a myth which for crudity of thought deserves to rank with the quaint fancies of the lowest savages.[5]

Frazer is referring to the Babylonian so-called "Epic of Creation". We there read how Tiamat the dragon of the waters, seeking vengeance on the younger gods for killing her husband Apsu, organised a host of monsters. She defeats the first champion of the gods, who then appeal to Marduk. He undertakes to save them, if he is promised kingship over the whole world. Exalted as a great god, he kills the dragon and imprisons her monsters in the lower world. He then splits her body in half to make sky and earth; fixes the regions of the world-order, and assigns the three provinces of heaven, earth, and sea to Anu, Enlil, and Ea. He orders the year and the signs of the Zodiac and other heavenly bodies. There is a long description of the constellations.

Here we have, in its oldest known form, the lifting-up of the starry heaven from the earth followed by the ordering of the stars and of the provinces in the cosmos. We have seen how all this is rationalised in Genesis i and reduced to the formation of the firmament, the creation of the heavenly bodies, the separation of land and sea.

Now the link connecting the Babylonian myth with Genesis i is provided by references in the Psalms and Prophets to the myth of Jahweh slaying the dragon Rahab or Leviathan. Here is one of many:

> God is my king of old, working salvation in the midst of the earth.
> Thou didst divide the sea by thy strength; thou brakest the heads
>   of the dragons in the waters.
> Thou breakest the heads of leviathan in pieces. . . .
> The day is thine, the night also is thine; thou hast prepared the
>   light and the sun.
> Thou hast set all the borders of the earth: thou hast made summer
>   and winter.[6]

Here the dividing of the waters by the firmament is equated with the breaking of the dragon in pieces. It is followed by the creation of light and the sun, the ordering of the seasons, and fixing of the borders of the earth.

Now in Hesiod, one of the most exciting episodes is the slaying of the dragon by Zeus. This is one of the passages which the editors condemn on account of some inconsistency and dislocation. Among the descendants of Pontos we find the half-human dragon Echidna, who in marriage with Typhaon

---

[5] *The Dying God*, p. 105.
[6] Ps. lxxiv. 12–17.

produces a brood of monsters (*Theog.* 295 ff.). Later (820), after the expulsion of the Titans from heaven, comes the battle of Zeus with the dragon Typhoeus, here the child of Earth and Tartarus. The whole of nature is involved in the turmoil of this terrific struggle. After his victory, Zeus, like Marduk, is established as king over the gods, and apportions to them their stations in the world-order.

On the strength of the Hebrew and Babylonian parallels (not to mention others), I claim that the battle of Zeus and the dragon Typhoeus is an original feature of the Greek Creation myth, which should be followed by the lifting up of the sky and the formation of the heavenly bodies. Of this sequel just a trace remains in the cosmogony, where the earth gives birth to the heaven and the shining stars – the second of those two separations of heaven and earth which we have noted.

It is now possible to explain why this separation occurs twice. In the rationalised cosmogonies it is inexplicable; but the reason appears in the myth. There the work of creation is the exploit of a personal god – Marduk, Jahweh, Zeus – who can bring light out of darkness, order out of formlessness, only by first triumphing over the powers of evil and disorder embodied in the dragon of the waters and her brood of monsters.[7] But this exploit must happen *somewhere*: the drama requires a stage. Also the hero must have a birth and history; and if he is to be the son of Heaven and Earth, his parents must have become distinct before they could marry and have a child.

Hence the necessity that the whole story should begin with the gap coming into being. In Hesiod's cosmogony, this simply happens: the first event has no cause behind it. But in myth all events are apt to have personal causes. So we find that Ouranos and Gaia are forced apart by Cronos, before the gods can be born, including Zeus himself. The result is this curious duplication. Heaven and earth are first separated in order to give birth to the god, who will create the world by separating heaven from earth as the two parts of the dragon.

But it is high time for me to fulfil the promise of my title which suggests that Hesiod's *Theogony* is, in the last resort, based on ritual. So far I have only argued that his all-but philosophical cosmogony is a rational reflection of his mythical hymn of Zeus, just as Genesis i is a reflection of the myths of Jahweh and Marduk. But I have only dealt with two episodes in the myth. In the light of the oriental material we can now go further and ask whether other episodes in the hymn of Zeus will not fit into a connected pattern, and whether this pattern may not be referred ultimately to a sequence of ritual acts.

It is now certainly established that the killing of Leviathan by Jahweh or of Tiamat by Marduk was not what Frazer called a "quaint fancy" of primitive and problematical savages, sitting round the fire and speculating on the origin

---

[7] Roscher, *Lex.* s.v. "Ophion". Jensen suggested that the battle of $X\rho\acute{o}\nu os$-$K\rho\acute{o}\nu os$ with Ophioneus in Pherecydes' cosmogony is equivalent to the battle of Marduk and Tiamat.

of the world. Nor was this conflict an isolated event without a context. Biblical students[8] have made out that the Psalm celebrating it belong to a group of liturgical songs, which were recited, as part of the Temple worship, at the Feast of Tabernacles. This feast inaugurated the New Year; and in its dramatic ritual the events these Psalms describe were annually re-enacted.

It is inferred from the Psalms that the fight with the dragon was one episode in the drama, in which, as throughout the festival, the part of Jahweh was taken by the king. There was also a triumphal procession, conducting the divine king in his chariot up the hill of Zion to be enthroned in the temple. Emblems of new vegetation, fertility, and moisture were carried and waved as a charm to secure a sufficiency of rain for the coming year. There are also signs that, at some point in the king's progress, there was another ritual combat. The procession was assailed by the powers of darkness and death, who are also the enemies of Israel, the kings of the earth who took counsel together against the Lord's anointed. The god who wields the thunder intervened to save his royal son and to dash his enemies in pieces. This episode has a parallel in the annual ritual at Abydos in Egypt. The procession conducting Osiris to his shrine was attacked by a band representing Set and his followers, who were repelled by a company led by Horus. At Jerusalem there was probably also a sacred marriage in a grove, commemorated by the booths made of branches from which the festival took its name, Tabernacles.

It appears, then, that the slaying of the dragon by the king-god, which was the initial act of creation, was one feature in the dramatic ritual of the New Year festival. What is the connection between a New Year festival and the myth of Creation?

This question has been convincingly answered by oriental scholars. The festival was much more than the civic inauguration of another year. It was in the first place a ceremony whose magical efficacy was to secure, during the coming year, the due supply of rain and the consequent fertility of plants and animals, on which man's life depends. This purpose was never forgotten. It is stated in the simplest terms by the prophet Zechariah (xiv. 16), who foretells that, when the Lord is King over the whole earth, every one that is left of all the nations which came against Jerusalem shall go up from year to year to worship the King, the Lord of Hosts, and to keep the feast of Tabernacles – "And it shall be, that whoso will not come up . . . *upon them shall be no rain.*"

So the central figure in the New Year rites was the rain-maker, the divine king. But at the advanced stage of civilisation we are now considering in Babylon, Egypt, and Palestine, the king has become much more than a rain-making magician. To control the rain is to control the procession of the seasons and their powers of drought and moisture, heat and cold; and these again are linked with the orderly revolutions of sun, moon, and stars. The king is thus

---

[8] Prof. W. O. E. Oesterley in *Myth and Ritual*, chap. VI; A. R. Johnson in *The Labyrinth*.

regarded as the living embodiment of the god who instituted this natural order and must perpetually renew and maintain its functioning for the benefit of man. The king embodies that power and also the life-force of his people, concentrated in his official person. He is the maintainer of the social order; and the prosperity of the nation depends upon his righteousness, the Hebrew *Sedek*, the Greek δίκη. He protects his people from the evil powers of death and disorder, as well as leading them in war to victory over their enemies.

The purpose of the New Year festival is to renovate – to recreate – the ordered life of the social group and of the world of nature, after the darkness and defeat of winter. The power which gives one more turn to the wheel of the revolving year is vested in the king, but derived from the god whom he embodies, the god who first set the wheel in motion. So the rites are regarded as an annual re-enactment of Creation.

Commenting on the features common to the New Year festivals of Babylon and Egypt, Professor Oesterley remarks[9] that, while there are many gods,

> there is one who assumes supremacy in the role of productive creator; and the earthly king is identified with him. Osiris among the Egyptians, and Marduk among the Babylonians, are the supreme gods, and in each case the earthly king is identified with his god. During the annual New Year Festival held in honour of the deity he is proclaimed king; and this is graphically set forth in the drama of his ascent upon his throne; he is thereby acknowledge as lord of creation. The mystery-rite not only symbolised, but was believed actually to bring about, the revivification of Nature.
>
> Now, what Osiris was to the Egyptians, and what Marduk was to the Babylonians, that Jahweh was to the Israelites. The New Year Festival of the Israelites was held on the first day of the Feast of Tabernacles (Sukkoth), when the Kingship of their God Jahweh was celebrated, and he was worshipped and honoured as Lord of Creation. By his will . . . the produce of the soil during the coming year would be abundant; thus, annually there was the renewed manifestation of His creative power, so that every New Year Festival was a memorial of the Creation, since at each New Year the land was recreated. . . . It may be said that the New Year Festival was, as it were, a repetition of the Creation.

To the same effect Professor Hooke has written of the Babylonian ceremony:

> It was, in a literal sense, the making of a New Year, the removal of the guilt and defilement of the old year, and the ensuring of security and prosperity for the coming year. By this ceremony was secured the due functioning of all things, sun, moon, stars, and seasons, in their appointed order. Here lies the ritual meaning of Creation: there is a new creation year by year, as a result of these ceremonies. The conception of creation in this stage of the evolution of religion is not cosmological but ritual. It has not come into existence in answer to

---

[9] *Myth and Ritual*, p. 123.

speculations about the origin of things, but as a ritual means of maintaining the necessary order of things essential for the well-being of the community.[10]

We can now define the relation between the Creation myth and the New Year rites. It is the relation called "aetiological". Here the Babylonian evidence is conclusive. We possess a large part of the myth in the tablets now misleadingly entitled "The Epic of Creation". This is not an epic, but a hymn. Epics do not reflect ritual action; nor were they recited as incantations to reinforce the efficacy of a rite every time it was performed. This document is a hymn to Marduk, recounting his exploits in creating and ordering the world of gods and men.

We know, moreover, that, on the fourth day of the New Year festival of the spring equinox, this hymn was recited, from beginning to end, by the high priest, shut up alone in the sanctuary. This was done before the king arrived to take the leading part in the principal ceremonies.

Further, fragments of a priestly commentary on the ritual explain that a whole series of actions performed by the king symbolised the exploits of Marduk in the story of Creation. That story is, in fact, the aetiological myth of the New Year festival.

Now we know that an aetiological myth is not really the historical record of a supernatural series of events instituting the rite which professes to re-enact these events on a miniature scale. The rite itself is the only historical event, repeated annually. Every spring the king-god actually recreates the natural and social order. The myth is a transcription of that performance on a higher plane, where the corresponding actions are imagined as performed once for all by the god whom the king is conceived to embody and represent. But that god is simply a projection, made up of the official character and functions of the king, abstracted from the accidental human personality who is invested with those functions so long as his vitality lasts in full vigour. When he grows old or dies, the divine character is transmitted to a successor. The god is related to the individual king as the Platonic Idea to a series of particulars which for a time manifest its character. The myth is similarly the universalised transcript of the recurrent ritual action, projected on to the superhuman plane.

It follows that the contents of the Creation myth are not "quaint fancies", or baseless speculations; nor are they derived from the observation of natural phenomena. Starting from the given appearance of the starry sky above our heads and the broad earth at our feet, no one but a lunatic under the influence of hashish could ever arrive at the theory that they were originally formed by splitting the body of a dragon in half. But suppose you start with a ritual drama, in which the powers of evil and disorder, represented by a priestly actor with a dragon's mask, are overcome by the divine king, as part of a

---

[10] *Origins of Early Semitic Ritual*, p. 19.

magical regeneration of the natural and social order. Then you may compose a hymn, in which this act is magnified, with every circumstance of splendour and horror, as a terrific battle between the king of the gods and the dragon of the deep. And you will recite this hymn, every time the ritual drama is performed, to reinforce its efficacy with all the majesty of the superhuman precedent.

Now so long as the myth remains part of a living ritual, its symbolic meaning is clear. But when the ritual has fallen into disuse, the myth may survive for many centuries. The action will now appear crude, grotesque, monstrous; and yet a poet may instinctively feel that the story is still charged with significance, however obscure, owing to the intense emotions that went to its making when it was part of vitally important religious action. Symbols like the dragon still haunt the dreams of our most civilised contemporaries.

The suggestion, then, to which all this intricate argument has led, is that the mythical element in the *Theogony* consists mainly in the debris of a Creation myth which is also a hymn to Zeus. By Hesiod's time it had long been detached from the ritual it once reflected, and the episodes have naturally suffered some dislocation. Also, since Hesiod was unaware of the ritual origin which alone makes them intelligible, the outlines are sometimes blurred. But if we pass them briefly in review, the ancient pattern can still be traced.

(1)   Hesiod's myth is linked with the preceding cosmogony by the marriage of Ouranos and Gaia, parents of the elder gods; the Cyclopes, who will furnish Zeus with his thunder; the Hundred-Armed, who will fight for him against the Titans; and the Titans themselves.

Ouranos hates his children, who cannot get born until Cronos castrates his father and forces the pair apart.

In the Babylonian myth the first parents are the male and female powers of the primaeval deep, Apsu and Tiamat, whose waters at first were mingled together. Apsu wishes to destroy his children, the elder gods. Ea plots against Apsu, kills him, and castrates his messenger, Mummu.

(2)   Here follow in Hesiod three genealogies. The children of Night include Death and all the evils that plague mankind. Among the descendants of Pontos is the dragon Echidna with her consort Typhaon and their brood of monsters.

In the Babylonian hymn, Tiamat plans to avenge Apsu, with the help of monsters born of the sea. She exalts Kingu among her first-born to be king over her other children, much as Gaia chose Cronos to take the lead among the Titans.

(3)   Both poems then tell of the birth of the young God – Marduk, Zeus – who is to become king and order the world of men and gods.

This part of the story of Zeus is of Cretan origin. Once more the old king tries to destroy his sons who will rob him of his kingship, and is defeated by a stratagem.

It will be remembered how in the Palaikastro hymn the fertility aspect of the young Zeus appears when he leads the dancing Kouretes, and is invoked to bring fruitfulness for the coming year.

In Hesiod Zeus releases the Hundred-Armed and the Cyclopes, who give him the thunder that will assure his kingship.

As Nilsson remarks, a fertility god who is annually reborn must also die annually. The death of Zeus was a part of the Cretan myth which the Greeks suppressed.

It is noteworthy that the death of Marduk does not figure in the Creation myth; but we possess tablets recording the ritual of his death and resurrection, which somehow accompanied the New Year festival. The ritual resembled that of Tammuz; and, while Bel-Marduk was in the underworld, the hymn of Creation was sung as an incantation to secure his return to life.

(4) Hesiod's story is here interrupted by the genealogy of Iapetus, which leads to the cheating of Zeus by Prometheus, the theft of fire, and the creation of woman to plague mankind. These events, which imply that man has already been created, are obviously out of place. At line 617 Hesiod goes back to the release of the Hundred-Armed. Zeus gives them the food of immortality, and they undertake to fight the Titans, who are attacking Olympus. The battle is indecisive until Zeus, now armed with the thunder, intervenes. The Titans are blasted and imprisoned in Tartarus.

These Titans who assail Olympus can hardly be the same as the children of Ouranos called Titans in the earlier genealogy. We cannot believe that the lovely Tethys, the gold-crowned Phebe, and two brides of Zeus, Themis and Mnemosyne, can have been battered with rocks, blasted by the lightning, and permanently chained in Tartarus.

This story has grown out of the ritual combat in which the forces of death and disorder, the followers of Set, the kings of the earth, attack the company of the young king, and are defeated by the god whom he represents. If this is so, the Titanomachy perpetuates a feature of New Year ritual.

(5) In the Babylonian myth the enemies of the younger gods are Tiamat and her host of monsters. She defeats their first champion, Anu. The gods then appeal to Marduk, who undertakes to save them if he is promised kingship over the whole world. The gods do homage to him and invest him with the insignia of royalty. There is a terrific battle, told at great length. Tiamat is slain and her monsters imprisoned.

Marduk then splits her body to make heaven and earth, fixes the regions of the world-order, and assigns heaven, earth, and sea to Anu, Enlil, and Ea as their provinces. (Compare the δασμός of these same regions to the three sons of Cronos.)

Marduk orders the year, the signs of the Zodiac, and the other heavenly bodies.

Man is created by Ea from the blood of Tiamat's consort, Kingu.

Marduk then gives laws to the gods and fixes their prerogatives. In gratitude, they build the temple of E-Sagila, where they assemble every year for the
New Year festival – that very festival of which this hymn reflects the ritual.

In Hesiod the battle with the dragon Typhoeus comes after the expulsion of
the Titans, as the last exploit of Zeus. It cannot be followed by the work of
Creation, since the formation of the world-order has already been described in
the cosmogony prefixed to the whole myth and Hesiod is too logical to repeat
it here. But it is followed by the final recognition of Zeus as king over the gods,
to whom he apportions their prerogatives.

Thus Zeus institutes the natural and social order. This royal function is
allegorically expressed by the marriage of Zeus with Themis (social order) and
the birth of their children, the Seasons (whose names are Good Government,
Justice, and Peace) and the Moirai, who give men their portions of good and
evil.

So the last event in the hymn of Marduk is that the seven gods of fate fix the
destinies for all mankind.

The parallel I have drawn might be illustrated in much greater detail. But
perhaps there is now a *prima facie* case for the thesis that Hesiod's hymn
of Zeus is not a genealogy interrupted by unconnected episodes, but reflects
the features of an ancient New Year ritual of recreation, in which the king
impersonated Zeus. The myth may have been for a long time detached from
the ritual. Hesiod cannot have been aware of its origin; but he must have
been dimly conscious that just these episodes were relevant to the story of
Creation. Further research in Crete and Asia Minor may show whether there
is any ground for the guess that the New Year festival in question was once
performed in the palace of King Minos.

Note

*The following is added at the end of the MS. of this essay, with a note saying that it
was occasioned by a criticism of Prof. A. B. Cook to the effect that it ought to be
possible to point to a ritual on Greek soil, of which the myth discussed might be the
aetiology. (W.K.C.G.)*

I am wondering whether this New Year festival is not the original parent of a lot of
festivals, including the Dionysia (New Year festivals need not be in spring), which have
diverged by emphasising different features of the original until they may seem to have
as little in common as a horse's leg, the human forearm and hand, and a bird's wing.
Thus the death and resurrection element may be almost entirely suppressed in one
form (as at Babylon, where it survived only as an extraneous rite and in the humiliation

of the divine king by the high priest, of which there is a trace still in the coronation rite). Elsewhere this feature might become central and all-important: then you have the ritual which yields tragedy and comedy. Hocart's *Kingship* suggests that you might derive from the one source also the coronation ritual and the initiation ceremonies of Eleusinian type (which were agricultural–fertility rites, *not* tribal initiations). In Osiris's case the death and resurrection *motif* is central, but other features survive.

There is only one fundamental theme behind all these: renewal of life; rebirth; the young king superseding the old.

What excited me was the idea (which I got from Hooke's books) that early philosophic cosmogony is not only a transcription of mythical cosmogony, but finally has its root in *ritual*, something tangibly existing, not baseless "fancies" and speculation.

7

NEW Year FESTIVALS

Ivan Engnell

The Swedish biblicist Ivan Engnell (1907–1964), who taught at the University of Uppsala, was the most radical member of the Scandinavian myth-ritualists. Like the English myth-ritualists headed by Hooke, the Scandinavians sought to identify a myth and ritual pattern in the ancient Near East. The key question was always how fully Israel fit the pattern, and the key question in the case of Israel was how nearly divine the king was. The stock, nonritualist answer has been that the Israelite king was a mere human being. Engnell argues uncompromisingly that the king was outright divine. Even Hooke, from whom Engnell takes unaltered his myth-ritualist pattern, is more cautious. Indeed, the key difference between Engnell and Hooke is that where for Hooke the king may be merely playing the role of god, for Engnell the king is god. Like Hooke, Engnell distances himself from Frazer, who in fact is his ultimate source. The chief difference between Engnell and Frazer, like that between Hooke and Frazer, is that Engnell restricts himself to the ancient Near East where Frazer postulates myth-ritualism worldwide. In the following selection from his collection of essays (*A Rigid Scrutiny*, ed. and tr. John T. Willis [Nashville: Vanderbilt University Press, 1969]; retitled *Critical Essays on the Old Testament* [London: SPCK, 1970], ch. 7), Engnell ties the Israelite New Year Festival to the abdication and restoration – not the killing and replacement – of the king and in turn of vegetation. See also his *Studies in Divine Kingship in the Ancient Near East* (1st edn, Uppsala: Almqvist & Wiksells, 1943). On Engnell see Christopher R. North, "Ivan Engnell: an Appreciation," in Engnell, *Studies in Divine Kingship in the Ancient Near East*, 2nd edn (Oxford: Blackwell, 1967), xvii–xxi; and Helmer Ringgren, Foreword to Engnell, *A Rigid Scrutiny*, ix–xi.

Original publication: Ivan Engnell, "New Year Festivals," in his *A Rigid Scrutiny*, edited and translated by John T. Willis (Nashville: Vanderbilt University Press, 1969), ch. 7 (pp. 180–4).

The New Year is a crucial and important time for mankind and all nature – and this may be said of humanity in general, since it is reflected in the most divergent cultures. At this time, the cosmos itself (the right order of nature, its "righteousness") is in jeopardy, and victory over the powers of evil and destruction can be guaranteed only by the intervention of the gods and especially by their worshippers – people who, through their cultic activities, contribute to the victory and "determine destinies"[1] – "create" order, fertility, and blessing for the time to come. In Israel, this "creation of destiny" is accomplished by the central rite of "making the covenant" between Yahweh and his people, who are represented by the king.[2] This dramatic concept of the New Year is expressed in the New Year festivals, which exhibit certain fundamental and recurring characteristics and rites in various places around the world. These rites both depict and affect the process by which nature is born again in the victory of life and order over the powers of death and chaos. To some extent, we can reconstruct the contents and ideology of the New Year festivals from the ceremony of the festival ritual, which was presented mimetically and dramatically. Since the New Year and the New Year festivals are almost always connected with the solstices and the return of the sun,[3] there are often two New Year festivals every year. This is true, to a great extent, in the Semitic world, both in the East, in the cities of Uruk and Ur, and in the West, as in Israel. Because of this special connection with the sun and light, fire rituals often play a prominent rôle in these festivals as, in the Semitic world, in the Accadian *akītu* festival, in the autumn festival at Ras Shamra, and in the Israelite *sukkôth*, the Feast of Booths.

The intensely dramatic character of the New Year festivals is reflected in particular in a sham fight[4] between groups of cultic actors who represent the powers of chaos and the powers of cosmos. In this battle, the king (or the ruler) is the central figure, as head of those who represent the powers of order and life. But the dramatic presentation also characteristically includes a portrayal of the state of chaos which precedes the victory of cosmos. The destructive powers enjoy a temporary victory. Chaos reigns, either in the form of an unbridled frenzy, often of an ecstatic sexual type – a "Witches' Sabbath" – or

---

This essay appears in *Svenskt Bibliskt Uppslagsverk*, 2nd edn, vol. II, cols. 336–340, under the title "Nyårsfester."

[1] The term is derived from an element in the Babylonian *akītu* festival.

[2] Cf. H. Ringgren, *Israelite Religion* (Philadelphia: Fortress Press, 1966), pp. 192 f.

[3] The expression is somewhat obscure. New Year festivals often fall at the equinoxes, too. Cf. T. H. Gaster, *Thespis*, second edition (Garden City, N. Y. Doubleday, 1961), pp. 47 f.

[4] Sham fight or "ritual combat" is a fight or battle enacted in a ritual in order to illustrate a battle told of in a myth; the result of this battle is the destruction of the enemies of the cosmic order or of the life of the community. Cf. I. Engnell, *Studies in Divine Kingship in the Ancient Near East*, second edition (Oxford: Basil Blackwell, 1967), Index, *s.v.* "Sham fight." See also Gaster, op. cit., pp. 37 ff.

in the form of a "Death Sabbath." The "Witches' Sabbath" depicts a condition in which everything is turned upside down:[5] law and order are abolished, the weak are exalted and the mighty are subdued, the slave becomes a lord and the lord becomes a slave. Where there is a sacral kingship, we often find a transitory regency of the so-called mock king.[6] The "Death Sabbath" is so called because all life in the world of nature and men stops and death reigns completely: the temple lies in ruins, priests and cultic servants are eradicated, and "the youthful god" himself descends into Sheol.[7] In most cases, these two blocks of ideas are found together. But finally, the victory of life is assured by sacrifices and other rites; and so, next come joyful processions, such as rites of enthronement, the sacred marriage, rites of harvest and fertility. Throughout the ancient Near East, which is characterized by a more or less homogeneous cultural level dominated by the institution and ideology of the sacral kingship, the unique characteristic of the New Year festivals above all is the central rôle which the king plays in them. He leads the fight against the power of chaos, is temporarily defeated, "dies," and "descends into Sheol," but "rises" again and brings home the victory, ascends the throne, celebrates his *hieros gamos*, and "determines the destinies" – creates fertility and blessing, prosperity and good years – by certain symbolic rites; and he does all this in his capacity as the incarnate "youthful god."[8] Since this renewal of the cosmos has the character of a renewal of the first creation, it is only natural for the creation epic to occupy a prominent place in the New Year festivals. It is the cultic text recited in these festivals. This is best known from Babylon, where the *Enūma eliš*, the Accadian creation epic, has this central rôle in the *akītu*, the New Year Festival. Texts like Genesis, chapter 1, and Pss. 74:12 ff., 89:9 ff. allow us to suppose that there was an analogous situation in Israel. As far as this is concerned, it is no exaggeration to speak of a common pattern in the ancient Near Eastern New Year festivals,[9] although everyone admits that this pattern in its complete form is a synthetic construction and therefore that, in every reconstruction of these different forms, we must allow for local variations which depend on different factors, including national and religious peculiarities. There are great differences between the New Year festivals in the important Eastern Semitic centers themselves; and these differ even more from their counterparts in western Semitic royal cities and peasant society. But now, thanks to the Ras

[5] J. G. Frazer and T. H. Gaster, *The New Golden Bough* (New York: Criterion Books, 1959), pp. 559 ff.

[6] Ibid., pp. 231 ff., 559 ff.

[7] The reference is primarily to the Tammuz ritual, especially as described by M. Witzel, *Tammuz-liturgien und Verwandtes* (Roma: Pontificio istituto biblico, 1935).

[8] This is more or less the fundamental thesis of Engnell's *Studies in Divine Kingship*; see, especially, pp. 33 ff.

[9] See S. H. Hooke, editor, *Myth and Ritual* (London: Oxford University Press, 1933), especially the introductory essay.

Shamra material, we know what an extraordinary rôle the New Year Festival
(especially the Autumn Festival) played in the West.[10] Because of the central
position which the enthronement of the divine king occupies in the ancient
Near Eastern New Year festivals, they are usually called *Enthronement Festivals*,
but this is not a very happy term. It is better to speak simply of the New Year
Festival and of its double form as a Spring Festival and an Autumn Festival.
Further, it should be observed that the ideas of sin, judgment, and atonement
were closely associated with the above-mentioned ideas and rites[11] and that the
New Year festivals were also characterized by strong social relations, by communion with the dead, and by national fellowship which was renewed by the
achievement of the king.

There can be no doubt whatsoever that the New Year was celebrated in the
land of Canaan and Israel and that the New Year festivals were dominant
throughout the country. This cannot be denied in spite of the fact that the
source material is rather meagre. In the land of Canaan, Judg. 9:27 testifies
to a New Year Festival (*'āsîph*) in Shechem connected with *Ba'al b'rîth*, "the
lord of the covenant," and celebrated "in the field"[12] in conjunction with a
sacrificial meal and carousal. Accordingly, the reconstruction of these New
Year festivals must be based on extrabiblical material and on forms of the New
Year Festival from later periods which may be used to work out the nature of
these festivals at an earlier time. This approach is not only permissible, but
also justified from a methodological point of view. We sometimes hear it
said that no "enthronement festival" was known in Israel.[13] Not only is this
hyper-skeptical, but we now know that it is clearly erroneous, insofar as the
"enthronement festival" is taken to mean the same as the New Year Festival
for, in its double form, this festival is as well attested in the Old Testament
as one could wish: the Spring Festival in the *pesaḥ-maṣṣôth*, the Passover and
the Feast of Unleavened Bread, and the Autumn Festival in the *'āsîph-sukkôth*,
the Feast of Harvest and Booths. The same thing applies to the three forms
of the Autumn Festival in a later period: the Feast of Booths, the New Year
Festival (in a limited sense) or *rō'sh hashshānāh*, and the Day of Atonement.
But when we see the connection between these different forms of the ancient
Annual Festival and realize their connection with its earlier form, it is also
erroneous to admit that there was a *Jewish* New Year Festival and still regard
it as a late innovation. This conclusion is due to a complete misinterpretation

---

[10] Engnell, op. cit., pp. 97 ff.

[11] E.g., the Israelite Day of Atonement, the humiliation of the king, and the purification of the
temple court during the Babylonian *akītu* festival.

[12] The expression "in the field" is emphasized because part of the Babylonian festival was
celebrated in the *akītu* house "in the field" (*ina ṣēri*) outside the city.

[13] The reference is probably to the criticism of Mowinckel's theory of an enthronement
festival. However, this festival, as described by Mowinckel, is supposed to have been a festival of
the enthronement and kingship of Yahweh, which is not exactly the same.

of the Old Testament psalm material,[14] for the so-called Enthronement Psalms constitute perhaps the most important foundation for the reconstruction of the earlier Israelite Annual Festival.

On the other hand, there can be no doubt that the uniquely Israelitic New Year festivals were influenced from without. But the question of when and how this influence took place is complicated. First of all, it is clear that we must assume that there was such influence at a very early period: Israel's New Year festivals are principally taken over from and mediated by ancient Canaan, which in turn had already been influenced by Eastern religions in the pre-Israelite period. But this does not mean that we should not look first to Israel and Canaan in order to determine the independent and highly unique form of the festival within the framework of the general pattern.

---

[14] N. H. Snaith, *The Jewish New Year Festival* (London: S.P.C.K., 1947); H. J. Kraus, *Die Königsherrschaft Gottes im Alten Testament* (Tübingen: J. C. B. Mohr [Paul Siebeck], 1951).

Part IV

APPLICATION OF THE THEORY WORLDWIDE

8

THE LIFE-GIVING MYTH

A. M. Hocart

The English anthropologist A. M. Hocart (1883–1939), who was Professor of Sociology at the University of Cairo, helped extend the myth-ritualist theory worldwide. For Hocart, as for Frazer, Hooke, and Harrison, myth provides the script for ritual, which is thus the enactment of myth. The function of myth is, as for Frazer above all, to provide food and other necessities. Hocart does not quite explain how ritual accomplishes its end. Presumably, ritual works magically, as for Frazer, Hooke, and Harrison. Hocart employs a skeleton version of myth-ritualism. He considers neither vegetation gods nor kings. The following selection originally appeared in one of Hooke's symposia on myth-ritualism (*The Labyrinth* [1935], ch. 8) and is taken here from its reprinting as the title essay of Hocart's *The Life-giving Myth and Other Essays* (ed. Lord Raglan [London: Methuen, 1952], ch. 1). See also chs 4 and 5 of *The Life-giving Myth and Other Essays; The Progress of Man* (London: Methuen, 1937), chs 13, 19; and *Kingship* (Oxford: Oxford University Press, 1927), where Hocart links kingship to ritual but not to myth. On Hocart see Lord Raglan, Introduction to Hocart, *The Life-giving Myth and Other Essays*, 6–8; Rodney Needham, "Biographical Introduction" to his *A Bibliography of Arthur Maurice Hocart* (Oxford: Blackwell, 1967), 13–16; and Needham, Introduction to Hocart, *Kings and Councillors* (Chicago: University of Chicago Press, 1970), xiii–xcix.

The Renaissance was an age of discovery: it discovered not only America, not only the course of the earth round the sun; it discovered Greek art and literature, and with them the Greek myth. It first discovered the myth, however, in the pages of Ovid, Virgil, Horace, and other late authors who had long since ceased to believe in their myths; who looked upon them merely as stories

Original publication: A. M. Hocart, "The Life-giving Myth" (1935), in his *The Life-giving Myth and Other Essays*, ed. Lord Raglan (London: Methuen, 1952), ch. 1 (pp. 9–27).

which it is good form not to question, or still more as good themes for literature, mines of plots and poetic ornaments. Far from bearing any relation to real life, those myths were rather a welcome escape from reality. The poet, jaded by the bustle and drabness of the city, found an idyllic retreat in the company of nymphs and dryads, ranging the sylvan wildness of his fantasy.

In the course of their explorations, the scholars of the Renaissance came upon Sophocles and Æschylus, but they interpreted the drama of those times as they interpreted their own stage – that is, as literature enacted. They failed to realise that the early Greek drama, literary as it might be, was still something more than mere theatricals, that it was still part of the national ritual, and that the myths were enacted not merely to amuse, but because the religion demanded it. This connection of drama with religion is now generally known, but it is doubtful if it is generally realised – to most scholars the Greek drama remains literature pure and simple.

The Renaissance scholars learned from Homer, the greatest of all mythologists. He was still earlier than Æschylus, nearer to the supposed age of myth. Homer's legends, however, are not Greek but Achæan. They were traditions passed on to the Greeks by their predecessors, just as the Arthurian Cycle was inherited by the English from a pre-Roman civilisation. The *Iliad* and the *Odyssey* are as Greek as the *Morte d'Arthur* is English. It is as vain to look to Homer for the primitive significance of the myth as it would be to seek it in Malory.

Thus everything conspired to persuade classical scholars that the myth is nothing but the creation of fancy, a kind of Midsummer Night's Dream. Several centuries of purely literary studies have allowed this conception of the myth to drive in its roots so deeply that it cannot be uprooted in a day. These roots have now spread beyond the Græco-Roman world into the East.

When the nineteenth century extended the sphere of discovery to Biblical lands and beyond, scholars naturally approached the myths of Egypt, Babylonia, and India in the spirit they had imbibed from their classical studies. They picked out the myths from the texts in which they were embedded, arranged them into neat systems of mythology after the fashion of the Hellenistic mythologists, and threw the rest of the text on the rubbish-heap.

In India they had this excuse, that they first became acquainted with its literary language, Sanskrit, in its late form, which is known as classical Sanskrit, and with works belonging to the centuries after Christ, contemporary with the break-up of the Roman Empire or even later. This classical form was a dead language carried on from a bygone civilisation, just as the Middle Ages continued to write Latin after the fall of Rome. With this dead language the Hindus inherited a store of dead myths. Some of these made good copy, so they were worked into epics such as the *Ramayana* and the *Puranas*. These epics did not assume their present form till long after Alexander had opened the gates of India to Hellenistic influence – not till that influence had had time to permeate Indian art, as it began to do in the first century of our era. It is difficult to believe that Indian literature escaped an influence which affected Indian art, and that the Indian epic owes nothing to Greek models.

If we want to study the real myth, not the literary exercise; if we want to know what the myth meant for mankind at large, not merely for poets, we shall no more look to the *Ramayana* or the *Vishnu Purana* than we should to Milton's *Paradise Lost* or Morris's *Earthly Paradise*. We shall turn rather from the Sanskrit which was a dead language to that Sanskrit which was still a living language about 800 BC, a thousand or more years earlier. That Sanskrit, known as the Vedic, has a very different character from the classical. Instead of being florid, ingenious, subtle, unreal, it is simple and direct, because it wants to convey information and not to display literary skill. It is concerned not to amuse or astonish, but to impart that knowledge which is necessary for the welfare of the community.

What really mattered to the ancient Brahman, as it does to us and to everyone, was life; not merely keeping alive, but living well, enjoying bodily vigour for the full span allotted to man. To have life it is necessary to have food, to escape sickness and the wiles of enemies, and to have stalwart sons. The Brahmans' quest, in the words of the first hymn of the *Rigveda*, is "wealth day by day, prosperity, glorious and abounding in heroes." They pray to Soma to save them from disease, to prolong their years as the sun the days of spring, not to abandon them according to the desire of their foe, to save them from disease.

Life depends on many things – on food, and food on rain and sun; on victory, and victory on skill and strength; on unity, and unity on wise rules and obedience. An elaborate ritual grew up designed to secure all these good things, all that contributed to the full life. This ritual became so elaborate that its accurate transmission became more and more difficult. One or two recitals were not enough; it had to be committed to memory, and its meaning and its reasons had to be expounded in lesson after lesson. Schools were formed, and from those schools issued the voluminous literature which is known as the *Brahmanas*.

The ritual was then, as it is now, based on precedent. If we have a king to crown, our experts search the old records to find out exactly what was done at previous coronations so that it may be done again. So the ancient Indians had their precedents. The sacrificer – that is, the man who presided over the ritual and was consecrated by it – acted strictly according to precedent; his actions merely repeated the actions of other sacrificers before him.

Thus one of the highest sacraments consists in setting up a mound, or altar, which represents the world. The sacrificer by the ritual recreates the earth, but he recreates it by the same methods as were used by the original creator. That original creation is first recalled in a myth, which tells how the creator brought forth foam from the waters, earth from the foam, and gradually built up this world. Then the sacrificer proceeds to imitate the creator by dissolving clay in water and producing foam from it, and then moulding the clay into a pan of which the bottom is the earth, the lower part of the sides the air, and the upper part the sky.

The relation of myth to ritual is best illustrated in the words of the Indian ritualist himself. He discusses the rite of carrying round Soma, the plant from which the sacrificial beverage is made. Soma is a god and a king, as well as a plant and a drink. He is carried round the way of a clock, or of port after dinner. Our authority states the precedent on which the rite is based in these words: "The gods and Titans strove together for these worlds. They strove for this eastern quarter. The Titans beat them thence. They strove for the southern quarter. The Titans beat them thence." And so they went fighting round the compass until "They strove for the north-eastern quarter: they were not beaten thence. This quarter is the unconquerable . . . the gods said, 'Through our lack of a king they beat us: let us make a king'. They made Soma king. With Soma as king they conquered all the quarters. He who sacrifices has Soma as king. They place Soma on the cart as it stands facing east: he conquers the east. They carry him round by the south: thereby he conquers the southern quarter," and so on round the compass. The conclusion is: "By Soma, the king, he conquers all the quarters who knows this." The text, like most of these texts, is not easy to understand. It is tempting to put the blame on the writer, or rather the lecturer (for there were no written records in those days); but we must remember that he was addressing his own people in his own time and not recording the facts for the scholars of a foreign race centuries later. He could assume in his hearers a knowledge which we lack, a knowledge of the ritual, the social organisation, the nature of the gods. He had only to expound the points which were not known to his pupils. The general outlook he could take for granted, but unfortunately we do not possess that outlook; we must reconstruct the principles from the applications which follow one another with deadly monotony.

We gradually come to realise that the sacrificer's object is to get control of the whole world – not temporal but ritual control; that is, he seeks to bend the forces of Nature to his will, so that they may produce plenty for him. The world consists of four quarters, and whoever secures the parts secures the whole. So the sacrificer proceeds to the supernatural conquest of the parts in a fixed order, that in which the sun goes round the earth. To succeed, however, a divine king must lead them. That king is the plant and god Soma, under whose leadership they take one quarter after another. That is the proper way to proceed, because once upon a time the gods under the leadership of Soma recovered one by one the quarters which they had lost to their rivals, the Titans, in the ritual struggle for power over the world. As the gods did, so must the sacrificer, for the sacrificer and his acolytes represent the gods. It is necessary that he should know the myth which describes how the gods succeeded.

The slaying of the serpent Vritra by Indra is the chief myth in Vedic mythology, as is the slaying of the monster Tiamat by Marduk in Babylonia. It is the theme of hymn after hymn to the glory of Indra, the wielder of the thunderbolt. "He slew the serpent; he released the water; he split open the bellies of the mountains. He slew the serpent lying in the mountains. Tvashitri fashioned his whizzing thunderbolt. . . . His missile the Bountiful One (Indra) grasped, and smote that first-born of serpents. When, Indra, that smotest the first-born of serpents, thou didst set at naught the enchantments of the enchanters; then bringing forth the sky, dawn, at that time thou foundest no enemy at all. Indra slew Vritra . . . with his thunderbolt, that great weapon of death. . . . Indra, the lightning armed, is the king of him that goes and him that rests and of tame cattle; yea, he rules over busy men as felly encloses the spokes." Such is the myth as told, or rather alluded to, in the *Rigveda*. One incident is omitted in this hymn but is referred to in others. All the gods deserted Indra except the Maruts, a troop of gods who are the gods of the commons, as Indra is the kingly god. This episode is thus commented on by the teacher: "Indra, being about to slay Vritra, addressed all the deities 'Do you support me, call to me.' – 'So be it' they said. They ran foward with intent to slay him (Vritra). He realised: 'They are running to slay me. Come, let me terrify them.' He snorted at them. At his snorting all the gods ran away in haste. The Maruts did not foresake him, saying: 'Smite, Blessed One, strike, put forth thy might.' Speaking these words they supported him. . . . He realised: 'These are indeed my friends; they showed me love. Well, let me give them a share in this litany.' He gave them a share in this litany. Up to that time both litanies were entirely his." Such is the myth which explains why in the time of the lecturer the officiating priest "draws a draught of Soma for the Maruts, sings an introductory stanza for the Maruts, sings a hymn for the Maruts." The reason is "wherever with them he (Indra) conquered, wherever he showed strength, by mentioning that also, he (the sacrificer) makes them fellow-drinkers of Soma with Indra." It comes to this, that in the course of the ritual of which Indra is the central figure an offering is made to the Maruts, a cup of Soma is drawn for them, a hymn sung, and a formula recited, of which the verses are still preserved for us in *Rigveda*, iii, 47, 4. The reason for this practice is given in the myth, that whereas all the other gods deserted Indra in his fight with the Serpent, the Maruts stood by him. It was apparently not a physical struggle, and the Maruts did not support him by force of arms, but by calling out to him, by uttering a formula which strengthened Indra. Therefore, the Maruts have a share in Indra's ritual. Now, as we are told over and over again, the sacrificer impersonates Indra. He has therefore to act exactly as Indra acted. He re-enacts the myth, even to giving the Maruts a share in the libations and the litanies.

In other words, the myth is the precedent. It is not a tale told to while away an idle moment, nor is it a deep and purely inquisitive speculation about the phenomena of nature. Nothing could be less entertaining than these myths, and nothing could shed less light on the sun, the moon, and the beginning of the world. A collection of these myths would, as the reader can see from these specimens, be dreary in the extreme; that is why they do not figure in the handbooks of Indian mythology, or only in a readable abstract. The handbooks confine themselves to those myths which approximate to the Greek standard, such as make good stories and have artistic possibilities. The rest is swept into the dustbin as so much nonsense spun by the subtle brains of priests. Such is the artistic tyranny of Greece, that scholars reject what is dull because it is real, because it pursues the prosaic needs of food, health and progeny, while they write volumes on gorgeous but unreal fantasies.

Let us stick to the real myth, the myth which has some relation to the serious business of life. It is a precedent, but it is more than that. Knowledge is essential for the success of the ritual. "He who knows this," ends our first myth, "conquers all the quarters." That is the conclusion which winds up myth after myth. The myth itself confers, or helps to confer, the object of men's desire – life.

The myth is necessary because it gives the ritual its intention. Thus if the Maruts are to have a share in the sacrifice along with Indra, it is necessary that the sacrificer should know the myth which relates how they earned that share. "Thus by mentioning that also," says the text, "he makes them share in the Soma drink with Indra."

It must be remembered that the sacrificer impersonates Indra; he is Indra; but only because he has been made so. His consecration has made him Indra. The myth reciting the exploits of Indra has to be recited in order that his action may be identified with the actions of Indra in the past. It is not sufficient just to carry Soma round the compass. The myth has to make it plain what the intention of this circumnambulation is; just as it is not sufficient for a Christian pilgrim to walk round the church; he must have the intention of repeating the stations of the cross. The mere sightseer gains no religious merit.

Knowledge is essential; it bestows life. The following passage will illustrate this. "For this death is the same as the year. For he destroys by nights and days the life of mortals; so they die. Therefore he is death. He who knows this death to be a year, death does not destroy his life by days and nights before old age. He attains the fullness of life." Thus he who knows the nature of death, that it is the same as the year which by the passage of time wears out our lives that man holds the secret of a long life. This knowledge protects him from an untimely death. This teaching is turning towards the mystical, but there is no doubt that it goes back to the old idea of Nature's dying with the year. When the attention of a leading Assyriologist was drawn to this passage from the *Satapatha Brahmana* he at once remarked, "Why, that is the Babylonian conception of the dying year."

The increasing mysticism of the later ritual books lays increasing stress on knowledge. Towards the end of that period we are told, "Here there is this verse, 'By knowledge they ascend where desires are vanished: thither sacrificial gifts go not, nor ascetics without knowledge;' for indeed he who does not know this does not attain to that world either by sacrificial gifts or by austerities; but to them who know this does that world belong." In the end knowledge alone is necessary. But knowledge without works cannot long survive; cut off from the realities of the world it pines away and degenerates. The myth was doomed once it became divorced from action. About 500 BC movements took place which broke away from the old mythology. Of these movements Buddhism is the most famous. It taught salvation by knowledge, but not by knowledge of the myth: it was knowledge of psychological causes. Like our modern psychological schools, it taught that one can escape pain and sorrow by tracing them to their source. It substituted scientific knowledge for the traditional knowledge which had lost contact with reality.

At first sight it looks as if Buddhism had killed the myth. It has its legends, but they are scarcely alluded to in the ritual, nor are they represented as necessary to a higher life. On the contrary, knowledge of causes is constantly insisted upon as the only way. But tradition is stronger than consistency, and survives underground when it is driven from the surface. If we look beneath the surface we find that the myth is not dead after all. When the writer was following the services at the Temple of the Tooth in Kandy the officiating priest volunteered the information that the service was repeating the daily attendance on the Buddha while he was alive. Thus the Buddhist ritual is really re-enacting the life of the Master. It is the Buddhist legend enacted for the welfare of the people.

Such is the Indian point of view. That point of view is regarded by those bred in Hellenic traditions as being merely a priestly view. The fantastic story, it is argued, is the original myth, the myth of the people, and the ritual myth is a distortion of it by priests obsessed by ritual. The priests, we are told, appropriate everything. They pluck the fresh blossoms from the free-growing fancy of the people, to wither in the musty atmosphere of their pedantry. We may ask how it is, then, that in India the ritual myth antedates the epic myth by many centuries. But the way of chronology is long and full of pitfalls, so we will leave it and go to the people to find out what is their conception of myth.

In Malaysia we are still in the Indian world. The Malay may be nominally a Mohammedan, but his culture is basically Hindu. In all his undertakings – marriage, cultivation, hunting, or whatever they may be – he seek success with the aid of charms. A striking feature of these charms is that they involve the recitation of, or at least allusion to, a myth. Whatever he is dealing with, the Malay has to recall its mythical origin. Thus in mining tin, when a tin-bearing stratum is reached, the ore is addressed in these words:

> Peace be with you O Tin-Ore,
> At the first it was dew that turned into water,
> And water that turned into foam,
> And foam that turned into rock,
> And rock that turned into tin-ore, . . .[1]

and so on. You will recognise at once the Indian creation myth as it was told and enacted some 800 years BC. But the Malay miner is not renovating the whole earth; he is only preparing tin-ore for extraction, so he is content to trace the genealogy, the ritual genealogy, of tin only; to affiliate it to the earth, and thereby derive the efficacy of his rite from that of the all-embracing ritual of creation. He is tracing but one line of the ritual pedigree, leaving the wider issue of general prosperity to the priest.

Such spells of origin, as we may call them, abound in the Finnish epic of the *Kalevala*. They are also used in Assyrian medicine, as is shown by the following incantation for toothache:

> After Anu made the heavens, the heavens made the earth, the earth made the rivers, the rivers made the canals, the canals made the marsh, the marsh made the Worm. The Worm came weeping unto Samas, unto Ea, her tears flowing: "What wilt thou give me for my food, and what wilt thou give me to destroy?". "I will give the dried figs and apricots." "Forsooth what are these dried figs to me or apricots? Set me amid the teeth and let me dwell in the gums, that I may destroy the blood of the teeth, and of the gums chew their marrow. So shall I hold the latch of the door." "Since thou has said this, O Worm, may Ea smite thee with his mighty fist."[2]

This spell also harks back to the creation, and tacks a particular disease on to it. The trouble can be controlled if you know its pedigree.

The same intimate relation between the myth and the affairs of everyday life is to be seen in Fiji, far from India and from the region of professional priests. There we find the striking fact that almost every myth is told in connection with some custom still observed. A myth may be told to explain why two tribes behave towards one another with insolent familiarity, call each other names, play tricks on one another, and even take each other's property. Thus two clans belonging to two different tribes in the North-east behave in this manner on account of their gods Wandamu and Vanda. "Wandamu went to beg for wild yams to plant. Vanda baked them, wrapped them up, and gave them to Wandamu. When Wandamu unwrapped the yams they were already cooked. Vanda came to beg for bananas; so the god of Nandaranga (Wandamu) brought in suckers of wild bananas from the jungle (not true bananas). Vanda planted

---

[1] W. Skeat, *Malay Magic*, p. 265.
[2] R. Campbell Thomson, *Proc. Roy. Soc. Medicine*, xix, p. 59.

them, and when they grew he found that they were not true bananas." To this day if the descendants of Wandamu go over to visit those of Vanda they are feasted on the very kind of yam over which Vanda tricked his friend.

Why do the people of Tunuloa and Nanggelelevu hoax one another? Because "Nggala, the god of Tunuloa, went to climb a palm stealthily. But Matawalu, the god of Nanngelelevu, had eight eyes, and saw him, and was angry, and drove him away, throwing after him coconut husks which became reefs between Nanngelelevu and Tunuloa. This is the cause: they are cousins because they abused one another and stole."

At bottom the idea is the same as in India; the living behave as the ancestors did. The gods cheated and abused one another, and therefore their descendants must do the same. This behaviour is not so obviously connected with life as it is in India, yet the connection is indicated. The plundering of one clan by another is done under divine sanction. The guests on arrival must make an offering to the chief of the village, the representative of the gods, before they can exercise their right to kill the fowls and pigs of their hosts. If they neglect to do this, the ancestor-god makes them ill, as he does any one of the hosts who resent being plundered. The whole procedure is of a ritual nature.

Custom and myth are as inseparable in Fiji as in early Brahmanic India, though the myth does not play quite as important a part in Fiji as in India. This is not because they have no priests, for we find the ritual myth in full vigour in Australia.

In his manner of making a livelihood the Australian Black has not progressed beyond Palæolithic man. He does not sow, nor spin, nor make pots, and lives from hand to mouth by hunting or digging up anything which can be eaten. The struggle for life admits of no specialisation, and no one is released from the quest of food in order to devote himself to study and speculation. There are no priests.

Let us take, for example, a tribe exposed to the most rigorous conditions in the arid central lands. The Aranda have their myths. What do these myths tell us? Not the doughty deeds of heroes, nor the movements of sun and stars. They are content to tell how the divine ancestors went about performing ceremonies, which they taught, and which are still performed. These myths are inexpressibly dull to us; there is none of that free flight of fancy which is supposed to be characteristic of myths. It takes some determination to wade through Strehlow's collection of myths. But that is not, of course, how the Aranda approaches his myths; he does not collect them, but learns them in connection with the ceremonies to which they relate, exactly as did the Brahman's pupil. They have for him a practical value which makes them interesting; they show him what to do and explain to him why. They contain the precedents for the ceremonies which help him to live.

These ceremonies take up a great part of his time. We wonder how he can spare so much from the struggle for existence to spend on mere ceremonies, but he does so precisely because existence is so uncertain; the ritual aims at abolishing that uncertainty. There are years when kangaroos, snakes, grubs, yams are scarce, when pools dry up. The ritual is designed to ensure a supply. For every species of food there is a ceremony which causes its increase. That ceremony's performance by an ancestor is recorded in the myth. The performers of to-day reproduce the ancestor's actions and, like him, identify themselves with the animal or plant to be increased. The myth is not merely a record of the precedent, but has to be chanted in the course of the dance to make it effective. On the other hand, the complete myth, as told to candidates for admission to the ritual, includes a detailed account of the ritual. Thus the myth is part of the ritual, and the ritual part of the myth. The myth describes the ritual, and the ritual enacts the myth. However much the Aranda myth may differ from the Brahmanic in detail, the principle is the same: the myth completes the desired identification of man and god for the attainment of plenty. It is not then the barren pedantry of the Brahmans which created the ritual myth, since it is found where there are no priests.

Aranda myth and ritual are so closely interwoven that it would seem impossible to separate them. But our chief authority, Strehlow, had, like all of us, been brought up on Greek and Roman mythologies. In order to conform to the traditions of the schools he cut all the descriptions of ritual out of the myths, and inflicted on his reader a wearisome succession of meaningless tales. We should never have known how closely the two were associated had he not in the course of one myth remarked: "Here follows a detailed account of the ritual which I shall reproduce elsewhere."[3] How can we make any progress in the understanding of cultures, ancient or modern, if we persist in dividing what the people join and in joining what they keep apart?

The connection between myth and life is even more apparent in North America. Each Winnebago clan has its own myth of origin, and if a man wants to know the myth he asks "about the origin of life." He is not told it without more ado, as one might be told a tale, but has to give gifts or make offerings. It is not that the teller is rapacious, for he will not tell it even to his own children without a fee. "It is really essential," a Winnebago told Mr P. Radin, "to make a gift." The applicant is told the myth not publicly but alone. "Then," says an informant, "the old man who had the right to tell the origin myth would announce subsequently at a feast that he had told So-and-so the story of the origin of the clan, and that if any one wished to be told of the same he should, in the future, when he himself had died, go to this young man and ask him in the proper way. Remember . . . that before everything else it is the duty of an individual to try and learn the origin of his clan." We may ask why it should be anyone's duty to learn a story. Because it is not a mere story, but a thing of power that affects the fortunes of the individual and of the clan. "My

---

[3] C. Strehlow, *Die Aranda etc.*, I, i, 20.

son," said an old man to an applicant, "he who makes the most gifts obtains life therewith." Then again, when the gifts are complete, "My son, you have done well – very well indeed – for the life that I am to give you is holy; and as you know, even if one was loved very much, they would not tell him this merely because they loved him, as it is holy." The origin myth cannot be told at a public feast "because it is sacred and it must not be told without proper ceremony, for the telling of it would injure the individual."[4] Thus the myth itself confers life, but it cannot be recited without ritual; the two are inseparable.

Nowhere is the oneness of myth and ritual more evident than it is among the Yuma of California. Professor Daryll Forde tells us that "The mourning ceremony of the Yuma is intended to perpetuate a ritual taught by the first men after the death of the creator Kukumat. . . . Informants constantly tend to refer to the activities of the existing rites in terms of the original. The Yuma, in other words, does not clearly distinguish between the mythological foundation and the existing ceremonial; and it was at first a matter of some difficulty to analyse and compare the two."[5] The Yuma funeral then is enacted myth, the myth a description of an ancient funeral. The Yuma myth is not a fable; it is a record which claims to be true, a claim which there is not the slightest reason to question. If the Yuma now perform certain funeral rites, why should not their forefathers have done so? If the present rites agreed in every detail, we might suspect that the myth was merely modern practice ascribed to the past, but there are slight differences. The only possible explanation is that the rites have changed since the time to which the myth refers.

The word "myth" has unfortunately become synonymous in our language with fiction. That is merely because it has become associated with a certain set of traditions in which we do not believe. It is necessary to go back to the original meaning – a sacred story; a story which purports to be true, and which research shows more and more to be true in essentials, however much the details may become distorted. It is a true record of ritual.

This ritual myth is not the result of perversion by that bugbear of scholars, an all-grasping priesthood. It flourishes most where there is no professional priesthood, because there it remains in contact with reality. The myth detached from reality can continue to exist only in a society which is itself divorced from reality, one which has such a reserve of wealth that it can afford to maintain an intelligentsia exempt from the pursuit of bare life, and free to devote all its energies to intellectual play, to poetry, and to romance. Such a society was the Hellenic, which had so far freed itself from mere labour that it had come to despise it. For Aristotle leisure, not work, was the end of a gentleman's life. The myth fell in with this conception of life; it was no longer required to give bare life, but to adorn it with the elegancies of fancy.

[4] P. Radin, 37th Rept. Bureau of Amer. Ethnology, pp. 226 ff.
[5] C. D. Forde, *Univ. Cal. Publ. in Archæology and Ethnology*, vol. xxviii, p. 214.

When a myth has reached that stage it is doomed. Myths, like limbs, atrophy and perish when they no longer work. The allegories of Plato were really an attempt to save the myth by giving it something to do. They were put to the task of educating the mind and improving morals. But allegories did not save the Greek myths; they went down before the impact of new myths which came out of the East and promised life to the believer.

To understand the animus of the early Christians against the pagan myths, which seem to us so beautiful and harmless, we must put ourselves in their position. The Roman peace had made daily bread secure, but it had raised mental problems such as always arise where there is idleness and luxury. The old myths and traditions had become the playthings of dilettantes, and the contemporaries of St Paul, like the contemporaries of the Buddha five hundred years earlier, found no help in them. They turned to those Eastern myths which offered them not health of the body, as their own myths had once done, but health of the soul. The Christian myth offers quite a different life from that conferred by the earlier myths. A Christian may be lusty and strong yet, in the words of Malory, "dead of sin"; he may be sickly, like St Paul, yet living in faith.

Here is a mighty revolution in mythology, but it was not accomplished in a day. We are all familiar with the story that Constantine, the night before the battle with Maxentius, "was admonished in a dream to inscribe the shields of his soldiers with the *celestial* sign of God, the sacred monogram of the name of Christ; that he executed the commands of heaven; and that his valour and obedience were rewarded by the decisive victory of the Milvian Bridge." "There is still extant a medal of the Emperor Constantius where the standard of the labarum is accompanied by these memorable words, BY THIS SIGN THOU SHALT CONQUER."[6] This is a standpoint little removed from that of the Vedic kings, or the Fijian chief who turned Christian because the missionary succeeded in healing his daughter.

Such a conception of the myth was still very strong in the Middle Ages side by side with the Pauline. We read in the *Morte d'Arthur* of how King Evelake was about to do battle with the Saracens, but was told by Joseph son of Joseph of Aramathea that he would be defeated and slain unless he accepted the new law. "And then he showed him the right belief of the Holy Trinity, to the which he agreed with all his heart; and there this shield was made for King Evelake, in the name of him that died upon the Cross. And then through his good belief he had the better of King Tolleme."

The Christian conception of life as a better life, and of the myth as bestower of that better life, is not as anciently established among us as we may be inclined to imagine. We need not go many centuries back to find our fore-fathers still clinging to a myth not very different in intention from that of the

---

[6] Gibbon's *Decline and Fall*, ii. 30.

Vedic Indians and Winnebagoes, the myth which confers health, wealth and victory over one's enemies. Perhaps if we look up from our books and glance round we may find that myth still flourishing. Many years ago the writer obtained in Heidelberg a "Powerful prayer whereby one can protect and preserve oneself from bullet and dagger, from visible and invisible enemies, as well as from all possible Evil." This preamble is followed by the myth: "Count Philip of Flanders had a man who had forfeited his life, and as the executioner (tried) to execute him, no sword could cut him. Then the Count was astonished and spoke, 'How am I to understand this? Show me the thing and I will grant thee thy life.' Then he showed him the letter, and copied it out (for him) together with all his servants." There follows an enumeration of all the evils against which this letter is a protection: law suits, loss of master's favour, childbirth, nose-bleeding and so on. The charm itself is full of allusions to the Christian myth: "Make their weapons as weak as the blood which Jesus Christ shed on Mount Olive" and so on. Every effect of the charm is linked up with some episode in the Christian story, which is made to confer not spiritual benefits or a mystical life, but life as the Winnebagoes, the Fijians and the rest understand it.

Thus we have gone round the world in search of the true myth, the myth that is bound up with life. We have found it in India, beneath the Southern Cross, in the plains of North America. We have come home to find it at our door.

9

THE BEGINNINGS OF RELIGION

E. O. James

Far more prolific than Hocart in applying myth-ritualism worldwide was the English historian of religion E. O. James (1888–1972), who was Professor of the History and Philosophy of Religion at the University of London. Like Hooke, James combines Frazer's focus on the death and rebirth of the vegetation god with Frazer's alternative focus on the killing and replacement of the king, who for James is eventually rejuvenated rather than replaced. To Frazer's myth-ritualism James adds a sociological dimension that comes from Bronislaw Malinowski: myth and ritual function to support society as well as to secure food. In addition to James' *The Beginnings of Religion* (London: Hutchinson, 1948), ch. 7, which is reprinted here, see his *Christian Myth and Ritual* (London: Murray, 1933); *The Old Testament in the Light of Anthropology* (London: SPCK, 1935), ch. 4; *Comparative Religion* (1st edn, London: Methuen, 1938), ch. 4; "Myth and Ritual," *Eranos-Jahrbüch* 17 (1949), 79–120; "The Nature and Function of Myth," *Folk-Lore* 68 (1957), 474–82; and *Myth and Ritual in the Ancient Near East* (London: Thames and Hudson, 1958), esp. ch. 9. On James see *The Saviour God: Comparative Studies in the Concept of Salvation Presented to Edwin Oliver James*, ed. S. G. F. Brandon (Manchester: Manchester University Press; New York: Bames & Noble, 1963).

Myth and Ritual

At all times and everywhere man's intense desire and determination to destroy death and "put on immortality" has found expression not only in his ritual behaviour but also in his mythology. Thus, one has only to consult such a book

Original publication: E. O. James, *The Beginnings of Religion* (London: Hutchinson, 1948), ch. 7 (pp. 135–56).

as the late Sir James Frazer's *Folk-lore in the Old Testament* to see how world-wide are the stories telling how the human race originally was created immortal but by some accident, ruse or device it lost this priceless boom and became a victim of death and all the other ills to which stricken humanity has been heir throughout the ages. In our own sacred literature inherited from the Jews and given a new interpretation in Christianity, this theme is predominant and affords an illuminating example of the nature and function of myth and ritual in giving stability to faith and practice.

The nature and function of myth and ritual

When the Jewish priests retold the Babylonian story of creation in terms of the monotheistic beliefs inculcated by the Prophets after the return of the exiles to Palestine in the sixth century BC, they did so primarily to provide a supernatural sanction for the observance of the seventh day of the week as the Sabbath. By referring back the new ritual institution to the alleged cessation of divine creative activity at the end of the first momentous week at the beginning of time, they transformed an ecclesiastical regulation into a divine decree binding on the conscience of all Jews. "For in six days the Lord made heaven and earth and rested the seventh day; wherefore the Lord blessed the Sabbath day and hallowed it." So the Genesis version of the creation myth lived on in the ritual of the nation. The Christian Church through the influence of St Paul carried the process a stage further by reinterpreting the earlier account of the Eden disaster in relation to its own doctrine of redemption. Death being swallowed up in the victory of the Cross, paradise lost, it declared, had become paradise regained. This theme in its turn was given ritual expression in the Eucharistic sacrifice as the perpetual memorial of the supreme recreative event in the history of the world, and it became the guiding principle in the ethical conduct of the faithful. In this way the sacred story, having become incorporated in the religious and social organization of the community, lives on from age to age in its faith and practice, continually undergoing changes in meaning and signifi-cance but never ceasing to determine its worship, theology, social sanctions and morality by affording a spiritual authority and precedent for the things believed, ordered and done.

Since in primitive society the spoken word is thought to exercise super-natural power in its utterance and repetition, it gives efficacy to the actions performed and the episodes recounted as an "uttered rite". Emotional situ-ations of continual recurrence require perpetual satisfaction, and around certain fundamental dogmas, such as the creation of the world, the loss of immortal-ity and the salvation and destiny of man, a sacred narrative has developed in which the providential ordering and sustaining of all things is affirmed, and power is liberated to enable man to overcome his disabilities and shortcomings through the magic of the sacred word. The stories told and repeated with regular precision usually relate to certain events of outstanding importance which have a permanent significance in the moral, social and religious organization of society. They are not concerned with purely theoretical questions or metaphysical speculations about the ultimate beginnings of things, and they draw only to a very limited extent, if at all, upon matters of purely scientific and historical interest. Primitive people, of course, are perfectly capable of accurate observation and are constantly experimenting, improvising and improving upon their techniques, but they do not theorize or tell stories about these every-day matter-of-fact occurrences. Again, it has yet to be proved that myths represent the day-dreams of the human race giving conscious expression through an elaboration of psychoanalytic symbolism to subconscious desires, conflicts, fears and phobias. In short, primitive man is neither a philosopher, a scientist nor a neurote. He is just a plain unsophisticated practical person living in a precarious environment and continually confronted with perplexing situations which he endeavours to meet as well as he is able by natural and supernatural means. His interest in the past is confined to the bearing of former events on present affairs, and when it becomes articulate in myth it is in the belief that the spoken word is an oracle the repetition of which sets free the creative and re-creative power with which it is replete.

Myths of origin

Thus, the many stories about the way in which the present order of events came into being which recur all over the world, are certainly not the result of an innate inquisitiveness regarding the way in which the natural order has arisen, as has been supposed;[1] neither are they imaginative episodes such as Plato had recourse to when at the end of an arduous quest for truth he felt that pure intellect had shot its bolt and yet something remained unsaid. In primitive thought myth is not called into play at the point where abstract ratiocination can go no further, any more than it is a poetic creation of fancy and of romantic story-telling like the heroic legends of Homer, Hesiod and the Epic cycle, or the body of tradition that has grown up around our British hero, Arthur, or the career of Rama in Indian lore. These are themes which lies outside the range of savage mentality, and are, in fact, the product of a long process of development and transformation. Thus, the Homeric poems are Achæan in origin and the Arthurian Cycle has come down from a pre-Roman civilization, while the great Sanskrit epic has been a national possession for at least two thousand years. As a literary production the *Mahabharata* was derived from the type of ancient legendary tale called *purana*, and the *Ramayana*

---

[1] Cf. A. Lang, *Myth, Ritual and Religion* (London, 1899), vol. i, p. 162.

from the class of artificial epic known as *kavya*, in which the poetic form is regarded as more important than the story.

The genuinely primitive myth being neither speculation nor poem, explanation nor philosophy, its ritual efficacy is the centre of interest. What happened in "the brave days of old", and at the creation of the world, is of practical importance because it has had a permanent effect on subsequent behaviour and the structure of society. Thus, in Australia a number of initiated males are set apart for the express purpose of acting as the custodians of the tribal lore, its ritual and sacred sites. It is their business to safeguard its transmission, interpretation and correct enactment in the manner prescribed by the heroes and ancestors when they lived on the earth in the Dream Time of long ago and gave the country occupied by each group its local configuration, and ordered its laws, customs and beliefs.

This mythical past is as far back as the native traditions go, and it serves the practical purposes for which it was designed. In describing the paths along which the ancestors are supposed to have travelled, and indicating the places at which they halted to perform ceremonies, the sacredness of the existing totemic centres is affirmed and established for all time. Moreover, not only does this mythological topography "confirm the faith" respecting the things done at the cult-centres, but it links the group with its tribal territory and provides intertribal common routes leading to the waterholes and the various sacred rites which have to be visited from time to time. The approach to them must be made along the same paths as those taken by the ancestors in the Alcheringa, or Dream Times, and as long as this course is followed the "pilgrims," provided they keep strictly to the peaceful purpose of their journey, are afforded protection and hospitality like those in medieval Europe en route for Santiago de Compostella (the most sacred spot in Spain which incidentally took its origin in all probability from a prehistoric megalithic monument and was approached along very ancient sacred ways).

Therefore, the myth of the wandering ancestors promotes friendly intercourse and security between local clans and tribes, and facilitates intertribal relationships. It also makes the various local groups mutually dependent for their cult-life. Each tribe is the custodian of a particular tradition and is responsible for the enactment of the myth and ritual associated with the sites in its area, thereby making its own contribution to the cultus and mythology as a composite whole. In this way the sacred lore and its rites become a consolidating force in society, grounded in the ancient past and its heroes. What they did during their wanderings and sojourn on earth in the Dream Time must be done now by their descendants because upon the due performance of this ancestral cultus at the proper places depends the well-being of the tribe. So the myth lives on in its ritual, and the creative period of long ago is an everpresent reality, reenacted in the traditional manner on the great ceremonial occasions.

By grounding the established order in a mythological supernatural reality, stability is given to the social structure and religious organization, making them proof against the disintegrating forces of change and decay. So long as it is believed that the regulations respecting marriage, for example, were laid down once and for all by the ancestors in the beginning, no departure from the rules is possible, any more than in the performance of the traditional rites which have been similarly prescribed and rationalized in the current mythology. If the complicated rules governing the kinship system came into being in this way, that is sufficient reason in the native mind for their observance and continuance, because the laws ordained at the threshold of human history must be observed having then been fixed for all time. This is the essence of tribal morality of which mythology is the guardian.

Cosmological myths

Closely connected with the mythology of a formative period in which the laws, institutions, customs and beliefs were bestowed upon mankind by ancestral beings, is the creation story describing the transformation of the earth into its present form by a beneficent Originator or Transformer, who assumes the rôle either of a Culture hero or of a Supreme Being. Since, as we have seen, the High God tends to be remote and little concerned with the government and sustenance of the world, he figures less prominently in this type of traditional lore than the more intimate subordinates to whom he delegates his creative functions.

Not infrequently in these cosmological myths, as in the Hebrew story of the Garden of Eden, the existence of the earth, or of the material universe, is taken for granted. Moreover, as the problem of ultimate origins and the idea of creation *ex nihilo* lies outside the range of the primitive mind, it is usually assumed that all things have come into being out of existing materials, such as the primeval ocean from which the earth was "fished up", or fashioned in some way or another. According to the Crow Indians of Montana in North America, "long ago there was no earth, only water. The only creatures in the world were the ducks and Old Man" (i.e., the Sun as the Supreme Being who has become merged with the Transformer known as the Coyote). "He came down to meet the ducks and said to them, 'My brothers, there is earth below us. It is not good for us to be alone'". They were then told to dive into the waters and out of the mud collected in the webbed feet of one of them he created the earth. "Now that we have created the earth," he said, "there are others who wish to be animate". Immediately a wolf appeared and the world was peopled with living creatures.

In Central California, where the Coyote figures very prominently in the mythology as a co-creator, transformer, evil genius and puck-like trickster, both he and the Supreme Being are generally represented as appearing on the primeval waters in a mysterious manner, as if from nowhere. This is the nearest approach to the idea of creation *ex nihilo*, except perhaps in the Uitoto myth of Colombia, South America, in which it is asserted that in the beginning only "appearance" existed as a phantasm out of which Nainema, "He who is appearance only," brought all things into being through a dream. In California among the Achomawi both the Creator and Coyote emerged in the condensation of a primeval fog, while in the neighbouring Maidu, who lived formerly in the Sacramento Valley and the Sierra Nevada, they descended upon the waters in a canoe.

On the West Coast of Southern Australia darkness and silence are said to have reigned over the mountains and valleys concealing static forms of life until the Great Spirit awoke the Sun-goddess and whispered to her to animate the universe. Thereupon she took a great breath that caused the atmosphere to vibrate, opened her eyes and her whole body became flooded with light. Darkness disappeared and when she made her home on the plain her vitalizing influence began to be felt upon the cold life of earth. As she walked in a Westerly direction the shrubs and trees sprang up in her footprints. She repeated her journeys all over the earth until it was covered with vegetation. Next she set out to take warmth and brightness to the cold regions in the caverns out of which emerged snakes and lizards. Butterflies, beetles and animals of all shapes, sizes and colours began to appear, and the seasonal changes, together with the succession of light and darkness, were ordained. Her work completed, the goddess returned to the sky and stood smiling upon them from her celestial abode, moving from East to West, and finally disappeared as darkness fell at night. She appointed the morning star to rule as her son, and the moon as the lady of the night to help him to shine in the darkness as his wife. They brought forth children who took their places in the sky as stars.

These cosmological myths of Southern and Eastern Australia in which sky heroes play the principal rôles, perform the same sociological functions as those of the Alchera ancestors in the Central and North-western regions. In these stories the work of creation was completed by a single figure, the First Father, to whom the Sun-goddess gave all power to finish the task she had begun. Sometimes he is equated with the moon which waxes and wanes like the first mortal who lives, dies and is restored. He is also symbolized under the form of semi-mythical animals, as in the case of the hares, rabbits, snakes and lizards which renew their youth by changing their skins, or some similar device. In his creative capacity, however, he has become equated with the Supreme Being and assumed many of his attributes so that it is often difficult to distinguish the one from the other. In a Yuki myth in California, for instance, the vault of the sky is stretched out by the combined efforts of the High God and the Culture-hero and supported on four great pillars at the cardinal points. A path is left for the sun and openings for the rain and mist to descend on the earth. Man is moulded out of clay and then the sun and moon, wind and rain are called into being. A flood destroys all men and animals, and the work is finished by the re-creation of life, and to the complete satisfaction of the Creator and his faithful dog. In another version of the story, a being called Thunder is said to have lived alone in the upper sky-world until he found a baby wrapped in leaves who became the progenitor of the human race, very much as among the Wichita of Texas the High God only bestowed the potentialities of all things in the beginning leaving it to the First Man to cause the sun and moon to appear, acting under a divine impulse.

The same theme recurs in a Pawnee tale in the state of Nebraska. When the all-powerful sky-chief, Tirawa, decided to create the earth he disclosed his plans to the gods and gave them their several stations. The sun was told to stand in the east to give light and warmth to the earth; the moon was to stand in the west to give light during the hours of darkness; and the evening star was to be there also as the Mother of all things, for through her all things would be created. This was accomplished by the four gods singing and so producing a cloud into which Tirawa dropped a pebble. The space was filled with water out of which the four gods made the world and prepared it for habitation. Animals and plants having been created, the first men and women came down from the sky, the son of the Sun and the daughter of the Evening-star, the sky-goddess. From them the human race is descended and has derived its rites and customs. Thus, while the High God is the ultimate source of creative activity, he employs intermediaries to exercise his powers and dispense his gifts in the world he and his associates have called into being. "All the powers that are in the heavens and all those that are upon the earth are derived," we are told, "from the mighty power of Tirawa. He is the father of all things visible and invisible. He is the father of all the powers represented by the Hako . . . and perpetuates the life of the tribe through the gift of children".[2]

Therefore, this ceremony, called the Hako, is held in the spring when the birds are mating, in the summer when they are rearing their young, in the autumn when they are flocking, and in the winter when they are asleep, to obtain from the High God "the gift of life, of strength, of plenty and of peace". Embodied in some twenty rituals consisting of dances, songs and mimetic actions, is the dramatization of the creation story reproducing on earth the world of the gods as it existed when the present order was established. This is made clear in a ceremony which the Skidi group of the Pawnee perform in their sacred enclosure portraying the community of the gods in the sky. In the centre is a fireplace surrounded by four posts placed respectively to the north-east, south-east, south-west and north-west. At the west end is a raised altar of earth inside the enclosure, and at the east end outside the enclosure is a

---

[2] A. Fletcher, *22nd Report of the Bureau of American Ethnology* (Washington, 1904), part II, p. 107.

mound. A priest is stationed at each of the posts and at the fireplace imperson-ating the gods at the cardinal points in the creation story.[3] Fire being the earthly counterpart of the sun, the symbol of life and of the orderly sequence of events,[4] the sacred fireplace occupies the central position in the rite and its setting, while the posts represent the supports of the domed roof of the sky, symbolised in the mount outside the enclosure.

This symbolism, in fact, may still be observed in many churches in our own land where the altar, taking the place of the fireplace in the Pawnee ceremonial ground, often is enclosed by four riddel posts and surmounted with a dome-like canopy, or *ciborium*, painted with stars on a blue surface on the underside in imitation of the sky. In ascending the steps of the sanctuary the sacred ministers go as it were into the heavenly sphere to "join with angels and archangels and the whole company of heaven" in offering the Holy Sacrifice in union with the eternal High Priest, who, having passed through the veil, is exalted at the right hand of the Majesty on high. It is this theme, or something very like it, that underlies the Pawnee ceremonial.

The rite is believed to have been given to the ancestors of the tribe at the threshold of its history, as in the case of the Australian mysteries, and in it is re-enacted the drama of creation exactly as it was handed down from the mysterious powers above. None of the actions or songs can be changed, for the gestures and words must be repeated precisely in the form in which they were delivered by the gods in the beginning as the means whereby the potency of Tirawa was bestowed upon mankind through his intermediaries, as the centre and source of fertility and of the tribal unity. Thus, the primeval drama lives on in the prescribed ritual and makes it an efficacious sign of creative activity and the consolidating force in the social structure.

Creation to the primitive mind does not convey the idea of a "First Cause" in the sense understood, for instance, by the Deists in the seventeenth and eighteenth centuries of our era; still less that of a beginning *in* time or *of* time. It involves rather the notion of renovating and revivifying the existing order of things to render the earth habitable and serviceable for human needs and organized for the well-being of society. The sacred order being the ground and support of the world and not merely its beginning, without it it could not exist at any moment. For this reason it sees the operation of divine forces in every natural event, and by referring institutional observances back to their original source in the transcendental world recreative energy is liberated. The repeti-tion of the myth of creation and its re-enactment in a sacred drama revital-izes and renews the face of the earth. To tell how a beneficent Providence as the giver of the laws of life and of all that is good exercised his functions in

---

[3] J. R. Murie, *Anthropological Papers of the Natural History of America*, vol. XI, 1916, p. 351 ff.

[4] E.g., in the Vedic ritual in India fire is equated both with the sun and with the ritual and moral order of the universe established creatively through sacrifice.

the beginning, is to impart a new vigour to the creative processes when it is believed that a spoken narrative possesses decisive efficacious power in its repetition, comparable to that of the sacred action. The essence of myth, in fact, lies in its being repeatedly told anew to give intention to the things done, and release in perpetuity the initial power recalled by the narrative of past events, celebrated as a living reality in the present.

Seasonal mythology

Thus, the daily course of nature and the regular succession of the seasons are given mythological form and expression in agricultural communities in relation to the vegetation cultus. The sequence upon which the growth of the crops depends must be maintained and its vitality retained by the celebration of the cult-drama in which the events which are supposed to have happened in primeval times are recalled in a myth and re-enacted in a ritual to renew the processes of fertility and stabilize the social and religious organization on which the community depends for its well-being and sustenance. The same methods are employed, and often the same words are repeated, as those supposed to have been used by the original Creator or Transformer in the formative period of the world's history to release their potency by recapitulation.

In the great collection of myths and liturgies that recur in the texts belonging to the third and second millenia BC in Asia Minor, Mesopotamia, Egypt, and Palestine, the victory of the beneficent forces at the threshold of creation is set forth and enacted in terms of a primeval struggle between gods. In the Tammuz liturgies, for example, the death of the king-god, Tammuz, at the hands of a supernatural adversary is described, followed by his imprisonment in the underworld, the lamentation of his sister-wife, Ishtar, who went to the nether regions in search of her lover, and his triumphant return to earth, symbolizing the yearly decay and revival of vegetation. In the urban civilization of Babylonia, as we have seen, the myth is re-enacted at the Annual Festival called *Akitu* with Marduk having replaced Tammuz and the ancient Sumerian Creation Epic, which goes back to about 3000 BC, occupying a central position as the basic myth of the New Year ritual.

In this later version, known as the *Enuma elish*, as set forth in the cuneiform texts of the eighth century BC, it has undergone a good deal of revision at the hands of the Babylonian priests to bring it into line with the story and significance of Marduk as a solar city-god, but its main theme and purpose remains essentially unchanged as an integral part of a seasonal drama, the ceremonial of which belongs at least to the time of Sargon (*c.*2500 BC). In the Babylonian festival it was recited to give life to the god (Marduk), to re-install and re-invigorate the king as his human representative, and to fix the "destinies" (i.e., maintain the cosmic order) for the coming year, just as in the original rite

Tammuz, or Dumu-zi, "the true son of the waters" (i.e., the life-giver), put an end to blight, dearth and death by rising from a watery grave by the aid of Ishtar, reborn from the underworld.

In the Babylonian epic of the adventures of the hero Gilgamesh, king of Erech, with whom Ishtar is said to have fallen in love, the story of the deluge has been incorporated as an incident in his search for immortality. Behind the narrative and its Sumerian prototypes, there would appear to have been a historical situation since archæological excavation has now brought to light evidence of an extensive flood in Mesopotamia in the neighbourhood of Ur and Kish about 3000 BC of a magnitude unparalleled in local experience.[5] But in its mythological form the event is interpreted as a sort of *rite de passage* in which Ut-Napishtim, the ancestor of Gilgamesh, passed through the waters of death in order to attain immortality. Therefore, apparently it acquired a ritual significance as part of the death and resurrection drama, the hero rising to newness of life like Tammuz emerging from the waters. Moreover, in the Sumerian version we are told that "after the Flood kingship again descended from heaven", while in the subsequent Hebrew record in the book of Genesis, the deluge is represented as a re-creative act in which Yahweh initiated a new post-diluvian epoch in the history of the world with Noah as the ancestor of the new humanity (Gen. ix, 1, 8 ff.).

In the ritual texts recently discovered at Ras Shamra on the north Syrian coast, written in an alphabetic script closely allied to Hebrew and ascribed to the fourteenth century BC, or perhaps earlier (*c*.1500), the Tammuz cult-drama recurs, probably in the form of a liturgy. The dying and rising god reappears in the guise of a fertility deity, Aleyan son of Baal, who is killed in the spring by his enemy Mot, the god of the harvest and son of El, the Lord of the underworld. This produces the drought of summer, and in order to ensure the return of the fertilizing showers of autumn, Aleyan-Baal has to be restored to life after the harvest, and Mot in his turn is killed and his flesh is scattered over the fields as a kind of manure, like that of the dismembered body of Osiris in the Egyptian myth. The "fixing of the destinies" in the Tammuz-Marduk story has its counterpart in the Ras Shamra texts in the acquisition of certain magical objects called teraphim to secure the proper functioning of the processes of nature, and there are several indications of a sacred marriage having been celebrated in honour of the victory of the god.[6]

The persistence and widespread distribution of this myth and ritual are to be explained by the fact that they represent a recurrent situation of profound emotional significance in the life of agricultural communities dependent upon the weather and the seasons for their subsistence. Therefore, whether the dying and reviving god was called Tammuz, Adonis, Aleyan-Baal, Osiris or

[5] C. L. Woolley, *Ur of the Chaldees* (London, 1929), pp. 22 ff.
[6] Cf. Hooke, *The Origins of Early Semitic Ritual* (Oxford, 1935), pp. 28 ff.

Dionysos, the same drama was enacted to regenerate nature at its most vital centre, symbolized by the death and revival of the divine hero and his earthly embodiment, the king. But in Egypt, as we have seen, Osiris was the Lord of the dead as well as the personification of growth and fertility, and in the other versions of the theme the underworld figures prominently. This doubtless explains why the mystery cultus, when it spread to Greece in the sixth century BC, acquired a more individual character as the means whereby the initiates were assured of a blessed resurrection after death.

Folk drama

These cults survived in Western Europe until the opening centuries of the Christian era, and before they were finally submerged in the new faith and practice they had exercised considerable influence on Christian doctrine and ritual. The Mass became the sacred drama *par excellence* as the perpetual commemoration of the death and resurrection of Christ, the renewal day by day of His redemptive sacrifice, and the "medicine of immortality" dispensed in Holy Communion. But, as has been pointed out in another connexion, the liturgy in due course gave rise to dramatic performances, ostensibly sacred in character and origin, but which tended to become secularised in the course of time. At first they were held in church, then in the churchyard, and eventually in the market-place, where more and more they lost their original content, until at length they merged with the rustic revels which survived in the peasant culture, little changed from the beginnings of agricultural civilization.

Thus, for example, as recently as 1906 Professor Dawkins discovered in Thrace a folk play in which the ancient Dionysiac myth and ritual were still performed annually at the carnival in the villages round Veza, between Adrianople and Estanbul. Two men in goatskins and masks visited all the houses, knocking on the doors with a fertility symbol in the form of a phallus, and carrying a cross-bow. Two boys dressed as brides danced outside the house, while a gipsy man and his wife performed an obscene pantomime and pre-tended to forge a ploughshare. A man, disguised as an old unmarried woman in rags, called "Babo," carrying in a cradle (*liknon*) a mock baby supposed to be seven months old and illegitimate, appeared on the scene at this point. The play opened with the child growing at great pace, developing an enormous appetite and demanding a wife. A mock marriage ensued with one of the "brides," and the bridegroom was then shot with the bow by the second of the two goatskin men. Loud lamentation followed and the "corpse" was lifted up as if to be carried to the grave, but instead the dead man suddenly came to life and jumped up on his feet.

The death and resurrection drama ended, a ploughshare was again supposed to be fashioned by the gipsy man, and two small boys were yoked to a real plough which they dragged twice round the village square widdershins (i.e., against the sun). At its tail walked one of the goatskin men, at the front the other man similarly attired, while a third man followed scattering seed from a *liknon* (basket). On the third round the gipsy and his wife replaced the boys, and the people shouted, "May wheat be ten piastres the bushel. Amen O God, that the poor folk may eat! Yea, O God that the poor folk be filled!"[7]

That this Thracian play held in the spring just before Lent was the dramatization of the Dionysiac celebrated in ancient Greece at Athens at the end of February, is suggested by the wonder-child born of an unmarried mother and laid in a winnowing fan, or *liknon*, as Dionysos was called *Liknites*, "he of the cradle". Its illegitimacy may be a relic of the miraculous birth of the divine hero, and his death, resuscitation and espousal to a bride, simulates the union of heaven and earth for the renewal of life in the spring "that the poor may eat." The phallic procession, the obscene pantomime, the circumstances surrounding the child, the combat, the re-animation ceremony and the marriage, have their counterparts not only in Dionysian myth and ritual but in folk drama everywhere.

Thus, in the Mumming plays the central act is the fight between two or more opponents, usually called the King, or St George, and Turkey Knight, one or all of whom are killed or wounded amid loud lamentation and then restored to life by a Doctor. The play ends with universal rejoicing. As a serio-comic survival of the seasonal drama it has preserved the main theme, viz., the death and resurrection of the royal hero-god, and added burlesque characters, such as the doctor's man, Jack Finney, the Man-woman, Beelzebub (Belzey Bob), Bob Slasher, Little Johnnie Jack, Little David Dout, Father Christmas and so on, devoid of any obvious function. The leaders of the once mighty forces of good and evil have become farcical figures, sometimes carrying a club or a dripping pan, while the tremendously serious sacred marriage has degenerated into a functionless "man-woman", or "boy-girl" character. The fallen hero has descended to the level of a farcical St George, and the masked impersonators of the gods are merely clowns with bladders, blackened faces and calves' tails. The hobby-horse may belong to the same category, unless it represents the last relic of animal sacrifice. But it is the combat and its sequel that give the clue to the original meaning and purpose of Folk drama and the Sword dance.

When myth and ritual no longer exercise their proper function in society in the formation and maintenance of the social order, they rapidly degenerate into idle tales told for amusement and conventional ceremonial which at best is merely quaint and picturesque, or an excuse for healthy exercise, as in the case of the folk dance. Around historical figures, *legends* (as distinct from myths) tend to cling, providing heroes with a halo of romance, just as they enhance the

---

[7] R. M. Dawkins, *Journal of Hellenic Studies*, XXVI, 1906, pp. 192–201.

prestige of saints and sanctuaries. Being attached to actual persons and places they preserve a considerable element of fact, whereas when a myth ceases to be a reality lived, embodied in a rite and in the social structure, it has no other useful purpose to fulfil. Consequently, it either lives on as an adjunct of peasant culture in the form of folklore, or it comes to an end ingloriously as burlesque or superstition.

Folklore

The term "Folklore" was coined in 1846 by T. H. Thoms to take the place of the rather awkward expression "Popular Antiquities", which hitherto had been used to describe the oral traditions and culture of the unlettered classes in civilized communities, comprising beliefs, customs, institutions, pastimes, sayings, songs, ballads, stories and arts and crafts, both as regards their origin and their present social functions. In this rich field of inquiry, John Aubrey had led the way as early as 1686 when, in his *Remaines of Gentilisme and Judaisme* he gave an account of such practices current in his day as "sin-eating" and making offerings in kind at funerals. In 1725 Henry Bourne recorded in a little book entitled *Antiquitates Vulgares* the "opinions and ceremonies" observed in the neighbourhood of Newcastle-on-Tyne. From this unpretentious beginning, half a century later sprang the volumes which subsequently were known as John Brand's *Observations on Popular Antiquities in Great Britain*. These were followed, in 1826, by Hone's *Everyday Book*, and in Germany by the remarkable collections of folk-tales, or *märchen*, in Jakob Grimm's *Deutsche Mythologie* (1812–15).

It was left, however, to the well-known Sanskrit scholar Max Müller and to A. Kuhn to make the study of mythology a crucial issue by tracing its origin to a "disease of language". From a comparative study of the Indian Rig Veda, the Iranian Avesta, the Scandinavian Edda and the Homeric literature, they endorsed the view of the brothers Grimm that both mythology and language are rooted deep in the heart of the common people, and are not the creation of the higher ranks in society. The explanation of myths is to be sought, they supposed, in nature and the heavenly bodies, notably the sun, and this it was claimed could be established by a philological analysis of mythical names. Wilhelm Mannhardt, on the other hand, having set himself systematically to collect, compare and explain the living customs and beliefs of the peasantry, concentrated attention upon the vegetation cultus of the farmer and the woodman. It now appeared that the oldest material was to be found not in the solar myths but in analogies of the classical stories with the German woodmaidens and the animistic spirits of the corn and of the wild. In England the parallel movement, initiated by the animistic theory of Tylor which influenced Mannhardt's interpretation of rural customs and beliefs, reached its climax in Frazer's monumental work, *The Golden Bough*, the first edition of which appeared in 1890.

In seeking to elucidate the unexplained rule of the Arician priesthood of Diana at her sylvan shrine on the banks of lake Nemi in the Alban hills, Frazer found in the sacrifice of the divine king the secret of the mysterious figure of the guardian of the "golden bough", or mistletoe, reigning in lonely seclusion "beneath Aricia's trees" as "the priest who slew the slayer, and shall himself be slain". The attempt to settle this question, however, raised many more problems, and step by step the indefatigable author was lured on, as he tells us, into far-spreading fields of primitive thought which had been little explored by his predecessors.

The evidence brought to light by Frazer, Tylor, Mannhardt and Andrew Lang, and their collaborators, destroyed once and for all the philological speculations of Max Müller and his followers, but no serious attempt was made to distinguish the lore of the folk embedded in civilizations from the myth and ritual of the savage living under genuinely primitive conditions. It remained for the late Sir Lawrence Gomme to draw this distinction, and to insist that the historical development of each culture must be taken into account before any analysis, classification or comparison is made between their customs, rites and beliefs.[8] It is unscientific, he maintained, to compare observances and traditions found among the European peasantry with those of the aboriginal populations on the fringes of civilization, although the religious institutions of both may have had a common origin. In the process of development, the divergence between the two cultures has been too great to make possible a legitimate comparison between the resultant products. On the other hand, a belief found among the folk may well be compared, in his opinion, with a belief recorded in classical mythology, the Rig Veda or the Avesta, since the cultural level, he thought, was much the same.

Apart from the vexed question of the historical value of folk material, its importance as an integral element in a *living* culture can hardly be over-emphasized. As a vital part of the life of the peasantry, arising out of their religious, social and economic tradition, customs, songs, stories, arts and crafts, reveal their mind and creative genius. Under modern conditions this phase of culture is so rapidly disappearing everywhere that it is ceasing to be the direct expression of its subject-matter, and tending more and more to become either interesting "bygones" or unedifying superstitions devoid of any serious meaning and purpose, like palmistry, crystal gazing, and beliefs about "luck". Unorganized and detached survivals from a former state of organic development, as in the case of the vermiform appendix and similar vestigial organs, are a cause of embarrassment to the organism unless they can be utilized in some beneficial manner and so acquire a functional value. Rites which were

[8] *Folk-lore as an Historical Science* (London, 1908).

once "faith" but which, from a later and higher cultural standpoint, have simply "remained over," become the equivalent of the Latin *"superstitio,"* which perhaps is best translated by the English term "survival" rather than "superstition". But however the phenomenon be defined, it ceases to exercise its proper function in detachment from the life of the community in which it occurs.

The efforts made in recent years to resuscitate the Folk-play, the Folk-dance and the Folk-song can hardly hope to restore their original significance in society. The drama often has been derived from printed sources and the actors may be no longer men of the soil, while even rural festivals, like folk-tales, are apt to lose their spontaneity and become an escape from life rather than a reproduction of it. The folk-dance frequently is now a pastime of the sophisticated, as is the folk-song, but, nevertheless, the fact that they make such a ready appeal in a mechanized age, so far removed from the culture in which they arose, is an indication of their vitality and the continuity of the emotions to which they give expression in action and words. Beneath the very thin veneer of modernity the living pulse of the folk still can be felt.

Moreover, in rural communities traditional ways of life and thought still survive as an integral part of a living culture, while many trades and industries have retained their own beliefs, customs and institutions (e.g., fisherfolk, sailors, landworkers, miners, etc.), which are as illuminating as they are culturally significant. In the material sphere, folk arts and crafts throw valuable light on the life and work of a people before the Industrial Revolution, and, therefore, the establishment of Folk Museums – an enterprise in which the Scandinavian countries have taken the lead – is to be welcomed as illustrating the evolution of society in its more material aspects for several hundred years. From these visible expressions of the folk mind valuable hints often can be obtained concerning the lore, learning and religion of former ages. For all these reasons, in the elucidation of the nature and origin of human institutions and beliefs the same care should be given to the study of the European peasant cultures, and their counterparts elsewhere, as to those of the more remote primitive peoples in Australia, Africa and the Pacific.

While there is no master key which will release all the secrets of the beginnings of religion, and much must remain hidden away in obscurity, lost forever in the remote recesses of primeval origins, a judicial use of the data made available in recent years by archæological excavation, anthropological inquiry and the investigation of the folk cultures of modern civilized communities, renders it possible to arrive at certain general conclusions respecting the raw material of religion and the function it has fulfilled in the development of society and in laying the foundation of the spiritual understanding of mankind. If at this stage ritual dominates the situation, this is only because the deepest emotions of the human heart, and the most profound convictions of the mind, find expression in actions before they are given utterance in words and elaborated in systematized theologies and philosophies, ætiological mythologies, spiritualized worship and ethical rules of conduct. Our purpose in this volume has been to determine the rudimentary ideas of religion and its fundamental practices in their historical, sociological and psychological context, leaving it to the other writers in this series to tell the rest of the fascinating story of the quest of the human spirit for fellowship with the transcendental source of its being, and of all becoming starting from these lowly beginnings.

10

MYTH IN PRIMITIVE PSYCHOLOGY

Bronislaw Malinowski

The famous Polish-born anthropologist Bronislaw Malinowski (1884–1942), Professor of Anthropology at the London School of Economics, helped pioneer the social functionalist approach to myth. For Malinowski, myth serves to spur obedience to the rules, customs, and institutions of society. Myths trace the origin of present-day social phenomena back to antiquity and thereby bestow on those phenomena the clout of tradition. Rituals are among the phenomena bolstered by myths. Where for Smith myths arise to explain and thereby support rituals only once the point of rituals has been lost, for Malinowski myths presumably arise to explain and support rituals from the outset. Where for Smith myths make sense of rituals that might well continue to be practiced anyway, for Malinowski myths ensure the continuing practice of rituals that might otherwise be abandoned as a burden. The following excerpt on the rituals of magic is from sections IV–V of Malinowski's classic essay on myth, "Myth in Primitive Psychology," which was originally published as a book (London: Routledge & Kegan Paul; New York: Norton, 1926) and was reprinted in his *Magic, Science and Religion and Other Essays* (Glencoe, IL: Free Press, 1948), 72–124. See also his *Argonauts of the Western Pacific* (London: Routledge, 1922), ch. 12; "Magic, Science and Religion," in *Science, Religion and Reality*, ed. Joseph Needham (London: Sheldon Press; New York: Macmillan, 1925), esp. 76–8 (reprinted in his *Magic, Science and Religion and Other Essays*, 7–71); "The Role of Myth in Life," *Psyche* 6 (1926), 29–39; "Anthropology," *Encyclopaedia Britannica*, 13th edn (1926), First Supplementary Volume, esp. 135–7; "Culture," *Encyclopaedia of the Social Sciences* 4 (1931), esp. 634–42; and *Malinowski and the Work of Myth*, ed. Ivan Strenski (Princeton:

Original publication: Bronislaw Malinowski, "Myth in Primitive Psychology" (1926), in his *Magic, Science and Religion and Other Essays* (Garden City, NY: Doubleday Anchor Books, 1954 [1948]), sections IV–V (pp. 138–48).

Princeton University Press, 1992). On Malinowski see *Man and Culture*, ed. Raymond Firth (London: Routledge & Kegan Paul, 1957); Edmund Leach, "Frazer and Malinowski: A CA Discussion," *Current Anthropology* 7 (1966), 560–76; and *Malinowski Between Two Worlds*, ed. Roy Ellen et al. (Cambridge: Cambridge University Press, 1988).

Myths of Magic

Let me discuss in more detail another class of mythical stories, those connected with magic. Magic, from many points of view, is the most important and the most mysterious aspect of primitive man's pragmatic attitude towards reality. It is one of the problems which are engaging at present the most vivid and most controversial interests of anthropologists. The foundations of this study have been laid by Sir James Frazer, who has also erected a magnificent edifice thereon in his famous theory of magic.

Magic plays such a great part in northwest Melanesia that even a superficial observer must soon realize its enormous sway. Its incidence, however, is not very clear at first sight. Although it seems to crop up everywhere, there are certain highly important and vital activities from which magic is conspicuously absent.

No native would ever make a yam or taro garden without magic. Yet certain important types of planting, such as the raising of the coconut, the cultivation of the banana, of the mango, and of the breadfruit, are devoid of magic. Fishing, the economic activity only second in importance to agriculture, has in some of its forms a highly developed magic. Thus the dangerous fishing of the shark, the pursuit of the uncertain *kalala* or of the *to'ulam* are smothered in magic. The equally vital, but easy and reliable method of fishing by poison has no magic whatever. In the construction of the canoe – an enterprise surrounded with technical difficulties, requiring organized labor, and leading to an ever-dangerous pursuit – the ritual is complex, deeply associated with the work, and regarded as absolutely indispensable. In the construction of houses, technically quite as difficult a pursuit, but involving neither danger, nor chance, nor yet such complex forms of co-operation as the canoe, there is no magic whatever associated with the work. Wood-carving, an industrial activity of the greatest importance, is carried on in certain communities as a universal trade, learnt in childhood, and practiced by everyone. In these communities there is no magic of carving at all. A different type of artistic sculpture in ebony and hardwood, practiced only by people of special technical and artistic ability all over the district, has, on the other hand, its magic, which is considered as the main source of skill and inspiration. In trade, a ceremonial form of exchange known as the *Kula* is surrounded by important magical ritual; while on the other hand, certain minor forms of barter of a purely commercial nature are without any magic at all. Pursuits such as war and love, as well as certain forces of destiny and nature such as disease, wind, and weather are in native belief almost completely governed by magical forces.

Even this rapid survey leads us to an important generalization which will serve as a convenient starting point. We find magic wherever the elements of chance and accident, and the emotional play between hope and fear have a wide and extensive range. We do not find magic wherever the pursuit is certain, reliable, and well under the control of rational methods and technological processes. Further, we find magic where the element of danger is conspicuous. We do not find it wherever absolute safety eliminates any elements of foreboding. This is the psychological factor. But magic also fulfills another and highly important sociological function. As I have tried to show elsewhere, magic is an active element in the organization of labor and in its systematic arrangement. It also provides the main controlling power in the pursuit of game. The integral cultural function of magic, therefore, consists in the bridging-over of gaps and inadequacies in highly important activities not yet completely mastered by man. In order to achieve this end, magic supplies primitive man with a firm belief in his power of succeeding; it provides him also with a definite mental and pragmatic technique wherever his ordinary means fail him. It thus enables man to carry out with confidence his most vital tasks, and to maintain his poise and his mental integrity under circumstances which, without the help of magic, would demoralize him by despair and anxiety, by fear and hatred, by unrequited love and impotent hate.

Magic is thus akin to science in that it always has a definite aim intimately associated with human instincts, needs, and pursuits. The magic art is directed towards the attainment of practical ends; like any other art or craft it is also governed by theory, and by a system of principles which dictate the manner in which the act has to be performed in order to be effective. Thus magic and science show a number of similarities, and with Sir James Frazer, we can appropriately call magic a pseudo science.

Let us look more closely at the nature of the magic art. Magic, in all its forms, is composed of three essential ingredients. In its performance there always enter certain words, spoken or chanted; certain ceremonial actions are always carried out; and there is always an officiating minister of the ceremony. In analyzing, therefore, the nature of magic, we have to distinguish the formula, the rite, and the condition of the performer. It may be said at once that in the part of Melanesia with which we are concerned, the spell is by far the most important constituent of magic. To the natives, knowledge of magic means the knowledge of the spell; and in any act of witchcraft the ritual centers round the utterance of the spell. The rite and the competence of the performer are merely conditioning factors which serve for the proper preservation and launching of the spell. This is very important from the point of view of our present discussion, for the magical spell stands in close relation to traditional lore and more especially to mythology.[1]

In the case of almost all types of magic we find some story accounting for its existence. Such a story tells when and where that particular magical formula entered the possession of man, how it became the property of a local group, how it passed from one to another. But such a story is not the story of magical origins. Magic never "originated"; it never was created or invented. All magic simply *was* from the beginning, as an essential adjunct to all those things and processes which vitally interest man and yet elude his normal rational efforts. The spell, the rite, and the object which they govern are coeval.

Thus the essence of all magic is its traditional integrity. Magic can only be efficient if it has been transmitted without loss and without flaw from one generation to the other, till it has come down from primeval times to the present performer. Magic, therefore, requires a pedigree, a sort of traditional passport in its travel across time. This is supplied by the myth of magic. The manner in which myth endows the performance of magic with worth and validity, in which myth blends with the belief in magical efficiency, will be best illustrated by a concrete example.

As we know, love and the attractions of the other sex play an important role in the life of these Melanesians. Like many races of the South Seas they are very free and easy in their conduct, especially before marriage. Adultery, however, is a punishable offense, and relations with the same totemic clan are strictly forbidden. But the greatest crime in the eyes of the natives is any form of incest. Even the bare idea of such a trespass between brother and sister fills them with violent horror. Brother and sister, united by the nearest bond of kinship in this matriarchal society, may not even converse freely, must never joke or smile at one another, and any allusion to one of them in the presence of the other is considered extremely bad taste. Outside the clan, however, freedom is great, and the pursuit of love assumes a variety of interesting and even attractive forms.

All sexual attraction and all power of seduction are believed to reside in the magic of love. This magic the natives regard as founded in a dramatic occurrence of the past, told in a strange, tragic myth of brother and sister incest, to which I can only refer briefly here.[2] The two young people lived in a village with their mother, and by an accident the girl inhaled a strong love decoction, prepared by her brother for someone else. Mad with passion, she chased him and seduced him on a lonely beach. Overcome by shame and remorse, they forsook food and drink, and died together in a grotto. An aromatic herb grew

---

[1] Cf. *Argonauts of the Western Pacific*, pp. 329, 401, et seq., and pp. 69–78 of "Magic, Science and Religion" in *Science, Religion and Reality*, Essays by Various Authors (1925).

[2] For the complete account of this myth see the author's *Sex and Repression in Primitive Society* (1926), where its full sociological bearings are discussed.

through their inlaced skeletons, and this herb forms the most powerful ingredient in the substances compounded together and used in love magic.

It can be said that the myth of magic, even more than the other types of savage myth, justifies the sociological claims of the wielder, shapes the ritual, and vouches for the truth of the belief in supplying the pattern of the subsequent miraculous confirmation.

Our discovery of this cultural function of magical myth fully endorses the brilliant theory of the origins of power and kingship developed by Sir James Frazer in the early parts of his *Golden Bough*. According to Sir James, the beginnings of social supremacy are due primarily to magic. By showing how the efficacy of magic is associated with local claims, sociological affiliation, and direct descent, we have been able to forge another link in the chain of causes which connect tradition, magic, and social power.

Conclusion

Throughout this book I have attempted to prove that myth is above all a cultural force; but it is not only that. It is obviously also a narrative, and thus it has its literary aspect – an aspect which has been unduly emphasized by most scholars, but which, nevertheless, should not be completely neglected. Myth contains germs of the future epic, romance, and tragedy; and it has been used in them by the creative genius of peoples and by the conscious art of civilization. We have seen that some myths are but dry and succinct statements with scarcely any nexus and no dramatic incident; others, like the myth of love or the myth of canoe magic and of overseas sailing, are eminently dramatic stories. Did space permit, I could repeat a long and elaborate saga of the culture hero Tudava, who slays an ogre, avenges his mother, and carries out a number of cultural tasks.[3] Comparing such stories, it might be possible to show why myth lends itself in certain of its forms to subsequent literary elaboration, and why certain other of its forms remain artistically sterile. Mere sociological precedence, legal title, and vindication of lineage and local claims do not lead far into the realm of human emotions, and therefore lack the elements of literary value. Belief, on the other hand, whether in magic or in religion, is closely associated with the deepest desires of man, with his fears and hopes, with his passions and sentiments. Myths of love and of death, stories of the loss of immortality, of the passing of the Golden Age, and of the banishment from Paradise, myths of incest and of sorcery play with the very elements which enter into the artistic forms of tragedy, of lyric, and of romantic narrative.

---

[3] For one of the main episodes of the myth of Tudava, see pp. 209–210 of the author's "Complex and Myth in Mother Right" in *Psyche*, vol. V., Jan. 1925.

Our theory, the theory of the cultural function of myth, accounting as it does for its intimate relation to belief and showing the close connection between ritual and tradition, could help us to deepen our understanding of the literary possibilities of savage story. But this subject, however fascinating, cannot be further elaborated here.

In our opening remarks, two current theories of myth were discredited and discarded: the view that myth is a rhapsodic rendering of natural phenomena, and Andrew Lang's doctrine that myth is essentially an explanation, a sort of primitive science. Our treatment has shown that neither of these mental attitudes is dominant in primitive culture; that neither can explain the form of primitive sacred stories, their sociological context, or their cultural function. But once we have realized that myth serves principally to establish a sociological charter, or a retrospective moral pattern of behavior, or the primeval supreme miracle of magic – it becomes clear that elements both of explanation and of interest in nature must be found in sacred legends. For a precedent accounts for subsequent cases, though it does so through an order of ideas entirely different from the scientific relation of cause and effect, of motive and consequence. The interest in nature, again, is obvious if we realize how important is the mythology of magic, and how definitely magic clings to the economic concerns of man. In this, however, mythology is very far from a disinterested and contemplative rhapsody about natural phenomena. Between myth and nature two links must be interpolated: man's pragmatic interest in certain aspects of the outer world, and his need of supplementing rational and empirical control of certain phenomena by magic.

Let me state once more that I have dealt in this book with savage myth, and not with the myth of culture. I believe that the study of mythology as it functions and works in primitive societies should anticipate the conclusions drawn from the material of higher civilizations. Some of this material has come down to us only in isolated literary texts, without its setting in actual life, without its social context. Such is the mythology of the ancient classical peoples and of the dead civilizations of the Orient. In the study of myth the classical scholar must learn from the anthropologist.

The science of myth in living higher cultures, such as the present civilization of India, Japan, China, and last but not least, our own, might well be inspired by the comparative study of primitive folklore; and in its turn civilized culture could furnish important additions and explanations to savage mythology. This subject is very much beyond the scope of the present study. I do, however, want to emphasize the fact that anthropology should be not only the study of savage custom in the light of our mentality and our culture, but also the study of our own mentality in the distant perspective borrowed from Stone Age man. By dwelling mentally for some time among people of a much simpler culture than our own, we may be able to see ourselves from a distance, we may be able to gain a new sense of proportion with regard to our own institutions, beliefs, and customs. If anthropology could thus inspire us with some sense of proportion, and supply us with a finer sense of humor, it might justly claim to be a very great science.

I have now completed the survey of facts and the range of conclusions; it only remains to summarize them briefly. I have tried to show that folklore, these stories handed on in a native community, live in the cultural context of tribal life and not merely in narrative. By this I mean that the ideas, emotions, and desires associated with a given story are experienced not only when the story is told, but also when in certain customs, moral rules, or ritual proceedings, the counterpart of the story is enacted. And here a considerable difference is discovered between the several types of story. While in the mere fireside *tale* the sociological context is narrow, the *legend* enters much more deeply into the tribal life of the community, and the *myth* plays a most important function. Myth, as a statement of primeval reality which still lives in present-day life and as a justification by precedent, supplies a retrospective pattern of moral values, sociological order, and magical belief. It is, therefore, neither a mere narrative, nor a form of science, nor a branch of art or history, nor an explanatory tale. It fulfills a function *sui generis* closely connected with the nature of tradition, and the continuity of culture, with the relation between age and youth, and with the human attitude towards the past. The function of myth, briefly, is to strengthen tradition and endow it with a greater value and prestige by tracing it back to a higher, better, more supernatural reality of initial events.

Myth is, therefore, an indispensable ingredient of all culture. It is, as we have seen, constantly regenerated; every historical change creates its mythology, which is, however, but indirectly related to historical fact. Myth is a constant by-product of living faith, which is in need of miracles; of sociological status, which demands precedent; of moral rule, which requires sanction.

We have made, perhaps, a too ambitious attempt to give a new definition of myth. Our conclusions imply a new method of treating the science of folklore, for we have shown that it cannot be independent of ritual, of sociology, or even of material culture. Folk tales, legends, and myths must be lifted from their flat existence on paper, and placed in the three-dimensional reality of full life. As regards anthropological field work, we are obviously demanding a new method of collecting evidence. The anthropologist must relinquish his comfortable position in the long chair on the veranda of the missionary compound, Government station, or planter's bungalow, where, armed with pencil and notebook and at times with a whisky and soda, he has been accustomed to collect statements from informants, write down stories, and fill out sheets of paper with savage texts. He must go out into the villages, and see the natives at work in gardens, on the beach, in the jungle; he must sail with them to distant sandbanks and to foreign tribes, and observe them in fishing, trading, and ceremonial overseas expeditions. Information must come to him full-flavored from his own observations of native life, and not be squeezed out of reluctant informants as a trickle of talk. Field work can be done first or secondhand even among the savages, in the middle of pile dwellings, not far from actual cannibalism and head-hunting. Open-air anthropology, as opposed to hearsay note-taking, is hard work, but it is also great fun. Only such anthropology can give us the all-round vision of primitive man and of primitive culture. Such anthropology shows us, as regards myth, that far from being an idle mental pursuit, it is a vital ingredient of practical relation to the environment.

The claims and merits, however, are not mine, but are due once more to Sir James Frazer. *The Golden Bough* contains the theory of the ritual and sociological function of myth, to which I have been able to make but a small contribution, in that I could test, prove, and document in my field work. This theory is implied in Frazer's treatment of magic; in his masterly exposition of the great importance of agricultural rites; in the central place which the cults of vegetation and fertility occupy in the volumes of *Adonis, Attis, Osiris*, and in those on the *Spirits of the Corn and of the Wild*. In these works, as in so many of his other writings, Sir James Frazer has established the intimate relation between the word and the deed in primitive faith; he has shown that the words of the story and of the spell, and the acts of ritual and ceremony are the two aspects of primitive belief. The deep philosophic query propounded by Faust, as to the primacy of the word or of the deed, appears to us fallacious. The beginning of man is the beginning of articulate thought and of thought put into action. Without words, whether framed in sober rational conversation, or launched in magical spells, or used to entreat superior divinities, man would not have been able to embark upon his great Odyssey of cultural adventure and achievement.

11

MYTH AND REALITY

Mircea Eliade

The Romanian-born Mircea Eliade (1927–1986), Professor of the History of Religions at the University of Chicago, credited myth with several functions. Myth serves to explain the origin of the world – the world as a whole and all phenomena in it. Myth serves to justify phenomena by tracing them back to a primordial origin and thereby, as for Malinowski, conferring on them the sanctity of antiquity. On the one hand rituals are among the many phenomena justified by myth. On the other hand myth is itself ritually enacted. When enacted, myth serves as a time machine, carrying one back to the time of the origin of the phenomenon explained and justified. By returning one to the time when, it is believed, god was nearer to humanity than god is now, myth serves its ultimate, distinctively religious function: providing proximity to god. In addition to Eliade's *Myth and Reality* (tr. Willard R. Trask [New York: Harper & Row, 1963]), from which the following selection (ch. 3) is taken, see his *The Sacred and the Profane*, tr. Willard R. Trask (New York: Harcourt, Brace, 1959 [1957]), ch. 2; *The Myth of the Eternal Return* (or *Cosmos and History*), tr. Willard R. Trask (New York: Pantheon, 1954 [1949]); and *Patterns in Comparative Religion*, tr. Rosemary Sheed (London: Sheed and Ward, 1958 [1949]), esp. ch. 15; "The Prestige of the Cosmogonic Myth," tr. Elaine P. Halperin, *Diogenes* 23 (1958), 1–13; "Myth," *Encyclopaedia Britannica*, 14th edn (1970), XV, 1132–42; and "Myth in the Nineteenth and Twentieth Centuries," in *Dictionary of the History of Ideas*, ed. Philip P. Wiener (New York: Scribner, 1973–74), III, 307–18. On Eliade see *Myths and Symbols: Studies in Honor of Mircea Eliade*, eds Joseph M. Kitagawa and Charles H. Long (Chicago: University of Chicago Press, 1969); Guilford Dudley III, *Religion on Trial* (Philadelphia: Temple University Press, 1977); Douglas Allen, *Structure and Creativity in Religion* (Hague: Mouton, 1978); Ivan Strenski, *Four Theories of Myth in*

Original publication: Mircea Eliade, *Myth and Reality*, tr. Willard R. Trask (New York: Harper Torchbooks, 1968 [1963]), ch. 3 (pp. 39–53).

Twentieth Century History (Iowa City: University of Iowa Press; London: Macmillan, 1989), chs 4–5; and Bryan S. Rennie, *Reconstructing Eliade* (Albany: State University of New York Press, 1996).

Myths and Rites of Renewal

A. M. Hocart had observed that in Fiji the king's enthronement ceremony is called "creation of the world," "fashioning the land," or "creating the earth."[1] On the accession of a sovereign the cosmogony was symbolically repeated. The idea is rather widespread among agricultural peoples. According to a recent interpretation, the installation of the Indian king, the *rajasūya*, included re-creating the Universe. And in fact the various phases of the ritual successively brought about the future sovereign's reversion to the embryonic state, his gestation for a year, and his mystical rebirth as Cosmocrator, identified with both Prajāpati (the All-God) and the Cosmos.

The future sovereign's embryonic period corresponded to the maturation process of the Universe and, in all probability, was originally related to the ripening of crops. The second phase of the ritual completes the formation of the sovereign's new ("divine") body. The third phase of the *rajasūya* comprises a series of rites whose cosmogonic symbolism is sufficiently emphasized by the texts. The king raises his arms; he is symbolizing the raising of the *axis mundi*. When he is anointed he stands on the throne, arms lifted; he is incarnating the cosmic axis fixed in the navel of the Earth (that is, the throne, the Center of the World) and touching the Heavens. The aspersion is connected with the Waters that come down from the Heavens along the *axis mundi* (that is, the king) to fertilize the Earth.[2]

In the historical period the *rajasūya* was performed only twice – the first time to consecrate the king and the second to ensure him universal sovereignty. But in protohistorical times the *rajasūya* was probably an annual rite, performed to regenerate the Cosmos.

Such was the case in Egypt. The coronation of a new pharaoh, Frankfort writes, "can be regarded as the creation of a new epoch after a dangerous interruption of the harmony between society and nature – a situation, therefore, which partakes of the quality of the creation of the universe. This is well illustrated by a text containing a curse on the king's enemies who are compared with Apophis, the snake of darkness whom Re destroys at dawn. But there is a curious addition to the comparison: 'They will be like the serpent Apophis

---

[1] *The Myth of the Eternal Return*, pp. 80 ff.
[2] M. Eliade, "Dimensions religieuses de renouvellement cosmique," *Eranos-Jahrbüch* (Zurich, 1960), vol. XXVIII, pp. 269 ff.

on New Year's morn.' The qualification 'on New Year's morn' can only be explained as an intensification: the snake is defeated at every sunrise, but the New Year celebrates creation and daily renewal as well as the opening of the new annual cycle."[3]

It is clear how the cosmogonic scenario of the New Year can be incorporated into the coronation ceremony of a king. The two ritual systems pursue the same end – cosmic renewal. "But the *renovatio* accomplished at the coronation of a king had important consequences in the later history of humanity. On the one hand, the ceremonies of renewal become movable, break away from the rigid frame of the calendar; on the other, the king becomes in a manner responsible for the stability, the fecundity, and the prosperity of the entire Cosmos. This is as much as to say that universal renewal is no longer bound to the cosmic rhythm and is connected instead with historical persons and events."[4]

Renewing the world

It is easy to understand why the installation of a king repeated the cosmogony or took place at the New Year. The king was believed to renew the entire Cosmos. The greatest of renewals takes place at the New Year, when a new time cycle is inaugurated. But the *renovatio* effected by the New Year ritual is, basically, a reiteration of the cosmogony. Each New Year begins the Creation over again. And it is by myths – both cosmogonic myths and origin myths – that man is reminded how the World was created and what happened afterward.

The world is always "our world," the world in which one lives. And although the mode of being of human existence is the same among the Australians as among modern Westerners, the cultural contexts in which human existence is apprehended vary widely. It is obvious, for example, that the "World" of the Australians, who live by gathering and small-game hunting, is not the same as that of the Neolithic agriculturalists; just as the World of the latter is neither that of the city dwellers of the ancient Near East nor the "World" in which the peoples of Western Europe and the United States live today. The differences are too great to require pointing out. We have mentioned them only to avoid a misunderstanding: in citing examples representing different types of culture, we have no intention of returning to a "confusionistic"

---

[3] H. Frankfort, *Kingship and the Gods* (Chicago, 1948), p. 150.

[4] M. Eliade, op. cit., pp. 270–271. "It is in this conception that we find the source for future historical and political eschatologies. For in the course of time cosmic renewal, the 'Salvation' of the World, came to be expected from a certain type of King or Hero or Saviour or even political leader. Although in strongly secularized form, the modern world still keeps the eschatological hope of a universal *renovatio* to be brought about by the victory of a social class or even of a political party or personality" (ibid., p. 271).

comparatism in the manner of Frazer. The historical context of each example we give is implied. But we think it unnecessary, in the case of every tribe cited, to define its social and economic structure and state with what tribes it can or cannot be compared.

The "World," then, is always the world that one knows and in which one lives; it differs from one type of culture to another; hence there are a considerable number of "Worlds." But what is significant for our study is the fact that, despite the differences in their socioeconomic structure and the variety of their cultural contexts, the archaic peoples believe that the World must be annually renewed and that this renewal is brought about by following a model – the cosmogony, or an origin myth that plays the role of a cosmogonic myth.

Obviously, the "Year" is variously conceived by primitives, and the dates of the "New Year" differ in accordance with climate, geographical setting, type of culture, and so on. But there is always a cycle, that is, a period of time that has a beginning and an end. Now, the end of one cycle and the beginning of the next are marked by a series of rituals whose purpose is the renewal of the World. As we said, the *renovatio* is a re-creation after the model of the cosmogony.

The simplest examples are found among the Australians. They are origin myths that are re-enacted annually. The animals and plants created *in illo tempore* by the Supernatural Beings are ritually re-created. In Kimberley the rock paintings, which are believed to have been painted by the Ancestors, are repainted in order to reactivate their creative force, as it was first manifested in mythical times, that is, at the beginning of the World.[5]

For the Australians, this re-creation of food animals and food plants is equivalent to re-creating the World. And this is so not only because, with a sufficient food supply, they hope to live through another year, but above all because the World really came to birth when the animals and plants first made their appearance in the Dream Times. Animals and plants are among the creative works accomplished by the Supernatural Beings. Feeding oneself is not merely a physiological act but is equally a "religious" act; one eats the creations of the Supernatural Beings, and one eats them as they were eaten by the mythical ancestors for the first time, at the beginning of the World.[6]

Among the Australians the cosmogony is limited to the creation of the territory with which they are familiar. This is their "World," and it must be periodically renewed or it may perish. The idea that the Cosmos is threatened with ruin if it is not annually re-created provides the inspiration for the chief festival of the Californian Karok, Hupa, and Yurok tribes. In the respective

---

[5] Helmut Petri, *Sterbende Welt in Nordwest Australien* (Braunschweig, 1954), pp. 200 ff.; A. P. Elkin, *The Australian Aborigines* (London, 1954), pp. 220 ff.

[6] On the religious value of food, cf. Eliade, "Dimensions religieuses du renouvellement cosmique," p. 273.

languages the ceremony is called "repair" or "fixing" of the world, and, in English, "New Year." Its purpose is to re-establish or strengthen the Earth for the following year or two years. Among some Yurok tribes the strengthening of the World is accomplished by ritually rebuilding the steam cabin, a rite that is cosmogonic in structure and of which other examples will be given later. The essential part of the ceremonial consists in long pilgrimages undertaken by the priest to all the sacred sites, that is, to the places where the Immortals performed certain acts. These ritual peregrinations continue for ten or twelve days. During all this time the priest incarnates the Immortals. As he walks, he thinks: "The ixkareya animas (i.e., one of the Immortals) walked over this in mythical times." When he comes to one of the sacred sites he begins to sweep it, saying: "Ixkareya yakam is sweeping this time, sweeping all the sickness out of this world." Afterward he climbs a mountain. There he finds a branch, which he makes into a walking stick, saying: "This world is cracked, but when I pick up and drag the stick, all the cracks will fill up and the earth will become solid again." Going down to the river, he finds a stone, which he sets solidly in place, saying: "The earth, which has been tipped, will be straight again. People will live to be stronger." He sits down on the stone. "When I sit on the stone," he explained to Gifford, "the earth will never get up and tip again." The stone has been there since the time of the Immortals, that is, since the beginning of the World.[7]

"Taken together, the rituals we have reviewed make up a cosmogonic scenario. In mythical Times, the Immortals created the World in which the California Indians were to live: they traced its outlines, established its Center and its foundations, ensured an abundant supply of salmon and acorns, and exorcised sicknesses. But this World is no longer the atemporal and unchangeable Cosmos in which the Immortals dwelt. It is a living world – inhabited and used by creatures of flesh and blood, subject to the law of becoming, of old age and death. Hence it requires a periodical repairing, a renewing, a strengthening. But the only way to renew the World is to repeat what the Immortals did *in illo tempore*, is to reiterate the creation. This is why the priest reproduces the exemplary itinerary of the Immortals and repeats their acts and words. In short, the priest ends by incarnating the Immortals. In other words, at the time of the New Year the Immortals are believed to be present on earth once again. This explains why the ritual of annually renewing the World is the most important religious ceremony among these California tribes. The World is not only made more stable and regenerated, it is also sanctified by the symbolic presence of the Immortals. The priest, who incarnates them, becomes – for a

---

[7] A. L. Kroeber and E. W. Gifford, *World Renewal, a Cult System of Native Northwest California*, Anthropological Records, vol. XIII, no. I (University of California, Berkeley, 1949), pp. 6 ff., 14–17, 19 ff., summarized in "Dimensions religieuses du renouvellement cosmique," pp. 259 ff.

certain length of time – an 'immortal person,' and, as such, he must be neither looked at nor touched. He performs the rites far from other men, in absolute solitude, for when the Immortals performed them for the first time there were yet no men on earth."[8]

Differences and similarities

The mythico-ritual scenario of periodic renewal of the World is also found among other Californian tribes – for example, the *aki* ceremony of the Hill Maidu, the *hesi* of the Plains Maidu, the *kuksu* of the Eastern Pomo.[9] In all these examples the renewal of the World forms part of a cult complex that includes honoring the Supreme Being, ensuring a good harvest, and the initiation of youths. This Californian scenario may be compared with the Shawnee ritual "The Cabin of New Life" (which forms part of the Sun Dance) and the "Big House" ceremonies of the Lenape. In both cases we find a cosmogonic ritual, a renewal of the World and rebirth of Life. Among the Shawnee the priest renews Creation; among the Lenape the New Year's ceremony reiterates the first creation of the World, to the end of recovering the fullness of the beginnings.[10]

We may add that the building or periodic repairing of the ritual cabin also has a cosmogonic meaning. The sacred cabin represents the Universe. Its roof symbolizes the vault of heaven, the floor the Earth, the four walls the four directions of cosmic space. The Dakotas say: the "Year is a circle around the World," that is, around the initiation cabin.[11] We may also add that the interdependence between the Cosmos and cosmic Time ("circular" Time) was so strongly felt that in several languages the term for "World" is also used to mean "Year." For example, certain California tribes say "The world is past," or "The earth is passed," to mean that "a year has passed."[12]

If we now turn to the New Year rituals that obtain among peoples practicing protoagriculture (i.e., cultivation of tubers) we are struck by the differences. We first note two new elements: the collective return of the dead and orgiastic excesses. But the outstanding difference is in religious atmosphere. Instead of the Karok priest's solitary pilgrimage, meditations, and prayers, we find a collective festival of the highest intensity. We need only think of the *milamala* festival of the Trobrianders, described by Malinowski. V. Lanternari has devoted

---

[8] Eliade, "Dimensions religieuses . . . ," pp. 261–262.
[9] Werner Müller, *Weltbild und Kult der Kwakiutl-Indianer* (Wiesbaden, 1955), p. 120.
[10] Werner Müller, *Die Religionen der Waldlandindianer Nordamerikas* (Berlin, 1956), pp. 306, 317.
[11] Werner Müller, *Die blaue Hütte. Zum Sinnbild der Perle bei nordamerikanischen Indianern* (Wiesbaden, 1954), p. 133.
[12] A. L. Kroeber, *Handbook of the Indians of California* (Washington, 1925), pp. 177, 498.

a whole book to a study of this mythico-ritual complex, and we, too, have
discussed it briefly in connection with the Melanesian prophetic cults.[13] There
is no need to give all the results of these studies here. We will only say that,
despite the differences between the mythico-ritual systems of the North American tribes cited above and those of the Melanesians, the structures of the two
systems can be homologized. In both cases the Cosmos must be periodically
re-created and the cosmogonic scenario through which the renewal is accomplished is related to the new harvest and the sacramentalization of food.

New Year and cosmogony in the ancient Near East

It is significant that similar ideas are found in the religions of the ancient Near
East, though of course with the inevitable differences between societies in the
pre- and protoagricultural stage and fully agricultural and urban societies, such
as Mesopotamia and Egypt. Yet one fact – and it seems to us an essential fact
– remains. The Egyptians, the Mesopotamians, the Jews, and other peoples
of the ancient Near East felt the need to renew the World periodically. The
renewal consisted in a cult scenario the chief rite of which symbolized the
reiteration of the cosmogony. The facts and their interpretation will be found
in the copious specialized literature on the subject[14] and in one chapter of
The Myth of the Eternal Return (pp. 51 ff.). However, we will repeat that in
Mesopotamia the Creation of the World was ritually reiterated during the New
Year festival (*akītu*). A series of rites re-enacted the fight between Marduk
and Tiamat (the Dragon symbolizing the primordial Ocean), the victory of
the God, and his cosmogonic labors. The "Poem of Creation" (*Enuma elish*)
was recited in the Temple. As H. Frankfort puts it, "each New Year shared
something essential with the first day when the world was created and the cycle
of the seasons started."[15] But examining the New Year rites more closely, we
realize that the Mesopotamians felt that the *beginning* was organically connected with an *end* that preceded it, that this "end" was of the same nature
as the "Chaos" preceding Creation, and that hence the end was indispensable
for every new beginning.

As we mentioned above, among the Egyptains too the New Year symbolized the Creation. As to the Jewish New Year scenario, Mowinckel writes that
"one of the chief ideas was the enthronement of Yahweh as king of the world,
the symbolic representation of His victory over His enemies, both the forces
of chaos and the historical enemies of Israel. The result of this victory was
the renewal of creation, election, and the covenant, ideas and rites from the

---

[13] Vittorio Lanternari, *La Grande Festa* (Milan, 1959); M. Eliade, "Dimensions religieuses du
renouvellement cosmique," pp. 243 ff.

[14] Cf. some bibliographical references in *The Myth of the Eternal Return*, p. 57, n. 7.

[15] H. Frankfort, op. cit., p. 319.

old fertility festivals which lay behind the historical festival."[16] Later, in the eschatology of the prophets, the restoration of Israel by Yahweh was taken to be a New Creation that implied a sort of return of Paradise.[17]

Obviously, the symbolic reiterations of the cosmogony at the New Year in Mesopotamia and in Israel cannot be put on the same plane. Among the Jews the archaic scenario of the periodic renewal of the World was progressively historicized, while still preserving something of its original meaning. Wensinck had shown that the New Year ritual scenario, which signified the passage from Chaos to Cosmos, was applied to such historical events as the exodus and the crossing of the Red Sea, the conquest of Canaan, the Babylonian captivity and the return from exile, etc.[18] Von Rad, for his part, proved that a single historical event, such as "the constitution of Israel at Mount Sinai through Yahweh and his servant Moses, when it becomes effective in the order of the people, does not have to remain in the sphere of remembrance through oral tradition or written narrative, but can be submitted to ritual renewal in a cult in the same manner as the cosmological order of the neighboring empires."[19] Eric Voegelin rightly stresses the fact that "the symbolic forms of the cosmological empires and of Israel are not mutually exclusive. . . . The ritual renewal of order, one of the symbolic elements developed within the cosmological civilizations, for instance, runs through the history of mankind from the Babylonian New Year festival, through Josiah's renewal of the Berith and the sacramental renewal of Christ, to Machiavelli's *ritornar ai principij*, because the fall from the order of being, and the return to it, is a fundamental problem in human existence."[20]

The "perfection of the beginnings"

Hence, however great the differences between the Mesopotamian and Jewish cult systems, they still obviously share a common hope for the annual or periodic regeneration of the World. In general, there is a belief in the possibility of recovering the absolute "beginning" – which implies the symbolic destruction and abolition of the old world. Hence the end is implied in the beginning and vice versa. There is nothing surprising in this, for the exemplary image of this beginning preceded and followed by an end is the Year, circular cosmic Time, as it can be perceived in the rhythm of the seasons and the regularity of celestial phenomena.

[16] S. Mowinckel, *He That Cometh*, trans. by G. W. Anderson (New York, 1956), p. 26.

[17] Ibid., p. 144.

[18] A. J. Wensinck, "The Semitic New Year and the Origin of Eschatology," *Acta Orientalia*, vol. I (1923), pp. 159–199.

[19] Von Rad, summarized in Eric Voegelin, *Order and History, I: Israel an Revelation* (Louisiana State University Press, 1956), p. 294.

[20] Ibid., p. 299.

But here a distinction must be made. If it is probable that the intuition of the "Year" as a cycle is at the bottom of the idea of a Cosmos that periodically renews itself, in the mythico-ritual New Year scenarios[21] another idea, an idea different in origin and structure, is discernible. It is the idea of the "perfection of the beginnings," the expression of a more intimate and deeper religious experience, nourished by the imaginary memory of a "Lost Paradise," of a state of bliss that preceded the present human condition. It is possible that the mythico-ritual New Year scenario has played such an important role in the history of humanity principally because, by ensuring renewal of the Cosmos, it also offered the hope that the bliss of the "beginnings" could be recovered. The image of the "Year-Circle" became charged with an ambivalent cosmico-vital symbolism, at once "optimistic" and "pessimistic." For the flux of Time implies an ever greater distance from the "beginnings," and hence loss of the original perfection. Whatever endures wastes away, degenerates, and finally perishes. Obviously, we here have a "vitalistic" expression of Reality; but it must not be forgotten that, for the primitive, being reveals itself – and expresses itself – in terms of life. Fullness and force are at the beginning; this is what we might call the "pessimism" inherent in the conception. But we must immediately add: fullness, though very quickly lost, is periodically recoverable. The Year has an end, that is to say, it is automatically followed by a new beginning.

The idea that perfection was at the beginning appears to be quite old. In any case, it is extremely widespread. Then too, it is an idea capable of being indefinitely reinterpreted and incorporated into an endless variety of religious conceptions. We shall have occasion to discuss some of these valuations. We may say at once that the idea of the perfection of the beginnings played an important role in the systematic elaboration of ever more embracing cosmic cycles. The ordinary "Year" was vastly extended by producing a "great Year" or cosmic cycle of incalculable duration. In proportion as the cosmic cycle became longer, the idea of the perfection of the beginnings tended to imply a complementary idea: that, *for something genuinely new to begin, the vestiges and ruins of the old cycle must be completely destroyed.* In other words, to obtain an *absolute* beginning, the end of a World must be total. Eschatology is only the prefiguration of a cosmogony to come. But every eschatology insists on this fact: the New Creation cannot take place before this world is abolished once and for all. There is no question of regenerating what has degenerated; nothing will serve but to destroy the old world so that it can be re-created *in toto*. The obsession with the bliss of the beginnings demands the destruction of all that has existed – and hence has degenerated – since the beginning of the World; there is no other way to restore the initial perfection.

To be sure, all these nostalgias and beliefs are already present in the mythico-ritual scenarios of the annual renewal of the World. But from the proto-

---

[21] As also, be it added, in countless other cosmogonic and origin myths.

agricultural stage of culture on, there was a growing acceptance of the idea that there are also *real* (not merely ritual) destructions and re-creations of the World, that there is a "return to the origin" in the literal sense, that is, a relapse of the Cosmos to the amorphous, chaotic state, followed by a new cosmogony.

This conception is best illustrated by the myths of the End of the World. We shall study them in the next chapter – not only for their intrinsic interest, but also because they can cast light on the function of myths in general. Until now we have dealt only with cosmogonic and origin myths, with myths telling *what has already taken place*. It is now time to see how the idea of the "perfection of the beginnings" was also projected into a timeless future. The myths of the End of the World have certainly played an important role in the history of mankind. They have shown that the "origin" is "movable." For, after a certain moment, the "origin" is no longer found only in a mythical past but also in a fabulous future. This, of course, is the conclusion that the Stoics and Neo-Pythagoreans reached by systematically elaborating the idea of "eternal return." But the notion of the "origin" is primarily bound up with the idea of perfection and bliss. So it is in conceptions of eschatology understood as a cosmogony of the future that we find the sources of all beliefs that proclaim the Age of Gold to be not merely (or no longer) in the past but also (or only) in the future.

Part V

APPLICATION OF THE THEORY TO LITERATURE

12

THE HERO OF TRADITION

Lord Raglan

The English folkorist Lord Raglan (1885–1964) extended Frazer's mythritualism to hero myths. Raglan employs the version of Frazer's myth-ritualism which centers on the king. Where Frazer identifies the king with the god of vegetation, Raglan in turn identifies the king with the hero. For Frazer, the king's willingness to die for the sake of the community may be heroic, but Raglan outright labels the king a hero. Frazer presents a simple pattern for the myth of the god of vegetation: the god dies and is reborn. Raglan works out a detailed pattern for the myth of the hero. By making the heart of hero myths not the gaining of the throne but the losing of it, Raglan is able to match the myth of the hero with the Frazerian ritual of the toppling of the king. The myth that Raglan links to ritual is not, then, that of the god but that of the hero. Raglan's hero myth pattern constitutes the myth-ritualist counterpart to Otto Rank's Freudian hero myth pattern (*The Myth of the Birth of the Hero* [1909, tr. 1914]) and Joseph Campbell's Jungian hero myth pattern (*The Hero with a Thousand Faces* [1949]). The following essay (from *Folk-Lore* 45 [1934] 212–31) is Raglan's first presentation of his hero myth pattern and is incorporated in his best-known book, *The Hero* (London: Methuen, 1936), chs 16–17. Raglan does not limit myth-ritualism to hero myths and insist that all myths are connected to rituals. See also his *Jocasta's Crime* (London: Methuen, 1933); *Death and Rebirth* (London: Watts, 1945); *The Origins of Religion* (London: Watts, 1949), esp. chs 9–10; and "Myth and Ritual," *Journal of American Folklore* 68 (1955), 454–61. On Raglan see William Bascom, "The Myth-Ritual Theory," *Journal of American Folklore* 70 (1957), 103–14; Joseph Fontenrose, *The Ritual Theory of Myth* (Berkeley: University of California Press, 1966), ch. 1; Victor Cook, "Lord Raglan's Hero – A Cross Cultural Critique," *Florida Anthropologist* 18 (1965), 147–54; Francis Lee Utley, *Lincoln Wasn't There, or Lord Raglan's Hero*, CEA Chap Book

Original publication: Lord Raglan, "The Hero of Tradition," *Folk-Lore* 45 (1934), pp. 212–31.

(Washington, DC: College English Association, 1965); and my introduction to Otto Rank et al., *In Quest of the Hero* (Princeton: Princeton University Press, 1990), esp. xi–xii, xxiii–xxvi.

Some years ago I had occasion to study the story of Oedipus, and to try to analyse it. I was struck by the fact that a number of the incidents of the story were remarkably similar to incidents in the stories of Theseus and Romulus. I then studied the stories of a number of other Greek traditional heroes, and found that when these stories were divided into separate incidents there were certain types of incidents which ran through all, or most, of the stories.

Whether these parallels have any significance, or whether they are merely accidental coincidences, or the kind of things that might happen to any hero, is a question to which we shall come later. My first task is to show that these parallels exist, and for that purpose it is necessary to tabulate and number them. What I have done is to take a dozen heroes whose stories are narrated in sufficient detail, to tabulate the incidents in their careers, and to take as typical those incidents which occur in the majority of the stories. Some of these incidents are miraculous, while others might seem insignificant, but everything that seemed to me to be part of the pattern, for I have been convinced that there is a pattern, has been included. Having arrived at this pattern, I then tried it on heroes from outside the classical world, and I hope that the results will seem as striking to you as they have done to me. The pattern is as follows:

Story of the Hero of Tradition

1. His mother is a royal virgin.
2. His father is a king, and
3. Often a near relative of his mother, but
4. The circumstances of his conception are unusual, and
5. He is also reputed to be the son of a god.
6. At birth an attempt is made, often by his father, to kill him, but
7. He is spirited away, and
8. Reared by foster-parents in a far county.
9. We are told nothing of his childhood, but
10. On reaching manhood he returns or goes to his future kingdom.
11. After a victory over the king and/or a giant, dragon or wild beast,
12. He marries a princess, often the daughter of his predecessor, and
13. Becomes king.
14. For a time he reigns uneventfully, and
15. Prescribes laws, but
16. Later he loses favour with the gods and/or his subjects, and

17 Is driven from the throne and city.
18 He meets with a mysterious death,
19 Often at the top of a hill.
20 His children, if any, do not succeed him.
21 His body is not buried, but nevertheless
22 He has one or more holy sepulchres.

Oedipus

His mother Jocasta is (1) a princess, and his father is (2) King Laius, who has sworn to have no connection with her but (4) does so when drunk, probably (5) in the character of Dionysus. Laius (6) tries to kill him, but (7) he is spirited away, and (8) reared by the king of Corinth. (9) We hear nothing of his childhood, but (10) on reaching manhood he returns to Thebes, gaining (11) victories over his father and the Sphinx. He (12) marries Jocasta and (13) becomes king. (14) For some years he reigns uneventfully, but (16) later comes to be regarded as the cause of a plague, and (17) is deposed and driven into exile. He meets with (18) a mysterious death at (19) a place near Athens called the Steep Pavement. (20) He is succeeded by Creon, by whose means he was deposed, and (21) though the place of his burial is uncertain, he has (22) several holy sepulchres.

He scores twenty points out of twenty-two.

Theseus

His mother, Aethra, is (1) a royal virgin, and his father is (2) King Aegeus, who is induced (4) to have intercourse with her by a trick. He is also (5) reputed to be the son of Poseidon. At birth he is (6) hidden from the Pallantidae, who wish to kill him, and (8) reared by his maternal grandfather. We hear (9) nothing of his childhood, but (10) on reaching manhood he proceeds to Athens, (11) killing monsters on the way. He marries (12) two heiress princesses in succession, but (13) succeeds his father, whose death (11) he causes. For a time (14) he reigns peacefully, and (15) prescribes laws, but (16) later becomes unpopular, is (17) driven from Athens, and (18) thrown or falls from (19) a high cliff by order of (20) Menestheus, his successor, who is no relation. His burial place is unknown (21) but bones alleged to be his are (22) laid in a holy sepulchre at Athens.

He scores twenty.

Romulus

His mother, Rhea, is (1) a royal virgin, and his father is (2) King Amulius, who is (3) her uncle, and (4) visits her in armour. He is also (5) reputed to be the son of Mars. At birth (6) his father tries to kill him, but (7) he is wafted away, and (8) he is brought up by foster-parents at a distance. On reaching manhood he (10) returns to his birthplace, and having (11) killed his father and gained a magical victory over his brother, (12) founds Rome and becomes king. His marriage is uncertain, and he is said to have performed some feats after his accession, but he (15) prescribes laws, and (16) later becomes unpopular. Leaving the city (17) after his deposition had been decided upon, he was (18) carried to the sky in a chariot of fire. His successor was a stranger (20). His body not having been found (21), he was worshipped in a Temple.

We can give him seventeen points.

Heracles

His mother, Alemene, is (1) a royal virgin. Her husband is (2) King Amphitryon, who is (3) her first cousin, but Heracles is reputed to be (5) the son of Zeus, who (4) visited her in the guise of Amphitryon. At his birth (6) Hera tries to kill him. On reaching manhood he (11) performs feats and wins victories, after which he proceeds (10) to Calydon, where he marries (12) the king's daughter, and (13) becomes ruler. (14) He remains there quietly for some years, after which an accidental manslaughter compels him (17) to flee from the country. He disappears from a funeral pyre (18), on the top of Mt. Oeta (19). His sons do not succeed him (20). His body is not found (21) and he is worshipped in temples.

He scores seventeen points.

Perseus

His mother, Danae, is (1) a royal virgin, and his father is (5) Zeus, who visits her in a shower of gold. His grandfather (6) tries to kill him at birth, but (7) he is wafted away and (8) reared by the King of Seriphos. We are told (9) nothing of his childhood, but on reaching manhood he overcomes monsters and returns to his birthplace (10), where he kills his father (11) or uncle, marries a princess (12) and (13) becomes king in his place. (14) We hear nothing of his reign, and his end is variously related (18), though in one version he is killed by his successor. His children do not succeed him (20). His burial place is unknown (21) but (22) he is worshipped at shrines.

He scores sixteen points.

Jason

His mother, name uncertain, is (1) a princess, and his father is (2) King Aeson. His uncle Pelias (6) tries to kill him at birth, but (7) he is spirited away, and (8) brought up elsewhere by Chiron. We hear nothing (9) of his childhood, but on reaching manhood he makes a journey in which he (11) wins the Golden Fleece, marries (12) a princess, kills (11) his uncle, and (13) becomes king. He is (17) driven from the throne and city. His death is (18) obscure, and his children (20) do not succeed him. His burial place (21) is unknown, but he has several shrines (22).

He scores fourteen points.

Bellerophon

His mother, Eurymede, is (1) a princess, and his father is (2) King Glaucus, but he is also (5) reputed to be the son of Poseidon. We hear (9) nothing of his childhood, but on reaching manhood he (10) travels to his future kingdom, (11) overcomes a monster, (12) marries the king's daughter and (13) becomes king. (14) We hear nothing of his reign, but later he (16) becomes hated by the gods, and (17) goes into exile. His fate is (18) obscure, though it includes (19) an attempted ascent to the sky. His children (20) do not succeed him, his burial place (21) is unknown, but (22) he was worshipped at Corinth.

He scores sixteen points.

Pelops

His mother, Dione, is (1) a goddess and his father is King Tantalus (2), but he is also reputed to be the son of (5) Poseidon. His father (6) kills and cooks him, but the gods restore him to life. We hear nothing (9) of his childhood, but (10) on reaching manhood he journeys to his future kingdom, (11) defeats and kills the king, (12) marries his daughter, and (13) becomes king. We hear (14) very little of his actions when king, except that (15) he regulates the Olympic Games. We are not told (18) about his death, but (20) his children do not succeed him, and (22) he has a holy sepulchre at Olympia.

He scores fourteen points.

Asclepius

His mother, Coronis, is (1) a royal virgin, and his father is (5) Apollo, who (6) nearly kills him at birth. He is (7) spirited away, and (8) reared by Chiron at a distance. On reaching manhood (11) he overcomes death, becomes a man of power (13) and (15) prescribes the laws of medicine, but (16) incurs the enmity of Zeus, who (18) destroys him with a flash of lightning. His burial place is unknown (21) but he has a number of alleged tombs (22).

He scores at least twelve points.

Dionysus

His mother, Semele, is (1) a royal virgin, and his father is (5) Zeus, who (3) was Semele's uncle by marriage, and who visits her (4) in a thunderstorm. Hera (6) tries to kill him at birth, but he is (7) miraculously saved, and (8) brought up in a remote spot. We hear (9) nothing of his childhood, but on reaching manhood he (10) travels into Asia, (11) gains victories, and becomes a ruler (13). For a time (14) he rules prosperously, and prescribes (15) laws of agriculture, etc., but later (17) is carried into exile. He (18) goes down to the dead, but later (19) ascends Olympus. He seems (20) to have no children. He had no burial place (21), but numerous shrines and temples (22).

We can give him nineteen points.

Apollo

His mother, Leto, is (1) a royal virgin, and his father is (5) Zeus, who is (3) her first cousin. At birth he is (6) in dangèr from Hera, but his mother (7) escapes with him, and (8) he is reared at Delos. We hear nothing (9) of his childhood, but on reaching manhood he (10) goes to Delphi, where he kills the Python (11), becomes king (13) and prescribes (15) the laws of music etc.

We hear no more, but he has scored eleven points.

Zeus

Is the son of Rhea and Cronus, who are goddess and god (1 and 5) and also brother and sister (3). At birth (6) his father tries to kill him, but (7) he is spirited away, and (8) reared in Crete. We hear nothing (9) of his childhood, but on reaching manhood he sets forth (10) for Olympus, (11) defeats the Titans, (12) marries his sister, and (13) becomes king in succession to his father. He reigns supreme (14), and prescribes laws (15). Nevertheless he has a holy sepulchre in Crete (22), and hilltops are particularly sacred to him (19). He scores fifteen points.

Joseph

His mother, Rachel, is (1) the daughter of a patriarch, and his father, Jacob, is (2) a patriarch and (3) her first cousin. His mother conceives him (4) by eating mandrakes. In his childhood his brothers (6) attempt to kill him, but he is saved by a stratagem (7), and reared (8) in Egypt. On reaching manhood he is the victor in a contest in dream-interpretation and weather forecasting (11), is married to a lady of high rank (12), and becomes (13) ruler of Egypt. He reigns prosperously (14) and prescribes laws (15), but we are told nothing of the latter part of his life.

He has scored twelve points.

Moses

His parents (1 and 2) were of the principal family of the Levites, and (3) near relatives. He was also (5) reputed to be the son of Pharaoh's daughter. Pharaoh (6) attempts to kill him at birth, but (7) he is wafted away, and (8) reared secretly. We are told (9) nothing of his childhood, but on reaching manhood he kills a man (11) and goes to Midian (10), where (12) he marries the ruler's daughter. Returning to Egypt, he gains (11) a series of magical victories over Pharaoh, after which he becomes a ruler (13). For a time his rule (14) is successful and he prescribes laws (15), but later he loses (16) the favour of Jehovah, is deposed (17) from his leadership, and (18) disappears mysteriously from (19) the top of a mountain. His children (20) do not succeed him. He has no burial place (21), but nevertheless has a holy sepulchre (22).

He scores twenty-one points.

Elijah

After (11) a victory in a rainmaking contest, he becomes a sort of dictator (13). After a period of success (14) there is a plot (16) against him. He flees to

Beersheba (17), and later (18) disappears mysteriously. His successor, Elisha, (20) is no relation. (21) Though not buried, he has (22) a holy sepulchre.

We do not know the circumstances of his birth, but we can give him nine points.

Sigurd or Siegfried

His mother, Sieglinde, is (1) a princess, and his father (2) King Siegmund, who is her brother (3), and whom she visits (4) in the guise of another woman. On reaching manhood he (11) kills a dragon, (12) marries a princess, and (13) becomes a ruler. For a time (14) he prospers, but later (16) there is a plot against him and he is killed.

He scores nine only, but I believe the whole story is there and has been cut up.

Arthur

His mother, Igraine, is (1) a princess, and her husband is (2) the Duke of Cornwall. He is, however, reputed to be (5) the son of Uther Pendragon, who (4) visited Igraine in the Duke's likeness. At birth he is apparently in no danger, but nevertheless is (7) spirited away, and (8) reared in a distant part of the country. We hear (9) nothing of his childhood, but (10) on reaching manhood he travels to London, wins (11) a magical victory, and is (13) chosen king. After other victories he marries Guenever (12), the heiress of the Round Table. After this he reigns (14) uneventfully, but later (17) goes abroad, and is (16) dethroned in his absence. (18) He meets with a mysterious death. His children (20) do not succeed him.

He scores sixteen points.

Nyikang

Nyikang is the traditional hero of the Shilluk of the White Nile, and his story conforms in some respects to the type. He is the son of (2) a king and (1) his mother Nyikaia was apparently a crocodile princess.

We hear nothing (9) of his childhood, but on reaching manhood his brother defeats him and threatens his life, whereupon he goes to (10) another country, and (12) marries a king's daughter. After (11) a number of victories, magical and actual, he becomes king. For a time he reigns prosperously (14), and (15) prescribes laws, but at last the people began to complain against him (16). Distressed at this (18) he disappears mysteriously. His body was not buried (21), but nevertheless he has (22) a holy sepulchre.

He scores twelve points.

The fact that the life of a hero of tradition can be divided up into a large number of incidents – I have taken twenty-two, but one could easily make it more – has suggested to me that the story of the hero of tradition is the story, not of real incidents in the life of a real man, but of ritual incidents in the career of a ritual personage. It does not necessarily follow from this that none of the heroes whom I have cited had any real existence, but it does, I think, follow that if they really did exist their activities were largely of a ritual character, or else that their stories were altered to make them conform to type.

I shall have something more to say about that later; what I propose to do now is to go through these incidents – what I regard as these typical incidents – in the life of the hero of tradition, and make some suggestions as to their significance.

The first point that we note is that the incidents fall definitely into three groups – those connected with the hero's birth, those connected with his accession to the throne, and those connected with his death. They correspond, that is to say, with the three principal *rites de passage*, that is to say the rites at birth, initiation and death. I shall have more to say on this when we reach point 9; now I will start at the beginning.

The first fact we note is that, except in the case of Moses, for whom there were no actual royalties available, the hero is always the son of royal parents; that in nearly every case he is the first child of his mother, and, except where his father is a god, of his father, and that with very few exceptions his father never marries twice. There is, of course, nothing very wonderful in all this – many kings have been the eldest child of monogamous parents – but I have laid stress on it because it seems definitely to be part of the pattern. There is a type of folk tale in which the hero, though he wins a princess and a throne, is of humble birth, but I suspect this of being a derived form, in which merely the central group of incidents is narrated, and in which the hero's birth therefore becomes unimportant.

The fact that in many cases the hero's parents are near relatives brings to mind the widespread custom by which kings marry their sisters, and with which I have dealt elsewhere.

The circumstances in which our hero is begotten are very puzzling. When, as in the case of Heracles, a god takes the form of the hero's father, we are reminded that the Pharaoh, on particular occasions, approached his queen in the guise of a god. In our stories however, the disguises assumed by the god are extremely varied. He may appear as a thunderstorm, a swan, or a shower of gold. We may conclude that the attribution of divine descent to a hero has nothing to do with his heroism, but is associated with the ritual union of a princess to her own husband, disguised as a god. It is not at all clear how a man disguised himself as a shower of gold; one can guess at the explanation, i.e., that in a darkened room the sunlight was allowed to fall on him alone, but this is merely a guess.

We now come to the attempt on the hero's life at birth, which happens in almost every case, and is quite clearly part of the pattern. We are all familiar with such rites as the Phoenician one, by which the eldest son was burnt as a sacrifice to Moloch. In our stories, it would seem, a pretence is made of sacrificing the child, and in some cases an animal is sacrificed instead. It is often the father who tries to kill the infant hero, and this fact brings the stories into line with that of Abraham and Isaac. The attempt on the life of Moses, like that on the other heroes, was made at birth, but the story of Abraham and Isaac suggests that at one period the Hebrews performed this rite at puberty. We may note that while a ram was sacrificed in place of Isaac, Jacob appeared before his father wearing the skin of kid, and Joseph wore a special garment which was soaked in goat's blood. We may perhaps suppose that a pretence was made of killing the child, which was wrapped in the skin of a sacrificed goat and soaked in its blood. Such a rite accounts for some of our stories, such as that of Pelops, and also for the widespread story of the Faithful Hound. In the case of Romulus, Moses and Perseus, however, as in the Japanese myth, the infant hero is set afloat. We must suppose that the pretence sacrifice took various forms, but that it was normally the father who performed the rite.

Having suffered a pretence death, our heroes are all removed to a distance and brought up either by another king, or in the cases of Jason and Asclepius, by Chiron. The latter is easy to understand, if we may suppose that Chiron was a title given to a prince's official tutor, but in most cases the foster-father is the king of another country or city. This suggests several possibilities. The first is that it was actually the practice for kings to send their sons to be brought up by other kings, as we read of in the story of Hakon Adalstein's fostri. The second, which I have put forward elsewhere, but which I am by no means confident about, is that princes succeeded their fathers-in-law, but became their sons by formal adoption. This might necessitate a pretence that they had been removed at birth. The third is the opposite of the second. It is that in theory princes could not succeed their fathers, but in practice did so, but were reared at a distance from the capital, and represented to be foreigners. The question requires much more investigation than I have been able to give it.

We next come to point No. 9, that we are told nothing of the hero's childhood. This may seem unimportant, since there are, of course, many great men of whose childhood we know nothing. In such cases, however, we equally know nothing of the circumstances of their birth. We may know the place and date, but that is all. With our heroes it is quite different. Their birth is the central feature in a series of highly dramatic incidents; incidents which are related in considerable detail, and such incidents as seldom, if ever, occur in the lives of real people. The most surprising things happen to our hero at birth; the most surprising things happen to him as soon as he reaches manhood, but in the meanwhile nothing happens to him at all. If, as I suppose, our hero is a figure, not of history, but of ritual, this is just what one would expect, since as a general rule children take no part in ritual between the rites at their birth and those at puberty or initiation. The story of the hero of tradition, if I understand it aright, is the story of his ritual progress, and it is therefore appropriate that those parts of his career in which he makes no ritual progress should be left blank. I would compare the blank which occurs during his childhood with the blank which usually occurs after his installation as king is complete.

The fact that on reaching manhood the hero sets out forthwith on a journey from the land of his upbringing to the land where he will reign is of course involved in the problem which I have discussed under point 8. It is, however, a remarkable fact that the hero's victories almost always take place either on the journey to which I have alluded or else immediately on arrival at his destination. He makes a definite progress from a foreign country to the throne, and all his feats and victories are connected with that progress.

This brings us to the hero's victories, and I wish to emphasise the point which I have just mentioned, namely that the victories of the hero of tradition, unlike those of the hero-king of history, always take place before his accession to the throne. Another remarkable fact is that the hero of tradition never wins a battle. It is very rarely that he is represented as having any army at all, and when he has one he never seems to train it or direct it in any way. In history the king as warrior means the king as commander, and this applies to savages as well as to the civilised. When we think of the great victors of history we think of serried ranks, of the Argyraspides, of the Tenth Legion, and so on. But the hero of tradition is never a commander. All his victories, when they are actual fights and not merely magical contests, are single combats against other kings, or against giants, dragons or especially noted wild animals. He never fights with ordinary men, or even with ordinary animals. And the king with whom he fights is the king whom he will succeed; in the case of Oedipus and Romulus his own father, and in other cases his future father-in-law. It is also possible that the giant or monster with whom the hero fights is merely the reigning king in disguise, or in other words that the reigning king had to wear a particular costume or mask in which to defend his title and his life. I will touch on this later, but will first pass on to the magical contest, which seems sometimes to be more important than the actual fight. Oedipus wins his throne by guessing a riddle; Theseus by escaping from a maze. The magical victories of the three Jewish heroes are all connected with rain-making. Joseph successfully prognosticates the weather; Moses is successful in a series of magical contests in which rain-making is included, and Elijah defeats the prophets of Baal in a rain-making contest. Power over the elements is the most unvarying characteristic of the divine king, and it would seem that in many cases the candidate for the throne had to pass in a rain-making test.

Our hero, then, has to qualify for the throne in two ways. He must pass an examination in such subjects as rain-making and riddle-guessing, and he must win a victory over the reigning king. Whether this was a real fight or a mock contest in which the conclusion was foregone we cannot be certain. There have undoubtedly been many cases in which the king was put to death at the end of a fixed term, or when his powers began to wane. There may have been cases in which there was a fair fight with equal weapons between the king and his challenger, but the evidence for them is rather uncertain. What several of the stories suggest is that the old king was ritually killed, and that his successor had to kill an animal – wolf, boar or snake, into which his spirit was supposed to have entered.

After passing his tests and winning his victories the hero marries the daughter, or widow, of his predecessor, and becomes king. It has often been assumed from this that the throne always went in the female line, and that the reigning queen, or heiress princess, as the case might be, could confer it upon her husband simply by marrying him; in other words that any man who managed to marry the queen became king automatically, whatever his antecedents, and that the only way in which any man could lawfully become king was by marrying the queen. Such an assumption is going a great deal beyond the evidence of the stories, which suggest that the new king established his claim to the throne by his pedigree, his upbringing and his victories. There were, it would seem, recognised qualifications for the kingship, just as there were recognised qualifications for the queenship. We do not know for certain that the new queen was really the old king's daughter, any more than we know for certain that the new king was really the old king's son. There may have been a ceremony of adoption in both cases. Anyhow the fact that our hero marries a princess and at the same time ascends the throne is far from proving that he ascends the throne in virtue of his marriage. It may merely indicate what we know from other sources to be a fact, namely that a *hieros gamos* normally formed an essential and highly important feature of the coronation or installation ceremony. I know of no case, in any age or in any country, in which a man has become king simply by marrying the queen; he must, so far as I can learn, always first have qualified for the throne, either by birth or by performing some feat or passing some test. Our heroes seem all to have qualified in all these ways. Even to-day in Europe marriage never confers the right to a throne. Princes or princesses who marry unqualified persons, who contract, that is to say, what are called morganatic marriages, not merely fail to raise their partners to the throne but lose their own right to it. It is difficult to believe that the rules were less strict in ages in which the ritual functions of the king and queen were far more important than they are to-day. Our hero, then, as part of his installation ritual, marries the daughter, or widow, of his predecessor. And what does he do then? It might be supposed that, having shown himself so brave and enterprising before coming to the throne, he would forthwith embark upon a career of conquest, found an empire and a dynasty, build temples and palaces, possess a large harem, and behave generally as the conquerors of history have behaved, or attempted to behave. The hero of tradition, however, in this as in all other respects, is totally unlike the hero of history.

He never goes to war, never extends the boundaries of his kingdom, never builds anything. In fact he does nothing at all. The only memorial of his reign, apart from the traditional story of the events which begin and end it, is the traditional code of laws which is often attributed to him. As a fact, however, a code of laws is always the product of hundreds or thousands of years of gradual development, and is never in any sense the work of one man. One man, a Justinian or a Napoleon, may cause laws to be codified, or alter their incidence, but it has never been suggested that all, or even any, of the laws in such codes were devised by the monarchs in question. It is well known, in fact, that they were not. On the other hand it has been clearly shown by Sir James Frazer that the Ten Commandments, in their familiar form, could have had nothing to do with Moses, since the original Ten Commandments, whoever first wrote them down, were entirely different. It seems clear, then, that the attribution of laws to a hero of tradition is merely a way of saying that they are very old and sacred. We next come to the important fact that the hero of tradition, unlike the hero of the fairy tale and many heroes of history, ends his career by being deposed, driven from his kingdom, and mysteriously put to death. This happens to the majority of our heroes, and when it does not their end is usually left uncertain. Even in the case of Joseph we are told of nothing that happened between his father's death and his own. We may conclude that deposition and mysterious death is the normal fate of a hero of tradition. There is one very puzzling feature, however, which is that the hero is never actually defeated in a fight. As he has gained the throne by winning a fight, one might expect that he would lose it by losing a fight, but this he never does.

Oedipus kills his father and marries his mother; one might expect that one of his sons, or some other prince, would kill him and marry Jocasta, or if she were too old Antigone, and become king. Creon, however, who succeeds him, does so by turning the oracle against him, and we find in several other cases that the hero falls out with a god and of course gets the worst of it. Perhaps the explanation is that when he began to grow old, or his tenure of the kingship, which Sir James Frazer puts at eight years in prehistoric Greece, had expired, there was a magical contest in which he was foredoomed to defeat. It is to be noted that the hero's fall from favour is sudden and not gradual; at one moment he is apparently at the height of his power and popularity and at the next moment both gods and men are against him.

The next point to note is that the heroes I have cited never meet their fate inside their cities. In many cases they are actually deposed and driven out, in others they have left it on some sacred mission. Then there is the hill-top, which appears in the stories of Oedipus, Theseus, Heracles, Bellerophon, Dionysus and Moses. Taken in conjunction with the chariot of fire in which Romulus and Elijah disappear, and the lightning-flash which kills Asclepius, we may conclude that in the most usual form of the rite the divine king was burned, either alive or dead, on a pyre erected on top of a hill, and that he was believed to ascend to the sky, in some form or other, in the smoke and flame. In that case it is clear that the person or animal defeated and killed by his successor could not have been himself, but must have been an assumed reincarnation.

The fact that the hero is very seldom succeeded by his son might be explained by supposing that the descent went in the female line. In that case he would be succeeded by his daughter, but he is not. If the king reigned for eight or nine years only, and married at his coronation, it would obviously be impossible for his children to succeed him, since they would be too young, but they might succeed his successor, and this is what seems sometimes to have happened. The story of Creon is not easy to follow, but he seems to have preceded and succeeded Oedipus, and also to have succeeded his sons. Perseus is said to have killed and succeeded Proetus, and to have been killed and succeeded by his son. Aegisthus kills and succeeds Agamemnon, and eight years later Orestes kills and succeeds Aegisthus. There are similar incidents in the stories of Theseus and Jason. There were two ruling families at Sparta, each of which found one of the two kings, and it seems possible that in prehistoric times each city had two ruling families which produced a king alternately.

The last point in the hero's career is that although he is usually supposed to have vanished mysteriously, yet nevertheless he has a holy sepulchre, if not several. I have attempted to explain this vanishing as being cremation, but if kings were cremated, they could hardly have a sepulchre or burial-place in the usual sense of the term, for we know that in all forms of religion the essential feature of a sepulchre, or shrine, is that it is supposed to contain the bones, or at any rate some of the bones, of the holy person to whom it is dedicated. A great deal has of course been written on the customs of the Greeks with regard to the disposal of the dead and their beliefs as to the other world, but I am here concerned chiefly to consider the existence, or possible existence, of rites in connection with the hero stories, and what they suggest to me, that while ordinary people were buried, the bodies of kings were burnt, but not burnt thoroughly, so that the bones were left, and could be buried. I believe that this view was put forward, though on different grounds, by Dorpfeld some thirty years ago, though I have not seen what he wrote. Anyhow similar customs are found in various parts of the world.

I have, I hope, now convinced you that the parallels between the stories of the various heroes of tradition are too numerous to be mere coincidences; and that they can be explained as incidents in ritual. Are we to conclude that all these heroes are mythical? In my own opinion most of them at any rate are purely mythical, but I have arrived at this opinion on somewhat different grounds. It by no means necessarily follows from the facts which I have just put before you. When we are told that Alexander the Great was the son of Zeus, who approached his mother in the form of a serpent, we do not conclude that he was mythical, nor when we read in Herodotus that the maternal grandfather of Cyrus ordered him to be killed at birth, do we conclude that Cyrus was mythical. What we conclude, at least I do, is that the pattern career for a hero was generally known, and that either from flattery, or from a genuine belief that the career of a hero must conform to type, mythical incidents were introduced into the story of genuinely historical heroes. It follows from this, however, that the earlier heroes must have been mythical, else the mythical type could not have arisen. The only possible alternative, and one that seems to me highly improbable, is that Oedipus was a really historical character, who killed his father, married his mother, and so on, but did it all as part of a fixed ritual.

As for the Freudian explanation, it is to say the least inadequate, since it only takes into account two incidents out of at least twenty-two, and we find that the rest of the story is the same whether the hero marries his mother, his sister or his first cousin.

The fault to which we are all of us liable, but which I have done my best to avoid, is to concentrate on one particular incident or one particular aspect, and to disregard everything else. This is what has been done by many classical scholars. Brought up on Homer and the Attic dramatists, they tend to concentrate not on what the heroes of tradition are actually alleged to have done, but on the words which the poets have put into their mouths. On these they base character studies of the heroes, oblivious of the fact that the whole art of the great poets lay in putting new words into the mouths of old characters. The fact is, I am afraid, that classical scholars as a whole are romantically rather than scientifically minded. The reading of the *Iliad* or of the *Seven Against Thebes* fills them with emotion, but they are unwilling to admit that it is emotion of exactly the same type as that experienced by the small boy who reads *Treasure Island*, and therefore they conceal it under a veil of pseudo-history. This veil takes the form of a belief in a "Heroic Age", in which, apparently, the principal features of life were single combats, elopements and dragons. In my view it is just as reasonable to suppose that there was once a "Comic Age" in which life consisted of backchat and disguises, and a "Tragic Age", in which lovers always came to an untimely end. Our knowledge of all three is derived from the poets, and the poets are not interested in historical truth. Very few people are. It is always assumed by historians that people prefer fact to fiction, but they need only go as far as the nearest lending library to find out that there is not the slightest foundation for this assumption. Homer is read, not because his readers are eager for historical accuracy, but because he wrote good stories, and he will still be read when it has come to be generally realised that these stories have not the slightest historical foundation.

13

FROM RITUAL TO ROMANCE

Jessie L. Weston

Jessie L. Weston (1850–1928) was an English expert on the Arthurian legends who late in life embraced Frazer's myth-ritualism and applied it to the Grail legend. In *From Ritual to Romance* (Cambridge: Cambridge University Press, 1920), from which the following selection (ch. 5) is taken, she argues that the roots of the Grail legend are neither Celtic nor Christian – the conventional alternatives – but primitive. Following Frazer, Weston assumes that for ancients and primitives the fertility of the land depends on the fertility of their king, in whom resides the god of vegetation. For Frazer, the key primitive ritual is the sacrifice of an ailing king. For Weston, however, the aim of the Grail quest is the rejuvenation of the king – an irenic view of myth-ritualism found also in James, among other Frazerians. The myth enacted by the ritual is that of the death – or sickness – and rejuvenation of the god of vegetation. While Weston never specifies how the ritual manages to revive the king, her linkage of ritual to king to god to vegetation is consummately Frazerian. At the same time, she adds an ethereal, spiritual side to the quest which transcends Frazer. The aim of the quest turns out to be mystical oneness with god as well as food from god. It is this spiritual dimension of the legend that inspired T. S. Eliot to use Weston in "The Waste Land." Like other literary myth-ritualists, Weston is not reducing the Grail legend to primitive myth and ritual but only tracing the legend back to primitive myth and ritual. The legend itself is literature, not myth. On Weston see Stanley Edgar Hyman, "Jessie Weston and the Forest of Broceliande," *Centennial Review* 9 (1966), 509–21; and my foreword to a reprint of *From Ritual to Romance* (Princeton: Princeton University Press, 1993), xix–xxxv.

Original publication: Jessie L. Weston, *From Ritual to Romance* (Cambridge: Cambridge University Press, 1920), ch. 5 (pp. 52–64).

Medieval and Modern Forms of Nature Ritual

Readers of the foregoing pages may, not improbably, object that, while we have instanced certain curious and isolated parallels from early Aryan literature and tradition, and, what, from the point of view of declared intention, appears to be a kindred group of religious belief and practice in pre-Historic and Classical times, the two, so far, show no direct signs of affiliation, while both may be held to be far removed, in point of date, alike from one another, and from the romantic literature of the twelfth century.

This objection is sound in itself, but if we can show by modern parallels that the ideas which took form and shape in early Aryan Drama, and Babylonian and Classic Ritual, not only survive to our day, but are found in combination with features corresponding minutely with details recorded in early Aryan literature, we may hold the gulf to be bridged, and the common origin, and close relationship, of the different stages to be an ascertained fact. At the outset, and before examining the evidence collected by scholars, I would remind my readers that the modern Greeks have retained, in many instances under changed names, no inconsiderable portion of their ancient mythological beliefs, among them the "Adonis" celebrations; the "Gardens of Adonis" blossom and fade to-day, as they did many centuries ago, and I have myself spoken with a scholar who has seen "women, at the door of their houses, weeping for Adonis."[1]

For evidence of the widespread character of Medieval and Modern survivals we have only to consult the epoch-making works of Mannhardt, *Wald und Feld-Kulte*, and Frazer, *The Golden Bough*;[2] in the pages of these volumes we shall find more than sufficient for our purpose. From the wealth of illustration with which these works abound I have selected merely such instances as seem to apply more directly to the subject of our investigation.[3]

Thus, in many places, it is still the custom to carry a figure representing the Vegetation Spirit on a bier, attended by mourning women, and either bury the figure, throw it into water (as a rain charm), or, after a mock death, carry the revivified Deity, with rejoicing, back to the town. Thus in the Lechrain a man in black women's clothes is borne on a bier, followed by men dressed as professional women mourners making lamentation, thrown on the village dung-heap, drenched with water, and buried in straw.[4]

---

[1] *Ancient Greek Religion, and Modern Greek Folk-Lore*, J. C. Lawson, gives some most interesting evidence as to modern survivals of mythological beliefs.

[2] *Wald und Feld-Kulte*, 2nd edition, 2 vols, Berlin, 1904. Cf. vol. II. p. 286. *The Golden Bough*, 3rd edition, 5 vols.

[3] I cite from Mannhardt, as the two works overlap in the particular line of research we are following: the same instances are given in both, but the honour of priority belongs to the German scholar.

[4] Op. cit. vol. I. p. 411.

In Russia the Vegetation or Year Spirit is known as Yarilo,[5] and is represented by a doll with phallic attributes, which is enclosed in a coffin, and carried through the streets to the accompaniment of lamentation by women whose emotions have been excited by drink. Mannhardt gives the lament as follows: "Wessen war Er schuldig? Er war so gut! Er wird nicht mehr aufstehen! O! Wie sollen wir uns von Dir trennen? Was ist das Leben wenn Du nicht mehr da bist? Erhebe Dich, wenn auch nur auf ein Stündchen! Aber Er steht nicht auf, Er steht nicht auf!"[6]

In other forms of the ritual, we find distinct traces of the resuscitation of the Vegetation Deity, occasionally accompanied by evidence of rejuvenation. Thus, in Lausitz, on Laetare Sunday (the 4th Sunday in Lent), women with mourning veils carry a straw figure, dressed in a man's shirt, to the bounds of the next village, where they tear the effigy to pieces, hang the shirt on a young and flourishing tree, "schöne Wald-Baum," which they proceed to cut down, and carry home with every sign of rejoicing. Here evidently the young tree is regarded as a rejuvenation of the person represented in the first instance by the straw figure.[7]

In many parts of Europe to-day the corresponding ceremonies, very generally held at Whitsuntide, include the mock execution of the individual representing the Vegetation Spirit, frequently known as the King of the May. In Bohemia the person playing the rôle of the King is, with his attendants, dressed in bark, and decked with garlands of flowers; at the conclusion of the ceremonies the King is allowed a short start, and is then pursued by the armed attendants. If he is not overtaken he holds office for a year, but if overtaken, he suffers a mock decapitation, head-dress, or crown, being struck off, and the pretended corpse is then borne on a bier to the next village.[8]

Mannhardt, discussing this point, remarks that in the mock execution we must recognize "Ein verbreiteter und jedenfalls uralter Gebrauch." He enumerates the various modes of death, shooting, stabbing (in the latter case a bladder filled with blood, and concealed under the clothes, is pierced); in Bohemia, decapitation, occasionally drowning (which primarily represents a rain charm), is the form adopted.[9] He then goes on to remark that this ceremonial death must have been generally followed by resuscitation, as in Thuringia, where the "Wild Man," as the central figure is there named, is brought to life again by the Doctor, while the survival, in the more elaborate Spring processions of this latter character, even where he plays no special rôle, points to the fact that his part in the proceedings was originally a more important one.

That Mannhardt was not mistaken is proved by the evidence of the kindred Dances, a subject we shall consider later; there we shall find the Doctor

---

[5] See G. Calderon, "Slavonic Elements in Greek religion," *Classical Review*, 1918, p. 79.
[6] Op. cit. p. 416.
[7] Op. cit. pp. 155 and 312.
[8] Op. cit. p. 353.
[9] Op. cit. p. 358.

playing his old-time *rôle*, and restoring to life the slain representative of the Vegetation Spirit.[10] The character of the Doctor, or Medicine Man, formed, as I believe, at one time, no unimportant link in the chain which connects these practices with the Grail tradition.

The signification of the resuscitation ceremony is obscured in cases where the same figure undergoes death and revival without any corresponding change of form. This point did not escape Mannhardt's acute critical eye; he remarks that, in cases where, e.g., in Swabia, the "King" is described as "ein armer alter Mann," who has lived seven years in the woods (the seven winter months), a scene of rejuvenation should follow – "diese scheint meistenteils verloren gegangen; doch vielleicht *scheint* es nur so." He goes on to draw attention to the practice in Reideberg, bei Halle, where, after burying a straw figure, called the Old Man, the villagers dance round the May-Pole, and he suggests that the "Old Man" represents the defunct Vegetation Spirit, the May Tree, that Spirit resuscitated, and refers in this connection to the "durchaus verwandten Asiatischen Gebrauchen des Attis, und Adonis-Kultus."[11]

The foregoing evidence offers, I think, sufficient proof of the, now generally admitted, relationship between Classical, Medieval, and Modern forms of Nature ritual.

But what of the relation to early Aryan practice? Can that, also, be proved?

In this connection I would draw attention to Chapter 17 of *Mysterium und Mimus*, entitled, *Ein Volkstümlicher Umzug beim Soma-Fest*. Here Professor von Schroeder discusses the real meaning and significance of a very curious little poem (*Rig-Veda*, 9. 112); the title by which it is generally known, *Alles läuft nach Geld*, does not, at first sight, fit the content of the verse, and the suggestion of scholars who have seen in it a humorous enumeration of different trades and handicrafts does not explain the fact that the Frog and the Horse appear in it.

To Professor von Schroeder belongs the credit of having discovered that the *personnel* of the poem corresponds with extraordinary exactitude to the Figures of the Spring and Summer "Fertility-exciting" processions, described with such fulness of detail by Mannhardt. Especially is this the case with the Whitsuntide procession at Värdegötzen, in Hanover, where we find the group of phallic and fertility demons, who, on Prof. von Schroeder's hypothesis, figure in the song, in concrete, and actual form.[12] The Vegetation Spirit appears

---

[10] Op. cit. p. 358.

[11] Op. cit. p. 359. Cf. the Lausitz custom given *supra*, which Mannhardt seems to have overlooked.

[12] In the poem, besides the ordinary figures of the Vegetation Deity, his female counterpart, and the Doctor, common to all such processions, we have Phallus, Frog, and Horse; in the Folk-procession, Laubfrosch, combining the two first, and Horse. Cf. Mannhardt, *Mythol. Forsch.* pp. 142–43; *Mysterium und Mimus*, pp. 408 *et seq.*; also, pp. 443–44. Sir W. Ridgeway (op. cit. p. 156) refers slightingly to this interpretation of a "harmless little hymn" – doubtless the poem is harmless; until Prof. von Schroeder pointed out its close affinity with the Fertility processions it was also meaningless.

in the song as an Old Man, while his female counterpart, an Old Woman, is described as "filling the hand-mill." Prof. von Schroeder points out that in some parts of Russia the "Baba-jaga" as the Corn Mother is called, is an Old Woman, who flies through the air in a hand-mill. The Doctor, to whom we have referred above, is mentioned twice in the four verses composing the song; he was evidently regarded as an important figure; while the whole is put into the mouth of a "Singer" evidently the Spokesman of the party, who proclaims their object, "Verschiednes könnend suchen wir Gute Dinge," i.e., gifts in money and kind, as such folk processions do to-day.

The whole study is of extraordinary interest for Folklore students, and so far as our especial investigation is concerned it seems to me to supply the necessary proof of the identity, and persistence, of Aryan folk-custom and tradition.

A very important modification of the root idea, and one which appears to have a direct bearing on the sources of the Grail tradition, was that by which, among certain peoples, the rôle of the god, his responsibility for providing the requisite rain upon which the fertility of the land, and the life of the folk, depended, was combined with that of the King.

This was the case among the Celts; McCulloch, in *The Religion of the Celts*, discussing the question of the early Irish *geasa* or taboo, explains the *geasa* of the Irish kings as designed to promote the welfare of the tribe, the making of rain and sunshine on which their prosperity depended. "Their observance made the earth fruitful, produced abundance and prosperity, and kept both the king and his land from misfortune. The Kings were divinities on whom depended fruitfulness and plenty, and who must therefore submit to obey their '*geasa.*'"[13]

The same idea seems to have prevailed in early Greece; Mr A. B. Cook, in his studies on *The European Sky-God*, remarks that the king in early Greece was regarded as the representative of Zeus: his duties could be satisfactorily discharged only by a man who was perfect, and without blemish, i.e., by a man in the prime of life, suffering from no defect of body, or mind; he quotes in illustration the speech of Odysseus (*Od.* 19. 109 ff.). " 'Even as a king without blemish, who ruleth god-fearing over many mighty men, and maintaineth justice, while the black earth beareth wheat and barley, and the trees are laden with fruit, and the flocks bring forth without fail, and the sea yieldeth fish by reason of his good rule, and the folk prosper beneath him.' The king who is without blemish has a flourishing kingdom, the king who is maimed has a kingdom diseased like himself, thus the Spartans were warned by an oracle to beware of a 'lame reign.' "[14]

A most remarkable modern survival of this idea is recorded by Dr Frazer in the latest edition of *The Golden Bough*,[15] and is so complete and suggestive that

[13] Op. cit. chap. 17, p. 253.
[14] Cf. *Folk-Lore*, vol. xv. p. 374.
[15] Op. cit. vol. v. *The Dying God*, pp. 17 *et seq.*

I make no apology for transcribing it at some length. The Shilluk, an African tribe, inhabit the banks of the White Nile, their territory extending on the west bank from Kaka in the north, to Lake No in the south, on the east bank from Fashoda to Taufikia, and some 35 miles up the Sohat river. Numbering some 40,000 in all, they are a pastoral people, their wealth consisting in flocks and herds, grain and millet. The King resides at Fashoda, and is regarded with extreme reverence, as being a re-incarnation of Nyakang, the semi-divine hero who settled the tribe in their present territory. Nyakang is the rain-giver, on whom their life and prosperity depend; there are several shrines in which sacred Spears, now kept for sacrificial purposes, are preserved, the originals, which were the property of Nyakang, having disappeared.

The King, though regarded with reverence, must not be allowed to become old or feeble, lest, with the diminishing vigour of the ruler, the cattle should sicken, and fail to bear increase, the crops should rot in the field and men die in ever growing numbers. One of the signs of failing energy is the King's inability to fulfil the desires of his wives, of whom he has a large number. When this occurs the wives report the fact to the chiefs, who condemn the King to death forthwith, communicating the sentence to him by spreading a white cloth over his face and knees during his mid-day slumber. Formerly the King was starved to death in a hut, in company with a young maiden but (in consequence, it is said, of the great vitality and protracted suffering of one King) this is no longer done; the precise manner of death is difficult to ascertain; Dr Seligmann, who was Sir J. G. Frazer's authority, thinks that he is now strangled in a hut, especially erected for that purpose.

At one time he might be attacked and slain by a rival, either of his own family, or of that of one of the previous Kings, of whom there are many, but this has long been superseded by the ceremonial slaying of the monarch who after his death is revered as Nyakang.[16]

This survival is of extraordinary interest; it presents us with a curiously close parallel to the situation which, on the evidence of the texts, we have postulated as forming the basic idea of the Grail tradition – the position of a people whose prosperity, and the fertility of their land, are closely bound up with the life and virility of their King, who is not a mere man, but a Divine re-incarnation. If he "falls into languishment," as does the Fisher King in *Perlesvaus*, the land and its inhabitants will suffer correspondingly; not only will the country suffer from drought, "*Nus près n'i raverdia*," but the men will die in numbers:

"Dames en perdront lor maris"

we may say; the cattle will cease to bear increase:

"Ne se n'i ot beste faon,"

[16] See Dr Seligmann's study, *The Cult of Nyakang and the Divine Kings of the Shilluk* in the Fourth Report of Wellcome Research Laboratories, Khartum, 1911, vol. B.

and the people take drastic steps to bring about a rejuvenation; the old King dies, to be replaced by a young and vigorous successor, even as Brons was replaced by Perceval.

Let us now turn back to the preceding chapter, and compare the position of the people of the Shilluk tribe, and the subjects of the Grail King, with that of the ancient Babylonians, as set forth in their Lamentations for Tammuz.

There we find that the absence of the Life-giving deity was followed by precisely the same disastrous consequences; Vegetation fails –

> "The wailing is for the plants; the first lament is they grow not.
> The wailing is for the barley; the ears grow not."

The reproductive energies of the animal kingdom are suspended –

> "For the habitation of flocks it is; they produce not.
> For the perishing wedded ones, for perishing children it is;
> the dark-headed people create not."

Nor can we evade the full force of the parallel by objecting that we are here dealing with a god, not with a man; we possess the recorded names of "kings who played the *rôle* of Tammuz," thus even for that early period the commingling of the two conceptions, god and king, is definitely established.

Now in face of this group of parallels, whose close correspondence, if we consider their separation in point of time (3000 BC; 1200 AD; and the present day), is nothing short of astonishing, is it not absolutely and utterly unreasonable to admit (as scholars no longer hesitate to do) the relationship between the first and last, and exclude, as a mere literary invention, the intermediate parallel?

The ground for such a denial may be mere prejudice, a reluctance to renounce a long cherished critical prepossession, but in the face of this new evidence does it not come perilously close to scientific dishonesty, to a disregard for that respect for truth in research the imperative duty of which has been so finely expressed by the late M. Gaston Paris. – "Je professe absolument et sans réserve cette doctrine, que la science n'a d'autre objet que la vérité, et la vérité pour elle-même, sans aucun souci des conséquences, bonnes ou mauvaises, regrettables ou heureuses, que cette vérité pourrait avoir dans la pratique."[17] When we further consider that behind these three main parallels, linking them together, there lies a continuous chain of evidence, expressed alike in classical literature, and surviving Folk practice, I would submit that there is no longer any shadow of a doubt that in the Grail King we have a romantic literary version of that strange mysterious figure whose presence hovers in the shadowy background of the history of our Aryan race; the figure

---

[17] Cf. Address on reception into the Academy when M. Paris succeeded to Pasteur's *fauteuil*.

of a divine or semi-divine ruler, at once god and king, upon whose life, and unimpaired vitality, the existence of his land and people directly depends.

And if we once grant this initial fact, and resolve that we will no longer, in the interests of an outworn critical tradition, deny the weight of scientific evidence in determining the real significance of the story, does it not inevitably follow, as a logical sequence, that such versions as fail to connect the misfortunes of the land directly with the disability of the king, but make them dependent upon the failure of the Quester, are, by that very fact, stamped as secondary versions? That by this one detail, of capital importance, they approve themselves as literary treatments of a traditional theme, the true meaning of which was unknown to the author?

Let us for a moment consider what the opposite view would entail; that a story which was originally the outcome of pure literary invention should in the course of re-modelling have been accidentally brought into close and detailed correspondence with a deeply rooted sequence of popular faith and practice is simply inconceivable, the re-modelling, if re-modelling there were, must have been intentional, the men whose handiwork it was were in possession of the requisite knowledge.

But how did they possess that knowledge, and why should they undertake such a task? Surely not from the point of view of antiquarian interest, as might be done to-day; they were no twelfth century Frazers and Mannhardts; the subject must have had for them a more living, a more intimate, interest. And if, in face of the evidence we now possess, we feel bound to admit the existence of such knowledge, is it not more reasonable to suppose that the men who first told the story were the men who *knew*, and that the confusion was due to those who, with more literary skill, but less first-hand information, re-modelled the original theme?

In view of the present facts I would submit that the problem posed in our first chapter may be held to be solved; that we accept as a *fait acquis* the conclusion that the woes of the land are directly dependent upon the sickness, or maiming, of the King, and in no wise caused by the failure of the Quester. The "Wasting of the land" must be held to have been antecedent to that failure, and the *Gawain* versions in which we find this condition fulfilled are, therefore, prior in origin to the *Perceval*, in which the "Wasting" is brought about by the action of the hero; in some versions, indeed, has altogether disappeared from the story.

Thus the position assigned in the versions to this feature of the Waste Land becomes one of capital importance as a critical factor. This is a point which has hitherto escaped the attention of scholars; the misfortunes of the land have been treated rather as an accident, than as an essential, of the Grail story, entirely subordinate in interest to the *dramatis personae* of the tale, or the objects, Lance and Grail, round which the action revolves. As a matter of fact I believe that the "Waste Land" is really the very heart of our problem; a rightful appreciation of its position and significance will place us in possession of the clue which will lead us safely through the most bewildering mazes of the fully developed tale.

Since the above pages were written Dr Frazer has notified the discovery of a second African parallel, equally complete, and striking. In *Folk-Lore* (vol. XXVI.) he prints, under the title *A Priest-King in Nigeria*, a communication received from Mr P. A. Talbot, District Commissioner in S. Nigeria. The writer states that the dominant Ju-Ju of Elele, a town in the N.W. of the Degema district, is a Priest-King, elected for a term of seven years. "The whole prosperity of the town, especially the fruitfulness of farm, byre, and marriage-bed, was linked with his life. Should he fall sick it entailed famine and grave disaster upon the inhabitants." So soon as a successor is appointed the former holder of the dignity is reported to "die for himself." Previous to the introduction of ordered government it is admitted that at any time during his seven years' term of office the Priest might be put to death by any man sufficiently strong and resourceful, consequently it is only on the rarest occasions (in fact only one such is recorded) that the Ju-Ju ventures to leave his compound. At the same time the riches derived from the offerings of the people are so considerable that there is never a lack of candidates for the office.

From this and the evidence cited above it would appear that the institution was widely spread in Africa, and at the same time it affords a striking proof in support of the essential soundness of Dr Frazer's interpretation of the Priest of Nemi, an interpretation which has been violently attacked in certain quarters, very largely on the ground that no one would be found willing to accept an office involving such direct danger to life. The above evidence shows clearly that not only does such an office exist, but that it is by no means an unpopular post.

14

THE ARCHETYPES OF LITERATURE

Northrop Frye

Famed Canadian literary critic Northrop Frye (1912–1991), who taught English at the University of Toronto, argued that literature derives from myth – specifically, from the myth of the hero. Frye associates the life cycle of the hero with that of god, vegetation, and the sun. The linkage of hero to god to vegetation comes from Frazer. The linkage to the sun comes from elsewhere. Rather than deriving from myth a single work of literature or even a single literary genre like tragedy, Frye derives from the myth of the hero all the main literary genres: romance, comedy, and satire as well as tragedy. (Innocently calling the genres "archetypes," Frye has ever since been mislabeled a Jungian.) The connection of literature to myth-ritualism and not merely to myth is that the myths which give rise to literature were once tied to rituals. Like other literary myth-ritualists, Frye is not reducing literature to myth but only rooting literature in myth. In the following programmatic essay (from *Kenyon Review* 13 [1951] 92–110), Frye sketches in part the section on myth in his subsequent grand work, *Anatomy of Criticism* (Princeton: Princeton University Press, 1957), 131–239. See also his "Myth, Fiction, and Displacement," *Daedalus* 90 (1961), 587–605; "Literature and Myth," in *Relations of Literary Study*, ed. James Thorpe (New York: Modern Language Association, 1967), 27–55; "Symbolism of the Unconscious" (1957) (on Frazer), in his *Northrop Frye on Culture and Literature*, ed. Robert D. Denham (Chicago: University of Chicago Press, 1978), 84–94; "Myth," *Antaeus* 43 (1981), 64–84; and "The Koine of Myth: Myth as a Universally Intelligible Language" and "The Mythical Approach to Creation," in his *Myth and Metaphor*, ed. Robert D. Denham (Charlottesville: University Press of Virginia, 1990), 3–17 and 238–54. On Frye see *Northrop Frye in Modern Criticism*, ed. Murray Krieger (New York: Columbia University Press, 1966); Robert D. Denham, *Northrop Frye and Critical* Method (University Park:

Original publication: Northrop Frye, "The Archetypes of Literature", *Kenyon Review* 13 (1951), pp. 92–110.

Pennsylvania State University Press, 1970); A. C. Hamilton, *Northrop Frye* (Toronto: University of Toronto Press, 1990); *The Legacy of Northrop Frye*, eds Alvin A. Lee and Robert D. Denham (Toronto: University of Toronto Press, 1994); and Jonathan Hart, *Northrop Frye* (London and New York: Routledge, 1994).

Every organized body of knowledge can be learned progressively; and experience shows that there is also something progressive about the learning of literature. Our opening sentence has already got us into a semantic difficulty. Physics is an organized body of knowledge about nature, and a student of it says that he is learning physics, not that he is learning nature. Art, like nature, is the subject of a systematic study, and has to be distinguished from the study itself, which is criticism. It is therefore impossible to "learn literature": one learns about it in a certain way, but what one learns, transitively, is the criticism of literature. Similarly, the difficulty often felt in "teaching literature" arises from the fact that it cannot be done: the criticism of literature is all that can be directly taught. So while no one expects literature itself to behave like a science, there is surely no reason why criticism, as a systematic and organized study, should not be, at least partly, a science. Not a "pure" or "exact" science, perhaps, but these phrases form part of a 19th Century cosmology which is no longer with us. Criticism deals with the arts and may well be something of an art itself, but it does not follow that it must be unsystematic. If it is to be related to the sciences too, it does not follow that it must be deprived of the graces of culture.

Certainly criticism as we find it in learned journals and scholarly monographs has every characteristic of a science. Evidence is examined scientifically; previous authorities are used scientifically; fields are investigated scientifically; texts are edited scientifically. Prosody is scientific in structure; so is phonetics; so is philology. And yet in studying this kind of critical science the student becomes aware of a centrifugal movement carrying him away from literature. He finds that literature is the central division of the "humanities," flanked on one side by history and on the other by philosophy. Criticism so far ranks only as a subdivision of literature; and hence, for the systematic mental organization of the subject, the student has to turn to the conceptual framework of the historian for events, and to that of the philosopher for ideas. Even the more centrally placed critical sciences, such as textual editing, seem to be part of a "background" that recedes into history or some other non-literary field. The thought suggests itself that the ancillary critical disciplines may be related to a central expanding pattern of systematic comprehension which has not yet been established, but which, if it were established, would prevent them from being centrifugal. If such a pattern exists, then criticism would be to art what philosophy is to wisdom and history to action.

Most of the central area of criticism is at present, and doubtless always will be, the area of commentary. But the commentators have little sense, unlike the researchers, of being contained within some sort of scientific discipline: they are chiefly engaged, in the words of the gospel hymn, in brightening the corner where they are. If we attempt to get a more comprehensive idea of what criticism is about, we find ourselves wandering over quaking bogs of generalities, judicious pronouncements of value, reflective comments, perorations to works of research, and other consequences of taking the large view. But this part of the critical field is so full of pseudo-propositions, sonorous nonsense that contains no truth and no falsehood, that it obviously exists only because criticism, like nature, prefers a waste space to an empty one.

The term "pseudo-proposition" may imply some sort of logical positivist attitude on my own part. But I would not confuse the significant proposition with the factual one; nor should I consider it advisable to muddle the study of literature with a schizophrenic dichotomy between subjective-emotional and objective-descriptive aspects of meaning, considering that in order to produce any literary meaning at all one has to ignore this dichotomy. I say only that the principles by which one can distinguish a significant from a meaningless statement in criticism are not clearly defined. Our first step, therefore, is to recognize and get rid of meaningless criticism: that is, talking about literature in a way that cannot help to build up a systematic structure of knowledge. Casual value-judgments belong not to criticism but to the history of taste, and reflect, at best, only the social and psychological compulsions which prompted their utterance. All judgments in which the values are not based on literary experience but are sentimental or derived from religious or political prejudice may be regarded as casual. Sentimental judgments are usually based either on non-existent categories or antitheses ("Shakespeare studied life, Milton books") or on a visceral reaction to the writer's personality. The literary chit-chat which makes the reputations of poets boom and crash in an imaginary stock exchange is pseudo-criticism. That wealthy investor Mr Eliot, after dumping Milton on the market, is now buying him again; Donne has probably reached his peak and will begin to taper off; Tennyson may be in for a slight flutter but the Shelley stocks are still bearish. This sort of thing cannot be part of any systematic study, for a systematic study can only progress: whatever dithers or vacillates or reacts is merely leisure-class conversation.

We next meet a more serious group of critics who say: the foreground of criticism is the impact of literature on the reader. Let us, then, keep the study of literature centripetal, and base the learning process on a structural analysis of the literary work itself. The texture of any great work of art is complex and ambiguous, and in unravelling the complexities we may take in as much history and philosophy as we please, if the subject of our study remains at the center. If it does not, we may find that in our anxiety to write about literature we have forgotten how to read it.

The only weakness in this approach is that it is conceived primarily as the antithesis of centrifugal or "background" criticism, and so lands us in a somewhat unreal dilemma, like the conflict of internal and external relations in philosophy. Antitheses are usually resolved, not by picking one side and refuting the other, or by making eclectic choices between them, but by trying to get past the antithetical way of stating the problem. It is right that the first effort of critical apprehension should take the form of a rhetorical or structural analysis of a work of art. But a purely structural approach has the same limitation in criticism that it has in biology. In itself it is simply a discrete series of analyses based on the mere existence of the literary structure, without developing any explanation of how the structure came to be what it was and what its nearest relatives are. Structural analysis brings rhetoric back to criticism, but we need a new poetics as well, and the attempt to construct a new poetics out of rhetoric alone can hardly avoid a mere complication of rhetorical terms into a sterile jargon. I suggest that what is at present missing from literary criticism is a co-ordinating principle, a central hypothesis which, like the theory of evolution in biology, will see the phenomena it deals with as parts of a whole. Such a principle, though it would retain the centripetal perspective of structural analysis, would try to give the same perspective to other kinds of criticism too.

The first postulate of this hypothesis is the same as that of any science: the assumption of total coherence. The assumption refers to the science, not to what it deals with. A belief in an order of nature is an inference from the intelligibility of the natural sciences; and if the natural sciences ever completely demonstrated the order of nature they would presumably exhaust their subject. Criticism, as a science, is totally intelligible; literature, as the subject of a science, is, so far as we know, an inexhaustible source of new critical discoveries, and would be even if new works of literature ceased to be written. If so, then the search for a limiting principle in literature in order to discourage the development of criticism is mistaken. The assertion that the critic should not look for more in a poem than the poet may safely be assumed to have been conscious of putting there is a common form of what may be called the fallacy of premature teleology. It corresponds to the assertion that a natural phenomenon is as it is because Providence in its inscrutable wisdom made it so.

Simple as the assumption appears, it takes a long time for a science to discover that it is in fact a totally intelligible body of knowledge. Until it makes this discovery it has not been born as an individual science, but remains an embryo within the body of some other subject. The birth of physics from "natural philosophy" and of sociology from "moral philosophy" will illustrate the process. It is also very approximately true that the modern sciences have developed in the order of their closeness to mathematics. Thus physics and astronomy assumed their modern form in the Renaissance, chemistry in the 18th Century, biology in the 19th, and the social sciences in the 20th. If systematic criticism, then, is developing only in our day, the fact is at least not an anachronism.

We are now looking for classifying principles lying in an area between two points that we have fixed. The first of these is the preliminary effort of criticism, the structural analysis of the work of art. The second is the assumption that there is such a subject as criticism, and that it makes, or could make, complete sense. We may next proceed inductively from structural analysis, associating the data we collect and trying to see larger patterns in them. Or we may proceed deductively, with the consequences that follow from postulating the unity of criticism. It is clear, of course, that neither procedure will work indefinitely without correction from the other. Pure induction will get us lost in haphazard guessing; pure deduction will lead to inflexible and over-simplified pigeon-holding. Let us now attempt a few tentative steps in each direction, beginning with the inductive one.

The unity of a work of art, the basis of structural analysis, has not been produced solely by the unconditioned will of the artist, for the artist is only its efficient cause: it has form, and consequently a formal cause. The fact that revision is possible, that the poet makes changes not because he likes them better but because they are better, means that poems, like poets, are born and not made. The poet's task is to deliver the poem in as uninjured a state as possible, and if the poem is alive, it is equally anxious to be rid of him, and screams to be cut loose from his private memories and associations, his desire for self-expression, and all the other navel-strings and feeding tubes of his ego. The critic takes over where the poet leaves off, and criticism can hardly do without a kind of literary psychology connecting the poet with the poem. Part of this may be a psychological study of the poet, though this is useful chiefly in analysing the failures in his expression, the things in him which are still attached to his work. More important is the fact that every poet has his private mythology, his own spectroscopic band or peculiar formation of symbols, of much of which he is quite unconscious. In works with characters of their own, such as dramas and novels, the same psychological analysis may be extended to the interplay of characters, though of course literary psychology would analyse the behavior of such characters only in relation to literary convention.

There is still before us the problem of the formal cause of the poem, a problem deeply involved with the question of genres. We cannot say much about genres, for criticism does not know much about them. A good many critical efforts to grapple with such words as "novel" or "epic" are chiefly interesting as examples of the psychology of rumor. Two conceptions of the genre, however, are obviously fallacious, and as they are opposite extremes, the truth must lie somewhere between them. One is the pseudo-Platonic conception of genres as existing prior to and independently of creation, which confuses them with mere conventions of form like the sonnet. The other is that pseudo-biological conception of them as evolving species which turns up in so many surveys of the "development" of this or that form.

We next inquire for the origin of the genre, and turn first of all to the social conditions and cultural demands which produced it – in other words to the material cause of the work of art. This leads us into literary history, which differs from ordinary history in that its containing categories, "Gothic," "Baroque," "Romantic," and the like, are cultural categories, of little use to the ordinary historian. Most literary history does not get as far as these categories, but even so we know more about it than about most kinds of critical scholarship. The historian treats literature and philosophy historically; the philosopher treats history and literature philosophically; and the so-called "history of ideas" approach marks the beginning of an attempt to treat history and philosophy from the point of view of an autonomous criticism.

But still we feel that there is something missing. We say that every poet has his own peculiar formation of images. But when so many poets use so many of the same images, surely there are much bigger critical problems involved than biographical ones. As Mr Auden's brilliant essay *The Enchafèd Flood* shows, an important symbol like the sea cannot remain within the poetry of Shelley or Keats or Coleridge: it is bound to expand over many poets into an archetypal symbol of literature. And if the genre has a historical origin, why does the genre of drama emerge from medieval religion in a way so strikingly similar to the way it emerged from Greek religion centuries before? This is a problem of structure rather than origin, and suggests that there may be archetypes of genres as well as of images.

It is clear that criticism cannot be systematic unless there is a quality in literature which enables it to be so, an order of words corresponding to the order of nature in the natural sciences. An archetype should be not only a unifying category of criticism, but itself a part of a total form, and it leads us at once to the question of what sort of total form criticism can see in literature. Our survey of critical techniques has taken us as far as literary history. Total literary history moves from the primitive to the sophisticated, and here we glimpse the possibility of seeing literature as a complication of a relatively restricted and simple group of formulas that can be studied in primitive culture. If so, then the search for archetypes is a kind of literary anthropology, concerned with the way that literature is informed by pre-literary categories such as ritual, myth and folk tale. We next realize that the relation between these categories and literature is by no means purely one of descent, as we find them reappearing in the greatest classics – in fact there seems to be a general tendency on the part of great classics to revert to them. This coincides with a feeling that we have all had: that the study of mediocre works of art, however energetic, obstinately remains a random and peripheral form of critical experience, whereas the profound masterpiece seems to draw us to a point at which we can see an enormous number of converging patterns of significance. Here we begin to wonder if we cannot see literature, not only as complicating itself in time, but as spread out in conceptual space from some unseen center.

This inductive movement towards the archetype is a process of backing up, as it were, from structural analysis, as we back up from a painting if we want to see composition instead of brushwork. In the foreground of the grave-digger scene in *Hamlet*, for instance, is an intricate verbal texture, ranging from the puns of the first clown to the *danse macabre* of the Yorick soliloquy, which we study in the printed text. One step back, and we are in the Wilson Knight and Spurgeon group of critics, listening to the steady rain of images of corruption and decay. Here too, as the sense of the place of this scene in the whole play begins to dawn on us, we are in the network of psychological relationships which were the main interest of Bradley. But after all, we say, we are forgetting the genre: *Hamlet* is a play, and an Elizabethan play. So we take another step back into the Stoll and Shaw group and see the scene conventionally as part of its dramatic context. One step more, and we can begin to glimpse the archetype of the scene, as the hero's *Liebestod* and first unequivocal declaration of his love, his struggle with Laertes and the sealing of his own fate, and the sudden sobering of his mood that marks the transition to the final scene, all take shape around a leap into and return from the grave that has so weirdly yawned open on the stage.

At each stage of understanding this scene we are dependent on a certain kind of scholarly organization. We need first an editor to clean up the text for us, then the rhetorician and philologist, then the literary psychologist. We cannot study the genre without the help of the literary social historian, the literary philosopher and the student of the "history of ideas," and for the archetype we need a literary anthropologist. But now that we have got our central pattern of criticism established, all these interests are seen as converging on literary criticism instead of receding from it into psychology and history and the rest. In particular, the literary anthropologist who chases the source of the Hamlet legend from the pre-Shakespeare play to Saxo, and from Saxo to nature myths, is not running away from Shakespeare: he is drawing closer to the archetypal form which Shakespeare recreated. A minor result of our new perspective is that contradictions among critics, and assertions that this and not that critical approach is the right one, show a remarkable tendency to dissolve into unreality. Let us now see what we can get from the deductive end.

Some arts move in time, like music; others are presented in space, like painting. In both cases the organizing principle is recurrence, which is called rhythm when it is temporal and pattern when it is spatial. Thus we speak of the rhythm of music and the pattern of painting; but later, to show off our sophistication, we may begin to speak of the rhythm of painting and the pattern of music. In other words, all arts may be conceived both temporally and spatially. The score of a musical composition may be studied all at once; a picture may be seen as the track of an intricate dance of the eye. Literature seems to be intermediate between music and painting: its words form rhythms which approach a musical sequence of sounds at one of its boundaries, and form patterns which approach the hieroglyphic or pictorial image at the other. The attempts to get as near to these boundaries as possible form the main body of what is called experimental writing. We may call the rhythm of literature the narrative, and the pattern, the simultaneous mental grasp of the verbal structure, the meaning or significance. We hear or listen to a narrative, but when we grasp a writer's total pattern we "see" what he means.

The criticism of literature is much more hampered by the representational fallacy than even the criticism of painting. That is why we are apt to think of narrative as a sequential representation of events in an outside "life," and of meaning as a reflection of some external "idea." Properly used as critical terms, an author's narrative is his linear movement; his meaning is the integrity of his completed form. Similarly an image is not merely a verbal replica of an external object, but any unit of a verbal structure seen as part of a total pattern or rhythm. Even the letters an author spells his words with form part of his imagery, though only in special cases (such as alliteration) would they call for critical notice. Narrative and meaning thus become respectively, to borrow musical terms, the melodic and harmonic contexts of the imagery.

Rhythm, or recurrent movement, is deeply founded on the natural cycle, and everything in nature that we think of as having some analogy with works of art, like the flower or the bird's song, grows out of a profound synchronization between an organism and the rhythms of its environment, especially that of the solar year. With animals some expressions of synchronization, like the mating dances of birds, could almost be called rituals. But in human life a ritual seems to be something of a voluntary effort (hence the magical element in it) to recapture a lost rapport with the natural cycle. A farmer must harvest his crop at a certain time of year, but because this is involuntary, harvesting itself is not precisely a ritual. It is the deliberate expression of a will to synchronize human and natural energies at that time which produces the harvest songs, harvest sacrifices and harvest folk customs that we call rituals. In ritual, then, we may find the origin of narrative, a ritual being a temporal sequence of acts in which the conscious meaning or significance is latent: it can be seen by an observer, but is largely concealed from the participators themselves. The pull of ritual is toward pure narrative, which, if there could be such a thing, would be automatic and unconscious repetition. We should notice too the regular tendency of ritual to become encyclopedic. All the important recurrences in nature, the day, the phases of the moon, the seasons and solstices of the year, the crises of existence from birth to death, get rituals attached to them, and most of the higher religions are equipped with a definitive total body of rituals suggestive, if we may put it so, of the entire range of potentially significant actions in human life.

Patterns of imagery, on the other hand, or fragments of significance, are oracular in origin, and derive from the epiphanic moment, the flash of instantaneous comprehension with no direct reference to time, the importance of which is indicated by Cassirer in *Myth and Language*. By the time we get them, in the form of proverbs, riddles, commandments and etiological folk tales, there is already a considerable element of narrative in them. They too are encyclopedic in tendency, building up a total structure of significance, or doctrine, from random and empiric fragments. And just as pure narrative would be unconscious act, so pure significance would be an incommunicable state of consciousness, for communication begins by constructing narrative.

The myth is the central informing power that gives archetypal significance to the ritual and archetypal narrative to the oracle. Hence the myth *is* the archetype, though it might be convenient to say myth only when referring to narrative, and archetype when speaking of significance. In the solar cycle of the day, the seasonal cycle of the year, and the organic cycle of human life, there is a single pattern of significance, out of which myth constructs a central narrative around a figure who is partly the sun, partly vegetative fertility and partly a god or archetypal human being. The crucial importance of this myth has been forced on literary critics by Jung and Frazer in particular, but the several books now available on it are not always systematic in their approach, for which reason I supply the following table of its phases:

1.   The dawn, spring and birth phase. Myths of the birth of the hero, of revival and resurrection, of creation and (because the four phases are a cycle) of the defeat of the powers of darkness, winter and death. Subordinate characters: the father and the mother. The archetype of romance and of most dithyrambic and rhapsodic poetry.

2.   The zenith, summer, and marriage or triumph phase. Myths of apotheosis, of the sacred marriage, and of entering into Paradise. Subordinate characters: the companion and the bride. The archetype of comedy, pastoral and idyll.

3.   The sunset, autumn and death phase. Myths of fall, of the dying god, of violent death and sacrifice and of the isolation of the hero. Subordinate characters: the traitor and the siren. The archetype of tragedy and elegy.

4.   The darkness, winter and dissolution phase. Myths of the triumph of these powers; myths of floods and the return of chaos, of the defeat of the hero, and Götterdämmerung myths. Subordinate characters: the ogre and the witch. The archetype of satire (see, for instance, the conclusion of *The Dunciad*).

The quest of the hero also tends to assimilate the oracular and random verbal structures, as we can see when we watch the chaos of local legends that results from prophetic epiphanies consolidating into a narrative mythology of departmental gods. In most of the higher religions this in turn has become the same central quest-myth that emerges from ritual, as the Messiah myth became the narrative structure of the oracles of Judaism. A local flood may beget a folk tale by accident, but a comparison of flood stories will show how quickly such tales become examples of the myth of dissolution. Finally, the tendency of both ritual and epiphany to become encyclopedic is realized in the definitive body of myth which constitutes the sacred scriptures of religions. These sacred scriptures are consequently the first documents that the literary critic has to study to gain a comprehensive view of his subject. After he has understood their structure, then he can descend from archetypes to genres, and see how the drama emerges from the ritual side of myth and lyric from the epiphanic or fragmented side, while the epic carries on the central encyclo-pedic structure.

Some words of caution and encouragement are necessary before literary criticism has clearly staked out its boundaries in these fields. It is part of the critic's business to show how all literary genres are derived from the quest-myth, but the derivation is a logical one within the science of criticism: the quest-myth will constitute the first chapter of whatever future handbooks of criticism may be written that will be based on enough organized critical knowledge to call themselves "introductions" or "outlines" and still be able to live up to their titles. It is only when we try to expound the derivation chrono-logically that we find ourselves writing pseudo-prehistorical fictions and the-ories of mythological contract. Again, because psychology and anthropology are more highly developed sciences, the critic who deals with this kind of material is bound to appear, for some time, a dilettante of those subjects. These two phases of criticism are largely undeveloped in comparison with literary history and rhetoric, the reason being the later development of the sciences they are related to. But the fascination which *The Golden Bough* and Jung's book on libido symbols have for literary critics is not based on dilettantism, but on the fact that these books are primarily studies in literary criticism, and very important ones.

In any case the critic who is studying the principles of literary form has a quite different interest from the psychologist's concern with states of mind or the anthropologist's with social institutions. For instance: the mental response to narrative is mainly passive; to significance mainly active. From this fact Ruth Benedict's *Patterns of Culture* develops a distinction between "Apollonian" cultures based on obedience to ritual and "Dionysiac" ones based on a tense exposure of the prophetic mind to epiphany. The critic would tend rather to note how popular literature which appeals to the inertia of the untrained mind puts a heavy emphasis on narrative values, whereas a sophisticated attempt to disrupt the connection between the poet and his environment produces the Rimbaud type of *illumination*, Joyce's solitary epiphanies, and Baudelaire's conception of nature as a source of oracles. Also how literature, as it develops from the primitive to the self-conscious, shows a gradual shift of the poet's attention from narrative to significant values, this shift of attention being the basis of Schiller's distinction between naive and sentimental poetry.

The relation of criticism to religion, when they deal with the same documents, is more complicated. In criticism, as in history, the divine is always treated as a human artifact. God for the critic, whether he finds him in *Paradise Lost* or the Bible, is a character in a human story; and for the critic all epiphanies are explained, not in terms of the riddle of a possessing god or devil, but as mental phenomena closely associated in their origin with dreams. This once established, it is then necessary to say that nothing in criticism or art compels the critic to take the attitude of ordinary waking consciousness towards the dream or the god. Art deals not with the real but with the conceivable; and criticism, though it will eventually have to have some theory of conceivability, can never be justified in trying to develop, much less assume, any theory of actuality. It is necessary to understand this before our next and final point can be made.

We have identified the central myth of literature, in its narrative aspect, with the quest-myth. Now if we wish to see this central myth as a pattern of meaning also, we have to start with the workings of the subconscious where the epiphany originates, in other words in the dream. The human cycle of waking and dreaming corresponds closely to the natural cycle of light and darkness, and it is perhaps in this correspondence that all imaginative life begins. The correspondence is largely an antithesis: it is in daylight that man is really in the power of darkness, a prey to frustration and weakness; it is in the darkness of nature that the "libido" or conquering heroic self awakes. Hence art, which Plato called a dream for awakened minds, seems to have as its final cause the resolution of the antithesis, the mingling of the sun and the hero, the realizing of a world in which the inner desire and the outward circumstance coincide. This is the same goal, of course, that the attempt to combine human and natural power in ritual has. The social function of the arts, therefore, seems to be closely connected with visualizing the goal of work in human life. So in terms of significance, the central myth of art must be the vision of the end of social effort, the innocent world of fulfilled desires, the free human society. Once this is understood, the integral place of criticism among the other social sciences, in interpreting and systematizing the vision of the artist, will be easier to see. It is at this point that we can see how religious conceptions of the final cause of human effort are as relevant as any others to criticism.

The importance of the god or hero in the myth lies in the fact that such characters, who are conceived in human likeness and yet have more power over nature, gradually build up the vision of an omnipotent personal community beyond an indifferent nature. It is this community which the hero regularly enters in his apotheosis. The world of this apotheosis thus begins to pull away from the rotary cycle of the quest in which all triumph is temporary. Hence if we look at the quest-myth as a pattern of imagery, we see the hero's quest first of all in terms of its fulfillment. This gives us our central pattern of archetypal images, the vision of innocence which sees the world in terms of total human intelligibility. It corresponds to, and is usually found in the form of, the vision of the unfallen world or heaven in religion. We may call it the comic vision of life, in contrast to the tragic vision, which sees the quest only in the form of its ordained cycle.

We conclude with a second table of contents, in which we shall attempt to set forth the central pattern of the comic and tragic visions. One essential principle of archetypal criticism is that the individual and the universal forms of an image are identical, the reasons being too complicated for us just now. We proceed according to the general plan of the game of Twenty Questions, or, if we prefer, of the Great Chain of Being:

1. In the comic vision the *human* world is a community, or a hero who represents the wish-fulfillment of the reader. The archetype of images of symposium, communion, order, friendship and love. In the tragic vision the human world is a tyranny or anarchy, or an individual or isolated man, the leader with his back to his followers, the bullying giant of romance, the deserted or betrayed hero. Marriage or some equivalent consummation belongs to the comic vision; the harlot, witch and other varieties of Jung's "terrible mother" belong to the tragic one. All divine, heroic, angelic or other superhuman communities follow the human pattern.

2. In the comic vision the *animal* world is a community of domesticated animals, usually a flock of sheep, or a lamb, or one of the gentler birds, usually a dove. The archetype of pastoral images. In the tragic vision the animal world is seen in terms of beasts and birds of prey, wolves, vultures, serpents, dragons and the like.

3. In the comic vision the *vegetable* world is a garden, grove or park, or a tree of life, or a rose or lotus. The archetype of Arcadian images, such as that of Marvell's green world or of Shakespeare's forest comedies. In the tragic vision it is a sinister forest like the one in *Comus* or at the opening of the *Inferno*, or a heath or wilderness, or a tree of death.

4. In the comic vision the *mineral* world is a city, or one building or temple, or one stone, normally a glowing precious stone – in fact the whole comic series, especially the tree, can be conceived as luminous or fiery. The archetype of geometrical images: the "starlit dome" belongs here. In the tragic vision the mineral world is seen in terms of deserts, rocks and ruins, or of sinister geometrical images like the cross.

5. In the comic vision the *unformed* world is a river, traditionally fourfold, which influenced the Renaissance image of the temperate body with its four humors. In the tragic vision this world usually becomes the sea, as the narrative myth of dissolution is so often a flood myth. The combination of the sea and beast images gives us the leviathan and similar water-monsters.

Obvious as this table looks, a great variety of poetic images and forms will be found to fit it. Yeats's "Sailing to Byzantium," to take a famous example of the comic vision at random, has the city, the tree, the bird, the community of sages, the geometrical gyre and the detachment from the cyclic world. It is, of course, only the general comic or tragic context that determines the interpretation of any symbol: this is obvious with relatively neutral archetypes like the island, which may be Prospero's island or Circe's.

Our tables are, of course, not only elementary but grossly over-simplified, just as our inductive approach to the archetype was a mere hunch. The important point is not the deficiencies of either procedure, taken by itself, but the fact that, somewhere and somehow, the two are clearly going to meet in the middle. And if they do meet, the ground plan of a systematic and comprehensive development of criticism has been established.

15

THE RITUAL VIEW OF MYTH
AND THE MYTHIC

Stanley Edgar Hyman

The most fervent evangelist for myth-ritualism was the American literary critic Stanley Edgar Hyman (1919–70), who taught at Bennington College. Hyman maintains that all myths are connected to rituals, but his version of myth-ritualism, which he attributes to Harrison, is spare. For him, as for Harrison and others, myth is the spoken correlate of ritual. But unlike Harrison, he postulates no specific ritual for myth and, unlike Frazer and Raglan, postulates no connection to kingship or to divinity. As a literary critic, Hyman is interested more in the mythic origin of literature than in myth in its own right. For him, as for Frye, all literature comes from myth. Indeed, for him seemingly all culture comes from myth. At the same time, he, like other literary myth-ritualists, distinguishes literature from myth. In the following essay (from *Journal of American Folklore* 68 [1955], 462–72) Hyman, with typical zeal, celebrates the spread of the myth-ritualist approach to literary and cultural studies. See also his "Myth, Ritual, and Nonsense," *Kenyon Review* 11 (1949), 455–75; "Leaping for Goodly Themis" (on Harrison), *New Leader* 45 (October 29, 1962), 24–5; *The Promised End* (Cleveland: World Publishing, 1963), 198–212, 249–70, 278–94 (which reprints "The Ritual View of Myth and the Mythic"), 356–67; *The Tangled Bank* (New York: Atheneum, 1962), 189–291 (on Frazer); and *The Critic's Credentials*, ed. Phoebe Pettingell (New York: Atheneum, 1978), 284–97 (on Weston), 298–304. On Hyman see Pettingell, Introduction to *The Critic's Credentials*, vii–xviii; and Joseph Fontenrose, *The Ritual Theory of Myth* (Berkeley: University of California Press, 1966), ch. 2.

The ritual approach comes directly out of Darwin, and thus, I suppose, ultimately from Heraclitus, whose *panta rei* seems to be the ancestor of any

Original publication: Stanley Edgar Hyman, "The Ritual View of Myth and the Mythic," *Journal of American Folklore* 68 (1955), pp. 462–72.

dynamic account of anything. When Darwin concluded *The Origin of Species* (1859) with a call for evolutionary treatment in the sciences of man, he opened the door to a variety of genetic studies of culture, and when he showed in *The Descent of Man* (1871) that human evolution was insignificant organically although vastly speeded up culturally (we might not be so quick to say "ethically" as he was), he made cultural studies the legitimate heirs of evolutionary biology. The same year as *The Descent*, in response to *The Origin*, E. B. Tylor's *Primitive Culture* appeared, drawing an immediate fan letter from Darwin. It staked off quite a broad claim to cultural studies in its subtitle "Researches into the Development of Mythology, Philosophy, Religion, Language, Art, and Custom." Tylor's general principle, almost his law, is that survivals are significant because they embody, sometimes in trivial or playful form, the serious usages of earlier stages. In material culture, it meant that such important tools as the bow and arrow, the fire drill, and the magician's rattle evolved into the toys of children; in non-material culture, it meant that myths were based on rites, although, like many rationalists before him, Tylor believed that they had been consciously devised as explanations.

Tylor's evolutionary anthropology, carried on by such successors as R. R. Marett and Henry Balfour, became the central tradition of British anthropology, but the emphasis gradually shifted from Tylor's concern with belief and custom to the more tangible areas of social organization, economics, and material culture. Meanwhile, at Cambridge, a classicist named James G. Frazer had found *Primitive Culture* a revelation, and his interest in ancient survivals was broadened and extended by his friend William Robertson Smith's studies of religion, in which Smith made use of the comparative method, invented by Montesquieu and developed by German philology. Weaving together the two main strands of Tylor's evolutionary survivals and Smith's comparative method, in 1885 Frazer began publishing a series of periodical articles on custom. When one of them, on a curious priesthood at Nemi in Italy, tied in with Smith's ideas about the slain god and outgrew article size, he kept working on it and in 1890 published it as the first edition of *The Golden Bough* in two volumes, dedicated to Smith. For Frazer in *The Golden Bough*, myth is still Tylor's rationalist "a fiction devised to explain an old custom, of which the real meaning and origin had been forgotten,"[1] and the evolution of custom is still Tylor's "to dwindle from solemn ritual into mere pageant and pastime,"[2] but Frazer constantly approaches, without ever quite stating, a synthesis of the two, with myths not consciously-devised rational explanations, but the actual dwindling or later form of the rite. Long before 1915, when the third and final edition of *The Golden Bough* appeared, that synthesis had been arrived at.

---

[1] J. G. Frazer, *The Golden Bough*, IV (London, 1915), 153.
[2] Frazer, *The Golden Bough*, IV, 214.

Since 1882, Jane Ellen Harrison, Frazer's contemporary at Cambridge, had been writing on Greek mythology and art, and in 1903, after she had seen a clay seal at Cnossos with its sudden revelation that the Minotaur was the king of Crete in a bull mask, she published *Prolegomena to the Study of Greek Religion*, which clearly stated the priority of ritual over myth or theology. Her book acknowledged the cooperation of Gilbert Murray at Tylor's Oxford, and Frazer, F. M. Cornford, and A. B. Cook at Cambridge. Cook, whose book, *Zeus*, did not begin to appear for another decade, began publishing parts of it in periodicals about that time, and his important series "Zeus, Jupiter, and the Oak" in the *Classical Review* (1903) took an approach similar to Harrison's. By the time Murray published *The Rise of the Greek Epic* (1907), reading such mythic figures as Helen and Achilles as ritual concretizations, he was able to draw on some of this Cambridge work his earlier writings had influenced. By 1908, when the Committee for Anthropology at Oxford sponsored six lectures, published under Marett's editorship later that year as *Anthropology and the Classics*, with the aim of interesting students of the humanities in "the lower culture,"[3] students of the humanities at the sister university had been turning their attention to the lower cultures for two decades, and the seed Tylor planted had flowered elsewhere.

The watershed year was 1912, when Harrison published *Themis*, a full and brilliant exposition of the chthonic origins of Greek mythology, including an excursus on the ritual forms underlying Greek tragedy by Murray (to whom the book is dedicated), a chapter on the ritual origin of the Olympic Games by Cornford, and copious material from Cook's forthcoming work. (Curiously, this book too had been inspired by a visit to Crete, where Harrison encountered the "Hymn of the Kouretes," which suggested that ritual magic, specifically the rite of a year-daimon, was the central element in early Greek religion.) In *Themis*, Harrison made three important points with great clarity: that myth arises out of rite, rather than the reverse;[4] that it is "the spoken correlative of the acted rite, the thing done; it is *to legomenon* as contrasted with or rather as related to *to dromenon*"[5] (a Greek definition of myth is *ta legomena epi tois dromenois* "the things said over a ritual act"); and that it is not anything else nor of any other origin.[6]

Basic to this view, as Harrison makes clear, is a dynamic or evolutionary conception of process whereby rites die out, and myths continue in religion, literature, art, and various symbolic forms with increased misunderstanding of the ancient rite, and a compensatory transformation for intelligibility in new terms. Thus myths are never the record of historical events or people, but freed from their ritual origins they may attach to historical events or people

---

[3] *Anthropology and the Classics*, ed. R. R. Marett (Oxford, 1907), p. 5.
[4] J. E. Harrison, *Themis* (Cambridge, 1912), p. 13.
[5] Harrison, *Themis*, p. 328.
[6] Harrison, *Themis*, p. 331.

(as Alexander was believed to be, or claimed to be, a god and the son of a snake, because mythic Greek kings like Cecrops had been ritual snake gods); they never originate as scientific or aetiological explanations of nature, but freed from their ritual origins may be so used (as stars have their positions in the sky because the mythic hero threw them there, but *his* origin is in rite, not primitive astronomy).

The ritual approach to mythology, or any form based on myth, thus cannot limit itself to genetic considerations. In the artificial division I have found most handy, it must deal with the three related problems of Origin, Structure, and Function. If the origin is the ancient anonymous collective one of ritual, the structure is intrinsically dramatic, the *dromenon* or thing done, but that form ceaselessly evolves in time in the chain of folk transmission. Here the considerations are not historic nor anthropological, but formal in terms of literary structure, principles of *Gestalt* organization, and dynamic criteria. In folk transmission, the "folk work" involves operations comparable to those Freud found in the "dream work" – splitting, displacement, multiplication, projection, rationalization, secondary elaboration, and interpretation – as well as such more characteristically aesthetic dynamics as Kenneth Burke's principle of "completion" or the fulfillment of expectations, in the work as well as in the audience. In regard to function, as the myth or text alters, there is at once a changing social function, as the work satisfies varying specific needs in the society along Malinowskian lines, and an unchanging, built-in function best described by Aristotle's *Poetics* and Freudian psychology, carrying with it its own context, taking us through its structural rites. In other words, the book of Jonah in the reading satisfies our need to be reborn in the belly of the great fish as efficiently as the initiatory rites from which it presumably derived satisfied the same need in the initiates. If these are now as then "fantasy gratifications," they are the charismatic experiences of great art now, as they were the charismatic experiences of organic religion then.

In a relatively short time, the ritual approach to folk study has met with remarkable success. There had of course been individual ritual studies in various areas long before 1912. Most of them were in the field of children's lore, where ritual survivals, after Tylor had called attention to them, were readily apparent. Some of the earliest studies were William Wells Newell's *Games and Songs of American Children* (1883), Henry Carrington Bolton's *The Counting-Out Rhymes of Children* (1888), Alice Gomme's *The Traditional Games Of England, Scotland and Ireland* (1894), and Lina Eckenstein's *Comparative Studies in Nursery Rhymes* (1906). Much of this work has never been superseded, and similarly, the most impressive ritual studies we have of the Bible appeared at the turn of the century: for the Old Testament, William Simpson's *The Jonah Legend* (1899), and for the New, John M. Robertson's series of books on the mythic Jesus, beginning with *Christianity and Mythology* (1900).

All of these people seem to have operated in relative isolation, independently working through to conclusions about their own material without knowing what was going on in other areas or recognizing the general application of their conclusions.

With the appearance of *Themis*, a powerful general statement of the theory buttressed by a prodigy of scholarship in several complicated areas of Greek culture, a "Cambridge" or "ritual" approach became generally available. Within a few years, its application to Greek studies had been enormously widened: Cornford's *From Religion to Philosophy* (1912) traced the ritual origins of some basic philosophic ideas; Harrison's *Ancient Art and Ritual* (1913) turned her theory on Greek plastic and pictorial arts; Murray tested his ritual forms on one tragic dramatist in *Euripides and His Age* (1913), (both it and *Ancient Art and Ritual* as popularizations for the Home University Library); Cornford tested the same forms on Greek comedy in *The Origin of Attic Comedy* (1914); and the first volume of Cook's enormous storehouse of ritual interpretation, *Zeus*, appeared (1914).

The first application of the theory outside Greek studies was Murray's 1914 Shakespeare Lecture, "Hamlet and Orestes,"[7] a brilliant comparative study in the common ritual origins of Shakespeare and Greek drama. 1920 saw the appearance of Jessie Weston's *From Ritual to Romance*, treating the Grail romances as the "misinterpreted" record of a fertility rite, and Bertha Phillpotts' *The Elder Edda and Ancient Scandinavian Drama*, tracing the ritual sources of Northern epic poetry. The next year Margaret Murray's *The Witch-Cult in Western Europe* appeared, claiming a real "Dianic cult," the survival of the old pagan religion, persecuted by Christianity as witchcraft, the book constituting the first substantial excursion of the theory into history. In 1923, the widening ripples took in fairy tales, in P. Saintyves' *Les Contes de Perrault et les Récits Parallèles*; folk drama, in R. J. E. Tiddy's editing *The Mummers' Play*; and law, in H. Goitein's *Primitive Ordeal and Modern Law*. In 1927, A. M. Hocart's *Kingship* appeared, tracing a great variety of material to a basic royal initiatory ceremony, and in 1929 Scott Buchanan's *Poetry and Mathematics* (the first American work along these lines in the third of a century since Bolton) boldly proposed a treatment of experimental science in ritual terms, and imaginatively worked some of it out.

In the thirties, S. H. Hooke edited two important symposia, *Myth and Ritual* (1933) and *The Labyrinth* (1935), in which a number of prominent scholars studied the relationships of myth and ritual in the ancient Near East; Lord Raglan published *Jocasta's Crime*, a ritual theory of taboo (1933), and his enormously influential *The Hero* (1936), which broadly generalized the ritual origins of all myth, as against the historical; Enid Welsford investigated the sources of an archetypal figure in *The Fool* (1935); Allen, Halliday, and Sikes

---

[7] In Gilbert Murray, *The Classical Tradition in Poetry* (Cambridge, Mass., 1927), pp. 205–240.

published their definitive edition of *The Homeric Hymns* (1936), extending previous considerations of Greek epic and dramatic poetry into sacred lyric; and in the late thirties William Troy began publishing his as yet uncollected ritual studies of such writers as Lawrence, Mann, and Fitzgerald.

By the forties, old subjects could be gone back over with greatly augmented information. George Thomson combined a ritual and Marxist approach in *Aeschylus and Athens* (1941) and *Studies in Ancient Greek Society* (the first volume of which appeared in 1949); Rhys Carpenter amplified Murray's earlier treatment of Homer in *Folk Tale, Fiction and Saga in the Homeric Epics* (1946); Lewis Spence brought Newell, Bolton, and Lady Gomme somewhat up to date in *Myth and Ritual in Dance, Game, and Rhyme* (1947); and Hugh Ross Williamson expanded Margaret Murray's brief account (in *The God of the Witches*, 1931) of the deaths of Thomas à Becket and William Rufus as Dianic cult sacrifices in *The Arrow and the Sword* (1947). Venturing into fresh fields, Gertrude Rachel Levy in *The Gate of Horn* (1948) traced some ritual sources of culture down from the stone age, paying considerable attention to plastic and pictorial art; and in 1949 there were two important literary applications: Francis Fergusson's *The Idea of a Theater*, a reading of modern drama in terms of the ritual patterns exemplified in Sophocles' *Oedipus the King*, and John Speirs' "Sir Gawain and the Green Knight," in *Scrutiny*, Winter 1949, the first of an important series of ritual studies of medieval English literature.

So far in the fifties half a dozen new territories have been explored and to some extent colonized. Theodor H. Gaster's *Thespis* (1950) generalized a ritual origin for the whole body of Near East sacred literature; Gertrude Kurath's articles on dance in the Funk and Wagnalls' *Dictionary of Folklore* the same year embraced a body of primitive and folk dance forms in the same approach; Cornford's luminous "A Ritual Basis for Hesiod's *Theogony*" was published posthumously in *The Unwritten Philosophy* (1950, although it had been written in 1941); and C. L. Barber published an ambitious exploration of Shakespeare in "The Saturnalian Pattern in Shakespeare's Comedy" in *The Sewanee Review*, Autumn 1951. Since then we have had the publication of Levy's second volume, *The Sword from the Stone* (1953), a ritual genesis of epic; Herbert Weisinger's *Tragedy and the Paradox of the Fortunate Fall* (1953), a similar treatment of tragedy; and Margaret Murray's third book on the Dianic cult, *The Divine King in England* (1954). In this listing I have made no attempt at completeness, confining it to those writers with whose work I am most familiar, and only one or two titles by each (Murray, Cornford, and Harrison have written about a dozen books each), but the breadth and variety of even this truncated list should make it obvious that the "Cambridge" view has gone far beyond the confines of Greek mythology, and that it is apparently here to stay.

Since the ritual approach to myth and literature does not claim to be a theory of ultimate significance, but a method of study in terms of specific significances, it can cohabit happily with a great many other approaches. If its anthropology has historically been Frazerian, the comparative generalization across many cultures, many of its most successful works, from *Themis* to Speirs on Gawain, have stayed narrowly within one area, and where it deals with social function, its anthropology is most profitably Malinowskian (if an unusually historical Malinowskian). The Boas tradition in American anthropology, with its bias against cross-cultural generalization and evolutionary theory, in favor of empirical cultural studies and known history, has often seemed inimical to the ritual approach at those key points. Many of the Boas rigidities, however, seem to have softened in the decade since his death: the new culture and personality anthropology from Ruth Benedict's *Patterns of Culture* (1934) to E. Adamson Hoebel's *The Law of Primitive Man* (1954) seems as cheerfully comparative as *The Golden Bough*; we are all neo-evolutionists once again; and *Primitive Heritage* (1953), Margaret Mead's anthology with Nicholas Calas, calls for "the restoration of wonder," and means, apparently, let us take Frazer and Crawley more seriously. If out of this comes a neo-Frazerian generalizing anthropology, based, not on dubious material wrenched out of its configuration, but on detailed and accurate field studies done with Boasian rigor, no one would welcome it more than the ritualists.

In regard to psychology, the ritual approach can draw centrally on Freudian psychoanalysis, informed by new knowledge and less circumscribed by ethnocentric patterns. This requires modernization without the loss of Freud's central vision, which is tragic where such rebels as Adler and Jung and such revisionists as Fromm and Horney are cheery faith-healers; unshrinking where they bowdlerize; stubbornly materialist where they are idealist and mystic; and dynamic, concerned with process, where they are static and concerned with one or another variety of timeless *élan vital*. After we have brought the Frazerian anthropology of *Totem and Taboo* up to date and restored Freud's "vision" of the Primal Horde, in Burke's terms, to its place as "essence" rather than "origin," the book remains our most useful and seminal equation of primitive rite with neurotic behavior, and thus the bridge to Burke's own "symbolic action," the private, individual symbolic equivalent for the ancient collective ritual. In the form of "symbolic action," psychoanalytic theory gives us the other dimension of function, the wish-fulfillment or fantasy gratification, and can thus answer some of our questions about the origins of origins.

As Jung's work increasingly seems to move toward mystic religion and away from analytic psychology, it appears to be of increasingly little use to a comparative and genetic approach. Strong as Jungian psychology has been in insisting on the universal archetypal identity of myth and symbol, its explanation of this identity in terms of the collective unconscious and innate awareness militates directly against any attempt to study the specific forms by which these traits are carried and transmitted in the culture (as did Freud's own "memory traces"). As Jung is used in the work of Maud Bodkin[8] or Joseph Campbell, as a source of suggestive insights, it seems far more to our purposes, and we can readily utilize Campbell's universal "great myth" or "monomyth," a concept itself derived from Van Gennep's *rites de passage*: "a separation from the world, a penetration to some source of power, and a life-enhancing return."[9] We must first, however, put the Jungian myth back on its roots, either a specific myth and text (literary study) or a specific culture and rite (anthropology). The ritual approach is certainly compatible with varieties of mysticism, as the conclusions of Weston's *From Ritual to Romance* or Harrison's *Epilegomena to the Study of Greek Religion* (1921) make clear, and Harrison was herself strongly drawn to Jung as well as to Bergson. Despite their examples, and the opinions of even so impressive a ritual poet as William Butler Yeats, the job of mythic analysis would seem to require a basic rational materialism, and a constant pressure in the direction of science and scholarship, away from mysticism and the occult. Within these limits of naturalism, and on the frame of this central concern with ritual, all possible knowledge and all approaches to myth, from the most meticulous motif-classification to the most speculative reconstruction of an *ur*-text, can be useful, with pluralism certainly the desirable condition.

There are only two varieties of approach, I think, with which the ritual view cannot usefully coexist. One is the euhemerist, the idea that myths are based on historic persons or events. This theory has been driven back from rampart to rampart over the years, but it stubbornly holds to each new defensive position: if it is forced to give up a historic William Tell, it retreats to a historic Robin Hood; if the historic Orpheus even Harrison's *Prolegomena* accepted in 1903 seems no longer tenable, perhaps Moses is; if there was no Leda and no egg, could there not have been a real Helen? By now, in regard to the great myths, we know that none of these is possible, even at those key points the Trojan War and the figure of Jesus. With stories unquestionably made up about real people, whether fictions about Napoleon or Eleanor Roosevelt jokes, it becomes a simple matter of definition, and if the euhemerists of our various schools want to call those stories myths, they are welcome to them. We find it more useful to apply some other term, insofar as the distinction between myth and history is a real and a basic one.[10]

The other approach to mythology that seems to offer no point of juncture with the ritual view is the cognitionist idea that myths derive from a quest for knowledge. In its nineteenth century forms, the theories that myths were personifications of nature, or the weather, or the sun and moon, it seems substantially to have died out; in various insidious twentieth century forms, the

---

[8] Maud Bodkin, *Archetypal Patterns in Poetry* (London, 1934), and *Studies of Type-Images in Poetry, Religion, and Philosophy* (London, 1951).

[9] Joseph Campbell, *The Hero with a Thousand Faces* (New York, 1949), pp. 10, 35.

[10] Myth must also be distinguished from all the other things we loosely call by its name: legend, tale, fantasy, mass delusion, popular belief and illusion, and plain lie.

theories that myths are designed to answer aetiological questions about how death came into the world or how the bunny got his little furry tail, or that taboo is primitive hygiene or primitive genetics, it is still pervasive. Again, all one can say is that myths do not originate in this fashion, that primitive peoples are speculative and proto-scientific, surely, but that the lore they transmit is another order of knowledge. If they knew that the tabooed food carried trichinosis or that the tabooed incestuous marriage deteriorated the stock, they would not save the first for their sacred feasts and the second for their rulers. Once more, if our various cognitionists want to call myth what is unquestionably primitive proto-science, like techniques for keeping a pot from cracking in the firing or seasonal lore for planting and harvesting, that is their privilege. The Alaskan Eskimos who took the Russian explorers for cuttlefish "on account of the buttons on their clothes," as Frazer reports,[11] obviously had speculative minds and a sense of continuity between the animal and human orders not unlike that informing Darwin's theory, but the difference between their myth of "The Great Cuttlefish That Walks Like a Man" (if they had one) and *The Origin of Species* is nevertheless substantial.

If we keep clearly in mind that myth tells a story sanctioning a rite, it is obvious that it neither means nor explains anything; that it is not science but a form of independent experience, analogous to literature. The pursuit of cognition in myth or folk literature has led to all the worst excesses of speculative research, whether the political slogans and events Katherine Elwes Thomas found hermetically concealed in nursery rhymes in *The Real Personages of Mother Goose* (1930), the wisdom messages, deliberately coded and jumbled, that Robert Graves uncoded in *The White Goddess* (1948), or, most recently, the secret fire worship Flavia Anderson discovered hidden behind every myth in *The Ancient Secret* (1953).

Among the important problems facing the ritual view at present is an adequate working-out of the relationship between ritual, the anonymous regular recurrence of an action, and history, the unique identifiable experience in time. The problem is raised dramatically in the latest book by Margaret Murray, one of the pioneers of ritual studies. Called *The Divine King in England*, it is the third in her series on the Dianic cult and easily her wildest. Where *The Witch-cult in Western Europe* named two historical figures, Joan of Arc and Gilles de Rais, as voluntary sacrificial figures in the cult, and her second book, *The God of the Witches*, added two more, Thomas à Becket and William Rufus, the new book makes the bold claim on English history that "at least once in every reign from William the Conqueror to James I the sacrifice of the Incarnate God was consummated either in the person of the king or in that of his substitute,"[12]

[11] Frazer, "Some Primitive Theories of the Origin of Man," *Darwin and Modern Science*, ed. A. C. Seward (Cambridge, 1909), p. 159.

[12] M. A. Murray, *The Divine King in England* (London, 1954), p. 13.

generally in a regular seven-year cycle. Since I have already reviewed the book at length for a forthcoming issue of *Midwest Folklore*, I can here only briefly summarize the problem. Murray's historical excursion is not only dubious history (as reviewers have pointed out, showing the errors of dates and durations by which she gets her seven-year victims, the number jugglery by which she gets her covens of thirteen), it is totally unnecessary history. She is certainly right about survivals of the old religion into modern times, but she seems to be basically in error about the manner in which it survives, to be confusing origins with events. As the ancient rites die out in literal practice, their misunderstood and transformed record passes into myth and symbol, and that is the form in which they survive and color history, without being themselves the events of history. In English history, assuming as she does that the primitive divine king was once slain every seven years, the monarch and his subjects might very well feel an ominousness about each seventh anniversary, and might welcome the death of the king or some high personage, but the step from that to the idea that the dead man was therefore the voluntary victim of a sacrificial cult is the unwarranted one. Murray's witch cult was a genuine worship of the old gods, surviving into modern times in a distorted form, but her Royal Covens are only the travesty of historical scholarship.

If the fallacy of historicity is still with us, the fallacy of aetiology may finally be on its way out. In *Themis*, as far back as 1912, Harrison wrote:

> The myth is not at first aetiological, it does not arise to give a reason; it is representative, another form of utterance, of expression. When the emotion that started the ritual has died down and the ritual though hallowed by tradition seems unmeaning, a reason is sought in the myth and it is regarded as aetiological.[13]

In his recent posthumous volume edited by Lord Raglan, *The Life-giving Myth* (1952), A. M. Hocart finally shows the process whereby myth goes beyond explaining the ritual to explaining other phenomena in nature, thus functioning as general aetiology. In Fiji, he reports, the physical peculiarities of an island with only one small patch of fertile soil are explained by a myth telling how Mberewalaki, a culture hero, flew into a passion at the misbehavior of the people of the island and hurled all the soil he was bringing them in a heap, instead of laying it out properly. Hocart points out that the myth is used aetiologically to explain the nature of the island, but did not originate in that attempt. The adventures of Mberewalaki originated, like all mythology, in ritual performance, and most of the lore of Hocart's Fijian informants consisted of such ritual myths. When they get interested in the topography of the island or are asked about it, Hocart argues, they do precisely what we would do, which is ransack their lore for an answer. Our lore might include a body of

---

[13] Harrison, *Themis*, p. 16.

geological process, and we would search through it for an explanation; theirs has no geology but tells the acts and passions of Mberewalaki, and they search through it similarly and come up with an explanation. It should take no more than this one pointed example, I think, to puncture that last survival of the cosmological origin theories, the aetiological myth, except as a category of function.

After the relationship to history and to science or cognition, we are left with the relationship of ritual theory to belief. For Harrison, as for Frazer, ritual studies were part of comparative religion, and a hoped-for result, if not the ultimate aim, was finding a pattern in which a person of sense or sensibility could believe. Harrison concludes her essay in the Darwin centenary volume: "It is, I venture to think, towards the apprehension of such mysteries, not by reason only, but by man's whole personality, that the religious spirit in the course of its evolution through ancient magic and modern mysticism is ever blindly yet persistently moving."[14] In the course of his researches, Darwin himself lost most of his faith, but for Asa Gray, as for some Darwinians since, the doctrine of evolution celebrated God's powers and strengthened Christian faith. For John M. Robertson, the demolition of the historicity of Jesus was a blow against Christianity on behalf of free-thought; for W. B. Smith and Arthur Drews it was a way of purifying Christianity by purging it of legendary accretions. William Simpson seems to have hit on the idea of Jonah as an initiation ritual because he was preoccupied with such matters as a Freemason. There is apparently no necessary correlation between knowledge and belief; to know all is to believe all, or some, or none.

Most contemporary ritual students of myth, I should imagine, are like myself unbelievers, and it would seem to get progressively more difficult to acknowledge the essential identity of religious myths, and their genesis from the act of worship itself, the god out of the machinery, while continuing to believe in the "truth" of any one of them (or of all of them, except in the woolliest and most Jungian fashion). On the other hand, in *Cults and Creeds in Graeco-Roman Egypt* (1953), we saw Sir Harold Idris Bell, a professional papyrologist, produce a learned and impressive study of the pragmatic competition of religions in Hellenistic Egypt, with the constant proviso that one of those systems, Christianity, was not only morally superior to the others, but was the divinely inspired true faith. So perhaps to know all *is* to believe all.

Finally, then, a number of technical problems remain. In its brief history, the ritual view has illuminated almost the whole of Greek culture, including religion, philosophy, art, many of the forms of literature, and much else. It has done the same for the games, songs, and rhymes of children; the Old and New

[14] Harrison, "The Influence of Darwinism on the Study of Religions," *Darwin and Modern Science*, ed. A. C. Seward, p. 511.

Testaments, epic and romance, edda and saga, folk drama and dance, folktale and legend, Near East religion, modern drama and literature, even problems in history, law, and science. A few forms of folk literature have not yet been explored in ritual terms, prominent among them the English and Scottish popular ballads (the present writer has made a tentative foray in that direction)[15] and the American Negro blues. A ritual origin for the ballads presumes a body of antecedent folk drama, from which they evolve as narrative songs (as it in turn derives from ritual sacrifice), which hardly exists except in a few late poor fragments such as Robin Hood plays, and which must consequently be conjectured. Such conjecture is not impossible, but it is a hard job involving heavy reliance on that frail reed analogy, and it still awaits its doer. The blues raise serious problems. If they are a true folksong of ancient anonymous collective ritual origin, rather than a folk-transmitted song of modern composition, then they precede any American conditions experienced by the Negro and must have an African source. No trouble here, except that nothing like them has ever been found in Africa, perhaps because it does not exist, perhaps because it would look so different before its sea change that no one has yet identified it. In any case, a ritual origin for the blues constitutes a fascinating problem, although not a critical issue (too much obviously convincing ritual interpretation has been produced for the theory to stand or fall on any single form). A ritual account of the ballads and the blues would close two large chinks, and might keep out drafts even in the coldest climate of opinion.

The relationship of ritual and ritual myth to formal literature has hardly yet been touched. The brilliant work that should have inaugurated such a movement in literary criticism was Murray's 1914 Shakespeare Lecture, "Hamlet and Orestes," in which he showed the essential identity of the two dramatic heroes, not as the result of any direct linkage between the two, but because Shakespeare's Hamlet, through a long Northern line of Amlethus, Amlodi, and Ambales, derived from precisely the same myth and rite of the Winter King – cold, mad, death-centered, bitter, and filthy – that Orestes derived from in his warmer clime. The plays are neither myth nor rite, Murray insists, they are literature, but myth and rite underly their forms, their plots, and their characters. (Greek drama itself represents a fusion of two separate derivations from ritual: the forms of Attic tragedy arise out of the sacrificial rites of tauriform or aegiform Dionysos, the plots of Attic tragedy come mostly from Homer; and the bloody plots fit the ritual form so well, as Rhys Carpenter showed most fully, because the Homeric stories themselves derive from similar sacrificial rites far from Mount Olympus.) In the four decades since Murray's lecture, literary criticism has scarcely noticed it. A student of Murray's, Janet Spens, published a ritual treatment of Shakespeare, *An Essay on Shakespeare's Relation to Tradition* (1916), which I have never seen, but which Barber

---

[15] S. E. Hyman, "The Raggle-Taggle Ballads O," *The Western Review*, XV (1951), 305–313.

describes with serious reservations, and until his own essay almost nothing had been done along that line. Troy and Fergusson have dealt with a handful of novels and plays in ritual terms, Carvel Collins has written several essays on Faulkner, and the present writer has similarly tackled Thoreau and a few others, but there has been very little else.

The chief difficulty seems to lie in the need to recognize the relationship of literature to folk tradition, while at the same time drawing Murray's sharp line between them. Literature is analogous to myth, we have to insist, but is not itself myth. There has been a great deal of confusion on this point, best exemplified by Richard Chase's *Quest for Myth* and *Herman Melville* (both in 1949). Chase simply equates the two, defining myth in the former as "the aesthetic activity of a man's mind,"[16] turning Melville's works in the latter into so many myths or mythic organizations. Here we ought to keep in mind a number of basic distinctions. Myth and literature are separate and independent entities, although myth can never be considered in isolation, and any specific written text of the protean myth, or even fixed oral text, can fairly be called folk literature. For literary purposes, all myths are not one, however much they may be one, the monomyth or ur-myth, in essence or origin. What such modern writers as Melville or Kafka create is not myth but an individual fantasy expressing a symbolic action, equivalent to and related to the myth's expression of a public rite. No one, not even Melville (let alone Moritz Jagendorf) can invent myths or write folk literature.

The writer can use traditional myths with varying degrees of consciousness (with Joyce and Mann perhaps most fully conscious in our time), and he often does so with no premeditated intention, working from symbolic equivalents in his own unconscious. Here other arts closer to origins, like the dance, where the ritual or symbolic action is physically mimed, can be profoundly instructive. Just as there are varying degrees of consciousness, so are there varying degrees of fruitfulness in these uses of traditional patterns, ranging from dishonest fakery at one extreme to some of the subtlest ironic and imaginative organizations in our poetry at the other. The aim of a ritual literary criticism would be the exploration of all these relations, along with missionary activity on behalf of some of the more fruitful ones.

What begins as a modest genetic theory for the origin of a few myths thus eventually comes to make rather large claims on the essential forms of the whole culture. If, as Schroedinger's *Nature and the Greeks* (1954) shows, the patterns of Greek myth and rite have been built into all our physics until the last few decades, perhaps ritual is a matter of some importance. Raglan and Hocart argue that the forms of social organization arise out of it, Goitein throws in the processes of law, Cornford and Buchanan add the forms of philosophic and scientific thinking (perhaps all our thinking follows the ritual

---

[16] Richard Chase, *Quest for Myth* (Baton Rouge, La., 1949), p. vii.

pattern of *agon* or contest, *sparagmos* or tearing apart, then *anagnorisis* or discovery and *epiphany* or showing-forth of the new idea). Even language itself suggests at many points a ritual origin. From rites come the structures, even the plots and characters, of literature, the magical organizations of painting, the arousing and fulfilling of expectation in music, perhaps the common origin of all the arts. If ritual is to be a general theory of culture, however, our operations must get more tentative and precise in proportion as our claims become more grandiose. We then have to keep distinctions even clearer, know so much more, and use every scrap of fact or theory that can be used. Having begun so easily by explaining the myth of the Sphinx, we may yet, working humbly in cooperation with anyone who will and can cooperate, end by reading her difficult riddle.

16

THE IDEA OF A THEATER

Francis Fergusson

Francis Fergusson (1904–86), an esteemed American drama critic who taught at Bennington College, Princeton University, and Rutgers University, extended the literary applications of myth-ritualism by Harrison and Murray to the concept of drama per se. Fergusson argues that the story of the suffering and redemption of the tragic hero derives from the Frazerian myth of the killing and replacement of the king. For example, Oedipus, King of Thebes, must sacrifice his throne, though not his life, for the sake of his subjects. Only with his abdication will the plague cease. But for Fergusson the renewal sought by Thebes is less physical than spiritual, and Oedipus seeks it for himself as well as for his people. In addition to his classic *The Idea of a Theater* (Princeton: Princeton University Press, 1949), from which the following selection (ch. 1) is taken, see also *Dante's Drama of the Mind* (Princeton: Princeton University Press, 1953) and "'Myth' and the Literary Scruple," *Sewanee Review* 64 (1956), 171–85, which is included in his collection of essays: *The Human Image in Dramatic Literature* (Garden City, NY: Doubleday Anchor Books, 1957). On Fergusson see *The Rarer Action: Essays in Honor of Francis Fergusson*, eds Alan Cheuse and Richard Koffler (New Brunswick, NJ: Rutgers University Press, 1970); and Wallace Fowlie, "Francis Fergusson and *The Idea of a Theater*," *Sewanee Review* 90 (1982), 150–8.

Oedipus Rex: The Tragic Rhythm of Action

> . . . *quel secondo regno*
> *dove l'umano spirito si purga.*
> – Purgatorio, CANTO I

Original publication: Francis Fergusson, *The Idea of a Theater* (Princeton: Princeton University Press, 1949), ch. 1 (pp. 13–41).

I suppose there can be little doubt that *Oedipus Rex* is a crucial instance of drama, if not *the* play which best exemplifies this art in its essential nature and its completeness. It owes its position partly to the fact that Aristotle founded his definitions upon it. But since the time of Aristotle it has been imitated, rewritten, and discussed by many different generations, not only of dramatists, but also of moralists, psychologists, historians, and other students of human nature and destiny.

Though the play is thus generally recognized as an archetype, there has been little agreement about its meaning or its form. It seems to beget, in every period, a different interpretation and a different dramaturgy. From the seventeenth century until the end of the eighteenth, a Neoclassic and rationalistic interpretation of *Oedipus*, of Greek tragedy, and of Aristotle, was generally accepted; and upon this interpretation was based the dramaturgy of Corneille and Racine. Nietzsche, under the inspiration of Wagner's *Tristan und Isolde*, developed a totally different view of it, and thence a different theory of drama. These two views of Greek tragedy, Racine's and Nietzsche's, still provide indispensable perspectives upon *Oedipus*. They show a great deal about modern principles of dramatic composition; and they show, when compared, how central and how essential Sophocles' drama is. In the two essays following, the attempt is made to develop the analogies, the similarities and differences, between these three conceptions of drama.

In our day a conception of *Oedipus* seems to be developing which is neither that of Racine nor that of Nietzsche. This view is based upon the studies which the Cambridge School, Frazer, Cornford, Harrison, Murray, made of the ritual origins of Greek tragedy. It also owes a great deal to the current interest in myth as a way of ordering human experience. *Oedipus*, we now see, is both myth and ritual. It assumes and employs these two ancient ways of understanding and representing human experience, which are prior to the arts and sciences and philosophies of modern times. To understand it (it now appears) we must endeavor to recapture the habit of significant make-believe, of the direct perception of action, which underlies Sophocles' theater.

If *Oedipus* is to be understood in this way, then we shall have to revise our ideas of Sophocles' dramaturgy. The notion of Aristotle's theory of drama, and hence of Greek dramaturgy, which still prevails (in spite of such studies as Butcher's of the *Poetics*) is largely colored by Neoclassic taste and rationalistic habits of mind. If we are to take it that Sophocles was imitating action before theory, instead of after it, like Racine, then both the elements and the form of his composition appear in a new light.

In the present essay the attempt is made to draw the deductions, for Sophocles' theater and dramaturgy, which the present view of *Oedipus* implies. We shall find that the various traditional views of this play are not so much wrong as partial.

Oedipus, Myth and Play

When Sophocles came to write his play he had the myth of Oedipus to start with. Laius and Jocasta, King and Queen of Thebes, are told by the oracle that their son will grow up to kill his father and marry his mother. The infant, his feet pierced, is left on Mount Kitharon to die. But a shepherd finds him and takes care of him; at last gives him to another shepherd, who takes him to Corinth, and there the King and Queen bring him up as their own son. But Oedipus – "Clubfoot" – is plagued in his turn by the oracle; he hears that he is fated to kill his father and marry his mother; and to escape that fate he leaves Corinth never to return. On his journey he meets an old man with his servants; gets into a dispute with him, and kills him and all his followers. He comes to Thebes at the time when the Sphinx is preying upon that City; solves the riddle which the Sphinx propounds, and saves the City. He marries the widowed Queen, Jocasta; has several children by her; rules prosperously for many years. But, when Thebes is suffering under a plague and a drought, the oracle reports that the gods are angry because Laius' slayer is unpunished. Oedipus, as King, undertakes to find him; discovers that he is himself the culprit and that Jocasta is his own mother. He blinds himself and goes into exile. From this time forth he becomes a sort of sacred relic, like the bones of a saint; perilous, but "good medicine" for the community that possesses him. He dies, at last, at Athens, in a grove sacred to the Eumenides, female spirits of fertility and night.

It is obvious, even from this sketch, that the myth, which covers several generations, has as much narrative material as *Gone with the Wind*. We do not know what versions of the story Sophocles used. It is the way of myths that they generate whole progenies of elaborations and varying versions. They are so suggestive, seem to say so much, yet so mysteriously, that the mind cannot rest content with any single form, but must add, or interpret, or simplify – reduce to terms which the reason can accept. Mr William Troy suggests that "what is possibly most in order at the moment is a thoroughgoing refurbishment of the medieval four-fold method of interpretation, which was first developed, it will be recalled, for just such a purpose – to make at least partially available to the reason that complex of human problems which are embedded, deep and imponderable, in the Myth."[1] It appears that Sophocles, in his play, succeeded in preserving the suggestive mystery of the Oedipus myth, while presenting it in a wonderfully unified dramatic form; and this drama has all the dimensions which the fourfold method was intended to explore.

Everyone knows that when Sophocles planned the plot of the play itself, he started almost at the end of the story, when the plague descends upon the City

---

[1] "Myth, Method and the Future," by William Troy. *Chimera*, Spring, 1946.

of Thebes which Oedipus and Jocasta had been ruling with great success for a number of years. The action of the play takes less than a day, and consists of Oedipus' quest for Laius' slayer – his consulting the Oracle of Apollo, his examination of the Prophet, Tiresias, and of a series of witnesses, ending with the old Shepherd who gave him to the King and Queen of Corinth. The play ends when Oedipus is unmistakably revealed as himself the culprit.

At this literal level, the play is intelligible as a murder mystery. Oedipus takes the role of District Attorney; and when he at last convicts himself, we have a twist, a *coup de théâtre*, of unparalleled excitement. But no one who sees or reads the play can rest content with its literal coherence. Questions as to its meaning arise at once: Is Oedipus really guilty, or simply a victim of the gods, of his famous complex, of fate, of original sin? How much did he know, all along? How much did Jocasta know? The first, and most deeply instinctive effort of the mind, when confronted with this play, is to endeavor to reduce its meanings to some set of rational categories.

The critics of the Age of Reason tried to understand it as a fable of the enlightened moral will, in accordance with the philosophy of that time. Voltaire's version of the play, following Corneille, and his comments upon it, may be taken as typical. He sees it as essentially a struggle between a strong and righteous Oedipus, and the malicious and very human gods, aided and abetted by the corrupt priest Tiresias; he makes it an anti-religious tract, with an unmistakable moral to satisfy the needs of the discursive intellect. In order to make Oedipus "sympathetic" to his audience, he elides, as much as possible, the incest motif; and he adds an irrelevant love story. He was aware that his version and interpretation were not those of Sophocles but, with the complacent provinciality of his period, he attributes the difference to the darkness of the age in which *Sophocles* lived.

Other attempts to rationalize *Oedipus Rex* are subtler than Voltaire's, and take us further toward an understanding of the play. Freud's reduction of the play to the concepts of his psychology reveals a great deal, opens up perspectives which we are still exploring. If one reads *Oedipus* in the light of Fustel de Coulanges' *The Ancient City*, one may see it as the expression of the ancient patriarchal religion of the Greeks. And other interpretations of the play, theological, philosophical, historical, are available, none of them wrong, but all partial, all reductions of Sophocles' masterpiece to an alien set of categories. For the peculiar virtue of Sophocles' presentation of the myth is that it preserves the ultimate mystery by focusing upon the tragic human at a level beneath, or prior to any rationalization whatever. The plot is so arranged that we see the action, as it were, illumined from many sides at once.

By starting the play at the end of the story, and showing onstage only the last crucial episode in Oedipus' life, the past and present action of the protagonist are revealed together; and, in each other's light, are at last felt as one. Oedipus' quest for the slayer of Laius becomes a quest for the hidden reality of his own past; and as that slowly comes into focus, like repressed material under psychoanalysis – with sensory and emotional immediacy, yet in the light of acceptance and understanding – his immediate quest also reaches its end: he comes to see himself (the Savior of the City) and the guilty one, the plague of Thebes, at once and at one.

This presentation of the myth of Oedipus constitutes, in one sense, an "interpretation" of it. What Sophocles saw as the essence of Oedipus' nature and destiny, is not what Seneca or Dryden or Cocteau saw; and one may grant that even Sophocles did not exhaust the possibilities in the materials of the myth. But Sophocles' version of the myth does not constitute a "reduction" in the same sense as the rest.

I have said that the action which Sophocles shows is a quest, the quest for Laius' slayer; and that as Oedipus' past is unrolled before us his whole life is seen as a kind of quest for his true nature and destiny. But since the object of this quest is not clear until the end, the seeking action takes many forms, as its object appears in different lights. The object, indeed, the final perception, the "truth," looks so different at the end from what it did at the beginning that Oedipus' action itself may seem not a quest, but its opposite, a flight. Thus it would be hard to say, simply, that Oedipus either succeeds or fails. He succeeds; but his success is his undoing. He fails to find what, in one way, he sought; yet from another point of view his search is brilliantly successful. The same ambiguities surround his effort to discover who and what he is. He seems to find that he is nothing; yet thereby finds himself. And what of his relation to the gods? His quest may be regarded as a heroic attempt to escape their decrees, or as an attempt, based upon some deep natural faith, to discover what their wishes are, and what true obedience would be. In one sense Oedipus suffers forces he can neither control nor understand, the puppet of fate; yet at the same time he wills and intelligently intends his every move.

The meaning, or spiritual content of the play, is not to be sought by trying to resolve such ambiguities as these. The spiritual content of the play is the tragic action which Sophocles directly presents; and this action is in its essence *zweideutig*: triumph and destruction, darkness and enlightenment, mourning and rejoicing, at any moment we care to consider it. But this action has also a shape: a beginning, middle, and end, in time. It starts with the reasoned purpose of finding Laius' slayer. But this aim meets unforeseen difficulties, evidences which do not fit, and therefore shake the purpose as it was first understood; and so the characters suffer the piteous and terrible sense of the mystery of the human situation. From this suffering or passion, with its shifting visions, a new perception of the situation emerges; and on that basis the purpose of the action is redefined, and a new movement starts. This movement, or *tragic rhythm of action*, constitutes the shape of the play as a whole; it is also the shape of each episode, each discussion between principals with the chorus following. Mr Kenneth Burke has studied the tragic rhythm in his

Philosophy of Literary Form, and also in *A Grammar of Motives*, where he gives the three moments traditional designations which are very suggestive: *Poiema*, *Pathema*, *Mathema*. They may also be called, for convenience, Purpose, Passion (or Suffering), and Perception. It is this tragic rhythm of action which is the substance or spiritual content of the play, and the clue to its extraordinarily comprehensive form.

In order to illustrate these points in more detail, it is convenient to examine the scene between Oedipus and Tiresias with the chorus following it. This episode, being early in the play (the first big agon), presents, as it were, a preview of the whole action and constitutes a clear and complete example of action in the tragic rhythm.

Hero and Scapegoat: The Agon between Oedipus and Tiresias

The scene between Oedipus and Tiresias comes after the opening sections of the play. We have seen the citizens of Thebes beseeching their King to find some way to lift the plague which is on the City. We have had Oedipus' entrance (majestic, but for his tell-tale limp) to reassure them, and we have heard the report which Creon brings from the Delphic Oracle: that the cause of the plague is the unpunished murder of Laius, the former king. Oedipus offers rewards to anyone who will reveal the culprit, and he threatens with dire punishment anyone who conceals or protects him. In the meantime, he decides, with the enthusiastic assent of the chorus, to summon Tiresias as the first witness.

Tiresias is that suffering seer whom Sophocles uses in *Antigone* also to reveal a truth which other mortals find it hard and uncomfortable to see. He is physically blind, but Oedipus and chorus alike assume that if anyone can see who the culprit is, it is Tiresias, with his uncanny inner vision of the future. As Tiresias enters, led by a boy, the chorus greets him in these words:[2]

> CHORUS: But the man to convict him is here. Look: they are bringing the one
> human being in whom the truth is native, the godlike seer.

Oedipus is, at this point in the play, at the opposite pole of experience from Tiresias: he is hero, monarch, helmsman of the state; the solver of the Sphinx's riddle, the triumphant being. He explains his purpose in the following proud clear terms:

[2] I am responsible for the English of this scene. The reader is referred to *Oedipus Rex*, translated by Dudley Fitts and Robert Fitzgerald (New York: Harcourt, Brace and Co., 1949), a very handsome version of the whole play.

OEDIPUS: O Tiresias, you know all things: what may be told, and the unspeakable: things of earth and things of heaven. You understand the City
(though you do not see it) in its present mortal illness – from which to save
us and protect us, we find, Lord, none but you. For you must know, in case
you haven't heard it from the messengers, that Apollo, when we asked him,
told us there was one way only with this plague: to discover Laius' slayers,
and put them to death or send them into exile. Therefore you must not
jealously withhold your omens, whether of birds or other visionary way, but
save yourself and the City – save me, save all of us – from the defilement of
the dead. In your hand we are. There is no handsomer work for a man, than
to bring, with what he has, what help he can.

This speech is the prologue of the scene, and the basis of the agon or
struggle which follows. This struggle in effect analyzes Oedipus' purpose;
places it in a wider context, reveals it as faulty and dubious. At the end of
the scene Oedipus loses his original purpose altogether, and suffers a wave of
rage and fear, which will have to be rationalized in its turn before he can
"pull himself together" and act again with a clear purpose.

In the first part of the struggle, Oedipus takes the initiative, while Tiresias,
on the defensive, tries to avoid replying:

TIRESIAS: Oh, oh. How terrible to know, when nothing can come of knowing!
Indeed, I had lost the vision of these things, or I should never have come.
OEDIPUS: What things? . . . In what discouragement have you come to us here!
TIR: Let me go home. I shall endure this most easily, and so will you, if you
do as I say.
OED: But what you ask is not right. To refuse your word is disloyalty to the
City that has fed you.
TIR: But I see that your demands are exorbitant, and lest I too suffer such a –
OED: For the sake of the gods, if you know, don't turn away! Speak to us, we
are your suppliants here.
TIR: None of you understands. But I – I never will tell my misery. Or yours.
OED: What are you saying? You know, but tell us nothing? You intend treachery
to us, and death to the City?
TIR: I intend to grieve neither myself nor you. Why then do you try to know?
You will never learn from me.
OED: Ah, evil old man! You would anger a stone! You will say *nothing*? Stand
futile, speechless before us?
TIR: You curse my temper, but you don't see the one that dwells in you; no,
you must blame me.
OED: And who would *not* lose his temper, if he heard you utter your scorn of
the City?
TIR: It will come. Silent though I be.
OED: Since it will come, it is your duty to inform me.
TIR: I shall say no more. Now, if you like, rage to your bitter heart's content.

OED:　Very well: in my "rage" I shall hold back nothing which I now begin to
see. I think you planned that deed, even performed it, though not with your
own hands. If you could see, I should say that the work was yours alone.

In the last speech quoted, Oedipus changes his tack, specifying his purpose
differently; he accuses Tiresias, and that makes Tiresias attack. In the next
part of the fight the opponents trade blow for blow:

TIR:　You would? I charge you, abide by the decree you uttered: from this day
forth, speak neither to these present, nor to me, unclean as you are, polluter
of the earth!
OED:　You have the impudence to speak out words like these! And now how do
you expect to escape?
TIR:　I have escaped. The truth strengthens and sustains me.
OED:　Who taught you the truth? Not your prophet's art.
TIR:　You did; you force me against my will to speak.
OED:　Speak what? Speak again, that I may understand better.
TIR:　*Didn't* you understand? Or are you goading me?
OED:　I can't say I really grasp it: speak again.
TIR:　I say you are the murderer of the man whose murderer you seek.
OED:　You won't be glad to have uttered that curse twice.
TIR:　Must I say more, so you may rage the more?
OED:　As much as you like – all is senseless.
TIR:　I say you do not know your own wretchedness, nor see in what shame you
live with those you love.
OED:　Do you think you can say that forever with impunity?
TIR:　If the truth has power.
OED:　It has, with all but you: helpless is truth with you: for you are blind, in
eye, in ear, in mind.
TIR:　You are the impotent one: you utter slanders which every man here will
apply to you.
OED:　You have your being only in the night; you couldn't hurt me or any man
who sees the sun.
TIR:　No. Your doom is not to fall by me. Apollo suffices for that, he will bring
it about.
OED:　Are these inventions yours, or Creon's?
TIR:　Your wretchedness is not Creon's, it is yours.
OED:　O wealth, and power, and skill – which skill, in emulous life, brings low
– what envy eyes you! if for this kingly power which the City gave into my
hands, unsought – if for *this* the faithful Creon, my friend from the first, has
stalked me in secret, yearning to supplant me! if he has bribed this juggling
wizard, this deceitful beggar, who discerns his profit only, blind in his own
art!

Tell me now, tell me where you have proved a true diviner? Why, when the
song-singing sphinx was near, did you not speak deliverance to the people?
Her riddles were not for any comer to solve, but for the mantic art, and you

were apparently instructed neither by birds nor by any sign from the gods. Yet when I came, I, Oedipus, all innocent, I stopped her song. No birds taught me, by my own wit I found the answer. And it is I whom you wish to banish, thinking that you will then stand close to Creon's throne.

You and your ally will weep, I think, for this attempt; and in fact, if you didn't seem to be an old man, you would already have learned, in pain, of your presumption.

In this part the beliefs, the visions, and hence the purposes of the antagonists are directly contrasted. Because both identify themselves so completely with their visions and purposes, the fight descends from the level of dialectic to a level below the rational altogether: it becomes cruelly *ad hominem*. We are made to see the absurd incommensurability of the very beings of Oedipus and Tiresias; they shrink from one another as from the uncanny. At the end of the round, it is Oedipus who has received the deeper wound; and his great speech, "O wealth and power," is a far more lyric utterance than the ordered exposition with which he began.

The end of this part of the fight is marked by the intervention of the chorus, which endeavors to recall the antagonists to the most general version of purpose which they supposedly share: the discovery of the truth and the service of the gods:

CHORUS: To us it appears that this man's words were uttered in anger, and yours too, Oedipus. No need for that: consider how best to discharge the mandate of the god.

The last part of the struggle shows Tiresias presenting his whole vision, and Oedipus, on the defensive, shaken to the depths:

TIR: Although you rule, we have equally the right to reply; in that I too have power. Indeed, I live to serve, not you, but Apollo; and I shall not be enrolled under Creon, either. Therefore I say, since you have insulted even my blindness, that though you have eyesight, you do not see what misery you are in, nor where you are living, nor with whom. Do you know whence you came? No, nor that you are the enemy of your own family, the living and the dead. The double prayer of mother and father shall from this land hound you in horror – who now see clearly, but then in darkness.

Where then will your cry be bounded? What part of Kitharon not echo it quickly back, when you shall come to understand that marriage, to which you sailed on so fair a wind, homelessly home? And many other evils which you do not see will bring you to yourself at last, your children's equal.

Scorn Creon, therefore, and my words: you will be struck down more terribly than any mortal.

OED: Can I really hear such things from him? Are you not gone? To death? To punishment? Not fled from this house?

TIR: I should never have come if you hadn't called me.

OED: I didn't know how mad you would sound, or it would have been a long time before I asked you here to my house.

TIR: This is what I am; foolish, as it seems to you; but wise, to the parents who gave you birth.

OED: To whom? Wait: *who* gave me birth?

TIR: This day shall give you birth, and death.

OED: In what dark riddles you always speak.

TIR: Aren't you the best diviner of riddles?

OED: Very well: mock that gift, which, you will find, is mine.

TIR: That very gift was your undoing.

OED: But if I saved the City, what does it matter?

TIR: So be it. I am going. Come, boy, lead me.

OED: Take him away. Your presence impedes and trips me; once you are gone, you can do no harm.

TIR: I shall go when I have done my errand without fear of your frowns, for they can't hurt me. I tell you, then, that the man whom you have long been seeking, with threats and proclamations, Laius' slayer, is here. He is thought to be an alien, but will appear a native Theban, and this circumstance will not please him. Blind, who once could see; destitute, who once was rich, leaning on a staff, he will make his way through a strange land. He will be revealed as brother and father of his own children; of the woman who bore him, both son and husband; sharer of his father's bed; his father's killer.

Go in and ponder this. If you find it wrong, say then I do not understand the prophetic vision.

Oedipus rushes off-stage, his clear purpose gone, his being shaken with fear and anger. Tiresias departs, led by his boy. The chorus is left to move and chant, suffering the mixed and ambivalent feelings, the suggestive but mysterious images, which the passion in which the agon eventuated produces in them:

CHORUS

Strophe I: Who is it that the god's voice from the Rock of Delphi says
Accomplished the unspeakable with murderous hands?
Time now that windswift
Stronger than horses
His feet take flight.
In panoply of fire and lightning
Now springs upon him the son of Zeus
Whom the dread follow,
The Fates unappeasable.

Antistrophe I: New word, like light, from snowy Parnassus:
Over all the earth trail the unseen one.
For in rough wood,
In cave or rocks,
Like bull bereft – stampeded, futile
He goes, seeking with futile foot to

Flee the ultimate
Doom, which ever
Lives and flies over him.
Strophe II: In awe now, and soul's disorder, I neither accept
The augur's wisdom, nor deny: I know not what to say.
I hover in hope, see neither present nor future.
Between the House of Laius
And Oedipus, I do not hear, have never heard, of any feud:
I cannot confirm the public charge against him, to help
Avenge the dark murder.
Antistrophe II: Zeus and Apollo are wise, and all that is mortal
They know: but whether that human seer knows more than I
There is no way of telling surely, though in wisdom
A man may excel.
Ah, never could I, till I see that word confirmed, consent to blame him!
Before all eyes the winged songstress, once, assailed him;
Wise showed he in that test, and to the City, tender; in my heart
I will call him evil never.

The chorus is considered in more detail below. At this point I merely wish to point out that Oedipus and Tiresias show, in their agon, the "purpose" part of the tragic rhythm; that this turns to "passion," and that the chorus presents the passion and also the new perception which follows. This new perception is that of Oedipus as the possible culprit. But his outlines are vague; perhaps the vision itself is illusory, a bad dream. The chorus has not yet reached the end of its quest; that will come only when Oedipus, in the flesh before them, is unmistakably seen as the guilty one. We have reached merely a provisional resting-place, the end of the first figure in which the tragic rhythm is presented. But this figure is a reduced version of the shape of the play as a whole, and the fleeting and unwelcome image of Oedipus as guilty corresponds to the final perception or epiphany, the full-stop, with which the play ends.

Oedipus: Ritual and Play

The Cambridge School of Classical Anthropologists has shown in great detail that the form of Greek tragedy follows the form of a very ancient ritual, that of the *Enniautos-Daimon*, or seasonal god.[3] This was one of the most influential discoveries of the last few generations, and it gives us new insights into *Oedipus* which I think are not yet completely explored. The clue to Sophocles' dramatizing of the myth of Oedipus is to be found in this ancient ritual, which had a similar form and meaning – that is, it also moved in the "tragic rhythm."

[3] See especially Jane Ellen Harrison's *Ancient Art and Ritual*, and her *Themis*, which contains an "Excursus on the Ritual Forms Preserved in Greek Tragedy" by Professor Gilbert Murray.

Experts in classical anthropology, like experts in other fields, dispute innumerable questions of fact and of interpretation which the layman can only pass over in respectful silence. One of the thornier questions seems to be whether myth or ritual came first. Is the ancient ceremony merely an enactment of the Ur-Myth of the year-god – Attis, or Adonis, or Osiris, or the "Fisher-King" – in any case that Hero-King-Father-High-Priest who fights with his rival, is slain and dismembered, then rises anew with the spring season? Or did the innumerable myths of this kind arise to "explain" a ritual which was perhaps mimed or danced or sung to celebrate the annual change of season?

For the purpose of understanding the form and meaning of *Oedipus*, it is not necessary to worry about the answer to this question of historic fact. The figure of Oedipus himself fulfills all the requirements of the scapegoat, the dismembered king or god-figure. The situation in which Thebes is presented at the beginning of the play – in peril of its life; its crops, its herds, its women mysteriously infertile, signs of a mortal disease of the City, and the disfavor of the gods – is like the withering which winter brings, and calls, in the same way, for struggle, dismemberment, death, and renewal. And this tragic sequence is the substance of the play. It is enough to know that myth and ritual are close together in their genesis, two direct imitations of the perennial experience of the race.

But when one considers *Oedipus* as a ritual one understands it in ways which one cannot by thinking of it merely as a dramatization of a story, even that story. Harrison has shown that the Festival of Dionysos, based ultimately upon the yearly vegetation ceremonies, included *rites de passage*, like that celebrating the assumption of adulthood – celebrations of the mystery of individual growth and development. At the same time, it was a prayer for the welfare of the whole City; and this welfare was understood not only as material prosperity, but also as the natural order of the family, the ancestors, the present members, and the generations still to come, and, by the same token, obedience to the gods who were jealous, each in his own province, of this natural and divinely sanctioned order and proportion.

We must suppose that Sophocles' audience (the whole population of the City) came early, prepared to spend the day in the bleachers. At their feet was the semicircular dancing-ground for the chorus, and the thrones for the priests, and the altar. Behind that was the raised platform for the principal actors, backed by the all-purpose, emblematic façade, which would presently be taken to represent Oedipus' palace in Tbebes. The actors were not professionals in our sense, but citizens selected for a religious office, and Sophocles himself had trained them and the chorus.

This crowd must have had as much appetite for thrills and diversion as the crowds who assemble in our day for football games and musical comedies, and Sophocles certainly holds the attention with an exciting show. At the same time his audience must have been alert for the fine points of poetry and dramaturgy, for *Oedipus* is being offered in competition with other plays on the same bill. But the element which distinguishes this theater, giving it its unique directness and depth, is the *ritual expectancy* which Sophocles assumed in his audience. The nearest thing we have to this ritual sense of theater is, I suppose, to be found at an Easter performance of the *Mattias Passion*. We also can observe something similar in the dances and ritual mummery of the Pueblo Indians. Sophocles' audience must have been prepared, like the Indians standing around their plaza, to consider the playing, the make-believe it was about to see – the choral invocations, with dancing and chanting; the reasoned discourses and the terrible combats of the protagonists; the mourning, the rejoicing, and the contemplation of the final stage-picture or epiphany – as imitating and celebrating the mystery of human nature and destiny. And this mystery was at once that of individual growth and development, and that of the precarious life of the human City.

I have indicated how Sophocles presents the life of the mythic Oedipus in the tragic rhythm, the mysterious quest of life. Oedipus is shown seeking his own true being; but at the same time and by the same token, the welfare of the City. When one considers the ritual form of the whole play, it becomes evident that it presents the tragic but perennial, even normal, quest of the whole City for its well-being. In this larger action, Oedipus is only the protagonist, the first and most important champion. This tragic quest is realized by all the characters in their various ways; but in the development of the action as a whole it is the chorus alone that plays a part as important as that of Oedipus; its counterpart, in fact. The chorus holds the balance between Oedipus and his antagonists, marks the progress of their struggles, and restates the main theme, and its new variation, after each dialogue or agon. The ancient ritual was probably performed by a chorus alone without individual developments and variations, and the chorus, in *Oedipus*, is still the element that throws most light on the ritual form of the play as a whole.

The chorus consists of twelve or fifteen "Elders of Thebes." This group is not intended to represent literally all of the citizens either of Thebes or of Athens. The play opens with a large delegation of Theban citizens before Oedipus' palace, and the chorus proper does not enter until after the prologue. Nor does the chorus speak directly for the Athenian audience; we are asked throughout to make-believe that the theater is the agora at Thebes; and at the same time Sophocles' audience is witnessing a ritual. It would, I think, be more accurate to say that the chorus represents the point of view and the faith of Thebes as a whole, and, by analogy, of the Athenian audience. Their errand before Oedipus' palace is like that of Sophocles' audience in the theater: they are watching a sacred combat, in the issue of which they have an all-important and official stake. Thus they represent the audience and the citizens in a particular way – not as a mob formed in response to some momentary feeling, but rather as an organ of a highly self-conscious community: something closer to the "conscience of the race" than to the overheated affectivity of a mob.

According to Aristotle, a Sophoclean chorus is a character that takes an important role in the action of the play, instead of merely making incidental music between the scenes, as in the plays of Euripides. The chorus may be described as a group personality, like an old Parliament. It has its own traditions, habits of thought and feeling, and mode of being. It exists, in a sense, as a living entity, but not with the sharp actuality of an individual. It perceives; but its perception is at once wider and vaguer than that of a single man. It shares, in its way, the seeking action of the play as a whole; but it cannot act in all the modes; it depends upon the chief agonists to invent and try out the detail of policy, just as a rather helpless but critical Parliament depends upon the Prime Minister to act but, in its less specific form of life, survives his destruction.

When the chorus enters after the prologue, with its questions, its invocation of the various gods, and its focus upon the hidden and jeopardized welfare of the City – Athens or Thebes – the list of essential *dramatis personae*, as well as the elements needed to celebrate the ritual, is complete, and the main action can begin. It is the function of the chorus to mark the stages of this action, and to perform the suffering and perceiving part of the tragic rhythm. The protagonist and his antagonists develop the "purpose" with which the tragic sequence begins; the chorus, with its less than individual being, broods over the agons, marks their stages with a word (like that of the chorus leader in the middle of the Tiresias scene), and (expressing its emotions and visions in song and dance) suffers the results, and the new perception at the end of the fight.

The choral odes are lyrics but they are not to be understood as poetry, the art of words, only, for they are intended also to be danced and sung. And though each chorus has its own shape, like that of a discrete lyric – its beginning, middle, and end – it represents also one passion or pathos in the changing action of the whole. This passion, like the other moments in the tragic rhythm, is felt at so general or, rather, so deep a level that it seems to contain both the mob ferocity that Nietzsche felt in it and, at the other extreme, the patience of prayer. It is informed by faith in the unseen order of nature and the gods, and moves through a sequence of modes of suffering. This may be illustrated from the chorus I have quoted at the end of the Tiresias scene.

It begins (close to the savage emotion of the end of the fight) with images suggesting that cruel "Bacchic frenzy" which is supposed to be the common root of tragedy and of the "old" comedy: "In panoply of fire and lightning/ The son of Zeus now springs upon him." In the first antistrophe these images come together more clearly as we relish the chase; and the fleeing culprit, as we imagine him, begins to resemble Oedipus, who is lame, and always associated with the rough wilderness of Kitharon. But in the second strophe, as though appalled by its ambivalent feelings and the imagined possibilities, the chorus sinks back into a more dark and patient posture of suffering, "in awe," "hovering in hope." In the second antistrophe this is developed into something like the orthodox Christian attitude of prayer, based on faith, and assuming the possibility of a hitherto unimaginable truth and answer: "Zeus and Apollo are wise," etc. The whole chorus then ends with a new vision of Oedipus, of the culprit, and of the direction in which the welfare of the City is to be sought. This vision is still colored by the chorus's human love of Oedipus as Hero, for the chorus has still its own purgation to complete, cannot as yet accept completely either the suffering in store for it, or Oedipus as scapegoat. But it marks the end of the first complete "purpose-passion-perception" unit, and lays the basis for the new purpose which will begin the next unit.

It is also to be noted that the chorus changes the scene which we, as audience, are to imagine. During the agon between Oedipus and Tiresias, our attention is fixed upon their clash, and the scene is literal, close, and immediate: before Oedipus' palace. When the fighters depart and the choral music starts, the focus suddenly widens, as though we had been removed to a distance. We become aware of the interested City around the bright arena; and beyond that, still more dimly, of Nature, sacred to the hidden gods. Mr Burke has expounded the fertile notion that human action may be understood in terms of the scene in which it occurs, and vice versa: the scene is defined by the mode of action. The chorus's action is not limited by the sharp, rationalized purposes of the protagonist; its mode of action, more patient, less sharply realized, is cognate with a wider, if less accurate, awareness of the scene of human life. But the chorus's action, as I have remarked, is not that of passion itself (Nietzsche's cosmic void of night) but suffering informed by the faith of the tribe in a human and a divinely sanctioned natural order: "If such deeds as these are honored," the chorus asks after Jocasta's impiety, "why should I dance and sing?" (lines 894, 895). Thus it is one of the most important functions of the chorus to reveal, in its widest and most mysterious extent, the theater of human life which the play, and indeed the whole Festival of Dionysos, assumed. Even when the chorus does not speak, but only watches, it maintains this theme and this perspective – ready to take the whole stage when the fighters depart.

If one thinks of the movement of the play, it appears that the tragic rhythm analyzes human action temporally into successive modes, as a crystal analyzes a white beam of light spatially into the colored bands of the spectrum. The chorus, always present, represents one of these modes, and at the recurrent moments when reasoned purpose is gone, it takes the stage with its faith-informed passion, moving through an ordered succession of modes of suffering, to a new perception of the immediate situation.

Sophocles and Euripides, the Rationalist

Oedipus Rex is a changing image of human life and action which could have been formed only in the mirror of the tragic theater of the Festival of Dionysos.

The perspectives of the myth, of the rituals, and of the traditional *hodos*, the way of life of the City – "habits of thought and feeling" which constitute the traditional wisdom of the race – were all required to make this play possible. That is why we have to try to regain these perspectives if we are to understand the written play which has come down to us: the analysis of the play leads to an analysis of the theater in which it was formed.

But though the theater was there, everyone could not use it to the full: Sophocles was required. This becomes clear if one considers the very different use which Euripides, Sophocles' contemporary, makes of the tragic theater and its ritual forms.

Professor Gilbert Murray has explained in detail how the tragic form is derived from the ritual form; and he has demonstrated the ritual forms which are preserved in each of the extant Greek tragedies. In general, the ritual had its agon, or sacred combat, between the old King, or god or hero, and the new, corresponding to the agons in the tragedies, and the clear "purpose" moment of the tragic rhythm. It had its *Sparagmos*, in which the royal victim was literally or symbolically torn asunder, followed by the lamentation and/or rejoicing of the chorus: elements which correspond to the moments of "passion." The ritual had its messenger, its recognition scene, and its epiphany; various plot devices for representing the moment of "perception" which follows the "pathos." Professor Murray, in a word, studies the art of tragedy in the light of ritual forms, and thus, throws a really new light upon Aristotle's *Poetics*. The parts of the ritual would appear to correspond to parts of the plot, like recognitions and scenes of suffering, which Aristotle mentions, but, in the text which has come down to us, fails to expound completely. In this view, both the ritual and the more highly elaborated and individualized art of tragedy would be "imitating" action in the tragic rhythm; the parts of the ritual, and the parts of the plot, would both be devices for showing forth the three moments of this rhythm.

Professor Murray, however, does not make precisely these deductions. Unlike Aristotle, he takes the plays of Euripides, rather than Sophocles' *Oedipus*, as the patterns of the tragic form. That is because his attitude to the ritual forms is like Euripides' own: he responds to their purely theatrical effectiveness, but has no interest or belief in the prerational image of human nature and destiny which the ritual conveyed; which Sophocles felt as still alive and significant for his generation, and presented once more in *Oedipus*. Professor Murray shows that Euripides restored the literal ritual much more accurately than Sophocles – his epiphanies, for example, are usually the bodily showing-forth of a very human god, who cynically expounds his cruel part in the proceedings; while the "epiphany" in *Oedipus*, the final tableau of the blind old man with his incestuous brood, merely conveys the moral truth which underlay the action, and implies the anagoge: human dependence upon a mysterious and divine order of nature. Perhaps these distinctions may be summarized as follows:

Professor Murray is interested in the ritual forms in abstraction from all content; Sophocles saw also the spiritual content of the old forms: understood them at a level deeper than the literal, as imitations of an action still "true" to life in his sophisticated age.

Though Euripides and Sophocles wrote at the same time and for the same theater, one cannot understand either the form or the meaning of Euripides' plays on the basis of Sophocles' dramaturgy. The beautiful lyrics sung by Euripides' choruses are, as I have said, incidental music rather than organic parts of the action; they are not based upon the feeling that all have a stake in the common way of life and therefore in the issue of the present action. Euripides' individualistic heroes find no light in their suffering, and bring no renewal to the moral life of the community: they are at war with the very clear, human, and malicious gods, and what they suffer, they suffer unjustly and to no good end. Where Sophocles' celebrated irony seems to envisage the *condition humaine* itself – the plight of the psyche in a world which is ultimately mysterious to it – Euripides' ironies are all aimed at the incredible "gods" and at the superstitions of those who believe in them. In short, if these two writers both used the tragic theater, they did so in very different ways.

Verrall's *Euripides the Rationalist* shows very clearly what the basis of Euripides' dramaturgy is. His use of myth and ritual is like that which Cocteau or, still more exactly, Sartre makes of them – for parody or satirical exposition, but without any belief in their meaning. If Euripides presents the plight of Electra in realistic detail, it is because he wants us to feel the suffering of the individual without benefit of any objective moral or cosmic order – with an almost sensational immediacy: he does not see the myth, as a whole, as significant as such. If he brings Apollo, in the flesh, before us, it is not because he "believes" in Apollo, but because he disbelieves in him, and wishes to reveal this figment of the Greek imagination as, literally, incredible. He depends as much as Sophocles upon the common heritage of ritual and myth: but he "reduces" its form and images to the uses of parody and metaphorical illustration, in the manner of Ovid and of the French Neoclassic tradition. And the human action he reveals is the extremely modern one of the psyche caught in the categories its reason invents, responding with unmitigated sharpness to the feeling of the moment, but cut off from the deepest level of experience, where the mysterious world is yet felt as real and prior to our inventions, demands, and criticisms.

Though Sophocles was not using the myths and ritual forms of the tragic theater for parody and to satirize their tradition, it does not appear that he had any more naïve belief in their literal validity than Euripides did. He would not, for his purpose, have had to ask himself whether the myth of Oedipus conveyed any historic facts. He would not have had to believe that the performance of *Oedipus*, or even the Festival of Dionysos itself, would assure the Athenians a good crop of children and olives. On the contrary he must have felt that the tragic rhythm of action which he discerned in the myth, which he felt as underlying the forms of the ritual, and which he realized in so many ways in his play, was a deeper version of human life than any particular manifestation of it, or any conceptual understanding of it, whether scientific and rationalistic, or theological; yet potentially including them all. If one takes Mr Troy's suggestion, one might say, using the Medieval notion of fourfold symbolism, that Sophocles might well have taken myth and ritual as literally "fictions," yet still have accepted their deeper meanings – trope, allegory, and anagoge – as valid.

Oedipus: The Imitation of an Action

The general notion we used to compare the forms and spiritual content of tragedy and of ancient ritual was the "imitation of action." Ritual imitates action in one way, tragedy in another; and Sophocles' use of ritual forms indicates that he sensed the tragic rhythm common to both.

But the language, plot, characters of the play may also be understood in more detail and in relation to each other as imitations, in their various media, of the one action. I have already quoted Coleridge on the unity of action: "not properly a rule," he calls it, "but in itself the great end, not only of the drama, but of the epic, lyric, even to the candle-flame cone of an epigram – not only of poetry, but of poesy in general, as the proper generic term inclusive of all the fine arts, as its species."[4] Probably the influence of Coleridge partly accounts for the revival of this notion of action which underlies the recent studies of poetry which I have mentioned. Mr Burke's phrase, "language as symbolic action," expresses the idea, and so does his dictum: "The poet spontaneously knows that 'beauty *is* as beauty *does*' (that the 'state' must be embodied in an 'actualization')." (*Four Tropes.*)

This idea of action, and of the play as the imitation of an action, is ultimately derived from the *Poetics*. This derivation is explained in the Appendix. At this point I wish to show how the complex form of *Oedipus* – its plot, characters, and discourse – may be understood as the imitation of a certain action.

The action of the play is the quest for Laius' slayer. That is the over-all aim which informs it – "to find the culprit in order to purify human life," as it may be put. Sophocles must have seen this seeking action as the real life of the Oedipus myth, discerning it through the personages and events as one discerns "life in a plant through the green leaves." Moreover, he must have seen this particular action as a type, or crucial instance, of human life in general; and hence he was able to present it in the form of the ancient ritual which also presents and celebrates the perennial mystery of human life and action. Thus

---

[4] The essay on *Othello*.

by "action" I do not mean the events of the story but the focus or aim of psychic life from which the events, in that situation, result.

If Sophocles was imitating action in this sense, one may schematically imagine his work of composition in three stages, three mimetic acts: 1. He makes the plot: i.e., arranges the events of the story in such a way as to reveal the seeking action from which they come. 2. He develops the characters of the story as individualized forms of "quest." 3. He expresses or realizes their actions by means of the words they utter in the various situations of the plot. This scheme, of course, has nothing to do with the temporal order which the poet may really have followed in elaborating his composition, nor to the order we follow in becoming acquainted with it; we start with the words, the "green leaves." The scheme refers to the "hierarchy of actualizations" which we may eventually learn to see in the completed work.

1. The first act of imitation consists in making the plot or arrangement of incidents. Aristotle says that the tragic poet is primarily a maker of plots, for the plot is the "soul of a tragedy," its formal cause. The arrangement which Sophocles made of the events of the story – starting near the end, and rehearsing the past in relation to what is happening now – already to some degree actualizes the tragic quest he wishes to show, even before we sense the characters as individuals or hear them speak and sing.

(The reader must be warned that this conception of the plot is rather unfamiliar to us. Usually we do not distinguish between the plot as the form of the play and the plot as producing a certain effect upon the audience – excitement, "interest," suspense, and the like. Aristotle also uses "plot" in this second sense. The mimicry of art has a further purpose, or final – as distinguished from its formal – cause, i.e., to reach the audience. Thinking of the Athenian theater, he describes the plot as intended to show the "universal," or to rouse and purge the emotions of pity and terror. These two meanings of the word – the form of the action, and the device for reaching the audience – are also further explained in the Appendix. At this point I am using the word *plot* in the first sense: as the form, the first actualization, of the tragic action.)

2. The characters, or agents, are the second actualization of the action. According to Aristotle, "the agents are imitated mainly with a view to the action" – i.e., the soul of the tragedy is there already in the order of events, the tragic rhythm of the life of Oedipus and Thebes; but this action may be more sharply realized and more elaborately shown forth by developing individual variations upon it. It was with this principle in mind that Ibsen wrote to his publisher, after two years' of work on *The Wild Duck*, that the play was nearly complete, and he could now proceed to "the more energetic individuation of the characters."

If one considers the Oedipus-Tiresias scene which I have quoted, one can see how the characters serve to realize the action of the whole. They reveal, at any moment, a "spectrum of action" like that which the tragic rhythm spread before us in temporal succession, at the same time offering concrete instances of almost photographic sharpness. Thus Tiresias "suffers" in the darkness of his blindness while Oedipus pursues his reasoned "purpose"; and then Tiresias effectuates his "purpose" of serving his mantic vision of the truth, while Oedipus "suffers" a blinding passion of fear and anger. The agents also serve to move the action ahead, develop it in time, through their conflicts. The chorus meanwhile, in some respects between, in others deeper, than the antagonists, represents the interests of that resolution, that final chord of feeling, in which the end of the action, seen ironically and sympathetically as one, will be realized.

3. The third actualization is in the words of the play. The seeking action which is the substance of the play is imitated first in the plot, second in the characters, and third in the words, concepts, and forms of discourse wherein the characters "actualize" their psychic life in its shifting forms, in response to the everchanging situations of the play. If one thinks of plotting, characterization, and poetry as successive "acts of imitation" by the author, one may also say that they constitute, in the completed work, a hierarchy of forms; and that the words of the play are its "highest individuation." They are the "green leaves" which we actually perceive; the product and the sign of the one "life of the plant" which, by an imaginative effort, one may divine behind them all.

At this point one encounters again Mr Burke's theory of "language as symbolic action," and the many contemporary studies of the arts of poetry which have been made from this point of view. It would be appropriate to offer a detailed study of Sophocles' language, using the modern tools of analysis, to substantiate my main point. But this would require the kind of knowledge of Greek which a Jebb spent his life to acquire; and I must be content to try to show, in very general terms, that the varied forms of the poetry of *Oedipus* can only be understood on a histrionic basis: i.e., as coming out of a direct sense of the tragic rhythm of *action*.

In the Oedipus-Tiresias scene, there is a "spectrum of the forms of discourse" corresponding to the "spectrum of action" which I have described. It extends from Oedipus' opening speech – a reasoned exposition not, of course, without feeling but based essentially upon clear ideas and a logical order – to the choral chant, based upon sensuous imagery and the "logic of feeling." Thus it employs, in the beginning, the principle of composition which Mr Burke calls "syllogistic progression," and, at the other end of the spectrum, Mr Burke's "progression by association and contrast." When the Neoclassic and rationalistic critics of the seventeenth century read *Oedipus*, they saw only the order of reason; they did not know what to make of the chorus. Hence Racine's drama of "Action as Rational": a drama of static situations, of clear concepts and merely illustrative images. Nietzsche, on the other hand, saw only the passion of the chorus; for his insight was based on *Tristam*, which is composed essentially in sensuous images, and moves by association and contrast according to the logic of feeling: the drama which takes "action as passion." Neither point of view enables one to see how the scene, as a whole, hangs together.

If the speeches of the characters and the songs of the chorus are only the foliage of the plant, this is as much as to say that the life and meaning of the whole is never literally and completely present in any one formulation. It takes *all* of the elements – the shifting situation, the changing and developing characters, and their reasoned or lyric utterances, to indicate, in the round, the action Sophocles wishes to convey. Because this action takes the form of reason as well as passion, and of contemplation by way of symbols; because it is essentially moving (in the tragic rhythm); and because it is shared in different ways by all the characters, the play has neither literal unity nor the rational unity of the truly abstract idea, or "univocal concept." Its parts and its moments are one only "by analogy"; and just as the Saints warn us that we must believe in order to understand, so we must "make believe," by a sympathetic and imitative act of the histrionic sensibility, in order to get what Sophocles intended by his play.

It is the histrionic basis of Sophocles' art which makes it mysterious to us, with our demands for conceptual clarity, or for the luxury of yielding to a stream of feeling and subjective imagery. But it is this also which makes it so crucial an instance of the art of the theater in its completeness, as though the author understood "song, spectacle, thought, and diction" in their primitive and subtle roots. And it is the histrionic basis of drama which "undercuts theology and science."

Analogues of the "Tragic Rhythm"

In the present study I propose to use *Oedipus* as a landmark, and to relate subsequent forms of drama to it. For it presents a moving image at the nascent moment of highest valency, of a way of life and action which is still at the root of our culture.

Professor Buchanan remarks, in *Poetry and Mathematics*, that the deepest and most elaborate development of the tragic rhythm is to be found in the *Divine Comedy*. The *Purgatorio* especially, though an epic and not a drama, evidently moves in the tragic rhythm, both as a whole and in detail. The daylight climb up the mountain, by moral effort, and in the light of natural reason, corresponds to the first moment, that of "purpose." The night, under the sign of Faith, Hope and Charity, when the Pilgrim can do nothing by his own unaided efforts, corresponds to the moments of passion and perception. The Pilgrim, as he pauses, mulls over the thoughts and experiences of the day; he sleeps and dreams, seeing ambivalent images from the mythic dreaming of the race, which refer, also, both to his own "suppressed desires" and to his own deepest aspirations. These images gradually solidify and clarify, giving place to a new perception of his situation. This rhythm, repeated in varied forms, carries the Pilgrim from the superficial but whole-hearted motivations of childhood, in the Antipurgatorio, through the divided counsels of the growing soul, to the new innocence, freedom, and integrity of the Terrestrial Paradise – the realm of *The Tempest* or of *Oedipus at Colonos*. The same rhythmic conception governs also the detail of the work, down to the *terza rima* itself – that verse-form which is clear at any moment in its literal fiction yet essentially moving ahead and pointing to deeper meanings.

Because Dante keeps his eye always upon the tragic moving of the psyche itself, his vision, like that of Sophocles, is not limited by any of the forms of thought whereby we seek to fix our experience – in which we are idolatrously expiring, like the coral animal in its shell. But Professor Buchanan shows that the abstract shape, at least, of the tragic rhythm is to be recognized in other and more limited or specialized cultural forms as well. "This pattern," he writes, "is the Greek view of life. It is the method of their and our science, history and philosophy. . . . The Greek employment of it had been humanistic in the main. . . . The late Middle Ages and the Renaissance substituted natural objects for the heroes of vicarious tragedies, the experiments in the laboratory. They put such objects under controlled conditions, introduced artificial complications, and waited for the answering pronouncement of fate. The crucial experiment is the crisis of an attempt to rationalize experience, that is, to force it into our analogies. Purgation and recognition are now called elimination of false hypotheses and verification. The shift is significant, but the essential tragic pattern of tragedy is still there."

The tragic rhythm is, in a sense, the shape of Racinian tragedy, even though Racine was imitating action as essentially rational, and would have called the moments of the rhythm exposition, complication, crisis, and denouement, to satisfy the reason. It is in a way the shape of *Tristan*, though action in that play is reduced to passion, the principles of composition to the logic of feeling. Even the over-all shape of *Hamlet* is similar, though the sense of pathos predominates, and the whole is elaborated in such subtle profusion as can only be explained with reference to Dante and the Middle Ages.

The next two chapters are devoted respectively to *Bérénice* and *Tristan*. It is true that neither Racine nor Wagner understood the dramatic art in the exact spirit of Aristotle's definition, "the *imitation* of action." Wagner was rather expressing an emotion, and Racine was *demonstrating* an essence. But expression of emotion and rational demonstration may themselves be regarded as modes of action, each analogous to one moment in Sophocles' tragic rhythm.

17

THE MYTH AND RITUAL APPROACH TO SHAKESPEAREAN TRAGEDY

Herbert Weisinger

Like Murray and Fergusson, the American literary critic Herbert Weisinger (b. 1913), who taught English at Michigan State University and at the State University of New York, Stony Brook, applied myth-ritualism to tragedy. Like them, Weisinger parallels the fate of the tragic hero with that of the Frazerian king. At the same time, he distinguishes tragedy from myth and ritual on many grounds. Most important, the myth-ritualist quest for food from god becomes the tragic quest for reconciliation with god. Tragedy comes from myth-ritualism but is both more and other than myth-ritualism. Yet Weisinger surprisingly employs myth-ritualism not merely to account for tragedy but also to evaluate it: the more fully a tragedy fits the myth-ritualist pattern, the more successful it is as tragedy. In addition to the following essay on Shakespearean tragedy in particular (from *Centennial Review* 1 [1957] 142–66), see his *Tragedy and the Paradox of the Fortunate Fall* (London: Routledge & Kegan Paul; East Lansing: Michigan State College Press, 1953). Weisinger subsequently became somewhat skeptical of myth-ritualism yet continued to practice and defend it. See his collection of essays on myth, *The Agony and the Triumph* (East Lansing: Michigan State University Press, 1964), esp. 92–117 (which reprints "The Myth and Ritual Approach to Shakespearean Tragedy"), 118–33, 172–9, 213–40; and "An Examination of the Myth and Ritual Approach to Shakespeare," in *Myth and Mythmaking*, ed. Henry A. Murray (New York: Braziller, 1960), 132–40. On Weisinger see Stanley Edgar Hyman, review of *Tragedy and the Paradox of the Fortunate Fall*, *Journal of American Folklore* 67 (1954), 86–9; and Joseph Fontenrose, *The Ritual Theory of Myth* (Berkeley: University of California Press, 1966), 34–5.

Original publication: Herbert Weisinger, "The Myth and Ritual Approach to Shakespearean Tragedy," *Centennial Review* 1 (1957), pp. 142–66.

The "myth and ritual" approach to literature is now one of the high gods in the pantheon of contemporary criticism, and it numbers among its devotees not a few eminently respectable names. This was not always so, however, and even as Zeus himself had laboriously to struggle up the ladder of divine acceptance, so the myth and ritual approach to literature now grows fat on quarterly hecatombs. So much so, indeed, that the very word *myth* has acquired a mana of its own and has been elevated into a substitute, less precise, less bold, and I dare say, less honest, for religion, though in this guise it has given many the courage of their conversion. As with other methods for the study of literature, the myth and ritual approach has its values, and they are distinctive and useful, but it also has its limitations, for it is certainly not a panacea concocted to cure all critical complaints.

What I want to do in this paper is to describe the myth and ritual approach to literature as I understand it and to show what new light it can throw on Shakespeare's tragedies, and presumably to illuminate them afresh. For the purposes of this analysis, I take the myth and ritual pattern as fundamental and anterior to tragedy, and I pass Shakespeare's tragedies over this pattern, as tracings over the original drawing, in order to reveal his changes, modifications, and alterations of it; that is to say, I try to distinguish the uniquely Shakespearean from the generally tragic. But I do not wish to be understood as suggesting that the myth and ritual pattern is either the *ur*-tragedy from which all others descend or the ideal tragedy toward which all others tend. Nor would I want to give the impression that the myth and ritual approach to Shakespearean tragedy excludes other established methods of interpreting the plays. The character analysis in ethical terms of Bradley, the visualization of the plays in action on the stage of Granville-Barker, the linking of Elizabethan tragedy with medieval traditions of Farnham, the study of Shakespearean characterization in the light of Elizabethan psychology of Campbell, the examination of the images and image-clusters of the plays as clues to their meaning of Spurgeon, the close reading of the text for structure and texture of Empson, the probing of character in Freudian psychoanalytic categories of Jones, the working-out of the Elizabethan world picture and its role in the Shakespearean ethos of Tillyard, the re-estimation of the extent and use of Shakespeare's learning of Baldwin, the utilization of the new texts established by the scientific bibliographers, the application of Christian ritual to the understanding of the plays of Knight, the placing of Shakespeare within the practices and economy of Elizabethan acting companies of Chambers, the syncretism of the *Scrutiny*-Penguin group – the achievements of these schools of Shakespearean criticism the myth and ritual approach endeavors to assimilate within its own methodology.

Certainly I am not the first to suggest such a correlation; on the contrary, many critics have seen the connection and have in fact gone beyond the tragedies to the later plays in an effort to prove that the pattern of rebirth and reconciliation is fundamental to virtually the whole of Shakespeare's plays. But, while the myth and ritual pattern so used makes, if I may say so, a Christian Olympian out of Shakespeare, it does so only at the expense of the myth and ritual pattern and of the substance of the plays themselves. It is my contention that while the last plays of Shakespeare do indeed carry forward the tragic pattern established in *Hamlet, Othello, King Lear*, and *Macbeth*, they neither heighten nor deepen it but on the contrary reject and even destroy it. In fact, I would go so far as to argue that the tragic pattern in the tragedies themselves is scarely maintained equally strongly over each of the plays. For, on the basis of a comparison between the myth and ritual pattern as I have described it in *Tragedy and the Paradox of the Fortunate Fall* and the tragedies, I think that Shakespeare's tragic vision, which he was able to sustain but tentatively in *Hamlet*, most fully in *Othello*, barely in *King Lear*, and hardly at all in *Macbeth*, failed him altogether in the last plays, and that this failure is manifested by the use of the elements of the myth and ritual pattern as mere machinery, virtually in burlesque fashion, and not as their informing and sustaining spirit. The instinct of the critics in applying the myth and ritual pattern to the plays has been sound, but their superimposition of the pattern on the plays has been inexact and, I suspect, prompted more by religious rather than by critical motives, with the result that both the method and the plays have been falsified.

I

If I begin with some diffidence, it is because I am always acutely aware that the myth and ritual pattern, upon which the myth and ritual approach to literature must be founded, is as uncertain in its origins as it is unrealized in actuality. I have tried to account for the persistence and power of the myth and ritual pattern by retracing it generally to that initial impact of experience which produced the archetypes of belief, and specifically, to the archetype of rebirth as crystallized out of the archetype of belief. Unfortunately no real proof of this process is possible, for the events which generated the primary shock of belief are now too deep and too dim in the racial memory of man to be exhumed by archaelogical means, though the psychoanalytic probings of Freud have cleared a path through this labyrinth, with reluctant confirmation coming from the anthropologists and classicists. Similarly, we must not forget that there is really no such thing as the myth and ritual pattern *per se*; at best, it is a probable construction of many varieties and variations of a number of beliefs and actions so closely related to each other that it is reasonable to construct – reconstruct would be a misleading word here – an ideal form of the myth and ritual pattern more comprehensive and more realized than any variations of it which we actually possess.

The myth and ritual pattern of the ancient Near East, which is at least six thousand years old, centers in a divine king who was killed annually and who was reborn in the person of his successor. In its later development, the king was not killed, but went through an annual symbolic death and a symbolic rebirth or resurrection. Starting out as a magical rite designed to ensure the success of the crops in climates where the outcome of the struggle between water and drought meant literally the difference between life and death, the pattern was gradually transformed into a religious ritual, designed this time to promote man's salvation, and finally became an ethical conviction, freed now of both its magical and religious ritual practices but still retaining in spiritualized and symbolic form its ancient appeal and emotional certitude. Because it begins with the need to survive, the pattern never loses it force, for it is concerned always with survival, whether physical or spiritual. So far as can be ascertained at present, the pattern had a double growth, one along the lines of the ancient civilizations of the Near East, the Sumerian, the Egyptian, the Babylonian, both South and North, the Palestinian – first with the Canaanites, and then with the Hebrews – and from thence into Christianity; the other along the lines of the island civilizations of the Aegean, from Crete to the mainland of Greece, from thence to Rome, and once more into Christianity, the two streams of development flowing into each other and reinforcing themselves at this crucial juncture.

Despite the differences between the religions of the ancient Near East (as, for example, between those of Egypt and Mesopotamia, and between that of the Hebrews and of the others), nevertheless they all possessed certain significant features of myth and ritual in common. These features, in their turn, stemmed from the common bond of ritual, characteristic (in one form or another) of all together, though, as I have said, none possessed completely all the elements, which varied in some degree from religion to religion. In this single, idealized ritual scheme, the well-being of the community was secured by the regular performance of certain ritual actions in which the king or his equivalent took the leading role. Moreover the king's importance for the community was incalculably increased by the almost universal conviction that the fortunes of the community or state and those of the king were inextricably intermingled; indeed one may go so far as to say that on the well-being of the king depended the well-being of the community as a whole. On the basis of the evidence covering different peoples at different times, we know then that in the ancient Near East there existed a pattern of thought and action which gripped the minds and emotions of those who believed in it so strongly that it was made the basis on which they could apprehend and accept the universe in which they lived. It made possible man's conviction that he could control that universe for his own purposes; and it placed in his hands the lever whereby he could exercise that control.

From an analysis of the extant seasonal rituals, particularly the new year festivals, and from the coronation, initiation, and personal rituals of the ancient

Near East, it is possible to make a reconstructed model of the basic ritual form. Essentially the pattern contains these basic elements: 1. the indispensable role of the divine king; 2. the combat between the God and an opposing power; 3. the suffering of the God; 4. the death of the God; 5. the resurrection of the God; 6. the symbolic recreation of the myth of creation; 7. the sacred marriage; 8. the triumphal procession; and 9. the settling of destinies. We must remember, however, that the dying-rising-God theme constitutes but one illustration, so to speak, of the greater cycle of birth, death, and rebirth. The many and various rites connected with birth, with initiation, with mariage, and with death in the case of the individual, as well as the rites concerned with the planting, the harvesting, the new year celebrations, and with the installation ceremonies of the king in the case of the community, all these rites repeat each in its own way the deep-rooted and abiding cycle of death and rebirth. Not only do these rituals *symbolize* the passage from death to life, from one way of life to another, but they are the actual *means* of achieving the changeover; they mark the transition by which – through the processes of separation, regeneration, and the return on a higher level – both the individual and the community are assured their victory over the forces of chaos which are thereby kept under control.

The purpose of these rituals is by enaction to bring about a just order of existence in which God, nature, and man are placed in complete and final rapport with each other; they are both the defence against disorder and the guarantee of order. In the myth and ritual pattern, then, man has devised a mighty weapon by which he keeps at bay, and sometimes even seems to conquer, the hostile forces which endlessly threaten to overpower him. In the early stages of the development of the myth and ritual pattern, however, the best that man could hope for was an uneasy truce between himself and chaos, because the cycle merely returned to its beginnings; the God fought, was defeated, was resurrected, was momentarily triumphant, and thus ensured the well-being of the community for the coming year, but it was inevitable that in the course of the year he would again be defeated and would again have to go through his annual agony. Thus nothing new could be expected nor was anticipated, and year after year man could hope for no more than a temporary gain which he was sure would soon be turned into an inevitable loss. To achieve genuine faith, therefore, was an act of courage difficult and infrequent to attain, and it is no wonder that we detect in the myth and ritual pattern of the ancient Near East before the Hebraic-Christian tradition takes over, too strong a reliance on the mere machinery of ritual, ultimately leading not to faith but to superstition, as well as the melancholy notes of despair and pessimism. But the Hebraic-Christian tradition in the very process of adapting the pattern, transformed it, for by virtue of its unique and tenacious insistence on the mercy and judgment of its transcendent God, it introduced a new and vital element in the pattern, that of the dialectical leap from out of the endless circle on to a different and higher stage of understanding. The crucial moment in this transformation of the myth and ritual pattern comes when man, by himself, undertakes on his own to make the leap; to him remains the decision and his is the responsibility; by making the leap, he makes himself. The Hebraic-Christian tradition utilized the cycle of birth, life, death, and rebirth to conquer chaos and disorder, but it made its unique contribution to the pattern by giving man the possibility of defeating chaos and disorder by a single, supreme act of human will which could wipe them out at one stroke. In so doing it preserved the potency of the pattern and retained its ancient appeal and, at the same time, ensured its continued use by supplying the one element it had hitherto lacked to give it its permanent role as the means whereby man is enabled to live in an indifferent universe; it showed that man can, by himself, transcend that universe.

II

This, then, is the myth and ritual pattern as I understand it. What are its implications for tragedy? To start with, I would suggest that in the myth and ritual pattern we have the seedbed of tragedy, the stuff out of which it was ultimately formed. Both the form and content of tragedy, its architecture as well as its ideology, closely parallel the form and content of the myth and ritual pattern. But having said that, I must also say that the myth and ritual pattern and tragedy are not the same. Both share the same shape and the same intent, but they differ significantly in the manner of their creation and in the methods of achieving their purposes. The myth and ritual pattern is the group product of many and different minds groping on many and different levels over long and kaleidoscopic periods of time under the stimulus of motivations quite different from those which produce tragedy. I am not suggesting anything like the formerly accepted communal origin of the ballad, for we know that myth in its form as the complement to ritual must have been devised by the priest-astrologer-magicians of the ancient world. The intent of the myth and ritual pattern is control, its method that of mimetically reproducing the rhythm of birth, death, and birth again to gain that control. But imitation here means, not acting alike, as we think of the term – a parallel and similar yet at the same time a distinct and different attitude and behavior toward the thing imitated – but rather the interpenetration of and union with the imitator, the thing imitated, and the imitation, all three being one and the same thing.

Tragedy, on the other hand, is a creation compounded of conscious craft and conviction. If we describe the myth and ritual pattern as the passage from ignorance to understanding through suffering mimetically and at first hand, then we must describe tragedy as the passage from ignorance to understanding through suffering symbolically and at a distance. To speak of symbolic meaning is already to have made the leap from myth to art. In the myth and ritual pattern, the dying-reborn God-king, the worshippers for whom he suffers, and the action of his agony are identical; in tragedy, the tragic protagonist undergoes his suffering at an aesthetic distance and only vicariously in the minds of his audience. And for that reason does Aristotle tell us that tragedy is an imitation of an action. You participate in a ritual but you are a spectator of a play.

Moreover, tragedy reconstitutes the myth and ritual pattern in terms of its own needs. Of the nine elements which make up the myth and ritual pattern as I have described it, four have been virtually eliminated from tragedy, namely, the actual death of the God, the symbolic recreation of the myth of creation, the sacred marriage, and the triumphal procession; two elements, the indispensable role of the divine king and the settling of destinies, are retained only by implication and play rather ambiguous roles in tragedy; while the remaining three – combat, suffering (with death subsumed), and resurrection – now give tragedy its structure and substance. I have already noted that one of the characteristics of the myth and ritual pattern is its adaptability, its ability to change shape while retaining its potency, and we should therefore not be surprised to find the same process at work in its relation to tragedy. What is revealing, however, is the direction of change, for we find, first, that the theme of the settling of destinies which is the highest point in the myth and ritual pattern – the goal of the struggle, since without it the passion of the God would be in vain, and chaos and disorder would be triumphant – this theme, so elaborately explicated in the ritual practices of the ancient Near East, is no more than implied in tragedy, just as the correspondence between the well-being of the king and the well-being of the community, again so detailed in ritual, is only shadowed forth, as a condition to be aimed at but not to be achieved in reality.

Second, we discover that even greater emphasis is placed on the small moment of doubt in tragedy than in the myth and ritual pattern itself. In the rituals of the ancient Near East, at the point between the death of the God and his resurrection, all action is arrested as the participants fearfully and anxiously wait for the God to be revived. After the din of combat, this quiet moment of doubt and indecision is all the more awful, for there is no assurance that the God will be reborn: "For a small moment have I forsaken thee." "But," continues Isaiah, "with great mercies will I gather thee." It is no wonder that the small moment is followed in the pattern by creation, the sacred marriage, and the triumphal procession as the peoples' expression of joy that the death of the God has not been in vain and that for another year at least: "the earth remaineth, seedtime and harvest, and cold and heat, and summer and winter, and day and night shall not cease."

And, clearly spelling out the implications of the second change made by tragedy in the myth and ritual pattern is the third, the freedom of choice of the tragic protagonist and the responsibility for the consequences of making that choice. For in that small moment of doubt and indecision, when victory and defeat are poised in the balance, only the moral force of man wills him on in action to success. The tragic protagonist acts in the conviction that his action is right, and he accepts the responsibility for that action; for him to do less than that means the loss of his stature as a moral, responsible agent. The tragic occurs when by the fall of a man of strong character we are made aware of something greater than that man or even than mankind; we seem to see a new and truer vision of the universe.

But that vision cannot be bought cheaply. It cannot be bought by blind reliance on the mere machinery of the myth and ritual pattern, and it cannot be bought by fixing the fight, as Handel's librettist fatuously puts it:

> How vain is man who boasts in fight
> The valour of gigantic might,
> And dreams not that a hand unseen
> Directs and guides this weak machine.

Better the indifferent Gods of Lucretius than the busybody *deus ex machina* of Vine Street and Madison Avenue. Only the deliberate moral choice of the tragic protagonist confronted by two equal and opposite forces and fully aware of the consequences of his choice can bring off the victory, and then only at the expense of pain and suffering: "He is despised and rejected of men; a man of sorrows, and acquainted with grief." But suffering can be made bearable only when at the same time it is made part of a rational world order into which it fits and which has an understandable place for it:

> I cried by reason of mine affliction unto the Lord, and he heard me; out of the belly of hell cried I, and thou heardest my voice.
>
> For thou hadst cast me into the deep, in the midst of the seas; and the floods compassed me about: all thy billows and thy waves passed over me.
>
> Then I said, I am cast out of thy sight; yet I will look again toward thy holy temple.
>
> The waters compassed me about, even to the soul: the depth closed me round about, the weeds were wrapped about my head.
>
> I went down to the bottoms of the mountains; the earth with her bars was about me for ever: yet hast thou brought up my life from corruption, O Lord my God.
>
> When my soul fainted within me I remembered the Lord: and my prayer came in unto thee, into thine holy temple.
>
> They that observe lying vanities forsake their own mercy.
>
> But I will sacrifice unto thee with the voice of thanksgiving; I will pay that that I have vowed. Salvation is of the Lord. (*Jonah* 2. 2–9)

Salvation is indeed of the Lord, but Jonah must deliberately look to the holy temple and must remember the Lord of his own free will; *then* salvation is of the Lord.

Tragedy therefore occurs when the accepted order of things is fundamentally questioned only to be the more triumphantly reaffirmed. It cannot exist where there is no faith; conversely, it cannot exist where there is no doubt; it can exist only in an atmosphere of sceptical faith. The protagonist must be free to choose, and though he chooses wrongly, yet the result of the wrong choice is our own escape and our enlightenment. Yet nothing less than this sacrifice will do, and only the symbolic sacrifice of one who is like us can make possible our atonement for the evil which is within us and for the sins which we are capable of committing. Nevertheless, in western thought, if man is free to choose, in the end he must choose rightly. He is free to choose his salvation, but he is punished for his wrong choice. Man is free, but he is free within the limits set for him by his condition as a man. So great is the emphasis placed on freedom of choice in tragedy that the settling of destinies, which in the myth and ritual pattern is the tangible reward of victory, recedes more and more into the background, and the messianic vision implicit in the settling of destinies is personalized and humanized in tragedy in the form of heightened self-awareness as the end of the tragic agony. In short, what I have been saying is that the myth and ritual pattern pertains to religion which proceeds by assertion, tragedy to literature which proceeds by assessment.

To sum up, then, the structure of tragic form, as derived from the myth and ritual pattern, may be diagrammed in this way: the tragic protagonist, in whom is subsumed the well-being of the people and the welfare of the state, engages in conflict with a representation of darkness and evil; a temporary defeat is inflicted on the tragic protagonist, but after shame and suffering he emerges triumphant as the symbol of the victory of light and good over darkness and evil, a victory sanctified by the covenant of the settling of destinies which reaffirms the well-being of the people and the welfare of the state. In the course of the conflict there comes a point where the protagonist and the antagonist appear to merge into a single challenge against the order of God; the evil which the protagonist would not do, he does, and the good which he would, he does not; and in this moment we are made aware that the real protagonist of tragedy is the order of God against which the tragic hero has rebelled. In this manner is the pride, the presumption which is in all of us by virtue of our mixed state as man, symbolized and revealed, and it is this *hybris* which is vicariously purged from us by the suffering of the tragic protagonist. He commits the foul deed which is potentially in us, he challenges the order of God which we would but dare not, he expiates our sin, and what we had hitherto felt we had been forced to accept we now believe of our free will, namely, that the order of God is just and good. Therefore is the tragic protagonist vouchsafed the vision of victory but not its attainment:

> But the Lord was wroth with me for your sakes, and would not hear me: and
> the Lord said unto me, Let it suffice thee; speak no more unto me of this matter.

Get thee up into the top of Pisgah, and lift up thine eyes westward, and northward, and southward, and eastward, and behold it with thine eyes: for thou shalt not go over this Jordan. (*Deuteronomy* 3. 26–27)

III

Seen from this point of view, *Hamlet* is a particularly fascinating example of the relationship between the myth and ritual pattern and tragedy, because it shows within the action of the play itself the development of Shakespeare's awareness of tragedy as a heightened and secularized version of the pattern. Hamlet begins by crying for revenge, which is personal, and ends by seeking justice, which is social. Shakespeare deals with the problem of the play – how shall a son avenge the injustice done his father? – by presenting it to us in four different yet related ways simultaneously, each consistent within its pattern of behavior, yet each overlapping and protruding beyond the other, like the successive superimpositions of the same face seen from different angles in a portrait by Picasso. First, there is Hamlet-Laertes, who, incapable of seeking more than revenge, dies unchanged and unfulfilled, no better nor no worse than when he had begun. Then there is Hamlet the Prince, caught midway between revenge and justice, who passes from ignorance to understanding but too late. Third, there is Hamlet-Fortinbras, who avenges his father's wrongs by joining the warring kingdoms into a single nation under his able rule. And finally, containing all these Hamlets, is Hamlet the King, idealized by his son into the perfect king whom he must replace. From this dynastic destiny stems Hamlet's ambivalence towards his father: he loves him for the man he wants to be himself and hates him for the King who stands in the way of the Prince and for the father who stands in the way of the son. Seeking his father's murderer, Hamlet finds himself. The same necessity holds Hal and Hamlet alike, but where Hal sees a straight line between his father and himself – "You won it, wore it, kept it, gave it me; / Then plain and right must my possession be." (*II Henry IV*. IV.v.222–23) – and is therefore sure of himself and of his actions, Hamlet finds himself in a labyrinth whose walls are lined with trick doors and distorting mirrors: "O cursed spite, / That ever I was born to set it right!"

Hamlet's ambivalence is reflected in the fragmentation of his character; there are as many Hamlets as there are scenes in which he appears, and each person in the play sees a different Hamlet before him. But of the contradictions in his character, two stand out as the major symptoms of his incompleteness. The first is Hamlet's yearning to be able to act, not for the sake of action alone, but rightly, in the clear cause of justice; for while no tragic protagonist acts more frequently and more vigorously than Hamlet, he is more and more perplexed to discover that the more he would do good – that is, cleanse Denmark by avenging his father's death – the more evil he in fact accomplishes; hence his envy of Fortinbras' ability to act resolutely and without equivocation (IV.iv.). Second, though he is nominally a Christian, yet in the moments of sharpest crisis Hamlet turns instead to the consolations of Stoicism: "If it be now, 'tis not to come; if it be not to come, it will be now; if it be not now, yet it will come; the readiness is all. Since no man has aught of what he leaves, what is't to leave betimes?" (V.ii.231–35). And it is not enough: his mission succeeds only by mischance, his cause is still not understood, and with his dying breath he calls on Horatio, the true Stoic, to tell his story to the unsatisfied. Hamlet's vision is still clouded at his death – "Things standing thus unknown"; Horatio's own version of the events is surprisingly but an advertisement for a tragedy by Seneca (V.ii.391–97); and there is something too cold and callous in the way Fortinbras embraces his fortune. In short, the myth and ritual elements have not been completely assimilated into the tragedy: the suffering of the tragic protagonist is neither altogether deserved nor altogether understood by him, the rebirth is not quite inevitable nor necessary, and the settling of destinies in the person of Fortinbras is somewhat forced and mechanical. The genuine sense of tragic loss is somewhat vulgarized into regret: Hamlet has been too-fascinating.

In *Othello*, Shakespeare mixed his most perfect amalgam of the myth and ritual elements with tragedy. Where in *Hamlet* he was almost too fecund and profusive in characterization – invention inundating integration – in *Othello* he ruthlessly simplified and organized; if *Hamlet* is linear, proceeding by the method of montage and multiple exposure, *Othello* is monolithic and nuclear: the opposites of good and evil in human nature are forcibly split and then fused together in the fire of suffering. By overvaluing human nature, Othello destroys the balance between good and bad which is the condition of man; by undervaluing human nature, Iago brings about the same destruction from the equal and opposite direction. Each in his own way is an incomplete man: where Othello responds emotionally, Iago reasons; where Othello feels that men are better than they are, Iago knows that they are worse; each, in short, believes only what he wants to, and they are alike only in that both lack tolerance and understanding. Othello must be made to realize that the perfect love which he demands – "My life upon her faith!" "And when I love thee not, Chaos is come again." – is nothing more than the perfect hate which Iago practices:

> *Othello*:   Now art thou my lieutenant.
> *Iago*:   I am your own for ever.
>   (III.iii.478–89)

If Iago is motivated by pride, will, and individualism, so then is Othello in his own way. Iago is the external symbol of the evil in Othello, for everything that

Othello would stand for is negated and reversed in Iago: the subverter of the order of God whose coming is after the working of Satan, the man who rejects principle, and who denies virtue, love, and reputation. To him, ideals are but a mask which conceals the sensuality, the brutality, and the greed for money, power, and sex, which he believes constitute man's true nature.

As the opposites of character in Othello and Iago meet and merge in Act III, scene iii, Othello becomes for the moment Iago: he reverts to paganism and calls on the stars for help, he orders his friend murdered, he spies on and humiliates and at the last repudiates his wife: "She's like a liar, gone to burning hell." But this is for him the bottom of the pit, and by a supreme effort of will he purges the Iago from within him; and in that awful moment of self-awareness, he recreates himself as he might have been, he realizes his potential as a human being. Having by his rashness put the well-being of the people and the welfare of the state in jeopardy, as Brabantio had foretold, perhaps better than he knew, –

> Mine's not an idle cause. The Duke himself,
> Or any of my brothers of the state,
> Cannot but feel this wrong as 'twere their own;
> For if such actions may have passage free,
> Bond-slaves and pagans shall our statesmen be.
> (I.ii.95–99)

– Othello is inevitably punished. And Iago is defeated by the one force which he is incapable of understanding, the power of principle. What he fails to see is that Othello's love for Desdemona is the symbol of Othello's faith in the goodness and justice of the world. What Othello seeks, therefore, when that faith is called into question, is not revenge, which is Iago's goal, but the cleansing of evil and the reaffirmation of goodness and justice: "It is the cause, my soul." From the depth of his self-awareness, bought at so dear a price, there emerges the theme of the settling of destinies, not embodied in the person of a successor, but filling as it were with its vision the entire stage, the sign of evil purged and the good restored, the image of man in his full stature as responsible man: "Speak of me as I am." "And when man faces destiny," Malraux writes, "destiny ends and man comes into his own."

IV

Both *Hamlet* and *Othello* possess three features in common which by contrast are not present in *Lear* and *Macbeth*. First, both *Hamlet* and *Othello* are for the Elizabethan audience contemporary plays laid in contemporary or nearly contemporary settings. No great historical distance separates them from their audience as it does in *Lear* and *Macbeth*, which are laid in pre-Christian England and Scotland. Second, both *Hamlet* and *Othello* operate within the Christian framework, recognized and apprehended as such by the audience for which they were written. But in *Lear* and *Macbeth* the pagan background is insistent. From the depth of their suffering Lear and Gloucester can appeal no higher than to the heathen gods: "As flies to wanton boys, are we to th' gods,/ They kill us for their sport" (IV.i.38–39); and Edgar's wisdom is but cold comfort in the Stoic manner: "Bear free and patient thoughts" (IV.vi.80). In *Macbeth*, the witches play the same role as do the gods in *Lear*:

> But 'tis strange;
> And oftentimes, to win us to our harm,
> The instruments of darkness tell us truths,
> Win us with honest trifles, to betray's
> In deepest consequence.
>
> (I.iii.122–26)

Finally, the theme of the settling of destinies – present directly in *Hamlet* and indirectly in *Othello* – fades away in *Lear* and disappears altogether in *Macbeth*. These changes reveal a significant shift in Shakespeare's use of the myth and ritual pattern and seem to be symptomatic of his increasing inability to bear the burden of the tragic vision. Having confronted the face of evil in *Othello* with an intensity unmatched even by the man staring at Death in Michelangelo's "Last Judgment," and having in the face of that evil been able to reassert the good, Shakespeare seems to have fallen back exhausted, so to speak, the effort of holding off evil weakening with each successive play.

Lear begins with the abdication of responsibility already accomplished; that a king could even contemplate, let alone achieve, the division of his kingdom must have struck an Elizabethan audience with fear and horror. By his own act, Lear deliberately divests himself of power and retains only the trappings of power, which in turn are one by one inexorably stripped from him until he stands naked on the heath in the rain. The waters of heaven give him wisdom, but his insight into the hypocrisy of this great stage of fools comes to him only in his madness, and he realizes at last that clothes – the symbols of his *hybris* – make neither the king nor the man. Having been purged of the pride of place, he sees himself as he is:

> I am a very foolish fond old man,
> Fourscore and upward, not an hour more nor less;
> And, to deal plainly,
> I fear I am not in my perfect mind.
>
> (IV.vii.60–63)

But this moment of illumination, of heightened self-awareness, so like Othello's, occurs not at the end of Act V, where it would be normally expected, but at the end of Act IV. Having said "Pray you now, forget and forgive; I am old and foolish" (IV.vii.85), what is left for Lear to say? Yet Shakespeare forces the action on to the shambles of the Grand Guignol of Act V, completely cancelling the calming and cleansing effect of the tragic vision already attained with Lear's self-awareness. The play ends not with the hope that this suffering has not been in vain, but with the defeatism of Kent's "All's cheerless, dark, and deadly" and Edgar's "The oldest hath borne most; we that are young/ Shall never see so much, nor live so long." The order of nature has been turned topsy-turvy; the old who cannot bear suffering have endured too much of it; the young who should be able to bear it are too weak.

But at least *Lear* gives us the consolation of the settling of destinies, mis-handled and misplaced as it is. There is none in *Macbeth*. The action of the play begins with the figure of the bloody man and ends with the figure of the dead butcher, and nothing between mitigates the endless horrors of the pro-gression from one to the other. Macbeth accepts the evil promise of the witches' prediction because they so neatly match the evil ambition already in him. Nor does his desire for the crown even pretend that it is for the well-being of the people and the welfare of the state, that excuse which gives some color to Bolingbroke's ambition: "I have no spurs/ To prick the sides of my intent," Macbeth confesses to himself, "but only/ Vaulting ambition." The country suffers under Macbeth's iron rule; "Things bad begun make strong themselves by ill" (III.ii.55), says Macbeth, and Malcolm confirms him:

> I think our country sinks beneath the yoke;
> It weeps, it bleeds; and each new day a gash
> Is added to her wounds.
>
> (IV.iii.39–41)

More – while Malcolm stands behind Macbeth as Fortinbras stands behind Hamlet, can we seriously accept him as the doctor who can "cast/ The water of my land, find her disease,/ And purge it to a sound and pristine health" (V.iii.50–52)? What are we to make of a potential successor to the throne whose own ambivalence towards himself confounds even his strongest supporter? Is Macduff – are we – really persuaded that Malcolm is in fact capable of exhibit-ing "The king-becoming graces,/ As justice, verity, temp'rance, stableness,/ Bounty, perseverance, mercy, lowliness,/ Devotion, patience, courage, forti-tude" (IV.iii.91–94)? Surely his black scruples, coupled with his innocence and inexperience, bode ill for Scotland, whatever the outcome, so that when at last Malcolm is hailed King of Scotland, and, like Hal and Fortinbras, emerges as the symbol of the settling of destinies, our eyes do not see the vision of peace rising from suffering, and our ears hear only the echo –

> for, from this instant,
> There's nothing serious in mortality.
> All is but toys; renown and grace is dead;
> The wine of life is drawn, and the mere lees
> Is left this vault to brag of.
>
> (II.iii.96–101).

– repeated in the dying close of Macbeth's reply to Seyton. The witches have indeed triumphed:

> He shall spurn fate, scorn death, and bear
> His hopes 'bove wisdom, grace, and fear;
> And, you all know, security
> Is mortals' chiefest enemy.
>
> (III.v.30–33)

Man's security, for which he has fought so feverishly, the guarantee of rebirth, has at the very last moment been snatched away from him. Tragedy may be much more and much different from what I have been suggesting here, but one thing it cannot be and that is a tale signifying nothing.

V

A few words must be said about the Roman tragedies. Though *Timon of Athens* and *Coriolanus* provide almost too easy confirmation of the point I am making, *Julius Caesar* and *Antony and Cleopatra* would seem substantial stumbling-blocks in the path of my argument. But the obstructions are not in the plays themselves so much as in our uncritical acceptance of the liberal view of Brutus as the champion of liberty laying down his life to free Rome from the shackles of tyranny, and of the romantic adulation of Antony and Cleopatra as lovers whose passion is so much beyond the ordinary that it justifies their indifference to mere mundane obligation. Having learned to read the histories as an aesthetic and ideological unity, so we must read *Julius Caesar* and *Antony and Cleopatra* as the continuous exposition of a single theme, that of the responsibility of rule. The clue to the Elizabethan judgment of Brutus is to be found in Canto 34 of the Inferno, where, in Judecca, "quite covered by the frozen sheet," and ceaselessly devoured by Satan, hang the ultimate traitors to sworn allegiance – Judas and Brutus and Cassius. For, whatever his defects – and Shakespeare does not minimize them – Caesar is the embodiment of legitimate authority, the source and guarantor of the order and stability of the state. He is, in Elizabethan terms, the anointed king, God's vicar on earth, from whom flow the blessings of peace, justice, and security to his grateful people; and if we want to see the problem of power through Elizabethan eyes, we must not permit our vision to be blurred by our own political preconceptions. By his pride and arrogance, then, by his insistence that he can set his judgment above that of his ruler and try him and condemn him, by his vanity, by his susceptibility to flattery, by his obstinacy – all traits which Shakespeare is at pains to make clear again and again – Brutus murders Caesar and thereby destroys the continuity and stability of the state. Into the vacuum left by the death of Caesar pour hatred, jealousy, and betrayal, and from the Senate House of Rome death spreads in ever-widening circles to the utmost confines of the Empire.

The imminent dissolution of the then known world is the backdrop against which Antony and Cleopatra play out their passion, and it is in terms of the responsibilities of rule which this setting imposes on them that they are judged and found wanting. Four claimants to the authority that was Caesar's now confront each other: Lepidus, Pompey, Antony, and Octavius. Each is brought to the test of power and the first two fail quickly, Lepidus because he cannot raise his eyes above his ledgers, Pompey because he is a credulous fool. Antony and Octavius remain, and the very first lines of the play foretell Antony's inevitable failure:

> Nay, but this dotage of our general's
> O'erflows the measure. Those his goodly eyes,
> That o'er the files and musters of the war
> Have glow'd like plated Mars, now bend, now turn
> The office and devotion of their view
> Upon a tawny front; his captain's heart,
> Which in the scuffles of great fights hath burst
> The buckles on his breast, reneges all temper,
> And is become the bellows and the fan
> To cool a gipsy's lust.
>
> (I.i.1–10)

There is no one who does not share this opinion of Cleopatra. Even "the noble ruin of her magic" reviles her: "I found you as a morsel cold upon/ Dead Caesar's trencher." But Antony is besotted by the passion of his last love: "Come,/ Let's have one more gaudy night." The luxury of Egypt has corrupted the Roman virtues, and Octavius, that calculating and priggish youth looking down his nose at human weakness ("the wild disguise hath almost/ Antick'd us all"), so like Hal and Fortinbras, alone remains at the end to wield the power of Caesar. The peace of Augustus is about to heal an empire diseased by pride and passion.

But, as with *Lear*, the construction of *Julius Caesar* and *Antony and Cleopatra* is at variance with their content. *Julius Caesar* presents the strange spectacle of a conflict between a ghost representing an idea and a man of flesh and blood, for though Caesar is the protagonist of the play, his early death removes his physical presence from the stage and forces Brutus into the center of our interest. The result of this unsuccessful dramaturgic experiment is that for half the play the antagonist is able to claim and gain our sympathy; the belated appearance of Caesar's ghost cannot turn the flow of our increasing affection for Brutus; and the motifs of *Antony and Cleopatra* already dominate *Julius Caesar*. And if the last act of *Lear* disturbs us as intellectually unnecessary, what are we to say of the end of *Antony and Cleopatra* from Act IV, scene 14 on? Defeated by Cleopatra's betrayal, Antony seeks an honorable death, yet he can find no one to kill him. He attempts his own life and even here he fails, and, as he lies mortally wounded, he begs the guards to end his misery; they refuse. The sight of the great Antony, dying of a self-inflicted wound, crying in vain for release, is surely one of the most moving and most bitter scenes in all Shakespeare. Nor is this the end of his trial: he is deceived by Cleopatra once more, he is ignominiously hauled up to her tower, and even his last words are all but silenced by Cleopatra's false lamentations. No wonder Caesar, on being informed of Antony's death, exclaims: "The breaking of so great a thing should make/ A greater crack." Yet, with Antony dead, the play continues for another act, an act which makes the death of Antony appear noble in comparison, which degrades both Cleopatra and Octavius, and makes a mockery of the promise of his forthcoming reign.

VI

The limitations of the subject of this paper prevent me from showing that the disintegration of the tragic pattern which we have seen take place in the major tragedies is paralleled in the three middle comedies, *Troilus and Cressida, All's Well That Ends Well*, and *Measure for Measure*, and comes to its culmination in the four last plays, *Pericles, Cymbeline, The Winter's Table*, and *The Tempest*. Nevertheless, I think that the configuration of Shakespeare's thought was for the most part sympathetically conformable to the shape of the myth and ritual pattern. Yet having raised the pattern to the heights of its most moving and significant expression, Shakespeare was unable to hold it there for long. This does not mean that we must regard him as less than, say, Sophocles or Milton, neither of whom seems to have given way to doubt, nor does it mean that the myth and ritual pattern is inadequate either to its purposes or as a means of elucidating tragedy. On the contrary, the application of the pattern to Shakespeare's plays discriminates between them with nicety, it intensifies our awareness of the unique qualities of the individual plays, and it enables us to respond to Shakespeare on a most profound level of understanding. Recent critics of Shakespeare have enjoyed many a laugh at the expense of their predecessors who labored to box Shakespeare's plays under the neat labels "in the work-shop," "in the world," "out of the depths," and "on the heights" – to use Dowden's terms – but I cannot see that they themselves have done anything more than to say the same thing in perhaps more fashionable language. But the myth and ritual approach converts a Progress into a Calvary.

Shakespeare paid for the cost of the tragic vision by its loss. He looked long and directly into the face of evil. In the end, he shut his eyes. Writing of another artist who found himself in the same dilemma, Sir Kenneth Clark says: "The perfect union of Piero's forms, transcending calculation, rested on confidence in the harmony of creation; and at some point this confidence left him." As it seems to me, at some point Shakespeare too lost his confidence in the harmony of creation. I do not know when Shakespeare reached that point, but I think that it perhaps came at the moment of his greatest expression of faith in the harmony of creation, in *Othello* when he realized that he had left Iago standing alive on the stage. When in the bottommost circle of Hell, Virgil steps aside from Dante and reveals to him that creature fairest once of the sons of light: "Behold now Dis!", the poet is moved to cry out: "This was not life, and yet it was not death." So in the end Iago: "Demand me nothing; what you know, you know./ From this time forth I never will speak word." The rest is silence.

18

WHAT IS A MYTH?

René Girard

The French critic René Girard (b. 1923), Professor of French at Stanford University, maintains that the prime human desire is imitative, or mimetic. Human beings covet not the possessions but the desires of those whom they choose as their models. Desiring whatever their models desire in order to become like them, humans turn models into rivals and rivalry into violence. Society must redirect the violence to survive. The redirected object of violence is an innocent victim, who is blamed for the woes of society and killed. The scapegoat can range from the most helpless member of society to the most elevated, including the king. The killing of a king for the good of his society harks back to Frazer. But for Girard the goal is peace, not food. Girard is a full-fledged myth-ritualist: all myths arise from sacrificial rituals. But instead of arising to explain ritual, as for other myth-ritualists, myth for Girard arises to hide it. Myth disguises the sacrifice of the victim in various ways – by making the killing deserved, by making the death accidental, by turning the death into a tamer fate such as exile, and above all by turning the hated victim into a revered savior and indeed into a god. The following selection from *The Scapegoat* (tr. Yvonne Freccero [London: Athlone Press; Baltimore: Johns Hopkins University Press, 1986 [1982], ch. 3) sums up Girard's myth-ritualism. See also his *Violence and the Sacred*, tr. Patrick Gregory (London: Athlone Press; Baltimore: Johns Hopkins University Press, 1977 [1972]); *"To double business bound"* (London: Athlone Press; Baltimore: Johns Hopkins University Press, 1978); *Things Hidden since the Foundation of the World*, trs Stephen Bann and Michael Metteer (London: Athlone Press; Stanford: Stanford University Press, 1987 [1978]); and *Job, the Victim of his People*, tr. Yvonne Freccero (London: Athlone Press; Stanford: Stanford University Press, 1987 [1985]); and "Generative

Original publication: René Girard, "What Is a Myth?", in his *The Scapegoat*, tr. Yvonne Freccero (London: Athlone Press; Baltimore: Johns Hopkins University Press, 1986), ch. 3 (pp. 24–44).

Scapegoating," in *Violent Origins*, ed. Robert G. Hamerton-Kelly (Stanford: Stanford University Press, 1987), 73–105. On Girard see the special issue on Girard in *Diacritics* 8 (Spring 1978); "René Girard and Biblical Studies," *Semeia*, no. 33 (1985); *Violence and Truth*, ed. Paul Dumouchel (London: Athlone Press, 1988 [1985]); James G. Williams, *The Bible, Violence, and the Sacred* (San Francisco: HarperSanFrancisco, 1991); Richard J. Golsan, *René Girard and Myth* (New York: Garland Publishing, 1993); and Cesáreo Bandera, *The Sacred Game* (University Park: Pennsylvania State University Press, 1994).

Each time an oral or written testament mentions an act of violence that is directly or indirectly collective we question whether it includes the description of a social and cultural crisis, that is, a generalized loss of differences (the first stereotype), crimes that "eliminate differences" (the second stereotype), and whether the identified authors of these crimes possess the marks that suggest a victim, the paradoxical marks of the absence of difference (the third stereotype). The fourth stereotype is violence itself, which will be discussed later.

The juxtaposition of more than one stereotype within a single document indicates persecution. Not all the stereotypes must be present: three are enough and often even two. Their existence convinces us that (1) the acts of violence are real; (2) the crisis is real; (3) the victims are chosen not for the crimes they are accused of but for the victim's signs that they bear, for everything that suggests their guilty relationship with the crisis; and (4) the import of the operation is to lay the responsibility for the crisis on the victims and to exert an influence on it by destroying these victims or at least by banishing them from the community they "pollute."

If this pattern is universal it should be found in virtually all societies. Historians do in fact find it in all the societies included in their studies which today embrace the entire planet, but previously were confined to Western society and prior to that specifically to the Roman Empire. And yet ethnologists have never come to recognize this pattern of persecution in the societies they study. Why is that? Two answers are possible. "Ethnological" societies are so little given to persecution that the type of analysis applied to Guillaume de Machaut is not applicable to them. Contemporary neoprimitivism which tends toward this solution places the superior humanity of all other cultures in opposition to the inhumanity of our society. But no one dares argue that persecution fails to exist in non-Western societies. The second possible answer is that persecution exists but we do not recognize it, either because we are not in possession of the necessary documents, *or because we do not know how to decipher the documents we do possess.*

I consider the second of these two hypotheses to be the correct one. Mythical, ritualistic societies are not exempt from persecution. We possess documents that allow us to prove this: they contain the stereotypes of persecution that I have named, they emerge from the same total pattern as the treatment of the Jews in Guillaume de Machaut. If our logic is consistent we should apply the same type of interpretation to them. These documents are myths.

To make my task easier I shall begin with a myth that is exemplary. It contains all the stereotypes of persecution and nothing else, and it contains them in a startling form. It is Sophocles' account of the myth of Oedipus in *Oedipus Rex*. I shall then turn to myths that reproduce the pattern of persecution but in a form that is harder to decipher. Finally, I shall turn to myths that reject this pattern but do so in such an obvious way as to confirm its relevance. By proceeding from easy to more difficult I intend to show that all myths must have their roots in real acts of violence against real victims.

I begin with the myth of Oedipus. The plague is ravaging Thebes: here we have the first stereotype of persecution. Oedipus is responsible because he has killed his father and married his mother: here is the second stereotype. The oracle declares that, in order to end the epidemic, the abominable criminal must be banished. The finality of persecution is explicit. Parricide and incest serve openly as the intermediaries between the individual and the collective; these crimes are so oblivious of differences that their influence is contagious to the whole society. In Sophocles' text we establish that to lack difference is to be plague-stricken.

The third stereotype has to do with the signs of a victim. The first is disability: Oedipus limps. This hero from another country arrived in Thebes unknown to anyone, a stranger in fact if not in right. Finally, he is the son of the king and a king himself, the legitimate heir of Laius. Like many other mythical characters, Oedipus manages to combine the marginality of the outsider with the marginality of the insider. Like Ulysses at the end of the *Odyssey* he is sometimes a stranger and a beggar and sometimes an all-powerful monarch.

The only detail without an equivalent in historical persecutions is the exposed infant. But the whole world agrees that an exposed infant is a victim at an early stage, chosen because of the signs of abnormality which augur badly for his future and which evidently are the same as the signs that indicate the selection of a victim mentioned above. The fatal destiny determined for the exposed child is to be expelled by his community. His escape is only ever temporary, his destiny is at the best deferred, and the conclusion of the myth confirms the infallibility of the signs of the oracle that dedicate him, from earliest infancy, to collective violence.

The more signs of a victim an individual bears, the more likely he is to attract disaster. Oedipus's infirmity, his past history of exposure as an infant, his situation as a foreigner, newcomer, and king, all make him a veritable conglomerate of victim's signs. We would not fail to observe this if the myth were a historical document, and we would wonder at the meaning of all these signs, together with other stereotypes of persecution. There would be no doubt about the answer. We would certainly see in the myth what we see in

Guillaume de Machaut's text, an account of persecution told from the perspective of naïve persecutors. The persecutors portray their victim exactly as they see him – as the guilty person – but they hide none of the objective traces of their persecution. We conclude that there must be a real victim behind the text, chosen not by virtue of the stereotypical crimes of which he is accused, crimes which never spread the plague, but because of all the characteristics of a victim specified in that text which are most likely to project on him the paranoiac suspicion of a crowd tormented by the plague.

In the myth, as in Guillaume and in the witchcraft trials, the accusations are truly *mythological*: parricide, incest, the moral or physical poisoning of the community. These accusations are characteristic of the way in which frenzied crowds conceive of their victims. But these same accusations are juxtaposed with criteria for the selection of a victim which may well be real. How can we not believe that a real victim lies behind a text which presents him in this way and which makes us see him, on the one hand, as the persecutors generally see him and, on the other hand, as he should really be to be chosen by real persecutors. For even greater certainty, his banishment is said to take place in a time of extreme crisis which favors real persecution. All the conditions are present that will automatically prompt the modern reader, as we have described above for *historical* texts, to reach the same interpretation we would make of texts written from the perspective of persecutors. Why do we hesitate in the case of myths?

Just as in medieval persecutions, stereotypical persecutors are always found in myths and are statistically too prevalent to ignore. The myths are too numerous for us to be able to attribute the repetition of the model to anything but real persecutions. Any other conclusion would be as absurd as to think that Guillaume de Machaut's account of the Jews was pure fiction. As soon as we are confronted with a text that is perceived to be historical we know that only the behavior of a persecutor, seen through a persecutor's mind, can generate the collection of stereotypes we find in many myths. Persecutors believe they choose their victims because of the crimes they attribute to them, which make them in their eyes responsible for the disasters to which they react by persecution. Actually, the victims are determined by the criteria of persecution that are faithfully reported to us, not because they want to inform us but because they are unaware of what they reveal.

In the case of a text written by the persecutors the only elements of it that should be believed are those that correspond (1) to the real circumstances of the texts coming into being, (2) to the characteristic traits of its usual victims, and (3) to the results that normally follow collective violence. If these authors describe not merely parricide and incest as the cause of plagues but also everything that goes with this type of belief in the real world and all the resulting sorts of behavior, then they are probably right on all these points because they are wrong about the first one. These are our four stereotypes of persecutors, the same combination of the likely and the unlikely that we saw in the historical texts, and we cannot expect it to have another significance than the one stated above. It is the partly accurate and partly false perspective of persecutors who are convinced of their own persecution.

This conclusion is not the result of naïveté. Real naïveté is buried under the extremes of skepticism, which is incapable of identifying the stereotypes of persecution and of resorting to the daring yet legitimate interpretation they require. The myth of Oedipus is not just a literary text, or a psychoanalytic text, but a persecution text and should be interpreted as such. It will be objected that an interpretive method that was invented in and for history cannot be applied to myth. I agree, but as I have shown above, genuine historical evidence plays no more than a secondary role in deciphering representations of persecution. If they had been dependent on history, they would never have been deciphered, a process that has only just begun in the modern era.

If we consider that the victims mentioned by the witch-hunters are real, we do not usually do so because we have information on them from independent, unbiased sources. Admittedly, we place the text in a framework of knowledge, but that framework would not exist if we treated historical persecution texts as we treat the myth of Oedipus.

As already mentioned, we do not know exactly where the events described by Guillaume de Machaut took place; even if we knew almost nothing, including the existence of the Black Death, we would still conclude that such a text must reflect a phenomenon of real persecution. Just the combination of persecutor stereotypes would give sufficient indication. Why is the situation different in the case of myth?

My hypothesis relies on nothing historical in the critics' sense. It is purely "structural" as in our interpretation of historical representations of persecution. We assert that certain texts are based on a real persecution because of the nature and the disposition of the persecutor stereotypes they portray. Without this origin it is impossible to explain why and how the same themes keep recurring in the same pattern. If we accept this thesis the obscurity of the text is immediately dispelled. The themes are all easily explained and no serious objection can be raised. For this reason we have unhesitatingly accepted the thesis as the origin of all the historical texts that follow the pattern of persecution we have described. As a result we no longer see it as controversial but as the pure and simple truth of these texts. And we have good reason. It remains to find out why such a solution does not occur to us in the case of a myth like that of Oedipus.

That is the real problem. The lengthy analysis I have just given of the type of interpretation that automatically results in the identification of stereotypes of persecution was necessary in order to understand that problem. As long as we are talking of historical texts the interpretation presents no problem, and there is no need to detail each step of the process. But this attitude is precisely the obstacle to our taking the necessary step backward to reflect on our *under-standing* of the representations of persecution. We have not completely mastered that understanding because it has never been made totally explicit.

Everything I have said about mythology would appear to be obvious, almost too obvious in the case of a "historical" document. If my readers are not convinced I shall convince them now by a very simple example. I am going to draw a rough sketch of the story of Oedipus; I shall remove his Greek clothing and substitute Western garb. In so doing, the myth will descend several steps on the social ladder. I will give no details of the place or the precise date of the event. The reader's good will will provide the rest. My tale falls naturally into some part of the Christian world between the twelfth and thirteenth centuries; that is all that is needed to release, like a spring, the operation that no one has thought of applying to a myth, as long as we have been calling it precisely that, a myth.

> Harvests are bad, the cows give birth to dead calves; no one is on good terms with anyone else. It is as if a spell had been cast on the village. Clearly, it is the cripple who is the cause. He arrived one fine morning, no one knows from where, and made himself at home. He even took the liberty of marrying the most obvious heiress in the village and had two children by her. All sorts of things seemed to take place in their house. The stranger was suspected of having killed his wife's former husband, a sort of local potentate, who disappeared under mysterious circumstances and was rather too quickly replaced by the newcomer. One day the fellows in the village had had enough; they took their pitchforks and forced the disturbing character to clear out.

No one will have the slightest hesitation in this instance. Everyone will instinctively give the explanation I have mentioned. Everyone understands that the victim most certainly did not do what he was accused of but that everything about him marked him as an outlet for the annoyance and irritation of his fellow citizens. Everyone will understand easily the relationship between the likely and unlikely elements in this little story. No one will suggest that it is an innocent fable; no one will see it as a casual work of poetic imagination or of a wish to portray "the fundamental mechanisms of man's thought."

And yet nothing has changed. It has the same structure as the myth since it is a rough sketch of it. Thus the interpretation does not rest on whether it is or is not set in a framework of historical detail. A change of setting is enough to redirect the interpreter to a reading that he indignantly rejects when the text is presented in a "true" mythological form. If we transported our story to the Polynesians or American Indians we would see the same ceremonious respect that the Hellenists had for the Greek version of the myth, accompanied by the same obstinate refusal to have recourse to the most effective interpretation. The latter is reserved exclusively for our historical universe, for reasons we shall try to uncover later.

We are dealing with cultural schizophrenia. My hypothesis would have served a purpose if it had only revealed just that. We interpret texts not by what they really are but by their external trappings (I am almost tempted to call it their commercial wrapping). A slight modification of the presentation of a text is enough to inhibit or release the only truly radical demystification available to us, and no one is aware of the situation.

So far I have only spoken of a myth that I myself recognize to be exemplary in regard to representations of persecution. Those myths that are not must also be discussed. They do not bear an obvious resemblance to persecution texts, but if we look for the four stereotypes we shall find plenty of them without difficulty, though in a rather more transfigured form.

Often the beginning of the myth can be reduced to a single characteristic. Day and night are confused; heaven and earth communicate; gods move among men and men among gods. Among god, man, and beast there is little distinction. Sun and moon are twins; they fight constantly and cannot be distinguished one from the other. The sun moves too close to the earth; drought and heat make life unbearable. At first sight, there is nothing in these beginnings of myth that has any connection with reality. Clearly, however, myth involves a lack of differentiation. The great social crises that engender collective persecutions are experienced as a lack of differentiation. This is the characteristic that I uncovered in the preceding chapter. We might well ask whether this is not our first stereotype of persecution, in an extremely stylized and transfigured form, reduced to its simplest expression.

Lack of differentiation in myth sometimes has idyllic connotations, of which I will speak later. Usually, its character is catastrophic. The confusion of day and night signifies the absence of sun and the withering of everything. The sun's too close proximity to the earth indicates that existence is equally unbearable but for the opposite reason. Myths that are thought to "invent death" in reality invent nothing but rather distinguish it from life when "in the beginning" both are confused. I believe this to mean that it is impossible to live without dying or, once again, that existence is unbearable.

"Primordial" lack of differentiation and the "original" chaos conflict strongly in character. Those elements that are indistinguishable often have conflictual connotations. This theme is particularly developed in the post-Vedic texts of Brahman India. Everything always begins with an interminable, indecisive battle between gods and demons who are so alike one can hardly tell them apart. In short, that too rapid and visible evil reciprocity makes all behavior the same in the great crises of society that are apt to trigger collective persecutions. The undifferentiated is only a partially mythical translation of this state of affairs. We must associate with it the theme of twins or fraternal enemies who illustrate the conflict between those who become undifferentiated in a particularly graphic fashion. No doubt this is why the theme provides the most classic beginning for myths everywhere.

Lévi-Strauss was the first to identify the unity of numerous mythical begin-nings in terms of a lack of differentiation. For him the undifferentiated is purely rhetorical; it serves as a background for the display of differences. There is no question of relating this, then, to real social conditions. And until now there would seem to be no evidence of any hope of finding in myth any concrete relationship with reality. Our four stereotypes of persecution have now modified this state of affairs. If we find three of them in the myths which begin in the way I have described, we might legitimately conclude that the initial lack of differentiation constitutes a schematic but nevertheless recogniz-able version of the first.

We need not dwell on this. All the crimes that persecutors attribute to their victims can generally be found in myths. In certain, especially Greek, mytholo-gies these crimes are often not treated as crimes; they are seen as mere pranks; they are excused and made light of but they are nevertheless present and, at least in letter if not in spirit, they correspond perfectly to our stereotype. In the myths that appear most "primitive" – if I dare use the term – the chief characters are formidable criminals and are treated as such. Because of this they incur a punishment that bears a strange resemblance to the fate of the victims of collective persecutions (it is often a question of lynching). On this one main point the myths which I call "primitive" are even closer than the myth of Oedipus to the crowd phenomena with which I am comparing them.

There is only one stereotype we must find in these myths: the mark that identifies the selection of a victim for persecution. I need not point out that world mythology swarms with the lame, the blind, and the crippled or abounds with people stricken by the plague. As well as the heroes in disgrace there are those who are exceptionally beautiful and free of all blemish. This means not that mythology literally is meaningless but that it usually deals in extremes; and we have already noted that this is a characteristic of the polarization of persecution.

The whole range of victim signs can be found in myths, a fact unnoticed because we focus on the victim's ethnic or religious minority. That particular sign cannot appear in the same form in mythology. We find neither persecuted Jews nor blacks. But their equivalent can be found in a theme that plays a central role in all parts of the world, that of the *foreigner* banished or assassi-nated by the community.[1]

The victim is a person who comes from elsewhere, a well-known stranger. He is invited to a feast which ends with his lynching. Why? He has done something he should not have done; his behavior is perceived as fatal; one of his gestures was misinterpreted. Here again we have only to imagine a real victim, a real stranger, and everything becomes clear. If the stranger behaves in a strange or insulting way in the eyes of his hosts, it is because he conforms

[1] See the three myths examined in *Des choses cachées depuis la fondation du monde*, pp. 114–40.

to other customs. Beyond a certain threshold of ethnocentrism, the stranger becomes, for better or worse, truly mythological. The smallest misunderstanding can be disastrous. Beneath this myth of an assassinated stranger who is made a god we can trace a form of "provincialism" so extreme that we can no longer identify it, just as we no longer can see the sounds and colors of an electromagnetic wave beyond a certain length. Again, to bring our overphilosophical interpretations down to earth, we need only place these mythical themes against a Western, rural background. One immediately grasps the meaning, just as in the transposition of the Oedipus myth a moment ago. A little suitable intellectual gymnastics, and especially a little less icy veneration for all that does not belong to the modern Western world, and we will quickly learn how to enlarge our field of recognition and understanding in mythology.

A close examination of myths is not necessary to establish that a great number of them contain our four stereotypes of persecution; there are others, of course, that contain only three, two, one or even none. I do not overlook them but am not yet able to analyze them successfully. We are beginning to see that the representations of persecution we have already deciphered are for us an Ariadne's thread to guide us through the labyrinth of mythology. They will enable us to trace the real origin in collective violence of even the myths that contain no stereotypes of persecution. We shall see later that, instead of gainsaying our thesis or demanding questionable feats to maintain it, those myths that are entirely void of stereotypes of persecution will provide us with the most astounding verification. For the time being we must continue our analysis of the myths that contain our stereotypes but under a form that is less easy to identify, because it is somewhat more transfigured, than in the medieval persecutions or the myth of Oedipus. This more extreme transfiguration does not create an insurpassable abyss between myths and persecutions that have already been deciphered. One word is sufficient to define the type to which they belong: monstrous.

Ever since the romantic movement we have tended to see in the mythological monster a true creation ex nihilo, a pure invention. Imagination is perceived as an absolute ability to conceive of forms that exist nowhere in nature. Examination of mythological monsters reveals no such thing. They always consist of a combination of elements borrowed from various existing forms and brought together in the monster, which then claim an independent identity. Thus the Minotaur is a mixture of man and bull. Dionysus equally, but the god in him commands more attention than the monster or than the mixture of forms.

We must think of the monstrous as beginning with the lack of differentiation, with a process that, though it has no effect on reality, does affect the perception of it. As the rate of conflictual reciprocity accelerates, it not only gives the accurate impression of identical behavior among the antagonists but it also disintegrates perception, as it becomes dizzying. Monsters are surely the result of a fragmentation of perception and of a decomposition followed by a recombination that does not take natural specificity into account. A monster is an unstable hallucination that, in retrospect, crystallizes into stable forms, owing to the fact that it is remembered in a world that has regained stability.

We saw earlier that the representations of historical persecutions resemble mythology. A transition to the monstrous is made in the extreme representations we have mentioned, such as in the crisis caused by the lack of differentiation, or in signs like deformity that mark a victim for persecution. There comes a point at which physical monstrosity and moral monstrosity merge. The crime of bestiality, for example, engenders monstrous mixtures of men and animals; in the hermaphroditism of a Tiresias, physical monstrosity cannot be distinguished from moral monstrosity. The stereotypes themselves merge, in other words, to form the mythological monsters.

In the mythological monster the "physical" and the "moral" are inseparable. The two are so perfectly combined that any attempt to separate them seems doomed to failure. Yet, if I am right, there is a distinction to be made. Physical deformity must correspond to a real human characteristic, a real infirmity. Oedipus's wounds or Vulcan's limp are not necessarily less real in their origins than the characteristics of medieval witches. Moral monstrosity, by contrast, actualizes the tendency of all persecutors to project the monstrous results of some calamity or public or private misfortune onto some poor unfortunate who, by being infirm or a foreigner, suggests a certain affinity to the monstrous.

My analysis may seem strange, for the monstrous character is generally perceived as being the final proof of the absolutely fictitious and imaginary character of mythology. Yet in the monster we recognize the false certainty and the true possibility that I have been discussing. It will be said that the presence of stereotypes in such confusion discounts my argument. If they are examined all at once, however, they do form a sort of unity; they create a particular climate that is specific to mythology, and we should do nothing to dissociate the elements even for aesthetic reasons. Nor have our best interpreters ever separated them, though some scholars are moving in the direction of a definitive separation of the (imaginary) crimes of the victims and the (possibly real) signs that indicate a victim. Here is a representative text, of Mircea Eliade's on Greek mythology, that begins with the latter and ends with the former:

[the heroes] are distinguished by their *strength* and *beauty* but also by *monstrous characteristics* ([gigantic] stature – Heracles, Achilles, Orestes, Pelops – but also stature [much shorter] than the average); or they are [theriomorphic] (Lycaon, the "wolf") or able to *change themselves into animals*. They are *androgynous* (Cecrops), or *change their sex* (Teiresias), or *dress like women* (Heracles). In addition, the heroes are characterized by numerous *anomalies* (*acephaly* or *polycephaly*; Heracles has *three rows of teeth*); they are apt to be *lame, one-eyed* or *blind*. Heroes often fall victim to *insanity* (Orestes, Bellerophon, even the exceptional Heracles, when he *slaughtered his sons* by Megara). As for their *sexual behavior*, it is *excessive* or *aberrant*: Heracles *impregnates the fifty daughters of Thespius in one night*; Theseus is famous for his *numerous rapes* (Helen, Ariadne, etc.); Achilles *ravishes Stratonice*. The heroes commit *incest with their daughters or their mothers* and indulge in *massacres* from envy or anger or often for no reason at all: *they even slaughter their fathers and mothers or their relatives*.[2]

This text is important because it contains so many relevant traits. Under the sign of the monstrous the author unites the marks that identify a victim and the stereotypical crimes without mixing them. Something here seems to resist conflating the two rubrics. There is an actual, though not justified, separation.

Physical and moral monstrosity go together in mythology. Their connection seems normal, and is even suggested by language. But in a similar situation in our historical universe we would not exclude the possibility of the victims being real, making the perpetual juxtaposition of the two kinds of monstrosity odious; we would suspect that its origin lay in the mentality of persecution. But what else could be its source? What other force might always be responsible for converging the two themes? For reassurance it is attributed to the *imagination*. We always rely on the imagination in order to avoid reality. Yet I'm not referring to the imagination of the aesthetician but, rather, to that of Guillaume de Machaut's at its most confused, to the sort of imagination, which, precisely because it is confused, brings us back to the real victims. It is always the imagination of the persecutors. Physical and moral monstrosity are heaped together in myths that justify the persecution of the infirm. The fact that other stereotypes of persecution surround them leaves no room for doubt. If this were a rare conjunction it might be dubious, but innumerable examples can be found; it is the daily fare of mythology.

Except in the case of certain exemplary myths, that of Oedipus in particular, mythology cannot be *directly* assimilated to the pattern of representations of persecution that can be decoded, but it can be so *indirectly*. Instead of bearing certain faintly monstrous characteristics, the victim is hard to recognize as a victim because he is totally monstrous. This difference should not lead us to decide that the two types of texts cannot have a common source.

After detailed examination it becomes clear that we are dealing with a single principle of distorted presentation, though in mythology the mechanism operates in a higher register than in history. It is undeniably and universally true that the less rational the persecutors' conviction the more formidable that conviction becomes. But in historical persecutions the conviction is not so overwhelming as to conceal its character and the process of accusation from which it stems. Admittedly, the victim is condemned in advance; he cannot

---

[2] Mircea Eliade, *A History of Religious Ideas* (Chicago: University of Chicago Press, 1978), 1:288 (italics mine).

defend himself, his trial has already taken place, but at least there is a trial no matter how prejudiced. The witches are hunted legally; even the persecuted Jews are explicitly charged, charged with crimes that are less unlikely than those of the mythical heroes. The desire for relative probability which conjures up "the poisoning of rivers," paradoxically helps us to make the distinction between truth and falsity. Mythology demands the same operation, though in a more daring form because the circumstances are more confused.

In historical persecutions the "guilty" remain sufficiently distinct from their "crimes" for there to be no mistake about the nature of the process. The same cannot be said of myth. The guilty person is so much a part of his offense that one is indistinguishable from the other. His offense seems to be a fantastic essence or ontological attribute. In many myths the wretched person's presence is enough to contaminate everything around him, infecting men and beasts with the plague, ruining crops, poisoning food, causing game to disappear, and sowing discord around him. Everything shrivels under his feet and the grass does not grow again. He produces disasters as easily as a fig tree produces figs. He need only be himself.

The definition of victim as sinner or criminal is so absolute in myth, and the causal relationship between crime and collective crisis is so strong, that even perceptive scholars have as yet failed to disassociate these details and to identify the accusatory process. The persecution text, whether medieval or modern, provides the needed Ariadne's thread. Even those historical texts that retain the strongest sense of persecution reflect only very slight conviction. The more relentlessly they struggle to demonstrate the justice of their wrongdoing, the less convincing they sound. If the myth were to state "Undoubtedly Oedipus killed his father; it is certain that he had intercourse with his mother," we would recognize the type of lie it embodies; it would be written in the style of historical persecutors, from a basis of belief. But it speaks tranquilly of an unquestionable fact: "Oedipus killed his father; he had intercourse with his mother," in the same tone one would say: "Night follows day" or "The sun rises in the East."

The distortions in persecution become weaker as we move from myths to persecutions in the Western world. This weakening has in fact allowed us to decipher the latter. Our task is to use this decoding in order to gain access to mythology. I will use as my guide the text of Guillaume de Machaut and the others we have already encountered because they are easier to read, to help interpret the myth of Oedipus, first of all, and then increasingly more difficult texts. As we proceed we will recognize all the stereotypes of persecution and so reach the conclusion that there are real acts of violence and real victims behind themes that seem so fantastic that it is difficult to think that one day we may no longer consider them purely and simply imaginary.

Our medieval ancestors took the most incredible fables seriously – the poisoning of fountains by the Jews or by lepers, ritual infanticide, witches' broomsticks, and moonlight diabolical orgies. The mixture of cruelty and credulity seems insurpassable to us. And yet myths surpass them; historical persecutions are the result of degraded superstitions. We think we are free of mythical illusions because we have sworn not to be hoodwinked by them.

We are in the habit of considering necessarily fictional even the most plausible characteristics of mythological heroes because of their association with other improbable characteristics. Similarly, if we were to permit it, the same false notion of prudence and the same attitude toward fiction would prevent us from recognizing the reality of the anti-Semitic massacres in Guillaume de Machaut. We do not doubt the reality of the massacres on the excuse that they are juxtaposed with all sorts of more or less significant fables. There is equally no good reason to doubt the reality in the case of myths.

The face of the victim shows through the mask in the texts of historical persecutions. There are chinks and cracks. In mythology the mask is still intact; it covers the whole face so well that we have no idea it is a mask. We think there is no one behind it, neither victim nor persecutor. We are somewhat like Polyphemus's brothers, the Cyclopes, to whom he calls in vain for help after Ulysses and his companions blinded him. We save our only eye, if we have one, for what we call history. As for our ears, if we have them, they only hear this *no one, no one* . . . that is so deeply embedded in collective violence that we take it for nothing, nonexistent, pure fabrication by a Polyphemus in a vein of poetic improvisation.

We no longer consider mythological monsters as a supernatural or even natural species; there are no longer theological or even zoological genres. They belong instead to the quasi-genres of the imaginary, "archetypes" of fable heaped in an unconsciousness that is even more mythical than the myths themselves. There was a time when no one could read even the distortions of persecution found in our own history. Finally we did learn. We can put a date to this achievement. It goes back to the beginning of the modern era and seems to constitute only the first stage in a process that has never really been interrupted but has been marking time for centuries because it lacked a truly fruitful direction that would stretch back to mythology.

Now we must discuss an essential dimension of myth that is almost entirely absent from historical persecutions: that of the sacred. Medieval and modern persecutors do not worship their victims, they only hate them. They are therefore easy to identify as victims. It is more difficult to spot the victim in a supernatural being who is a cult object. Admittedly, the glorious adventures of the hero can hardly be distinguished from the stereotypical crimes of collective victims. Like those victims, moreover, the hero is hunted and even assassinated by his own people. But the experts are in agreement that such annoying incidents are not important. They are merely minor escapades in a career that is so noble and transcendental it is poor taste to notice them.

Myths exude the sacred and do not seem comparable with texts that do not.
No matter how striking the similarities mentioned in the preceding pages they
pale before this dissimilarity. I am trying to explain myths by discovering in
them more extreme distortions of persecution than those of historical persecutors as they recall their own persecutions. The method has been successful
until now since I have uncovered in myths the warped forms of everything that
appears equally in persecution texts. We may wonder whether we are missing
the essential. Even if on a lower level mythology is vulnerable to my comparative method, idealists will say that at a higher level it escapes through the
transcendental dimension that is beyond reach.

This is not so for the following two reasons. Beginning with the similarities
and differences between our two types of texts, the nature of the sacred and
the necessity of its presence in myths can literally be deduced by a simple
process of reasoning. I will go back to the persecution texts and show that,
despite appearances, they contain traces of the sacred that correspond exactly
to what is to be expected, if we were to recognize, as I did earlier, the degenerated and half-decomposed myths in these texts.

In order to understand that existence of the sacred, we must begin by
recognizing a true belief in what I have called the stereotype of accusation, the
guilt and the apparent responsibility of the victims. Guillaume de Machaut
sincerely believed that the rivers were poisoned by the Jews. Jean Bodin sincerely believed that France was exposed to danger by sorcery in his day. We
do not have to sympathize with the belief by admitting its sincerity. Jean Bodin
was an intelligent man and yet he believed in sorcery. Two centuries later such
a belief makes people of even mediocre intelligence laugh. What, then, is the
source of the illusions of a Jean Bodin or a Guillaume de Machaut? Clearly,
they are social in nature. They are illusions shared by a great number of
people. In most societies belief in witchcraft is not the act of certain individuals
only, or even of many, but the act of everyone.

Magical beliefs flourish amid a certain social consensus. Even though it was
far from unanimous in the sixteenth and even in the fourteenth century, the
consensus was broad, at least in certain milieus. It acted as a sort of constraint
on people. The exceptions were not numerous, and they were not influential
enough to prevent the persecutions. The representation of these persecutions
retains certain characteristics of a collective representation in the sense used by
Durkheim. We have examined the makeup of this belief. Vast social groups
found themselves at the mercy of terrifying plagues such as the Black Death or
sometimes less visible problems. Thanks to the mechanism of persecution,
collective anguish and frustration found vicarious appeasement in the victims
who easily found themselves united in opposition to them by virtue of being
poorly integrated minorities.

We owe our comprehension of this to the discovery of stereotypes of persecution in a text. Once we understand we almost always exclaim: *The victim is*

a scapegoat. Everyone has a clear understanding of this expression; no one has any hesitation about its meaning. Scapegoat indicates both the innocence of the victims, the collective polarization in opposition to them, and the collective end result of that polarization. The persecutors are caught up in the "logic" of the representation of persecution from a persecutor's standpoint, and they cannot break away. Guillaume de Machaut no doubt never participated himself in collective acts of violence, but he adopts the representation of persecution that feeds the violence and is fed in return. He shares in the collective effect of the scapegoat. The polarization exerts such a constraint on those polarized that the victims cannot prove their innocence.

We use the word "scapegoat" therefore to summarize all that I have said so far on collective persecutions. By mentioning "scapegoat" when discussing Guillaume de Machaut we indicate that we are not taken in by his representation and that we have done what is necessary to break down the system and substitute our own reading. "Scapegoat" epitomizes the type of interpretation I would like to extend to mythology. Unfortunately, the expression and the interpretation suffer the same fate. Because everyone uses it no one bothers to determine its exact significance, and the misconceptions multiply. In the example of Guillaume de Machaut and persecution texts in general, this use has no direct connection with the rite of the scapegoat as described in Leviticus, or with other rites that are sometimes described as belonging to the "scapegoat" because they more or less resemble that of Leviticus.

As soon as we begin to study the "scapegoat" or think about the expression apart from the context of the persecutor, we tend to modify its meaning. We are reminded of the rite; we think of a religious ceremony that unfolds on a fixed date and is performed by priests; we imagine a deliberate manipulation. We think of skillful strategists who are fully aware of the mechanisms of victimization and who knowingly sacrifice innocent victims in full awareness of the cause with Machiavellian ease.

Such things can happen, especially in our time, but they cannot happen, even today, without the availability of an eminently manipulable mass to be used by the manipulators for their evil purposes, people who will allow themselves to be trapped in the persecutors' representation of persecution, people capable of belief where the scapegoat is concerned. Guillaume de Machaut is obviously no manipulator. He is not intelligent enough. If manipulation exists in his universe, he must be numbered among the manipulated. The details that are so revealing in his text are not revealing for him, evidently, but only for those who understand their real significance. Earlier I spoke of naïve persecutors; I could have spoken of their lack of awareness.

Too conscious and calculating an awareness of all that the "scapegoat" connotes in modern usage eliminates the essential point that the persecutors believe in the guilt of their victim; they are imprisoned in the illusion of persecution that is no simple idea but a full system of representation. Imprisonment in this system allows us to speak of an unconscious persecutor, and the proof of his existence lies in the fact that those in our day who are the most proficient in discovering other people's scapegoats, and God knows we are past masters at this, are never able to recognize their own. Almost no one is aware of his own shortcoming. We must question ourselves if we are to understand the enormity of the mystery. Each person must ask what his relationship is to the scapegoat. I am not aware of my own, and I am persuaded that the same holds true for my readers. We only have legitimate enmities. And yet the entire universe swarms with scapegoats. The illusion of persecution is as rampant as ever, less tragically but more cunningly than under Guillaume de Machaut. *Hypocite lecteur, mon semblable, mon frère . . .*

If we are at the point where we compete in the penetrating and subtle discovery of scapegoats, both individual and collective, where was the fourteenth century? No one decoded the representation of persecution as we do today. "Scapegoat" had not yet taken on the meaning we give it today. The concept that crowds, or even entire societies, can imprison themselves in their own illusions of victimage was inconceivable. Had we tried to explain it to the men of the Middle Ages, they would not have understood. Guillaume de Machaut was much more influenced by the scapegoat effect than we are. His universe was more deeply immersed in its unawareness of persecution than we are, but even so, it was less so than the world of mythology. In Guillaume, as we have seen, just a small portion, and not the worst, of the Black Death is blamed on scapegoats: in the myth of Oedipus it is the entire plague. In order to explain epidemics, mythological universes have never needed anything more than stereotypical crimes and of course those who are guilty of them. Proof can be found in ethnological documents. Ethnologists are shocked by my blasphemies yet for a long time they have had at their disposal the necessary evidence to confirm them. In so-called ethological societies the presence of an epidemic immediately rouses the suspicion that there has been an infraction of the basic rules of the community. We are not permitted to call such societies primitive, yet we are expected to describe as primitive everything that perpetuates the mythological type of beliefs and behaviors that belong to persecution in our universe.

The representation of persecution is more forceful in myths than in historical accounts and we are disconcerted by that strength. Compared with such granitelike belief ours seems paltry. The representations of persecution in our history are always vacillating and residual, which is why they are so quickly demystified, at least within several centuries, instead of lasting for millennia, like the myth of Oedipus, which toys with our efforts to understand it. Such formidable belief is foreign to us today. At best we can try to imagine it by tracing it in the texts. We are led, then, to the determination that the sacred forms a part of that blind and massive belief.

Let us examine this phenomenon, beginning with the conditions that make it possible. We do not know why this belief is so strong, but we suspect that it corresponds to a more effective scapegoat mechanism than our own, to a system of persecution that functions at a higher level than our own. To judge by the numerical preponderance of mythological universes, this higher system is more the norm for humanity than our own society which constitutes the exception. Such a strong belief could not be established and perpetuated, after the death of the victim, in the persecutors' commemoration in their myths, if there were any doubt left in the relationships at the heart of the community, in other words if there were not total reconciliation. In order for all the persecutors to be inspired by the same faith in the evil power of their victim, the latter must successfully polarize all the suspicions, tensions, and reprisals that poisoned those relationships. The community must effectively be emptied of its poisons. It must feel liberated and reconciled within itself. This is implied in the conclusion of most myths. We see the actual return to the order that was compromised by the crisis, or even more often the birth of a completely new order in the religious union of a community brought to life by its experience.

The perpetual conjunction in myths of a very guilty victim with a conclusion that is both violent and liberating can only be explained by the extreme force of the scapegoat mechanism. This hypothesis in fact solves the fundamental enigma of all mythology: the order that is either absent or compromised by the scapegoat once more establishes itself or is established by the intervention of someone who disturbed it in the first place. It is conceivable that a victim may be responsible for public disasters, which is what happened in myths as in collective persecutions, but in myths, and only in myths, this same victim restores the order, symbolizes, and even incarnates it.

Our specialists have not yet gotten over this. The transgressor restores and even establishes the order he has somehow transgressed in anticipation. The greatest of all delinquents is transformed into a pillar of society. In some myths this paradox is diminished, censured, or camouflaged, no doubt by the faithful whom it scandalizes almost as much as our contemporary ethnologists, but it is no less transparent beneath the camouflage. This is eminently characteristic of mythology. Plato was troubled by this precise enigma when he complained of the immorality of the Homeric gods. Interpreters have stumbled over this enigma for centuries. It is identical with the enigma of the *primitive* sacred, the beneficial return from the harmful omnipotence attributed to the scapegoat. To understand this return and solve the enigma, we have to reexamine our conjunction of themes, our four stereotypes of persecution, somewhat deformed, *plus* the conclusion that reveals for us the persecutors reconciled. *They really must be reconciled.* There is no reason to doubt it since they commemorate their experiences after the death of the victim and always attribute them unhesitatingly to him.

On further thought this is not surprising. How could the persecutors explain their own reconciliation and the end of the crisis? They cannot take credit for it. Terrified as they are by their own victim, they see themselves as completely passive, purely reactive, totally controlled by this scapegoat at the very moment when they rush to his attack. They think that all initiative comes from him. There is only room for a single cause in their field of vision, and its triumph is absolute, it absorbs all other causality: it is the scapegoat. Thus nothing happens to the persecutors that is not immediately related to him, and if they happen to become reconciled, the scapegoat benefits. There is only one person responsible for everything, one who is absolutely responsible, and he will be responsible for the cure because he is already responsible for the sickness. This is only a paradox for someone with a dualistic vision who is too remote from the experience of a victim to feel the unity and is too determined to differentiate precisely between "good" and "evil."

Admittedly, scapegoats cure neither real epidemics nor droughts nor floods. But the main dimension of every crisis is the way in which it affects human relations. A process of bad reciprocity is its own initiator; it gains nourishment from itself and has no need of external causes in order to continue. As long as external causes exist, such as an epidemic of plague for example, scapegoats will have no efficacy. On the other hand, when these causes no longer exist, the first scapegoat to appear will bring an end to the crisis by eliminating all the interpersonal repercussions in the concentration of all evildoing in the person of one victim. The scapegoat is only effective when human relations have broken down in crisis, but he gives the impression of effecting external causes as well, such as plagues, droughts, and other objective calamities.

Beyond a certain threshold of belief, the effect of the scapegoat is to reverse the relationships between persecutors and their victims, thereby producing the sacred, the founding ancestors and the divinities. The victim, in reality passive, becomes the only effective and omnipotent cause in the face of a group that believes itself to be entirely passive. If groups of people can, as a group, become sick for reasons that are objective or that concern only themselves, if the relationships at the heart of these groups can deteriorate and then be reestablished by means of victims who are unanimously despised, obviously these groups will commemorate these social ills in conformance with the illusory belief that the scapegoat is omnipotent and facilitates the cure. The universal execration of the person who causes the sickness is replaced by universal veneration for the person who cures that same sickness.

We can trace in myths a system of representation of persecutions similar to our own but complicated by the effectiveness of the process of persecution. We are not willing to recognize that effectiveness because it scandalizes us on the levels of both morality and intelligence. We are able to recognize the first evil transfiguration of the victim, which seems normal, but we cannot recognize the second beneficent transfiguration; it is inconceivable that it can unite with the first without destroying it, at least initially.

People in groups are subject to sudden variations in their relationships, for better or worse. If they attribute a complete cycle of variations to the collective victim who facilitates the return to normal, they will inevitably deduce from this double transference belief in a transcendental power that is both double and will bring them alternatively both loss and health, punishment and recompense. This force is manifest through the acts of violence of which it is the victim but is also, more importantly, the mysterious instigator.

If this victim can extend his benefits beyond death to those who have killed him, he must either be resuscitated or was not truly dead. The causality of the scapegoat is imposed with such force that even death cannot prevent it. In order not to renounce the victim's causality, he is brought back to life and immortalized, temporarily and what we call the transcendent and supernatural are invented for that purpose.[3]

---

[3] René Girard, *Violence and the Sacred* (Baltimore: Johns Hopkins University Press, 1972) pp. 85–88; *Des choses cachées depuis la fondation du monde*, pp. 32–50.

Part VI

REVISIONS OF THE THEORY

19

THESPIS

Theodor H. Gaster

Theodor H. Gaster (1906–92), an English-born Semiticist who taught at Barnard College and other American universities, proposed a brand of myth-ritualism intended to accord myth the same importance as ritual. Gaster's myth-ritualist scenario, which he painstakingly seeks to reconstruct for the ancient Near East, derives from Frazer, whose dual version of myth-ritualism Gaster combines in a fashion akin to Hooke and James. The king, who either is god or represents god, is literally or symbolically killed and replaced annually. The killing and replacing of the king parallel the death and rebirth of the god of vegetation and, by magical imitation, cause the rebirth of the god. But for Gaster the myth does more than explain the ritual. By itself, ritual somehow operates on only the human plane. Myth elevates ritual to the divine plane. The renewal sought thereby becomes spiritual and not merely physical. Rather than simply explicating the inherent, physical meaning of ritual, as for Frazer, Harrison, Hooke, and James, myth for Gaster gives ritual its spiritual meaning. The following selection comes from the revised edition of Gaster's major work, *Thespis* (Garden City, NY: Doubleday, 1961 [1950]), 17–19, 23–5. See also his "Divine Kingship in the Ancient Near East: A Review Article," *Review of Religion* 9 (1945), 267–81; "Semitic Mythology," in *Funk & Wagnalls Standard Dictionary of Folklore, Mythology, and Legend*, ed. Maria Leach (New York: Funk & Wagnalls, 1950), II, 989–96; "Myth and Story," *Numen* 1 (1954), 184–212; *The New Golden Bough* (New York: Criterion, 1959), 462–4; "Myth, Mythology," in *Interpreter's Dictionary of the Bible*, ed. George A. Buttrick (New York and Nashville: Abingdon, 1962), II, 481–7; and *Myth, Legend, and Custom in the Old Testament* (New York: Harper & Row, 1969), I, xxv–xxvii. On Gaster see the special issue of the *Journal of the Ancient Near Eastern Society of Columbia University* 5 (1973); and Ronald L. Grimes, "Ritual Studies:

Original publication: Theodor H. Gaster, *Thespis*, rev. edn (Garden City, NY: Doubleday, 1961), Synopsis (pp. 17–19), and ch. 1 (pp. 23–5).

A Comparative Review of Theodor Gaster and Victor Turner," *Religious Studies Review* 2 (1976), 13–25.

Synopsis

Seasonal *rituals* are functional in character. Their purpose is periodically to revive the *topocosm*, that is, the entire complex of any given locality conceived as a living organism. But this topocosm possesses both a punctual and a durative aspect, representing, not only the actual and present community, but also that ideal and continuous entity of which the latter is but the current manifestation. Accordingly, seasonal rituals are accompanied by *myths* which are designed to present the purely functional acts in terms of ideal and durative situations. The interpenetration of the myth and ritual creates *drama*.

In most parts of the world, seasonal rituals follow a common pattern. This pattern is based on the conception that life is vouchsafed in a series of leases which have annually to be renewed. The renewal is achieved, however, not through divine providence alone but also through the concerted effort of men; and the rituals are designed primarily to recruit and regiment that effort. They fall into the two clear divisions of *Kenosis*, or Emptying, and *Plerosis*, or Filling, the former representing the evacuation of life, the latter its replenishment. Rites of Kenosis include the observance of fasts, lents, and similar austerities, all designed to indicate that the topocosm is in a state of suspended animation. Rites of Plerosis include mock combats against the forces of drought or evil, mass mating, the performance of rain charms and the like, all designed to effect the reinvigoration of the topocosm.

The rites originally performed by the community as a whole tend in time to be centered in a single representative individual, viz., the king. It is the king who then undergoes the temporary eclipse, who fights against the noxious powers, and who serves as the bridegroom in a "sacred marriage."

What the king does on the punctual plane, the god does on the durative. Accordingly, all the ceremonies performed by the king are transmuted, through the medium of myth, into deeds done by the god. This transmutation in turn gives rise to the idea that the king and the other performers of the seasonal rites are merely impersonating acts originally performed by the gods, and the tendency develops to represent what is really a parallel situation on the durative plane as something that happened primordially – the archetype of what may be periodically repeated with the same effect. Presentation then becomes representation; the ritual turns into drama.

The Seasonal Pattern may be traced in many of the calendar festivals of the Ancient Near East. Representative instances are the Akitu (New Year) Festival of the Babylonians and Assyrians and the New Year-Day of Atonement-Feast of Ingathering complex of the Israelites. It may be recognized also in Egypt and among the Hittites, and – at least vestigially – in the Asianic mysteries of Attis.

In course of time, as new conceptions evolve, the urgency of the primitive seasonal rituals tends to recede. But the Pattern lingers on in increasingly meaningless folk customs and in the conventions of literary style. Recent studies have shown that it may be recognized behind the conventional structure of Greek tragedy and comedy and behind the European mummers' play. Using the same approach, it is here shown that several mythological texts which have come down to us from the Ancient Near East likewise ascend to the Seasonal Pattern, reflecting in their general themes and in the sequence of their episodes the basic motifs and sequence of acts in the primitive ritual. It is fully conceded, however, that most of the texts in question now stand a long way from the primitive form and have been subjected to considerable literary and artistic development. What is at issue is, in fact, the history of the literary genre as a whole, not of the particular compositions.

The mythological texts in which the Pattern is here detected are the following:

The CANAANITE poems of *Baal*, *Aqhat*, and *The Gracious Gods*, from Ras Shamra-Ugarit;

The BABYLONIAN Epic of Creation (*Enuma Elish*);

The HITTITE myths of *Hahhimas* and *Telipinu* and of *The Snaring of the Dragon*. The last-named was, in fact, the cultic myth of the annual Puruli Festival;

The EGYPTIAN "dramatic" texts from Edfu and from the Ramesseum, and the so-called "Memphite Creation Play" inscribed on the celebrated "Shabaka Stone."

The texts revolve around different elements of the primitive Seasonal Pattern, some of them concentrating on the ritual combat, others on the eclipse and renewal of kingship, and others again on the disappearance and restoration of the genius of topocosmic vitality. Moreover, while some (i.e., the Hittite texts) are actually accompanied by ritual directions, and must therefore have been recited at public ceremonies, others appear to be purely literary compositions, and one of them (viz., the Canaanite *Poem of the Gracious Gods*) even verges on the burlesque, in the manner of the English mummers' play and of the modern Carnival dramas of Northern Greece. All of these compositions, except the Babylonian *Epic of Creation* and the Egyptian Edfu drama, are here presented in translation, with running commentaries setting forth their relation to the seasonal ritual and elucidating them in the light of comparative religion and folklore. They are grouped according to their various dominant themes.

The Seasonal Pattern survived not only in formal myths but also – albeit in severely attenuated guise – in the hymns and chants associated with the liturgy. It may be recognized in the structure of several Biblical psalms, while sophisticated literary developments of it may be detected in the same way in the choral odes of the *Bacchae* of Euripides, in the Homeric *Hymn to Demeter*, and even in some of the hymns of the medieval Church.

Ritual and Myth

§1.   All over the world, from time immemorial, it has been the custom to usher in years and seasons by means of public ceremonies. These, however, are neither arbitrary nor haphazard, nor are they mere diversions. On the contrary, they follow everywhere a more or less uniform and consistent pattern and serve a distinctly *functional* purpose. They represent the mechanism whereby, at a primitive level, society seeks periodically to renew its vitality and thus ensure its continuance.

From the standpoint of a primitive community, life is not so much a progression from cradle to grave as a series of leases annually or periodically renewed and best exemplified in the revolution of the seasons. The renewal, however, is not effected by grace of superior providence or by any automatic law of nature; for of such the primitive has no conception. Rather has it to be fought for and won by the concerted effort of men. Accordingly, a regular program of activities is established, which, performed periodically under communal sanction, will furnish the necessary replenishment of life and vitality. This program constitutes the pattern of the seasonal ceremonies.

§2.   The activities fall into two main divisions which we may call, respectively, rites of Kenosis, or Emptying, and rites of Plerosis, or Filling. The former portray and symbolize the eclipse of life and vitality at the end of each lease, and are exemplified by lenten periods, fasts, austerities, and other expressions of mortification or suspended animation. The latter, on the other hand, portray and symbolize the revitalization which ensues at the beginning of the new lease, and are exemplified by rites of mass mating, ceremonial purgations of evil and noxiousness (both physical and "moral"),[1] and magical procedures designed to promote fertility, produce rain, relume the sun, and so forth.

---

[1] In primitive thought, of course, the two categories are not rigidly distinguished. Morality, or the social code, is identified and validated as the innate structural order of the world – the same order which governs its physical phenomena and which is determined by the gods.

§3.   Basic to the entire procedure is the conception that what is in turn eclipsed and revitalized is not merely the human community of a given area or locality but the total corporate unit of all elements, animate and inanimate alike, which together constitute its distinctive character and "atmosphere." To this wider entity we may assign the name *topocosm*, formed (on the analogy of *microcosm* and *macrocosm*) from Greek *topos*, "place," and *cosmos*, "world, order."[2] The seasonal ceremonies are the economic regimen of this topocosm.

From the outset, however, they are more than mere ritual. The essence of the topocosm is that it possesses a twofold character, at once real and punctual, and ideal and durative, the former aspect being necessarily immerged in the latter, as a moment is immerged in time. If it is bodied forth as a real and concrete organism in the present, it exists also as an ideal, timeless entity, embracing but transcending the here and now in exactly the same way that the ideal America embraces but transcends the present generation of Americans.[3] The successive leases of its life therefore exist not only in the reality of the present but also in a kind of infinite continuum of which the present is but the current phase. Accordingly, the seasonal ceremonies which mark the beginnings and ends of those leases possess at once a punctual and a transcendent aspect. In the former, they serve as effective mechanisms for articulating immediate situations and satisfying immediate needs. In the latter, however, they objectify, in terms of the present, situations which are intrinsically durative and sempiternal. Thus they are, from the start, not only direct experiences but also and at the same time representations – not only rituals but also dramas.

§4.   The connecting link between these two aspects is myth. The function of myth (so obstinately misunderstood) is to translate the real into terms of the ideal, the punctual into terms of the durative and transcendental. This it does by projecting the procedures of ritual to the plane of ideal situations, which they are then taken to objectify and reproduce. Myth is therefore an essential ingredient in the pattern of the seasonal ceremonies; and the interpenetration of ritual and myth provides the key to the essential nature of drama.

In this context, myth is not, as Robertson Smith maintained, a mere outgrowth of ritual, an artistic or literary interpretation imposed later upon sacral acts; nor is it merely, as Jane Harrison insisted, the spoken correlative of "things done." Rather, it is the expression of a parallel aspect inherent in them from the beginning; and its function within the scheme of the Seasonal Pattern is to translate the punctual into terms of the durative, the real into those of the ideal.

---

[2] That the social unit embraces more than the mere human community was already recognized by Robertson Smith in his classic exposition of the subject in *Religion of the Semites*, 271 ff.; but while he perceived its spatial extension beyond that community, he missed the essential point that it extends in time as well as in space, embracing past, present, and future in one ideal, durative entity.

[3] Symbols of the topocosmic concept in modern thought are Alma Mater, La France, etc.

Moreover, the impulse which inspires myth is no mere flight of literary or artistic fancy, nor can mythology itself be defined in terms of its articulation. To do so is to mistake the form for the essence; it is as if one were to define prayer solely in terms of litany, or music in those of score and scale. Mythology is a function of religio-social behavior, not a department of literature or art; the latter are merely its vehicles or instruments.

20

MYTHS AND RITUALS: A GENERAL THEORY

Clyde Kluckhohn

The American anthropologist Clyde Kluckhohn (1905–60), who taught at Harvard University, introduced a looser, less dogmatic variety of myth-ritualism. Instead of insisting that myths and rituals always operate together, he allows for the independence of each. He claims only that myths and rituals tend to come together. Instead of insisting that when myths and rituals come together, they work in a single manner, he allows for varying forms of interaction. He claims only that myths and rituals, operating separately or together, serve a psychological function: alleviating anxiety, anxiety arising from the physical world, from society, and from oneself. Myths reduce anxiety by providing fixed ways of understanding; rituals, by providing fixed ways of behaving. The alleviation of anxiety abets society as much as individuals – an echo of Malinowski. Kluckhohn draws most of his examples from the Navaho, the culture where he did repeated field work. The following essay (from *Harvard Theological Review* 35 [1942] 45–79), is Kluckhohn's classic formulation of myth-ritualism. See also Kluckhohn and Dorothea Leighton, *The Navaho*, rev. edn (Cambridge, MA: Harvard University Press, 1974 [1946]), 229–40; and Kluckhohn, *Anthropology and the Classics* (Providence: Brown University Press, 1961). On Kluckhohn see the obituary by Talcott Parsons and Evon Z. Vogt in *American Anthropologist* 64 (1962), 140–61, reprinted in Kluckhohn, *Navaho Witchcraft* (Boston: Beacon Press, 1967 [1944]), ix–xx.

I

Nineteenth century students strongly tended to study mythology apart from associated rituals (and indeed apart from the life of the people generally).

Original publication: Clyde Kluckhohn, "Myths and Rituals: A General Theory," *Harvard Theological Review* 35 (1942), pp. 45–79.

Myths were held to be symbolic descriptions of phenomena of nature.[1] One prominent school, in fact, tried to find an astral basis for all mythic tales. Others, among whom Andrew Lang was prominent, saw in the myth a kind of primitive scientific theory. Mythology answered the insistent human HOW? and WHY? How and why was the world made? How and why were living creatures brought into being? Why, if there was life must there be death? To early psychoanalysts such as Abraham[2] and Rank[3] myths were "group phantasies," wish-fulfillments for a society strictly analogous to the dream and day-dream of individuals. Mythology for these psychoanalysts was also a symbolic structure par excellence, but the symbolism which required interpretation was primarily a sex sym-bolism which was postulated as universal and all-pervasive. Reik[4] recognized a connection between rite and myth, and he, with Freud,[5] verbally agreed to Robertson Smith's proposition that mythology was mainly a description of ritual. To the psychoanalysts, however, mythology was essentially (so far as what they did with it is concerned) societal phantasy material which reflected impulse repression.[6] There was no attempt to discover the practical function of mythology in the daily behaviors of the members of a society[7] nor to demonstrate specific interactions of mythology and ceremonials. The interest was in supposedly pan-human symbolic meanings, not in the

Based upon a paper read at the Symposium of the American Folklore Society at Chicago in December, 1939. My thanks are due to W. W. Hill, Florence Kluckhohn, A. H. Leighton, Arthur Nock, E. C. Parsons, and Alfred Tozzer for a critical reading and a number of suggestions, to Ruth Underhill and David Mandelbaum for supplying unpublished material on the Papago and Toda respectively.

[1] Professor Nock has called my attention to the fact that the naturalistic theory actually works very well for the Vedic material.

[2] See Traum und Mythus (Vienna, 1909). Rank's final conclusion was that "myths are relics from the infantile mental life of the people, and dreams constitute the myths of the individual" (Selected Papers of Karl Abraham, London, 1927, p. 32). Cf. also Traum und Mythus, pp. 69, 71.

[3] See Otto Rank, Psychoanalytische Beiträge zur Mythenforschung (Vienna and Leipzig, 1919) and Der Mythus von der Geburt des Helden (2nd edition, Leipzig and Vienna, 1922). Rank attempts to show that hero myths originate in the delusional structures of paranoiacs.

[4] Theodor Reik, Das Ritual (Leipzig, Vienna, Zurich, 1928).

[5] Cf. Freud's statement in his introduction to Reik, op. cit., p. 11.

[6] Many psychoanalysts today consider myths simply "a form of collective day-dreaming." I have heard a prominent psychoanalyst say "Creation myths are for culture what early memories (true or fictitious) are to the individual."

[7] This has been done, even by anthropologists, only quite recently. Boas, as early as 1916 (Tsimshian Mythology, Bureau of American Ethnology, Annual Report for 1909–10, vol. 31, pp. 29–1037), did attempt to show how the origin of all folklore must be sought in imaginings based upon the ordinary social life of the society in question. But in this (as in his later publication on the Kwakiutl) he showed how mythology reflected social organization – not how mythology preserved social equilibrium or symbolized social organization.

relation of a given myth or part of a myth to particular cultural forms or specific social situations.[8]

To some extent the answer to the whole question of the relationship between myth and ceremony depends, of course, upon how wide or how restricted a sense one gives to "mythology." In ordinary usage the Oedipus tale is a "myth," but only some Freudians believe that this is merely the description of a ritual! The famous stories of the Republic are certainly called "μῦθος," and while a few scholars[9] believe that Plato in *some* cases had reference to the Orphic and/or Eleusinian mysteries there is certainly not a shred of evidence that all of Plato's immortal "myths" are "descriptions of rituals." To be sure, one may justifiably narrow the problem by saying that in a technical sense these are "legends," and by insisting that "myths" be rigorously distinguished from "legends," "fairy-tales," and "folk-tales." If, however, one agrees that "myth" has Durkheim's connotation of the "sacred" as opposed to the "profane" the line is still sometimes hard to draw in concrete cases. What of "creation myths"? In some cases (as at Zuni) these are indeed recited[10] during ritual performances (with variations for various ceremonies). In other cases, even though they may be recited in a "ritual" attitude, they do not enter into any ceremonial. Nevertheless, they definitely retain the flavor of "the sacred." Moreover, there are (as again at Zuni) exoteric and esoteric forms of the same myth. Among the Navaho many of the older men who are not ceremonial practitioners know that part of a myth which tells of the exploits of the hero or heroes but not the portion which prescribes the ritual details of the chant. Granting that there are sometimes both secular and sacred versions of the same tale and that other difficulties obtrude themselves in particular cases, it still seems possible to use the connotation of the sacred as that which differentiates "myth" from the rest of folklore.[11] At least, such a distinction appears workable to a rough first approximation and will be followed throughout this paper.

But defining "myth" strictly as "sacred tale" does not carry with it by implication a warrant for considering mythology purely as a description of

---

[8] Dr. Benedict in her Zuni Mythology (New York, 1935) follows a form of explanation which draws heavily from psychoanalytic interpretations. Thus, (p. xix) in discussing the compensatory functions of mythology, she speaks of "folkloristic day-dreaming." But her treatment lacks the most objectionable features of the older psychoanalytic contributions because she does not deal in universalistic, *pan*-symbolic "meanings" but rather orients her whole presentation to the richly documented Zuni materials and to the specific context of Zuni culture.

[9] Cf. e.g., R. H. S. Crossman, Plato Today (London, 1937), p. 88.

[10] There are Aranda, Fijian, and Winnebago chants which are almost purely recitals of an origin myth.

[11] This covers the differentia which is often suggested: namely, that myth is distinguished from legend or folktale by the circumstance that some (or perhaps most) of the actors in a myth must be supernatural beings – not simply human beings of however great a legendary stature. There are, of course, other distinctions which could – for other purposes – profitably be entered

correlative rituals. Rose[12] quite correctly says "among myths there are many whose connection with any rite is a thing to be proved, not assumed." What is needed is a detailed comparative analysis of actual associations. Generally speaking, we do seem to find rich ritualism and a rich mythology together. But there are cases (like the Toda)[13] where an extensive ceremonialism does not appear to have its equally extensive mythological counterpart and instances (like classical Greece) where a ramified mythology appears to have existed more or less independent of a comparatively meagre rite-system.[14] For example, in spite of the many myths relating to Ares the rituals connected with Ares seem to have been few in number and highly localized in time and space.[15] The early Romans, on the other hand, seemed to get along very well without mythology. The poverty of the ritual which accompanies the extremely complex mythology of the Mohave is well known.[16] Kroeber indeed says "Public ceremonies or rituals as they occur among almost all native Americans cannot be said to be practised by the Mohave."[17] The Bushmen likewise had many

---

into. Thus, Professor Nock has suggested to me that there are differences of some consequence between an oral mythology and a written theology. "A true myth," he says, "never takes form with an eye to the pen or to the printed page."

These refinements are undoubtedly interesting and important, but they do not seem directly relevant to the issues dealt with in this paper. Here only the major contrast of sacred and profane appears crucial. Any segregation of myth from folktale, legend, fairytale, etc. which rests upon hair-splitting or upon special premises must be avoided. Thus Róheim's recent stimulating discussion (Myth and Folk-Tale, American Imago, vol. 2, 1941, pp. 266–279) is acceptable only insofar as one grants the major postulates of orthodox Freudian psychoanalysis. Róheim says: "A folktale is a narrative with a happy end, a myth is a tragedy; a god must die before he can be truly divine" (p. 276). "In the folk tale we relate how we overcome the anxiety connected with the 'bad parents' and grew up, in myth we confess that only death can end the tragic ambivalence of human nature. Eros triumphs in the folk-tale, Thanatos in the myth" (p. 279).

[12] H. J. Rose, Review of "The Labyrinth" (Man, vol. 36, 1936, no. 87, p. 69).

[13] Dr. Mandelbaum writes me: "For the Todas do not have complex myths; myth episodes which take hours and days in the telling among Kotas, are told by Todas in less than three minutes." Cf. M. Emeneau, The Songs of the Todas (Proceedings of the American Philosophical Society, vol. 77, 1937, pp. 543–560); "... the art of story-telling is almost non-existent. In fact, imaginative story-telling hardly exists and the stories of traditional events in the life of the tribe do not seem to be popular.... Some of the songs are based on legendary stories, but even in the case of these some of my informants knew the songs without knowing the stories" (p. 543).

[14] I am thinking here of public (non-cultist) mythology and of official and public ritual. Orphic ritual may have been more closely connected to the complicated Orphic myth. Cf. W. K. C. Guthrie, Who Were the Orphics? (Scientia, vol. 67, 1937, pp. 110–121), esp. pp. 119–120.

[15] Cf. L. R. Farnell, The Cults of the Greek States, vol. IV (Oxford, 1909), pp. 396–407.

[16] A. L. Kroeber, Handbook of the Indians of California (Washington, 1925), p. 660.

[17] Ibid., p. 755. The Mohave are, of course, also a classic case where myths, at least according to cultural theory, are dreamed. But even though we recognize the cultural patterning of the "dreaming" this in no sense justifies the inference that the myths are derived from the meagre rituals. Indeed Kroeber points out (p. 770) that some myths are not sung to – i.e., are not even ritualized to the extent of being connected with song recitals.

myths and very little ritual. On the other hand, one can point to examples like the Central Eskimo, where every detail of the Sedna myth has its ritual analogue in confessional, other rites, or hunting tabus, or, for contrast, to the American Indian tribes (especially some Californian ones) where the creation myth is never enacted in ceremonial form. In different sectors of one culture, the Papago, all of these possibilities are represented. Some myths are never ceremonially enacted. Some ceremonies emphasize content foreign to the myth. Other ceremonies consisting only of songs have some vague place in the mythological world; between these and the myths "there is a certain tenuous connection which may be a rationalization made for the sake of unity. . . ."[18]

The anthropology of the past generation has tended to recoil sharply from any sort of generalized interpretation. Obsessed with the complexity of the historical experience of all peoples, anthropologists have (perhaps over-much) eschewed the inference of regularities of psychological reaction which would transcend the facts of diffusion and of contacts of groups. Emphasis has been laid upon the distribution of myths and upon the mythological patterning which prevailed in different cultures and culture areas. Study of these distributions has led to a generalization of another order which is the converse of the hypothesis of most nineteenth century classical scholars[19] that a ritual was an enactment of a myth. In the words of Boas:[20] "The uniformity of many such rituals over large areas and the diversity of mythological explanations show clearly that the ritual itself is the stimulus for the origin of the myth. . . . The ritual existed, and the tale originated from the desire to account for it."

While this suggestion of the primacy of ritual over myth is probably a valid statistical induction and a proper statement of the modal tendency of our evidence, it is, it seems to me, as objectionably a simple unitary explanation (if pressed too far) as the generally rejected nineteenth century views. Thus we find Hocart[21] recently asking: "If there are myths that give rise to ritual where do these myths come from?" A number of instances will shortly be presented in which the evidence is unequivocal that myths did give rise to ritual. May I only remark here that – if we view the matter objectively – the Christian Mass, as interpreted by Christians, is a clear illustration of a ritual based upon a sacred story. Surely, in any case, Hocart's question can be answered very simply: from a dream or a waking phantasy or a personal habit system of

[18] Personal communication from Dr. Ruth Underhill.

[19] Certain contemporary classical scholars take a point of view which is very similar to that adopted in this paper. Thus H. J. Rose (Modern Methods in Classical Mythology, St. Andrews, 1930, p. 12) says ". . . I postulate . . . a reciprocal influence of myth and ceremony. . . ." Cf. also L. R. Farnell, The Value and the Methods of Mythologic Study (London, 1919), p. 11, ". . . occasionally myth is the prior fact that generates a certain ritual, as for instance the offering of horses to St. George in Silesia was suggested by the myth of St. George the horseman. . . ."

[20] F. Boas and others, General Anthropology (New York, 1938), p. 617.

[21] A. M. Hocart, Myth and Ritual (Man, vol. 36, no. 230), p. 167.

some individual in the society. The basic psychological mechanisms involved would seem not dissimilar to those whereby individuals in our own (and other) cultures construct private rituals[22] or carry out private divination[23] – e.g., counting and guessing before the clock strikes, trying to get to a given point (a traffic light, for instance) before something else happens. As DuBois[24] has suggested, "the explanation may be that personal rituals have been taken over and socialized by the group." These "personal rituals" could have their genesis in idiosyncratic habit[25] formations (similar to those of obsessional neurotics in our culture) or in dreams or reveries. Mrs. Seligman[26] has convincingly suggested that spontaneous personal dissociation is a frequent mechanism for rite innovations. The literature is replete with instances of persons "dreaming" that supernaturals summoned them, conducted them on travels or adventures, and finally admonished them thereafter to carry out certain rites (often symbolically repetitive of the adventures).

Moreover, there are a number of well documented actual cases where historical persons, in the memory of other historical persons, actually instituted new rituals. The ritual innovations of the American Indian Ghost Dance cult[27] and other nativistic cults of the New World[28] provide striking illustration. In these cases the dreams or phantasies – told by the innovators before the ceremonial was ever actualized in deeds – became an important part of traditionally accepted rite-myths. Lincoln[29] has presented plausible evidence that dreams are the source of "new" rituals. Morgan,[30] on the basis of Navaho material, says:

[22] Cf. A. M. Tozzer, Social Origins and Social Continuities (New York, 1934), pp. 242–267, esp. pp. 260 ff.

[23] R. R. Willoughby gives good examples and discussions of these culturally unformalized divinatory practices. See Magic and Cognate Phenomena: An Hypothesis (In: A Handbook of Social Psychology, Carl Murchison, ed., Worcester, Mass., 1935, pp. 461–520), pp. 480–482.

[24] C. DuBois, Some Anthropological Perspectives on Psychoanalysis (Psychoanalytic Review, vol. 24, 1937, pp. 246–264), p. 254.

[25] In other words, in terms of patterns of behavior which are distinctive of an individual, not as a representative of a particular cultural tradition, but as a differentiated biological organism who – either because of inherited constitutional differences or because of accidents of the conditioning process – behaves differently in major respects from most individuals of the same age, sex, and status acculturated in the same culture.

[26] B. Z. Seligman, The Part of the Unconscious in Social Heritage (In: Essays Presented to C. G. Seligman, London, 1934, pp. 307–319).

[27] I am, of course, well aware that the rites of the Ghost Dance were not by any means identical in all tribes. But in spite of wide variations under the influence of pre-existent ideal and behavioral patterns *certain* new ritual practices which must be connected with the visions of the founder may be found in almost every tribe.

[28] See A. F. Chamberlain, New Religions among the North American Indians (Journal of Religious Psychology, 1913, vol. 6, pp. 1–49).

[29] J. S. Lincoln, The Dream in Primitive Cultures (Baltimore, 1935).

[30] William Morgan, Human Wolves Among the Navaho (Yale University Publications in Anthropology, no. 11, 1936), p. 40. Dr. Henry A. Murray of the Harvard Psychological Clinic informs me that there is clinical evidence that an individual can be conditioned (in the technical psychological sense) by a dream.

... delusions and dreams ... are so vivid and carry such conviction that any attempt to reason about them afterwards on the basis of conscious sense impressions is unavailing. Such experiences deeply condition the individual, sometimes so deeply that if the experience is at variance with a tribal or neighborhood belief, the individual will retain his own variation. There can be no doubt that this is a very significant means of modifying a culture.

Van Gennep[31] asserts that persons went to dream in the sanctuary at Epidaurus as a source for new rites in the cult of Asclepius. To obtain ceremony through dream is, of course, itself a pattern, a proper traditional way of obtaining a ceremony or power. I do not know of any cases of a society where dreaming is generally in disrepute, as at Zuni, and where ceremony has yet demonstrably originated through dream. But where dreaming is accepted as revelation it must not be assumed that the content (or even, entirely, the structure) of a new myth and its derived ceremony will be altogether determined by pre-existent cultural forms. As Lowie[32] has remarked, "That they themselves (dreams) in part reflect the regnant folklore offers no ultimate explanation." Anthropologists must be wary of what Korzybski calls "self-reflexive systems" – here, specifically, the covert premise that "culture alone determines culture."

The structure of new cultural forms (whether myths or rituals) will undoubtedly be conditioned by the pre-existent cultural matrix. But the rise of new cultural forms will almost always be determined by factors external to that culture: pressure from other societies, biological events such as epidemics, or changes in the physical environment. Barber[33] has recently shown how the Ghost Dance and the Peyote Cult represent alternative responses of various American Indian tribes to the deprivation resultant upon the encroachment of whites. The Ghost Dance was an adaptive response under the earlier external conditions, but under later conditions the Peyote Cult was the more adaptive response, and the Ghost Dance suffered what the stimulus-response psychologists would call "extinction through non-reward." At any rate the Ghost Dance became extinct in some tribes; in others it has perhaps suffered only partial extinction.

There are always individuals in every society who have their private rituals; there are always individuals who dream and who have compensatory phantasies. In the normal course of things these are simply deviant behaviors which are ridiculed or ignored by most members of the society. Perhaps indeed one should not speak of them as "deviant" – they are "deviant" only as carried to extremes by a relatively small number of individuals, for everyone probably

---

[31] A. van Gennep, La Formation des Légendes (Paris, 1910), p. 255. The peyote cult is, of course, an outstanding case where dreams determine variation in ritual.

[32] R. H. Lowie, The History of Ethnological Theory (N. Y., 1937), p. 264.

[33] Bernard Barber, Acculturation and Messianic Movements (American Sociological Review, vol. 6, 1941, pp. 663–670); A Socio-Cultural Interpretation of the Peyote Cult (American Anthropologist, 1941, vol. 43, pp. 673–676).

has some private rituals and compensatory phantasies. When, however, changed conditions happen to make a particular type of obsessive behavior or a special sort of phantasy generally congenial, the private ritual is then socialized by the group, the phantasy of the individual becomes the myth of his society. Indeed there is evidence[34] that when pressures are peculiarly strong and peculiarly general, a considerable number of different individuals may almost simultaneously develop substantially identical phantasies which then become widely current.

Whether belief (myth) or behavior (ritual) changes first will depend, again, both upon cultural tradition and upon external circumstances. Taking a very broad view of the matter, it does seem that behavioral patterns more frequently alter first. In a rapidly changing culture such as our own many ideal patterns are as much as a generation behind the corresponding behavioral patterns. There is evidence that certain ideal patterns (for example, those defining the status of women) are slowly being altered to harmonize with, to act as rationalizations for, the behavioral actualities. On the other hand, the case of Nazi Germany is an excellent illustration of the ideal patterns ("the myth") being provided from above almost whole cloth and of the state, through various organizations, exerting all its force to make the behavioral patterns conform to the standards of conduct laid down in the Nazi mythology.

Some cultures and sub-cultures are relatively indifferent to belief, others to behavior. The dominant practice of the Christian Church, throughout long periods of its history, was to give an emphasis to belief which is most unusual as seen from a cross-cultural perspective. In general, the crucial test as to whether or not one was a Christian was the willingness to avow belief in certain dogmas.[35] The term "believer" was almost synonymous with "Christian." It is very possibly because of this cultural screen that until this century most European scholars selected the myth as primary.

II

To a considerable degree, the whole question of the primacy of ceremonial or mythology is as meaningless as all questions of "the hen or the egg" form. What is really important, as Malinowski has so brilliantly shown, is the intricate interdependence of myth (which is one form of ideology) with ritual and many other forms of behavior. I am quite aware that I have little to add

[34] See Marie Bonaparte, Princess of Greece, The Myth of the Corpse in the Car (The American Imago, 1941, vol. 2, pp. 105–127).

[35] Ruth Benedict in the Article "Myth" (Encyclopaedia of the Social Sciences, vol. IX, 1933) makes a similar point but distorts it by the implication that belief in a certain *cosmology* was the single crucial test of Christianity.

conceptually to Malinowski's discussion in "The Myth in Primitive Psychology."[36] There he examines myths not as curiosa taken out of their total context but as living, vitally important elements in the day to day lives of his Trobrianders, interwoven with every other abstracted type of activity. From this point of view one sees the fallacy of all unilateral explanations. One also sees the aspect of truth in all (or nearly all) of them. There are features which seem to be explanatory of natural phenomena.[37] There are features which reveal the peculiar forms of wish fulfillments characteristic of the culture in question (including the expression of the culturally disallowed but unconsciously wanted). There *are* myths which are intimately related to rituals, which may be descriptive of them, but there are other myths which stand apart. If these others are descriptive of rituals at all, they are, as Durkheim (followed by Radcliffe-Brown and others) suggested, descriptions of rituals of the social organization. That is, they are symbolic representations of the dominant configurations[38] of the particular culture. Myths, then, may express not only the latent content of rituals but of other culturally organized behaviors. Malinowski is surely in error when he writes[39] ". . . myth . . . is not symbolic. . . ." Durkheim and Mauss[40] have pointed out how various non-literate groups (notably the Zuni and certain tribes of southeastern Australia) embrace nature within the schema of their social organization through myths which classify natural phenomena precisely according to the principles that prevail in the social organization. Warner[41] has further developed this type of interpretation.

Boas,[42] with his usual caution, is sceptical of all attempts to find a systematic interpretation of mythology. But, while we can agree with him when he writes

---

[36] London, 1926.

[37] Radcliffe-Brown's explanation, though useful, strikes me as too narrow in that it seems to deny to nonliterate man *all* bare curiosity and any free play of fancy, undetermined by societal necessities. He says (Andaman Islanders, Cambridge, England, 1933, pp. 380–381): "Natural phenomena such as the alternation of day and night, the changes of the moon, the procession of the seasons, and variations of the weather, have important effects on the welfare of the society . . . a process of bringing within the circle of the social life those aspects of nature that are of importance to the well-being of the society."

[38] "Configuration" is here used as a technical term referring to a structural regularity of the covert culture. In other words, a configuration is a principle which structures widely varying contexts of culture content but of which the culture carriers are minimally aware. By "configuration" I mean something fairly similar to what some authors have meant by "latent culture pattern" as distinguished from "manifest culture pattern." The concept is also closely akin to what Sumner and Keller call a cultural "ethos." For a fuller discussion of "configuration" and "covert culture" see Clyde Kluckhohn, Patterning as Exemplified in Navaho Culture (In: Language, Culture, and Personality, L. Spier, ed., Menasha, 1941, pp. 109–131), esp. pp. 109, 124–129.

[39] Op. cit., p. 19.

[40] De Quelques formes primitives de classification (L'Année Sociologique, vol. 6).

[41] W. L. Warner, A Black Civilization (New York, 1937), esp. pp. 371–411.

[42] See especially F. Boas, Review of G. W. Locher, "The Serpent in Kwakiutl Religion: a Study in Primitive Culture" (Deutsche Literaturzeitung, 1933, pp. 1182–1186; reprinted in Race, Language, and Culture, New York, 1940, pp. 446–450).

". . . mythological narratives and mythological concepts should not be equal-
ized; for social, psychological, and historical conditions affect both in different
ways,"[43] the need for scrupulous inquiry into historical and other determinants
must not be perverted to justify a repudiation of all attempts to deal with the
symbolic processes of the all-important covert culture. At all events, the factual record is perfectly straightforward in one respect: neither myth nor ritual
can be postulated as "primary."

   This is the important point in our discussion at this juncture, and it is
unfortunate that Hooke and his associates in their otherwise very illuminating
contributions to the study of the relations between myth and ritual in the Near
East have emphasized only one aspect of the system of interdependences which
Malinowski and Radcliffe-Brown have shown to exist. When Hooke[44] points
out that myths are constantly used to justify rituals this observation is quite
congruent with the observed facts in many cultures. Indeed all of these data
may be used toward a still wider induction: man, as a symbol-using animal,
appears to feel the need not only to act but almost equally to give verbal or
other symbolic "reasons" for his acts.[45] Hooke[46] rightly speaks of "the vital
significance of the myth as something that works," but when he continues
"and that dies apart from its ritual" he seems to imply that myths cannot exist
apart from rituals and this, as has been shown, is contrary to documented
cases. No, the central theorem has been expressed much more adequately
by Radcliffe-Brown:[47] "In the case of both ritual and myth the sentiments
expressed are those that are essential to the existence of the society." This
theorem can be regarded as having been well established in a general way, but
we still lack detailed observations on change in myths as correlated with changes
in ritual and changes in a culture generally.[48] Navaho material gives certain
hints that when a culture as a whole changes rapidly its myths are also substantially and quickly altered.

   In sum, the facts do not permit any universal generalizations as to ritual
being the "cause" of myth or vice versa. Their relationship is rather that of
intricate mutual interdependence, differently structured in different cultures

---

   [43] Ibid., p. 450.
   [44] S. H. Hooke, The Origins of Early Semitic Ritual (London, 1938), pp. 2, 3, 8. See also
Myth and Ritual (London, 1933).
   [45] This statement is not to be interpreted as credence in "the aetiological myth" if by this
one means that a myth "satisfies curiosity." We are not justified, I believe, in *completely* excluding
the aetiological (in this sense) motive in every case, but Whitehead's statement (Religion in the
Making, New York, 1926) probably conforms to a rough induction: "Thus the myth not only
explains but reinforces the hidden purpose of the ritual which is emotion" (p. 25).
   [46] S. H. Hooke (ed.) The Labyrinth (New York, 1935), p. ix.
   [47] Op. cit., p. 405.
   [48] The best documentation of the fact that myths are constantly undergoing revision is probably to be found in various writings of Boas. See, for example, Race, Language, and Culture
(New York, 1940), pp. 397–525, passim.

and probably at different times in the same culture. As Benedict[49] has pointed out, there is great variation in the extent to which mythology conditions the religious complex – "the small role of myth in Africa and its much greater importance in religion in parts of North America." Both myth and ritual satisfy the needs of a society and the relative place of one or the other will depend upon the particular needs (conscious and unconscious) of the individuals in a particular society at a particular time. This principle covers the observed data which show that rituals are borrowed without their myths,[50] and myths without any accompanying ritual. A ritual may be reinforced by a myth (or vice versa) in the donor culture but satisfy the carriers of the recipient culture simply as a form of activity (or be rationalized by a quite different myth which better meets their emotional needs).[51] In short, the only uniformity which can be posited is that there is a strong tendency for some sort of interrelationship between myth and ceremony and that this interrelationship is dependent upon what appears, so far as present information goes, to be an invariant function of both myth and ritual: the gratification (most often in the negative form of anxiety reduction) of a large proportion of the individuals in a society.

If Malinowski and Radcliffe-Brown (and their followers) turned the searchlight of their interpretations as illuminatingly upon specific human animals and their impulses as upon cultural and social abstractions, it might be possible to take their work as providing a fairly complete and adequate general theory of myth and ritual. With Malinowski's notion of myth as "an active force" which is intimately related to almost every other aspect of a culture we can only agree. When he writes:[52] "Myth is a constant by-product of living faith which is in need of miracles; of sociological status, which demands precedent; of moral rule which requires sanction," we can only applaud. To the French sociologists, to

---

[49] Op. cit., p. 180.

[50] This appears to be the Papago case. (Underhill, personal communication.)

[51] There are many striking and highly specific parallels between Navaho and Hopi ceremonial practices. For example, the mechanical equipment used in connection with the Sun's House phase of the Navaho Shooting Way chants has so much in common with similar gadgets used in Hopi ceremonials that one can hardly fail to posit a connection. Dr. Parsons has documented the intimate resemblances between the Male Shooting Way chant and Hopi Flute and Snake-Antelope ceremonies (A Pre-Spanish Record of Hopi Ceremonies; American Anthropologist, 1940, vol. 42, pp. 541–543, fn. 4, p. 541). The best guess at present would be that the Hopi was the donor culture, but the direction of diffusion is immaterial here: the significant point is that the supporting myths in the cases concerned show little likeness. For instance, Dr Parsons regards the Flute Ceremony as a dramatization of the Hopi emergence myth, but the comparable ritual acts in Navaho culture are linked to chantway legends of the usual Holy Way pattern and not to the emergence story. In contrast, the White Mountain Apache seem to have borrowed *both* Snake myth and ritual from the Hopi. See E. C. Parsons, Pueblo Indian Religion (Chicago, 1939), p. 1060 and G. Goodwin, Myths and Tales of the White Mountain Apache (Memoirs of the American Folklore Society, vol. 33, New York, 1939), p. vii.

[52] Op. cit., p. 92.

Radcliffe-Brown, and to Warner we are indebted for the clear formulation of the symbolic principle. Those realms of behavior and of experience which man finds beyond rational and technological control he feels are capable of manipulation through symbols.[53] Both myth and ritual are symbolical procedures and are most closely tied together by this, as well as by other, facts. The myth is a system of word symbols, whereas ritual is a system of object and act symbols. Both are symbolic processes for dealing with the same type of situation in the same affective mode.

But the French sociologists, Radcliffe-Brown, and − to a lesser extent − Malinowski are so interested in formulating the relations between conceptual elements that they tend to lose sight of the concrete human organisms. The "functionalists" do usually start with a description of some particular ritualistic behaviors. Not only, however, do the historical origins of this particular behavioral complex fail to interest them. Equally, the motivations and rewards which persons feel are lost sight of in the preoccupation with the contributions which the rituals make to the social system. Thus a sense of the specific detail is lost and we are soon talking about myth in general and ritual in general. From the "functionalist" point of view specific details are about as arbitrary as the phonemes of a language are with respect to "the content" of what is communicated by speech. Hence, as Dollard[54] says, "What one sees from the cultural angle is a drama of life much like a puppet show in which 'culture' is pulling the strings from behind the scenes." The realization that we are really dealing with "animals struggling in real dilemmas" is lacking.

From this angle, some recent psychoanalytic interpretations of myth and ritual seem preferable. We may regard as unconvincing Róheim's[55] attempts to treat myths as historical documents which link human phylogenetic and ontogenetic development, as we may justly feel that many psychoanalytic discussions of the latent content of mythology are extravagant and undisciplined. Casey's[56] summary of the psychoanalytic view of religion ". . . ritual is a sublimated compulsion; dogma and myth are sublimated obsessions" may well strike us as an over-simplified, over-neat generalization, but at least our attention is drawn to the connection between cultural forms and impulse-motivated organisms. And Kardiner's[57] relatively sober and controlled treatment does "point at individuals, at bodies, and at a rich and turbulent biological life"

[53] That is, forms of behavior whose value or meaning is assigned by human beings − not inherent in the intrinsic properties of the words or acts.

[54] John Dollard, Culture, Society, Impulse, and Socialization (American Journal of Sociology, vol. 45, pp. 50–64), p. 52.

[55] G. Róheim, The Riddle of the Sphinx (London, 1934), esp. pp. 173–174.

[56] R. P. Casey, The Psychoanalytic Study of Religion (Journal of Abnormal and Social Psychology, vol. 33, 1938, pp. 437–453), p. 449.

[57] A. Kardiner, The Individual and His Society (New York, 1939), esp. pp. 182–194, 268–270.

– even though that life is admittedly conditioned by social heredity: social organization, culturally defined symbolic systems, and the like.

In a later section of this paper, we shall return to the problem of how myths and rituals reinforce the behavior of individuals. But first let us test the generalities which have been propounded thus far by concrete data from a single culture, the Navaho.[58]

III

The Navaho certainly have sacred tales which, as yet at all events, are not used to justify associated rituals. A striking case, and one where the tale has a clear function as expressing a sentiment "essential to the existence of the society," is known from different parts of the Navaho country.[59] The tales differ in detail but all have these structural elements in common: one of "the Holy People" visits one or more Navahos to warn them of an impending catastrophe (a flood or the like) which will destroy the whites – but believing Navahos will be saved if they retire to the top of a mountain or some other sanctuary. It is surely not without meaning that these tales became current at about the time that the Navahos were first feeling intensive and sustained pressure (they were not just prisoners of war as in the Fort Sumner epoch) from the agents of our culture.[60]

[58] Some Navaho material has, of course, already been presented. See pp. 47, 51, 57, supra.

[59] E. L. Hewett (The Chaco Canyon and Its Monuments, Albuquerque, 1936, p. 139) records the dissemination of this tale among the Chaco Canyon Navaho. Drs. A. and D. Leighton and I have obtained independent evidence that the same story was told, and believed by many, among the Ramah Navaho (two hundred odd miles away) at the same time. Those who believed the tale carried out ceremonials but not new ceremonials. Rather the old ceremonials (especially Blessing Way rites) were carried out in unusual frequency. In 1936 in the Huerfano country a young woman reported that she had been visited by White Shell Woman who had been given instructions for Blessing Ways to be held – but with special additional procedures. These rites were widely carried out in the northeastern portion of the Navaho area. (See article by Will Evans in the Farmington, N. M., Times Hustler, under date-line of February 21, 1937.) Also in 1936 a woman in the Farmington region claimed to have been visited by Banded Rock Boy (one of the Holy People) and a similar story spread over the Reservation. A famous singer, Left-handed, refused to credit the tale and many Navahos attributed his death (which occurred soon thereafter) to his disbelief. See Mesa Verde Notes, March, 1937, vol. 7, pp. 16–19. F. Gilmor (Windsinger, New York, 1930) has used a story of the same pattern, obtained from the Navaho of the Kayenta, Arizona region as a central episode in a novel.

[60] Jane Harrison (Themis, Cambridge, England, 1912) says: "It is this collective sanction and solemn purpose that differentiate the myth alike from the historical narrative and the mere conte or fairy-tale . . ." (p. 330), and many agreeing with her will doubtless assert that my argument here is invalid because these tales though unquestionably having "solemn purpose" lack "collective sanction." Some would also contend that since living persons claim to have seen the supernatural beings these stories must be called "tales" or, at any rate, not "myths." I see these points and, since I wish to avoid a purely verbal quarrel, I would agree, so far as present data go, that

Father Berard Haile[61] has recently published evidence that Navaho ceremonials may originate in dreams or visions rather than being invariably post
hoc justifications for existent ritual practices. A practitioner called "son of
the late Black Goat" instituted a new ceremonial "which he had learned in
a dream while sleeping in a cave." Various informants assured Father Berard
that chantway legends originated in the "visions" of individuals.[62] We have,
then, Navaho data for (*a*) the existence of myths without associated rituals, (*b*)
the origin of both legends and rituals in dreams or visions.

It is true that all ceremonial practice among the Navaho is, in cultural
theory, justified by an accompanying myth. One may say with Dr. Parsons[63] on
the Pueblos: "Whatever the original relationship between myth and ceremony,
once made, the myth supports the ceremony or ceremonial office and may
suggest ritual increments." One must in the same breath, however, call attention to the fact that myth also supports accepted ways of secular behavior. As
Dr. Hill[64] has pointed out, "Women are required to sit with their legs under
them and to one side, men with their legs crossed in front of them, because it
is said that in the beginning Changing Woman and the Monster Slayer sat in
these positions." Let this one example suffice for the many which could easily
be given.[65] The general point is that in both sacred and secular spheres myths

---

Navaho myths (in the narrow sense) are uniformly associated with ritual behaviors. Actually, *the*
myth which most Navaho call their most sacred (the emergence story) is associated with rites only
in a manner which is, from certain points of view, tenuous. The emergence myth is not held to
be the basis for any single ceremonial, nor is it used to justify any very considerable portion of
ceremonial practice. The emergence myth (or some part of it) *is* often prefaced to the chantway
legend proper. In any case, I must insist (granting always that the line between secular and sacred
folk literature must not be drawn too sharply) that the stories dealt with above are not part of the
"profane" folklore of the Navaho in the sense in which the Coyote tales, for example, are. The
origin legends of the various clans are certainly not secular literature, but I imagine that a purist
would maintain that we must call these "legends" as lacking "solemn purpose" (in Harrison's
sense). Nevertheless I repeat that "myths" in the broad sense of "sacred tale" are, among the
Navaho, found quite dissociated from ritual.

[61] A Note on the Navaho Visionary (American Anthropologist, vol. 42, 1940, p. 359). This
contains still another reference to the flood motif.

[62] The assertion that ceremonials sometimes have their genesis in dreams and the like does
not imply that this, any more than that between myth and ritual, is a one-way relationship.
One can by no means dispose of the matter simply by saying "dreams cause myths and myths
cause ceremonies." William Morgan (Navaho Dreams, American Anthropologist, vol. 34, 1932,
pp. 390–406), who was also convinced that some Navaho myths derive from dreams (p. 395),
has pointed out the other aspect of the interdependence: ". . . myths . . . influence dreams; and
these dreams, in turn, help to maintain the efficacy of the ceremonies. . . . Repetitive dreams do
much to strengthen the traditional beliefs concerning dreams" (p. 400).

[63] E. C. Parsons, Pueblo Indian Religion (Chicago, 1939), p. 968, footnote.

[64] W. W. Hill, The Agricultural and Hunting Methods of the Navaho Indians (New Haven,
1938), p. 179.

[65] Dr. Parsons has suggested (personal communication) an analogue from our own culture:
"It was argued that because Eve was made from Adam's rib women should not have the vote."

give some fixity to the ideal patterns of cultures where this is not attained by the printed word. The existence of rituals has a similar effect. Although I cannot agree with Wissler[66] that "the primary function" of rituals is "to perpetuate exact knowledge and to secure precision in their application," there can be no doubt that both myths and rituals are important agencies in the transmission of a culture and that they act as brakes upon the speed of culture change.

Returning to the connections between myth and rite among the Navaho, one cannot do better than begin by quoting some sentences from Washington Matthews:[67] "In some cases a Navajo rite has only one myth pertaining to it. In other cases it has many myths. The relations of the myth to the ceremony is variable. Sometimes it explains nearly everything in the ceremony and gives an account of all the important acts from beginning to end, in the order in which they occur; at other times it describes the work in a less systematic manner. . . . Some of the myths seem to tell only of the way in which rites, already established with other tribes, were introduced among the Navajos. . . . The rite-myth never explains all of the symbolism of the rite, although it may account for all the important acts. A primitive and underlying symbolism which probably existed previous to the establishment of the rite, remains unexplained by the myth, as though its existence were taken as a matter of course, and required no explanation."

To these observations one may add the fact that knowledge of the myth is in no way prerequisite to carrying out of a chant. Knowledge does give the singer or curer prestige and ability to expect higher fees, and disparaging remarks are often heard to the effect "Oh, he doesn't know the story," or "He doesn't know the story very well yet." And yet treatment by a practitioner ignorant of the myth[68] is regarded as efficacious. Navahos are often a little cynical about the variation in the myths. If someone observes that one singer did not carry out a procedure exactly as did another (of perhaps greater repute) it will often be said "Well, he says *his* story is different." Different forms of a rite-myth tend to prevail in different areas of the Navaho country and in different localities. Here the significance of the "personality" of various singers may sometimes be detected in the rise of variations. The transvestite[69] "Left-handed" who died a few years ago enjoyed a tremendous reputation as a singer. There

---

[66] C. Wissler, The Function of Primitive Ritualistic Ceremonies (Popular Science Monthly, vol. 87, pp. 200–204), p. 203.

[67] Washington Matthews, Some Illustrations of the Connection between Myth and Ceremony (International Congress of Anthropology, Memoirs, Chicago, 1894, pp. 246–251), p. 246.

[68] How much a practitioner knows of both legend and ceremonial depends upon the demands he made upon his instructor during his apprenticeship. The instructor is not supposed to prompt his pupil. Many practitioners are satisfied with quite mechanical performances, and there is no doubt that much information (both legendary and ritualistic) is being lost at present owing to the fact that apprentices do not question their instructors more than superficially.

[69] A transvestite is an individual who assumes the garb of the other sex. Transvestites are often, but apparently not always, homosexuals.

is some evidence[70] that he restructuralized a number of myths as he told them to his apprentices in a way which tended to make the hermaphrodite be?gočidí a kind of supreme Navaho deity – a position which he perhaps never held in the general tradition up to that point.[71] I have heard other Navaho singers say that sandpaintings and other ceremonial acts and procedures were slightly revised to accord with this tenet. If this be true, we have here another clear case of myth-before-ritual.

Instances of the reverse sort are also well documented. From a number of informants accounts have been independently obtained of the creation (less than a hundred years ago) of a new rite: Enemy Monster Blessing Way. All the information agreed that the ritual procedures had been devised by one man who collated parts of two previously existent ceremonials and added a few bits from his own fancy. And three informants independently volunteered the observation "He didn't have any story. But after a while he and his son and another fellow made one up."[72] This is corroborated by the fact that none of Father Berard's numerous versions of the Blessing Way myth mention an Enemy Monster form.[73]

Besides these notes on the relations between myth and rite I should like to record my impression of another function of myth – one which ranges from simple entertainment to "intellectual edification." Myth among the Navaho not only acts as a justification, a rationale for ritual behavior and as a moral reinforcement for other customary behaviors. It also plays a role not dissimilar to that of literature (especially sacred literature) in many literate cultures. Navahos have a keen expectation of the long recitals of myths (or portions of them) around the fire on winter nights.[74] Myths have all the charm of the familiar. Their very familiarity increases their efficacy, for, in a certain broad and loose sense, the function of both myths and rituals is "the discharge of the emotion of individuals in socially accepted channels." And Hocart[75] acutely

---

[70] See W. W. Hill, The Status of the Hermaphrodite and Transvestite in Navaho Culture (American Anthropologist, vol. 37, 1935, pp. 273–280), p. 279.

[71] For a hint, however, that be?gočidí was so considered at an earlier time, see W. Matthews, Navaho Legends (New York, 1897), p. 226, footnote 78.

[72] Cf. Clyde Kluckhohn and Leland C. Wyman, An Introduction to Navaho Chant Practice (Memoir 53, American Anthropological Association, 1940), pp. 186–187.

[73] Personal communication.

[74] Why may the myths be recited only in winter? In Navaho feeling today this prohibition is linked in a wider configuration of forbidden activities. There is also, as usual, an historical and distributional problem, for this same prohibition is apparently widely distributed in North America. For example, it is found among the Berens River Salteaux (see A. I. Hallowell, Fear and Anxiety as Cultural and Individual Variables in a Primitive Society, Journal of Social Psychology, vol. 9, 1938, pp. 25–48, p. 31) and among the Iroquois (Dr William Fenton: personal conversation). But I wonder if in a certain "deeper" sense this prohibition is not founded upon the circumstance that only winter affords the leisure for telling myths, that telling them in summer would be unfitting because it would interfere with work activities.

[75] A. M. Hocart, Ritual and Emotion (Character and Personality, vol. 7, 1939, pp. 201–211), p. 208.

observes: "Emotion is assisted by the repetition of words that have acquired a strong emotional coloring, and this coloring again is intensified by repetition." Myths are expective, repetitive dramatizations – their role is similar to that of books in cultures which have few books. They have the (to us) scarcely understandable meaningfulness which the tragedies had for the Greek populace. As Matthew Arnold said of these, "their significance appeared inexhaustible."

IV

The inadequacy of any simplistic statement of the relationship between myth and ritual has been established. It has likewise been maintained that the most adequate generalization will not be cast in terms of the primacy of one or the other of these cultural forms but rather in terms of the general tendency for the two to be interdependent. This generalization has been arrived at through induction from abstractions at the cultural level. That is, as we have sampled the evidence from various cultures we have found cases where myths have justified rituals and have appeared to be "after the fact" of ritual; we have also seen cases where new myths have given rise to new rituals. In other words, the primary conclusion which may be drawn from the data is that myths and rituals tend to be very intimately associated and to influence each other. What is the explanation of the observed connection?

The explanation is to be found in the circumstance that myth and ritual satisfy a group of identical or closely related needs of individuals. Thus far we have alluded only occasionally and often obliquely to myths and rituals as cultural forms defining individual behaviors which are adaptive or adjustive[76] responses. We have seen how myths and rituals are adaptive from the point of view of the society in that they promote social solidarity, enhance the integration of the society by providing a formalized statement of its ultimate value-attitudes, afford a means for the transmission of much of the culture with little loss of content – thus protecting cultural continuity and stabilizing the society. But how are myth and ritual rewarding enough in the daily lives of individuals so that individuals are instigated to preserve them, so that myth and ritual continue to prevail at the expense of more rational responses?

A systematic examination of this question, mainly again in terms of Navaho material, will help us to understand the prevailing interdependence of myth and ritual which has been documented. This sketch of a general theory of myth and ritual as providing a cultural storehouse of adjustive responses for

---

[76] This useful distinction I owe to my colleague, Dr Hobart Mowrer. "Adaptation" is a purely descriptive term referring to the fact that certain types of behavior result in survival. "Adjustment" refers to those responses which remove the motivation stimulating the individual. Thus suicide is adjustive but not adaptive.

individuals is to be regarded as tentative from the writer's point of view. I do not claim that the theory is proven – even in the context of Navaho culture. I do suggest that it provides a series of working hypotheses which can be tested by specifically pointed field procedures.

We can profitably begin by recurring to the function of myth as fulfilling the expectancy of the familiar. Both myth and ritual here provide cultural solutions to problems which all human beings face. Burke has remarked, "Human beings build their cultures, nervously loquacious, upon the edge of an abyss." In the face of want and death and destruction all humans have a fundamental insecurity.[77] To some extent, all culture is a gigantic effort to mask this, to give the future the simulacrum of safety by making activity repetitive, expective – "to make the future predictable by making it conform to the past." From one angle our own scientific mythology is clearly related to that motivation as is the obsessive, the compulsive tendency which lurks in all organized thought.

When questioned as to why a particular ceremonial activity is carried out in a particular way, Navaho singers will most often say "because the diyin diné – the Holy People – did it that way in the first place." The *ultima ratio* of non-literates[78] strongly tends to be "that is what our fathers said it was." An Eskimo said to Rasmussen:[79] "We Eskimos do not concern ourselves with solving all riddles. We repeat the old stories in the way they were told to us and with the words we ourselves remember." The Eskimo saying "we keep the old rules in order that we may live untroubled" is well-known. The Navaho and Eskimo thus implicitly recognize a principle which has been expressed by Harvey Ferguson[80] as follows:

> . . . man dreads both spontaneity and change, . . . he is a worshipper of habit in all its forms. Conventions and institutions are merely organized and more or less sanctified habits. These are the real gods of human society, which transcend and outlive all other gods. All of them originate as group expedients which have some social value at some time, but they remain the objects of a passionate adoration long after they have outlived their usefulness. Men fight and die for them. They have their high priests, their martyrs, and their rituals. They are the working gods, whatever the ostensible ones may be.

These principles apply as well to standardized overt acts as to standardized forms of words. Thus Pareto considered the prevalence of ritual in all human

---

[77] Cf. Malinowski (op. cit., p. 78): "They would screen with the vivid texture of their myths, stories, and beliefs about the spirit world, the vast emotional void gaping beyond them."

[78] There is, to be sure, at least a rough parallel in our own culture in "the Bible says so" and similar phrases.

[79] Knud Rasmussen, Intellectual Culture of the Hudson Bay Eskimos (Copenhagen, 1938), p. 69.

[80] Modern Man (New York, 1936), p. 29.

cultures as perhaps the outstanding empirical justification for his thesis of the importance of non-logical action. Merton[81] writes:

> . . . activities originally conceived as instrumental are transmuted into ends in themselves. The original purposes are forgotten and ritualistic adherence to institutionally prescribed conduct becomes virtually obsessive. . . . Such ritualism may be associated with a mythology which rationalizes these actions so that they appear to retain their status as means, but the dominant pressure is in the direction of strict ritualistic conformity, irrespective of such rationalizations. In this sense ritual has proceeded farthest when such rationalizations are not even called forth.

Goldstein,[82] a neurologist, recognizes a neurological basis for the persistence of such habit systems and writes: "The organism tends to function in the accustomed manner, as long as an at least moderately effective performance can be achieved in this way."

Nevertheless, certain objections to the position as thus far developed must be anticipated and met. It must be allowed at once that the proposition "man dreads both spontaneity and change" must be qualified. More precisely put, we may say "most men, most of the time, dread both spontaneity and change in most of their activities." This formulation allows for the observed fact that most of us *occasionally* get irked with the routines of our lives or that there are certain sectors of our behavior where we fairly consistently show spontaneity. But a careful examination of the totality of behavior of any individual who is not confined in an institution or who has not withdrawn almost completely from participation in the society will show that the larger proportion of the behavior of even the greatest iconoclasts is habitual. This must be so, for by very definition a socialized organism is an organism which behaves mainly in a predictable manner. Even in a culture like contemporary American culture which has made an institutionalized value of change (both for the individual and for society), conformity is at the same time a great virtue. To some extent, this is phrased as conformity with the latest fashion, but Americans remain, by and large, even greater conformists than most Europeans.

Existence in an organized society would be unthinkable unless most people, most of the time, behaved in an expectable manner. Rituals constitute a guarantee that in certain societally organized behaviors touching upon certain "areas of ignorance" which constitute "tender spots" for all human beings, people can count upon the repetitive nature of the phenomena. For example, in Zuni society (where rituals are highly calendrical) a man whose wife has left him or whose crops have been ruined by a torrential downpour can yet look forward to the Shalako ceremonial as something which is fixed and immutable. Similarly, the personal sorrow of the devout Christian is in some measure mitigated

---

[81] R. K. Merton, Social Structure and Anomie (American Sociological Review, vol. 3, 1938, pp. 672–683), p. 673.

[82] Kurt Goldstein, The Organism (New York, 1939), p. 57.

by anticipation of the great feasts of Christmas and Easter. Perhaps the even turn of the week with its Sunday services and mid-week prayer meetings gave a dependable regularity which the Christian clung to even more in disaster and sorrow. For some individuals daily prayer and the confessional gave the needed sense of security. Myths, likewise, give men "something to hold to." The Christian can better face the seemingly capricious reverses of his plans when he hears the joyous words "lift up your hearts." Rituals and myths supply, then, fixed points in a world of bewildering change and disappointment.

If almost all behavior has something of the habitual about it, how is it that myths and rituals tend to represent the maximum of fixity? Because they deal with those sectors of experience which do not seem amenable to rational control and hence where human beings can least tolerate insecurity. That very insistence upon the minutiae of ritual performance, upon preserving the myth to the very letter, which is characteristic of religious behavior must be regarded as a "reaction formation" (in the Freudian sense) which compensates for the actual intransigeance of those events which religion tries to control.

To anticipate another objection: do these "sanctified habit systems" show such extraordinary persistence simply because they are repeated so often and so scrupulously? Do myths and rituals constitute repetitive behavior par excellence not merely as reaction formations but because the habits are practiced so insistently? Perhaps myths and rituals perdure in accord with Allport's "principle of functional autonomy"[83] – as interpreted by some writers? No, performances must be rewarded in the day to day lives of participating individuals. Sheer repetition in and of itself has never assured the persistence of any habit. If this were not so, no myths and rituals would ever have become extinct except when a whole society died out. It is necessary for us to recognize the somewhat special conditions of drive and of reward which apply to myths and rituals.

It is easy to understand why organisms eat. It is easy to understand why a defenceless man will run to escape a charging tiger. The physiological bases of the activities represented by myths and rituals are less obvious. A recent statement by a stimulus-response psychologist gives us the clue:[84] "The position here taken is that human beings (and also other living organisms to varying degrees) can be motivated either by organic pressures (needs) that are currently felt *or* by the mere anticipation of such pressures and that those habits tend to be acquired and perpetuated (reinforced) which effect a reduction in either of these two types of motivation." That is, myths and rituals are reinforced because they reduce the anticipation of disaster. No living person has

[83] As a matter of fact, Allport has made it plain (Motivation in Personality: Reply to Mr. Bertocci, Psychological Review, 1940, vol. 47, pp. 533–555) that he contends only that motives may be autonomous in respect to their origins but never in respect to the satisfaction of the ego (p. 547).

[84] O. H. Mowrer, A Stimulus-Response Analysis of Anxiety and its Role as a Reinforcing Agent (Psychological Review, vol. 46, 1939, pp. 553–566), p. 561.

died – but he has seen others die. The terrible things which we have seen happen to others may not yet have plagued us, but our experience teaches us that these are at least potential threats to our own health or happiness.

If a Navaho gets a bad case of snow-blindness and recovers after being sung over, his disposition to go to a singer in the event of a recurrence will be strongly reinforced. And, by the principle of generalization, he is likely to go even if the ailment is quite different. Likewise, the reinforcement will be reciprocal – the singer's confidence in his powers will also be reinforced. Finally, there will be some reinforcement for spectators and for all who hear of the recovery. That the ritual treatment rather than more rational preventatives or cures tends to be followed on future occasions can be understood in terms of the principle of the gradient of reinforcement. Delayed rewards are less effective than immediate rewards. In terms of the conceptual picture of experience with which the surrogates of his culture have furnished him, the patient *expects* to be relieved. Therefore, the very onset of the chant produces some lessening of emotional tension – in technical terms, some reduction of anxiety. If the Navaho is treated by a white physician, the "cure" is more gradual and is dependent upon the purely physico-chemical effects of the treatment. If the native wears snow goggles or practices some other form of prevention recommended by a white, the connection between the behavior and the reward (no soreness of the eyes) is so diffuse and so separated in time that reinforcement is relatively weak. Even in those cases where no improvement (other than "psychological") is effected, the realization or at any rate the final acceptance that no help was obtained comes so much later than the immediate sense of benefit[85] that the extinction effects are relatively slight.[86]

Navaho myths and rituals provide a cultural storehouse of adjustive[87] responses for individuals. Nor are these limited to the more obvious functions

---

[85] I have attended hundreds of Navaho ceremonials and I have never yet seen a case where the patient at some point, at least, during the ceremonial did not profess to feel an improvement. This applies even to cases where the patient was actually dying.

[86] The theory of this paragraph has been stated in the language of contemporary stimulus-response psychology. But it is interesting to note that E. S. Hartland (Ritual and Belief, New York) expressed essentially the same content in 1916: "Recurrence of the emotional stress would tend to be accompanied by repetition of the acts in which the reaction has been previously expressed. If the recurrence were sufficiently frequent, the form of the reaction would become a habit to be repeated on similar occasions, even where the stress was less vivid or almost absent. It can hardly be doubted that many rites owe their existence to such reactions" (pp. 116–117).

[87] It is not possible to say adaptive here because there are not infrequent occasions on which ceremonial treatment aggravates the condition or actually brings about death (which would probably not have supervened under a more rational treatment or even if the patient had simply been allowed to rest). From the point of view of the society, however, the rituals are with little doubt adaptive. Careful samples in two areas and more impressionistic data from the Navaho country generally indicate that the frequency of ceremonials has very materially increased concomitantly with the increase of white pressure in recent years. It is tempting to regard this as an adaptive response similar to that of the Ghost Dance and Peyote Cult on the part of other American Indian tribes.

of providing individuals with the possibility of enhancing personal prestige through display of memory, histrionic ability, etc. Of the ten "mechanisms of defence" which Anna Freud[88] suggests that the ego has available, their myths and rituals afford the Navaho with institutionalized means of employing at least four. Reaction-formation has already been briefly discussed. Myths supply abundant materials for introjection and likewise (in the form of witchcraft myths) suggest an easy and culturally acceptable method of projection of hostile impulses. Finally, rituals provide ways of sublimation of aggression and other socially disapproved tendencies, in part, simply through giving people something to *do*.

All of these "mechanisms of ego defence" will come into context only if we answer the question "adjustive with respect to what?" The existence of motivation, of "anxiety" in Navaho individuals must be accounted for by a number of different factors. In the first place – as in every society – there are those components of "anxiety," those "threats" which may be understood in terms of the "reality principle" of psychoanalysis: life *is* hard – an unseasonable temperature, a vagary of the rainfall does bring hunger or actual starvation; people *are* organically ill. In the second place, there are various forms of "neurotic" anxiety. To some extent, every society tends to have a type anxiety. In our own society it is probably sexual, although this may be true only of those segments of our society who are able to purchase economic and physical security. In most Plains Indians sexual anxiety, so far as we can tell from the available documents, was insignificant. There the basic anxiety was for life itself and for a certain quality of that life (which I cannot attempt to characterize in a few words).

Among the Navaho the "type anxiety" is certainly that for health. Almost all Navaho ceremonials (essentially every ceremonial still carried out today) are curing ceremonials. And this apparently has a realistic basis. A prominent officer of the Indian Medical Service stated that it was his impression that morbidity among the Navaho is about three times that found in average white communities. In a period of four months' field work among the Navaho Drs. A. and D. Leighton found in their running field notes a total of 707 Navaho references to "threats" which they classified under six headings.[89] Of these, sixty per cent referred to bodily welfare, and are broken down by the Leightons as follows:

> Disease is responsible for sixty-seven per cent, accidents for seventeen per cent, and the rest are attributed to wars and fights. Of the diseases described, eighty-one per cent were evidently organic, like smallpox, broken legs, colds, and sore throats; sixteen per cent left us in doubt as to whether they were organic or functional; and three per cent were apparently functional, with symptoms

[88] Anna Freud, The Ego and the Mechanisms of Defence (London, 1937).

[89] See A. H. and D. C. Leighton, Some Types of Uneasiness and Fear in a Navaho Indian Community (to appear in the American Anthropologist, April, 1942).

suggesting depression, hysteria, etc. Of all the diseases, forty per cent were incapacitating, forty-three per cent were not, and seventeen per cent were not sufficiently specified in our notes to judge. From these figures it can easily be seen that lack of health is a very important concern of these Navahos, and that almost half of the instances of disease that they mentioned interfered with life activities.

While I am inclined to believe that the character of this sample was somewhat influenced by the fact that the Leightons were white physicians – to whom organic illnesses, primarily, would be reported – there is no doubt that these data confirm the reality of the health "threat." In terms of clothing and shelter which are inadequate (from our point of view at least), of hygiene and diet which similarly fail to conform to our health standards, it is not altogether surprising that the Navaho need to be preoccupied with their health.[90] It is unequivocally true in my experience that a greater proportion of my Navaho friends are found ill when I call upon them than of my white friends.

The Navaho and Pueblo Indians live in essentially the same physical environment. But Pueblo rituals are concerned predominantly with rain and with fertility. This contrast to the Navaho preoccupation with disease cannot (in the absence of fuller supporting facts) be laid to a lesser frequency of illness among the Pueblos, for it seems well documented that the Pueblos, living in congested towns, have been far more ravaged by endemic diseases than the Navaho. The explanation is probably to be sought in terms of the differing historical experience of the two peoples and in terms of the contrasting economic and social organizations. If one is living in relative isolation and if one is largely dependent (as were the Navaho at no terribly distant date) upon one's ability to move about hunting and collecting, ill health presents a danger much more crucial than to the Indian who lives in a town which has a reserve supply of corn and a more specialized social organization.

That Navaho myths and rituals are focussed upon health and upon curing has, then, a firm basis in the reality of the external world. But there is also a great deal of uneasiness arising from inter-personal relationships, and this undoubtedly influences the way the Navaho react to their illnesses. Then, too, one type of anxiousness always tends to modify others. Indeed, in view of what the psychoanalysts have taught us about "accidents" and of what we are learning from psychosomatic medicine about the psychogenic origin of many "organic" diseases we cannot regard the sources of disease among the Navaho as a closed question.[91]

[90] It remains amazing that their population could have increased at such an extraordinary rate if health conditions have been so poor. Dr. A. Leighton suggests to to me that it is conceivable that when the land was less crowded their health was better.

[91] It does not seem implausible that some disorders (especially perhaps those associated with acute anxieties) are examples of what Caner has called "superstitious self-protection." See G. C. Caner, Superstitious Self-Protection (Archives of Neurology and Psychiatry, 1940, vol. 44, pp. 351–361).

Where people live under constant threat from the physical environment, where small groups are geographically isolated and "emotional inbreeding" within the extended family group is at a maximum, inter-personal tensions and hostilities are inevitably intense. The prevalence of ill health which throws additional burdens on the well and strong is in itself an additional socially disrupting force.[92] But if the overt expression of aggressive impulses proceeds very far the whole system of "economic" co-operation breaks down and then sheer physical survival is more than precarious. Here myths and rituals constitute a series of highly adaptive responses from the point of view of the society. Recital of or reference to the myths reaffirms the solidarity of the Navaho sentiment system.[93] In the words of a Navaho informant: "Knowing a good story will protect your home and children and property. A myth is just like a big stone foundation – it lasts a long time." Performance of rituals likewise heightens awareness of the common system of sentiments. The ceremonials also bring individuals together in a situation where quarrelling is forbidden. Preparation for and carrying out of a chant demands intricately ramified co-operation, economic and otherwise, and doubtless thus reinforces the sense of mutual dependency.

Myths and rituals equally facilitate the adjustment of the individual to his society. Primarily, perhaps, they provide a means of sublimation of his anti-social tendencies. It is surely not without meaning that essentially all known chant myths take the family and some trouble within it as a point of departure. Let us look at Reichard's[94] generalization of the chant myth:

> A number of chant legends are now available and all show approximately *the same* construction. People are having a hard time to secure *subsistence or have some grievance. A boy of the family is forbidden* to go somewhere or to do some particular thing. He does not observe the warnings and does that which was forbidden, whereupon he embarks upon a series of adventures which keep him away from home so long that *his family despairs of his return.* . . . After the

---

[92] Dr. A. Leighton has pointed out to me that these disruptive tendencies are reinforced by one of the techniques for survival which those Navahos who have intimate and competitive relations with whites have developed. He writes: "A group threatened by a stronger group can swing to one of two poles. (*a*) They can coalesce and form a highly efficient, highly integrated unit that can act with swiftness, power, and precision, and in which all individuals stand or fall together. (*b*) They can disperse like a covey of quail so as never to present a united target to the foe. This is the Navaho method of dealing with the whites. It is every man for himself, and though individuals may fall, enough escape to survive. You don't rush to help your tribesman when trouble comes, you stay out of it, you 'let it go.' Such an attitude, however, does lead to mutual mistrust."

[93] Cf. Radcliffe-Brown (op. cit., p. 330): ". . . tales that might seem merely the products of a somewhat childish fancy are very far indeed from being merely fanciful and are the means by which the Andamanese express and systematize their fundamental notions of life and nature and the sentiments attaching to those notions."

[94] Gladys Reichard, Navajo Medicine Man (New York, 1939), p. 76. Italics mine.

dramatic episodes, the hero returns to his home bringing with him the ritualistic lore which he teaches to *his brother*. He has been away so long and has become so accustomed to association with deity that *his own people seem impure* to him. He corrects that fault by teaching them the means of purification. . . . He has *his brother* conduct the ritual over *his sister* . . . he vanishes into the air.

While as a total explanation the following would be over-simple, it seems fair to say that the gist of this may be interpreted as follows: the chant myth supplies a catharsis for the traumata incident upon the socialization of the Navaho child. That brother and sister are the principal *dramatis personae* fits neatly with the central conflicts of the Navaho socialization process. This is a subject which I hope to treat in detail in a later paper.

Overt quarrels between family members are by no means infrequent, and, especially when drinking has been going on, physical blows are often exchanged. Abundant data indicate that Navahos have a sense of shame[95] which is fairly persistent and that this is closely connected with the socially disapproved hostile impulses which they have experienced toward relatives. It is also clear that their mistrust of others (including those in their own extended family group) is in part based upon a fear of retaliation (and this fear of retaliation is soundly based upon experience in actual life as well as, possibly, upon "unconcious guilt"). Certain passages in the myths indicate that the Navaho have a somewhat conscious realization that the ceremonials act as a cure, not only for physical illness, but also for anti-social tendencies. The following extract from the myth of the Mountain Top Way Chant will serve as an example: "The ceremony cured Dsiliyi Neyani of all his strange feelings and notions. The lodge of his people no longer smelled unpleasant to him."[96]

Thus "the working gods" of the Navaho are their sanctified repetitive ways of behavior. If these are offended by violation of the culture's system of scruples, the ceremonials exist as institutionalized means of restoring the individual to full rapport with the universe: nature and his own society.[97] Indeed "restore" is the best English translation of the Navaho word which the Navaho constantly use to express what the ceremonial does for the "patient." The

[95] This is significantly reflected in ceremonial lore. Torlino, a singer of Beauty Way, said to Washington Matthews: "I am ashamed before the earth; I am ashamed before the heavens; I am ashamed before the dawn; I am ashamed before the evening twilight; I am ashamed before the blue sky; I am ashamed before the sun; *I am ashamed before that standing within me which speaks with me* (*my conscience*). Some of these things are always looking at me. I am never out of sight." Washington Matthews, Navaho Legends (American Folklore Society, Memoirs, 5, 1897), pp. 58–59. Italics are mine.

[96] W. Matthews, The Mountain Chant (Annual Report of the Bureau of American Ethnology, vol. 5, Washington, 1887, pp. 379–467), p. 417.

[97] Cf. A. R. Radcliffe-Brown, Taboo (Cambridge, England, 1939), p. 44. "The primary value of ritual . . . is the attribution of ritual value to objects and occasions which are either themselves objects of important common interests linking together the persons of a community or are symbolically representative of such objects."

associated myths reinforce the patient's belief that the ceremonial will both truly cure him of his illness and also "change" him so that he will be a better man in his relations with his family and his neighbors. An English-speaking Navaho who had just returned from jail where he had been put for beating his wife and molesting his stepdaughter said to me: "I am sure going to behave from now on. I am going to be changed – just like somebody who has been sung over."

Since a certain minimum of social efficiency is by derivation a biological necessity for the Navaho, not all of the hostility and uneasiness engendered by the rigors of the physical environment, geographical isolation, and the burdens imposed by illness is expressed or even gets into consciousness. There is a great deal of repression and this leads, on the one hand, to projection phenomena (especially in the form of phantasies that others are practicing witchcraft against one[98]) and, on the other hand, the strong feelings of shame at the conscious level are matched by powerful feelings of guilt at the unconscious level. Because a person feels guilty by reason of his unconscious hostilities toward members of his family (and friends and neighbors generally), some individuals develop chronic anxieties. Such persons feel continually uncomfortable. They say they "feel sick all over" without specifying organic ailments other than very vaguely. They feel so "ill" that they must have ceremonials to cure them. The diagnostician and other practitioners, taking myths as their authority, will refer the cause of the illness to the patient's having seen animals struck by lightning, to a past failure to observe ritual requirements or to some similar violation of a cultural scruple. But isn't this perhaps basically a substitution of symbols acceptable to consciousness, a displacement of guilt feelings?

It is my observation that Navahos other than those who exhibit chronic or acute anxieties tend characteristically to show a high level of anxiety. It would be a mistake, however, to attribute all of this anxiety to intra-familial tensions, although it is my impression that this is the outstanding pressure. Secondary drives resultant upon culture change and upon white pressure are also of undoubted importance. And it is likewise true, as Mr. Homans[99] has recently pointed out, that the existence of these ritual injunctions and prohibitions (and of the concomitant myths and other beliefs) gives rise to still another variety of anxiety which Homans has well called secondary anxiety. In other words, the conceptual picture of the world which Navaho culture sets forth makes for a high threshold of anxiety in that it defines all manner of situation as fraught with peril, and individuals are instigated to anticipate danger on every hand.

But the culture, of course, prescribes not only the supernatural dangers but also the supernatural means of meeting these dangers or of alleviating their

---

[98] This view is developed with full documentation in a forthcoming publication to be issued by the Peabody Museum of Harvard University in the spring of 1942.

[99] G. C. Homans, Anxiety and Ritual (American Anthropologist, vol. 43, 1941), pp. 164–173.

effects. Myths and rituals jointly provide systematic protection against super-natural dangers, the threats of ill health and of the physical environment, anti-social tensions, and the pressures of a more powerful society. In the absence of a codified law and of an authoritarian "chief" or other father substitute, it is only through the myth-ritual system that Navahos can make a socially sup-ported, unified response to all of these disintegrating threats. The all-pervasive configurations of word symbols (myths) and of act symbols (rituals) preserve the cohesion of the society and sustain the individual, protecting him from intolerable conflict. As Hoagland[100] has recently remarked:

> Religion appears to me to be a culmination of this basic tendency of organisms to react in a configurational way to situations. We must resolve conflicts and disturbing puzzles by closing some sort of a configuration, and the religious urge appears to be a primitive tendency, possessing biological survival value, to unify our environment so that we can cope with it.

V

The Navaho are only one case.[101] The specific adaptive and adjustive responses performed by myth and ritual will be differently phrased in different societies according to the historical experience of these societies (including the specific opportunities they have had for borrowing from other cultures), in accord with prevalent configurations of other aspects of the culture, and with reference to pressures exerted by other societies and by the physical and biological environ-ment. But the general nature of the adaptive and adjustive responses per-formed by myth and ritual appears very much the same in all human groups. Hence, although the relative importance of myth and of ritual does vary greatly, the two tend universally to be associated.

For myth and ritual have a common psychological basis. Ritual is an obsessive repetitive activity – often a symbolic dramatization of the fundamental "needs" of the society, whether "economic," "biological," "social," or "sexual." Mythol-ogy is the rationalization of these same needs, whether they are all expressed in overt ceremonial or not. Someone has said "every culture has a type conflict and a type solution." Ceremonials tend to portray a symbolic resolvement of

[100] Hudson Hoagland, Some Comments on Science and Faith (In: Conference on Science, Philosophy, and Religion, New York, 1941, mimeographed), p. 5.
[101] But I was very much struck in reading Dr. Hallowell's recent article (A. I. Hallowell, The Social Function of Anxiety in a Primitive Society, American Sociological Review, vol. 6, Decem-ber, 1941, pp. 869–882) – which I read only when this paper was in proof – at the similarity not only in the interpretations he reached but at that in the data from the Saulteaux, when he says "fear of disease is a major social sanction" (p. 871) that fits the Navaho case precisely – as does "illness due to having done bad things or to transgression of a parent" (p. 873).

the conflicts which external environment, historical experience, and selective distribution of personality types[102] have caused to be characteristic in the society. Because different conflict situations characterize different societies, the "needs" which are typical in one society may be the "needs" of only deviant individuals in another society. And the institutionalized gratifications (of which rituals and myths are prominent examples) of culturally recognized needs vary greatly from society to society. "Culturally recognized needs" is, of course, an analytical abstraction. Concretely, "needs" arise and exist only in specific individuals. This we must never forget, but it is equally important that myths and rituals, though surviving as functioning aspects of a coherent culture only so long as they meet the "needs" of a number of concrete individuals, are, in one sense, "supra-individual." They are usually composite creations; they normally embody the accretions of many generations, the modifications (through borrowing from other cultures or by intra-cultural changes) which the varying needs of the group as a whole and of innovating individuals in the group have imposed. In short, both myths and rituals are cultural products, part of the social heredity of a society.

---

[102] This selective distribution of personality types may become established biologically, through the operation of genetic mechanisms, or through the processes of child socialization operative in the particular culture.

21
HOMO NECANS
Walter Burkert

Like Girard, Walter Burkert (b. 1931), Professor of Classical Philology at the University of Zurich, roots ritual in aggression. For Girard, the aggression that arises from rivalry with others is redirected in the form of the ritual killing of an innocent member of society. For Burkert, the innate aggression that initially expresses itself in hunting is preserved in the ritual sacrifice of first fruits and animals as well as of human beings. For Girard, myth arises after ritual to disguise the deed. For Burkert, myth arises after ritual to preserve the memory of the deed even more starkly than the ritual does. Hunting, itself ritualized, not merely vents aggression but enables humans to cope with the guilt and anxiety that killing stirs in them. In addition to Burkert's *Homo Necans* (tr. Peter Bing [Berkeley: University of California Press, 1983 [1972]), from which the following excerpt (pp. 29–34) is taken, see his *Structure and History in Greek Mythology and Ritual* (Berkeley: University of California Press, 1979), esp. 56–8, 99–101 (on Frazer); *Greek Religion*, tr. John Raffan (Cambridge, MA: Harvard University Press, 1985 [1977]), esp. 2–4, 8–9; *Ancient Mystery Cults* (Cambridge, MA: Harvard University Press, 1987), 73–8 (74–6 on Frazer); "The Problem of Ritual Killings," in *Violent Origins*, ed. Robert G. Hamerton-Kelly (Stanford: Stanford University Press, 1987), 149–76; and *Creation of the Sacred* (Cambridge, MA: Harvard University Press, 1996), ch. 3. On Burkert see Larry J. Alderink, "Greek Ritual and Mythology: The Work of Walter Burkert," *Religious Studies Review* 6 (1980), 1–13.

Myth and Ritual

Ritual, as a form of communication, is a kind of language. It is natural, then, that verbalized language, man's most effective system of communication, should

Original publication: Walter Burkert, *Homo Necans*, tr. Peter Bing (Berkeley: University of California Press, 1983), pp. 29–34.

be associated with ritual. Although the accomplishment of language resides in communicating some content and in projecting a model of reality, it is at the same time an extremely social phenomenon: it brings about reciprocal personal contact and preserves it; it determines who belongs to the group; indeed, the special peculiarities of grammar and phonetics almost seem made to keep the circle of members small. In many cases, that which is said seems less important in everyday life than that something is in fact said.[1] Being together in silence is almost unbearable.

Doubtless for this reason, ritual and language have gone hand in hand since language began. Any number of forms are conceivable for such a combination, and many are indeed attested; from a responsion of expressive cries during the ritual, to naming that which seems present in it and invoking it,[2] to a more or less direct account of what is happening there. This leads us to the problem of myth.

The theme of myth and ritual is still the subject of great controversy. While some see the ritual backdrop of a myth as the only acceptable meaning for something that at first appears absurd, others champion the cause of free fantasy and speculation. After Robertson Smith had determined "the dependence of myth on ritual," which Jane Harrison then distilled into the theory that myth is often just "ritual misunderstood,"[3] S. H. Hooke postulated on the basis of ancient Near Eastern and biblical material that there was a unity, a necessary connection between myth and ritual: myth is "the spoken part of the ritual."[4] The occasional claims that this thesis resolved the question

---

[1] See Morris (1967) 202–206 on "grooming talk."

[2] The divine names Paian (L. Deubner, "Paian," *NJb* 22 [1919], 385–406; Nilsson [1955] 543; see already the Mycenaean *pa-ja-wo-ne*, Gérard-Rousseau [1968] 164–65) and Iakchos (Foucart [1914] 111; Deubner [1932] 73; Nilsson [1955] 664) arose out of the cultic cries ἰήιε Παιάν and Ἴακχ᾽ ὦ Ἴακχε.

[3] W. R. Smith (1894) 17–20; for "absurd mythology" seen as "ritual misunderstood" see J. Harrison, *Mythology and Monuments of Ancient Athens* (1890), xxxiii. Cf. Harrison (1927) 327–31, where the meaning of myth is recognized once again: "the myth is the plot of the dromenon" (331). The connections between myth and ritual were already stressed by F. G. Welcker (*Die aeschylische Trilogie Prometheus und die Kabirenweihe zu Lemnos* [1824], esp. 159, 249–50) and Wilamowitz (e.g., *Euripides Herakles* I [1889], 85; "Hephaistos," *NGG* 1895, 234 = *Kl. Schr.* V 2, 23–24).

[4] S. H. Hooke, ed., *Myth and Ritual* (1933), 3: myth is "the spoken part of the ritual," "the story which the ritual enacts." As early as 1910, A. van Gennep stated that myth is "eine Erzählung . . . , deren Bestandteile sich in gleicher Sequenz durch religiös-magische Handlungen (Riten) äussern" (*Internationale Wochenschrift* 4, 1174). In the meantime, empirical ethnology had arrived on the scene: B. Malinowski, *Myth in Primitive Psychology* (1926). For an attempt at an overview see C. Kluckhohn, "Myths and Rituals: A General Theory," *HThR* 35 (1942), 45–79; also S. H. Hooke, *Myth, Ritual, and Kingship* (1958); and Th. H. Gaster, *Thespis: Ritual, Myth and Drama in the Ancient Near East* (1950, 1961²). Lord Raglan, *The Origins of Religion* (1949), and A. M. Hocart, *Social Origins* (1954), went so far as to reconstruct an Ur-ritual, rooted in ancient Near Eastern kingship.

absolutely have caused a variety of strong reactions,[5] but these have been unable to dampen the fascination occasioned by the myth-and-ritual theory. Because the concept of myth is even more vague than that of ritual, a solution satisfactory to all is virtually hopeless.

A radical way out is to say that the defining feature of myth, as opposed to saga, fairytale, and folktale, is its connection with ritual.[6] But empirical facts argue against this: stories that are obviously identical are sometimes accompanied by ritual, sometimes not. Likewise, in both ancient and modern cultures there are rituals without corresponding, explicatory myths.[7] And although one could attribute the lack of a correspondence in antiquity to incomplete documentation preserved by chance, it is hard to attack the proofs brought forward by ethnology.[8] One could, of course, argue that myths without rituals derive nonetheless from lost rituals, that myth is so much easier to transmit and takes so much less expense that it could spread and grow on its own. But this hypothesis cannot be verified. Ritual is far older in the history of evolution, since it goes back even to animals, whereas myth only became possible with the advent of speech, a specifically human ability. Myth, however, cannot be documented before the era in which writing was invented, although it was obviously present long before. Somewhere in between, in the vast reaches of the unknowable, are the "origins." We are left with the fact that stories are something new in relation to biologically observable ritual. To this extent, myth does not grow directly out of ritual. On the other hand, even critics do not dispute that ritual and myth came to be closely allied.

According to the broadest definition, a *myth* is a traditional tale.[9] This is already enough to dispose of the opinion, held from Xenophanes up through

---

Alongside this debate – carried on almost exclusively among English-speaking scholars – are parallel attempts in the early work of G. Dumézil (*Le crime des Lemniennes* [1924]; *Le problème des Centaurs* [1929]) on the one hand, and, on the other, in Germany where W. F. Otto, *Dionysos* (1933), 44, spoke of the "Zusammenfall von Kultus und Mythos," and O. Höfler (1934) derived the sagas about hordes of wild men and about werewolves from ritual.

[5] H. J. Rose, *Mnemosyne* n.s. 3 (1950), 281–87; M. P. Nilsson, *Cults, Myths, Oracles and Politics in Ancient Greece* (1951), 10, and cf. Nilsson (1955) 14n.; A. N. Marlow, *Bull. J. Ryland Libr.* 43 (1960/61), 373–402; Fontenrose (1959); idem, *The Ritual Theory of Myth* (1966); Kirk (1970) 12–29. In the surveys by J. de Vries, *Forschungsgeschichte der Mythologie* (1961), and K. Kerényi, *Die Eröffnung des Zugangs zum Mythos* (1967), the ritual theory appears only marginally. Cf. Burkert (1980).

[6] According to Harrison, Hooke, and Kluckhohn (nn. 3 and 4 above) and E. R. Leach, *Political Systems of Highland Burma* (1954), 13; for an opposing view see Kirk (1970) 28: "Myths and rituals overlap rather than being interdependent."

[7] Particularly in ancient Egypt: see E. Otto, "Das Verhältnis von Rite und Mythus im Ägyptischen," *SB Heidelberg* (1958), 1; C. J. Bleeker, *Egyptian Festivals, Enactments of Religious Renewal* (1967), 19.

[8] Kirk (1970) 25–28.

[9] For Kirk (1970), the "traditional tale" is in any case the framework within which the "myth" must be located (28, 73–75, 282); the distinction between myth and "folktale" remains hazy (41).

modern classicists, that myths were created by the poet's fancy, if not in historical times, then in prehistory.[10] Regardless of its origin, myth is characterized by its suitability for telling and retelling. Although it does not derive from empirical observation or individual experience and can be only partially verified, at best, myth is extraordinarily lucid. Its themes are often surprisingly constant, in spite of the many fantastic and paradoxical motifs that shape its unmistakable identity; even though slightly distorted, they return again and again. For this reason, psychoanalysis sees myth as a projection of specific structures in the soul, an elaboration of inborn psychological dispositions.[11] From a strictly evolutionary standpoint, however, we must suppose that even these archetypes, like valleys hollowed out by ancient streams, were created by a process of selection between various ways of life open to Palaeolithic man. And if the ways of life were determined by rituals, then from the very start they shaped the mythic patterns.

This is speculation. We can be certain, however, that myths and rituals successfully combine as forms of cultural tradition. There is no need for the myth itself to be part of the ritual, as the strict orientation of the myth-and-ritual school would have it. Continuous stories appear in ritual only exceptionally. The ritual can be discussed outside its own context, either in preparation or to explain it afterward; in this way, the Greeks connected almost every ritual with a story explaining in each case why a questionable custom was established.[12] Only the opposite question, whether in turn all Greek myths refer to rituals, is disputed. There have been attempts, of course, to distinguish etiological myths referring to cult from "genuine" myths,[13] but the distinction falls apart as soon as one can show in even a few cases that indisputably genuine

---

[10] "Der Mythos ... entsteht in der Phantasie des Dichters," Wilamowitz (1931) 42, a thesis restated programatically by E. Howald, *Der Mythos als Dichtung* (1937). To be sure, it is perfectly legitimate to investigate each particular individual manifestation of a myth, but it is no less legitimate to search for the underlying themes which are the given for every poet historically known to us.

[11] C. G. Jung, *Eranos-Jb.* (1938), 403–10, on archetypes as "Funktionsformen"; idem, *Man and His Symbols* (1964); J. Jacobi, *Komplex, Archetypus, Symbol in der Psychologie C. G. Jungs* (1957). Following A. E. Jensen (*Das religiöse Weltbild einer frühen Kultur* [1948], 131 ff.), even Kerényi (1967) xxiii–xxxiii has now distanced himself from Jung. Regarding the problem of myth and history, W. F. Jackson Knight stated: "Myth ... is used as a mental container to hold the facts of some new event. The container can be called an archetypal pattern" (*Cumaean Gates* [1936], 91).

[12] The earliest examples are Hesiod's Prometheus story (*Th.* 556–57), the possibly interpolated verses *Il.* 2.546–51, among the *Homeric Hymns* primarily those to Apollo (D. Kolk, *Der pythische Apollonhymnus als aitiologische Dichtung* [1963]), to Demeter (F. Wehrli, *ARW* 31 (1934), 77–104), and to Hermes (cf. I.2 at n. 13 above). On cultic etiologies in tragedy see W. Schmid, *Geschichte der griech. Literatur* I/3 (1940), 705.7, 776.8. Cf. Nilsson (1955) 27–29.

[13] E.g., A. E. Jensen, "Echte und ätiologische (explanatorische) Mythen," in K. Kerényi, *Die Eröffnung des Zugangs zum Mythos* (1967), 262–70 = *Mythos und Kult bei Naturvölkern* (1951), 87–91, 97–100, in which "mythical truth" is the criterion for what is genuine; cf. I.2.n. 38 above.

old myths are subordinate to cultic action, as, for instance, the myth of Pelops is to the festival at Olympia. Nor is it generally true that the Greeks saw a correspondence between speech and action, λεγόμενα and δρώμενα, only in mystery cults.[14] Piety was indeed in the Greek view a matter of ritual, but myth was nonetheless ubiquitous. The two were transmitted together because they explained and strengthened each other.

This is not to say that ritual is a theatrical dramatization of myth.[15] Nor can it be seen as arising from magical ideas with an alleged purpose. The relationship of the two becomes clear if we take ritual for what it is, if we accept that its function is to dramatize the order of life, expressing itself in basic modes of behavior, especially aggression. In its own way, too, myth clarifies the order of life.[16] As is well known, it frequently explains and justifies social orders and establishments,[17] and in so doing it is related to ritual, which occurs by means of social interaction. The most exciting themes in myth come from the realm of sexuality and aggression, and these are also prominent in ritual communication. The most fascinating stories concern the perils of death and destruction. These have their counterpart in sacrificial killing.

"The myth is the plot of the dromenon."[18] The mythical tale, as communication between participants within a single ritual tradition, does not, of course, provide an objective behavioral description of what occurs there. It names that which the ritual intends. Rituals are redirected patterns of behavior, with a displaced referent. Thus, the mythical naming, because it follows the original orientation and so fills the space left vacant, creates a quasi-reality which cannot be perceived with the senses but is directly experienced in the ritual. Human speech naturally refers to some subject, and thus ritual communication gives rise to mythical subjects. In hunting and then in sacrifice, aggressive modes of behavior between men are diverted onto animals; in the myth, on the other hand, is a human victim.[19] Fears are displayed in the preparatory rituals;

---

[14] Thus Nilsson (1955) 14n. It is true that the general terms (ἱερός) λόγος (Hdt. 2.47, 2.51, 2.81) or λεγόμενα and δρώμενα (Paus. 1.43.2, 2.38.2, 2.37.2, 9.30.12, 9.27.2) come up precisely in situations where the content of the story and ritual may not be described, that is, in the mysteries. So also, for instance, Euseb. *Praep. Ev.* 15.1.2 τελεταὶ καὶ μυστήρια σύμφωνα τοῖς τῶν προτέρων μυθικοῖς διηγήμασιν; Lact. *Div. inst.* 1.21.39 *quidquid est gestum in abscondendo puero, id ipsum per imaginem geritur in sacris* (mysteries of Kuretes); Steph. Byz. *s.v.* Ἄγρα ... μίμημα τῶν περὶ τὸν Διόνυσον. But the correspondence is not limited to these cases: on sacrifice generally see Firm. *Err.* 16.3: *ut acerbarum mortium casus cottidiano victimarum sanguine recrudescant.* Ach. Tat. 2.2.2 τῆς ἑορτῆς διηγοῦνται πατέρα μῦθον.

[15] See Fontenrose (1959) 464, who correctly states: "Whenever myth precedes ritual, then drama is produced."

[16] On the parallel functions of ritual and myth see Kluckhohn, "Myths and Rituals" (n. 4 above); Leach, *Political Systems*.

[17] Following Malinowski, *Myth in Primitive Psychology*, on "charter myths" see Kirk (1970) 154–57.

[18] Harrison (1927) 331.

[19] See I.2.n.35 above; cf. at n. 2 above.

the myth names someone who is to be feared. The ritual is shaped by gestures of guilt and submission; the myth tells of some stronger being and of his power. The myth develops what the gestures contain *in nuce*: a threatening gesture becomes murder, sorrow acted out becomes genuine mourning, erotic movements become a story of love and death. The as-if element in the ritual becomes mythical reality; conversely, the ritual confirms the reality of the myth. In this way, by mutually affirming each other, myth and ritual became a strong force in forming a cultural tradition, even though their origins were different.

To some extent myth can even supplant ritual, especially in its function of expressing the unity and organization of the group. Speech is far superior to ritual in its precision and dexterity. One word, one cry can replace a complicated war dance. But because of its very flexibility, language is also fickle. It can easily be abused or used to deceive. Therefore society always returns to ritual, even though it runs contrary to the rational acceleration of communication.[20] An agreement can be expressed quickly and clearly in words, but it is only made effective by a ritual gesture: open, weaponless hands stretched toward one another, grasping each other in a mutual handshake – a mutual display of aggression – sealing what had previously been merely spoken. Similarly, it may be possible to conceive of a religion without myths, but not of a religion using myth without ritual practice. There has yet to be a community without ritual.

---

[20] A. Portmann, *Das Tier als soziales Wesen* (1964), 340: "Das Ritual bleibt auch in Zukunft das gewaltige Instrument des Überindividuellen in allem höheren, d.h. sozialen Leben." On shaking hands see Eibl-Eibesfeldt (1970) 203–206.

22

STRUCTURE AND DIALECTICS

Claude Lévi-Strauss

Claude Lévi-Strauss (b. 1908), the famous French anthropologist, has long applied to myth the structuralist anthropology he pioneered. When, much less often, he turns to ritual, he finds the same structural relationship between ritual and myth that he finds between one myth and another, not to say between one part of a single myth and another. Where other myth-ritualists seek to show how myth and ritual mirror each other, Lévi-Strauss seeks to show how the two are the reverse of each other. Myth and ritual remain umbilically linked, but as opposing rather than parallel members of a pair. Reprinted here is Lévi-Strauss' Rey essay on myth and ritual, "Structure and Dialectics" (in his *Structural Anthropology*, trs. Claire Jacobson and Brooke Grundfest Schoepf [New York: Basic Books, 1963 (1958)], ch. 12). See also his "Comparative Religions of Non-literate Peoples," in his *Structural Anthropology II*, tr. Monique Layton (New York: Basic Books, 1976 [1973]), ch. 5. For Lévi-Strauss' theory of myth in itself see his "The Structural Study of Myth," *Journal of American Folklore* (1955), 428–44 (reprinted, slightly revised, in *Structural Anthropology*, ch. 11); "The Story of Asdiwal," tr. Nicholas Mann, in *The Structural Study of Myth and Totemism*, ed. Edmund Leach, A. S. A. Monographs, no. 5 (London: Tavistock, 1967), 1–47; *Introduction to a Science of Mythology*, trs John and Doreen Weightman, I (*The Raw and the Cooked*), II (*From Honey to Ashes*), III (*The Origin of Table Manners*), IV (*The Naked Man*) (New York: Harper & Row, 1969 [1964], 1973 [1966], 1978 [1968], 1981 [1971]); *The Jealous Potter*, tr. Bénédicte Chorier (Chicago: University of Chicago Press, 1988 [1985]); and *The Story of Lynx*, tr. Catherine Tihanyi (Chicago: University of Chicago Press, 1995 [1991]). On Lévi-Strauss see Mary Douglas, "The Meaning of Myth, with Special Reference to 'La Geste d'Asdiwal'," in *The Structural Study of Myth and Totemism*, ed. Leach, 49–69; Edmund

Original publication: Claude Lévi-Strauss, "Structure and Dialectics," in his *Structural Anthropology*, trs Claire Jacobson and Brooke Grundfest Schoepf (NY: Basic Books, 1963), ch. 12 (pp. 232–41).

Leach, *Claude Lévi-Strauss*, rev. edn (New York: Viking, 1974 [1970]); *Claude Lévi-Strauss*, ed. E. Nelson Hayes and Tanya Hayes (Cambridge and London: MIT Press, 1970); *The Unconscious in Culture*, ed. Ino Rossi (New York: Dutton, 1974); and Roland A. Champagne, *The Structuralists on Myth* (New York: Garland Publishing, 1992), esp. ch. 3.

From Lang to Malinowski, through Durkheim, Lévy-Bruhl, and van der Leeuw, sociologists and anthropologists who were interested in the interrelations between myth and ritual have considered them as mutually redundant. Some of these thinkers see in each myth the ideological projection of a rite, the purpose of the myth being to provide a foundation for the rite. Others reverse the relationship and regard ritual as a kind of dramatized illustration of the myth. Regardless of whether the myth or the ritual is the original, they replicate each other; the myth exists on the conceptual level and the ritual on the level of action. In both cases, one assumes an orderly correspondence between the two – in other words, a homology. Curiously enough, this homology is demonstrable in only a small number of cases. It remains to be seen why all myths do not correspond to rites and vice versa, and most important, why there should be such a curious replication in the first place.

I intend to show by means of a concrete example that this homology does not always exist; or, more specifically, that when we do find such a homology, it might very well constitute a particular illustration of a more generalized relationship between myth and ritual and between the rites themselves. Such a generalized relationship would imply a one-to-one correspondence between the elements of rites which seem to differ, or between the elements of any one rite and any one myth. Such a correspondence could not, however, be considered a homology. In the example to be discussed here, the reconstruction of the correspondence requires a series of preliminary operations – that is, permutations or transformations which may furnish the key to the correspondence. If this hypothesis is correct, we shall have to give up mechanical causality as an explanation and, instead, conceive of the relationship between myth and ritual as dialectical, accessible only if both have first been reduced to their structural elements.

The demonstration of such a hypothesis seems to me to constitute an appropriate tribute to the work and method of Roman Jakobson. He himself was concerned on several occasions with mythology and folklore; let us merely recall his article on Slavic mythology in the *Standard Dictionary of Folklore, Mythology and Legend*, and his valuable commentaries on *Russian Fairy Tales*.[1] Secondly, it is clear that the method I am employing is simply the extension to another field of structural linguistics, which is associated with the name of

---

[1] *Standard Dictionary of Folklore, Mythology and Legend*, vol. I (New York: 1949); *Russian Fairy Tales* (New York: 1945).

Jakobson. And finally, he was always concerned with the intimate relationship between structural analysis and dialectical method. He concluded his well-known work, *Prinzipien der historischen Phonologie*, by saying: "The relationship between statics and dynamics is one of the most fundamental dialectical antinomies which determine the idea of language." In attempting to clarify the mutual implications of the concept of structure and dialectical thought, I am merely following one of the paths which he himself charted.

In the work of G. A. Dorsey devoted to the mythology of the Pawnee Indians of the North American Plains,[2] we find a series of myths (numbered 77 through 116) which give an account of the origin of shamanistic powers. One theme recurs several times (see numbers 77, 86, 89, and *passim*); I shall call it, for purposes of simplification, the theme of the *pregnant boy*. Let us examine, for example, myth number 77.

An ignorant young boy becomes aware that he possesses magical powers that enable him to cure the sick. Jealous of the boy's increasing reputation, an old medicine man of established position visits him on several different occasions, accompanied by his wife. Enraged because he obtains no secret in exchange for his own teachings, the medicine man offers the boy a pipe filled with magical herbs. Thus bewitched, the boy discovers that he is pregnant. Full of shame, he leaves his village and seeks death among wild animals. The animals, moved to pity by his misfortune, decide to cure him. They extract the fetus from his body. They teach him their magical powers, by means of which the boy, on returning to his home, kills the evil medicine man and becomes himself a famous and respected healer.

A careful analysis of the text of this myth, which in one version alone takes up thirteen pages of Dorsey's work, discloses that it is built on a long series of oppositions: (1) *initiated shaman* versus *non-initiated shaman*, that is, the opposition between acquired power and innate power; (2) *child* versus *old man*, since the myth insists on the youth of one protagonist and the old age of the other; (3) *confusion of sexes* versus *differentiation of sexes*; all of Pawnee metaphysical thought is actually based on the idea that at the time of the creation of the world antagonistic elements were intermingled and that the first work of the gods consisted in sorting them out. The young child is asexual or, more accurately, the male and female principles co-exist in him. Conversely, in the old man the distinction is irrevocable – an idea clearly expressed in the myth by the fact that his wife is always with him – in contrast with the boy, who is alone but who harbors in himself both masculinity and femininity (he becomes pregnant); (4) *fertility of the child* (despite his virginity) versus *sterility of the old man* (notwithstanding his constantly mentioned marriage); (5) the irreversible relationship of the fertilization of the "son" by the "father" versus an equally irreversible relationship, namely the revenge of the "father" because the "son"

---

[2] *The Pawnee: Mythology*, part I (Washington: 1906).

does not reveal any secrets to him (he possesses none) in exchange for his own secrets; (6) the threefold opposition between, on the one hand, *plant* magic, which is *real*, that is, a drug by means of which the old man fertilizes the child (this magic, however, is *curable*) and, on the other hand, magic of *animal* origin, which is *symbolic* (manipulation of a skull), by means of which the child kills the old man *without any possibility of resurrection*; (7) magic which proceeds by *introduction* versus magic which proceeds by *extraction*.

The construction of the myth by oppositions also characterizes details of the text. The animals are moved to pity at the sight of the boy for two reasons, which are well defined in the text: He compounds the characteristics of man and woman, a combination expressed by the opposition between the leanness of his own body (he has been fasting for days) and the swelling of his abdomen (due to his condition). To induce a miscarriage, the *herbivorous* animals *vomit* the *bones*, while the *carnivorous* animals *extract* the *flesh* (threefold opposition). And finally, while the boy risks death from a swollen stomach (in myth number 89 the fetus is replaced by a ball of clay, which continues to grow until its bearer bursts), the medicine man actually dies of an abdominal constriction.

The version given in myth number 86 both retains and elaborates some of these oppositions. The murderer lowers his victim at the end of a rope down into the subterranean world (the abode of mammals, which are magical mammals) to pick up some eagle and woodpecker feathers, that is, feathers of sky-dwelling birds, the former specifically associated with the empyreal heavens and the latter with thunderstorms. This inversion of the system of the world is accompanied by a concomitant "rectification" of the inverted opposition (found in the "right-side-up" system of myth number 77) between carnivorous and herbivorous animals. As seems to be "normal," the former are now concerned with the bones of the fetus, the latter with its blood. We see, then, what a structural analysis of the myth content can achieve in itself: It furnishes rules of transformation which enable us to shift from one variant to another by means of operations similar to those of algebra.

At this point, however, I wish to consider another aspect of the problem. To what Pawnee ritual does the myth of the pregnant boy correspond? On first inspection, none. Whereas the myth emphasizes the opposition between generations, the Pawnee have no shamanistic societies based on age-grades. Membership in these societies is not subjected to trials or payments. According to Murie, "the usual way to become a medicine-man was to succeed one's teacher at his death."[3] The myth, on the contrary, is based upon a twofold concept of innate power, which, because it is *innate*, is denied the boy by the master; because the boy's power is not taught him by the master, the master refuses to acknowledge him as his successor.

---

[3] J. R. Murie, "Pawnee Societies," *Anthropological Papers of the American Museum of Natural History*, vol. XI (1916), pp. vii, 603.

Shall we say, therefore, that the Pawnee myth reflects a system which is correlated with and yet the reverse of the system which prevails in Pawnee ritual? This would be only partly correct, because the opposition would not be pertinent; that is, the concept of opposition is not heuristic here: It accounts for certain differences between the myth and the rite but leaves others unexplained. It especially neglects the theme of the pregnant boy, to which we nevertheless attributed a central position in the group of myths under consideration.

On the other hand, all the elements of the myth fall into place when we compare it, not with the corresponding Pawnee ritual, but rather with the symmetrical and inverse ritual that prevails among those tribes of the American Plains which conceive their shamanistic societies and the rules for membership in the reverse manner from that of the Pawnee themselves. As Lowie expresses it, "The Pawnee have the distinction of having developed the most elaborate system of societies outside the age-series."[4] In this respect they contrast with the Blackfoot and with such sedentary tribes as the Mandan and Hidatsa, which exemplify most elaborately the other type and to which they are related, not only culturally, but also geographically and historically through the Arikara, whose separation from the Skidi Pawnee (precisely those whose myths Dorsey collected) dates only from the first half of the eighteenth century.

Among these tribes, societies are based on age-grades. The transition from one to another is achieved by purchase, and the relationship between seller and buyer is conceived as a relationship between "father" and "son." Finally, the candidate always appears in the company of his wife, and the central motif of the transaction is the handing over of the "son's" wife to the "father," who carries out with her an ace of real or symbolic coitus, which is, however, always represented as a fertility act.

We thus rediscover all the oppositions already analyzed on the level of myth, but there is a reversal of the values attributed to each pair: initiated and noninitiated, youth and old age, confusion and differentiation of sexes, and so on. In fact, in the Mandan, Hidatsa, and Blackfoot rites, the "son" is accompanied by his wife, just as in the Pawnee myth the wife accompanied the "father." But whereas in the latter case she was a mere supernumerary, here it is she who plays the principal role: Fertilized by the "father" and conceiving the "son," she thus represents the bisexuality which the Pawnee myth ascribed to the "son." In other words, the semantic values are the same; they are merely permuted in relation to the symbols which express them. It is interesting to compare, in this respect, the objects which are considered to be fertilizing agents in the two systems. In the Pawnee myth, a pipe is transferred by the father and his wife to the son. In the Blackfoot rite, a wild turnip is first

---

[4] R. H. Lowie, "Plains-Indian Age-Societies: Historical and Comparative Summary." *Anthropological Papers of the American Museum of Natural History*, vol. XI (1916), pp. xiii, 890.

transferred by the father to the son's wife, then by the latter to the son. The pipe, a hollow tube, is the intermediary between the sky and the middle world; hence its role is symmetrical to, and the reverse of, the role ascribed to the wild turnip in Plains mythology – as is evident in the innumerable variants of the cycle called "Star-Husband," where the turnip is a plug, functioning as a circuit-breaker between the two worlds. The elements are expressed by different symbols when their order is reversed.

The extraordinary Hidatsa rite (whose archaic Chinese parallels were never, to my knowledge, pointed out), concerning the prestation of women in an arbor roofed over with dried meat, also corresponds to the Pawnee myth. A payment of meat is made, sometimes to the fertilizing fathers who own the magic, sometimes to the magical animals playing the role of non-fathers (that is, abortionists). But in the first case, meat is offered in the form of a container (hut covered with meat), whereas in the other it is specified that meat should be presented as content (satchels stuffed with meat). We could further pursue these comparisons, which would all lead to the same conclusion, namely, that the Pawnee myth reveals a ritual system which is the reverse, not of that prevailing among the Pawnee, but of a system which they do not employ and which exists among related tribes whose ritual organization is exactly the opposite of that of the Pawnee. Moreover, the relationship between the two systems has a contrapuntal character: If one system is considered as a progression, the other appears as a retrogression.

We have thus defined a Pawnee myth in terms of both its correlation with and its opposition to an alien ritual. It is remarkable that a relationship of the same type, but of a still more complex order, may be detected between this very myth and a ritual which, while not characteristic of the Pawnee alone, was the subject of a particularly elaborate study – namely, the Hako.[5]

The Hako is a ritual of alliance between two groups. In contrast to the Pawnee societies, whose position in the social structure is fixed, these groups may freely choose one another. By operating in this fashion, however, they place themselves in a father-son relationship that also defines the stable relationship between consecutive age-grades in the sedentary tribes. As Hocart once demonstrated, the father-son relationship upon which the Hako is based may be considered a permutation of an affinal relationship between paternal and maternal kin.[6] In other words, the myth of the pregnant boy, the Mandan and Hidatsa ritual of accession to the highest rank of a series of age-grades, and the Hako represent so many groups of permutations whose formula is an equivalence between the opposition *father/son* and the opposition *man/woman*. I, for one, am prepared to hold that this equation is based on the distinctive

---

[5] A. C. Fletcher and J. R. Murie, *The Hako: A Pawnee Ceremony*, Bureau of American Ethnology, 22nd Annual Report, Part II (Washington: 1900–1901 [1904]).

[6] A. M. Hocart, "Covenants," in *The Life-giving Myth* (London: 1952).

characteristics of the kinship system known as Crow-Omaha, in which the relationships between affinal groups are specifically formalized in terms of relationships between ascendants and descendants. But this aspect of the problem will have to be developed elsewhere.

I shall limit myself to examining briefly the last phases of the Hako ritual (16 to 19 in Fletcher's breakdown). These phases are invested with the most sacred character and offer a series of remarkable analogies with the myth of the pregnant boy. The father's group arrives in the village of the son. It symbolically captures a young child. The child's sex is immaterial, or, more accurately, he is of unidentified sex.[7] The group consecrates him by means of a series of anointings, in order to identify him with Tirawa, the supreme deity of the celestial world. Then the child is raised in a robe with his legs projecting forward, and in this position he is handled in the fashion of a phallus for a symbolic coitus with the world, represented by a circle outlined on the ground, into which he is to drop, like an egg, an oriole's nest: "The putting of the child's feet in the circle means the giving of new life . . . ," comments the native informer unambiguously.[8] Finally, the circle is erased and the anointments are removed from the child, who is sent away to join his playmates.

All these operations may be considered clearly as a permutation of the elements of the myth of the pregnant child. In the myth as well as the ritual, we have three protagonists:

Myth: son	father (or husband)	wife of father
Ritual: son (permutation of wife)	father (permutation of husband)	child (permutation of son)

In both myth and ritual, two protagonists are identified with respect to sex, and one is left unidentified (son or child).

In the myth, the lack of identification of the son enables him to be half-man and half-woman; in the ritual, he becomes fully a man (an agent of coitus) and fully a woman (he actually gives birth to a nest, which symbolizes an egg, in a circle, which symbolizes a nest).

The entire symbolism of the Hako implies that the father fertilizes the son by means of the ambivalent function of the child; just as in the myth, the ambivalent function of the couple (the medicine man and his wife) fertilizes the child and, similarly, in the ritual of the sedentary tribes, the father fertilizes the son through the ambivalent function of the son's wife. This ambiguity as to the sex of one of the protagonists is constantly emphasized regardless of context. Compare, in this respect, the sack from which the legs of the child emerge (Hako); the male child with protuberant abdomen (Pawnee myth); the

---

[7] Fletcher and Murie, op. cit., p. 201.

[8] Ibid., p. 245.

woman holding in her mouth a protuberant turnip (Blackfoot myth constituting the basis of the rite of access to the society of *Kit-foxes* by prestation of
the wife).

In another study[9] I attempted to show that the genetic model of the myth –
that is, the model which generates it and simultaneously gives it its structure
– consists of the application of *four* functions to *three* symbols. Here, the four
functions are defined by the twofold opposition *elder/younger* and *male/female*,
from which stem the father, mother, son, and daughter functions. In the myth
of the pregnant boy, the father and mother each use a different symbol, and
the functions of son and daughter are merged under the third available symbol,
the child. In the Mandan-Hidatsa ritual, it is the father and son who are distinguished, while the wife of the son embodies the functions of mother and
daughter. The Hako appears to be more complex, since here the symbols,
always three in number, require that besides the father and son a new figure
play a role – namely, the child (boy or girl) of the son. The reason for this is
that the allocation of functions to symbols requires here an ideal dichotomization
of the latter. As we noted before, the father is both father and mother; the
son, both son and daughter; and the child borrows from each of the other two
symbols one of their half-functions: fertilizing agent (father) and fertilized
object (daughter). It is remarkable that this more complex distribution of the
functions among the symbols characterizes the only one of the three systems
which is based on reciprocity. Although the purpose of each system is to
establish an alliance, this alliance is rejected in the first case, solicited in the
second, and negotiated only in the third.

The dialectical relationship between myth and ritual is based on considerations of structure which we cannot take up here, and we must refer the reader
to the study already cited. But we hope to have shown that in order to understand this relationship it is indispensable to compare myth and ritual, not only
within the confines of one and the same society, but also with the beliefs and
practices of neighboring societies. If a certain group of Pawnee myths represents a permutation of certain rituals, not only of the same tribe, but also of
other peoples, one cannot rest content with a purely formal analysis. Such
an analysis constitutes a preliminary stage of research, which is fruitful to the
extent that it permits the formulation of geographical and historical problems
in more rigorous terms than is customary. Structural dialectics does not con-
tradict historical determinism, but rather promotes it by giving it a new tool.
Along with Meillet and Troubetzkoy, Jakobson proved, moreover, on several
occasions that the phenomena of reciprocal influence between geographically
related linguistic areas cannot remain outside of structural analysis; this constitutes the well-known theory of linguistic affinities. I have attempted to
bring a modest contribution to this theory, which I applied in another field,

---

[9] "The Structural Study of Myth."

by emphasizing that the affinity can be seen not only in the diffusion of certain structural properties outside their area of origin or in their rejection, which impedes this propagation. The affinity may also be demonstrated by antithesis, which generates structures presenting the character of answers, cures, excuses, or even remorse. In mythology, as in linguistics, formal analysis immediately raises the question of *meaning*.

Part *VII*

EVALUATIONS OF THE THEORY

23

THE DRAMAS AND DRAMATIC DANCES OF NON-EUROPEAN RACES

William Ridgeway

The English classicist William Ridgeway (1853–1926), who was Professor of Archaeology at Cambridge University, argued that religion originated in the worship of dead ancestors and not of gods. He was an uncompromising euhemerist. He never disputed that tragedy originated in ritual, but for him the ritual was dancing in honor of dead human beings, not dancing to revive a dead god of vegetation. Ridgeway first presented his theory of tragedy in *The Origin of Tragedy* (Cambridge: Cambridge University Press, 1910) and then in *The Dramas and Dramatic Dances of Non-European Races* (Cambridge: Cambridge University Press, 1915), where, in the following selection (pp. 41–64), he attacks the views of Harrison and Murray. On Ridgeway see *Essays and Studies Presented to William Ridgeway*, ed. E. C. Quiggin (Cambridge: Cambridge University Press, 1913); A. Y. Campbell, "Professor Ridgeway and Greek Tragedy," *Cambridge Review* 24 (May 24, 1916), 326–9; R. S. Conway, "Sir William Ridgeway, 1853–1926," *Proceedings of the British Academy* 12 (1926), 327–36; and Robert Ackerman, *The Myth and Ritual School* (New York: Garland Publishing, 1991), 125–9.

Professor Murray's Theory of Tragedy

This latest theory of the origin of Tragedy – a mere modification of the Sun-myth, Vegetation spirit, and Seasonal drama – with which we have already

Original publication: William Ridgeway, *The Dramas and Dramatic Dances of Non-European Races* (Cambridge: Cambridge University Press, 1915), pp. 41–64.

dealt in the case of Dr Farnell, is set forth in Miss J. E. Harrison's *Themis*,[1] to which Mr F. M. Cornford and Professor G. G. Murray have each contributed a chapter. Miss Harrison draws her inspiration from Sir James Frazer, from Professor Murray's *Rise of the Greek Epic* (based in its turn on the theories of Drs v. Wilamowitz-Moellendorff and Bethe), from Professor Bergson's philosophy, from the psychology of primitive ritual as expounded by Drs Durkheim, Hubert, and Mauss, and from the *mana* theory of Dr R. R. Marett. She starts with the birth-story of Zeus in Crete in the newly-found hymn to the Curetes, in which Zeus is termed *Kouros*. This she assumes always means a *youth*, though it just as often, if not more often, means a *child* or a *babe*. As Zeus *the Kouros* is attended by his Curetes, so is Dionysus by his *Thiasos*. Miss Harrison proceeds to the death and rebirth of Zagreus in the Mysteries, assuming that this is primitive, although, as we have seen, Zagreus does not appear in the Mysteries of Eleusis until after 370 BC, whilst as in the case of the Sacred Marriage she relies on the statement of Christian writers who describe the practices and beliefs of their own time, thus her sole evidence for the Zagreus story is that of Clement of Alexandria. On the strength of this she essays to explain the ritual of death and rebirth by primitive rites of tribal initiation of youths at puberty,[2] in use amongst the aborigines of Australia. She also assumes that early Greek society was matrilinear, totemistic, and had no gods, all their religion being comprised in the supposed tribal mysteries of which we have spoken, that the essence of these was the death and rebirth of the initiated *Kouros*, and the continuous life of their tribe: it is further assumed that at this stage there is no individualism, self-consciousness, or desire for a separate immortality. The initiated *Kouroi*, following the Megistos Kouros, cherish certain *choses sacrées*, such as totem animals, thunderbolts, bull-roarers, and the like, from which they derive *mana*, and with which they perform magic, not as a *mimesis*, but as a "fore-doing" of the things they desired.

Group-thinking might project into the *chose sacrée*, or evolve from it a *daimon*, who by dying and rising again reflected the life of Nature and of the tribe, and in turn out of the *daimon* might be projected a *theos*, who got rid of his totem-form, refused the privileges of a recurring death, rose to the sky, claimed immortality, and was thereby, if he separated himself from his *thiasos*, "doomed to desiccate and die". The Kouros Megistos is thus nothing more than the projection of the Kouretes into a *chose sacrée*. Miss Harrison contemns the Olympian gods, who play so great a part in Homer, and she declares that he marks a stage when collective thinking and magic ritual are, if not dead, at least dying, when rationalism and the individualistic thinking to which it belongs are developed to a point not far behind that of the days of Pericles. Homer's attitude towards religion was sceptical, Ionian. What is meant by the

---

[1] Cambridge, 1912.
[2] *Themis*, p. 124.

individualism of Homer is seen very clearly in the case of the *Androktasiai* or "*Manslayings*". Dr Bethe has shown beyond the possibility of a doubt that the superabundant *Androktasiai*, which appear as single combats in the *Iliad*, really reflect not the fights of individual heroes at Troy, but the conflicts of tribes on the mainland of Greece. But I may remark parenthetically that Dr Bethe has no more proved this for Homer than he has for the numerous "manslayings" in Froissart's descriptions of Crécy and Poitiers. "When the tribes", she proceeds, "who waged this warfare on the mainland pass in the long series of migrations to Asia Minor and the Islands, the local sanctities, from which they are cut loose, are forgotten, and local *daimones*, eponymous heroes, and the like become individualized. Saga-heroes, Achilles, and Alexandros are tribal heroes – that is, collective conceptions of conflicting tribes of Thessaly. Hector, before, not after he went to Troy, was a hero-daemon in Boeotian Thebes; his comrade Melanippus had a cult in Thebes; Patroclus, whom he slew, was his near neighbour – like him, a local *daimon*. It is the life-stories of heroes such as these, cut loose by the migrations from their local cults, from their monotonous periodicity, that are the material of Attic drama, that forms its "free and plastic plots".[3] As we have already shown (p. 13) the untenable character of such theories of heroes, it is unnecessary to repeat the arguments here.

Miss Harrison then passes to the Dithyrambos,[4] the Dromenon, and the Drama. In Dionysus, to whom Euripides in his *Bacchae* (one of his latest plays and written in Thrace) applied the name *Dithyrambos*, with the meaning of "twice through the door" or "twice-born", she finds the Kouros and concludes not only that the Dithyrambos reflects the rite of rebirth, the Bacchants the mothers of a matriarchal society, and that Dionysus reflects his *thiasos* as the Megistos Kouros reflects his Kouretes, but that the Dithyrambos, like the Hymn of the Kouretes, is not only a song of human rebirth, it is the song of the rebirth of all Nature, all living things; it is the "Spring Song for the Year-Feast". Elsewhere she states: "The dithyramb, we have seen, is a Birth-song, a δρώμενον giving rise to the divine figures of Mother, Full-grown Son, and Child; it is a spring-song of magical fertility for the new year; it is a group-song, a κύκλιος χορός, later sung by a *thiasos*, a song of those who leap and dance rhythmically together." She then adopts Mr A. B. Cook's fantastic guess for the etymology of Dithyrambos, "Zeus-leap-song", the song that makes Zeus leap or beget. "Our Hymn of the Kouretes", she says, is "*the Dithyramb*". "The Dithyrambos is a bull-god reborn into his tribe, not only as a full-grown male, but as a sacred beast." Her argument thus depends upon both the derivation of Dithyrambus given by Euripides and that given by Mr Cook. But if one of them is right, the other must be wrong. As proof of this supposed spring festival of Dionysus she cites a Dithyrambic Paean to Dionysus recently

---

[3] Op. cit., p. 335.
[4] Ibid., pp. 202–4.

discovered at Delphi, and a well-known fragment of Pindar, in both of which there are allusions to the season of spring; and finally she cites the well-known invocation of the Elean women to Dionysus: "Come, O hero Dionysus," which Mr Cook has obligingly emended into "Come in the *spring*, O Dionysus".[5] She further adds that boys at puberty were initiated at this Year-Feast into a tribal mystery or Dromenon, and that out of this sprang the Drama. But there is not a scrap of evidence to show that in any state in ancient Greece boys were initiated at festivals, either in the Spring or at any other time. At Athens they certainly were not initiated at any of the four festivals connected with the name of Dionysus, two of which fell in the Spring. There was, however, a most ancient Ionic festival, the *Apaturia*, on the third day of which, termed *Koureotis*, fathers took the children born in that year, or such as were not registered, and introduced them to the assembled members of their respective Phratries, a victim being offered for each child. But so far from this festival taking its name from Kouroi initiated at the age of puberty, it derived its appellation from babes; and so far from being held in the Spring, it was celebrated on the 13th of Pyanepsion, i.e., the last days of October or the first days of November.

Again, festivals of Dionysus were not confined to Spring, as Miss Harrison assumes. Thus it was at midwinter that the Cynaethians of Arcadia held their famous festival in honour of Dionysus, which best illustrates Pindar's phrase "the ox-driving dithyramb of Dionysus".[6] For the men with their bodies greased with oil picked out from a herd of cattle "that bull which the god put into their heads to take, lifted him up bodily and carried him into the shrine for sacrifice".

The Dithyramb

As all theories of the origin of Tragedy take as their starting-point Aristotle's statement that "Tragedy arose from the leaders of the dithyramb", it is essential to ascertain what he meant by that term. Strange as it may seem, no scholar before the present writer essayed to settle this question. All writers had assumed that Aristotle regarded the dithyramb as peculiar to and restricted to Dionysus, and in reality the Dionysiac theory of the origin of Tragedy depends on this passage, the references to the Satyric drama and Satyric style which occurs a few lines lower down, and on some half-dozen references to the dithyramb in other authors. Let us first take the scattered references: (1) Archilochus (670 BC) declares that when "his brain is thunder-smitten with wine he knows how to lead a fair strain in honour of king Dionysus, a

---

[5] Plut. *Quaest. Graec.* xxxvi: ἐλθεῖν ἥρω Διόνυσε κτλ., which Mr Cook, on the ground that this voc. of ἥρως is not found elsewhere, emends into ἐλθεῖν ἥρ' ὦ Διόνυσε.

[6] Paus. viii. 19. 15; Ridgeway, *Origin of Tragedy*, p. 6.

dithyramb", but he does not say that when sober he would not have sung a dithyramb in honour of some other god or hero; (2) Arion trained a chorus at Corinth in the time of Periander to sing a dithyramb, but this does not prove that he did not or would not have composed dithyrambs on other heroes or gods; (3) this last view is supported by the fact that Simonides (born 567 BC) in the generation after Arion wrote a dithyramb on the hero Memnon; and (4) that Bacchylides, his nephew and younger contemporary, composed two dithyrambs on Theseus and one on Apollo; (5) Pindar in an allusion to Arion's dithyramb at Corinth-speaks of the "ox-driving dithyramb of Dionysus", but, as I have pointed out elsewhere, this phrase only refers to such a custom as that of the Cynaethians (*supra*, p. 44) and does not prove that Pindar thought that the dithyramb belonged only to Dionysus; (6) Pratinas, who introduced the Satyric drama into Athens, termed Dionysus *Thriambo-Dithyrambos*; and (7) Euripides called him *Dithyrambos*. But in the recently-found Delphic "Dithyrambic Paean" on which Miss Harrison builds so much, Dionysus is termed *Paean*. Yet on the strength of this neither she nor any one else would venture to maintain that the *paean* as a literary form belonged exclusively to Dionysus, for it was composed in honour of Apollo, Artemis, and various other gods. (8) Finally, Miss Harrison relies most on a passage in Plato,[7] in which, when discussing the various kinds of odes, he says: "some are prayers to the gods, and these are termed *hymnoi*; others of an opposite sort might best be called *threnoi*; another sort *paeans*, and another – the birth of Dionysus, I suppose (οἶμαι), is termed *dithyrambos*." His remark ("I suppose") shows that he is not at all clear on the point. In view, therefore, of these *loci classici*, we must conclude that at no time was the *dithyramb* any more the exclusive property of Dionysus than the *paean* was that of Apollo.

But what did Aristotle mean by the dithyramb from which he says that Tragedy arose? His words make it clear that he knew only of *one* kind of dithyramb, for he does not say that Tragedy arose from the worship of Dionysus either here or elsewhere in his voluminous writings, nor does he say that it arose from the dithyramb of Dionysus, or from the ancient dithyramb, or from the dithyramb of Archilochus or from that of Arion. Now, as all modern scholars admit the soundness of the principle by which difficulties in an author's meaning or in his use of words should, if possible, be explained from his own writings, it is important to discover what meaning Aristotle attached to the term *dithyrambos*. Did he regard it as restricted to Dionysus or as common to gods and heroes, as was certainly the view of Simonides and Bacchylides in the end of the sixth and the beginning of the fifth centuries BC? Fortunately we have the means of forming an opinion, and that too not from his other writings but from very definite passages in the *Poetic* itself.[8] Just a page before the

---

[7] *Legg.* 700 B.

[8] W. Ridgeway, "Three Notes on *Poetic* of Aristotle" (*Classical Quarterly*, 1912, pp. 241–2).

famous passage with which we are dealing, he describes[9] *dithyramboi* as a kind of *Mimesis*, and cites as an example of that form of literature the *Cyclops* of Timotheus, the famous dithyrambic poet and musician of Miletus (447–357 BC), who wrote some eighteen dithyrambs on various subjects, including one called the *Pang of Semele*. It may be said that the *Cyclops* was Dionysiac, since Euripides' play of that name was Satyric, but let us turn to another passage,[10] some five pages after that on the origin of Tragedy. He is discussing the question of *ēthos* in Tragedy and the need of consistency in the characters. As a breach of this rule, he cites the *threnos* of Odysseus in the *Scylla*, which was beyond doubt a dithyramb, and that too by Timotheus. It is therefore clear that Timotheus wrote dithyrambs on heroes, and not merely on Dionysus. It is also certain that Aristotle only knew one class of dithyrambs, *the* dithyramb, and that as he cites as examples of it the dithyrambs of Timotheus, which were addressed, like those of Simonides and Bacchylides, to heroes, as well as to Dionysus, he held that the dithyramb had for its themes heroes and gods other than Dionysus. Aristotle thus held that Tragedy sprang from a dithyramb which was not restricted to Dionysus, but was common to heroes and gods, and as such included Dionysus (termed *Heros*, as well as *theos*) amongst its themes. It cannot therefore be assumed any longer that because Aristotle makes Tragedy arise out of the *dithyramb* it therefore arose from the worship of Dionysus.

But it may be said that we do not know what Aristotle meant by heroes and gods. Yet there is no doubt that he held the same doctrine as that of all Greeks from Homer down to the latest times, and this cannot be better stated than in the words of Pausanias when speaking of Lycaon: "For the men of that time by reason of their righteousness and piety, were guests of the gods and sat with them at table; the gods openly visited the good with honour and the bad with their displeasure. Indeed men were raised to the rank of gods in those days and are worshipped down to the present time. Such were Aristaeus and the Cretan damsel Britomartis; and Heracles the son of Alcmena; and Amphiaraus son of Oecles, and moreover Pollux and Castor."[11]

Choses Sacrées

But Miss Harrison and her partners aver that such heroes, some of whom were deified, were "only projections" into *choses sacrées*. What is a *chose sacrée*? It is only the French for a "holy thing". But as soon as we examine the objects

---

[9] *Poetic*, 1448 *a* 14.
[10] 1454 *a* 30.
[11] viii. 2. 4.

which are deemed "holy things" by various peoples, both ancient and modern, we find that such "holy things" or "relics", to use the proper English term, are (1) either a portion of some loved or revered human personage, a lock of hair, a tooth, such as that of Buddha in Ceylon, numerous remains of mediaeval and even modern saints, such as the famous arm-bone of St Botolph, carried in procession in its silver case on great festivals at Bury St Edmunds. Greece was no exception to this practice. Great care was taken of the bones of famous men, such as Leonidas and Themistocles, and the possession of the bones of departed worthies, such as Orestes, Tisamenus, and Melanippus, was of great importance to their owners, whilst we know that in Arcadia the bones of the dead were regularly worshipped. (2) The next class of relics are objects worn by or once possessed by some loved or venerated person, e.g., Nelson's cocked hat that he wore at Trafalgar, the shirt in which Charles I was executed, the so-called Crown of Thorns worn by Christ on Calvary for which St Louis gave an enormous price and built the Sainte Chapelle at Paris. (3) A place or object at or in contact with or near which some famous or venerated person met his or her end, or into which his spirit is supposed to have passed, whether it be animal, tree, or stone, e.g., the Cross of Calvary, and the Sepulchre in which Christ lay. (4) Men also regard natural objects, such as rocks, mountains, trees, and rivers as sacred because they are thought to be inhabited by the spirits of the dead, and by a natural extension of this belief they frequently revere, as having magical powers, stones and other natural objects of unusual form or colour, such as crystals, or fossils – for example, belemnites, commonly deemed thunderbolts from heaven, or even stones wrought into axes and arrows, which amongst peoples who have reached the stage of metals, are universally believed to be thunderbolts or "elf-shots". Such are the *choses sacrées* of civilized races, and such we shall find to be those of barbarous races also. But it may be said that there are sham relics. Certainly, but unless people believed in the great importance of real ones, there would be no market for the forgeries.

It is therefore the human individual and not the *chose sacrée* which is primary and antecedent, for a *chose* can only become *sacrée* by being, or being believed to be, part of some human individual, or to have been once owned by or have been in close contact with his or her remains, or to be inhabited by his or her spirit or something analogous, and accordingly such relics are only secondary phenomena.

Mana

This will be the proper place to discuss the term *mana*, which has come into the nomenclature of Comparative Religion from Dr R. R. Marett's essay on

Pre-Animistic Religion.[12] His statements have not unreasonably been taken to mean that there was a pre-animistic stage in the evolution of Religion, though he now disclaims this interpretation,[13] yet hardly with success. He writes: "It would be untrue to deny that the term pre-animistic was used by me designedly and with chronological reference. What I would not be prepared to lay down dogmatically or even provisionally is merely that there was a pre-animistic era in the history of religion when animism was not and nevertheless religion of a kind existed. For all I know some sort of animism in Tylor's sense of the word was a primary condition of the most primitive religion of mankind. But I believe that there were other conditions no less primary. Moreover, I hold that it can be shown conclusively that in some cases animistic interpretations have been superimposed on what previously bore a non-animistic sense. I would go farther still. I hold that religion in its psychological aspect is fundamentally a mode of social behaviour." Elsewhere he adds with reference to his statement of his own theory: "In regard to religion thus understood, I say not that its evolution proceeds from abstract to concrete, which would be meaningless, but that it proceeds from indistinct to distinct, from undifferentiated to differentiated, from incoherent to coherent."[14]

Let us now examine his various contentions. (1) If *mana* is "no less primary" and is not more primary than animism, why does Dr Marett place *mana* under the head of "pre-animistic religion", in which he admits that the qualifying adjective is used "designedly" with a chronological reference? (2) The evidence presented by Dr Marett does not seem in any wise to substantiate his statement that "it can be shown conclusively that in some cases animistic interpretations have been superimposed on what previously bore a non-animistic sense". Even if it could, this by no means proves that animism did not precede in time the vague notions attached to certain objects which later received full animistic interpretation. (3) As Dr Marett holds that "religion in its psychological aspect is fundamentally a mode of social behaviour", let us test his other statement that "the evolution in religion proceeds from indistinct to distinct, from undifferentiated to differentiated, from incoherent to coherent" by an appeal to the facts of primitive society. In modern civilized communities consanguinity and relationships through marriage play so unimportant a part, that we are perfectly content with the word "uncle" for father's brother and mother's brother, with the word "aunt" for father's sister and for mother's sister, and so on. Yet the old civilized races, such as those of Rome, Greece, and India, were much more careful in differentiating these relationships and connexions, for they had one term for a father's brother, another for a mother's brother, one name for a father's sister, another for a mother's sister. The Greeks were not content

---

[12] *Folk-lore*, June, 1900, pp. 162–82.
[13] *Threshold of Religion*, pref. to ed. 1, p. ix.
[14] Ibid., p. xi.

with one name for half-brothers and half-sisters, but they had separate terms to express half-blood on the father's side and half-blood on the mother's, and they had special words to express "husband's brother's wife" and the like, and the same holds true in a still higher degree for Sanskrit, in which there is a host of terms for blood and marriage connexions for which we have no equivalents. Let us next examine the nomenclature of the lower races such as that of the Australians, amongst whom religion and social organization are inextricably bound up, and where, if Dr Marett is right, we should find in the highest degree vagueness and indefiniteness. But here we meet the very opposite, for they have separate terms for every one of the highly complicated relationships and connexions that result from their very elaborate tribal, clan, and totemic divisions. The fact is that mankind in the lower stages, so far from being vague, indefinite, and undifferentiating in matters of vital concern to his very existence, on the contrary has a power of discrimination and differentiation apparently as great, if not greater, because more concentrated and circumscribed in its action than that possessed by civilized men in regard to matters which they from their standpoint deem of vital importance. We may go further and point out that so far from the lower animals being vague and undifferentiating, they have in their own limited spheres a power of differentiation by sight, sound, and smell, in matters vital to them utterly unknown to civilized man, though found in some degree in such races as the Australians, whose powers in tracking men or animals is too well known to need elaboration. Dr Marett's hypothesis is therefore refuted by well-established facts. But is he more right in assuming that *mana* is as primary as animism? Let us turn to his own examples of what is termed *mana* by the men of the Pacific Isles. "Codrington", he writes,[15] "defines *mana* in its Melanesian sense as follows: 'a force altogether distinct from physical power, which acts in all kinds of ways for good and evil and which is of the greatest advantage to possess or to control.' Or again he says: 'it is a power or influence, not physical, and in a way supernatural, but it shows itself in physical force or in any kind of power or excellence a man possesses.' It is supernatural just in this way, that it is what works to effect everything which is beyond the ordinary power of men outside the common processes of nature." He illustrates this point by examples: "If a man has been successful in fighting, it has not been his natural strength of arm, quickness of eye, or readiness in resource, that has won success; he has certainly got the *mana* of a spirit of some deceased warrior to empower him conveyed in an amulet of a stone round his neck or a tuft of leaves in his belt, in a tooth hung upon a finger of his bow hand or in the form of words with which he brings supernatural assistance to his side. If a man's pigs multiply and his gardens are productive, it is not because he is industrious and looks after his property, but because of the stones full of *mana* for pigs and yams that

[15] Op. cit., p. 104.

he possesses." But in the first case cited, it is clear that it is only an ordinary case of relics and that *mana* depends on a primary belief in the existence of souls after the death of the body, and thus *mana* cannot be regarded as primary, but rather as secondary and dependent. In the second case, if it can be shown in the following pages that these very races and numbers more pray to their dead ancestors to make their pigs and yams prosper, and offer to the spirits of their dead the firstfruits, Dr Marett's second instance is no less fatal to his assumption, for the stones full of *mana* may be the dwelling-place of spirits of the dead.

"From Polynesia", Dr Marett proceeds, "comes much the same story. Tregear in his admirable comparative dictionary of the Polynesian dialects renders the word, which may be either noun or adjective, thus: 'supernatural power; divine authority, having qualities which ordinary persons or things do not possess.' He seems to distinguish, however, what might be called a secular sense, in which the term stands generally for authority or, as an adjective, for 'effectual, effective'. He cites copious instances from the various dialects to exemplify the supernatural mode of *mana*. Thus the word is applied in Maori to a wooden sword that has done deeds so wonderful as to possess a sanctity and power of its own; in Samoan to a parent who brings a curse on a disobedient child; in Hawaian to the gods, or to a man who by his death gives efficacy to an idol; in Tongan to whoever performs miracles or bewitches; in Mangarevan to a magic staff given to a man by his grandfather, or again to divination in general, and so forth. In short, its range is as wide as those of divinity and witchcraft taken together." As instances of the so-called secular use, Dr Marett cites the cases of a chief's tabu, a healer of maladies, a successful pleader, or the winner of a race. But in all these cases we have ordinary examples of animism. Thus the wooden sword and the magic staff fall under "relics", the "gods" we shall find to be only the spirits of the dead, the idol became the abode of the spirit of the man sacrificed to it, whilst the power of a chief, of a caster out of devils, of witches and the like all depend upon the same antecedent belief in the existence of disembodied human spirits. We shall find that the potency of all the secret societies of the Pacific and elsewhere rests entirely upon the general belief that their members have special communion with and control over the spirits of the dead, and that their initiation ceremonies are concerned with the latter. There is thus no reason for believing either that *mana* is pre-animistic in time, or that mankind proceeds from the undifferentiated to the differentiated in matters of religion any more than in those of society.

Miss Harrison and her partners argue that behind Dionysus there was never any human reality, but that the god was only the result of the group-thinking of his *thiasos* of Satyr *daimons* and Maenads. Yet they might as well argue that neither Dominic, nor Francis of Assisi, nor Muhammad, nor Christ himself ever existed, but that they are the mere "projections" of the "group-thinking" of the Dominicans, Franciscans, Muhammadans, and Christians respectively.

Nay, they might as well maintain that the German Kaiser has no material existence, but is a mere "projection" of the "group-thinking" of his *thiasos* of Prussian Guards. But to this point we will revert again.

As we have seen above, persons of exceptional prowess, wisdom, and virtue were deified and worshipped by the Greeks, and were honoured after their deaths by periodical celebrations at their tombs, and such too shall we find to be the case in Hindustan, Burma, China, and Japan, and from this practice the Greeks themselves held that the great games, such as those of Olympia, Pytho, Nemea, the Isthmus, the Panathenaea, Hyacinthia, and the like had their origin. Nor can it be maintained that such celebrations belonged to a misty antiquity, for when Timoleon, the liberator of Sicily, died in 336 BC, games were established in his honour, and the people of Amphipolis founded similar games in honour of Brasidas after his death in 422 BC. Yet under the spell of the Mannhardt-Frazer theory, my friends Mr A. B. Cook[16] and Mr F. M. Cornford[17] have sought to prove that the great games of Greece, such as those at Olympia, arose out of a contest similar to that for the priesthood at Nemi. Mr Cook holds that in mythical times the Olympic contest was a means of determining who should be king of the district and champion of the local tree-Zeus. The holder of the office for the time being was analogous to the *Rex Nemorensis* of the Golden Bough – an incarnation of the Tree- and Sky-god, and like his Italian parallel, defended his office against all comers until he was finally defeated and superseded by the successful combatant. Mr Cook bases this view on a statement of Plutarch[18] that the Olympic contests once included a monomachia, which had later been abolished. He goes still further, for he maintains that the Olympic victor was treated with special honour in his life-time and not infrequently worshipped as a hero after death, not because he was a successful athlete, but because he had once been an incarnate god. Mr Cornford accepts this last part of Mr Cook's hypothesis as "fundamentally correct", whilst he adopts the first part with certain modifications, as he thinks that the terms "king, god, incarnation of the tree-Zeus, may all be somewhat misleading", and he holds that "a weather magician like Oinomaos, though a late theology may see in him the temporary incarnation of a god, goes back to a time when there was no god to be incarnated", and that "the sky-god is only a projected reflex of this human figure of the magician who claims to command the powers of the sky and to call down its rain and thunder by virtue of his own *mana*".

"We shall be on safer ground if we restrict ourselves to the simple primitive group consisting of the weather magician, who wields the fertilizing influences of Heaven, and the tree which embodies the powers of the Earth – the

---

[16] *Themis*, p. 220.
[17] Ibid., pp. 220 *sqq.*
[18] *Quaest. Symp.*, p. 675.

vegetation which springs up when the thunder shower has burst, and Heaven and Earth are married in the life-giving rain. To this we must add the conception with which Dr Frazer has made us familiar, of the limited period of office enjoyed by such a personage. The individual on whose vigour and exceptional powers the fertility of earth depends, cannot be allowed to continue in office when his natural forces fall into decay. Hence the single combat, in which he has to make good his right to a renewed period or die at the hands of his more vigorous antagonist. Now in some cases at least this period of office was not merely limited by the duration of its holder's natural strength, but it bore some fixed relation to the year and to the seasonal cycle of vegetable life in nature. In other words the term of office was a 'year' – a term which, as we have seen, may denote a lunar or solar year, or a longer period of two, four, or eight solar years, a *trieteris, penteteris,* or *ennaeteris.* During this period, long or short as it might be, the tenant of the office represented, or rather *was,* the power which governed the rains of heaven and the fruits of earth; at the end of it he was either continued for a new *eniautos* or was violently dispossessed by his successor. Further, since the *eniautos* itself could be concretely conceived as a *daimon* carrying the horn of plenty, the contents and fruits of the year in the more abstract sense, we may think of the temporary 'king', as actually being the *eniautos-daimon,* or fertility spirit of his 'year'.

"When the year is fixed by the solar period, we get festivals of the type of the Roman Saturnalia, the Greek Κρόνια (with which the Saturnalia were regularly equated in ancient times), and the single combat appears as the driving out of winter or of the dying year by the vigorous young spirit of the New Year that is to come. It is as *eniautos-daimon,* not at first as 'incarnate god' or as king in the later political sense, that the representative of the fertility powers of nature dies at the hands of the New Year – in this combat we may see, in a word, the essential feature of a Saturnalian or a *Kronian festival.*"[19]

But formerly Mr Cornford, on the ground that the *Cronia* at Olympia were held at the vernal equinox, maintained that they were a Spring Vegetation festival. The present writer, however, pointed out that at Athens the *Cronia* were held in the end of July or the beginning of August, at Rhodes in the latter part of August or the first part of September, whilst the Thessalian *Peloria* identified with the *Cronia* synchronized with the Roman *Saturnalia,* and were thus held at midwinter. Mr Cornford has now changed his front, and without letting his reader know the facts about the Cronian celebrations at Olympia, Athens, and Rhodes, is no less dogmatic and lays down that it was a midwinter festival to celebrate the triumph of the New Year over the dying one. But was the year dying at the vernal equinox; was the New Year triumphing over its dead predecessor in July, August, and September? In view of these facts we must resolutely reject Mr Cornford's interpretation of the single combat at Olympia.

[19] Op. cit., pp. 222–3.

But we have seen (p. 7) how at the funeral games of Patroclus, the single combat nearly issued in the death of one of the champions. This offers a simple and natural reason for the abolition of such a contest at Olympia.[20] If it be urged by my opponents that a Homeric combat between heroes whom they assume to be mere embodiments of the Year-Daimon is worthless as evidence, I can point to the fact that such combats were in use amongst the Thracians of historical times, and that too at funeral celebrations (p. 7). I have also given reason for believing that the gladiatorial combats at Roman funerals were the survival of contests similar to those at Thracian funerals, and I cited the significant remark of Servius that this was in accord with the ancient belief that human blood should flow on the grave of a dead man. Finally, we saw reason for believing that the combat at Nemi itself on which Sir James Frazer, Mr Cook, Mr Cornford, and others raise such lofty structures may prove to have been in honour not of a Vegetation abstraction, but of a concrete dead man.

If the truth must be told, Mr Cook and Mr Cornford would find more solid ground for the theory of the incarnation of the Tree spirit in the Hangman of *Punch and Judy* than in the priest at Nemi, in Phorbas who hung his victims' heads on an oak, or in Sinis who tied his captives to a pine tree.[21] Had not the Hangman, too, his gallows *tree*, and had he not on it hung others, and in his turn was not he (like the priest at Nemi, Phorbas, and Sinis) doomed to be hung by that still more crafty ruffian Punch? In this case, they would have at all events a popular puppet-play, belonging to a class of great antiquity, of which we shall presently have much to say (pp. 157 *sqq.*), and they would not have been driven to so many conjectures and suppositions to fill up the story.

Elsewhere Mr Cornford describes Pelops as "the young year-god whose marriage was celebrated in the summer". The ritual would be appropriate to a seasonal feast of a Kronian (Saturnalian) character, at which the young year-god, standing for a young and growing thinking nature, was initiated or inaugurated as "King" for his Year, under the doom of "death and resurrection". Furthermore he takes as the true account of the foundation of the Olympic games one of the local myths which Pausanias heard at Olympia in the second half of the second century after Christ. According to this the Idaean Heracles set his brethren the Idaean Dactyls to run a race and crowned the victor with a branch of wild olive, of which they had such an abundance that they slept on heaps of its fresh green leaves. "There is no need", says Mr Cornford, "for lengthy comment. The games are traced back to an original foot-race held by young men (Kouretes) from Crete, presumably analogous to the young unmarried Karneatai of Sparta. The race, we may suppose, determined who should be *the* Kouros – the Greatest Kouros – of his year. The winner received not a

---

[20] *Quaest. Symp.*, p. 675.
[21] For a confutation of Mr A. B. Cook's theory of Phorbas and Sinis, see Mr E. M. W. Tillyard's "Theseus, Sinis, and the Isthmian Games" (*Jour. Hell. Stud.*, vol. xxxiii, 1913, pp. 296–312).

prize of commercial value such as was usual in funeral games, but a symbol of his office, as vegetation-*daimon* – the branch of the sacred tree. This branch reminds us of the golden bough and perhaps links the foot-race of the young men to the contest between the young and the old king. For in the famous wood at Nemi it was he who succeeded in tearing a bough from the sacred tree who had a right to contend in single combat with the King of the Wood for succession to his office."[22]

But this later local legend on which Mr Cornford builds so much was treated with contempt by Pausanias[23] himself, as we know from another passage (which I pointed out when Mr Cornford first put forward his view in public). When discussing the relative antiquity of the Lycaean and Panathenaic games he says: "I here leave out of account the Olympic games because they are traced back to a period earlier than the origin of man, the legend being that Cronus and Zeus wrestled at Olympia and that the first who ran there were the Curetes." This passage of itself is fatal to Mr Cornford's theory. But he has ignored a still more important authority. Pindar[24] more than six centuries before Pausanias explicitly declared that the Olympic games "were founded beside the ancient tomb of Pelops". It is obvious that any theories of the origin of the Olympic games, which rest only on a legend rejected by Pausanias its narrator, and on a fantastic interpretation of the single combats held at funeral games, must be summarily rejected.

But Mr Cornford's theory breaks down also in details as well as in principle. He finds an analogy between the race of the Curetes at Olympia and the plucking of the branch by the competitor at Nemi. Yet there is not the slightest reference to any foot-race in the various stories relating to that sacred spot. Again, he assumes that the wild olive at Olympia is parallel to the oak at Nemi, regardless of the fact that Sir James Frazer's theory depends on the assumption that the supreme god of the Aryans always dwelt in an oak tree, and that the King of the Wood was the incarnation not of any kind of tree spirit, but only of the oak-tree spirit, which was itself the Sky-god. He thus contravenes his master's teaching in one of its most vital points.

We have now disposed of the fundamental assumptions upon which Miss Harrison and her partners base their theory of the origin of Tragedy – the supposed primitive Sacred Marriage, or *Sacer Ludus* at Eleusis, with which also disappears Dieterich's theory of the origin of Tragedy, that the Dithyramb was a Spring vegetation ceremony in honour of the Year-*Daimon*, at which youths were initiated, that heroes and gods were only "projections" into *choses sacrées* by "group-thinking", and the views of Sir James Frazer, Mr Cook, and Mr Cornford respecting the origin of the Olympic games,

---

[22] *Themis*, pp. 235–6.

[23] viii. 2. 1.

[24] *Ol.* x. 30; cf. Miss W. M. L. Hutchinson's searching review of *Themis* (*Class. Rev.*, vol. xxvii, 1913, pp. 132–4).

whilst at the same time we have seen grave reasons for doubting the validity of Sir James Frazer's theory of the *Rex Nemorensis* at Nemi, on which so many and vast superstructures have been raised. We are now in a position to deal with Professor G. G. Murray's contribution – his modification of Dieterich's theory of the origin of Tragedy.

Let us hear his own account of the joint efforts of himself and his collaborators.[25]

"The following note presupposes certain general views about the origin and the essential nature of Greek Tragedy. It assumes that Tragedy is in origin a Ritual Dance, a *Sacer Ludus*, representing normally the Aition or supposed historical Cause, of some current ritual practice; e.g., the *Hippolytus* represents the legendary death of that hero regarded as the Aition of a certain ritual lamentation practised by the maidens of Troezen. Further, it assumes in accord with the overwhelming weight of ancient tradition that the Dance in question is originally or centrally that of Dionysus; and it regards Dionysus in this connexion as the spirit of the Dithyramb or Spring *Dromenon*, an 'Eniautos Daimon', who represents the cyclic death and rebirth of the world, including the rebirth of the tribe by the return of the heroes or dead ancestors. These conceptions, it will be seen, are in general agreement with the recent work of Dieterich,[26] also with those of Usener[27] as developed by Dr Farnell[28] and the indications of the Macedonian mummeries described by Mr Dawkins and others. I must also acknowledge a large debt to Professor Ridgeway's Tomb-theory, the more so since I ultimately differ from him on the main question, and seek to show that certain features in Tragedy which he regards as markedly foreign to Dionysus-worship are in reality natural expressions of it. It is of course clear that Tragedy, as we possess it, contains many non-Dionysiac elements. The ancients themselves have warned us of that. It has been influenced by the Epic, by hero cults, and by various ceremonies not connected with Dionysus. Indeed, the actual Aition treated in Tragedy is seldom confessedly and obviously Dionysiac. It is so sometimes. Sometimes it is the founding of a torch-race or the original reception of suppliants at some altar or sanctuary. But it is much more often the death or *Pathos* of some hero. Indeed, I think it can be shown that every extant Tragedy contains somewhere towards the end the celebration of a *tabu* tomb. This point we must gladly concede to Professor Ridgeway. I wish to suggest, however, that while the content has strayed far from Dionysus, the forms of Tragedy retain clear traces of the original drama of the Death and Rebirth of the Year Spirit."

Let us now examine the postulates on which Professor Murray's theory depends, and which of themselves are sufficient to raise doubts. He assumes

---

[25] *Themis*, pp. 341 *sqq.*
[26] *Archiv f. Religionswissenschaft*, vol. xi, pp. 163–96.
[27] Ibid., vii, pp. 303–13.
[28] *Cults*, vol. v, p. 235, note A.

(1) that mankind in its primitive stages has no individual thinking, but this is not supported by any cogent facts; (2) that man revered the abstract before the concrete, the Universal before the Particular, a proposition refuted (pp. 12–13) by the history of the whole human race; (3) that men did not worship or revere actual human heroes, such as Brasidas and Timoleon, and that those of whom we read in Homer and other early Greek literature never existed, but were mere "projections" into *choses sacrées* by "group-thinking" of pre-existing abstract conceptions of the Year Spirit. But we have shown (pp. 47–8) that a *chose sacrée* or relic derives regularly its sanctity or power (Dr Marett's *mana*) from having been a part of or having been closely connected with some human being, or from a belief that such is the case. (4) All depends on the assumption that the *Sacer Ludus* at Eleusis was primaeval. But as I have disproved this by irresistible facts, which have led Sir James Frazer to abandon it, the basis of the Dieterich-Harrison-Cornford-Murray theory is gone. (5) He assumes that the Dance or Dithyramb is originally or centrally that of Dionysus, and he regards Dionysus as the spirit of the Dithyramb or Spring *Dromenon*, an Eniautos Daimon, who represents the cyclic death and rebirth of the world. But we have shown above (pp. 45–7) that at no period was the Dithyramb peculiar to Dionysus, that his festivals were not confined to Spring (p. 44), and that Aristotle, on whom this assumption is really based, nowhere connects the origin of Tragedy proper with Dionysus. As we have already disposed of the theories of Dieterich, Usener, and Farnell, their agreement with Professor Murray's view weakens rather than strengthens it. There thus remains nothing of all Professor Murray's postulates but "Professor Ridgeway's Tomb-theory". Furthermore, he admits that "the content of Tragedy has strayed far from Dionysus", yet he wishes to suggest, however, that "the forms of Tragedy contain clear traces of the original drama of the Death and Rebirth of the Year Spirit".

What is this "original drama" of the Death and Rebirth of the Year Spirit? Nothing more than the sacred drama of Eleusis, on which Dieterich builds his theory. But we have already shown that so far from any drama of this kind being original at Eleusis, it did not make its appearance there until after the Christian era. The only primitive dramatization for which, as we saw, there is evidence at Eleusis was the mimetic search with torches for Persephone in which the descendants of Triptolemus as Torch-bearers took the leading part. But this is not claimed to be a case of the Death and Rebirth of the Year Spirit by Professor Murray or any one else. Its object was to honour Demeter by commemorating her grief for her lost daughter, who, be it remembered, was not recovered by that vain quest. But there is another question of principle before we proceed to deal with the details. Professor Murray's[29] account of the original drama of the Death and Rebirth of the Year Spirit is as follows: "If we examine this kind of myth which seems to underlie the various Eniautos'

[29] *Themis*, pp. 342–3.

celebrations, we shall find (1) an *Agon* or Contest, the Year against its enemy, Light against Darkness, Summer against Winter. (2) A *Pathos* of the Year-Daimon, generally a ritual or sacrificial death, in which Adonis or Attis is slain by the *tabu* animal, the Pharmakos stoned, Osiris, Dionysus, Pentheus, Orpheus, Hippolytus torn to pieces (σπαραγμός). (3) A *Messenger*. For this Pathos seems seldom or never to be actually performed under the eyes of the audience. (The reason of this is not hard to suggest.) It is announced by a messenger. The news comes that Pan the Great, Thammuz, Adonis, Osiris is dead, and the dead body is often brought in on a bier. This leads to (4) a *Threnos* or lamentation. Specially characteristic, however, is a clash of contrary emotions, the death of the old being also the triumph of the new. (5) and (6) An *Anagnorisis*, discovery or recognition, of the slain and mutilated Daimon followed by his Resurrection or Apotheosis or, in some sense, his Epiphany in glory. This I shall call by the general name, *The Theophany*. It naturally goes with a Peripeteia or extreme change of feeling from grief to joy." He next points out the only difficulty that he finds in Dieterich's theory (p. 41), that whereas the *Sacer Ludus* at Eleusis had a joyful *dénouement*, in the typical Greek tragedies the Reversal was from happiness to sorrow. To meet this Professor Murray tries to show that his supposed primitive ritual of the death and rebirth of the Year had a happy conclusion by the resurrection of the god. Traces of this he imagines he finds in the Satyric drama, which gave a joyous conclusion to the Tragic trilogy, but he fails to explain the fact that Thespis knew not the Satyric drama, which was first composed and brought to Athens by Pratinas of Phlius later than 535 BC, and he omits a fact no less important, that Aeschylus, who only began to write after 499 BC, was the first to exhibit trilogies. But it is on the *deus ex machina* of Euripides that he chiefly relies. Starting with the *Bacchae* he assumes (after some German) that Pentheus and Dionysus are one and the same person, or, as he would say, the spirit of the Year, and he finds in the reappearance of Dionysus at the end of the play Pentheus come to life. But he might as reasonably assume that William Rufus and Sir Walter Tyrrell, or Charles I and Oliver Cromwell, were one and the same individual as that Pentheus and Dionysus are identical simply because one killed the other. He next takes the *Hippolytus* in which that hero is killed by his own horses, and in Artemis who appears at the close Professor Murray sees the revived Hippolytus. But as it was not Artemis but his own horses that killed the hero, on his own principles Professor Murray must regard as identical Hippolytus, a pair of horses, and Artemis. Again he points out that the trilogy of Aeschylus of which the *Suppliants* was the second play, ended with the appearance of Aphrodite. But he omits to point out that the *Sparagmos* in this case was the slaying of forty-nine sons of Aegyptus by their respective brides. Again, on Professor Murray's own principles Aphrodite must be identical with forty-nine young men. It is needless to give any other examples, as we have cited what he considers his strongest cases.

But a moment's reflection will convince the reader that the features which Professor Murray takes as characteristic of this ancient ritual drama of the death and rebirth of the Year can be found not only at any moment in human life, but in the whole realm of nature. For example, on a garden lawn is a happy family, two old sparrows feeding their young; enter the lady's favourite cat; she pounces on a baby sparrow (*Peripeteia*); a short struggle (*Agon*), speedy death (*Pathos*), and the cat retires rending her victim (*Sparagmos*). All under the eyes of little Tommy, who (*Messenger*) runs in to tell his mother what the naughty cat has done; meantime the parent sparrows are expressing their grief (*Threnos*) in unmistakable terms; the lady comes forth and discovers (*Anagnorisis*) the cat (*Theophany*) returning (possibly with an eye to another of the brood), her former victim lodged comfortably inside, the two now in process of forming one body, if not one personality.

Professor Murray proceeds:[30] "Lastly, there are some plays in which our supposed Year-Daimon makes his Epiphany not as a celestial god, but as a ghost or hero returned from the grave. It is obvious that he is quite within his rights in so appearing; he is essentially a being returned from the dead, and his original ritual Epiphany was a resurrection."

Most readers will be astonished to find that in obedience to the exigencies of a preconceived hypothesis Darius, son of Hystaspes, one of the best authenticated personages in all history, is turned into a mere manifestation of the Year-Daimon. "The hero or as he is called the God ($\theta\epsilon\acute{o}s$, 644 &c., $\delta\alpha\acute{\iota}\mu\omega\nu$, 642) Darius is evoked from his sacred tomb." "After the Pathos related by the Messenger comes a Threnos and an *evocation* of the dead king or god, Darius." This strange conclusion is due to the fact that Professor Murray and his partners follow Sir James Frazer in assuming that not only Dionysus, Adonis, Attis, and Osiris were mere phases of the Vegetation or Year spirit, but also in assuming that mankind first grieved and lamented for the supposed sorrows of these mere abstractions, and that only later they began to grieve and lament for their own woes and disasters.

Is it seriously maintained that in the Balkans, Asia Minor, and Egypt, of old the seats of the cults of Dionysus, Adonis, and Osiris, women only learned to wail and beat their breasts for the loved child or husband, from ritual lamentations in honour of empty abstractions? But we have already seen that the concrete in human life always precedes the abstract, the Captain Boycott before the verb to boycott, and so *ad infinitum*. The One in the Many – the Universal that runs through all Particulars – was only discovered by the philosophers, like Socrates and Plato, but certainly formed no part of the mental furniture of the ordinary Athenians of their time, much less of the early Greeks or of any other primitive race.

---

[30] *Themis*, pp. 348–50.

But another of the main supports of the edifice reared by Professor Murray and his partners – Sir James Frazer's doctrine that Dionysus, Adonis, Attis, and Osiris were mere names for the abstract Vegetation spirit – has suddenly given way, and thus involves the downfall of their airy castle. Sir James Frazer in the preface to the third edition of *Adonis, Attis, Osiris* (1914), now writes: "Following the example of Dr Wallis Budge, I have indicated certain analogies which may be traced between the worship of Osiris and the worship of the dead, especially of dead kings, among the modern tribes of Africa. The conclusion to which these analogies appear to point is that under the mythical pall of the glorified Osiris, the god who died and rose again from the dead, there once lay the body of a dead man," and though he endeavours to save some fragments of his theory by trying to draw a distinction between the stories of Adonis and Attis and that of Osiris, I have hopes that the evidence given in this work (pp. 86–93) will show that there is no better reason for still regarding the two former as abstract Vegetation or Year spirits than there is for Osiris. But if "under the mythical pall of the glorified Osiris" once lay the body of a dead man, may not the same hold true for Dionysus, who is termed by the Greeks not only *theos* but also *heros*, i.e., one who had been a real human personage, but treated with divine honours after his death? The fact that Dionysus had an oracle at his oldest sanctuary, that on the top of the Pangaean range in Thrace, in the light of evidence to be cited later (p. 376) will point clearly to the same conclusion.

What now becomes of Professor Murray's theory of the origin of Tragedy? What becomes of the doctrine that Ajax, Achilles, Agamemnon, Odysseus, and all the other Greek heroes, and even Archelaus, king of Macedon, and Darius, son of Hystaspes, were mere "projections" into *choses sacrées* by "group-thinking"? What becomes of his theory of the *Sparagmos* of Osiris, Dionysus, Pentheus, Orpheus, and Hippolytus if his mainstay Osiris turns out to have been a real human being? There is nothing left of the elements with which he started to frame his hypothesis except "Professor Ridgeway's Tomb-theory", i.e., the worship of the dead.

That a certain ancient ritual can be detected in Greek tragedies I gladly admit, for I have maintained that such there is, and that it arose out of the funeral rites and periodical celebrations to honour the good and noble or to appease the malevolent. But such burial rites, including the representation of the dead man himself (as at Rome), solemn dances, and athletic contests were practised by mankind in Mediterranean lands, and all the world over in some form or other before the cult of Dionysus had issued from Thrace or Zagreus had been given a place in the Mysteries of Eleusis.

We have already seen that these ancient rites were regarded by the Greeks as an offering of firstfruits, i.e., harvest-thanksgiving, that the oldest part of the ceremonial was the worshipping of the dead succeeded by races, like those

regularly held at actual funeral and periodic celebrations of historical personages, such as Brasidas and Timoleon. It may turn out in our investigations
that the Mysteries of Eleusis arose out of the custom of offering the first-fruits
of the harvest to the spirits of the dead, before the living partook of them. It
may also turn out that wherever initiatory Mysteries such as those on which
Miss Harrison and her partners rely are to-day held amongst savage races,
the essential part of the initiation is the presentation or introduction of the
youths to the ancestors of the tribe.

This is not the place to treat of the origin of Comedy, but Mr F. M.
Cornford in the preface to his recently published *Origin of Attic Comedy* (1914)
has put forward the hypothesis that "these traditional forms" still traceable
in the content of the Aristophanic play were inherited from a ritual drama,
the contents of which can be reconstructed, and that "the ritual drama lying
behind Comedy proves to be essentially of the same type as that in which
Professor Gilbert Murray has sought the origin of Tragedy". But what that
ritual was not, and also what it really was, has been made clear in the preceding
pages – primitive funerary rites. Even if Mr Cornford could prove that it was
not mere obscene buffoonery, but a Dionysiac fertility ritual which lay behind
these phallic songs, still common in certain cities in the days of Aristotle, and
out of which he states that Comedy arose, this Dionysiac ritual would be nothing more than the worship of one who had been once a human being, and of
certain of his parts or imitations thereof. This proposition will be made clear
in our section on Uganda, pp. 381, 384.

In the following pages I propose to test the truth or falsehood of the propositions set forth above – that Vegetation, Corn and Tree spirits, as well as those
of rocks, mountains, and rivers, and what are collectively termed Totemistic
beliefs, are not primary phenomena, totally independent of the belief in the
continued existence of the human soul after the death of the body, but are
merely secondary and dependent on the primary belief in the immortality or
durability of the soul: that men first pray to the dead and not to abstract spirits
for rain and good crops; that in gratitude they make offerings of the firstfruits
to the dead; that it is only at a late stage that Corn, or Maize mothers, Harvest
and Food goddesses, i.e., generalizations, appear; that mankind has sought and
still seeks to win the favour of the dead by periodical offerings, athletic contests, and mimetic dances which refer to the lives of the departed, and that
Tragedy arose out of these dramatic dances in honour of the dead. If the facts
derived from the history and living practices of non-European races, civilized
as well as barbarous, should establish these propositions, we may rest assured
that Greek Tragedy also arose in the worship of the dead.

24

INTRODUCTION TO APOLLODORUS, THE LIBRARY

James Frazer

James Frazer, by far the most celebrated of all myth-ritualists, was himself ambivalent toward the theory. His own disparate versions of myth-ritualism aside, he was a fervent intellectualist and, like Ridgeway, a euhemerist as well as a myth-ritualist. While never abandoning myth-ritualism, Frazer moved further and further away from it. In the following brief excerpt from his introduction to his translation of the Library of Apollodorus, who amassed Greek myths and other stories, Frazer not only touts intellectualism but also castigates myth-ritualism. The brand of myth-ritualism he spurns is not, however, that of his apparent targets, the Cambridge Ritualists, but the long superseded version of his friend and mentor, Smith. For Frazer, myth is an explanation of the world – primarily the physical world, as for Tylor, but also the social world. Frazer does not deny that myth explains ritual. He denies that it explains only ritual. Elsewhere in his introduction he espouses euhemerism, while in The Golden Bough the reigning theory of myth is myth-ritualism. On Frazer's fluctuating and inconsistent views of myth see Robert Ackerman, "Frazer on Myth and Ritual," Journal of the History of Ideas 36 (1975), 115–34; and Ackerman, The Myth and Ritual School (New York: Garland Publishing, 1991), 55–60.

By myths I understand mistaken explanations of phenomena, whether of human life or of external nature. Such explanations originate in that instinctive curiosity concerning the causes of things which at a more advanced stage of knowledge seeks satisfaction in philosophy and science, but being founded on ignorance and misapprehension they are always false, for were they true they would cease to be myths. The subjects of myths are as numerous as the objects which present themselves to the mind of man; for everything excites

Original publication: James Frazer, "Introduction to Apollodorus, The Library," Loeb Classical Library (London: Heinemann; New York: Putnam's, 1921), vol. I, pp. xxvii–xxviii.

his curiosity, and of everything he desires to learn the cause. Among the larger questions which many peoples have attempted to answer by myths are those which concern the origin of the world and of man, the apparent motions of the heavenly bodies, the regular recurrence of the seasons, the growth and decay of vegetation, the fall of rain, the phenomena of thunder and lightning, of eclipses and earthquakes, the discovery of fire, the invention of the useful arts, the beginnings of society, and the mystery of death. In short, the range of myths is as wide as the world, being coextensive with the curiosity and the ignorance of man.[1]

---

[1] By a curious limitation of view some modern writers would restrict the scope of myths to ritual, as if nothing but ritual were fitted to set men wondering and meditating on the causes of things. As a recent writer has put it concisely, *"Les mythes sont les explications des rites"* (F. Sartiaux, "La philosophie de l'histoire des religions et les origines du Christianisme dans le dernier ouvrage de M. Loisy," *Revue du Mois*, Septembre–Octobre, 1920, p. 15 of the separate reprint). It might have been thought that merely to open such familiar collections of myths as the *Theogony* of Hesiod, the *Library* of Apollodorus, or the *Metamorphoses* of Ovid, would have sufficed to dissipate so erroneous a conception; for how small is the attention paid to ritual in these works! No doubt some myths have been devised to explain rites of which the true origin was forgotten; but the number of such myths is small, probably almost infinitesimally small, by comparison with myths which deal with other subjects and have had another origin.

25

THE EVIDENCE OF DIVINE KINGS IN GREECE

H. J. Rose

The English classicist H. J. Rose (1883–1961), who was Professor of Greek at the University of St Andrews, was intrigued by many theories of myth but skeptical of nearly all of them. In the following selection (in *The Sacral Kingship* [Leiden: Brill, 1959], 371–8) Rose puts to the test the key assumption in Frazer's more popular version of myth-ritualism: that ancient and primitive kings were considered to be divine. Rose argues that at least in ancient Greece they were not. Insofar as he is prepared to theorize even provisionally about myth, Rose is a Tylorean: myth for him is a pre-scientific explanation of the world. See the introduction to his *A Handbook of Greek Mythology* (London: Methuen, 1928). In the first of his three lectures on *Modern Methods in Classical Mythology* (St Andrews: University of St Andrews Press, 1930), he speculates that myth is, as for Smith, an explanation of ritual but that, à la Tylor, it presupposes a religious explanation of the world.

I need not spend much time defining a "divine" or as I sometimes say a "Frazerian" king. He is a phenomenon common to many parts of the world and not a few centuries of man's history, and his characteristics are, that he is an incarnate god, that in consequence he can beneficially affect the life of his people, especially by bringing rain and fine weather as desired, that his powers depend upon his bodily vigour, and that in consequence his reign is limited, for either after a fixed period or on the approach of old age he is really or in a ceremonial pretence put to death, or at all events deposed, and his godhead with the concomitant earthly sovranty passes to a younger man. The question is, not whether such kings exist or have existed, for Frazer has proved beyond

Original publication: H. J. Rose, "The Evidence of Divine Kings in Greece," in *The Sacral Kinship/La Regalità Sacra*, VIIIth International Congress for the History of Religions (Leiden: Brill, 1959), pp. 371–8.

question that they do, or have done, but simply whether there is any sufficient reason for supposing that they were to be found at any time in classical Greece. If we can find kings who were gods, or who were notable weather-magicians by virtue of their office, or who were not allowed to reign longer than a certain period, we shall be obliged to answer more or less decidedly in the affirmative. If we can find none of these appurtenances to Greek royalty, we must say that either there were never any such kings there, or all trace of them has disappeared from our documents.

The most thorough-going and by far the most learned defence of the proposition that they did exist is found in that gigantic work of the late Prof. A. B. Cook which is entitled simply *Zeus*. I therefore take most of my material from it, feeling that if Cook's case for divine kings in Greece proves unsatisfactory, no other is likely to win favour before any impartial jury. For completeness' sake, I begin by saying a word about the most noteworthy pre-Hellenic kings, those of Minoan Crete. We have abundant archaeological evidence that a Minoan king was a very important person; the magnificence of his palace shows that. We also know that the palace contained a chapel full of sacred emblems and the like. But further, archaeology does not go. We do not, for instance, find in Minoan art any scene which clearly shows us what Oriental art often displays, the king in company with gods, or even sacrificing to them, or to the great and important goddesses whom the Minoans seem to have worshipped. The one piece of evidence which suggests that Crete may have known divine kings is in the *Odyssey*, where a well-known and often quoted passage tells us that Minos was king for nine years and was the speech-mate of great Zeus (τ 178–79). This may mean that his reign was limited and that he was in some sense divine; it may equally well mean that he was a priest-king in close connection with, presumably, the local "Zeus", the year-god, as he seems to have been, of whose cult we know about enough to tantalise us. In any case, it does not tell us anything about Greek kings proper.

Passing then to them, and trusting for our information partly to surviving kingships in historical times, such as those of Sparta, partly to what Epic and saga generally have to tell us of vanished sovranties, we find at once that kings had, at least in some cases, priestly functions, hence e.g., the priesthoods held by the Spartan kings, and the survival at Athens, not indeed of a real king, but of an annual magistrate who bore the title of king and had sacerdotal duties among others. In particular, his wife took part in the remarkable sacred marriage with Dionysos at the Anthesteria ([Dem.] lix, 76, Arist., Ἀθ. Πολ., 3,5). But as every householder had priestly functions of a kind in his family worship, and priesthood was not a separate status in Greece, but an office which practically any citizen not specially disqualified might fill, this gets us no nearer a divine king. We can only say that when there were kings at Athens, they had not only secular but sacred functions, which is about equivalent to saying that they were Greek magistrates. And if we pass from Athens to Elis and consider the tragic tale of Salmoneus and how he pretended to be Zeus and made imitation thunder and lightning until a real thunderbolt smote him for his presumption, although it has long been recognised that behind the moral legend there lies some ancient piece of weather-magic, nothing in the tradition hints that Salmoneus and no one else had by virtue of his sovranty the right to perform such magic, still less that he had aught of divinity in his person. The rite was carried out *pro populo*, as a Roman would say; priests who were no kings performed weather-magic on as large a scale for sundry communities (Fiedler, *Antiker Wetterzauber*, pp. 13 ff. for cxx.), and I have already mentioned the Greek kings had priestly functions. A better example, in the sense of being a rather nearer approach to a Frazerian king, is again given in the Odyssey (τ 109 ff.) in the famous description of the virtuous and godfearing monarch under whom the people prosper and earth and sea yield their fruits abundantly, ἐξ εὐηγεσίης "because of his good leadership", if that and not εὐεργεσίης is the right reading. But here again, the poet insists on the piety and justice of the king, and it is a commonplace that the gods reward such conduct. If one evil man can harm a whole city (Hesiod, *W.D.* 240), it is only fair that one good man, in a position to enforce just and pious dealings in the rest, should bring down the benediction of the gods he zealously worships.

Not much, I think, can be made of sundry legends to the effect that this or that king of old days was called by a divine title. It is to be noted that such stories mostly are of Hellenistic date, that is, of a time when the deifying of kings was a commonplace, often hardly more than a piece of formal loyalty. Let us examine one or two. Periphas, of whose legend Cook makes a great deal (*Zeus* II, pp. 1121 ff.), we know only from Antoninus Liberalis 6, who presumably got his information either from Boios, the source of the preceding and following items, or from some such author as Nikandros, therefore from a Hellenistic source. Ovid knows of the story, but just mentions it in passing, *Met.* vii, 399–400; again his source is very likely to be Alexandrian. Periphas then was, so to speak, a pre-Adamite king, for he was so very ancient that Kekrops had not yet been produced from the Earth. He was a pattern of justice and also extremely devoted to the worship of Apollo. His loving and admiring subjects made over to him the festivals and some at least of the titles of Zeus (the shadow of Euhemeros lurks somewhere in the background of this), and the real Zeus was minded to stop this impiety with a thunderbolt. However, at the instance of Apollo he compromised by turning Periphas into an eagle and his wife Phene into the bird of that name, a sort of vulture or lammergeyer, which is a bird of good omen to men. Now a king whose name means something like Very Brilliant and who ends by passing into the well-known Minoan avatar of a bird has certainly some claim to be considered divine, if the story really goes back to any old tradition. But the connection is, to my mind, anything but Frazerian. So far from seeing a divine king in Periphas, I incline rather to suppose him a faded god whose cult was later absorbed by that of

Zeus or perhaps of Apollo. All conjectures, however, must be uncertain, for we have nothing but the myth, no trace of this Periphas surviving in cult.

I have next to consider the fairly long list of figures, ranging, roughly, from Agamemnon to Asklepios, to whose names that of Zeus is reported on one authority or another to have been appended. For these I see no one explanation. Some probably are due to syncretism. For example, since Zeus is (among other titles) Soter and Soter is also a favourite title of Asklepios, I see no reason why the minor, but enormously popular god should not have been on occasion identified with the greater one. It makes no difference whether we assume Asklepios to have been originally a god or, what I consider more probable, a hero. In the former case we may compare Zeus Meilichios, certainly chthonian (like Asklepios) and certainly called Zeus wherever he was worshipped, in Greece and out of it. I would here remember that according to Aeschylus, for instance (*Supp.* 230–31) there is another Zeus in the lower world who judges men's sins after their death. The father of gods and men was, I think, early grown so great that, like the Hebrew Yahweh, the heaven of heavens could not contain him and his power spread to the lower world, where indeed, as art and literature alike testify, his grim brother Hades much resembled him in features: *uoltus est illi Iouis sed fulminantis* (Sen., *H.F.* 724–25). It would be easier still for the sky-god, whose titles include that of Georgos, to take within his scope a chthonian whose epithet of "kindly" suggests that he could and did bestow on men the benefits of the earth's increase. If on the other hand Asklepios was a hero to begin with, he was not the only one to have so great a title attached to him. Agamemnon, with much less reason, got the same honorific epithet in Hellenistic days; our first intimation of it is in Lykophron (*Alex.* 335, 1124, 1369) and Staphylos (*ap. Clem. Alex., Prot.* p. 28, 17–18 Stählin). How this came about, I do not know. If we had any real reason to suppose that early Greek kings were seriously taken to be divine (not merely "honoured even as a god", as Homer repeatedly says), the matter would be quite clear, of course, and that is how the supporters of that view do explain it. But this hypothesis does not account for the late date of our testimonies, which if it were correct ought to be early and supported by writers less open to the suspicion of judging other kings by the frequently deified Ptolemies than the historian and poet in question. But give their evidence its fullest possible weight; suppose that Zeus-Agamemnon not only was worshipped, as both Staphylos and Lykophron say, in Sparta, but had been worshipped there for centuries when they wrote; I still have never been convinced of the falsity of a suggestion I made many years ago (*C.R.* xxxv, pp. 147–59) that as the conception of Zeus broadened and gained in majesty in superior minds, the vulgar tended to make the name lose definite content and become little more than an epithet meaning something like "super-human", "non-human", or the like. But be that as it may; our earliest evidence of how kings were regarded, written in days when kings still had real power and were highly honoured, gives us no authority whatever for supposing that they were then considered divine, nor that they ever had been.

And here I would pass to a recurrent fallacy, as it seems to me, which the spread of anthropological knowledge has not yet eradicated from all classical scholars, a naïve misapplication of the Comparative Method. All civilised peoples have, beyond doubt, a savage past; from this truth it has been, and for some still is, far too easy to go on to the tacit, even unconscious, assumption that all civilised peoples have in their past any and every savage custom or belief which can be shown to exist, or lately to have existed, among existing backward cultures. A rather glaring instance is the readiness which is still shown in some quarters to assume the former existence of totemism for districts, such as Europe, from which there can be produced no sort of proof that it was ever in vogue. In like manner there have been and still are researchers, by no means lacking in either erudition or ingenuity, who blithely assume for Greece the former existence, and consequently the more or less fossilised survival, of practices which belong not only to a much lower level of culture than the classical Hellenic but also to a kind of culture the existence of which anywhere in the Greek area at any time is a thing to be cogently demonstrated, not lightly assumed. I quote as an example a recent work (it appeared in 1944 as one of the publications of the Faculty of Philosophy at Liège), by Marie Delcourt, entitled *Oedipe ou la légende du conquérant*. This work explains Oidipus as a "ritual" hero, an embodiment of a method of succession to kingship supposed once to have existed on Greek soil, which among other things involved the killing of the old king by the new, *le rite de la succession par meurtre*, as the author calls it. We are to suppose, that is, not only that there once was such a rite in Greece, which is the whole question at issue, but furthermore, that some vague memory of it survived long enough to colour the existing tales. But if we look at our material, we do indeed find stories of the deaths of kings, sometimes at the hands of their successors, but no hint that these were the result of anything but conquest or unscrupulous ambition or, as in the case of the death of Laios, a chance quarrel. To allow that now and then, as old stories assert, A killed B and took his throne is to assume what other evidence justifies us in supposing, that in pre-classical Greece there were times of disturbance and that στάσις was no more an unknown phenomenon then than it was in the sixth and fifth centuries BC, or in much more recent days. I can see no grounds for making any further assumption, certainly not for assuming sociological and religious practices totally foreign to everything in historical Greece of which we have clear proof. Nor am I at all impressed by statements, perfectly credible in themselves, to the effect that now and then an old king, feeling incapable of carrying out his ordinary secular duties in peace and especially in war, retired in favour of a younger man, like Laertes in the *Odyssey* and Kadmos in the *Bacchae*. It surely needs no belief in the divinity of kings to hold that a vigorous prince in his thirties or so will make a more efficient head of a little community liable to be at war any moment than one weakened by the oncoming of old age. That the old king was in no way obliged to retire is clear enough from the example of Nestor, who evidently still held the reins of government in his own hands when perhaps seventy years old or thereabouts, although when it came to actual fighting he could do no more than appear on the field to encourage the rest, and now and then to give them the dangerous task of rescuing him, while in peace one may suspect that much of the actual day-to-day business of governing was carried out by his sons under his supervision.

Much the same tacit and fallacious assumption seems to me to be illustrated by any such suggestion as that of A. B. Cook (*Zeus* III, p. 733), that the birth of Athena was in some sense a reminiscence of the killing of an aged king. It contradicts the entire tone of Greek myth, a fundamental assumption of which is that the gods do not die, and the details of that particular story, which never hints that Zeus was any the worse for the cleaving of his head by Hephaistos or some other skilled operator, or was even for a moment incapacitated for his divine functions. Furthermore, it supposes a vague consciousness (in this case, belonging to certain vase-painters who occasionally show Zeus grey-haired) of the supposed custom, whereof not a word is said in any Greek author, even in places where, if the least recollection of it existed, one would suppose some mention of it inevitable, notably in those few writers who mention the singular ritual of the Rex Nemorensis in Italy, which as is well known furnishes the text for Frazer's greatest and most famous work. And it is to be remembered that Greece, especially Hellenistic Greece, had a number of writers who were full of intelligent curiosity regarding ancient custom and legend, and made extensive and systematic researches, whereof considerable remains survive to this day. There were also numerous theorists who sought to give a rational account of the origins of religion and of the received opinions regarding the traditional gods. Their speculations were of the most varied character, and included the notorious theory of Euhemeros, that Zeus and all his kind were prehistoric kings given divine honours by admirers or flatterers. The *argumentum ex silentio* is I think valid here; why does neither Euhemeros himself nor any of his followers and imitators adduce any characteristic of the divine kings we know from Frazer? The Euhemeristic Zeus has an adventurous and successful career, but he neither controls the weather nor has his reign limited by anything like a ritual killing nor is by nature anything more than a daring and able ruler.

Such are all the serious arguments for "Frazerian" kings in Greece that I have been able to find. Of minor ones I take little account; I am for instance quite unimpressed by the circumstance that the royal (if mythical) name Akrisios resembles Ἀκρισίας, which according to Hesychios is a name (or title) of Kronos in Phrygia. To conclude that Akrisios "was the royal embodiment of a sky-god" (*Zeus* II, pp. 1155–56) seems to me merely a piece of unscientific temerity. Still less am I inclined to give any credit to the statement of a puzzle-headed Byzantine (Tzetzes, *Chil.* I, 474) that anciently all kings were called *Dies*, for which he gives an astrological reason, hence one which cannot be of earlier than Hellenistic date at best. Sundry arguments again adduced from traditional royal costume (e.g., the eagle on the sceptre) point to one thing only, the world-wide tendency to make a god resemble an earthly monarch. As with the Roman *triumphator*, it is not the king or magistrate who dresses like the god, but the god who is thought of as dressed like a king. I therefore hold confidently to the opinion that, whatever may be true for other countries, Greece from the earliest days in which its population was in any sense Greek down to the close of the classical epoch had no kings of the kind made famous by *The Golden Bough*.

26

THE MYTH AND RITUAL POSITION CRITICALLY EXAMINED

S. G. F. Brandon

In the following essay the English historian of religion S. G. F. Brandon (1907–71), who was Professor of Comparative Religion at the University of Manchester, questions how fully Hooke's pattern holds for all of the ancient Near East. Brandon asks whether all Near Eastern kings were considered to be divine; whether all chief gods in the Near East were vegetation gods; and, in the case of Israel, whether the emphasis was really cyclical and agricultural rather than linear and historical. To Hooke's credit, Brandon's essay appears in one of Hooke's own symposia on myth-ritualism: *Myth, Ritual, and Kingship* (Oxford: Clarendon Press, 1958), ch. 9. See also Brandon, "Divine Kings and Dying Gods," *Hibbert Journal* 53 (1955), 327–33. On Brandon see *Man and His Salvation: Essays in Memory of S. G. F. Brandon*, Eric J. Sharpe and John R. Hinnells, eds (Manchester: Manchester University Press; Totowa, NJ: Rowman & Littlefield, 1973).

Since the year 1795, when Charles-François Dupuis set forth the view[1] that behind the figures of Christ and Osiris, of Bacchus and Mithra, there lay a common tendency to personify the sun in its annual course, the comparative study of religions has been generally characterized by attempts to find some common interpretative principle which will account either for the origin of religion or for its essential structure. The motive behind such attempts is intelligible, and it may well be compared to the tendency manifest in many

Original publication: S. G. F. Brandon, "The Myth and Ritual Position Critically Examined," in *Myth, Ritual, and Kingship*, ed. S. H. Hooke (Oxford: Clarendon Press, 1958), pp. 261–91.

[1] *L'Origine de tous les cultes ou la religion universelle* (nouv. éd., Paris, 1822). On Dupuis see *La Grande Encyclopédie*, t. 15, p. 97. Cf. G. Berguer in *Histoire générale des religions*, ed. M. Gorce et R. Mortier, t. i (Paris, 1948), p. 8.

other disciplines to seek one simple formula which will explain an immense corpus of otherwise amorphous data. But these attempts, which have generally occurred successively and often in consequence of each other, have resulted in the history of the comparative study of religions assuming the appearance of a chronological record of the rise and fall of various so-called "schools", which are severally distinguished by the peculiar theories concerning the origin or nature of religion which their members advanced or defended. Thus, to name but a few representative examples: the so-called "Philological School" of Max Müller and his followers sought to account for religious origins in terms of a solar mythology by means of comparative philology;[2] the reactions which this line of interpretation provoked found a common expression in the efforts of those scholars who turned for a solution to anthropological research and of whom one of the earliest and most distinguished representatives, Sir Edward B. Tylor, set forth animism, i.e., "belief in Spiritual Beings", as what he termed "the minimum definition of Religion".[3] An even greater name in this "Anthropological School" is that of Sir James G. Frazer – indeed by reason of his prodigious labours in assembling material and in advancing certain hypotheses in the interpretation of it his name still remains, despite criticism and changing modes of thought, the most significant in this field of study. The work of Frazer, based as that of the "Anthropological School" generally on the assumption of the soundness of the evolutionary principle in the interpretation of culture,[4] was largely devoted to showing how profoundly the needs of the agriculturalist's life had affected religious concept and practice. The spectacle of the annual cycle of Nature's year, with its recurrent drama of the death and revival of vegetation, inspired, so he maintained, the pregnant idea of the dying-god, of which Adonis, Attis, and Osiris are the classic examples, and from which derived the institution of divine kingship, whereby communities at a certain level of cultural development believed that their well-being was essentially bound up with the well-being of their king, who impersonated or was the incarnation of the spirit of vegetation.[5]

Frazer in his interpretation of religious origins had also advanced the thesis that an "Age of Magic" had preceded the "Age of Religion",[6] and in support of this view he had cited a great abundance of evidence concerning the magical

[2] E.g., Max Müller, "Comparative Mythology" (1856), in *Chips from a German Workshop* ii (London, 1867). Cf. L. Spence, *Introduction to Mythology* (London, 1921), pp. 47–51.

[3] *Primitive Culture* i (London, 1929, 1st edn 1871), 424.

[4] But Frazer fully realized the complexity of the issue and the vital part played by cultural diffusion, cf. *Balder the Beautiful* (*Golden Bough, VIII*), i, Preface, pp. vi–vii; *Folklore in the Old Testament*, i. 106–7; "Sur l'étude des origines humaines" in *The Gorgon's Head and other Literary Pieces* (London, 1927), pp. 348–55.

[5] The theme in its various aspects finds expression throughout the constitutive parts of *The Golden Bough*.

[6] *The Dying God* (*Golden Bough*, iii. 1936), p. 2.

rites practised by primitive peoples whereby mainly by the action of miming they sought to cause the recurrence of phenomena advantageous to themselves. This evaluation of the importance of ritual was in due course so developed by the late Professor Gilbert Murray[7] and the late Dr Jane Harrison[8] in interpreting ancient Greek religion that the claims of ritual magic to be one of the primary factors in the origin of religious concept became generally recognized. Closely associated with this new appreciation of ritual came a re-evaluation of myth. In early times myth had been generally regarded either as the poetic imaginings of primitive peoples or it was interpreted aetiologically, i.e., as being the naïve explanations of natural phenomena concocted by the primitive mind. But now attention was given to the close connexion holding between ritual and myth, and since the former was generally believed to be prior in order of appearance, myth in its original form was held to be an explanation of the ritual, a kind of libretto designed to make intelligible sacro-magical acts when the original emotions which prompted them were no longer remembered or understood.[9]

It was in this setting, constituted by the trend of thought in the field of *Religionsgeschichte*, that the so-called "Myth and Ritual School" emerged in the third decade of the present century. As seen in that context, it appears as an intelligible derivation from the work of Frazer[10] and the new estimate of the function of ritual and myth, and it may also be fairly regarded as another instance of that same tendency to seek a formula which will neatly explain the origin or nature of a complex of religious faith and practice.

Intelligible though it be when seen in such a context, the "Myth and Ritual" thesis is not thereby adequately explained in the matter of original inspiration, and it would seem that there is yet another factor of considerable significance concerning which a reckoning must be made. A clue to the nature of this factor is surely to be found in the fact that the majority of those scholars who co-operated with Professor S. H. Hooke in the original publication of the thesis in 1933 were men who were Profoundly concerned with the interests of the Christian religion; most of them, moreover, were Old Testament

---

[7] "Excursus on Ritual Forms preserved in Greek Tragedy", in J. E. Harrison, *Themis* (Cambridge, 1912); *Five Stages of Greek Religion*, chap. i (the substance of the book was originally delivered as lectures in 1912).

[8] *Prolegomena to the Study of Greek Religion* (Cambridge, 1907); *Ancient Art and Ritual* (London, 1913).

[9] Cf. W. R. Smith, *Religion of the Semites* (3rd ed., London, 1927), pp. 17–20, see also S. A. Cook's notes, op. cit., pp. 500–3; A. N. Whitehead, *Religion in the Making* (Cambridge, 1927), pp. 8–17; E. O. James, *Comparative Religion* (London, 1938), pp. 97–100; G. van der Leeuw, *La Religion dans son essence et ses manifestations* (Paris, 1948), pp. 404–5; M. Éliade, *Traité d'histoire des religions* (Paris, 1949), pp. 350–73; Chantepie de la Saussaye, *Lehrbuch der Religionsgeschichte* (ed. A. Bertholet u. E. Lehman, Tübingen, 1925), i. 93–94; E. Cassirer, *An Essay on Man* (New Haven, 1944), pp. 79–83; T. H. Gaster, "Myth and Story", *Numen*, i (1954), pp. 184–212.

[10] The work of A. M. Hocart should also be noted in this connexion: his *Kingship* was published in 1927 and he contributed to the symposium *The Labyrinth*.

scholars.[11] It is, therefore, not altogether surprising that five out of the original eight lectures, which formed the symposium *Myth and Ritual*, were concerned with the various aspects of the so-called "Myth and Ritual pattern" as manifest in the cultures of Palestine, and as constituting issues which ultimately had significance for Christian theology.[12] And to what may be described as this general professional interest there may have been an even deeper-lying motive, which can be reasonably defined, although its existence cannot be demonstrated. It is that the "Myth and Ritual" thesis represents a reaction on the part of certain scholars to the great emphasis which had hitherto been laid upon the essential significance of the prophetic movement and tradition in the religion of Israel. The prophet had been exalted to the detriment of the priest, the inspirational element in religion at the expense of the cultic. Whether such considerations were consciously felt or subconsciously operative,[13] the "Myth and Ritual" thesis did in fact help to redress the balance by showing that in the cultus of Israel there was a factor which proved as influential as that of prophecy in shaping the thought and aspirations, not only of Israel, but also of Christianity, and it is surely significant that this tacit *apologia* for the cultus coincided with a renewed interest in this country and on the Continent in the liturgical heritage of the Christian Church.[14]

To complete the account of those factors which appear to have been influential in the genesis of the "Myth and Ritual" thesis consideration must also be given to the theory concerning the diffusion of culture propounded by Sir Grafton Elliot Smith and W. J. Perry, according to which certain fundamental inventions and institutions of human society, having been first achieved in Egypt, had gradually been diffused among the other peoples of the ancient world: among such institutions was notably that of divine kingship.[15] As will be noticed at greater length presently, the exponents of the "Myth and Ritual" thesis have variously based themselves upon the diffusionist and the evolutionary theories of culture; nevertheless it is evident in the earliest statements of the thesis that the view that the pharaonic kingship of Egypt had powerfully

[11] The Preface to *Myth and Ritual* (Oxford, 1933) by Canon D. C. Simpson is significant in this connexion.

[12] In the succeeding symphsium edited by S. H. Hooke entitled *The Labyrinth* (London, 1935) the same interest manifests itself in the majority of the essays.

[13] In his Preface to *Myth and Ritual*, pp. xiii–xiv, Dr Simpson was evidently conscious of the issue.

[14] The controversy aroused by the measures to revise the *Book of Common Prayer* in 1927 and 1928 and the publication by the S.P.C.K. of the symposium *Liturgy and Worship* in 1932 may be mentioned in this connexion.

[15] The chief works in which the diffusionist theory was expounded prior to 1933 were G. Elliot Smith, *The Ancient Egyptian and the Origins of Civilization* (London, 1911, 2nd edn 1923), *Human History* (London, 1930); W. J. Perry, *The Children of the Sun: a Study in the Early History of Civilization* (London, 1923); *The Growth of Civilization* (1924). Cf. A. J. Toynbee, *A Study of History* i (London, 1935), 424–40.

influenced the ideas and institutions of neighbouring peoples was accepted as virtually axiomatic.[16]

As seen now across more than twenty subsequent years of discussion, discovery, and research, the original exposition of the "Myth and Ritual" thesis may also be reckoned as the first notable effort to reap the harvest which the archaeology of the Near East had been steadily producing. From the discovery of the celebrated Amarna tablets in 1887 to the uncovering of the ancient city of Ugarit, at the modern Ras Shamra, in 1929, evidence had been accumulating to show that among the peoples occupying what the late Professor J. H. Breasted had aptly called the "Fertile Crescent" there had been a lively commerce, with its consequent intermingling of cultural elements and influences, so that justification was given for thinking of the ancient Near East as an integral culture-area.[17] Viewed in this light, similarities which were found to exist between the ideas and institutions of the various peoples dwelling in that area were naturally suggestive of a common attitude and response to certain situations. Moreover, this predisposition in particular was conducive to an appreciation of that which in the culture of Israel, traditionally regarded as the "peculiar people", attested the basic integration of Israelite culture with that which seemed common to the area. But, as will be shown in greater detail presently, by making of the undoubted similarities occurring in the cultures of the ancient Near East the basic assumption of the existence throughout the area of a common cultural tradition in the matter of the institution of kingship, the exponents of the "Myth and Ritual" thesis tended to disregard the equally or even more significant differences which existed in the *Weltanschauungen* of the cultures concerned.

With this basic assumption there was closely linked in the "Myth and Ritual" thesis another, namely, the validity of the concept of "culture-pattern" and the possibility of its effective diffusion outside the sphere in which it was created. In the two volumes in which the "Myth and Ritual" thesis was first published no formal definition of a "culture-pattern" was given,[18] but from

---

[16] *Myth and Ritual*, pp. 6, 8–9, 11–12, 71–73, 86 (S. H. Hooke), 87–88 (F. J. Hollis), 117, 118, 121, 123–4, 129 (W. O. E. Oesterley), 149 (E. O. James). It is significant that the Egyptologist, Prof. A. M. Blackman, who contributed to the volume, ends his essay by noting "an indication that the original 'pattern' was not a product of Egypt but was imported thither, possibly from Syria" (op. cit., p. 39).

[17] Cf. ed. Meyer, *Geschichte des Altertums* (Stuttgart u. Berlin, 1913), i. 680–3; A. Moret, *Des clans aux empires* (Paris, 1923), pp. 185–6, 246, 341–8, 401–3; W. F. Albright, *From the Stone Age to Christianity* (Baltimore, 1946), pp. 1–33, 35–36.

[18] In *Myth and Ritual*, p. 8, S. H. Hooke does give this partial definition: "The ritual pattern represents the things which were done to and by the king in order to secure the prosperity of the community in every sense for the coming year." In *The Labyrinth*, p. 260, E. O. James makes what may be deemed a definition of certain aspects of the "pattern": "Around the divine kingship a series of religious activities was set in motion in the great agricultural civilizations of the ancient East which had for their purpose the maintenance of the food supply and the prosperity of society in general, as well as the satisfaction of individual needs." Cf. E. O. James, *Comparative Religion*, pp. 94–95.

the use of the term in many passages it is evident that the authors believed that in certain cultures there can be perceived a number of interrelated ideas and practices which may be considered as constituting a unified whole which has its own logic and is expressive of a specific communal endeavour to deal with some situation which threatens the common good and/or which might be made to serve the common welfare. This complex of idea and practice, or in the "Myth and Ritual" terminology the "culture-pattern",[19] it is further maintained, can be, in fact has been, diffused from the culture in which it originated and established effectively within alien cultures or at least among alien peoples. Now the mode of such a diffusion is never explicitly described, and the most that may be inferred from various allusions and references is that such "culture-pattern," were diffused in consequence of war or trade or colonization. But the issue involved here is too important to permit the assumption to be passed without a closer scrutiny of its practical aspects. Accordingly it may be noted that in a pertinent passage Professor Hooke maintains that, just as the symbol of the winged sun-disk was diffused from Egypt to Assyria, Cappadocia and Persia, so "it is also possible to conceive of the carrying of the larger ritual pattern with its associated myth from one country to another by one of the various ways of 'culture spread', such as commerce, conquest, or colonization".[20] However, the very example which is here chosen in support of the theory does itself raise doubt about the soundness of that theory, because it is evident that, while Hittite, Assyrian, and Iranian artists did copy this famous Egyptian symbol, its original significance was not understood by them – quite obviously it was the general form of the symbol which impressed the foreigner and he reproduced it without insight into its intrinsic meaning, changing its pregnant details according to his own fancy or needs.[21] If this then happened in the transmission of the concrete symbol of the winged sun-disk of Egypt, the question may well be asked how far is the assumption justified that a complex of religious ideas and practice, such as that presupposed in the "Myth and Ritual" thesis, which had been created by a particular people in response to its experience of life in a given geographical environment, could be effectively transmitted to alien peoples? It will be well here to consider again the instance of the winged sun-disk, since it has further significance in this connexion. Because such a symbol was a visible object and could be seen by a traveller

---

[19] It is to be noted that often the term "ritual pattern" is used when its connotation is clearly meant to include other elements than the "ritual". Cf. R. F. Benedict, *Patterns of Culture* (New York, 1934), pp. 23–24, 46, 254. See also J. de Fraine, *L'Aspect religieux de la royauté israélite* (Roma, 1954), pp. 27–32; A. Bentzen, *Messias-Moses redivivus Menschensohn* (Zürich, 1948), p. 16; *King and Messiah* (London, 1955), p. 83 n. 8, p. 84 n. 11.

[20] *Myth and Ritual*, p. 4.

[21] An example of this can be noted in op. cit., fig. i, in the reproduction of the *uraeus* serpents by the foreign artists: quite clearly they did not appreciate this part of the symbol and treated it as a pair of decorative streamers. On the significance of the Egyptian winged sun-disk see H. Bonnet, *Reallexikon der ägyptischen Religionsgeschichte* (Berlin, 1952), *sub nominibus* "Behdeti" and "Uräus".

on many Egyptian buildings or on objects circulated outside Egypt through trade or diplomatic policy, it was easy for a foreign artist to reproduce it, or something like it, in his own land; but, if the foreigner had not been content merely with an approximate reproduction of such a symbol and had sought to understand its spiritual meaning, he would have been obliged to make special inquiry of the competent Egyptian authorities, an undertaking which would have required considerable knowledge of a foreign language and insight into alien modes of thought.[22] It may accordingly be asked who in the countries of the ancient Near East would have been sufficiently interested in, or capable of, surmounting such immense difficulties in order to transmit to their own people the esoteric "culture-pattern" of some alien folk? Merchants, soldiers, or colonists are certainly not cast for this role, and it is instructive to note what happened when educated men in the ancient world did specially seek to understand and interpret a culture alien to their own – the strange accounts which Herodotus gave of Egyptian customs and Plutarch's version of the Osirian myth have provided several generations of Egyptologists with a fascinating task of trying to identify their queer statements with what is known of ancient Egyptian faith and practice from the native records; and the general verdict is that these Greek savants utterly failed to apprehend the true nature of Egyptian religion.[23]

The assumption that "culture-patterns" existed and could be effectively disseminated from their original centre among the peoples of the ancient Near East prepares the way for the next assumption, namely, that there existed a definitive "culture-pattern" centred on the institution of divine kingship which was thus disseminated and which came to constitute a common tradition of faith and practice throughout that area. It is a crucial part of the "Myth and Ritual" thesis that this "culture-pattern" found dramatic expression at an annual festival in which the king played an essential part. The constitutive elements of the ritual enacted at this festival are defined as "the dramatic

[22] The Egyptians' fear of dying and being buried in a foreign land, which is graphically described in the Middle Kingdom story of Sinuhe (Erman–Blackman, *Literature of the Ancient Egyptians*, pp. 14–29), is evidence of their conviction that foreigners could not really understand the essentials of Egyptian religion. The Phoenician attempts at embalming the bodies of certain magnates and their burial in anthropoid sarcophagi were obviously inspired by knowledge of Egyptian funerary practice, but it is equally obvious that such imitation did not imply an intelligent adoption of the Egyptian mortuary faith; cf. G. Contenau, *La Civilisation phénicienne* (Paris, 1949), pp. 155–6, 197–202, plates xi, xii; E. A. W. Budge, *The Mummy* (Cambridge, 1925), p. 431. See also H. Frankfort *The Art and Architecture of the Ancient Orient* (London, 1954), pp. 66, 117, 157–61, 197–201.

[23] Cf. Sourdille, *Hérodote et la religion de l'Égypte* (Paris, 1910), pp. 363, 365–6, 401; W. Spiegelberg, *Die Glaubwürdigkeit der Herodots Berichte über Ägypten im Lichte der ägyptischen Denkmäler* (Heidelberg, 1926), pp. 16–18, 34–40; A. Erman, *Die Religion der Ägypter* (Berlin u. Leipzig, 1934), pp. 86–87, 333, 425–6; E. A. W. Budge, *Osiris and the Egyptian Resurrection* i (London, 1911), 18. Megasthenes's identification of two Indian gods with Dionysos and Herakles is also significant in this connexion; cf. C. Eliot, *Hinduism and Buddhism* ii (London, 1954), 137–8, 139 n. 1.

representation of the death and resurrection of the god"; "the recitation or symbolic representation of the myth of creation"; "the ritual combat, in which the triumph of the god over his enemies was depicted"; "the sacred marriage"; "the triumphal procession, in which the king played the part of the god followed by a train of lesser gods or visiting deities".[24] The clarity with which these liturgical moments are defined and their articulation in the assumed ἱερὸς λόγος demonstrated is certainly impressive, but when a search is made in the relevant expositions of the "Myth and Ritual" thesis for an account of the actual origin of this "ritual-pattern" and for evidence of its occurrence as such in the records of the various cultures concerned, the result is curiously vague and unsatisfactory. If the influence of the pharaonic kingship had been such as is assumed, it is reasonable to expect that in the Egyptian records there should be ample evidence of the existence of this "ritual pattern" as a regular feature of the state-religion of Egypt and, further, of its great antiquity. However, the essay which was contributed to the original symposium by the Egyptologist, Professor A. M. Blackman, despite its considerable value to Egyptological studies, is notable for its generally negative character in this respect. Although, by ranging throughout the whole course of Egyptian history, a number of instances were found which had a certain degree of correspondence to certain moments of the hypothetical "ritual-pattern", nowhere was it shown that there was a regular annual festival in Egypt which reproduced this "pattern" in its essential entirety and thus presumably provided the prototype of such a festival, which was diffused from the valley of the Nile throughout the lands of the Fertile Crescent.[25]

The most convincing evidence of the occurrence of such a "ritual-pattern" at an annual festival is actually provided by the records of the New Year festival at Babylon.[26] But the significance of this evidence may well be questioned; the actual documents concerned are relatively late in date and Babylon cannot, without qualification, be regarded as representative of Mesopotamia generally back to the era of Sumerian hegemony,[27] and still less may it be taken

---

[24] *Myth and Ritual*, p. 8 (S. H. Hooke).

[25] Cf. H. Frankfort, *Kingship and the Gods* (Chicago, 1948), pp. 34–35, 183–5. 204, 207–9. See also the account of Egyptian kingship given by Bonnet, op. cit., *sub nomin*. "Dreißigjahrfest", "Feste", "König", "Krönung", "Kult", "Theokratie"; see also under "Ernte". Reference might also be made to the account of H. W. Fairman ("Worship and Festivals in an Egyptian Temple", in *B.J.R.L.*, xxxvii. 1954) of the annual festivals, in which the king participated, at the Ptolemaic temple of Edfu: the sacred marriage there had nothing of the character of that assumed in the "Myth and Ritual" thesis (cf. op. cit., pp. 196–7, 200).

[26] Cf. C. J. Gadd, *Myth and Ritual*, pp. 47 ff.; S. H. Hooke, *The Origins of Early Semitic Ritual* (Schweich Lectures, 1935), pp. 8–19, *Babylonian and Assyrian Religion* (London, 1953), pp. 58–60, 103–11; I. Engnell, *Studies in Divine Kingship in the Ancient Near East* (Uppsala, 1943), pp. 18 ff.

[27] The Babylonian evidence for the sacred marriage is actually wanting and the "pattern" has to be completed in this respect from other sources, see Gadd, op. cit., p. 56. "La spéculation

as typical in the matter of the religious faith and practice of various states, not all of them of Semitic origin, lying far to the west and north, unless it can be shown that the culture of Babylon or of some older Mesopotamian state was effectively diffused throughout the area of the Near East.

This consideration leads back to an issue which has already been briefly noticed. It is that in the exposition of the "Myth and Ritual" thesis there appears to be some uncertainty as to whether an original "myth and ritual pattern" was diffused throughout the Near East from some single centre or whether in various places throughout that area similar "patterns" were independently evolved in response to the challenge of similar environments. Each of these alternatives has its own particular set of problems. Generally it would seem that the diffusionist view has prevailed, but with uncertainty as to the original source of the movement. The continuous reference which is made to the pharaonic monarchy as the supreme example of divine kingship suggests that often Egypt is regarded as the original source of the "myth and ritual pattern".[28] But no attempt is made to demonstrate this, which perhaps is not surprising in view of the fact just previously noticed that the Egyptian records provide no evidence of the hypothetical "cult-pattern" having existed as such in the state-religion of the land. That Mesopotamia is assumed to be the original point of diffusion seems to be indicated in certain other statements of the thesis,[29] but here again no definitive attempt has been made to prove that this was so; moreover, as has already been noted, there is a vagueness about the presumed place of origin of the "pattern" in Mesopotamia itself, which in view of the nature of the relevant data is understandable. It is, accordingly, found on examination that not only have the exponents of the "Myth and Ritual" thesis neglected to deal with the practical problems which the idea of a diffusion of an esoteric complex of religious concept and practice inevitably entails, but they themselves do not appear to be clear in their minds on the fundamental point of the location of the original centre from which the "pattern" was diffused.[30]

---

théologique doit adapter les anciens mythes au nouvel état politique et puisque rien n'existe en ce monde, si ce n'est par l'ordre des dieux et le destin qu'ils ont fixé, à l'élévation de Babylone au-dessus des autres cités doit répondre nécessairement l'exaltation de son dieu au-dessus de tous les autres dieux", L. Delaporte, *La Mésopotamie* (Paris, 1923), p. 154. Some allowance must also be made for the religious "reformation" effected about the time of Ḥammurabi, cf. Delaporte, *Le Proche-Orient Asiatique* (Paris, 1948), pp. 139–40.

[28] See the later references of E. O. James, *The Labyrinth*, pp. 244, 249–50, 253–4, *Christian Myth and Ritual* (London, 1937), pp. 1–6, 40–41, 58–62.

[29] Cf. *Myth and Ritual*, pp. 66 (Gadd), 70, 81, 86 (Hooke – in this essay a compromise sometimes seems to appear in the use of the term "Egyptian-Babylonian pattern"), 112–13, 120, 124, 129, 135 (Oesterley): Hooke, *Origins of Early Semitic Ritual*, p. 1.

[30] That the "pattern" might have been diffused from two separate centres, namely, Egypt and Mesopotamia, as some statements seem to imply, must encounter the objection either that it is very improbable that such a "pattern" would have been spontaneously and contemporaneously generated in two different places, or, that, if one of these centres had originally borrowed from the other, there is still the same "diffusionist" problem to be solved.

In the final paragraph of his contribution to the symposium *Myth and Ritual* Professor W. O. E. Oesterley suggested that, while the diffusionist theory accounted for the recurrence of the "pattern" among various peoples in what might be termed its classic form, the true cause of its being lay deeper. The passage deserves quotation:[31]

> Behind the central "pattern" with all its varying modifications in different centres among diverse peoples, there were certain underlying conceptions common to the entire world of the Near East, and beyond. Whether expressed in the developed and elaborate ritual of the city-god of Babylon, or in the somewhat similar rites in Erech and Asshur, or in those of the Egyptians on the morning of their New Year, or in those of the Zoroastrian *Naurūz* (New Year Festival), or in the celebrations in Jerusalem in honour of Jahweh, the underlying *motif*, expressed in various ways by different peoples, was the attempt to explain the mysteries of the dying vegetation at the approach of winter, and of the revival of Nature in the spring. While it is clear that in the case both of ideas and ritual the influence of more powerful and cultured peoples exerted itself on the less advanced, yet behind and beneath all was the insistent urge to answer the questions: Why does the vegetation die; how can it be revivified?

In this passage Dr Oesterley touches upon an issue which must be much in the mind of one who seeks to study religion with comparative reference when he finds himself confronted with the "Myth and Ritual" thesis. If the alleged recurrence of the so-called "pattern" is not to be explained by some theory of cultural diffusion but is regarded as constituting specific expressions of a common endeavour to answer some problem basic to the life of man (in this case that of the death and revival of vegetation), ought not similar manifestations of the "pattern" to be found among other peoples than those of the Near East, when they were at a similar state of cultural development and living under similar environmental conditions? A test case at once suggests itself, namely, ancient China, where civilized life was based on agriculture and where climatic conditions produced those tensions arising from the need of certain kinds of weather at different times of the year, which were such potent factors in the religious conception of the Near Eastern peoples. Here indeed the ruler had an essential part in securing the prosperity of the land and this role involved him in the performance of an elaborate ritual, which was regulated

---

[31] *Myth and Ritual*, p. 146. In this connexion the curiously obscure statement of Engnell (op. cit., p. 72) should be noted: "However, as a possible contrary conception one may consider the west-Semitic type as an autochthonous development of an otherwise homogeneous schedule that has actually never been brought together and worked out or, in a word, urbanized, but has remained standing half-way. . . . It offers greater possibilities of doing justice to the original features found in the western area. Yet I am fully aware of the fact that we have at the same time to reckon with an extraordinarily strong influence from abroad, from the Egyptian and the "Hittite", but far more still from the eastern Sumero-Accadian culture. We come, I think, nearest to the truth if we merely say that this western pattern is only an offshoot of the general Near East pattern."

by the calendar; he was, moreover, the "Son of Heaven", who alone could perform those sacrifices which, it was believed, were vital to the well-being of the state.[32] However, despite all this apparent similarity between Chinese kingship and that which existed in the Near East, in Chinese faith and practice there is no trace of those elements which are fundamental to the Near Eastern "ritual-pattern", namely, the concept of the "dying-rising god", the ritual combat, or the sacred marriage.[33] And it may further be noted that in ancient India at a comparable stage of cultural development the power of the Brahman caste effectively prevented the political rulers from acquiring and exercising sacerdotal status and function, and, so far as a claim was made to divinity, it was made pre-eminently by the Brahmans themselves.[34] Accordingly, it seems necessary to conclude that the so-called "ritual-pattern" cannot be regarded as the natural expression in cultic imagery and practice of human societies when living at a specific cultural level and faced with the common challenges of the agriculturist's life. The "pattern", as it has been defined, is clearly an artificial composition and as such it must have had its origin in some specific community of peculiar genius, which inference naturally points to the necessity of adopting some theory of diffusion to account for the alleged recurrence of the "pattern" in a number of different localities; but of the soundness of such a theory it has been found that serious doubt exists.

---

[32] Cf. M. Granet, *Chinese Civilization* (London, 1930), pp. 379–89, 400–2; L. Wieger, *History of Religious Beliefs and Philosophical Opinions in China* (Hsienhsien Press, 1927), pp. 57–60, 63–64; W. E. Soothill, *The Hall of Light* (London, 1950), *passim*. See also "The Mythico-Ritual Pattern in Chinese Civilization", by J. J. L. Duyvendak, and "Zur konfuzianischen Staatsmoral" by E. Haenisch in *Proceedings of the 7th Congress for the History of Religions* (Amsterdam, 1951). The issue here is discussed at length by D. H. Smith in an article entitled "Divine Kingship in Ancient China", which is due to appear in a future number of *Numen*.

[33] The thesis recently advanced by H. G. Quaritch Wales (*The Mountain of God*, London, 1953, pp. 38 ff.) that "a new religion, as part of a cultural pattern originating in Mesopotamia, was introduced to the Yellow River basin in the middle of the second millenium BC", must be considered improbable on two basic points: (i) its interpretation of the role of Enlil in Mesopotamian religion is not demonstrated, (ii) the diffusion of the "cultural pattern" from Mesopotamia to China is rather assumed than proved: indeed on the evidence available for that period it could not be otherwise.

[34] "Verily, there are two kinds of gods; for, indeed, the gods are the gods, and the Brahmans who have studied and teach sacred lore are the human gods", *Satapatha Brahmana*, 11. ii. 2–6, trans. J. N. Farquhar, *A Primer of Hinduism* (Madras, 1911), p. 19. "An examination of all passages in which the masculine *brahmán* is found shows that it denotes in general a distinct class, if not a caste, with their dependents, and is frequently used in direct contrast with the king", A. Hillebrandt in *Encyclopaedia of Religion and Ethics* (ed. J. Hastings), ii. 798a. Divinity was ascribed to kings in honorific titles, but the fact is without significance in the present context, cf. J. Filliozat in *Anthropologie religieuse* (ed. C. J. Bleeker, Leiden, 1955), pp. 115–17. Cf. L. H. Gray in *Encyclopaedia of Religion and Ethics*, vii. 720–1; A. L. Basham, *The Wonder that was India* (London, 1954), pp. 34, 81–93, who shows that ancient Indian kingship was essentially a political institution; see also pp. 120, 138, 141. It is also significant that the only instance of a "dying-god" in Hindu mythology, namely, the death of Krishna, appears in that part of his legend which contains other non-Indian *motifs*.

From this critical estimate of what might be called the assumptive basis of the "Myth and Ritual" thesis attention must now be turned to the interpretation of the data relevant to the establishment of that thesis. Here invaluable work has been done by Professor H. Frankfort in his great study entitled *Kingship and the Gods*[35] and in his Frazer Memorial Lecture;[36] and his demonstration of the fundamental difference between the institution of kingship in Egypt and in Mesopotamia is so satisfactory that the case may be deemed established, so that consideration may now be given to some other issues.[37]

The exponents of the "Myth and Ritual" thesis have rightly emphasized the essentiality of the connexion of the god Osiris with the pharaonic kingship. Osiris was indeed the vegetation god *par excellence* of Egypt, and his cultus, as it found expression in the royal ritual and in certain annual festivals, made manifest the Egyptian belief that the prosperity of the land was vitally integrated with the king's being and function. But to concentrate interest on this aspect of Osiris is to run the risk of misunderstanding or misrepresenting what appears to have been the greater significance of this deity for the inhabitants of the valley of the Nile. Osiris, the "dying-rising god" of Egypt, was pre-eminently the centre of one of the most remarkable mortuary cults ever practised by mankind.[38] Whatever may have been the origins of this deity and whatever part he had in the state cult as a vegetation god,[39] from the earliest documents of Egyptian thought Osiris is the god to whom the individual turned in fervent hope when confronted by the dread prospect of death. It is of the pharaoh's faith in this respect that we are first informed, but a process of democratization can be traced until by the New Kingdom period the ordinary man and woman sought salvation through Osiris.[40] The means by which it was believed that

[35] Chicago, 1948.

[36] *The Problem of Similarity in Ancient Near Eastern Religions* (Oxford, 1951). Cf. S. G. F. Brandon, "Divine Kings and Dying Gods", in *The Hibbert Journal*, liii (1955). For a criticism along somewhat different lines see de Fraine, op. cit., pp. 27–54.

[37] The evidence assembled by T. Fish in his article "Some Aspects of Kingship in the Sumerian City and Kingdom of Ur" (*B.J.R.L.*, xxxii. 1951) should also be noted in this connexion. The account of kingship which C. J. Gadd gives in his Schweich Lectures entitled *Ideas of Divine Rule in the Ancient East* (London, 1948), pp. 33 ff., is significant in view of the fact of his being one of the original contributors to *Myth and Ritual*.

[38] H. Kees, *Totenglauben und Jenseitsvorstellungen der alten Ägypter* (Leipzig, 1926), p. 190; Erman, *Die Religion der Ägypter*, pp. 40, 68–69, 217–21; G. Roeder, *Volksglaube im Pharaonenreich* (Stuttgart, 1952), pp. 156–60; Bonnet, op. cit., *sub nomin.* "Osiris", "Jenseitsglaube" (pp. 344b ff.); J. Vandier, *La Religion égyptienne* (Paris, 1949), pp. 81–107; J. Černý, *Ancient Egyptian Religion* (London, 1952), pp. 84–90.

[39] Cf. A. Moret, *Le Nil et la civilisation égyptienne* (Paris, 1926), pp. 92–112; Vandier, op. cit., pp. 67–69; Frankfort, *Kingship and the Gods*, pp. 200–3, 207–9.

[40] This was first done in a masterly way by the late J. H. Breasted in his *Development of Religion and Thought in Ancient Egypt* (London, 1912), lecture viii. Cf. Frankfort, *Ancient Egyptian Religion* (New York, 1948), pp. 103–5. There is evidence in the Pyramid Texts that Osiris was an ancient mortuary deity whose prestige the Heliopolitan priesthood sought to controvert in favour of their god Atum. Cf. H. Kees, "Das Eindringen des Osiris in die Pyramidtexte", Excursus XXVII in S. A. B. Mercer, *The Pyramid Texts* (London, 1952), iv. 123–39.

this salvation might be achieved was that of the magical assimilation of the deceased with the god, so that, as the devotee was identified with the god in death, he would be one with him in his resurrection.[41] And this death and resurrection was no piece of mystical symbolism, but was conceived of in the most realistic terms. Thus, the myth of Osiris is set forth essentially as a human drama, and the horrors of death are depicted with a brutal realism – for example in the *Pyramid Texts*, in a passage in which the ritual of embalmment is represented in terms of the Osirian drama, a spell against physical decomposition is provided for the deceased pharaoh Pepi:

> Isis comes and Nephthys: the one from the right and the other from the left. . . . They find Osiris, as his brother Set laid him low in *Ndi.t.* Then speaks Osiris Pepi: "Hasten thou to me!" and thus he exists in his name Sokaris. They prevent thee from perishing in thy name *inpw* (Anubis); they prevent thy putrefaction from flowing on the earth according to thy name *sꜣb šmꜥ*; they prevent the odour of thy corpse from being evil for thee in thy name of *Ḥrw ḫꜣti*. . . .[42]

Then:

> Isis brings a libation to thee, Nephthys cleanses thee; thy two great sisters restore thy flesh, they reunite thy members, they cause thy two eyes to appear in thy face.[43]

It is seen then that primarily for the Egyptians Osiris was not a vegetation deity, with whose being the king was intimately associated and whose life-cycle constituted critical points in the course of the year; rather Osiris was the saviour to whom men and women turned for the assurance of immortality and before whom they believed that they would be judged in the next world.[44] Hence, although he may have been solicited for a good harvest, the real significance of Osiris lay in his mortuary role, a fact which is graphically attested by his iconography, for he is ever represented as one who is embalmed for burial and yet holds the emblems of sovereignty and power.[45] And it is only by appreciating this aspect of Osiris that the peculiarity of the Egyptian *Weltanschauung* may be understood. Although the Egyptian was intensely concerned with the

---

[41] The pattern is set in the Pyramid Texts: see P.T., 167 (K. Sethe, *Die altägyptischen Pyramidtexten*, i. 93–94). Cf. G. Thausing, *Der Auferstehungsgedanke in ägyptischen religiösen Texten* (Leipzig, 1943), pp. 21–22.

[42] P.T., 1255–7 (text in Sethe, op. cit. ii. 210–11; trans. L. Speleers, *Les Textes des pyramides égyptiennes* (Bruxelles, 1923), i. 83; S. A. B. Mercer, *The Pyramid Texts*, i. 207). Cf. Thausing, op. cit., pp. 115–16. See also P.T. 722, 725.

[43] P.T. 1981 (text in Sethe, op. cit. i. 478; trans. Speleers, op. cit. i. 115; Mercer, op. cit. i. 295). Cf. Thausing, op. cit., p. 133; Mercer, op. cit. iii. 892.

[44] Eloquent witness of the reality of this judgement before Osiris is afforded by the vignettes to chapters 30 and 125 of the *Book of the Dead*. Cf. *The Book of the Dead: Facsimile of the Papyrus of Ani* (British Museum, 1894), sheet 3.

[45] Cf. Budge, *Osiris and the Egyptian Resurrection*, i. 30–54.

prosperity of his land and enthusiastically participated in those festivals which were designed to promote it, he was obsessed by the thought of his own personal fate when death should strike him down.[46] Consequently it is not strange that the vast bulk of the evidence which has survived of Egyptian life and thought is of a mortuary character, while little remains to illustrate concern with those issues which, according to the "Myth and Ritual" thesis, should have been primary.

This conclusion in respect of Egypt inevitably raises the question whether the impression created by the "Myth and Ritual" thesis in its interpretation of the Mesopotamian data may not similarly place too great an emphasis on certain aspects of religious faith and practice in that land and so obstruct the forming of a balanced estimate. If the New Year festival at Babylon, thus interpreted, were representative of a long-established tradition of faith and practice throughout that cultural area, it must next be asked to what degree was that tradition influential in the formation of the Mesopotamian *Weltanschauung*. At first sight it would appear that, in comparison with the Egyptian faith, religion in Mesopotamia was singularly deficient in encouraging those who professed it to look beyond the scope of this life – indeed, far to the contrary, its grim eschatology was calculated to invest death with the utmost terror.[47] However, despite the consequent concentration of interest on life in this world, it does not appear that state rituals, such as those in which the "Myth and Ritual pattern" presumably found expression, satisfied the spiritual needs of the people, however necessary they were felt to be to the well-being of the community as a whole. Instead the great mass of divinatory and exorcismal texts, which have been recovered by archaeological research, attests the preoccupation of the people with warding off all manner of ills which were believed to be due to the action of evil spirits.[48] And of particular significance is it that in those texts in which Dumu-zi or Tammuz, the dying-rising god of vegetation, is invoked, the deliverance which is sought through his instrumentality is

---

[46] Cf. S. G. F. Brandon, *Time and Mankind* (London, 1951), pp. 32–39; to the references there given add C. E. Sander-Hansen, *Der Begriff des Todes bei den Ägyptern* (Copenhagen, 1942); C. J. Bleeker, "Die Idee des Schicksals in der altägyptischen Religion", in *Numen*, ii (1955), pp. 28–46.

[47] See the *Epic of Gilgamesh*, Tab. VII, vol. iv. 31–41, Tab. XII, 84–153; *Ishtar's Descent to the Underworld* (trans. A. Heidel in *The Epic of Gilgamesh and Old Testament Parallels*, Chicago, 1949, pp. 60, 99–101, 119–28; A. Ungnad, *Die Religion der Babylonier und Assyrer*, Jena, 1921, pp. 86–87, 117–18, 142–50). Cf. A. Jeremias, *Die babylonisch-assyrischen Vorstellungen vom Leben nach dem Tode* (Leipzig, 1887); F. Jeremias in Chantepie de la Saussaye, *Lehrbuch der Religionsgeschichte* (Tübingen, edn 1925), i. 585–8; M. David, *Les Dieux et le destin en Babylonie* (Paris, 1949), pp. 39–40; T. Jacobsen, in *The Intellectual Adventure of Ancient Man* (Chicago, 1946), pp. 202–18, in *Before Philosophy* (Penguin Books), pp. 217–34.

[48] Cf. E. Ebeling, *Tod und Leben nach Vorstellungen der Babylonier* (Leipzig, 1931), pp. 122–62; Hooke, *Babylonian and Assyrian Religion*, pp. 77 ff.; Ed. Dhorme, *Les Religions de Babylonie et d'Assyrie* (Paris, 1945), pp. 260 ff.

never from the common fate after death but from some evil which spoilt the enjoyment of this life. Indeed, if the *Epic of Gilgamesh* may be taken, as it surely must be in view of its great popularity, as a faithful reflection of the Mesopotamian view of life, then the advice which Siduri gives to the hero in his quest constitutes the best comment on the matter at issue here:

> Gilgamesh, whither runnest thou?
> The life thou seekest thou wilt not find;
> (For) when the gods created mankind,
> They allotted death to mankind,
> But life they retained in their keeping.
> Thou, O Gilgamesh, let thy belly be full;
> Day and night be thou merry;
> Make every day (a day of) rejoicing.
> Let thy raiment be clean,
> Thy head be washed, (and) thyself bathed in water.
> Cherish the little one holding thy hand,
> (And) let thy wife rejoice in thy bosom.
> This is the lot of [mankind. . . .][49]

It has already been noted that many of the original exponents of the "Myth and Ritual" thesis were evidently profoundly concerned with the interests of Christian theology; indeed on consideration it may fairly be asked how far the idea of the "pattern" was itself suggested by the Christian *mythos*, because the form which that *mythos* had attained by the end of the first century reproduced in a remarkable way all the constitutive elements of the "pattern". The Christ was a god incarnate and of royal status by virtue of His Davidic descent; He had struggled with the power of evil and descended into Death but had revived again to a new and more glorious life; in triumph He had ascended into the heavens, where He reigned in majesty and dispensed new life to those who served Him. The *motif* of the sacred marriage was there too: the Bride of Christ was the Church and from that union was born the company of the faithful.[50] Indeed so complete did the parallels appear that Professor E. O. James was led to write:

Thus at the beginning of the Christian era the stage was set for a new act in the ancient drama of the divine kingship and its ritual pattern. . . . With the break-up of the Roman Empire the scattered fragments were again brought together, like the dismembered body of Osiris, this time round the figure of a spiritual Divine king "incarnated once and for all in order ever after to rule the souls of

---

[49] Tab. X, col. iii. 1–14; translated by A. Heidel, *The Epic of Gilgamesh and Old Testament Parallels* (University of Chicago Press, 1949), p. 70. For another recent translation see that of E. A. Speiser in *Ancient Near Eastern Texts* (ed. J. B. Pritchard, Princeton, 1955), p. 90a.

[50] Rev. xxi. 2, xxii. 17; cf. Eph. v. 23–32; 2 Cor. xi. 2. Cf. the vision of the Church as a woman in the *Shepherd of Hermes*.

men"; invested in a scarlet robe, a crown of thorns, and a reed for a sceptre, and dying to live on a cross which has become symbolized as the tree of life.[51]

The apparent fulfilment in the Christian *mythos* of the ancient "pattern" is truly impressive, and Professor James ably interpreted it as a notable instance of the *Praeparatio Evangelii*, but it must be recognized that it could with equal aptness be interpreted adversely to the orthodox Christian claim, in that it might be contended that the ancient "Myth and Ritual" pattern provided a set of inherited categories in terms of which Christian soteriology was inevitably formed. However, it appears on closer examination of the issues involved here that the definitive form which the Christian *mythos* achieved by the end of the first century is not to be explained primarily as due either to divine predestination or to the influence of inherited modes of thought, but as the outcome of a peculiar combination of events which can only be properly understood by a detailed investigation of the relevant data. Although such an investigation cannot be attempted here, a summary of a study published elsewhere[52] may be conveniently utilized to demonstrate the need of substantiating each alleged instance of the occurrence of the "Myth and Ritual" pattern by an adequate examination of its historical context.

In the history of Christian doctrine there is perhaps no more significant fact, although it has been consistently disregarded by Christian scholars, than St Paul's attestation that within some twenty years of the Crucifixion there were current two different and rival interpretations of the faith. This attestation is contained in two distinct passages in his Epistles, namely, Gal. i. 6–8 and 2 Cor. xi. 3–4. In view of the fundamental importance of the witness of these passages they must be quoted *in extenso*. In the Galatian passage Paul writes to his converts:

> I marvel that ye are so quickly removing from him that called you in the grace of Christ unto a different gospel (εἰς ἕτερον εὐαγγέλιον); which is not another gospel (ὃ οὐκ ἔστιν ἄλλο);[53] only there be some that trouble you, and would

[51] *Christian Myth and Ritual*, pp. 40–41. See also his essay in *The Labyrinth* entitled "The Sources of Christian Ritual". It should be noted that A. Ehrhardt has attempted to show that Christian myth and ritual originated in reaction to Roman emperor-worship (see "Myth and Ritual from Alexander to Constantine", in *Studi in onore di Pietro de Francisci* (Milano, 1955), iv, pp. 423–44.

[52] S. G. F. Brandon, *The Fall of Jerusalem and the Christian Church* (London, 1951, 2nd edn 1957).

[53] "This is not an admission in favour of the false teachers, as though they taught the one Gospel, however perverted (comp. Phil. i. 15, 18)", J. B. Lightfoot, *Saint Paul's Epistle to the Galatians* (London, 1881), p. 76. After a survey of the comparative meanings of ἄλλος and ἕτερος, Lightfoot concluded (ibid.); "Thus while ἄλλος is generally confined to a negative of identity, ἕτερος sometimes implies the negation of resemblance." Cf. K. Lake, *The Earlier Epistles of St Paul* (London, 1930), p. 267 n. 1. ἄλλος ein anderer v. Art'., W. Bauer, *Wörterbuch zum Neuen Testament* (Giessen, 1928), p. 61a, cf. p. 491a sub ἕτερος.

pervert the gospel of Christ. But though we, or an angel from heaven, should preach (unto you) any gospel other (or contrary to: παρ'ὅ) than that we preached unto you, let him be anathema.

In the other passage the Apostle writes in admonition to his Corinthian converts:

> But I fear, lest by any means, as the serpent beguiled Eve in his craftiness, your minds should be corrupted from the simplicity and the purity that is toward Christ. For if he that cometh preacheth another Jesus (ἄλλον Ἰησοῦν), whom we did not preach, or if ye receive a different spirit (πνεῦμα ἕτερον), which ye did not receive, or a different gospel (εὐαγγέλιον ἕτερον), which ye did not accept, ye welcome it (καλῶς ἀνέχεσθε).[54]

Quite clearly in these two places Paul acknowledges that the interpretation of the person and mission of Jesus, of which he was the protagonist, was being challenged in its authority for his converts by another interpretation, which seriously differed from it. Now the significance of the situation obviously depends upon the identity of the exponents of this rival version of the faith. Unfortunately Paul nowhere explicitly states who they were, but it is patent from the profound concern which he shows about their activities that they were no mere group of irresponsible heretics but men who were capable of challenging his authority among his own converts. On further investigation there can be little doubt that these exponents of the rival gospel were none other than the emissaries of the Church of Jerusalem, which means that their teaching represented the interpretation of the status and role of Jesus held by those original apostles and "eye-witnesses" who constituted the *Urgemeinde* of Christianity.[55]

That the teaching of the Mother Church of the faith differed so seriously from that of Paul is clearly a matter of supreme moment, but one also that is most unfortunately complicated by the fact that no documents of that church survived its obliteration when Jerusalem was destroyed by the Romans in AD 70. However, the situation is not completely hopeless, and it is possible by patient research to reconstruct the main tenets of its gospel from scattered allusions and references found in the writings of Paul, in the Acts of the Apostles, the Gospels, in the surviving fragments of Hegesippus, and in the Pseudo-Clementine literature. Accordingly it is found that Jesus was primarily proclaimed as the Messiah of Israel, who would shortly return with supernatural power and glory to "restore again the kingdom to Israel". This proclamation had apparently encountered the serious objection that Jesus had died the accursed death of the Law, and, to meet it, it had been necessary to

---

[54] Cf. A. Menzies, *The Second Epistle to the Corinthians* (London, 1912), p. 78.

[55] Cf. *Fall of Jerusalem*, chap. 4 and pp. 136–153; to the references given therein add M. Simon, *Les Premiers Chrétiens* (Paris, 1952), pp. 70–82.

elaborate an apologetic whereby it could be shown that this death had been foretold by the prophets, pre-eminently by Isaiah in the figure of the Suffering Servant of Yahweh. But such an apologetic, it must be noted, contained no elements of soteriology; the invocation of the Isaianic Servant as a prototype of the crucified Jesus was strictly a defensive move, for it could not have been otherwise in a Judaic milieu, where such an idea as that of the Messiah of Israel dying to save the Gentiles would have been an inconceivable, let alone an outrageous, thing. Consequently, in the definition of their gospel the Jerusalem Christians represented the Crucifixion as an unfortunate accident done in ignorance, but which had been anticipated by divine revelation; no emphasis was placed upon its significance and attention was directed instead to the imminent return of Jesus to redeem Israel. There seems to be evidence also for thinking that the prominence given to the Davidic descent of Jesus meant that his Messiahship was interpreted in a political sense.[56]

To this presentation of Jesus and His mission we know that Paul was vehemently opposed, but unfortunately no formal statement of his own gospel appears in his writings which have survived; however, it is possible to piece together from various parts of the Epistles a coherent outline of the contents of that gospel.

Of key importance is the fact that for Paul the Crucifixion was of supreme significance and its proclamation stood in the forefront of his message. To him it was a supernatural event preordained by God before the aeons. Its explanation was comprised in an esoteric doctrine of mankind's state and destiny which is briefly sketched in 1 Cor. ii. 6–8 and Gal. iv. 1–7. Herein man is represented as held in bondage by the daemonic powers which ruled in the present world-order and which were closely associated with the celestial phenomena; to rescue men from this dire condition God had sent a supernatural pre-existent being, a veritable *deuteros theos*, to earth in an incarnated human form, and the daemonic powers, not recognizing his true nature, had crucified him and so, presumably by exceeding their rights, they had forfeited their hold over man. Paul, of course, identified this divine saviour with the historical Jesus, whom he accordingly calls "the Son of God", *Kyrios* and *Soter*. Thus Paul's gospel was a soteriology of universal significance. The *mythos* also had its ritual expression, for in his references to baptism in Rom. vi. 2–5 it is evident that the Apostle taught that salvation was effected by the ritual assimilation, through the baptismal rite, of the neophyte to the saviour in both his death and resurrection.[57]

What would have been the outcome, if these two rival interpretations of the faith had been left to struggle together for the allegiance of the Church,

---

[56] Cf. *Fall of Jerusalem*, chap. 5; H. J. Schoeps, *Theologie und Geschichte des Judenchristentums* (Tübingen, 1949), pp. 71–73, 78–98, 157.

[57] Cf. op. cit., chap. 4.

is unknown. Judging by the resources of the rival exponents of them it would seem that victory must ultimately have gone to the Jerusalem leaders, because their authority and prestige as the first disciples far outweighed the claims of Paul. However, it was fated that the issue should be decided by extraneous forces. In the year 66 the Jewish nationalists revolted against the Roman suzerainty and four years later, after a disastrous struggle, the cause of Israel was lost with the utter destruction of Jerusalem and its Temple. In this catastrophe the Christian community of Jerusalem was in some way involved, because after AD 70 it disappears completely from the life of the Church. It was in the reconstruction of Christian life and thought which followed these shattering events that there was born that synthesis of the rival gospels of Paul and the Jerusalem *Urgemeinde* which constitutes the classic *mythos* of Christian soteriology and which first found expression in the Markan Gospel. Herein were fused into a single figure the picture of the historical Jesus, of royal descent, the Messiah of Israel, and the concept of the incarnated divine saviour of Paul, who by his vicarious death had redeemed mankind and whose mystic bride was the Church.[58] And thus in the Christ of Catholic theology was sublimely manifest the apparent fulfilment of those ancient adumbrations of a divine king who dies to give his people new life. But the fulfilment was apparent only, because it was not the achievement of forces of which the operation may be consistently traced; it was the fortuitous result of a combination of disparate and generically unconnected factors – yet to the eye of faith, it must be admitted, the fortuitous element here may be deemed providential and the events of AD 66–70 be seen as evidence of that divine intervention in history which is the basic concept of the Christian interpretation of the past.

The "Myth and Ritual" thesis by implication raises an important question in another field, but one which is also of vital concern for the comparative study of religion.

By postulating the "Myth and Ritual" complex as the basic religious pattern common to the cultures of the ancient Near East and by attempting to show that this pattern found expression in a series of annual festivals which were related to the course of Nature's year, a situation is implied from which it may reasonably be inferred on *a priori* grounds that a cyclic view of existence must have been held by those who practised such rituals.[59] That such a view was actually held there is a certain amount of confirmatory evidence in Egyptian[60]

---

[58] Cf. op. cit., chaps. 7, 9, 10.

[59] Cf. M. Éliade, *Traité d'histoire des religions* (Paris, 1949), pp. 332–49; *Ly Mythe de l'éternel retour* (Paris, 1949), pp. 83–99.

[60] "Re showeth himself in the morning, and Atum goeth down in Manu. Men beget, women conceive, and every nose breatheth air – day dawneth, and their children go one and all to their place." (Quoted from the so-called "Song of the Harper" of the New Kingdom period; Eng. trans. by A. M. Blackman in A. Erman's *Literature of the Ancient Egyptians* (Methuen, London, 1927), p. 252.)

and Mesopotamian[61] documents, although the fact leaves unanswered the question whether such a view had been inspired by some "myth and ritual" pattern or whether that pattern, if it existed, would have been a specific expression of a *Weltanschauung* which had been formed by the operation of other causes. However that may be, the vital issue here lies in the fact that among the cultures of the ancient Near East there were two of which the *Weltanschauungen* were notably teleological and not cyclic in outlook. The cultures concerned were the Iranian, as conditioned by Zarathustra's reform, and the Hebrew. Since in the present context the significance of the Iranian estimate is more peripheral, attention may be devoted to that of the Hebrews.

If the "Myth and Ritual" thesis be sound in its suggestion that the "pattern" had once an effective currency in Israel through the institution of kingship, it would appear that, not only did a cyclic view of the temporal process never establish itself there, but, on the contrary, the teleological interpretation emerged at a very early period.

The origin of what might justly be called the "Hebrew philosophy of History" is admittedly obscure, but there is reason for thinking that its roots are to be found in the propaganda of the Yahwist party which sought to maintain allegiance to Yahweh among the Israelite tribes after the settlement in Canaan.[62] If Professor Martin Noth's interpretation of the original confederacy of the Twelve Tribes on the analogy of the Greek and Italian amphictyonies be accepted,[63] and there is much reason for so doing, then a situation can reasonably be envisaged after the invasion of Canaan, in which the constituent tribes tended to revert to their former independence, which meant devotion to their own tribal deities and a corresponding forgetfulness of Yahweh, under whose patronage they had achieved their first successful lodgement in the Promised Land. This centrifugal movement had the effect of weakening the invaders militarily, the consequences of which were soon felt in terms of conquest by the reviving power of the Canaanites and perhaps by the newly-arrived Philistines. The situation provided the devotees of Yahweh with a unique opportunity to press the claims of their deity with considerable assurance of success. Their message to their compatriots naturally took the form of an appeal to the memory of the past – that, when they had been faithful, Yahweh

---

[61] Cf. A. Jeremias, *Handbuch der altorientalischen Geisteskultur* (Leipzig, 1913), pp. 193–204, in Hastings, *Encycl. Rel. and Ethics*, i. 185: A. Rey, *La Science orientale avant les Grecs* (Paris, 1930), pp. 155 ff. The decreeing of destinies for the ensuing year was an important factor in the Babylonian New Year festival as C. J. Gadd shows in *Myth and Ritual*, pp. 55–56. Cf. Éliade, *Le Mythe de l'éternel retour*, pp. 89–94; F. Jeremias in Chantepie de la Saussaye, *Lehrbuch der Religionsgeschichte* (Tübingen, 1925), i. 505–12.

[62] Cf. S. G. F. Brandon, *Time and Mankind* (London, 1951), pp. 63–72.

[63] M. Noth, *Das System der Zwölf Stämme Israels* (*Beiträge z. Wiss. v. Alt. u. N. Test.*, Vierte Folge, Heft 1, Stuttgart, 1930). Cf. W. F. Albright, *From the Stone Age to Christianity* (Baltimore, 1946), p. 215; H. H. Rowley, *From Joseph to Joshua* (Schweich Lectures, 1948, London, 1950), pp. 102 ff., 126; Brandon, op. cit., pp. 71–72.

had done mighty deeds for their fathers: if now they would return to their allegiance to him, he would forgive them and redeem them. The appeal rested on a sound military logic, for return to Yahweh meant the unification of their forces, and, hence, increased military strength and a better chance of victory against their oppressors.

Thus Yahwism acquired its characteristic preoccupation with history, or at least an accepted tradition about the past. In its earliest form this attitude probably found expression in cultic formulae[64] and the exhortations of prophets. Whether it would have survived long in such form is a matter for speculation, but its survival was guaranteed from about the ninth or tenth century by a creation which is quite unparalleled in any other ancient religion. A writer (or a school of writers), usually designated the Yahwist, composed out of various fragments of tradition, legend, and folk-lore, a unique conspectus of the past from the very act of Creation. The composition was a work of genius, because out of such disparate material a coherent narrative was fashioned in which Yahweh was shown as guiding the course of history in order to fulfil his promise to the nation's ancestor, Abraham, that of his descendants he would make a great people and settle them in the land of Canaan. Yahweh's character as the "Lord of History" was thus exhibited in a dramatic narrative and the Israelite tribes acquired thereby the sense of a common ancestry and a divinely guided past.[65]

The influence of this Yahwist achievement was profound, and it set the pattern for all subsequent Hebrew thought. Even the great vicissitudes of fortune which the nation subsequently suffered failed to shake its conviction in the providence of its god, and the darker Israel's political situation became the more fervent grew Israel's hopes that Yahweh would eventually intervene to save them and destroy their enemies. Accordingly, the distinctive Hebrew *Weltanschauung* was formed, whereby the passage of time was regarded teleologically as the gradual unfolding of the divine purpose and its irresistible achievement. Hence, whatever encouragement the periodic festivals of kingship may have given to a cyclic view of existence, that encouragement was too weak a thing to challenge the teleologically conceived *Weltanschauung* of Yahwism.

And the Yahwist teleological interpretation of the past was destined to exercise an even greater influence, outside the bounds of Judaism, through Christianity. The scheme of Jewish apocalyptic clearly shows itself in the earliest Christian documents, and from their testimony it is evident that primitive Christian thought was essentially teleological in outlook. Even the problem caused by the continued delay of the expected *Parousia* of Christ did not disturb this mode of thought, nor did the subsequent process of Hellenization,

[64] Cf. Brandon, op. cit., pp. 69, 72.
[65] Cf. Brandon, op. cit., pp. 63–84, and the references there given. See also G. Hölscher, *Geschichtsschreibung in Israel* (Lund, 1952), pp. 119, 134–5.

which might have introduced the cyclic view of time which was native to Greek thought. Indeed, far to the contrary, by utilizing Paul's apologetic theory of "Godly Remnant", which was the true Israel, the Church was able to lay claim to the traditional Jewish philosophy of History and so to formulate the theory of the two divine covenants, the Old and the New, which eventually found abiding expression in the chronology which divides the stream of time by the Incarnation into two parts, designated respectively the era "Before Christ" and that of the *anni domini*.[66]

Accordingly, it must be deemed remarkable, if the "myth and ritual pattern" had succeeded in establishing itself in both Hebrew religion and Christianity, that the influence of the concomitant cyclic view of existence never seriously challenged the dominance of that peculiar teleology of Yahwism which by its very genius was inimical to the premisses of the "myth and ritual" complex.

In the phenomenology of religion the ritual pattern envisaged in the "myth and ritual" thesis belongs to the class of seasonal rites which expresses a consciousness that human life is faced with recurrent crisis through the cyclic process of nature's year. In this sense it is to be distinguished from another class of ritual practice which is concerned with the perpetuation or re-creation of the efficacy of a unique event of the past.[67] The principle involved here may be described as the magical or ritual perpetuation of the past, and it represents a mode of primitive thought and action which has had a very long and remarkable history. It appears in Palaeolithic times in the famous painting of the so-called "Dancing Sorcerer" in the cavern of the Trois Frères in the *département* of Ariège. The motive behind the production of this picture would seem to be that of perpetuating the potency of a magical dance after the action of that dance had finished in time.[68] The idea which was thus adumbrated at this remote period finds some notable forms of expression in subsequent ages. One of the most remarkable is that enshrined in the Osirian mortuary ritual, which we have already noticed. Herein it was sought by the use of imitative magic to make available to the devotee, on whose behalf the rites were being celebrated, the efficacy of a past event, namely, the resurrection of Osiris.[69] The same principle found expression in the ritual of the Christian Eucharist; indeed it may truly be said that therein it achieved its classic form. The quintessence of the rite lies in a ritual re-presentation of the historical death of Christ on

[66] Cf. Brandon, op. cit., chap. viii and the references given therein.
[67] Cf. Brandon, op. cit., p. 23. "Le temps qui a vu l'événement commémoré ou répété par le rituel en question est *rendu* présent, 're-présenté' si l'on peut dire, si reculé qu'on l'imagine dans le temps", Éliade, *Traité d'histoire des religions*, p. 336.
[68] Cf. Brandon, op. cit., pp. 17–18. For a photograph and drawing of this figure, which is partly painted and partly engraved, see the Abbé Breuil, *Quatre cents siècles d'art pariétal* (Montignac, 1952), p. 166, see also pp. 176–7.
[69] Cf. Brandon, op. cit., pp. 29–30, 31.

Calvary for the purpose of pleading that Sacrifice again before God and for making its efficacy available to the faithful, then assembled, or on behalf of certain specified objects. Although in the course of the liturgical calendar this rite assumes the guise of a cyclically recurring festival, its reference to a unique historical event remains essential.[70]

In view of these considerations, doubt must again surely be felt about the presumed ubiquity of the so-called "Myth and Ritual" pattern in the ancient Near East and also about its supposed influence. Indeed it would be ironical, if the "Myth and Ritual" hypothesis be sound, that it was just in that cultural area in which the "pattern" was supposed to have originated and flourished that the tradition of a teleological *Weltanschauung* developed, while in India, where it had no such currency, a cyclic view of existence was generated to become the basic premiss of both Hinduism and Buddhism.

According to its terms of reference this essay has been consistently critical of the "Myth and Ritual" thesis. Moreover, since it is designed to be a contribution to a symposium on this subject, care has been taken not to enter too deeply into those fields which were being specifically covered by other contributors. Observance of these limitations has inevitably meant that little or no account has been given here of those aspects of the thesis which have met with general approval in the academic circles concerned and which have been very adequately and ably described by Professor Hooke and Professor Widengren in their papers. But the present contributor would not like the impression to be given by his own critical consideration of the thesis that he is not appreciative of the significance of those aspects and that he does not recognize the achievement of those scholars who originally expounded the thesis. He sees the "Myth and Ritual" thesis as one of the major developments in the comparative study of religion, and he believes that, despite all the opposition which it has encountered, when the final adjustments are made it will be found that its contribution has been of the highest importance and that its value is abiding.[71] To particularize, it would seem that the exponents of the thesis have established beyond all doubt the fundamental importance of kingship as a religious institution throughout the various cultures of the ancient Near East. Secondly, that they have succeeded in showing that kingship in Israel must be evaluated in this light, and that, if this is done, many hitherto obscure

[70] Ibid., pp. 169, 177–8, 180–1.

[71] A measure of the influence of the "Myth and Ritual" thesis is to be seen in the fact that the theme of the 7th International Congress for the History of Religions, held at Amsterdam in 1950, was "the mythical-ritual pattern in civilization", and that of the 8th Congress, held in Rome in 1955, was "the king-god and the sacral character of kingship". Cf. *Proceedings of the 7th Congress for the History of Religions* (Amsterdam, 1951); *Atti dell'VIII Congresso internazionale di Storia delle Religioni* (Florence, 1956). The full text of the relevant papers is to be published under the title of *La royauté sacrée*.

passages in Hebrew literature gain a new and convincing meaning, and truer appreciation of the peculiar genius of Israelite religion is thereby made possible. Another aspect of this contribution, which is of the highest import for the study of religion, is constituted by the demonstration which has thereby been given of the fundamental importance of the evidence of ritual and myth for understanding both the ethos and the *Weltanschauung* of ancient cultures.

But what is perhaps the most significant indication of the achievement of the "Myth and Ritual" thesis is to be found by way of a comparison. Between the years 1903 and 1921 the twelve volumes comprising Hastings's *Encyclopaedia of Religion and Ethics* were published. In this great corpus of information under "Ritual" only a cross-reference was given to "Prayer" and "Worship", while the article on "Mythology" treated the question of the ritual origin of myth solely from the aetiological point of view.[72] When one contemplates the great output of works which has been inspired by the "Myth and Ritual" thesis and the interest and reorientation of view which those works represent, it would seem that a veritable renaissance (or reformation) was inaugurated in this field of study in 1933, when Professor Hooke and his colleagues published their symposium.

---

[72] In vol. x, p. 666a of this work, some notice is given of the "myth versus ritual" controversy, reference being made to such books as W. R. Smith, *Religion of the Semites*. Reference to other standard works in the field of *Religionsgeschichte* is of significance in this connexion. The *Histoire générale des religions* (ed. M. Gorce et R. Mortier), 5 tomes, Paris, 1948–52, pays no attention to the "Myth and Ritual" thesis. In the 1950 edition of the *Encyclopaedia Britannica* an article is given under "Myth and Ritual", but it contains no reference to the thesis of Professor Hooke or the work of the so-called Uppsala school in this respect. The last (French) edition of G. van der Leeuw's great work on the phenomenology of religion (*La Religion dans son essence et ses manifestations*, Paris, 1948) takes no cognizance of the thesis. M. Éliade, in his *Traité d'histoire des religions* (Paris, 1949), accepts A. R. Johnson's interpretation of Yahweh's victory over Rahab (p. 343), but has nothing to say of the thesis as a whole beyond making a bibliographical reference to it (p. 371). The *Eranos-Jahrbuch*, Bd. XVII, 1949 (Zürich, 1950), contains a paper by E. O. James entitled "Myth and Ritual"; A. Bertholet in his *Wörterbuch der Religionen* (Stuttgart, 1952), pp. 327–8, says briefly that "die Begründung des Kultus durch den Mythus das Sekundäre ist". He does not apparently discuss "Myth and Ritual" as such. G. Mensching, in his *Vergleichende Religionswissenschaft* (Heidelberg, 1949), merely mentions *Myth and Ritual* in a bibliographical note (p. 100). It may also be noted that the "Myth and Ritual" thesis appears to have played no part in the "Entmythologisierung" controversy associated with Rudolf Bultmann. H.-C. Puech in the *Bibliographie générale* to the *Mana* collection on the History of Religion (printed in J. Vandier, *La Religion égyptienne*, Paris, 1948), after noticing the two fundamental studies, contents himself with a reference to C. Kluckhohn's estimate "Myth and Ritual" in the *Harvard Theological Review*, xxx (1942) (p. xxx). N. Turchi in his *Storia delle religioni*, 2 vols (Florence, 1954), merely gives a bibliographical reference under "Myth and Ritual" (vol. i, p. 73) to Kluckhohn's article in the *Harvard Theological Review* and to the *Eranos-Jahrbuch*, xvii (1949). No notice is taken of the "Myth and Ritual" thesis in the following general works: *De Godsdiensten der Wereld* (ed. G. van der Leeuw, Amsterdam, 1948, 2 vols); *Christus und die Religionen der Erde* (ed. F. König, 3 Bände, Vienna, 1951); *Christus* (*Manuel d'histoire des religions* (de. J. Huby, 8th edn, Paris, 1947); *Histoire des religions* (ed. M. Brillant et R. Aigrain, t. i, Paris, 1953); *Storia delle religioni* (ed. P. T. Venturi, 2 vols, Turin, 4th edn, 1954).

27

THE MYTH-RITUAL THEORY

William Bascom

In "The Myth-Ritual Theory" (*Journal of American Folklore* 70 [1957] 103–14), the American anthropologist and folklorist William Bascom (1912–81), who taught at Northwestern University and at the University of California at Berkeley, challenges the myth-ritualist theory, at least as represented by Raglan. Bascom attacks Raglan on multiple grounds. Raglan, contends Bascom, fails to prove that myth cannot arise from either history or imagination and must therefore arise from ritual. Raglan's pattern fails to fit many of the hero myths chosen by Raglan himself. And Raglan fails to distinguish myth from other genres of folklore. Bascom concludes not that myth is unrelated to ritual but that the case remains unproved. See Raglan's "Reply to Bascom," *Journal of American Folklore* 70 (1957), 359–60. See, in turn, Bascom's "Rejoinder to Raglan and Bidney," *Journal of American Folklore* 71 (1958), 79–80. See, too, the defense of Raglan by Stanley Edgar Hyman (*Journal of American Folklore* 71 [1958], 152–5) and Bascom's reply in the same issue (pp. 155–6). On myth in its own right see also Bascom, "Four Functions of Folklore," *Journal of American Folklore* 67 (1954), 333–49, and "The Forms of Folklore," *Journal of American Folklore* 78 (1965), 3–20.

The theory that various forms of folklore and literature are ultimately derived from ritual has been expounded at considerable length by an active group of scholars,[1] but has received very little attention from American folklorists. Some of our colleagues in related fields have assumed that the ritual theory has been accepted, apparently without demurrer, and it comes as something of a surprise to learn that this is not the case. If not, why have American folklorists

Original publication: William Bascom, "The Myth-Ritual Theory," *Journal of American Folklore* 70 (1957), pp. 103–14.

[1] The extensive literature of these scholars has been summarized by Stanley Edgar Hyman in "The Ritual View of Myth and the Mythic," *JAF*, LXVIII (1955), 462–472; and in an earlier review, *JAF*, LXVII (1954), 86–89.

not criticized or queried it, or challenged the vigorous campaign of such men as Lord Raglan and Stanley Edgar Hyman? It is only in the recent Myth issue of the *JAF*, to which both Raglan and Hyman contributed, that Stith Thompson has injected a few carefully chosen reservations. I propose to undertake an analysis of the ritual theory as presented in Raglan's *The Hero*, the broadest in scope and of most interest to folklorists of the many relevant publications.

Historicity

Raglan's argument is in large part that myths and tales must have their origin in ritual because they do not have them either in actual history or in folk imagination. Almost half of *The Hero* is devoted to an attack on scholars who assume myths and legends to be based on history and use them to supplement or interpret the available written documents. He disposes of the historicity of traditional family pedigrees, local traditions, Robin Hood, the Norse Sagas, King Arthur, Hengist and Horsa, Cuchulainn, the tale of Troy, and traditions of other lands. Much of this argument is based on demonstrating historical inaccuracies in verbal traditions. With this there can be no quarrel except as to the question of degree, which Raglan carries to the ultimate extreme. "Tradition never preserves historical facts." "There are no valid grounds for believing in the historicity of tradition." "As we must continue to point out, there is no good reason to believe that a myth or any other traditional narrative has ever embodied an historic fact."[2]

A major weakness in this argument is that the mass of evidence of historical inaccuracies in folklore, which could easily be extended, does not disprove the possibility of historical origins. If some myths and tales can have their origins in human social situations or other historical events, however inaccurately they may be reported, it is not necessary to look for their origins in ritual any more than in natural phenomena. The fact that verbal tradition is not an accurate historical account does not mean that it cannot have its basis in historical event. Raglan, however, says "If one traditional tale, told as a tale of fact, is completely devoid of fact, then the belief that such stories must have a historical basis is clearly ill-founded" (p. 44). Even the fact that one tale is completely contradicted by historical records does not prove that it, or any other tale, has no basis in historical events. Having been called a "neo-euhemerist" by Hyman on an earlier occasion,[3] I should state clearly that I do not maintain

---

[2] Quotations from Lord Raglan, *The Hero* (London, 1949; first published 1936), pp. 36, 120, 121, respectively. Subsequent page references, to the 1949 edition, are given parenthetically in the text.

[3] Stanley Edgar Hyman, "Dissent on a Dictionary," *Kenyon Review*, XII (1950), 726.

either that all tales have a historical basis or that any of them are completely accurate. But I do believe that some tales can have their origins in human social situations or other historical events, and that some historical facts are transmitted in verbal tradition.

Raglan maintains that peasants and non-literate peoples have no concept of history as such, and no interest in it. "History . . . is the recital in chronological sequence of events which are known to have occurred. Without precise chronology there can be no history, since the essence of history is the relation of events in their correct sequence" (p. 2). And without writing there can be no chronology (p. 4). "Since history depends upon written chronology, and the savage has no written chronology, the savage can have no history. And since interest in the past is induced solely by books, the savage can take no interest in the past; the events of the past are, in fact, completely lost" (p. 6).

Polynesian genealogies and traditions of exploration at once come to mind, as well as American Indian traditions of migration, African accounts of wars and succession of kings, and other legends. "Most illiterate communities have, of course, traditional stories, and these stories may seem to be memories of historical events. They tell of the journeys and victories of heroes, and with some rationalization and rearrangement these journeys and victories can be made to represent historical migrations and conquests. These stories, however, are really myths" (p. 8). Raglan quotes Alfred Nutt, who asked in 1891 and again in 1901, "Is there such a thing as historic myth at all? Do men commemorate tribal wanderings, settlements, conquests, subjugations, acquisitions of new forms of culture, or any other incidents in the collective life of a people in the form of stories about individual men and women? I do not deny the possibility of their so doing; all I ask for is evidence of the fact."[4] Raglan comments, "I cannot learn that anyone ever gave Mr Nutt the evidence for which he asked, no doubt for the very good reason that there is no such evidence" (p. 121).

Van Gennep stated that the French peasantry had completely forgotten the facts of Napoleon's career within fifty years of his death (p. 8), and believed than an incident which is not recorded in writing cannot be remembered more than 200 years. Raglan believes this is too long. "After much consideration I have fixed on the term of one hundred and fifty years as the maximum. I have arrived at this figure, which is of course approximate, in various ways. A careful study of what is known of my grandparents and great-grandparents has convinced me that any fact about a person which is not placed on record within a hundred years of his death is lost. Giving a person about fifty years of active life, we get a hundred and fifty years as the limit. Among ourselves the names of the dead are recorded in various ways, but I believe that among the illiterate, anyone who has been dead a hundred years is completely forgotten. Again I

---

[4] Raglan, *The Hero*, p. 121; Alfred Nutt, "History, Tradition, and Historic Myths," *Folk-Lore*, XII (1901), 339.

have known cases in which old men have succeeded in impressing incidents of their own lives upon children in such a way that the children remember them; but they cannot impress in this way incidents which have not made an impression upon themselves. Matter that is not part of the group tradition thus dies out in the second generation" (p. 12).

This of course does not prove that children upon whom the incidents of their fathers' lives have been impressed may not in turn impress these incidents on their own children. One may therefore ask what about matter which thus becomes a part of the verbal tradition and does not die out in the second, or third, or fourth generation? Raglan's position is clear: it does not exist. "The fact is that all history, except in so far as it has been recorded, or as it can be recovered by archaeologists, is completely lost" (p. 36). "Such evidence as I have been able to collect, then, shows firstly that the alleged historical facts embodied in local tradition are not facts at all, and secondly, that the real facts of history are never preserved by local tradition" (p. 37).

Most anthropologists who have attempted an ethnohistorical reconstruction of the past would probably agree that while an informant's accounts of events which happened during his lifetime can be accepted with the usual cautions, those going back farther than this are questionable but can often be verified by historical documents, and those beyond a century or two are highly suspect and often impossible to verify because of the absence of written documents. The question, however, is whether actual events beyond this point in time can be preserved in verbal traditions.

This is the crux of Raglan's anti-historical argument. He maintains that historical events cannot be remembered longer than 150 years, and that unless they are preserved longer than this they are not truly traditional. It is to the lore that is traditional in this sense that Raglan imputes a ritual origin. It is no problem to find legendary accounts of wars, migrations, and other historically verifiable events, but most of these are relatively recent. By implication Raglan admits that these forms, to which I refer as legends, and which constitute a sizeable portion of the folklore of many societies, have a historical basis. But the real answer to the question he raises must be sought in any historical event, whether perpetuated in verbal tradition or elaborated into myth, legend, or folktale, which has survived more than 150 years.

An answer is to be found in a recent dissertation by Charles Edward Fuller, "An Ethnohistoric Study of Continuity and Change in Gwambe Culture" (Northwestern University, 1955), based on a comparison of the early historical records with the contemporary culture of the Gwambe of Mozambique. The Gwambe, who call their present home Wutonga, claim "that their ancestors came to Wutonga from the Karanga country prior to or during the reign of Gamba, their early chief" (Fuller, p. 12). Recording the experience of the survivors of the shipwreck of the *Sao Thome* in 1589, Diago do Couto wrote "They went to the city of this King Gamba, who would be a league and a half from the river. He, knowing of their coming already, gave orders to receive them well, and to entertain them. The king and his children were Christians baptized by the Padre Goncalo da Silveira, of the Company of Jesuits, who in the year 1560–1561, travelled in these parts among the Barbarians, preaching the law of the Holy Gospel" (Fuller, p. 19). King Gamba's son was baptized in the port of Mozambique in 1559, and arranged for Fr. Goncalo da Silveira and his companion, Fr. Andre Fernandes, to visit Gwambe country, where they spent almost two years as guests of chief Gamba. In their letters they reported that the people of Gwambe were Makaranga from the highlands of the interior (Fuller, p. 16). "The wording of the account suggests that the chief Gamba, their host, had been the actual leader of the group which left Karanga, his father having been defeated by a stronger Karanga chief" (Fuller, p. 17). Because of a classificatory system of kinship terms, a person other than Gamba's biological father may be referred to, but written records document the fact that Gamba was actually the chief of the Gwambe 400 years ago, and that the tradition of Karanga origin has persisted for four centuries.

The Gwambe also occasionally tell legends about early European contacts, probably derived from the Tembe, Maputo, Inyaka, or other coastal neighbors. One reports a disagreement among the chiefs of the Delagoa Bay area as to whether Europeans should be refused permission to pass through their territories, since they were so dirty, disease ridden, and destructive. Another legend – according to a personal communication from Fuller – tells of the killing and prompt burial of white cannibals in the region south of Delagoa Bay. Both of these legends find confirmation in Portuguese records referring to historical events 400 years ago. "When the galleon, *S. Joao* was wrecked on May 25, 1553, off the Natal coast, over 500 persons, half slaves and half Europeans were saved. Their mistreatment of African benefactors on the coastal route north caused trouble which brought death to many. . . . Elsewhere, news of cannibalism, which occurred when Portuguese sailors sought relief from starvation, shocked natives, who killed the offenders who had eaten their fellow tribesmen. Word of this travelled over long distances, and persisted over many years, as other shipwrecked travellers learned later. . . . When, in 1554, the survivors of the *Sao Bento* travelled the same coast they found Africans remembering the ill treatment meted out to them earlier . . ." (Fuller, p. 17). Legendary accounts of mistreatments or hard bargains driven by Europeans might have originated in later periods. But it is most unlikely that the coastal chiefs would have continued for 250 years to debate whether or not to allow Europeans passage through their territories, after having established a precedent in the 1550's, or that they could have been able to persist in killing Europeans on the grounds of intra-tribal cannibalism, even if later European survivors had practiced it. These two historical events, which have been elaborated into legends, have clearly, according to the available evidence, persisted in the verbal traditions of the peoples near Delagoa Bay for far more than two centuries.

Imagination

The second part of Raglan's argument denies that folklore arises from imagination or creative fantasy. Raglan begins by disposing of the nature allegorical school, and then rejects the idea that myths are an attempt to explain nature and the world about him, citing Malinowski's criticism of the latter position (pp. 126–128). He then attacks the idea that the folktale or Märchen is a type of fiction and the product of creative imagination, offering four arguments (p. 133) against it.

First, "No popular story-teller has ever been known to invent anything." In support of this he cites several examples, such as the Eskimo, which show that the narrator is expected to recite a tale "as nearly as possible in the words of the original version" (p. 134). There are, however, societies such as Zuni, where this is clearly not the case. Originality and improvisation operate within certain limits, to be sure, but it cannot be maintained that creativity is lacking in all societies. Raglan continues "in illiterate communities the people as a whole not merely do not invent stories, but they do not even tell stories. The telling of stories may only be done by recognized story tellers, and . . . among many tribes they may tell only the particular stories which they have a recognized right to tell" (pp. 134–135). Granted that invention is an individual, not a group act, does this show that it cannot occur? Even if this statement were true for all societies, which it is not, it has no bearing on the proposition it is purported to support.

Second, "Not only are the incidents in folk-tales the same all over the world, but in areas of the same language they are commonly narrated in the same actual words." Raglan shows that "the fairy-tales of England and France contain not merely the same incidents, but the same or equivalent names" (p. 135) as in Bluebeard and Barbe-bleu, and Little Red Riding Hood and Le Petit Chaperon Rouge. "We must conclude," he says "that one set of tales is a translation" (p. 135), implying that all of the tales of either France or England were borrowed from the other country. "The above seems enough to show that the fairy-tales of one country are not of popular origin, and this being so, we have no reason to assume that the fairy-tales of another country are of popular origin" (p. 135). Here, I confess, I am again unable to follow his reasoning. If some, or even all, English tales are borrowed from France, this is no demonstration that some, or even all of them, were not originated in France. Yet he continues, "If we find reason to believe that a folk-story has been borrowed, even from the next village, its popular origin becomes suspect, since if one community borrows instead of inventing, another may well do the same, and if one item of what passes as folk-lore is borrowed, it is at least possible that all is borrowed" (p. 136).

Diffusion is of course a most important process, but every element in culture, and every plot and incident in folklore, must have been invented at least once, by some individual somewhere. To show that a plot or motif has spread by diffusion even as widely as the Magic Flight does not by any means establish that it could not have had a secular origin or have been the product of some individual's imagination.

Third, "Folk-tales deal as a rule with subjects of which the folk can have no knowledge." They deal, he says, with supernatural beings, kings and queens, princes and princesses; their scenes are laid in palaces and castles, not in the farmyard or the harvest field. If folktales were really composed by the folk, he maintains, they would deal with everyday subjects such as courtship and marriage, seed-time and harvest, or hunting and fishing, with which the folk are familiar, rather than heroic feats of arms and succession to kingdoms. "Even when the characters are supposed to be peasants, the situations and incidents are quite unreal" (p. 138), as in the story of Red Riding Hood. Two possible explanations of this can be put forward, neither of which involves ritual origins. One is that these European folktales originated in the palaces and castles, and eventually seeped down to the peasants. The other is that the peasants found the same gratification in tales of royalty that Americans find in movies about romance and success. Gossip about the affairs of the castle was probably as interesting as the latest romances and scandals of Hollywood or royalty are to Americans today. There is nothing surprising in the fact that people find enjoyment in talking about things that they will never have or about events that will never happen to them.

Raglan continues, "It seems to be supposed, though I have nowhere seen this clearly stated, that the peasant and the savage, although they are great hands at making up stories, are nevertheless incapable of making up the simplest story of the doings of ordinary human beings, and are therefore obliged to have recourse to ogres, fairies, talking animals, and people endowed with supernatural powers, to which conceptions they are led by some mysterious but universal force. It has been suggested that this force operates by means of dreams and hallucinations, but those who make this suggestion fail to realize that dreams and hallucinations cannot put new ideas into the mind" (p. 139). What Raglan seems clearly to be stating is that although they are great hands at making up ritual, the peasant and the savage are nevertheless incapable of making up even the simplest folktale. As Stith Thompson has said, "None of these writers tells us how the ritual itself evolved and how the inventive process which moved from ritual into a story about the gods and heroes is any easier than any other form of invention."[5] Nor does Raglan tell us why it requires greater genius to invent myths or folktales than the complex rituals from which they are claimed to be derived.

It is worth noting, also, that this argument is based on European folklore exclusively. The fact that kings and castles are not found in North American

---

[5] Stith Thompson, "Myths and Folktales," *JAF*, LXVIII (1955), 483.

Indian folklore is not surprising, but is most pertinent here. Moreover, although they involve a variety of wondrous events, one also finds descriptions of hunting, grinding meal, courtship and desertion, and other ordinary human activities. In fact, in most bodies of living folklore one can find enough descriptions of technology, economics, social and political organization, as well as religion and ritual, to extract a description of the daily life, as Boas did using Tsimshian myths.

Fourth, "The exercise of the imagination consists not in creating something out of nothing, but in the transmutation of matter already present in the mind." The argument presented here is that the teller of a folktale, like the architect who designs a house and the literary poet or author, largely reworks familiar materials. I agree with this, but not with Raglan's conclusions that genius and true originality are restricted to the literates, and that it is absurd to suppose the unlettered rustic capable of composing the story of Cinderella. "Every literary community has certain types of story outside which none but exceptional geniuses can venture. As for the folk, they may make minor alterations, mostly for the worse, in existing poems, stories, or plays, but they never compose them for themselves" (p. 143). If the aborigines of the Americas could invent the igloo, snowshoe, toboggan, smoking, *cire perdue* casting, the zero concept, and so forth, could they not also have composed a folktale?

Summarizing the argument thus far, Raglan states "The position which we have now reached is that the folk-tale is never of popular origin, but is merely one form of the traditional narrative; that the traditional narrative has no basis either in history or in philosophical speculation, but is derived from the myth; and that the myth is a narrative connected with a rite" (p. 144). Nothing is traditional unless it is more than 150 years old, and a myth by definition is "a narrative connected with a rite." Raglan cites Hooke's definition of a myth as "the spoken part of a ritual; the story which the ritual enacts," and Jane Harrison, who says "A *mythos* to the Greek was primarily just a thing spoken, uttered by the *mouth*. Its antithesis or rather correlative is the thing done, enacted. . . . The primary meaning of myth in religion is just the same as in early literature; it is the spoken correlative of the acted rite."[6] Like Stith Thompson, I do not believe that Raglan's argument is intended to be as circular as it seems, when he begins his recent article by saying that a myth is simply a narrative associated with a rite, and "then proceeds to show that a myth (that is, a narrative associated with a rite) is indeed associated with a rite."[7]

In support of the theory that all traditional narratives are connected with ritual, Raglan (p. 144) recapitulates five arguments: "(1) That there is no

[6] Raglan, *The Hero*, p. 128; S. H. Hooke, *Myth and Ritual* (Oxford, 1933), p. 3; J. E. Harrison, *Themis* (Cambridge, Eng., 1912), p. 328.
[7] Thompson, "Myths and Folktales," p. 484.

other satisfactory way in which they can be explained. . . . (2) That these narratives are concerned primarily and chiefly with supernatural beings, kings, and heroes. (3) That miracles play a large part in them. (4) That the same scenes and incidents appear in many parts of the world. (5) That many of these scenes and incidents are explicable in terms of known rituals." In my opinion Raglan has failed to demonstrate either that myths and tales cannot have their origin in actual events and situations, or that it is impossible to ascribe them to creative imagination. It is not necessary, therefore, to look to ritual as their only satisfactory explanation. But his evidence for this explanation remains to be examined.

Jocasta and Oedipus

The ritual with which Raglan and many of the others of this school are primarily concerned is that of the early inhabitants of the Nile, Euphrates, and the Indus valleys. It is described as a complex ritual, in which they pretended to destroy the old world and create a new one, and as the means by which the divine king insured the regular flooding of the rivers and general fertility and prosperity. It consisted of a "dramatic ritual representing the death and resurrection of the king, who was also the god, performed by priests and members of the royal family. It comprised a sacred combat in which was enacted the victory of the god over his enemies, a triumphal procession in which the neighbouring gods took part, an enthronement, a ceremony by which the destinies of the state for the coming year were determined, and a sacred marriage." "Whereas the existing accounts of the ritual of Egypt and Mesopotamia provide only for a pretence of killing the king, the traditions of Greece and less civilized countries point to a ritual in which the king was actually killed, either annually, at the end of some longer term, or when his strength fails."[8] An essential and equally potent part of this ritual was the recitation of the myth which outlined the ritual itself.

This ritual is viewed by Raglan not only as the probable origin of the flood myths, but also as the basis for the Oedipus myth. Oedipus, who kills his father Laius, marries his mother Jocasta, and himself becomes king, is the new king who must defeat his predecessor either in battle or mock contest, be enthroned, and enter into a sacred marriage. Raglan's theory substitutes regicide, based on ancient ritual, for Freudian patricide, based on innate sexual desires.

Yet there is no criticism of the Freudian interpretation of this myth. In *The Hero* the Oedipus complex is not even mentioned, all of the ammunition being spent on the theory of ancient Euhemerus. Earlier, in *Jocasta's Crime*

---

[8] Raglan, *The Hero*, p. 153; S. H. Hooke, *The Labyrinth* (London, 1935), v.

(London, 1933), Raglan devoted some pages (70–75) to a criticism of the "two different and indeed contradictory theories of the incest taboo" in Freud's *Totem and Taboo*, including a page-long discussion of the Oedipus complex. Raglan writes: "There seems to be no doubt that this complex occurs among European neurotics, and it may occur to some extent among normal Europeans; but even Freud's own followers have been unable to find it among savages, and have been reduced to the necessity of postulating a repressed repression in order to account for its apparent absence. . . . Among the classes from which Freud drew his data, women often retain their sexual attractiveness until after their sons have reached puberty. . . . Among savages, on the other hand, women age rapidly, and the result of this, combined with low birth-rate and high infant death-rate, is that by the time a boy reaches puberty his mother is normally a withered hag." Aside from the single sentence quoted previously from *The Hero* about dreams and hallucinations, I have found only one other reference to the Freudian interpretation of myths; in *Jocasta's Crime* (p. 136) Raglan mentions "the psychoanalysts, who produce myths from the subconscious much as conjurors produce rabbits from hats."

This is worth nothing, not only because Jocasta's crime and the Oedipus complex stem from the same myth, but also because the rest of Raglan's analysis of myths is closely paralleled by Rank's prior analysis in "The Myth of the Birth of the Hero."[9] As early as 1908 Rank had arrived at the following pattern, which he interprets in Freudian terms: "The hero is the child of most distinguished parents; usually the son of a king. His origin is preceded by difficulties, such as continence, or prolonged barrenness, or secret intercourse of the parents, due to external prohibition or obstacles. During the pregnancy, or antedating the same, there is a prophecy in form of a dream or oracle, cautioning against his birth, and usually threatening danger to the father, or his representative. As a rule, he is surrendered to the water, in a box. He is then saved by animals, or lowly people (shepards) and is suckled by a female animal, or by a humble woman. After he has grown up, he finds his distinguished parents, in a highly versatile fashion; takes his revenge on his father, on the one hand, and is acknowledged on the other, and finally achieves rank and honors" (Rank, p. 61).

In 1936, Raglan (pp. 178–179) compared the Oedipus myth with twenty others, abstracting a pattern of twenty-two points, of which the first thirteen are strikingly similar to Rank's analysis. "(1) The hero's mother is a royal virgin; (2) his father is a king, and (3) often a near relative of his mother, but (4) the circumstances of his conception are unusual, and (5) he is also reputed

---

[9] Otto Rank, *The Myth of the Birth of the Hero*, Nervous and Mental Disease Mono. Ser., no. 18 (New York, 1914). Page references are to this edition. This study had been published as *Der Mythus von der Geburt des Helden*, Schriften zur Angewanden Seelenkunde, V, ed. S. Freud (1908), with a second and enlarged edition in 1922. The English edition has been republished by R. Brunner (New York, 1952).

to be the son of a god. (6) At birth an attempt is made, usually by his father or maternal grandfather, to kill him, but (7) he is spirited away, and (8) reared by foster-parents in a far country. (9) We are told nothing of his childhood, but (10) on reaching manhood he returns or goes to his future kingdom. (11) After a victory over the king and/or a giant, dragon or wild beast, (12) he marries a princess, often the daughter of his predecessor, and (13) becomes king.

"(14) For a time he reigns uneventfully, and (15) prescribes laws, but (16) later he loses favour with the gods and/or his subjects, and (17) is driven from the throne and city, after which (18) he meets with a mysterious death, (19) often at the top of a hill. (20) His children, if any, do not succeed him. (21) His body is not buried, but nevertheless (22) he has one or more holy sepulchres."

Raglan applies this pattern to Oedipus and finds he scores the full twenty-two points. Theseus, Romulus, Heracles, Perseus, Jason, Bellerophon, Pelops, Asclepios, Dionysos, Apollo, and Zeus, also in classical mythology, are given scores ranging from eleven to twenty points. Elijah, Joseph, and Moses from the Old Testament score from nine to twenty points. Siegfried, Llew Llawgyffes, Robin Hood, and King Arthur from European folklore score from eleven to nineteen points. Nyikang, the cult hero of the Shilluk of Africa, scores fourteen and Wata Gunung, a Javanese hero, scores eighteen.

Rank's analysis, to which Raglan makes no reference, had included six of these myths. Rank had considered Oedipus, Romulus, Heracles, Perseus, Paris, Telephos, Kyros, Karna, Sargon, Gilgamos, Moses, Jesus, Siegfried, Tristan, and Lohengrin, with subsidiary analyses of Ion, Amphion and Zethos, Darab, Kaikhosrav, Zal, Feridun, Zoroaster, Abraham, Isaac, Judas, St. Gregory, Arthur, Tristram, Wolfdietrich, Horn, Wieland, Helias, and Sceaf. Rank interprets these heroes, all of whom come from Europe, the Middle East, and India, in terms of the Oedipus complex and the exposure of the child in a box, basket, or cave, which symbolizes not a return to the womb, but the process of birth (Rank, p. 70).

These two analyses confirm the pattern, but obviously neither of the two very different interpretations. As far as the Freudian interpretation is concerned, the hero marries his mother in only four of these forty-eight myths: Oedipus himself, Judas, St. Gregory, and Wata Gunung, who marries his mother and his sister. Zeus marries his sister, Theseus marries several princesses, St. Gregory is "the child of the incestuous union of royal lovers," Darab is the child of father-daughter incest, and Heracles' parents are parallel first cousins, suggesting the violation of taboos, but not the Oedipus complex. Rank himself (p. 88) notes that the myths emphasize the hostility toward the father or father surrogate, but not the sexual desire for the mother: "The mother, and her relation to the hero, appear relegated to the background in the myth of the birth of the hero."

Yet again, in only four of the forty-eight myths, Oedipus, Judas, Theseus, and Romulus, does the hero kill his father or cause his death. This supports neither the theory of patricide nor that of regicide. Perseus and Kaikhoarav kill their mother's father, Jason his father's brother, Heracles his foster father, Romulus his twin brother, but Amphion and Zethos kill their mother's father's brother's wife, Helias causes his father's mother to be burned, and Karna is himself killed by his brother. It is difficult to interpret all of these as father surrogates. In other cases the hero kills or overcomes monsters, performs feats, overcomes death, wins actual or magical victories or, in the case of Joseph, wins "a contest in dream-interpretation and weather-forecasting" (Raglan, p. 184). The pattern as abstracted by Raglan and Rank seems less compatible with Oedipal interpretations and ritual origins than with Hollywood's formulae. The hero overcomes insurmountable obstacles, marries a princess, and becomes a king. But many of the details and incidents would be censored by Hollywood.

In another very important point the theory of ritual regicide fails to account for the hero pattern outlined by Raglan, namely the fact that the hero himself is not slain by his successor, but is driven away after losing favor and meets a mysterious death on top of a hill. Raglan himself remarks, "We may conclude that deposition and a mysterious death is a part of the pattern, but a puzzling feature is that there is nothing to suggest that the hero suffers a defeat. As he has gained the throne by a victory, one would expect him to lose it by a defeat, but this he never does" (pp. 197–198). Raglan's only explanation is that the divine king may have been burned on a pyre erected on a hill-top, but he admits that there is nothing to suggest that before being burned he is compelled to fight with and be defeated by his successor. Yet if the death of the old king is to be found in ritual regicide, so must the death of the new king. Point 18 should equal point 11. Raglan himself says earlier, "History is what happens once, but things that happen once only are nothing to the ritualist, who is concerned only with things that are done again and again" (p. 150). The same criticism, of course, applies with equal force to the Freudian interpretation, since the Oedipus complex is held to be inherent in every man.

Nyikang and Wata Gunung

I do not propose an alternative theory of origin of Raglan or Rank's hero pattern. Perhaps its origin is in ritual regicide or sexual patricide, and perhaps it is in imaginative fantasy or actual human situations. I do not regard any of these as either proven or impossible. It is important to note, however, that all of Rank's heroes and all but two of Raglan's are derived from the societies of India, the Middle East and Europe, whose cultures are historically related. The similarities in these tales could be explained by diffusion from a common source, as Raglan suggests, and this might also account for Nyikang and Wata

Gunung. The Shilluk are not too remote from Mohammedan peoples, and perhaps this tale spread to Java along with either Islam or Buddhism. But, if similarities are due to diffusion from a single source, is there any reason to look for ritual origins to explain them? Documenting the similarities at least proves nothing about their origin in ritual, history, or fantasy, Freudian or otherwise.

In a recent paper, Lessa has discussed Oedipus-type tales in Sumatra, Java, and Lombok, and beyond the area of Buddhistic and Islamic influence, on Ulithi, Truk, Ponape, Kusaie, the Marshalls, Kapingamarangi, New Guinea, and the Marquesas.[10] In the Maori creation myth in which Tanemahuta severs his father and mother, Lang had found a close parallel to the Cronus myth,[11] and as other analogues had cited the Indian myth in which Indra severs Dyaus and Prthivi and the Chinese myth of Puang-ku to which Tylor had previously referred.[12] Lessa concludes that the Oedipus-type story spread by diffusion from the patriarchal Euro-Asiatic societies to Oceanic societies in which the Oedipal situation is lacking. Although I have as yet found no references to it in Burma, Siam, Indo-China, or Malaya, this is at least a reasonable hypothesis. Lessa says that "we find such stories limited to a continuous belt extending from Europe to the Near and Middle East and south-eastern Asia, and from there into the islands of the Pacific. It seems to be absent from such vast areas as Africa, China, central Asia, northeastern Asia, North America, South America, and Australia."[13]

Rank and other classical Freudians would explain these analogues in terms of innate Oedipal drives. Yet if these drives are innate and universal, why are not such myths found in all societies? And why are the Oedipus myths of closely related cultures more similar than those separated by greater time, space, and cultural differences?

Raglan apparently does not claim that all myths have a common source in a single ritual. "It may be urged," he writes, "that if all myths are derived from the royal ritual of the Nile-Indus region, then all myths should be alike. In fact, many myths are extremely widespread; this fact has been generally realized, except by exponents of the 'Aryan' theory, but has been attributed to the alleged similar working of the human mind. This theory breaks down, however, when it is realized that however widespread certain features of myth and ritual may be, other myths and rites have a distribution comparable, let us

[10] William A. Lessa, "Oedipus-Type Tales in Oceania," *JAF*, LXIX (1956), 63.

[11] Andrew Lang, *Custom and Myth* (New York, 1885), pp. 45–51.

[12] Edward B. Tylor, *Primitive Culture* (London, 1871), I, 294.

[13] Lessa, p. 68. Li Hwei has traced fifty-one flood myths in Formosa, South China, the Indo-China Peninsula, the Malay Archipelago, and westward to central India, in which a brother and sister survive by floating in "a wooden box, or the like." Being the only living beings, they mate with each other and give birth to the ancestors of mankind; see Li Hwei, "The Deluge Legend of the Sibling-Mating Type in Aboriginal Formosa and Southeast Asia," *Bull. of the Ethno. Soc.* (Taiwan, 1955), I, 205–206. Although not Oedipus-type myths, these would have to be considered in any comprehensive study, since they overlap in distribution and in at least one motif.

say, to that of the Moslem religion. Nobody asserts that, because we find in Java and in Nigeria men who marry four wives and pray five times a day, the human mind works naturally in the direction of four wives and five daily prayers. No belief or practice can be claimed as natural unless it is universal, and even the most widespread myths and rites are not that" (p. 150).

Yet he goes on to say, "The myth varies with the ritual, and both, especially among the illiterate, tend to reflect political and economic conditions. A ritual developed among a people who both kept cattle and cultivated the soil might spread on the one hand to pastoral nomads, and on the other to cultivators who kept no cattle. One part of the ritual would then die out, and as it would, of course, not be the same part, it might come to be supposed that the two rituals were quite independent. . . . The original, so far as can be judged from the general pattern, was based on the existence of a king who was killed and replaced annually. A hundred myths describe his death and the installation of his successor" (p. 151). I can only conclude that Raglan does not mean to imply that all myths have a single source, and that if he did, he has certainly not demonstrated this to be the case.

In his recent article, Raglan cites Parsons' statement that the Hopi Emergence myth is too explanatory of the ceremonial life to be told to rank outsiders.[14] Although in the same passage Parsons refers to it as less esoteric than Pueblo chants, this quotation suggests that it is a narrative of the events enacted in rituals. It is not clear from this passage whether the Emergence story, which among the Zuni differs markedly from one version to another in the details which are introduced,[15] is similar in this respect to what Parsons (I, 215) calls "the archeological or topographic legends." "Into this legendary frame a considerable number of narratives are embroidered and a few songs, for ritual recitation or for edification. Versions vary, for there will be stressed or introduced myth bearing upon the ceremony or organization the particular narrator is connected with." In similar accounts, which Benedict (I, xxxii, xxxix) refers to as "myths," the Zuni narrator is free to incorporate details of rituals of which he has special knowledge, drawing on his own personal experience. It is clear that the relation between these Zuni myths and ritual is secondary. Although these details are derived from rituals and are enacted in rituals, the myths are not. The passage cited by Raglan does not show that this is not also the case with regard to the Hopi Emergence myth.

In support of ritual associations, Raglan might better have quoted from Parsons' previous paragraph (I, 215): "As yet only a few ritual recitals or chants have been recorded, mostly Zuni. These ritual versions are known only to those in charge of them; even when recited semipublicly, like the Shalako

[14] Lord Raglan, "Myth and Ritual," *JAF*, LXVIII (1955), 461; Elsie Clews Parsons, *Pueblo Indian Religion* (Chicago, 1939), I, 216.

[15] Ruth Benedict, *Zuni Mythology*, Columbia Univ. Contr. to Anthro., no. 21 (New York, 1935), I, xxx.

and Sayatasha myths, they are not attended to by outsiders; they are merely part of the ceremony. In this respect these unique Zuni recitals suggest the all-night song myths of the Mohave which constitute Mohave ceremony or the Athapascan song myths which are also a part of the ceremony. In general, however, Pueblo mythology and ceremonial are far more separate than are Navaho-Apache song myths and ceremonial."

It is not difficult to recognize other myths, even in Raglan's special sense of narratives associated with rituals, in societies outside the stream of Western culture. The totemic myths of the Murngin of Australia, as described by Warner, also fulfill in detail the definitions of Harrison and Hooke. "A fundamental conceptual scheme runs through all the ceremonies; the various dramatic sections portray the myth by dance and song. For the Western European, this whole totemic ceremonial behavior might be compared to a Wagnerian opera, with the myth as libretto; the motifs, like that of the snake swallowing the women, first expressed in a phrase or two, are later elaborated; and certain motifs, highly elaborate in some of the ceremonies are only hinted at in others. For the reason that here we have ceremonies treated separately by the natives which they yet realize fit into a larger whole, the totality may, without too much stretching, be compared with the Nibelungen Ring. The fundamental difference is that the story is not a myth to them, but a dogma and has the same ceremonial significance to the Murngin as the Mass to a believing Catholic."[16]

These instances, and others which might be cited, are reason enough for anthropologists to pay more attention to the relation of myth to ritual, and to test cross-culturally what the ritual school often puts forth as its own dogma or at least as unsupported hypotheses.[17] Are what the ritualists define as myths universal in all societies? Or to restate the question, are all myths as more commonly defined connected with ritual? I would doubt that this is the case, but before these questions can be answered there must be some further agreement among the ritualists and a clearer statement of whether a myth is (1) a narrative which is recited as a part of a ritual, (2) a narrative, the events of which are enacted in a ritual, (3) a narrative which is both recited and enacted in a ritual, or (4) a narrative which is only indirectly and secondarily associated with ritual.

There is an equal need for anthropologists and folklorists, as a whole, to arrive at some agreement as to what they mean by myth, and at least some tentative distinctions between myth, legend, and folktale. In the American Indian field as a whole it is particularly difficult to distinguish between them, as Parsons' reference to legends and Benedict's reference to myths, for which

[16] W. Lloyd Warner, *A Black Civilization* (New York and London, 1937), p. 260.
[17] For example, Raglan's interpretation of William Tell and the tale of the Faithful Hound, "Myth and Ritual," p. 459.

she also uses the term folktales, indicate. Warner, in saying that what he has called myth is "not a myth, but a dogma," and Bidney, in defining myth as something which is untrue, have simply added to the confusion. This is no place to present my own system of classification, but in it myths are by definition regarded as true in the society in which they are told. They are regarded as fact, rather than fiction, while legends are also, folktales are not.

28

THE RITUAL THEORY OF MYTH

Joseph Fontenrose

In *The Ritual Theory of Myth* (Berkeley: University of California Press, 1966), the American classicist Joseph Fontenrose (1903–86), who taught at Berkeley, offers the most relentless critique to date of the myth-ritualist theory. Fontenrose attacks, in turn, Raglan, Frazer, Hyman, and Harrison. No aspect of their theories, factual or logical, goes unassailed, as the following selection on Raglan (ch. 1) evinces. There has been no formal rejoinder to Fontenrose. See also his *Python* (Berkeley: University of California Press, 1959), ch. 15. On Fontenrose see Stanley Edgar Hyman, review of *Python, Carleton Miscellany* 1 (1960), 124–7; and Fontenrose's reply, "Some Observations on Hyman's review of *Python*," *Carleton Miscellany* 2 (1961), 122–5.

Raglan's Royal Victim

If all myths have a ritual origin, do all myths arise ultimately from a single ritual, or do all rituals, and only rituals, have a myth-engendering power? The logically simpler alternative is Lord Raglan's choice: all myths are ritual texts and all myth-ritual complexes go back to a single ancient ritual. What about legends and folktales? For they have many of the same themes, patterns, and kinds of character that are found in myth. Lord Raglan sees no real differences among traditional tales: a legend or folktale is simply a myth cut loose from its ritual. As he sees it, all traditional tales, all existing rituals, all religious systems, and, in fact, a good deal else – magic, nursery rhymes, games, riddles, etiquette – are derived from a single Ur-ritual. Historical events, intellectual

Original publication: Joseph Fontenrose, *The Ritual Theory of Myth* (Berkeley: University of California Press, 1966), ch 1 (pp. 2–25) and bibliography (pp. 69–70).

curiosity, dreams, fantasies, poetic invention, have nothing to do with either the origin or the development of myths, or of any part of them.[1]

Sacrifice of the Divine King

Raglan's is a diffusionist theory of sweeping proportions: it purports to account for the religions and myths of pre-Columbian America as well as for those of the Old World.[2] What was this Ur-ritual which so powerfully stirred men's emotions and imaginations that in manifold forms it still sways men's minds today and has been the sole generator of religions, mythologies, and folklore? It was not the very first ritual in the world: Lord Raglan grants ritual to palaeolithic man, but does not believe that it had any effect on historic and known rituals (*OR* 51). "The original ritual," says Raglan, "so far as can be judged from the general pattern, was based on the existence of a king who was killed and replaced annually" (*H* xiii *fin.*). That is, the original myth-ritual pattern began with the annual sacrifice of a king and the installation of his successor. Raglan describes the evolution of the ritual as follows:

> In the first [stage] it was the divine king who was regularly sacrificed; in the second somebody else was regularly sacrificed as a substitute for the divine king; with the progress of civilization came a third stage, in which a human victim was sacrificed in times of emergency, but at other times a pretense was made of killing him, but some other victim was substituted. In the fourth stage the victim was never human, but was usually treated in such a way as to indicate that it once had been. (1955: 81)

In some late neolithic kingdom of the ancient Near East men thought it a good idea to kill their "divine king" every year; neighboring kingdoms took up the practice with alacrity, and it spread in ever-widening circles until it embraced the world – to everyone's satisfaction, it seems, except perhaps the divine king's.[3] And so charged with emotion was this ceremony that it not only colored but provided the whole mythico-religious structure of human society thereafter.

---

[1] Raglan 1936, 1949. His books are strange compounds of lucidity and absurdity, as pointed out by Edmund Leach in his review of Raglan's recent *The Temple and the House* (*New York Review of Books*, September 16, 1965, pp. 16–17).

[2] Raglan almost ignores the Americas; but three times he adduces Mexican parallels (*H* xv, xviii, xxi), once quotes Lang on Algonquin and Eskimo folktales (*H* xii), and once quotes MacCulloch on Algonquin myths (*H* xv).

[3] Raglan puts the place of origin in the ancient Near East without defining it more exactly (*H* xiv *init.*, *OR* 67–68). He seems to lean toward Egypt, since with some reservations he approves Elliot Smith's pan-Egyptian theory (*OR* 35). He may be further influenced by his own experiences in the Sudan and by the African evidence which he adduces.

In its first stage, apparently, the ancient ritual had become elaborate and dramatic. According to Raglan it consisted of six acts:

(*a*)   A symbolical destruction of the old world by flood and fire.

(*b*)   The killing of a sacred victim after a mock combat.

(*c*)   The dismemberment of the victim and construction of a "new world" from his members.

(*d*)   The making of a pair of human figures from clay and the victim's blood.

(*e*)   The coming to life of the images in the persons of a young man and woman who were, or were supposed to be, a brother and sister.

(*f*)   A sacred marriage between the pair, who were then regarded as the parents of the newly created race of men. (*OR* 68–69)

What is the evidence for this Ur-ritual? Raglan says, "There is evidence from the myths, and from recorded and existing rites," and it is plain that he has done his best to work in flood myths, combat myths, creation myths, and the sacred-marriage rite. He has in fact derived most of it from S. H. Hooke's festival program, which Hooke considers to be the basic ritual pattern of the ancient Near East:

(*a*)   The dramatic representation of the death and resurrection of the god.

(*b*)   The recitation or symbolic representation of the myth of creation.

(*c*)   The ritual combat, in which the triumph of the god over his enemies was depicted.

(*d*)   The sacred marriage.

(*e*)   The triumphal procession, in which the king played the part of the god followed by a train of lesser gods or visiting deities.[4]

Here the ritual has obviously reached Raglan's fourth stage of development. Oddly enough Hooke does not mention sacrifice as one of the elements; apparently the sacrifice is part of the first element (*a*). Applying a Frazerian interpretation to Hooke's pattern, Raglan derives his whole first stage from it, except for his first act. Logic suggests an old world destroyed before a new world created, and the flood myths offer Raglan what he needs. The "divine victim developed into the divine king," said Raglan in 1949 (*OR* 73). The first performers of the ritual had no kings as yet: the process is sacrificial victim > king = god (the first kings were not rulers). But in 1955, as we have seen, he said that in the first stage the king was sacrificed, in the second simply a human victim as substitute. Probably this is incomplete statement rather than inconsistency or revision of views. Raglan would diagram the whole process as human victim > divine king > substitute human victim > animal. But now we

---

[4] Hooke 1933: 8; see *H* xiv *init.*, *OR* 67; Hocart 1927: 70–71.

have the divine king developing out of a human victim (who is not yet a king) and then giving place to a human victim (who is no longer a king). We are back where we started; now, however, the human victim does not become a king, but gives place to an animal. Raglan also does not make evident any link between the powerless divine king and subsequent kings who ruled as absolute monarchs. Why should we call him *king?* If the earliest ruling kings took over a title formerly borne by sacrificed kings, what was the connection?

Raglan's whole structure, we perceive, rests on a single foundation, the annual sacrifice of a divine king or divine victim. What is the evidence for this sacrifice? Raglan insists that his opponents produce evidence for their views, and we have a right to expect him to be well provided with evidence for his own. He does indeed refer us to the appropriate section of *The Golden Bough* (part III, *The Dying God*), saying that Frazer "abundantly provides [the evidence] that all kings were once put to death at the end of a fixed term" (*OR* 71); and he refers us to the evidence collected by Hooke, Hocart, and their school for the ancient Near Eastern myth-ritual pattern. So in examining Raglan's evidence we are in fact looking at the evidence which Frazer, Hooke, and Hocart have to offer. This evidence falls into two general categories, the historical and the ethnographical.

Ancient Evidence for King Sacrifice

We must deal first with the historical evidence, since if this theory is sound it should have abundant support in surviving literature and art, and Frazer does appear to provide a good deal of evidence. We must look back to the ancient Near East first, to the earliest civilizations, in one of which Raglan and Hooke place the center of diffusion. These lands, especially Egypt, had divine kings (i.e., kings believed to be gods and worshipped as such). But do we find the periodic ritual sacrifice in Egypt or Mesopotamia? Do we find any king-killing at all whether at regular or irregular intervals? On Egyptian kingship, C. N. Deedes, one of Hooke's school, says, "The actual killing of the king-god, ... remains a mystery in Egyptian history"; the mystery is simply that "No account of it has ever yet been found." There is apparently no mystery about Sumer, where according to Deedes, "there are seals, dating back to about 3000 BC, on which is depicted the actual killing of the king."[5] Splendid evidence – if the seals are correctly interpreted. However, on consulting Frankfort's

[5] In Hooke 1935: 23. See also Moret 1927, who approves Frazer's theory and attempts to find king-killing in ancient Egypt. Like Frazer and Raglan, he can point only to the Osiris myth, the legend of King Bocchoris burned alive, the custom at Meroe (Diod. 3.5–7), and the ritual of the Sed festival; see Moret 1927: 47–52. The evidence is scanty and folkloristic in nature, and the case is far from cogent.

Cylinder Seals, I found that they represent the sun-god Shamash killing an enemy; it is not a sacrifice, and the enemy is not the king.[6]

In Mesopotamia, as in Egypt, there is no record of an annual or periodic killing of the king. Yet some Mesopotamian kingdoms had the institution of *shar-puhi*, substitute king. When omens indicated that danger threatened the king or the nation, the king made a show of abdicating and of turning over his office to a substitute, who took over the royal insignia and sat upon the throne.[7] The substitution was complete; otherwise it would be ineffective for its purpose. The substitute was really king for the period, except in one important respect; he had to leave the throne as soon as the dangers were declared at an end; he did not dare employ the prerogatives of his office in order to retain them.[8] And the *shar-puhi's* immediate surrender of the throne does not in any respect fit Frazer's or Hooke's ritual hypothesis. The substitute was not put to death at the end of his term, but returned entirely whole to his usual routine. Known records show but one *sharpuhi* who was put to death, Damqi, substitute for the late Assyrian king Esarhaddon.[9] On this occasion omens portended the king's death. That is, death threatened the *king*, the man who literally occupied the throne; and by killing a *shar-puhi*, who had been seated on the throne with all the trappings of royalty, the government could circumvent the fates. This occasion reveals the whole purpose of the institution: to deflect threatened dangers from the true king to the substitute king; if harm should strike, it would strike the man on the throne (ordinarily nothing happened to him). The institution can be simply and satisfactorily explained as a magical device for protecting the king. Furthermore the substitution was not periodic and did not occur as part of a New Year ritual (the hypothetical annual sacrifice marked a new year, according to Frazer and his successors).

[6] Henri Frankfort, *Cylinder Seals* (London: Macmillan, 1939), p. 100 and plates XVIII h, i, j, XIX b, c, d. Frankfort, moreover, assigns them to the Akkadian period. Deedes cites nothing to support his statement.

[7] See René Labat, *Le caractère religieux de la royauté assyro-babylonienne* (Paris: Adrien-Maisonneuve, 1939), pp. 103–105; Henri Frankfort, *Kingship and the Gods* (University of Chicago Press, 1948), pp. 262–264.

[8] Two chronicle entries tell the story of Enlil-bani, whom King Irra-imitti of Isin placed upon the throne, apparently to serve as *shar-puhi*, since the entries say "that the dynasty might not come to an end." Irra-imitti died during the substitution and Enlil-bani kept the kingship. See L. W. King, *Chronicles Concerning Early Babylonian Kings* (London: Luzac, 1907), II, 12–16, with discussion in I, 62–68; Labat, op. cit., pp. 103–104, 108–109. This appears to be the tale of Beleûs and Beletaras alluded to by Agathias *Hist.* 2.25, who cites Bion and Alexander Polyhistor. According to H. R. Hall (*The Ancient History of the Near East*, 10th edn [London: Methuen, 1947], p. 191, note 2), Enlil-bani reigned in Isin about 2184–2160; but the chronicles were composed around 500 BC. Agathias' Beletaras was identified with Sargon I before the Akkadian chronicles came to light; the mistake may point in the right direction: both Sargon and Enlil-bani were usurpers and a tale was told to legitimate the accession of each. The story of Enlil-bani can hardly be historical as told, since an ordinary *shar-puhi* would surely step down in any case. We may, if we wish, see in it Enlil-bani's plot to take the throne through deception of Irra-imitti.

[9] See Labat, op. cit., pp. 103, 359–360.

Frazer did not know about the *shar-puhi* when he wrote *The Golden Bough* (even in the final edition and in *Aftermath*, when he might have had information about this office, he makes no mention of it). He surely would have considered this custom to be his best evidence for an annual sacrifice of divine kings in Mesopotamia, where he was very anxious to find evidence of the institution. It would have provided him with the second stage of his conjectured development of the ritual: real king > substitute king > mock king. He had to be content with a mock king and with such ritual practices as the king's humiliation at the New Year festival. He found his mock king in the Sakaia festival (Frazer 1911*b*: 113–117), celebrated in Babylon under the Persian domination, and earlier too, if Frazer was right, for he insisted that Sakaia and the ancient Babylonian New Year Festival (the Akitu festival to which he referred as Zakmuk) were one and the same.[10] There are few sources for the Sakaia festival, almost nothing aside from three passages, one each in Strabo, Athenaeus (who cites Berosos and Ktesias), and Dion Chrysostom.[11] In his usual fashion Frazer runs all three together into a single consistent description, which he leads the reader to suppose is vouched for by Berosos, "who as a Babylonian priest spoke with ample knowledge." Frazer tells us that during the Sakaia, when masters and servants changed places in Saturnalian revelry, a condemned criminal was dressed in the king's robes, seated on the throne, and given the title *Zoganês*; for five days he ate and drank luxuriously, enjoyed the king's concubines, and gave any orders he liked (except, apparently, a commutation of his death sentence); on the fifth day he was stripped, scourged, and hanged. Berosos, however, as reported by Athenaeus, mentions only the date and number of days, the Saturnalian revelry, the title *Zoganês*, and Babylon as the place of celebration; he says nothing about the criminal or the execution. His Zoganês is one of the servants in a household (any household, and not the royal palace only), who ruled the house during the feast and wore royal dress for the period. The criminal mock king's fatal reign comes from Dion Chrysostom, who puts a description of the feast into the mouth of Diogenes the Cynic in conversation with the youthful Alexander. Andrew Lang rightly suspected Dion's picture to be fanciful, since it does not agree with either

[10] This meant placing the Sakaia at the vernal equinox, although Berosos (15 Schnabel, *ap.* Ath. 14.639C) placed its first day on the sixteenth of the Macedonian month Lōos, which the available evidence shows to be July or September, a summer month. Frazer (1911*b*: 116, note 1) seized upon the uncertainty between July and September (he mentions August and October also) to justify his placing the Sakaia in March–April, as his theory required. Andrew Lang (1901: 137–138, 144–146) adequately demonstrated the weakness of Frazer's case. Frazer would have done better to accept the September date and point to evidence that some Mesopotamian cities celebrated the New Year festival at the autumnal equinox; he would then have had to interpret Berosos' (or Athenaeus') *Babylon* as Babylonia. Any attempt at etymological identification of Sakaia and Zakmuk is vain.

[11] Berosos *loc. cit.*; Strabo 11.8.5, p. 512; Dion Chrys. 4.66–67; see also Hesych. *Σ* 65 and Steph. Byz. p. 296 Mein.

Berosos' or Strabo's testimony. According to Strabo, the festival was initiated
at Zela in honor of the goddess Anaitis, and was thereafter celebrated at every
shrine of Anaitis; and Zela, rather than Babylon, appears to be the main seat of
the festival. Strabo reports two fundamentally consistent accounts of the origin
of the Sakaia: (1) that when Scythians were celebrating at Zela, making use of
their spoils to do so, Persian generals set upon them at night and annihilated
them; (2) that when Scythians were revelling upon stores of food and wine
taken in a captured Persian camp, Cyrus and his Persians surprised them and
destroyed most of them.[12] Strabo says no more about the festival than that
Persian men and women, dressed in Scythian garb, did a good deal of drinking
and revelling in Bacchic fashion (ἡ τῶν Σακαίων ἑορτὴ Βακχεία τις); but
what he does say in no way contradicts the testimony of Berosos-Athenaeus.
For that matter it can be fitted to Dion's account, too; but Strabo says nothing about Babylon or a condemned criminal who was made mock king and put
to death.

Andrew Lang has thoroughly demonstrated both the weakness of the Sakaia
evidence for Frazer's case and Frazer's misuse of this evidence.[13] The festival
was Persian, as its very name indicates: Strabo and Dion call it Persian and say
nothing about Babylon; it is only Athenaeus, citing Berosos' *Babyloniaca*, who
mentions Babylon as the place of celebration; and, of course, Persian kings
reigned in Babylon for over two centuries (538–331).[14] And to find evidence
that Iranian kings were ever put to death annually or periodically is much more
difficult than it is to find evidence for the killing of Mesopotamian kings: there
is no evidence at all, unless one wishes to consider Dion's account of the Sakaia
as evidence.

[12] It is perhaps crass Euhemerism to accept Lang's view (1901: 119, 194–195) that the Sakaia
really celebrated a victory in war and was a patriotic festival like the Fourth of July or Guy
Fawkes Day. It should be noticed that Strabo's tale – how Cyrus abandoned a camp full of fine
food and wine to the Scythians and afterwards surprised them in the midst of drunken revels and
destroyed them – repeats Herodotos' tale of how Cyrus tricked the Massagetai (a Scythian
people) beyond the Araxes (1.211). In Strabo the scene is transferred from Turkestan to Pontos,
and Cyrus' success is not followed by his defeat and death. It is an historicized combat myth in
which food and drink are the means whereby either Antagonist or Champion is lured to his
doom. In Polyain. *Strat.* 8.28, Tomyris is a Judith who traps Cyrus in a camp full of food and
drink. See Fontenrose 1959: 89, 124, 137, 139–140, 259–260, 488–490.

[13] Lang 1901: 76–81, 118–160, 182–199. His criticism of Frazer's case is devastating. He
shows too how impossible it is to find the origin of Purim or of Easter in this Persian festival or
to show any apparentation of Sakaia, Akitu, Purim, and Easter. J. M. Robertson tried valiantly
but unconvincingly to rescue Frazer's case from Lang's attack; see *Pagan Christs*, 2nd edn (London: Watts, 1911, pp. 144–147); as another ritual theorist he wanted to prove a Judaic mystery
drama which gave rise to the Jesus story.

[14] The title *Zoganês* (which Dion does *not* give to the Sacaean mock king) is perhaps beyond
etymology, but certainly looks like a Greek rendition of a Persian term. Attempts to connect it
with Semitic words, as with Hebrew *sagan* (which means "captain" or "nobleman") are very
dubious; e.g., Robertson, op. cit., pp. 159–160.

Next to the Sakaia, Frazer's best evidence is drawn from the program of the Akitu festival. On the fifth day the king went with escort to the Esagil temple: there before Bel's image the high priest took the king's crown, sceptre, and sword from him, slapped his cheek, seized him by the ears, and forced him to bow down before Bel. The king then declared that he had done no wrongful acts during the old year, whereupon the priest returned his royal insignia to him. The priest struck the king's cheek again; if he brought tears to the king's eyes, Bel was favorable; if he did not, dangers impended.[15] This means, say Frazer and Raglan, that formerly the king was actually put to death and his successor installed. But in the absence of confirming evidence, such an interpretation of this ceremony is unnecessary. It can be more easily interpreted as a ceremonial vestige of annual terms for the chief magistrate in the early Mesopotamian city-state – an executive like the Athenian archon or Roman consul – who could be reappointed for another year (unlike the consul) if he could show that he had governed justly and wisely. That suggestion is pure conjecture, although no more so than Frazer's, and it saves the phenomena at least as well. More likely, this ceremony was purely magical in intent, to purify the king of all pollutions accumulated during the preceding year; there is nothing in the ritual text to indicate that it was ever anything but a ceremony of purification and renewal. And it is essential to Frazer's thesis that the king be Bel; but here, we notice, the king exculpates himself before Bel as before another person. He is manifestly not Bel, but Bel's agent.

Much the same conclusion can be drawn about the Egyptian Sed festival, traditionally celebrated after thirty years of a king's reign and then repeated at three-year intervals until his death. At this festival the king's coronation was re-enacted. Obviously the ceremony was meant to renew his powers, to give him a new lease of life; nothing in it suggests that it was an innocuous survival of a ritual in which the king was put to death.[16] Moret (1927: 51) goes beyond the evidence in interpreting the Sed ritual acts to signify a death and revival of the king.

Raglan, however, still relying principally on Frazer, claims abundant evidence that early Greece had kings who were slain periodically. He says, "But whereas the existing accounts of the ritual of Egypt and Mesopotamia provide only for a pretence of killing the king, the traditions of Greece and less civilized countries point to a ritual in which the king was actually killed, . . . annually, [or] at the end of some longer term, . . ." (*H* xiv). For Greece, he tells us, it was usually an eight-year term. His evidence is that section of *The Golden Bough* in which Frazer cites eight-year cycles in Greek rituals, customs, and myths (Frazer 1911*b*: 58–60, 68–83, 87–92). At best this is evidence for

[15] Text (trans. A. Sachs) in *Ancient Near Eastern Texts*, ed. J. B. Pritchard (Princeton University Press, 1950), pp. 331–334. See Fontenrose 1959: 436–446.

[16] On the Sed festival see Frankfort, *Kingship and the Gods*, pp. 79–88; see also J. Černy, *Ancient Egyptian Religion* (London: Hutchinson, 1952), pp. 122–123.

royal terms of eight years, but all of it is legendary or inferred from ritual practices – yet Raglan has strictly forbidden us to rely on legend as historical evidence, and the inferences alone lead to circular reasoning. There is no historical record of a Greek king who suffered a ritual death at the end of an eight-year term or any other kind of term; and there is absolutely no historical or archaeological evidence that in prehistoric Greece "the king must die." In fact, there is no mythical record either of just that. Frazer cites eight-year cycles in myth and tradition without any king-killing and mythical murders of kings that were not periodic or sacrificial; he gives the appearance of having a good deal of evidence for eight-year reigns by introducing long digressions on shooting stars, animal transformations, and the like.

There is, moreover, no record of divine kingship in ancient Greece. As H. J. Rose (1959: 371–378) admirably demonstrated in his examination of the case which A. B. Cook had made in his *Zeus* for Frazerian divine kings in early Greece, there is nothing besides the equivocal evidence of myths and legends (and little in them); that Greek kings exercised priestly functions proves nothing, especially since priests were not gods.[17] Rose ignores the occasional Homeric phrase in which it is said of a king that his people honored him as a god. Lest anyone see divine kings in this expression, it should be said that if the king were a god, the *as* (*hōs*) would not be used. This adverb plainly indicates a simile: it is not used appositively like the English *as*. The Homeric kings like Agamemnon and Odysseus are plainly mortal men on a lower level than the gods and are at the mercy of deity.

Ethnographic Evidence for King Sacrifice

In all the ancient world we find no record, clear or obscure, of an annual or periodic sacrifice of divine kings. That leaves us with the ethnographic evidence, the rituals and customs of contemporary and recent "savages," as Frazer and Raglan constantly call them. Raglan triumphantly tells us that Frazer cites hundreds of instances. True enough, Frazer (1911*b*: 14–58) offers a goodly number of examples of king-killing, mostly from Africa. He could, and would, have added many more examples if he had written *The Dying God*

---

[17] A. B. Cook, *Zeus: A Study in Ancient Religion* (Cambridge University Press, 1914–40), I, 12–14, 79–81; II, 794, 1073–1077, 1087–1089, 1121–1137, 1159–1160; III, 733–734. See Marlow 1961, who finds no good evidence of the Hooke-Raglan myth-ritual pattern nor of divine kings in early Greece, and who demolishes the theory of Raglan and others that the Homeric epics were ritual texts which accompanied a ritual performance called "Trojan War." I should also mention Arne Furumark, "Was There a Sacral Kingship in Minoan Crete?" (*Studies in the History of Religions*, IV [1959], 369–370); his answer to the question of his title is affirmative, but on inadequate and ambiguous evidence; and he interprets the Palaikastro hymn as a ritual text.

in recent years, for in Tor Irstam's *The King of Ganda* (1944) most of the relevant African material on king-killing is conveniently assembled – the practice is alleged for fifty African peoples. In none, however, is the king killed annually, and the examples of periodic king-killing are rare and dubious. Still, the ritualists say, here are kings put to death when their strength fails, a custom which preserves the original meaning of the ritual; the old rigidity and excessive caution of periodic sacrifice have given way to a more rational irregularity. And since the king-killing custom is so prevalent in Africa, they say, it must either have spread southward from Egypt or have had the same origin as the hypothetical Egyptian custom (Hamitic, according to Seligman 1934). And indeed the most remarkable instance attested occurs (or occurred) among the Shilluk of the Nilotic Sudan. Frazer depended upon the first studies of the Shilluk made by C. G. Seligman, who lived among them and reported that they still practiced king-killing, although no instance occurred during his stay. According to Seligman, the god Nyakang is immanent in every Shilluk king; the Shilluk believe that if the king should become sick or feeble, his weakness would infect the people, cattle, and crops; and "there is no doubt that the kings of the Shilluk were killed ceremonially when they began to show signs of old age or ill-health, . . ."[18] Seligman was told that in contemporary practice certain chiefs and nobles, having decided that the king (*reth*) must die, informed him of his fate and took him to a hut (especially built for the occasion) and strangled him (Seligman rejects another account received from informants, that the king's wives did the strangling). After two months the king-killing cabal broke the hut down, buried the king's bones, and then for the first time informed the Shilluk people of the king's death. The people wept, slaughtered cattle, and sacrificed a man and woman by drowning them. The Shilluk reported that five generations earlier they had abandoned a custom of walling the king and a "nubile maiden" in a hut without food or water.[19]

For the moment let us grant that the Shilluk kill (and have killed) their kings in the aforesaid ways. But where is that elaborate ritual which Raglan describes in great detail? Where are the symbolic destruction of the old world in flood or fire, the ritual combat, the construction of a new world and a new mankind from the dead king's body and blood, and the sacred marriage? There is no ritual to speak of: an aging or sick ruler is taken to a hut (apparently at night) and strangled. Everything is done in secret; there is no public fanfare

---

[18] See Seligman 1932: 90–93. This book is later than *The Dying God*, but it repeats the results of Seligman's studies that Frazer used. Notice the past tense in the quoted sentence and also the words, "the Shilluk kings are (or were) killed," which indicate uncertainty about its being a contemporary sacrifice.

[19] For this sacrifice Seligman cites Diedrich Westermann, *The Shilluk People* (Philadelphia: Board of Foreign Missions, United Presbyterian Church; Berlin: Reimer [Ernst Vohsen], 1912), p. 136, a text dictated by a Shilluk informant. In this text two girls are walled in a hut with the *dead* body of the king (the cause of his death is not given) and die there.

such as Frazer's or Raglan's theory demands. The later slaughter of cattle and of two persons, who were bound in a canoe that was loaded with various objects and then sunk in the river, hardly meets the hypothetical ritual; moreover Seligman owed his information about this sacrifice not to his own informants, but to a Shilluk folklore text in Westermann's collection. However the king dies, the king's successor is installed with great pomp after an interregnum of one year. Coronations are always splendid affairs, and this coronation can hardly be taken to be the enactment of resurrection or re-creation, as demanded by Raglan's ritual scheme. His whole ritual should take place in one festival, whereas among the Shilluk the old king's death, the human sacrifices (if the report be accepted), and the new king's installation take place at widely separate times, occupying a whole year from first to last. Seligman points to the report of a still more ancient custom in which we may see combat for the kingship between the king and a challenger. A royal son had the right to attempt the king's life, and if he killed the king, to reign in his stead. Royal sons made the attempt only at night when the king was alone and almost unguarded in his harem; but ever on the watch, like Frazer's King of the Woods, he prowled about all night, fully armed, ready for any challenger who should appear. If the report is anything more than traditional lore, it may be a memory of regicides and usurpations, which have nothing to do with king sacrifice; in any case we observe none of the ritual of periodic renewal that Hooke and Raglan have constructed.

Frazer (and his sources), Seligman, Irstam, and others cite identical or similar practices among other African peoples: Dinka, Konde, Bakitara, Bungoro, Kibanga, Zulu, and over forty others.[20] In all parts of the continent, it appears, kings, on showing signs of weakness, have been strangled or compelled to drink poison; as among the Shilluk, an interregnum of several months followed the king's death (not reported to the people for a time), ending with the installation of a successor. Thus there appears to be abundant evidence for the killing of kings in Africa, although it is hardly evidence for the Frazer-Hooke-Raglan rituals. Yet the reader should notice one constant statement made in the material on the killing of the divine king in Africa as reported by the aforesaid scholars. In every instance, save that of the Shilluk, the native informants said that the king *used to be* killed, and that the practice came to an end at some indefinite time in the past, two, three, or more generations back. If, then, the information is reliable, we should expect that African divine kings were meeting ritual deaths two or three centuries ago and that early visitors to Africa might have witnessed or heard about king-killing as a contemporary practice. But even the earliest European visitors were told that the killing of kings was

[20] Frazer 1911*b*: 14–41, Seligman 1934: 21–39, Irstam 1944: 142–146; Leo Frobenius, *Und Afrika Sprach* . . . III (Berlin: Vita, Deutsches Verlagshaus, 1913), pp. 84–87, 113, 140–143, 147, 255; E. J. and J. D. Krige, *The Realm of a Rain-Queen* (Oxford University Press, 1943), pp. 165–166.

a practice of earlier times. Dos Santos, a Portuguese traveller who visited Bantu tribes of Mozambique in the sixteenth century, reported concerning the king of Sofala that "It was formerly the custom of the kings of this land to commit suicide by taking poison when any disaster or natural physical defect fell upon them, such as impotence, infectious disease, . . ." (Seligman 1934: 30). In truth, we can go back another sixteen centuries to Diodoros of Sicily (3.5–7), whose testimony about the kings of Aethiopia has been used by Frazer and the ritualists as an important link between ancient Egyptian and modern African king-killing, especially since Diodoros' reference to kings and priests at Meroe brings us near to the Shilluk and Dinka. Diodoros, relying upon a source that might be some two centuries earlier, informs us that whenever the priests at Meroe took the notion, they sent a message to the king, instructing him to kill himself, since the gods had so ordered. Every king obeyed the divine behest until the time of Ptolemy II in Egypt, when King Ergamenes of Aethiopia refused to obey the command and killed the priests instead. Once more the custom *used to be* practiced; and the report contains a legend of how the practice came to an end. Diodoros (3.7) then goes on to report the court etiquette of Aethiopians. When a king lost the use of some part of his body, his companions gave up that member in sympathy. This custom, whether or not it is reliably reported, is directly contrary to the reported custom of killing kings when they failed in health or wholeness. Obviously an eyeless, toothless, or legless king would have a bad effect on his land and should be sacrificed as soon as possible; yet among a people who reputedly killed their kings, and in a section of Africa where king-killing has reputedly been traditional, Diodoros' lame kings lived out their lives and without objection imposed their own disabilities on their subjects.

So constantly is it said that the killing of kings "used to be," and so unverifiable is the rare report of contemporary king-killing, that one may conclude that the whole reported tradition of African king-killing is itself mythical, a fragment or memory of an ancient African myth. Such was the conclusion which I had already reached when I came upon Evans-Pritchard's *The Divine Kingship of the Shilluk of the Nilotic Sudan* (1948) and found it confirmed. In spite of Seligman's unhesitating acceptance of the Shilluk tradition that failing kings were put to death, Evans-Pritchard says, "I must confess that I consider [the Shilluk statements] of interest more as an indication of the mystical nature of the kingship than as evidence that the kings were, in fact, ever killed in the ways mentioned or for the reasons given" (p. 20). He found no convincing evidence that the Shilluk ever observed such a custom; therefore, he adds, "In the absence of other than traditional evidence of royal executions in Shilluk history and in view of the contradictory accounts cited I conclude that the ceremonial putting to death of kings is probably a fiction, . . ." (p. 21). Shilluk kings have, of course, been killed in the usual secular ways, by assassins or by rebels in battle. So if the case for Shilluk king-killing fails, it fails *a fortiori* for other African peoples. We look in vain for an authentic royal victim, whether real king or substitute king, whether strangled or poisoned or killed in combat by a sanctioned challenger. And even if the reports are true, we still do not see either Raglan's ritual pattern or any clear relation to rituals of the ancient Near East; nor, so far as I know, do we find any African myth which the reported king-killing has manifestly inspired. Indeed the African myths of kingship are quite otherwise.

Today we know more about African kingship than Frazer knew a half-century ago, when anthropologists gave little attention to primitive government. Recently several books on African tribal government have appeared, written by distinguished anthropologists.[21] These books necessarily say a good deal about the powers, terms, prerogatives, and duties of native kings and chieftains in those African societies which trained observers have studied; but one will hunt almost in vain for any mention of the institution which Frazer, Raglan, and others have emphasized so much. In *African Political Systems* (p. 137) we learn that the Mugabe of Ankole drank poison when his physical powers waned (an instance unknown to Frazer). This too is reported as a *former* custom. The Nyakyusa (southern Tanganyika) killing of a ritual king and the killing of a mock king at Nyoro accession ceremonies are likewise reported as *past* customs.[22] Frazer, moreover, who uncritically accepted the reports of unskilled observers, was wrong in some instances, e.g., concerning the Zulu. He believed (1911*b*: 36–37) that King Chaka was destined to a ritual death when his powers waned; but in fact the Zulu killed Chaka, not "ritually," but because he had oppressed his people. This is evidence of secular rebellion and regicide, not of the ritual death of a divine king, and similar instances can be adduced. According to Max Gluckman, even secular regicide is rare among Africans: "It required a long period of suffering before the people would turn against their rulers" (Fortes and Evans-Pritchard 1940: 42). Bantu and Nilote, we see, differ in no way from Frenchman and Russian in this respect (did Louis XVI and Nicholas II suffer ritual deaths?).

If one turns from recent anthropological studies of African tribal government to like studies of African tribal religion, one finds no firmer support for Frazer's case. In *African Traditional Religion* (1954), Geoffrey Parrinder mentions only the "destooling" of chiefs among the Ashanti and Dahomeans, and the Yoruba practice of "[giving a] chief parrot's eggs as a sign that he must commit suicide" (p. 74). These are not ritual deaths, as Parrinder reports them, but political devices for removing kings. Thus West African institutions offer Frazer no more comfort than do East and South African.

[21] Notably Fortes and Evans-Pritchard 1940; Mair 1962; I. Schapera, *Government and Politics in Tribal Societies* (London: Watts, 1956). Schapera's book is limited to South African peoples, Mair's to East African.

[22] See Mair 1962: 224–227. Reports of human sacrifices at Nyoro and Ganda accession ceremonies and at intervals in a reign to augment the king's strength (Mair 1962: 224–225) also refer to an obsolete custom.

Miss Mair, in fact, spends a few pages (229–233) on Frazer's theory and asserts that no "East African ruler . . . conforms at all points to Frazer's picture of the divine king," and we may extend her statement to all Africa. Africa has divinè kings and ritual kings; African kings have ritual duties; Africans believe that the king's health is sympathetically linked to his nation's welfare. But there is no evidence for the ritual killing of the divine king.

Miss Mair (226–227, 232) is inclined to accept the Nyakyusa tradition of a former killing of a ritual king in anticipation of his natural death on the ground that the old men give such circumstantial accounts of the act: "When a Nyakyusa king was dying his councillors stopped up the orifices of his body so that his soul should not escape and the fertility of the land with it." As Mair points out, "this happened *when he was dying* – not when he was simply thought to be not as strong as he was." What happened to the Nyakyusa ritual king (no one now holds the office), as Mair reports it, conforms very closely to a widespread African custom of not allowing a dying king to breathe out his last breath by himself. Edwin Loeb reports this custom among the Kuanyama: before the king can die "naturally" a faithful attendant smothers him and does so at the last moment possible. This is essentially what Mair reports as a former Nyakyusa practice: the Nyakyusa councillors prevented the king's soul, identified with the fertility of the land, from escaping. According to Loeb, the Kuanyama identify the king's last breath with his soul; and if they do not catch his soul, his successor will be weakened: "If the heir caused a dying king to be killed, he then possessed the king's soul and became, like his predecessors, the incarnation of Kalunga, the High God. If on the other hand a king was allowed to die an entirely natural death, his soul did not enter into his successor."[23] This practice of anticipating the king's last breath hardly supports Frazer's theory. This is not the killing of a king when he begins to show signs of weakness, but when he is all but dead; it is not periodic, and there is no ritual. The attendants observe rules of etiquette, and the king must be suffocated in a prescribed way: e.g., the Kuanyama smother him with a piece of lambskin. All this is very far from Frazer's or Hooke's or Raglan's sacrificial ritual. Even this killing of the dying king is generally reported as a former custom, although Loeb and others believe that it still prevails among some tribes. Granting this to be a genuine African custom, we can see in it a source of those traditions reported or collected by Seligman, Frazer, Irstam, and others.[24]

[23] Edwin M. Loeb, *In Feudal Africa* (Bloomington: Indiana University, Research Center in Anthropology, Folklore, and Linguistics, 1962), p. 28.

[24] I have grave doubts that the alleged anticipatory killing of a dying king is or has been a real custom; no one has actually confirmed it. I am inclined to believe that the reports of this custom too are part of African folklore, fragments of the king-killing myth conjectured above. In Ghana, for example, the Akan king's death meant that the cosmos had succumbed to chaos; however old or sick the king was, his death was not anticipated. The cemetery custodian was sometimes brought to a dying king's bed, for the Akan believed that this would cause the king to die sooner; the custodian, however, merely touched the king gently and spoke a word of sympathy. See Meyerowitz 1960: 186–196.

Another source may be assassinations and usurpations, when the man who challenges the reigning king and succeeds in killing him obviously has the power to win the nation's acceptance of himself as successor. That is, these traditions are the myths and beliefs that justify and validate (see below) the actual killing of kings by whatever method and for whatever reason. Out of this traditional lore came those fanciful reports that fill a large part of *The Dying God*.

If we look outside Africa for evidence of king-killing, Frazer's hypothesis fares no better. There is in fact little to be found. Frazer, relying on the reports of early travellers to southern India, cites kings of Quilacare and Calicut as rulers who had to kill themselves at the end of a twelve-year reign.[25] A Portuguese traveller in the early sixteenth century reported that a king in Quilacare, after reigning twelve years, feasted the Brahmans and then in their presence mounted a scaffold and started hacking away his own members and flesh, finally cutting his throat as he grew faint from loss of blood; then scaffold and corpse were burned. The traveller did not see this done; he reported only what he was told.[26] According to Hamilton, an English traveller who visited Malabar in 1695, this royal suicide had *once* been the custom in Calicut. As a contemporary custom, he reported a feast of ten or twelve days held every twelve years. At the end of the festival any four men who wished could try to kill the king in his tent and take the kingship. The catch was that thirty or forty thousand armed men guarded the king's tent; yet there were always a few men who were ready to commit suicide by attacking the king's guard on that day. Hamilton did not witness this event, although he was in the region at the time. This custom was last observed in 1743, according to Logan, who found a record of it in the royal archives of Calicut. Logan, however, makes no mention of an earlier royal suicide. The king's suicide is plainly another "used to be" custom and almost certainly a fiction. We cannot be certain, either, that the reported later custom is authentic; a description of it in royal archives is no guarantee of its actuality: Logan examined the archives more than a century after the alleged final observance. Nevertheless, let all reports be as true as you please; where is the Hooke-Hocart-Raglan ritual? We see only feasting followed by the king's suicide on a scaffold, followed in turn by cremation of the dead king's body and election of a new king. In the later custom we see only a futile attack on the king's bodyguard.

---

[25] Frazer (1911*b*: 46–51) relies on F. de Magalhâes, *A Description of the Coasts of East Africa and Malabar* (title of the English translation published by Hakluyt Society, London, 1866, vol. 35, pp. 172–173; the original has been wrongly attributed to Duarte Barbosa) and on A. Hamilton, *Account of the East Indies* in Pinkerton's *Voyages and Travels*, VIII, 374; also on William Logan, *Malabar* (Madras, 1887).

[26] We may notice that the Portuguese traveller speaks of kings in Quilacare, whereas Hamilton and Logan speak of kings in Calicut. In Quilacare it was the king of the province, who was subject to the king of Colam. Apparently the greater king suffered no ritual death.

Wherever we look we reach the same result. Frazer (1911*b*: 51–52) cites the king of Passier in Sumatra: he too was killed after a short reign *in former times*. Frazer's example of the kingship of Bengal (1911*b*: 51) points to frequent assassinations rather than to ritual deaths (reports on the kingship of Passier also look rather like assassinations and usurpations): not all kings were killed. In any land an assassin-usurper who succeeds in gaining power is likely to be accepted and acknowledged by palace attendants and subjects. Other examples of human victims (e.g., the Meriah of Khonds) that Frazer cites were not kings, chiefs, pontiffs, or rainmakers; nor is their any indication that the victims were royal surrogates. Outside of Africa and South Asia, Frazer found no evidence of king-killing which is not purely mythical or legendary. Moreover he cites many instances of temporary kings and mock kings who were not put to death.

Such is Frazer's evidence on which Raglan relies for his original ritual, and which has deeply impressed Raglan, Graves, Hyman, and many another. For Frazer's impressive accumulation of materials has overwhelmed them, as it has many readers (especially the earlier), and blinded them to his frequent non-sequiturs and to the weaknesses in his argument. But in the past quarter-century an increasing number of readers, especially anthropologists, folklorists, and classical scholars, have not been convinced.[27]

Primeval Origins

Thus *The Golden Bough* fails to provide Raglan with the evidence he needs for his Ur-ritual of king-killing. Raglan's own theory, in so far as he goes beyond Frazer in tracing all myth and religion back to a single origin in the ancient Near East, encounters obstacles which Frazer's did not. We must ask about the ages before Raglan's primeval ritual began. Was it derived from earlier rituals? Raglan grants that there were earlier rituals, e.g., among late palaeolithic men, "but the rituals of known religions are not derived from [them]" (*OR* 51). Yet our only reason for interpreting the sorcerer painting at Les Trois Frères Cave

---

[27] For critiques of Frazer see Lang 1901, Fontenrose 1962: 76–77, and E. R. Leach, "Golden Bough or Gilded Twig?," *Daedalus* (Spring 1961), pp. 371–387. The anonymous reviewer of Evans-Pritchard's *Essays in Social Anthropology* in the London *Times Literary Supplement* (September 20, 1963, p. 698) points out the fundamental reason for the persistent vogue of Frazer's views among non-specialists: Evans-Pritchard's "account of the Shilluk kingship . . . is more complex and, from a European point of view, more prosaic than Frazer's mystique of the dying priest-king yielding to a young successor who will restore the national vitality. It is not difficult to understand why many general readers will continue to prefer the Frazerian type of interpretation which provides them with instant poetry, to the better argued, better documented and intellectually more exacting constructs of modern students." Greenway (1964: 283) makes the same point. Error is indeed hard to combat and almost impossible to defeat finally, especially if the undisciplined consider it "poetic"; yet it always turns out to be as tinsel compared with gold.

(a man masked as a deer or elk) as a participant in a ritual is that persons so masked take part in known primitive rituals (which, according to Raglan, must be descended from the ancient Near Eastern ritual). But let Raglan have his way. His theory requires that there be no myth or ritual on hand in the ancient Near East when the first divine victim was sacrificed. This sacrifice occurred, he says, in an already centralized kingdom (*H* xiii *fin.*). So it could not have begun before 4000 BC (*OR* 68). If we allow his king-sacrifice to begin in a monarchical city-state we might push the date back toward 6000 BC (much too early). We must assume that in the preceding centuries and millennia men told no stories, since in Raglan's hypothesis all known traditional tales must be derived from his Ur-ritual and only from that; and if traditional tales were already current, how deny that they must have had some influence on the content of the myths which arose from the ritual? Could it be that men had speech and yet told no stories? When did human speech begin? Surely the cave painters had speech; and there is much in palaeolithic artifacts to indicate that their makers and users gave instructions in words.[28] We may safely assume that Magdalenian hunters were speaking in 12,000 BC. So if we allow the most favorable dates to Raglan's hypothesis at each end, we are left with 6,000 years in which men could talk but never told a story to one another.[29]

Raglan would grant, I suppose, that men reported exciting events to friends, who repeated them to others, and that these narratives became changed and distorted in transmission. Raglan tells us that this sort of thing can happen: "a garbled account becomes more garbled every time it is repeated"; "the stories of court life that get abroad today are always inaccurate and often quite untrue" (*H* i). He would probably grant that supernatural features can enter into such narratives. Then are not these narratives what we call legends (which Raglan derives only from myths)? No, Raglan replies; some people call them legends, but they are really pseudo-history; they die out of oral tradition in a century or so and never contribute anything to myth or ritual. It appears that myth and pseudo-history are mutually repulsive, never touching each other. Myth and legend, according to Raglan, never contain any historical truth or real persons: if the Mesopotamians or Egyptians of 6000–4000 BC told pseudo-historical tales, these had no effect on the momentous ritual text, i.e., myth, which they invented, even if some tales were told about the king.

[28] See Jacquetta Hawkes, *History of Mankind I: Prehistory* (New York: Harper & Row, 1963), pp. 108–113; Grahame Clark, *World Prehistory: An Outline* (Cambridge University Press, 1961), pp. 28–29, 33.

[29] Raglan has a ritual theory of language origin too (*OR* 44, 45–46). Ritualists are likely to seize on the gesture theory of speech origin to support their position; in doing so they identify all gesture with ritual, just as they sometimes incline to identify all speech with myth. But obviously, if all gesture is ritual and all speech is myth, the terms *ritual* and *myth* lose all distinctive meaning, and the ritual theory, embracing everything, becomes meaningless. Then we must start all over to study ceremonial acts as distinct from other acts, traditional tales of gods and heroes as distinct from all other forms of speech.

Still, Raglan must hedge. Attila, Theodoric, and Charlemagne were certainly historical persons, and yet they appear prominently as characters in medieval legends. Raglan says that they have slipped into the place of old hero-gods (*H* v). Recalling, however, what Raglan has said about Arthur, Robin Hood, Agamemnon, and other legendary figures, we know well that if the historicity of Attila, Theodoric, and Charlemagne were not guaranteed, Raglan (and Hyman too) would confidently assert that they were simply old gods and that anybody who thought otherwise would be a Euhemerist. That is, the only real persons who have ever become legendary figures are those whose historicity can be proved. I do not believe in the historicity of Arthur or Agamemnon either (I am not arguing for an origin of legends in real events and persons), but I believe that Raglan's way of proving them unhistorical is unsound.

Thomas Becket

The weakness of Raglan's theory is revealed when he deals with Thomas Becket and Guy Fawkes (1955). The murder of Becket in Canterbury Cathedral on December 29, 1170, is an historical event, described by five eyewitnesses who wrote accounts of the deed (Abbott 1898: I, 11–15). A cult of the Martyr Thomas (canonized as St. Thomas of Canterbury on February 21, 1173) began at once in Canterbury and flourished there until the Reformation. After 1220 the cathedral contained four shrines of St Thomas (Martyrdom, his tomb in the crypt, St. Thomas's crown, the great shrine).[30] Hither came thousands of pilgrims for three centuries and a half. A Canterbury pilgrimage provided Chaucer with the frame of his *Canterbury Tales*, and the poet lets us see vividly how

> . . . to Caunterbury they wende,
> The holy blisful martir for to seke,
> That hem hath holpen, whan that they were seke.
> (Prologue 16–18)

Thomas immediately acquired a healing cult; his first miracles, reported soon after his death (the very first is reported to have occurred the evening that followed his murder), are miracles of healing. Like Asklepios, he appeared to the sick in dreams and prescribed remedies to them. Thousands were healed, according to report, by drinking St. Thomas's water, which had remarkable powers; it was drawn from St. Thomas's well in the crypt and tinctured with what was reputed to be his blood. And, like Asklepios, Thomas even raised

---

[30] J. Charles Wall, *The Four Shrines of St. Thomas at Canterbury* (London: Talbot, 1932); John Morris, *The Life and Martyrdom of Saint Thomas Becket*, 2nd edn (London, New York, 1885), pp. 473–476.

men from death (so we are told by William of Canterbury and others).[31] He was also a savior and protector of sailors and seafarers, and thus his cult resembles those of Apollo and the Hemithea of Kastabos, who were also believed powerful for both healing and safe navigation.[32] Like Poseidon, Thomas could strike the earth with his staff and bring forth a spring. Like healing and marine deities of the pagans, he had prophetic powers: he had reputedly foreseen his violent death and he spoke prophecies in dreams after his death. The cult of St. Thomas of Canterbury (or of Acre) spread throughout England, and in France, Italy, Flanders, and elsewhere churches were dedicated to him. Relics of St. Thomas could be seen everywhere, and some can still be seen; the four shrines at Canterbury held his bones, his arms could once be seen in a nunnery in Lisbon, and churches at Mons and Florence still have parts of his arms.[33]

[31]   See Abbott 1898: I, 250–251; II, 18, 44, 51, 55. For the testimonies of the Asklepios cult at Epidauros, see Emma J. and Ludwig Edelstein, *Asclepius I: Testimonies* (Baltimore: Johns Hopkins Press, 1945).

[32]   *Hemithea* (Demigoddess) was a name or title of the Aegean sea-goddess commonly called Leukothea (White Goddess); see my *White Goddess and Syrian Goddess*, University of California Publications in Semitic Philology, XI (Berkeley and Los Angeles: University of California Press, 1951), 125–148, and Diod. 5.62, where we see Apollo as the divine patron of the three daughters of Staphylos who were translated into forms of the sea-goddess. In fact, the latter myth (or its type) appears to survive in several Canterbury miracle stories wherein a young woman replaces Hemithea. See e.g., Abbott 1898: II, 237–256: Salerna of Ifield stole cheese from her mother's larder, and in fear of punishment leaped into a well. The daughters of Staphylos fell asleep while guarding their father's wine (perhaps because they drank of it), and as they slept swine broke into the wine vat and destroyed its contents; in fear of punishment they leaped into the sea. St Thomas appeared to Salerna and protected her until rescue came; Apollo appeared to Staphylos' daughters in the sea and brought them safely to land. In the miracle tales of men who were buried under earth or submerged under water we may see Hemithea-Leukothea's male companion, son or brother, worshipped as Palaimon or Tenes or Anios, and closely related to Dionysos, Attis, and Adonis – the descent into earth or sea in the pagan myths means death, which is followed by resurrection and apotheosis. William of Gloucester, buried under a fall of earth from the tenth hour of one day to the third hour of the next (two days in archaic reckoning) emerged alive and unhurt with St Thomas's help, after the priest had celebrated his funeral rites (Abbott, II, 220–235); just so Herakles, who had the by-name Palaimon, emerged from the Nemean lion's cave to find King Molorchos making funeral offerings to the dead Herakles (see Fontenrose 1959: 357). John of Roxburgh, cast by his horse into the Tweed, descended into the depths of the stream to a rock-built hollow: *in quoddam concavum lapideum quod vel natura construxerat vel suo naufrago martyr excavaverat intrusus est* (William of Canterbury). He stayed underneath for many hours, saw visions, and finally was raised miraculously to land; he too had been given up for dead (Abbott, II, 259–270). Only in this sketchy way can I draw the parallels here; the correspondences of detail between these miracle stories and the indicated pagan myths are numerous and deserve careful study.

[33]   Latin texts and translations of the accounts of miracles compiled by Benedict and William of Canterbury are contained in Abbott 1898: II; for illustrative examples see 76–79, 80–102, 128–143, 146–160, 162–169. On the miracles in general see Abbott, I, 223–333, and II, 3–75; Morris, op. cit., pp. 454–465; Francis Watt, *Canterbury Pilgrims and Their Ways* (London: Methuen, 1917), pp. 24–34; H. Snowden Ward, *The Canterbury Pilgrimages* (London: Black, 1927), pp. 85–92. On relics, pilgrimages, and cult see Morris, pp. 466–477, 510–519; Watt, pp. 35–46, 160–174; Ward, pp. 100–107.

Although the cult of St. Thomas waned after Henry VIII destroyed the shrines and relics at Canterbury in 1538, it has by no means disappeared. The Roman Catholic Church maintains the cult: at Canterbury the Catholic church of St. Thomas contains a reproduction of the great shrine. Nor has the Church of England entirely forsaken him. Thirty-seven Anglican churches have preserved their dedications to St. Thomas of Canterbury (e.g., at Lapford in Devon), and the verger at Canterbury Cathedral now guides visitors to the sites of the former shrines. In several English towns and districts St. Thomas's Day, July 7, is still observed with fairs, feasts, and customs, either on the day itself or on the Sunday or Monday following.[34]

Myths and legends soon gathered about Thomas. Not only are the tales of miracles and cures abundant, but also marvelous features found their way into the saint's biography, even in the contemporary *vitae*. Marvels attended his birth, every phase of his life, and his death; obviously some biographers adapted Thomas's *vita* to the gospel narrative. The tale of the murder reached Iceland in the thirteenth century and became the subject of the *Thomas Saga*, a highly inconvenient fact for Lord Raglan, who contends that all Norse sagas have plots derived from the *Volsunga Saga* (*H* v).

So we see clearly that in the tradition of Thomas Becket an historical person became an object of worship and a figure of myth and legend. Obviously, if the historicity of Thomas Becket were not unassailable, Raglan would banish him from history as merely a medieval form of Asklepios or Apollo. In making this point I do not intend to say that gods and heroes were originally living men, or that we should look for the source of myths and legends in true history. I am *not* advocating "Euhemerism"; I am showing that historical persons sometimes become objects of cult and figures of legend, and that historical events may become episodes of legend. If we dismiss the miracle legends as pure fabrications, we still find legendary distortion of the murder narrative. For example, according to William Fitzstephen, when the four knights tried to drag Thomas from the cathedral, he struggled against them and his companions held him back; and so the knights killed him on the spot (Abbott 1898: I 102–104, 128). According to Edward Grim, Thomas clung to a pillar, so that the murderers could not move him (Abbot 1898: I, 101–102). According to an anonymous account, Edward Grim held Thomas back, thwarting the efforts of the assassins to drag him outside (Abbott 1898: I, 107). But in the *Thomas Saga* the knights could not budge Thomas, because the Holy Ghost made the

---

[34] On the modern cult see Watt, op. cit., pp. 274–276; Ward, op. cit., pp. 103–107; A. R. Wright and T. E. Lones, *British Calendar Customs, England III: Fixed Festivals* (London: Glaisher; Glasgow: Wylie, 1940), pp. 30–32. Wright describes the Bodmin Riding, celebrated at Bodmin in Cornwall on the Sunday and Monday after July 7 with a riding procession, offering of flowers at the Priory, and drinking of "the Riding-ale," which two young men, attended by musicians, carried around the town. The observance apparently died out in the nineteenth century, unless it has been revived, as such customs often are nowadays.

marble floor as soft as snow, so that Thomas's feet were firmly planted in the marble; and as evidence of this marvel, adds the *Saga*, his footprints may still be seen on the floor and receive the pilgrims' kisses (Abbott 1898: I, 114–115). The knight's first blow, dealt by Reginald Fitzurse, fell on Edward Grim's arm, which was nearly amputated (Abbott 1898: I, 128). No recovery of the arm is mentioned in contemporary sources; but according to pseudo-Grim, it was miraculously made whole a year later, after Grim had despaired of its healing, when the martyr appeared to him in a dream (Abbott 1898: II, 288). In the *Saga* Grim's arm was miraculously "whole and healed before the body of the Archbishop was cold on the floor" (Abbott 1898: I, 245).

In these accounts we notice the very process which Raglan and Hyman deny, the legendary distortion of an actual event and the introduction or addition of supernatural features to an historical narrative. In truth, we may plainly see two sources of legend in the Becket material. (1) The miracles and visions, which have no basis in actual events, were modelled on familiar patterns of Christian myth and legend: the Christ story and saints' legends directly affected the Thomas story. Old pagan myths, long since absorbed into Christian legend, affected it indirectly – myths of Asklepios, Leukothea-Hemithea, and Dionysos (see notes 31, 32). This is not to deny that these myth-types may have an ultimate ritual origin – that is the main question before us. (2) Most legends about Becket's life and death obviously arose from actual events, and some miracle legends possibly have a basis in fact (the Canterbury clergy made some attempt to verify the early cures, and the same question of authenticity arises as for tales of faith healings in general). We may grant that the historical narratives were gradually shaped into traditional forms of legend; but we must still allow that an actual event, or series of events, made Thomas Becket a figure of legend and shaped the central narrative of his death in those accounts that are legendary rather than historical.

We can hardly overvalue the Becket material for the study of myth and religion: it allows us to witness the birth and development of a deity, his cult, and his myth. Are we to say that Thomas's case is unique? That nothing of the sort happened in ancient times? We may observe, above all, that although the cult and myth grew up together, there is no correspondence whatever between the rituals of Thomas worship and the mythical events. We may overlook Lord Raglan's inconsistency and allow him to say that in this instance the myth recounts an historical event: "As the pilgrims performed the ritual of touring the cathedral and singing hymns or praying at spots connected with Becket's life and death, the story of these was recited. The story, since it explained the ritual, could properly be described as a myth" (1955: 76). But do the tour, hymns, and prayers re-enact the tale of murder in the cathedral? Or did the myth grow up with or develop out of the rituals as their spoken accompaniment, as Raglan says all myths do? Obviously in this case the myth is prior; and the processions, hymns, prayers, offerings, and masses at Canterbury were the long-established forms of Catholic worship. What Raglan needs at Canterbury is a dramatic ritual or ritual drama which enacted Becket's ministry, passion, death, and epiphany as a saint, out of which drama the myth as we know it took shape. No such thing occurred.

Guy Fawkes

If in the tradition of Thomas Becket we witness the making of a god (i.e., a benevolent deity), in the tradition of Guy Fawkes we witness the making of a demon (a malevolent deity).[35] Guy Fawkes was a real person who was convicted of complicity in a plot to blow up the Parliament House in 1605 and was hanged for it along with fellow conspirators. Since 1607, when the failure of the Gunpowder Plot was first commemorated at Bristol, November 5 has been Guy Fawkes Day in England, celebrated with the making of effigies called guys, which are burned in huge bonfires on the evening of that day (see the beginning of Hardy's *Return of the Native*). The guys and bonfires are constant features of the festival; otherwise each English town has its own way of observing the day. Frequent are fireworks, bell-ringing, making and eating of "tharfcakes" and "Parkin cakes," shouting and chanting of rhymes, and certain pranks associated elsewhere (and in England, too) with Hallowe'en: the wearing of grotesque masks and costumes, taking of gates and fences (sometimes burnt in the bonfires), breaking of windows, and "trick or treat."[36] Obviously this patriotic festival has taken over the rites and customs of older religious festivals, celebrated around the same time of year. Raglan informs us that "The fifth of November was the date of an ancient fire festival," and supposes that once the burning of a human victim was an important feature of it. In so speculating, Raglan ignores the simpler explanation that a people familiar with burning as a means of execution may find it appropriate to burn a criminal's

---

[35] We should notice too that Becket and Fawkes represent the same cause, that of the Catholic Church against the English king. We can understand fairly well why the slain Becket, in the twelfth century, became a saint and martyr, whereas the executed Fawkes and fellow-conspirators, in the seventeenth century, acquired an odious memory. Yet, though the demonic Fawkes is a Protestant creation (notice also Protestant hostility to Becket's memory beginning with Henry VIII), Catholics have never, so far as I know, remotely considered Fawkes or any other conspirator a candidate for sainthood; there have been at most attempts to clear his name and to debunk the Gunpowder Plot (see H. Ross Williamson, *The Gunpowder Plot* [London: Faber, 1951]). One of the executed, Father Garnet, whose guilt may be open to question, appears to have started on Becket's road, for his execution was immediately followed by a miracle: his blood on a straw which fell from the scaffold showed the outline of a face; in due time this became Garnet's face under "a martyr's crown and with the sign of the Cross on his forehead"; prints of the straw were thereafter sold on the continent (see Williamson, pp. 242–243). Worth study is why Fawkes became the arch-villian rather than Catesby, Winter, or some other.

[36] See Wright and Lones, op. cit., pp. 145–156.

effigy. To this simpler explanation Raglan may object (and he does point out) that Fawkes was not burned but hanged. Yet the hanging of effigies is also a well-known feature of harvest and other festivals.[37] The burning, after all, disposes of the guys.

After mentioning the true manner of Fawkes's execution, Raglan says, rather oddly for his general thesis, "but his story has nevertheless been adopted as the myth of this ritual" (1955: 76). He now wants to take the true and unchanged historical narrative as the "myth" of the November 5 rituals. He would rather allow a myth to be a true story than to be distorted history. And yet a distorted tradition that Fawkes was burned has really become the popular "myth" of the November 5 festivities. Here is unquestionably a real person who has become a figure of myth and who has also become an object of apotropaic rites (which bear little resemblance to the Fawkes story, true or distorted). Again what Raglan and Hyman say cannot happen has happened. They must grant the reality of Guy Fawkes, but we know very well that, if we had no record of the Gunpowder Plot, they would point to ancient fire festivals at harvest time, to the burning and hanging of effigies, and flatly deny that Fawkes could possibly be anything but an old deity (a harvest spirit in fox form, no doubt), and that the Gunpowder Plot could be anything but an ancient myth derived from the sacrifice of the divine king.[38] It would be perfectly obvious to them: here was an agent of the current Antichrist (Old Year, Winter, Drought, Death, Evil, ultimately the slain king), just about to kill the king (Christ's viceroy) and lords (and early in the new king's reign too), whom the king's officers rescued in the nick of time by capturing and killing the enemy for the good of the whole kingdom. They would point for confirmation to the record of a Guy Fawkes Day procession: a wagon carried an enthroned image of the Pope, behind which stood a person dressed as Satan, the Pope's privy-councillor, who caressed the effigy and gave advice to it, now in whispers, now in loud tones.[39] Yes, perfectly obvious, but quite wrong.

Raglan's Euhemerism

Many more instances of real men who have become subjects of myth and objects of cult or apotropaic rites can be found. Such apotheosis, of course,

[37] On rites of burning or hanging effigies, see Frazer, 1911b: 220–233 and *Adonis Attis Osiris*, 3rd edn (*Golden Bough* IV [London: Macmillan, 1914]), I, pp. 288–297.

[38] In his criticism of Frazer's theory Alfred C. Lyall, pointing to the rituals of Guy Fawkes and to those of Hasan and Hosein among the Shiite Moslems, says, "These and many other such ceremonies are only saved from annexation to mythologic cloudland by lying within the region of accepted history; while all that are found beyond that pale seem to be treated as fair prize by victorious analysis; . . . ," *Asiatic Studies Religious and Social*, 2nd edn, II (London: Murray, 1907), p. 209.

[39] See W. Carew Hazlitt, *Faiths and Folklore* (London: Reeves & Turner, 1905), p. 232.

does not justify us in finding a real person behind Zeus or Odin, or an historical event behind Thor's visit to Jötunheim. That is, we cannot accept either Euhemerism or Raglanism as a satisfactory theory of the origin of the concept of deity or of the origin of myths. I have said "Euhemerism or Raglanism," and Raglan would approve the disjunction, since he considers his ritual theory to be the polar opposite of Euhemerism. But is it? Our treatment of Becket and Fawkes warrants a discussion of Euhemerism, since the subject has provoked many misconceptions.

Although Raglan and Hyman have talked a good deal about Euhemerism and have made "Euhemerist" a term of reproach, they are not clear about what Euhemerism means and do not realize that Euhemerism is not inconsistent with a ritual theory of god and myth origins. According to Raglan, who consulted Smith's *Classical Dictionary* and Hastings' *Encyclopedia*, Euhemerism is the theory that the gods were originally kings and great men who received worship after their deaths (*H* xviii, *OR* 80). Raglan seizes upon the phrase "after death," supposing that the essence of Euhemerism is the worship of a dead king or benefactor. He has fallen into a common misconception of Euhemerism; for Euhemeros did *not* say that the first gods were dead kings: he said that they were *living* kings. Raglan and Hyman have not looked up Euhemeros' *Sacred History* to find out what it actually said. The book itself is lost, but Diodoros' history has a summary of it (5.41–46, 6.1). It was the story of an imaginary journey across the Indian Ocean to the Utopian land of Panchaia. There, says Euhemeros, he read an inscription, which informed him that Kronos and Zeus had been kings on earth; and while he was king, "Zeus received honor among all peoples and was called god (*theos*)" (Diod. 6. 1. 10). Euhemeros also tells us that "Others became gods on earth, who because of their benefactions to men won immortal honor and glory" (Diod. 6. 1. 2). That is, Zeus and other men became gods *while they lived on earth*. And this turns out to be a simpler form of Raglan's own theory. For Raglan, like Euhemeros, maintains that the first gods were living kings: "If [my] view is correct, then it follows that the earliest gods were not invisible beings, but men" (*OR* 73); ". . . from the divine king arose in course of time the idea of the god" (*OR* 70). Euhemeros differs from Raglan only in believing that a king named Zeus became the god so named; Raglan, somewhat less naively, believes that the god is the apotheosized kingship, and that the god's name is not necessarily that of any actual king. Raglan reveals his own Euhemerism when he asserts that "invisible gods are the spirits of dead men; not, as the Euhemerists believe, of individual dead men, but of royal dynasties."[40] He is here very careless in

[40] *OR* 90. According to Raglan (*OR* 73), we should expect the earliest gods to be men and not invisible beings, "for if gods had been thought of from the beginning as spiritual and invisible, it is difficult to imagine how people could have come to believe that a man was a god; the very fact that he was visible would make it obvious that he was not." Raglan takes no notice here of

expression, since he objects to others' speaking of gods as deified dead men; but he is really making a distinction between ancient and modern Euhemerism. In essence Euhemerism is the statement that gods developed from men who are now dead, and that is Raglan's position: "The king is worshipped when alive; he continues to be worshipped when dead, not because he is dead, but because he is believed to be in some way alive" (*OR* 80). So says Raglan, and all Euhemerists agree with him, even those who believe that the first gods were dead kings (for Raglan, after all, the first gods were dying kings).

In Raglan's eyes the arch-Euhemerist was William Ridgeway, who found the origins of drama in the worship of the dead, that is, in the cults of heroes and ancestors.[41] Ridgeway also thought that some gods and heroes had been real persons. What Raglan and Hyman fail to realize is that Ridgeway's theory is as much a theory of ritual origins as their own. Ridgeway said that "solemn songs and dances were part of the propitiatory rites performed at the tombs of heroes in order that they might protect their people, and that the earth, through their kindly interposition, might bring forth her fruits" (1910: 108). He further said that in Greece and elsewhere such dramatic rites developed into drama: "That a certain ancient ritual can be detected in Greek tragedies I gladly admit, for I have maintained that such there is, and that it arose out of the funeral rites and periodical celebrations to honour the good and noble or to appease the malevolent" (1915: 62). True enough, Ridgeway was speaking of the origins of drama; but for Raglan and Hyman the origin of myth and the origin of drama are much the same thing. Hyman, for example, constantly confuses tragic with myth origins. Ridgeway, furthermore, would probably not object to their interpretation of myth as ritual text; he objected only to deriving gods from projections of the rites and worshippers' emotions, to interpreting them as vegetation spirits or seasons, and to tracing all ritual drama back to king sacrifices and combats for the royal succession. Ridgeway was naive in his acceptance of the non-miraculous parts of legend as true history and in his supposing that every god or spirit was directly derived from some once living man who probably bore the same name. The point is that his theory is a ritual theory of myth origin. For there is no incompatibility between Euhemerism, however we define it, and the ritual theory; they are not polar opposites as

---

a god's power of taking bodily form or of vanishing as he wishes; but disregarding that omission, we should notice that he spends the next chapter in demonstrating that ghosts, spirits, and gods were always considered material and visible. Then why should the first gods not be a development of visible ghosts? I am not saying that they were; I am only pointing out that Raglan's alternatives are not mutually exclusive. Gods and ghosts are visible if present; but usually they are not present, and so are unseen.

[41] *H* iii, viii, xviii. Hyman (1962*a*: 242) adopts Raglan's view of Ridgeway. See Ridgeway 1910: chs i, ii; 1915: sect. i. I see no essential difference between Ridgeway's views and A. B. Cook's, who likewise derived myths from the rites attending dead kings (see note 17 above); yet Raglan and Hyman approve of Cook, who belonged to Jane Harrison's group.

Raglan and Hyman suppose.[42] Indeed, Raglan's own arguments might support Ridgeway's contention that the legends preserve a fairly accurate record of the actual deeds of men now dead, for Raglan maintains that nothing persists in oral tradition for more than 150 years at most, unless it is ritual-bound: the rituals, periodically reenacted, preserve the oral texts attached to them (*H* i, xi, xiii). If, then, a warrior's deeds were recited at his funeral rites, and if he became a hero or god with a permanent cult (the rites being repeated every year, for example), and if the rites included some mimicry or representation of the deeds, on Raglan's own showing a memory of true historical deeds might be preserved in oral tradition. I do not agree with Ridgeway that legends very often preserve historical fact; and I do not agree with Raglan that only ritual-bound narratives can endure in oral tradition. We know that many folktales have been transmitted over great expanses of space and time without ritual accompaniment, and have suffered only superficial changes in the process. For Raglan, folktales are myths detached from the rituals; but he can hardly deny that they continue to be preserved fairly intact in folk tradition after they have been cut loose from the supposed rituals. In any case, Raglan's and Ridgeway's theories fit nicely together on many points.

So Hyman could very well list Ridgeway in his calendar of ritualist saints rather than in his Euhemerist rogues' gallery.[43] And he could easily place Raglan among the rogues for deriving gods from real kings, which is the Euhemerism of Euhemeros. Raglan is also guilty of Euhemerism in the broader and looser sense that he and Hyman give to the term: the rationalist interpretation of myth as distorted history. This is Palaiphatism rather than Euhemerism: Palaiphatos' rather absurd *Peri Apistōn* (*On Incredible Tales*) is the principal surviving example of ancient attempts to extract true history from myths by translating mythic into possible events. Raglan too, less naively than Palaiphatos, derives history from myths and traditions. From them, and from no other evidence, as we have seen, he derives a recurring prehistoric (or early historic) event, the annual killing of a king and installation of his successor. And this he does after spending several chapters of *The Hero* in demonstrating that

---

[42] Hyman (1960: 127) maintains that the Euhemeristic theory makes myths into "trivial lies," whereas myths embody the "deepest and most profound truths" of a society, expressing "profound sociological and psychological truth." On the contrary, if myths spring from actual events (and I do not say that they do), they would contain some truth; and the theory is that the untruthful parts were not deliberate lies but the result of gradually accumulating errors. As for the profound truths in myths, Hyman and the ritualists never tell us what they are. The statements made in myths are almost without exception factually untrue (a myth might incidentally include a correct geographical or astronomical statement). Any sense in which they might be true is wholly Pickwickian. Truth and falsehood have nothing to do with their value for us: they are good stories.

[43] Among the saints Hyman should also list Robert Graves, who in his *Greek Myths* announces a ritualistic interpretation which centers on matriarchy; but he includes a good deal of "Euhemerism" too.

we must not look for any historical truth whatever in legend. To this Raglan
would reply that history is what happens once; recurring events are not history
– that is, coronations and presidential inaugurations are not history, nor, it
seems, are periodic executions, assassinations, and dethronements of kings.[44]
Such a distinction will not hold up for a moment; either myth and legend are
never veracious in any respect, or they preserve memories of both single and
repeated events, if they preserve any at all. The assassination of Becket was not
a repeated event.

Prehistoric Drama

Raglan's theory demands a well developed drama in the ancient Near East, and
afterwards in other lands when it had been diffused thence, since he spends
several chapters (*H* xx–xxvii) in pointing out the dramatic features of myths:
direct discourse, prophecies, agelessness of characters, unities of place and
time, and so forth. He is hardly right about all traditional tales, since Peleus,
Pelias, Tithonos, and Oedipus grew old, and Greek legendary cycles do not
come to an abrupt end, as Raglan maintains. In any case, these features are
narrative conventions the world over; that they were originally dramatic conventions and that all narrative arises from drama (as when one person tells
another the plot of a play that he has seen) remains for Raglan to demonstrate,
especially since the familiar sequence is just the other way: a novel is often
dramatized, whereas a play is seldom converted to narrative form (except
orally and casually). There is simply no evidence of a well developed drama in
the ancient Near East: festival programs and ritual texts survive, but there is
nothing truly dramatic in them (the Egyptian coronation drama, as it is called,
is in no real sense a drama). We may speak of dramatic rituals, but hardly of
ritual dramas in ancient Mesopotamia, Canaan, or Egypt: it is the difference
between the Mass and Passion Play. We can agree with Raglan (*H* xxvii) that
Athenian tragedy did not suddenly spring into existence in 534 BC; nobody,
indeed, has said that it did, and there is good evidence for earlier dramatic
performances in several parts of Greece (but not very much earlier; was there
anything like true drama before 700 BC?). Raglan's theory demands dramatic
performances all over the Near East at least two thousand years before 600 BC.
Did drama receive a high development in Mesopotamia or Egypt? There is no
record of it.

[44] See *H* xiii; Raglan says "things that happen once only are nothing to the ritualist [meaning
the ritual performer]." However, the Gunpowder Plot, the Battle of Kossovo, the American
declaration of independence in 1776, the Greek in 1821, are all examples of single events which
have meant something to ritual performers. In ancient times single events like victories and
foundations of cities gave rise to anniversary festivals.

Let us suppose that Babylon and Egypt had some fine plays which have completely disappeared: why then was Greek drama still primitive and elementary in the sixth century? Raglan, remember, allows no independent starts: all ritual drama and myth were diffused from one center. We find a development of true drama in Greece, India, China, Japan, and late medieval Europe, but hardly anywhere else. True enough, it probably did not have a spontaneous and independent origin in each country; diffusion and cultural influences were at work. But it appeared comparatively late everywhere, and Raglan must have a flourishing drama in the Near East in very early times.

Furthermore is it likely that an elaborate myth-ritual complex could have been transmitted intact from land to land in early times, as Raglan's theory demands? In an essay which surprisingly concludes Hooke's third collection of papers on the Near Eastern myth-ritual pattern (and delivers the *coup de grâce* to the theory built up in all three), S. G. F. Brandon shows that diffusion of such a complex was highly unlikely (Hooke 1958: 261–291); when such a simple device as the winged sun-disk symbol lost its whole significance in its migration from Egypt to Assyria, Persia, and Cappadocia, how can we suppose that the royal sacrificial ritual could preserve not only its whole program but its whole meaning? And who were the carriers? Not even Hooke and his school suppose that this was a proselytizing religion that sent forth missionaries like Christianity and Islam; they allege transmission through trade, war, and colonization. But, asks Brandon, were traders, soldiers, and colonists likely to be interested in spreading this particular cult? Finally he shows that Hooke bases his myth-ritual pattern mainly on the ritual program of the Akitu festival, which was not typical. And I have shown in *Python* (ch. xv) that the Babylonian myth of beginnings, as told in *Enuma elish*, which was recited at the Akitu festival, was not enacted or symbolized in the ritual program of that festival.

Hocart (1927) has built up a model coronation ritual of 26 parts, which he believes was adapted for use on other solemn occasions, so that other rituals (e.g., marriage and initiation) are derived from it. He explains that "A complete set of all the parts is not known to occur anywhere" (p. 70). The ancient Indian coronation ritual shows 18 parts or component acts, and the Fijian ceremony of installation of a chief shows 17; of the 25 Old World rituals which he analyzes, all others have fewer than 17 of the 26 components. In fact, the Indian coronation ritual, being the only ritual of the 25 that contains as many as 18 of the 26 acts, serves Hocart much as the Akitu ritual serves Hooke. Eleven rituals (44%) have 13 or more component acts (one half or more of the 26); eighteen (72%) have 9 or more (above one-third); seven (28%), then, show less than one-third of Hocart's pattern (the Malay marriage ritual has only two components). Component A which is really not an act but a belief (that the king dies and is reborn as a god) appears in 22 rituals, F in 20 ("The King is admonished to rule justly and promises to do so"), E in 19 ("The King must fight a ritual combat [1] by arms, or [2] by ceremonies, and [3] come out victorious"). Only these three components (under one-eighth) appear in more than three-fourths of the rituals; six (under one-fourth) appear in 17 or more (above two-thirds); nine (just above one-third) in 13 or more (above one-half); fifteen (under three-fifths) in 9 or more (above one-third); ten components (nearly two-fifths), therefore, are seen in fewer than 9 rituals (under one-third), and four of these ten in fewer than 6 rituals: component S (the king takes three steps in imitation of the rising sun) appears in only two and W (vassals and officials are consecrated with the king in either the ceremony or on the subsequent tour) in only one. This hardly looks like a well-established ritual pattern, even if we grant Hocart the validity of his analysis in every instance where he finds a pattern component in a particular ritual (correspondences are sometimes obscure or far-fetched).[45] If his case for a single ritual pattern fails, so must his case for deriving myths from it (Hocart 1952: ch. 1).

Conclusion of Critique of Raglan's Theory

Thus the scholarly foundations of Raglan's theory prove to be weak. William Bascom (1957) has undermined other supports, bringing forward damaging ethnographical and folkloristic facts. He admirably exposes the weaknesses, absurdities, and non-sequiturs of Raglan's arguments that myths must have a ritual origin because they do not have an historical or imaginative origin; that if one part of a legend is certainly unhistorical (as it is bound to be, if we call the story a legend), no part of it can have an historical origin; that no popular story-teller ever invents anything; that if the fairy tales of one country do not have a popular origin in that country (having been borrowed from another country) they do not have a popular origin in any country; and that folktales deal with subjects about which the folk have no knowledge (e.g., royal

---

[45] Ritual theorists may object that Hocart's case for his ritual pattern is as sound as the case for any myth pattern which scholars have constructed, e.g., the combat-myth pattern which I constructed in *Python* (1959: 9–11, 579–583, and tables on pp. 267–273, 359–364). If we make the same statistical analysis of the pattern, which contains 43 themes tabulated for 20 Old World myths, we get the following results. As many as 40 appear in the Python myth as tabulated (and all 43 might be claimed). Seven myths (35%) show 33–40 themes (above three-fourths); eleven (55%) show 29–40 (over two-thirds); fifteen (75%) show 22–40 (over one half); the least number of themes present in any myth is 17 (about 40%). Of the 43 themes, 3 appear in all twenty myths; 20 (nearly one half) in 15–20 myths (at least three-fourths); 22 (a bare majority) in 14–20 (over two-thirds); 30 (about 70%) in 10–20 (at least one half); 41 (95%) in 7–20 (over one-third); the remaining two appear in 6 myths (just under one-third). If one makes this analysis according to the 36 plot-components outlined in *Python* (262–265 and tables on pp. 270, 271, 361) instead of the themes, the results are approximately the same. I would say that this combat-myth pattern is much better established than Hocart's ritual pattern.

households).[46] Raglan has put us on our guard about reading history into legends – that is his one sound contribution.

References

A list of the books and articles referred to in text and notes by author's surname and publication year.

Abbott, Edwin A. 1898. *St Thomas of Canterbury: His Death and Miracles.* 2 vols; London.

Altheim, Franz 1930. *Griechische Götter im alten Rom.* In Religionsgeschichtliche Versuche und Vorarbeiten XXII, 1. Giessen: Töpelmann.

Bascom, William 1957. "The Myth-Ritual Theory," *JAF* 70: 103–114.

―― 1965. "The Forms of Folklore: Prose Narratives," *JAF* 78: 3–20.

Conway, R. S. 1928. *The Vergilian Age.* Cambridge, Mass.: Harvard University Press.

Evans-Pritchard, E. E. 1948. *The Divine Kingship of the Shilluk of the Nilotic Sudan.* Cambridge University Press.

Fontenrose, Joseph 1959. *Python: A Study of Delphic Myth and Its Origins.* Berkeley and Los Angeles: University of California Press.

―― 1961. "Some Observations on Hyman's Review of *Python,*" *Carleton Miscellany* II, 3: 122–125.

―― 1962. Review of Hyman, *The Tangled Bank. Carleton Miscellany* III, 4: 73–78.

Fortes, M., and E. E. Evans-Pritchard, editors 1940. *African Political Systems.* Oxford University Press.

[46] The Tory lord speaks often in Raglan's scholarly writing. According to him, only a few human beings are inventive or even intelligent, and they are royalty, nobility, or high clergy; no one else can even repeat anything correctly but must garble it (at the same time, it seems, they must tell a tale always in the same words without variation). I have known a humble miner who composed a ballad with refrain and elementary melody. D. H. Lawrence was fairly inventive in fiction for being the son of a miner. Raglan's upper-class bias appears in his remarks on the story of King Alfred and the cakes. The story cannot be true, he assures us, because "Even if the old woman had dared to whisper it to her cronies, they would not have believed her, and the King would never have recounted a story that would have exposed him to ridicule and lowered the prestige upon which his success depended" (*H* i). But of course the old woman would tell her friends, and they would readily believe her and spread the story; and good King Alfred would certainly tell the story as a joke on himself, since he did not take the kingship as seriously as Lord Raglan does. The story is probably untrue, but not for Raglan's reasons. Likewise Raglan's contention (*H* xi) that nobody who has beliefs about the supernatural can "give free rein to his imagination" concerning his deities, because "the freedom of his imagination must [be] trammelled by the nature of his belief," is not true for ancient Greece or any other land. Raglan is thinking about the Christian creed and the Thirty-Nine Articles; but myths are not creeds, and myth-tellers innovate as they please. Nor is his statement (*H* xi) that an atheist could not tell a myth imaginatively at all sound. Gods may have no existence for an atheist (Raglan's argument), but he knows about the concept of gods, and may hear, enjoy, and even tell myths.

Frazer, James George 1911a. *The Magic Art* (*The Golden Bough* I). 2 vols; 3rd edn; London: Macmillan.

―― 1911b. *The Dying God* (*The Golden Bough* III). London: Macmillan.

Gaster, Theodor 1950. *Thespis: Ritual, Myth and Drama in the Ancient Near East*. New York: Schuman.

Gordon, Arthur E. 1934. *The Cults of Aricia*. University of California Publications in Classical Archaeology, vol. 2, no. 1. Berkeley: University of California Press.

Greenway, John 1964. *Literature among the Primitives*. Hatboro: Folklore Associates.

Guarducci, Margherita 1939. "L'inno a Zeus Dicteo," *Studi e Materiali di Storia delle Religioni* XV: 1–22.

Harrison, Jane 1927. *Themis: A Study of the Social Origins of Greek Religion*. 2nd edn; Cambridge University Press.

Hocart, A. M. 1927. *Kingship*. London: Oxford University Press.

―― 1952. *The Life-giving Myth and Other Essays*. London: Methuen.

Hooke, S. H., editor 1933. *Myth and Ritual*. London: Oxford University Press.

―― 1935. *The Labyrinth*. London: SPCK; New York: Macmillan.

―― 1958. *Myth, Ritual, and Kingship*. Oxford University Press.

Hyman, Stanley Edgar 1948. *The Armed Vision*. New York: Knopf.

―― 1949. "Myth, Ritual, and Nonsense," *Kenyon Review* XI: 455–475.

―― 1955. "The Ritual View of Myth and the Mythic." In *Myth: A Symposium*, ed. Thomas Sebeok, pp. 84–94. Philadelphia: American Folklore Society.

―― 1960. Review of Fontenrose, *Python*. *Carleton Miscellany* I, 4: 124–127.

―― 1962a. *The Tangled Bank: Darwin, Marx, Frazer and Freud as Imaginative Writers*. New York: Atheneum.

―― 1962b. "Leaping for Goodly Themis," *New Leader* XLV, 22 (October 29, 1962): 24–25.

Irstam, Tor 1944. *The King of Ganda: Studies in the Institutions of Sacral Kingship in Africa*. The Ethnographical Museum of Sweden, Stockholm, n.s. 8. Lund: Ohlsson.

Kluckhohn, Clyde 1942. "Myths and Rituals: A General Theory," *Harvard Theological Review* XXXV: 45–79.

Lang, Andrew 1901. *Magic and Religion*. London, New York, Bombay: Longmans, Green.

Mair, Lucy 1962. *Primitive Government*. Baltimore: Penguin Books.

Malinowski, Bronislaw 1926. *Myth in Primitive Psychology*. London: Kegan Paul, Trench, Trubner.

Marlow, A. N. 1961. "Myth and Ritual in Early Greece," *John Rylands Library Bulletin* XLIII: 373–402.

Meyerowitz, Eva L. R. 1960. *The Divine Kingship in Ghana and Ancient Egypt*. London: Faber.

Moret, Alexandre 1927. *La mise à mort du dieu en Egypte*. Paris: Geuthner.

Morpurgo, Lucia 1903. "Nemus Aricinum," *Monumenti Antichi* XIII: 297–368 and Tables XIV–XVI.

Nilsson, Martin P. 1950. ·*The Minoan-Mycenaean Religion*. 2nd edn; Lund: Gleerup.

Raglan, Lord 1936. *The Hero: A Study in Tradition, Myth, and Drama*. London: Methuen.

―― 1949. *The Origins of Religion*. London: Watts.

―― 1955. "Myth and Ritual." In *Myth: A Symposium*, pp. 76–83 (see Hyman 1955).

Ridgeway, William 1910. *The Origin of Tragedy with Special Reference to the Greek Tragedians*. Cambridge University Press.

—— 1915. *The Dramas and Dramatic Dances of Non-European Races in Special Reference to the Origin of Greek Tragedy*. Cambridge University Press.

Rose, H. J. 1959. "The Evidence for Divine Kings in Greece." In *The Sacral Kingship*, Contributions to the Central Theme of the VIIIth International Congress for the History of Religions (Rome, April, 1955) – *Studies in the History of Religion* IV: 371–378. Leiden: Brill.

Seligman, C. G. 1932. *Pagan Tribes of the Nilotic Sudan* (with B. Z. Seligman). London: Routledge.

—— 1934. *Egypt and Negro Africa: A Study in Divine Kingship*. London: Routledge.

Willetts, R. F. 1962. *Cretan Cults and Festivals*. London: Routledge and Kegan Paul.

29

PROSPECTS

H. S. Versnel

In the concluding section (pp. 79–88) of his magisterial overview of the myth-ritualist theory "What Is Sauce for the Goose Is Sauce for the Gander: Myth and Ritual, Old and New" (1990, rev. 1993) (*Transition and Reversal in Myth and Ritual* [Leiden: Brill, 1993], ch. 1), H. S. Versnel (b. 1936), Professor of Ancient History at the University of Leiden, tries to reconcile the two main varieties of myth-ritualism that he has identified. Rather than focusing on differing views of the relationship between myth and ritual, he focuses on the differing kinds of rituals selected. Earlier myth-ritualists, beginning with Frazer, linked myths to New Year rituals. More recent myth-ritualists, notably Burkert, link myths to initiation rituals – a view first proposed by Harrison but not picked up by others till Burkert. Versnel seeks to harmonize the two approaches by stressing how both kinds of rituals function to provide transitions from one state – of the year or of the person – to another. In contrast to the other evaluations of myth-ritualism in this section, Versnel writes to promote, not to condemn, the theory.

So far I have essentially done no more than arrange, describe and, to a lesser degree, evaluate. The fact that the critical aspect was emphasized more forcibly in the latter part of the discussion may be explained by the fact that the first phase of the myth and ritual theory had long been concluded and assessed, whereas the most recent approach is still in full swing. That is why critical observations can certainly be useful, but never definitive. I do not want to conclude, however, without once more gathering in the lines we have observed so far. The resultant synthesis may no doubt strike the reader as sweeping. To make matters worse, the lack of space prevents me from arguing more

Original publication: H. S. Versnel, "Prospects," in his *Transition and Reversal in Myth and Ritual* (Leiden: Brill, 1993), pp. 79–88.

specifically. However, a few illustrations of what I mean will be given in later chapters. What I have to offer here is thus nothing but a tentative, somewhat intuitive suggestion that enables me to return to those complexes that up to now had been felt to be mutually exclusive: the myth and ritual complex of the New Year-sacral king-dying and rising god, on the one hand, and that of initiation, on the other.

Let us concentrate exclusively on the two complexes we have discussed – we might conceive of others, of course, but not many nor such easily recognizable ones – and consider the following questions:

What might be the reason that in the head of one person, Jane Harrison, the notions of two complexes could exist one after or beside the other, the divine protagonists changing effortlessly from one complex into the next (*Megistos Kouros*, Dionysos)?

How can we explain that some enthusiasts trace back the entire world-wide mythology to one myth and ritual complex, whereas others are reducing a considerable number of myths to the other complex?

How is it that some New Year specialists time and again point out resemblance, affinity or relation with initiation ideology, whereas initiation specialists are repeatedly drawing parallels with New Year elements?[1]

What do we infer from the fact that a myth and ritual theorist of the old stamp, A. M. Hocart, wrote a book about coronation rites of kings, whereas a representative of the recent trend, J. N. Bremmer, is seen to waver between boys' initiation and royal initiation?

Why is it that both types of approach claim primeval images like the flood[2]

---

[1] For these associations see for instance Burkert 1966, 25: "In den Initiationsriten erneuert sich das Leben der Gemeinschaft, in den daraus gewachsenen Neujahrsriten erneuert sich die Ordnung der Polis". Cf. *idem* on the legend of Romulus in: *Historia* 11 (1962) 356 ff.; Bremmer 1978b, 33 f. on elements of lustration as features of New Year festival and initiation; Eliade 1975 *passim*, especially ch. XII, XIII, p. 48; *idem, The Myth of the Eternal Return* (New York 1954) 62–73; Nouvel An, peau neuve, *Le Courier* 8 (1955) 7–32. In Egypt the coronation (initiation) of the new king is seen as the beginning of a new aeon and a new year: J. Bergman, *Ich bin Isis* (Uppsala 1968) 212 ff.

[2] There are relatively few examples of the primeval flood as a signal of initiation. Generally, the deluge theme is pre-eminently the image of chaos, seen as the obstacle to *kosmos*. The latter can only come to being after the victory over the chaotic deluge, a victory that is generally celebrated on New Year's day. Meuli 1975 I, 283–99, concludes: "Jene 'regénération totale du temps' ist von alten Völkern begriffen und dargestellt worden als das Auftauchen einer neuen, reinen Welt aus den Wassern der Sintflut" and he gives a substantiation of this statement in Meuli 1975 II, 1041 ff. The same ideas already in: H. Usener, *Sintflutsagen* (Bonn 1899) 36 ff. Cf. also: G. Piccaluga, *Lycaon* (Rome 1968) 69; Burkert 1983, index s.v. "Flood"; J. Rudhardt, Les mythes grecs relatifs a l'instauration du sacrifice. Les rôles corrélatifs de Prométhée et de son fils Deucalion, *MH* 27 (1970) 1–15; *idem, Le thème de l'eau primordiale dans la mythologie grecque* (Bern 1971). For a full discussion of the Greek material see: G. A. Caduff, *Antike Sintflutsgen* (Göttingen 1986): relationship with New Year festival: 229, 246, 255–8, 275 f. (with documentation), connection with initiation: 276 (without documentation). I agree with his predilection

and man-eating monsters,[3] beside numerous other elements such as role and status reversal, experience of anarchy, and so forth, for their own complex?[4]

How is one to explain that both can refer to word-wide materials, and, finally, how is it that so much attention was and still is paid to these two myth and ritual patterns and relatively little to others?

Now let us just give specific form to these questions once more. In the sequence of the epic of the *Odyssey* and the story of Troy connected with it, the hero leaves his country, has to wander, to wage war far from home, takes Troy by means of a stratagem, is threatened by water (sea), by man-eating and

---

for a more general interpretation of the victory over the Flood as a guarantee of "Ordnung". The theme has a central function in Near Eastern mythology: J. G. Frazer, *Folklore in the Old Testament* I (London 1918) 104–360, in the revised edition by Theodor H. Gaster, *Myth, Legend, and Custom in the Old Testament* (New York-London 1969, 1975[2]) 82–130; A. J. Wensinck, *The Ocean in the Literature of the Western Semites* (Amsterdam 1918); O. Kaiser, *Die mythische Bedeutung des Meeres in Aegypten, Ugarith und Israel* (Berlin 1962[2]); J. P. Lewis, *A Study of the Interpretation of Noah and the Flood in Jewish and Christian Literature* (Leiden 1968, 1978[2]). Generally on the symbolism of the Flood: H. Gollob, *Chrysaor. Mit einem Anhange über die Sintflutsage* (Vienna 1956). Cf. also the literature cited by Smith 1978, 98, and more recently on the "most studied narrative ever": A. Dundes (ed.), *The Flood Myth* (Berkeley 1988).

[3] On man-eating monsters and anthropophagy as symptoms of initiation: Bremmer 1978, 16 f. Cannibalism as a sign of (recurrent) periods of chaos and disturbance of order: A. J. Festugière, *Études de religion grecque et hellénistique* (Paris 1972) 145 ff.; M. Detienne, *Dionysos mis à mort* (Paris 1977) 5–60; C. Grottanelli, The Enemy King is a Monster. A Biblical Equation, *SSR* 3 (1979) 5 ff.; Versnel 1980, 591, and see below ch. II (p. 94). Chr. Sourvinou-Inwood, *BICS* 33 (1986) 42 n. 22, gives an extensive bibliography. Until very recently it was generally assumed that anthropophagy was practised, at least for ritual-cultic purposes, in prehistoric times. See for instance: H. Matjeka, Anthropophagie in der prähistorischen Ansiedlung bei Knowize und in der prähistorischen Zeit überhaupt, *Mitteilungen der Anthropologischen Gesellschaft Wien* 26 (1896) 129 ff.; W. Coblenz, Bandkeramischer Kannibalismus in Zauschwitz, *Ausgrabungen und Funde* 7 (1962) 67 ff.; J. Kneipp & H. Büttner, Anthropophagie in der jüngsten Bandkeramik der Wetterau, *Germania* 66 (1988) 489–97; R. Tannahill, *Flesh and Blood. A History of the Cannibal Complex* (1975). This belief is also professed in Hamerton-Kelly 1987, index s.v. Recently, however, serious doubts have been expressed. See for instance: *Nature* 348 (29 Nov. 1990) 395. The theories about cannibalism in Minoic Greece suffered the same fate: Hughes 1991, 18–24. This, of course, does not mean that W. Arens. *The Man-Eating Myth: Anthropology and Anthropophagy* (Oxford 1979) is right in rejecting *all* testimonies of man eating. Cf. R. Rosaldo in: Hamerton-Kelly 1987, 240: "I have spent three years in northern Luzon living with a group who are headhunters. Their headhunting is vastly exaggerated and overreported, but they do headhunt; there is no question about that"; cf. also: G. Weiss, *Elementarreligionen* (Vienna-New York 1987) 142–59. Recently, T. D. White, *Prehistoric Cannibalism at Mancos 5MTUMR-2346* (Princeton U. P. Lawrenceville 1992) has reopened the discusion and established cannibalism in a Colorado pueblo of around 1100 AD.

[4] It cannot be said that the fairy tales in which persons are swallowed up by a whale or dragon are necessarily connected with initiation ritual. For the widespread occurrence of this motif see: W. Fauth, Utopische Inseln in den "Wahren Geschichten" des Lukian, *Gymnasium* 86 (1979) 49 ff.; U. Steffen, *Das Mysterium von Tod und Auferstehung: Formen und Wandlungen des Jona-Motivs* (Göttingen 1963); *idem, Drachenkampf: Der Mythos vom Bösen* (Stuttgart 1984); N. Forsyth, *The Old Enemy: Satan and the Combat Myth* (Princeton UP 1987).

other monsters, returns home, is menaced again, is finally triumphant and becomes king (again).

If we had been obliged to decide, after reading the second section of the present chapter, which pattern had been transformed into a myth in this case, would not the New Year pattern of fall and return of the sacral king and the battling god have been an obvious choice? It was this choice that was made long ago by Lord Raglan and others, witness the way he manages to fit all details into his pattern. And if we had been asked the same question after the reading of section five, would we not have hesitated to answer the question, because the story, when you come to think of it, fits very well into the initiatory scheme as well?

Meanwhile, the reason for all this has become abundantly clear, and so the questions asked above have been essentially answered. Both situations, that of the New Year and that of initiation, have a firmly related ritual and social function and follow, in essence, identical basic patterns: the old situation has to be taken leave of (symbol of death, fall, farewell: the *séparation*); there is a period of transition between old and new (sojourn in death, underworld, labyrinth, flood, foreign countries, a monster's belly: the *marge*); the new situation is accepted (rebirth, resurrection, reinvestiture, return and reintegration: the *agrégation*). That one complex is embedded in a process of nature, the other in a social passage, is, seen from a structural point of view, not immediately relevant. What matters is the close relationship in the typically transitional situations and the mythical symbols in which they find their expression.

Here I could stop. I have suggested a tentative explanation for both the radical substitution and the persistent thematic intertwining in the history of the two major theories of myth and ritual of the last hundred years. Functional and (consequently) structural analogies are responsible. Hence acceptance of one of the theories does not entail the need to reject dogmatically the other one. However, what we have not considered so far is the question of what urged human culture to *ritualize* the two related passages so emphatically and, more precisely, why this was expressed in imagery which was so closely related, if not identical. In other words, if we accept that periods of transition – i.e., crisis – are inherent in natural and social life, and that they naturally provoke similar reactions, we still have not elucidated the baffling *formal* similarities in the ritual and mythical expressions. I would therefore not like to end without making a few suggestions. They should be seen, however, as an *encore*: what follows has no strict dependence of the previous argument.

This argument has its starting point in the similarity of the two myth and ritual complexes. Burkert's recent work has not yet been taken account of in the discussion. So let us now take the ultimate step: suppose we had not been asked the question about the interpretation of the Odysseus story until after reading section 6. Would we not be inclined to class it under the head of Propp's narrative structure and – as the next step – to consider, with Burkert, whether the story reveals references to deep-rooted biological and cultural schemes of action? If one checks it, again everything fits. That would mean that we have reached a deeper level of interpretation, which does not supersede the other two but supports and envelops them. We might conceive of it in this way: the most elementary and primordial scheme of (originally bio-sociological) functions has been conserved and transformed, in ritualized and mythicized form, at precisely those points where human society experiences primal crisis most intensely. Apart from incidental calamities like epidemics, wars, earthquakes and floods, these are precisely the critical and painful moments of transition that are experienced nowhere more keenly than during initiatory periods and at the turning points of the agricultural or social year. In this way the structural relationship between these two "crises" and their mythical-ritual representations is now placed in a historical evolutionary perspective. This seems to be implied in Burkert's clearly evolved view.[5] The author of "Kekropidensage und Arrhephoria: vom Initiationsritus zum Panathenäenfest" now writes (1979, 57): "The pattern called 'the girl's tragedy' *can* [my italics H.S.V.] be interpreted as reflecting initiation rituals; but these, in turn, are demonstrative accentuations of biologically programed crises, menstruation, defloration, pregnancy, birth". In the latter study, Odysseus and the Cyclops no longer have anything to do with initiation. Instead, they are related to very remote reminiscences from even palaeolithic action patterns (cf. the lance tempered in the fire). And when Burkert discusses phenomena of role reversal and sexual submission (pp. 29–30), initiation is found to play only a marginal role in the predominantly biologically oriented argument (apes also offer themselves in an act of submission).[6]

---

[5] One perceives traces of a shift in the frame of interpretation in later works of Burkert. Burkert 1980, 184, discusses the overtly Freudian theory of O. Rank, *Der Mythos der Geburt des Helden* (Vienna 1909), in which the "Aussetzung- und Rückkehrformel" is traced back to the "father-son conflict". Burkert considers this "eine der solidesten Leistungen" and states: "dies leuchtet weithin ein". The implications of this assessment are crucial: one of the traditional ingredients of the initiation theory has been detached from this context and is now exploited in a different type of interpretation. Very interesting on the neurobiological origins of the connections between myth and ritual: E. G. d'Aquili, Ch. D. Laughlin Jr, J. McManus, *The Spectrum of Ritual. A Biogenetic Structural Analysis* (New York 1979). More recently on the motif of exposure in legend and folk tale: Bremmer 1987b, 30, who now also seeks the function of this element outside the sphere of initiation. Cf. also Auffarth 1991, 457.

[6] Before Burkert this issue was already discussed by D. Fehling, *Ethologische Überlegungen auf dem Gebiet der Altertumskunde* (Munich 1974) 18 ff.: "Kopulations-verhalten als Rangdemonstration", which has been supplemented by recent studies on the social function of "institutionalized homosexuality". Though no doubt often connected with initiation-ritual, its application generally exceeds the strict boundaries of the period of initiation. Homosexual subjection appears to have a broader function as a powerful component of social hierarchy: it supports the status and position of older men over and against women and young men. See: G. W. Creed, Sexual Subordination: Institutionalized Homosexuality and Social Control in Melanesia, *Ethnology* 23 (1984) 157–76, and bibliographical references there; G. Herdt (ed.), *Ritualized Homosexuality in Melanesia* (Berkeley-Los Angeles 1984); *idem, The Sambia. Ritual and Gender in New Guinea* (1987).

No doubt not everybody who *is* perhaps prepared to acknowledge the structural affinity of the two complexes is willing to take this ultimate step. I would repeat that I consider it as no more than a suggestion, a suggestion, though, that deserves serious consideration. In a series of books – especially *The Hero with a Thousand Faces* (1949, 1975²) – , that have come in for a good deal of discussion, J. Campbell deals with a mythical complex "the adventure of the hero", whose structure he outlines as follows: 1. departure; 2. initiation; 3. return. This is a familiar scheme by now, but what is interesting is that Campbell proceeds totally independently of the scholars referred to above. He interprets the entire scheme with the help of Freud and Jung above all in terms of depth psychology, citing material from dreams. How these images get into our dreams is not explained, at least not explicitly, and here the recent movement of socio-biology, despite the criticisms it has received, might well be revelatory.[7]

[7] M. Eliade 1975, 128 (with a very hazy note on p. 165) suggests that the initiation scheme was prior and landed in dreams and myths, whereas at the same time he nevertheless concedes that "every human life is made up of a series of ordeals, of 'deaths' and of 'resurrections'". But if this is so, it is far more likely that these ordeals common to human life have given shape to both the initiation scenario and – independently – to the materials dreams and myths are made of. See on this and similar questions: H. von Beit, *Symbolik des Märchens. Versuch einer Deutung* (Bern 1952) and *Enzyklopädie des Märchens* s.v. "Aufgabe", where, conversely, the unfeasible assignment known from fairy tales is seen as the reflection of "Alptraumerfahrungen". Nor is it very likely that Snow White has borrowed her seven dwarfs from initiation ritual: H. Bausinger, Anmerkungen zu Schneewittchen, in: H. Brackert (ed.), *Und wenn sie nicht gestorben sind . . . Perspektiven auf das Märchen* (Frankfurt 1982²) 39–70. What Campbell omits has been made up by G. J. Baudy: *Exkommunikation und Reintegration. Zur Genese und Kulturfunktion frühgriechischer Einstellungen zum Tod* (Frankfurt 1980). He offers a psycho-ethological explanation of deep-seated fears, for instance the fear of voracious monsters, interpreting them as relics of primates' primordial fear of the "Artfeind" (the praedator; cf. in the same vein: d'Aquili *et alii o.c.* [above n. 168] 178: "When ritual works [. . .] it powerfully relieves man's existential anxiety and, at its most powerful, relieves him of the fear of death and places him in harmony with the universe"). On p. 33 f. he juxtaposes the initiand, who is in danger of being swallowed up, and the fairy tale hero in the same situation, as I have done, but does not suggest an evolutionary link between the two. On pp. 250 ff., however, he wishes to trace the fairy tale motif back to initiation (specifically, the shamanistic scenario), which seems unnecessary to me. Obviously similar problems of origin emerge in different fields: it is *the* basic problem of Freud's Oedipus theory. It plays an important role in the discussion between Henrichs and Winkler (above n. 144), where the latter – I think convincingly – refers to "patterns of narrative, the basic plots and formulae of popular entertainment", without, however, inquiring into the origins of these patterns. It also figures in the discussion between F. Ranke, *Kleinere Schriften* (Bern-Münster 1971), who explains the popular fancies of the "Wilde Heer" as "innerseeliche Vorgänge des numinösen Erlebnis" (especially as manifest in hysteria, epilepsy, etc.) and his fierce opponent O. Höffler, *Verwandlungskulte, Volkssagen und Mythen* (*Sitz. Ber. Oesterr. Ak. Wiss. Phil. -hist. Kl.* 279 [1973]), who traces this "wild army" back to historical, cultic *Jungmannschaften*. It is also present in the discussion on the origins of the Eleusinian and other mysteries. See for instance on the ambivalence of human initiation and agricultural fertility as the ultimate background of the mysteries: G. Casadio, Per un'indagine storico-religiosa sui culti di Dioniso in relazione alla fenomenologia dei misteri I, *SSR* 6 (1982) 209–34.

As regards our two myth and ritual complexes we thus find that what is
sauce for the goose is sauce for the gander, which is probably due to the fact
that both sauces are prepared by the same cook, who works with only one
recipe. The primordial "crisis", which is experienced continuously in the risks
of daily ventures, has a stereotyped program: leaving the relative safety of the
familiar environment – setting out for sheer superhuman enterprises and unspeakable dangers in a marginal landscape marked by monsters and every sort
of nameless terror, often to the very limits of death – returning in triumph.
These indispensable, successive actions are reflected in the imagery of our two
complexes *and* in fairy tales and myths of the *Odyssey* type. Equating the
sauces of goose and gander does *not* necessarily disqualify either of them. Nor
does it entail a depreciation of the remarkable progress made in our field
through the recent shift in our model of interpretation, as I hope to have made
clear and shall further elucidate in later chapters. While, as I remarked in the
Introduction, in the natural sciences some implications of Kuhn's concept of
"paradigm" are liable to criticism, the concept has proved helpful in analysing
developments in the social sciences. However, it has been pointed out recently
that in this sector paradigms are, as a rule, not radically exclusive. This tolerance has awarded anthropology the qualification: "polyparadigmatic". And this
is exactly my point.

Though the new paradigm introducing the social interpretation of myth and
ritual has cleared the way for explanations that were unheard of in the first half
of this century, – I am especially referring to the application of the concept of
"marginality", both in the rites of initiation and in the festivals of reversal –,
the new model by no means completely eradicates or replaces the old one.
First, I would not (and did not) deny that the presence of the two patterns
described by the myth and ritual theorists can actually be demonstrated. What
I oppose is the totalitarian, monolithic interpretation of such mythical patterns
from the point of view of just one of the complexes. Secondly, I do not doubt
that there are myths which, in the final analysis, go back to some New Year
scenario, nor that there are myths which derive their origin from initiatory
schemes. However, I think it unlikely that all the stories with the scenario
described above have developed in either one of these ways. Anyone who goes
to such lengths, while still acknowledging that everywhere – in both complexes
and in a great mass of myths, fairy tales, stories (and dreams) from all over the
world – we can discern a more or less identical basic pattern, has the right if
not the duty to try to find an explanation for this phenomenon. Perhaps this
can be done without the help of recent ethological and biological insights, but
it may be better to try to incorporate them. In any case – and that was my chief
aim – we can understand now why the champions of the two complexes have
so often encroached upon each others' territories.

To return to the Odysseus theme, I, for one, think that an origin in some
New Year scenario is less plausible than a descent from some initiatory scenario.

Much more plausible than either, though, is the interpretation of this story as a variation on the biological-cultural program of action, which may have been carried over into both complexes and which, *independently*, has become the material from which dreams, fairy tales and myths of a certain type have been fashioned. Of course, whoever thinks all this much too vague and prefers to sit down and reread the *Odyssey* itself is right, too.

In *The Golden Bough* IV (1914) p. vii, Frazer sighs: "The longer I occupy myself with questions of ancient mythology, the more diffident I become of success in dealing with them, and I am apt to think that we who spend our years in searching for solutions of these insoluble problems are like Sisyphos perpetually rolling his stone uphill only to see it revolve again into the valley".

This is a pessimistic expression of what I found more hopefully phrased by the anthropologist E. M. Ackerknecht:[8] "If anthropology returns to the comparative method" [and as we have seen, recent developments in the borderland of anthropology and the classics tend in that direction H.S.V.], "it will certainly not forget what it has learned meanwhile in general and what it has learned about the limitations of the method in particular. It will return only in that spiral movement, so characteristic of scientific thought, *arriving after half a century at the same point but at a higher level*. It will know better how and what to compare than it knew fifty years ago".

Sisyphus' stone rolling but landing at a higher level each time? Let us hope so, even if the stone turns out to obey Zeno's laws.

---

[8] I found this quotation in a book from which I have learned more than I have been able to account for within the scope of this paper: Smith 1978, 264.

FURTHER READING

Myth-Ritualist Theory and Application

Aijmer, Göran. "The Cultural Nature of Ritual and Myth." In *Symbolic Textures*, ed. Aijmer. Göteborg, Sweden: Acta Universitatis Gothoburgensis, 1987. Pp. 1–22.

Anderson, Roland F. "Structure, Myth, and Rite in *Oliver Twist*." *Studies in the Novel* 18 (1986), 238–57.

Bowie, A. M. *Aristophanes*. Cambridge: Cambridge University Press, 1993.

Carpenter, Rhys. *Folk Tale, Fiction, and Saga in the Homeric Epics*. Berkeley: University of California Press, 1946.

Chambers, E. K. *The Mediaeval Stage*. 2 vols. Oxford: Clarendon Press, 1903.

Graves, Robert. *The White Goddess*. 1st edn. London: Faber & Faber; New York: Creative Age Press, 1948.

———. *The Greek Myths*. 2 vols 1st edn. Harmond worth, Middlesex: Penguin, 1955.

Leach, E. R. *Political Systems of Highland Burma*. London: Bell; Cambridge, MA: Harvard University Press, 1954.

Levy, G. R. *The Gate of Horn*. London: Faber & Faber, 1948.

———. *The Sword from the Rock*. London: Faber & Faber, 1953.

Lindsay, Jack. *The Clashing Rocks*. London: Chapman & Hall, 1965.

Murray, Margaret A. *The Witch-Cult in Western Europe*. Oxford: Clarendon, 1921.

———. *The God of the Witches*. 1st edn. London: Faber & Faber, 1931.

———. *The Divine King in England*. London: Faber & Faber, 1954.

Phillpotts, Bertha S. *The Elder Edda and Ancient Scandinavian Drama*. Cambridge: Cambridge University Press, 1920.

Righter, Anne. *Shakespeare and the Idea of the Play*. London: Chatto & Windus, 1962.

Speirs, John. *Medieval English Poetry*. London: Faber & Faber, 1957.

Spens, Janet. *An Essay on Shakespeare's Relation to Tradition*. Oxford: Oxford University Press, 1916.

Thomson, George. *Aeschylus and Athens*. 1st edn. London: Lawrence & Wishart, 1941.

Tiddy, R. J. E. *The Mummers' Play*. Oxford: Clarendon Press, 1923.

Troy, William. "Thomas Mann: Myth and Reason." *Partisan Review* 5 (1938), 24–32, 51–64. James Burnham. "William Troy's Myths." *Partisan Review* 5 (1938), 65–8. William Troy. "A Further Note on Myth." *Partisan Review* 6 (1938), 95–100.

——. *Selected Essays*, ed. Stanley Edgar Hyman. New Brunswick, NJ: Rutgers University Press, 1967.

Versnel, H. S. *Transition and Reversal in Greek Religion.* Leiden: Brill, 1993. Chs 2–5.

Vickery, John B., ed. *Myth and Literature.* Lincoln: University of Nebraska Press, 1966.

——, and J'nan M. Sellery, eds. *The Scapegoat.* Boston: Houghton Mifflin, 1972.

——. *Myths and Texts.* Baton Rouge: Louisiana State University Press, 1983.

Watts, Harold H. "Myth and Drama." *Cross Currents* 5 (1955), 154–70.

History and Presentation

Dorson, Richard M. *The British Folklorists.* Chicago: University of Chicago Press; London: Routledge & Kegan Paul, 1968.

Gross, John J. "After Frazer: The Ritualistic Approach to Myth." *Western Humanities Review* 5 (1951), 379–91.

Harrelson, Walter. "Myth and Ritual School." In *Encyclopedia of Religion*, ed. Mircea Eliade. New York: Macmillan, 1987. Vol. 10, 282–5.

Jones, Robert Alun. "Robertson Smith and James Frazer on Religion: Two Traditions in British Social Anthropology." In *Functionalism Historicized*, ed. George W. Stocking, Jr. Madison: University of Wisconsin Press, 1984. Pp. 31–58.

Kaberry, Phyllis M. "Myth and Ritual: Some Recent Theories." *Bulletin of the Institute of Classical Studies* 4 (1957), 42–54.

Kurath, Gertrude P. "Ritual Drama." In *Funk & Wagnalls Standard Dictionary of Folklore, Mythology, and Legend*, ed. Maria Leach. New York: Funk & Wagnalls 1950. Vol. II, 946–9.

Leach, Edmund R. "Ritual." *International Encyclopedia of the Social Sciences* (1968), vol. 13, 520–6.

Payne, Harry C. "Modernizing the Ancients: The Reconstruction of Ritual Drama 1870–1920," *Proceedings of the American Philosophical Society* 122 (1978), 182–92.

——. "The Ritual Question and Modernizing Society, 1800–1945 – A Schema for a History." *Historical Reflections/ Réflexions Historigues* 11 (1984), 404–32.

Rogerson, J. W. *Myth in Old Testament Interpretation.* Berlin: De Gruyter, 1974.

Stocking George W., Jr. *Victorian Anthropology.* New York: Free Press; London: Collier Macmillan, 1987.

——. *After Tylor.* Madison: University of Wisconsin Press; London: Athlone, 1996.

Evaluation

Bynum, David E. "Myth and Ritual: Two Faces of Tradition." In *Oral Traditional Literature*, ed. John Miles Foley. Columbus: Slavica, 1981. Pp. 142–63.

Calder, William M., III, ed. *The Cambridge Ritualists Reconsidered.* Atlanta: Scholars Press, 1989.

Chase, Richard. "Notes on the Study of Myth." *Partisan Review* 13 (1946), 338–46.
——. "The Study of Myth." *Nation* 167 (1948), 635–7.
——. "Myth as Literature." *English Institute Essays, 1947.* New York: Columbia University Press, 1948. Pp. 3–22.
Else, Gerald F. *The Origin and Early Form of Greek Tragedy.* Cambridge, MA: Harvard University Press, 1965.
Graham-White, Anthony. "'Ritual' in Contemporary Theatre Criticism." *Educational Theater Review* 28 (1976), 318–24.
Hartmann, Geoffrey H. "Structuralism: The Anglo-American Adventure" (1966), in his *Beyond Formalism* (New Haven: Yale University Press, 1970), 3–23.
Kirby, E. T. "The Origin of the Mummers' Play." *Journal of American Folklore* 84 (1971), 275–88. E. C. Cawte, "More on the 'Mummers' Play'," *Journal of American Folklore* 85 (1972), 375–6. E. T. Kirby, "Mummers' Plays and the Calendar," *Journal of American Folklore* 86 (1973), 282–5. E. C. Cawte, "Even More about the Mummers' Play," *Journal of American Folklore* 87 (1974), 250–2.
Kirk, Geoffrey S. "Aetiology, Ritual, Charter: Three Equivocal Terms in the Study of Myths." *Yale Classical Studies* 22 (1972), 83–102.
Knox, Bernard. "Myth and Attic Tragedy," in his *Word and Action.* Baltimore: Johns Hopkins University Press, 1979. Ch. 1.
Manganaro, Marc. *Myth, Rhetoric, and the Voice of Authority.* New Haven: Yale University Press, 1992.
Phillips, C. Robert, III. "Misconceptualizing Classical Mythology." *Institute of Classical Studies Bulletin*, Supplement 58 (1991), 143–51.
Proceedings of the 7th Congress for the History of Religions, eds C. J. Bleeker, G. W. J. Drewes, and K. A. H. Hidding. 1950. Amsterdam: North-Holland, 1951.
Rahv, Philip. "The Myth and the Powerhouse." *Partisan Review* 20 (1953), 635–48.
The Sacral Kingship/La Regalità Sacra. VIIIth International Congress for the History of Religions, 1955. Leiden: Brill, 1959.
Smith, Hallett. *Shakespeare's Romances.* San Marino, CA: Huntington Library, 1972.
Webster, T. B. L. "Some Thoughts on the Pre-History of Greek Drama." *Institute of Classical Studies Bulletin*, no. 5 (1978), 43–8.

Bibliography

Accardi, Bernard et al. *Recent Studies in Myths and Literature, 1970–1990.* Westport, CT: Greenwood Press, 1991.
Arlen, Shelley. *The Cambridge Ritualists: An Annotated Bibliography.* Metuchen, NJ: Scarecrow Press, 1990.

INDEX